Mr. Lincoln's Forts

A Guide to the Civil War Defenses of Washington

New Edition

DEFENSES OF WASHINGTON
Extract of Military Map
of N. E. Virginia
SCALE OF MILES
0 ¼ ½ ¾ 1 2 Miles
N
Silver Spring
Brookeville Road
Rockville Road
River Road
Rock Cr.
Sligo Br.
North West Br.
Little Point Br.
Battery Smead
Fort DeRussy
Fort Stevens
Battery Kingsbury
Fort Slocum
Battery Reno
Fort Bayard
Battery Terrill
Fort Kearny
Fort Reno
Tennallytown
Fort Sumner
Bat. Bailey
Bat. Benson
Block-House
Langley
Reservoir
Pierce's Mill Road
Fort Totten
Bladensburg Road
Hyattsville
Bladensburg
Battery Vermont
Fort Gaines
Fort Marcy
Battery Martin Scott
Battery Kemble
Fort Slemmer
Fort Bunker Hill
Fort Saratoga
Fort Thayer
Fort Lincoln
Fort Ethan Allen
Pimmit Run
Kirby Road
Battery Parrott
Battery Cameron
Rock Creek
Seventh Street Road
Rock Creek Church Road
Old Bladensburg Road
Bladensburg Turnpike
Eastern Branch Road
BALTIMORE & OHIO R.R.
GEORGETOWN
Fort C.F. Smith
Fort Bennett
Fort Strong
Fort Corcoran
Fort Morton
Fort Haggerty
Fort Woodbury
Fort Cass
Fort Whipple
Fort Tillinghast
Fort McPherson
Soldiers Nat. Cemetery
Arlington
Benning's Bridge Road
Fort Mahan
Fort Chaplin
Fort Meigs
Fort Dupont
Fort Davis
Falls Church
Fort Taylor
Fort Buffalo
Fort Ramsay
Ball's Cross Roads
LOUDOUN & HAMPS. R.R.
Fort Craig
Fort Jackson
Long Bridge
POTOMAC RIVER
EASTERN BRANCH
Navy Yard
Poplar Pt.
Uniontown
Fort Albany
Fort Runyon
Fort Munson
Arlington Mills Sta.
Columbia Turnpike
Fort Richardson
Fort Berry
U.S. Arsenal
Fort Stanton
Fort Baker
Fort Wagner
Fort Ricketts
Ridge Road
Fort Barnard
Fort Scott
Giesborough Pt.
Cavalry Depot
Fort Snyder
Battery Garesche
Fort Reynolds
Leesburg and Alexandria Turnpike
Holmes Run
Fort Carroll
Oxon Run
Fort Ward
Fort Greble
Turkey Cock Br.
Fort Worth
Fort Williams
Fort Ellsworth
Little River Turnpike
ALEXANDRIA
Cameron R.
ORANGE & ALEXANDRIA R.R.
Back Lick R.
Fort Lyon
Fort Farnsworth
Fort Weed
Fort O'Rourke
Bat. Rodgers
Hunting Creek
Old Fairfax Road
Telegraph Road
Gravel Road
Accotink Turnpike
Fort Willard
Fort Foote

Mr. Lincoln's Forts

A Guide to the Civil War Defenses of Washington

New Edition

Benjamin Franklin Cooling III
Walton H. Owen II

Foreword by Edwin C. Bearss

THE SCARECROW PRESS, INC.
Lanham • Toronto • Plymouth, UK
2010

Published by Scarecrow Press, Inc.
A wholly owned subsidiary of The Rowman & Littlefield Publishing Group, Inc.
4501 Forbes Boulevard, Suite 200, Lanham, Maryland 20706
http://www.scarecrowpress.com

Estover Road, Plymouth PL6 7PY, United Kingdom

British Library Cataloguing in Publication Information Available

Library of Congress Cataloging-in-Publication Data

Cooling, B. Franklin.
Mr. Lincoln's forts : a guide to the Civil War defenses of Washington / Benjamin Franklin Cooling III, Walton H. Owen II ; foreword by Edwin C. Bearss. — Rev. ed.
p. cm.
Includes bibliographical references and index.
ISBN 978-0-8108-6759-8 (cloth : alk. paper) — ISBN 978-0-8108-6067-4 (pbk. : alk. paper) — ISBN 978-0-8108-6307-1 (ebook)
1. Fortification—Washington Region—Guidebooks. 2. Washington (D.C.)—Guidebooks. 3. Washington (D.C.)—History—Civil War, 1861–1865. 4. Washington Region—Guidebooks. I. Owen, Walton H., 1954– II. Title. III. Title: Mister Lincoln's forts. F195.C66 2010
973.7'453—dc22

2009018392

∞™ The paper used in this publication meets the minimum requirements of American National Standard for Information Sciences—Permanence of Paper for Printed Library Materials, ANSI/NISO Z39.48-1992.

Printed in the United States of America

Contents

Foreword

A broad constituency of readers—not limited to Civil War buffs, military historians, preservationists, and those who like to explore their neighborhoods—will hail the publication of *Mr. Lincoln's Forts: A Guide to the Civil War Defenses of Washington*. The first edition, a handsomely illustrated and well-written book sponsored by The Friends of Fort Ward, addressed a long-recognized need in an exciting and thought-provoking manner.

Even before I joined the National Park Service (NPS), I recognized that a great many sites associated with our nation's past are difficult to locate, and frequently, when visited, old-timers' tales of what happened on-site clash with the written records. In the years since 1955, I have found that many people like nothing better than visiting out-of-the-way historic sites and places, especially when they are associated with our Civil War battlefields and military past.

It has been demonstrated that, in the 127 years since the firing on Fort Sumter, interest in our Civil War, fittingly called "The American Iliad" by my friends Otto Eisenschiml and Ralph Newman, has been cyclic. A major manifestation of this phenomenon is a desire to visit sites associated with the Civil War, to walk in the footsteps of the soldiers and civilians of the 1860s, and to see and touch the landscapes, structures, and objects in a conscious effort to recapture the past.

The first great awakening of interest in the "War" began in the late 1880s and continued into the first years of the twentieth century. The most important and permanent evidence of this surge was the establishment by Congress of four national military parks—Chickamauga and Chattanooga, Shiloh, Gettysburg, and Vicksburg—and the Antietam National Battlefield site. The campaigns that resulted in these successes were spearheaded by veterans (many of whom had become politically and economically powerful), abetted by major railroads, and supported by the War Department. These parks were commemorative, with hundreds of memorials and markers, and sought to either preserve or recapture the historic scene, served as field classrooms for military staff rides, and interpreted the Civil War campaigns, battles, and leaders for the general public. Visits to these areas were enhanced through the publication of guidebooks.

The next renaissance of the public's interest in the Civil War began in the mid-1920s and continued into the years of Franklin D. Roosevelt's New Deal. In the years after World War I, Americans, disenchanted with the "Great Adventure," turned their backs on Europe to look at the history of their own country as a source of inspiration. The Great War and its aftermath brought the five-and-a-half-day workweek, paid two-week summer vacations, and the family car to much of middle-class America. With more leisure time, automobiles, and improved roads, the public took to the highways.

Responding to the pleas of aging but no longer politically powerful Civil War veterans, the travel industry, a harking back by many Americans to the years when the nation had successfully confronted its greatest challenge, and the desire to prime the pump to get the United States back to work by stimulating the economy, between 1924 and 1937 Congress (by legislation) and the president (by executive order) authorized or established eleven national Civil War parks and monuments. In August 1933, the administration of the Civil War areas (and associated national cemeteries) was transferred from the War Department to the NPS, a bureau of the Department of the Interior, which therefore was principally responsible for overseeing the nation's great natural parks.

Spokespeople for the NPS had buttressed arguments before Congress in support of consolidating park areas administered by the War and Agriculture departments in their bureau by stressing their proven ability to better interpret these parks and monuments for the public. As a principal medium for accomplishing this goal, the NPS, following the 1933 reorganization, published and distributed to park visitors twofold leaflets. These publications—most Civil War parks and monuments had these designed for them—had similar formats, featuring a history of the event or person commemorated and maps to enable the visitor to tour the area. The maps identified and described the principal interpretive stops in addition to locating park visitor centers, roads, and trails. For the more heavily visited areas, the NPS published and sold interpretive booklets, or handbooks. In addition to the maps found in the leaflets, these publications featured longer narratives and were better illustrated.

Also appearing in the New Deal years were Work Projects Administration guides to each of the forty-eight states, the territories, and Puerto Rico. The guidebooks, compiled by the "Workers of the Writers' Program," were and still are invaluable sources for locating historic sites and structures.

The approach of the Civil War Centennial and the implementation of the NPS's MISSION 66 development program and the inauguration of its handbook publication program coincided with another, third, great reawakening of interest by the American public at large in the Civil War. Several new parks were established to interpret, on-site, battles and events associated with that tragic era. MISSION 66 saw new or upgraded visitor centers, museum exhibits, waysides, and interpretive publications at the NPS's older Civil War areas. In 1955, Colonel Joseph B. Mitchell authored his heralded *Decisive Battles of the Civil War*, and Alice Cromie followed in 1964 with her *Tour Guide to the Civil War*. Mitchell's publication featured most NPS Civil War areas, narrative descriptions, and maps (many of them adapted from those found in NPS leaflets, with current roads and their designations added) to enable motorists to tour these parks and monuments. Cromie's guide included information on a great number of Civil War–related sites and structures, but her maps provided only general information on locations.

The planned five-year national commemoration of the Civil War Centennial had lost most of its interest and public support by 1963, killed by excessive hoopla and poorly conceived and executed reenactments. But by the late 1970s, a new surge in the public's on-and-off-again romance with the Civil War appeared. This was evidenced on a number of fronts. New book titles and reprints of old favorites and unit histories flooded the market; battlefield art appeared; living history and reenactment groups became highly sophisticated, popular, and relevant; battlefield preservation was championed; the number of Civil War roundtables and study groups, which had enjoyed spectacular growth during the late 1950s and early 1960s, only to see their strength erode, rebounded; organized battlefield tours became increasingly popular; and the Department of the Army reinstituted its staff rides that had been phased out in the early 1940s.

A number of authors and publishers have taken advantage of the return of interest in the "War" by site-oriented visitors to address this need and market their guidebooks. While several of these books are valuable additions to Civil War historiography, *Mr. Lincoln's Forts* is a classic, a publication against which future endeavors in this field will be measured. In making this assessment, I do so with some authority because I have been leading tours to battlefields and related historic sites and structures since 1961 and am familiar with guidebooks and related literature. One of my more popular tours, sponsored by the Smithsonian Resident Associates, focuses on the "Washington Forts," and information found in *Mr. Lincoln's Forts* provides invaluable anecdotal information that will be used to enrich future conducted tours.

The authors, Benjamin Franklin Cooling III and Walton H. Owen II, have similar backgrounds. Both became interested in the Civil War forts of Washington while growing up near them. Knowing the forts first as play sites, the authors became intrigued with their story. Their keen interest is reflected in this book. Cooling is also the author of *Symbol, Sword and Shield: Defending Washington during the Civil War*, published in 1975, a much-acclaimed study of the Washington fortifications, their role and significance in the defense of the nation's capital, and the strategy in the eastern theater of the war.

The background, interests, and education of the authors ensure that the narratives and site descriptions found in *Mr. Lincoln's Forts* are accurate, interestingly written, and certain to appeal to a broad spectrum of the public. The instructions for finding the forts—be they reconstructions, restorations, preserved structures, sites, or nearly forgotten sites—are succinct and understandable.

A special bonus that will fire the enthusiasm of all readers is the magnificent selection of illustrations. These photographs, maps, and drawings reinforce the value of this guide, which, in my opinion, would be a bargain at double its sale price.

Edwin C. Bearss
Chief Historian Emeritus
National Park Service

Acknowledgments

Various groups and individuals have made this guide possible. The Friends of Fort Ward originally sponsored the work. This nonprofit group remains dedicated to improving public awareness of Fort Ward Museum and Park in Alexandria, Virginia.

The professional staff of Fort Ward Museum have built on the pioneering leadership of former directors Colonel Joseph Mitchell (USA Ret.) and Mrs. Wanda Dowell. The present director, Ms. Susan Cumbey, and Mr. Walton Owen, as assistant director/curator, continue to serve the City of Alexandria, making this small museum and historic site the centerpiece for studying the Defenses of Washington. The authors have placed the guide's research files in the Fort Ward Library for public use. Any tour of the Defenses should begin at Fort Ward Museum.

The first edition of *Mr. Lincoln's Forts* was supported with a welcome research grant from the Mason-Dixon Relic Hunter's Association of Gettysburg, Pennsylvania. The Friends of Fort Ward sponsored the publication of the first edition, and this valuable organization, under current president Bill Schreiner, continues to promote the preservation of Fort Ward and the Defenses of Washington. To support the Defenses of Washington, membership information can be obtained by contacting Fort Ward Museum at 4301 West Braddock Road, Alexandria, VA 22304, or www.fortward.org.

Key current and former individuals working for the National Park Service merit special mention: Ed Bearss, George Vasjuta, Don Briggs, David Smith, Ted Alexander, Corky Mayo, Steve Potter, Bob Sonderman, Gary Scott, Vince Santucci, Brandon Bies, and Matt Virta have continually supported this project and have been helpful. Special thanks to Tammy Stidham and Ron Harvey, who contributed specialized information to the second edition. Louisa Arnold, Randy Hackenberg, and Michael Winey of the U.S. Army Military History Institute, Carlisle Barracks, Pennsylvania, took time to search for data and illustrations for the earlier editions, as did the late Pete Seaborg of Rock Creek bookshop in Washington, D.C. Richard Smith, Paul Conner, Bob Richardson, and Ray Cotton expedited maps at the Cartographic Branch of the National Archives and Records Administration. Jodi Myers assisted with the first-edition manuscript, and Denise Chauvette provided editorial review for the second-edition manuscript.

A special acknowledgment needs to go to those special individuals and families who donated copies of soldier letters and information to Fort Ward Museum that have been used in this guide to illuminate the lives of the soldiers who served in the Defenses of Washington. These individuals include David Gosling, Bruce Gosling, Rob Aronson, Robert Alexander, Virginia Pollock, Gary Hoover, Wes Clark, Steve Mayeux, Dale Floyd, and many others. Special thanks go to historian Ed Hendrickson for cataloging Fort Ward's Defenses of Washington research material—a never-ending process. Sharing materials, interest, enthusiasm, and curiosity with the authors during the development of the latest edition are the following: Jim Sorensen and Don Housley of the Maryland National Capital Park and Planning Commission; Jim Campi and Mary Goundrey Koik of the Civil War Preservation Trust; Tersh Boasberg and the Alliance for Preservation of the Defenses of Washington; the Arlington Heritage Alliance, which has worked to protect Fort Ethan Allen and Fort C. F. Smith and the Arlington Line; Burt Bostwick and the Old Glebe Citizen's Association; Liz Crowell and the staff of the Resource Management Division, Fairfax County, Virginia; archaeologist and historian Joseph Balicki; Patricia Tyson and the Military Road School Preservation Trust; Jane Freudel Levy and D.C. Cultural Tourism; and individuals such as Jason Hagy of Washington, D.C.; Fred Ray of Ashville, North Carolina; Art Edinger of Shelbyville, Kentucky; and Gil Barrett of New Bern, North Carolina.

Introduction: The State and the Fate of the Defenses of Washington

> The fortifications, so numerous in all this region and now so unsightly with their bare sides,—will remain as historic monuments, grass-grown and picturesque memorials of an epoch of terror and suffering; they will serve to make our country dearer and more interesting to us.
>
> The more historical associations we can link with our localities, the richer will be the daily life that feeds upon the past, and the more valuable are the things that have long been established: so that our children will be less foolish than their fathers in sacrificing good institutions. . . . Let us hope this grace may be found in the old footprints of the war.
>
> —Nathaniel Hawthorne,
> writing of Fort Ellsworth, 1862

Washington, D.C., was the most heavily fortified city in the nation during the Civil War. In 1871, Major General John Gross Barnard of the Corps of Engineers, the man most responsible for designing and creating the extensive system of forts that protected Washington, wrote a history of his work that was published as *Professional Papers of the Corps of Engineers U.S. Army, No. 20, A Report on the Defenses of Washington to the Chief of Engineers, U.S. Army*. Historians today simply refer to this work as "Barnard's Report." He declared that

> at the termination of the war in April 1865, the "defenses of Washington" consisted of 68 forts and batteries, having an aggregate perimeter of 22,800 yards (13 miles), and emplacements for 1,120 guns, 807 of which and 98 mortars were actually mounted; of 93 unarmed batteries for field-guns, having 401 emplacements; and of 35,711 yards (20 miles) of rifle trenches, and 3 blockhouses. Thirty-two miles of military roads, besides the existing roads of the District and the avenues of Washington, served as the means of communication from the interior to the defensive lines, and from point to point thereof. The entire circuit, including the distance across the Potomac from Fort Greble to Fort Lyon (four miles) was . . . thirty-seven miles.

A detailed examination of Plates 29 and 30 in Barnard's Report lists 164 armed and unarmed forts and batteries in the formal Defenses of Washington. They can be enumerated as follows: sixty-eight major forts and batteries (the forts listed with perimeters in Barnard's Report), plus Fort McPherson, Fort Jackson, battery at Chain Bridge, Battery Martin Scott, Battery Vermont, Battery Kemble, Battery Parrott, and Battery Cameron. There were eighty-eight named forts and batteries and seven blockhouses. Advanced forts in Fairfax County and early-warning fortified picket posts and camps are not included in these formal defenses. They included Fort Ramsay, Fort Buffalo, Fort Taylor, Freedom Hill Fort, the stockade or fortified picket posts at Annandale, Fairfax Court House, and the "Star" fort at Vienna. This massive fort-building effort was a result of President Abraham Lincoln's fear that the Confederacy would attack the nation's capital and his government.

At first, soldiers memorialized the forts and their own common everyday tasks in letters home. Journalists and illustrated-newspaper artists followed the armies to report on activities in the forts. Later, after the war, veterans would return to visit the forts where they were stationed in their youth to retrace their footsteps and to remember those comrades who did not return home. Today, only a fraction of these fortifications remain as monuments to their effort. Yet each year, families and individuals make a pilgrimage to the forts to walk in the footprints of their ancestors, sometimes stopping to read letters that were written from the very spot nearly 150 years earlier. The soldiers' camps, barracks, and outbuildings that served the fortifications have vanished. Streets and houses have supplanted the fields where the forts were built, and trees once again grow where great forests were clear-cut to open fields of fire for the cannon. An occasional modern street sign labeled "Military Road" in northwestern Washington and Arlington attests to their wartime antecedents. That any works remain at all is a tribute to early preservationist activities by the U.S. Army Corps of Engineers, a congressional commission at the turn of the twentieth century, the National Park Service, and the municipal governments of Arlington County, Fairfax County, Montgomery County, Maryland, and the City of Alexandria.

Over the years, hundreds of private citizens and amateur and professional historians have served on Defenses of Washington advisory groups and have worked to save or protect a historic fort in their neighborhood. Occasionally, even individual citizens will save an earthwork trace on their property without fully appreciating its significance or their own contribution to the preservation of these historic sites. The citizens of the Washington metropolitan area have paid significant sums in tax dollars for dozens of fort archaeological and planning reports. Their recommendations sit mostly ignored or unacted on by most local jurisdictions.

The current state of preservation found throughout the Defenses offers many challenges and opportunities to the entities in charge of their proper stewardship. Since the publication of *Mr. Lincoln's Forts* in 1988, even successful fort preservation initiatives have yielded meager interpretative results. Arlington County, Virginia, officials spent nearly $11 million to save the remnants of Fort C. F. Smith and create Fort C. F. Smith Park. Adhering to the "Arlington Way" of community public process, an extensive "Cultural Resource Master Plan" was written that emphasized education and historic site interpretation. Today, at Fort C. F. Smith Park, visitors will find a rental/meeting facility to generate revenue but little interpretation. Only in the past three years has Arlington County emerged from a six-year preservation controversy involving the Fort Ethan Allen Historic District. There, an unknowledgeable senior manager in the park's maintenance division placed a dog exercise area in the middle of the historic fort. Ignoring historic district guidelines that require oversight approval, the employee's decision and misstep nearly destroyed part of the historic site and ultimately pitted neighbor against neighbor, dog advocate against fort preservationist. The fight went through two different public processes and took six years to settle—longer than the Civil War. Visitors to Fort Ethan Allen will not find any meaningful interpretation but can admire a new $400,000 state-of-the-art dog park (restyled Community Canine Area) adjacent to the remains of the historic fort. An outlying gun battery that supported the fort during the war exists nearby in Fort Ethan Allen Park and features a Virginia Civil War Trails sign that describes not the battery but Fort Ethan Allen, which is nearly a block away from the location of the sign. At Fort Scott Park, the historic fort sits neglected adjacent to playground equipment, and even though the site has documented archaeological features, the fort is not protected by historic district status. Arlington County, along with many other jurisdictions and the National Park Service, does not know where its fortifications are located because it has not inventoried its extensive Civil War resources. It remains to be seen if interpretation will be included for Fort Jackson and Fort Runyon in Arlington County's new Long Bridge Park. A lack of preservation planning is not limited to Arlington County and can be seen in every jurisdiction in the region.

Fairfax County made significant progress toward preservation planning by creating an inventory of its Civil War resources but continues to struggle to meaningfully preserve and interpret Fort Willard in the well-to-do community of Belle Haven, south of Alexandria, Virginia. There, in public meetings, some local residents openly voiced concern about improved interpretation at the fort because "it might bring the wrong kind of people into the neighborhood." In Mt. Eagle Park, Fairfax County, what was a pristine example of an unmanned battery in 1988 has now been affected by irresponsible development that includes the extension of a ball field on the north side of the battery with improper grading and high-density townhouse development adjacent to the earthworks.

The National Park Service manages the largest number of forts in Washington (as well as Maryland and Virginia). Inadequate budgets, an organizational structure that divides oversight of the forts among three different National Park Service superintendents, competing priorities, and unknowledgeable staff and bureaucratic disinterest have created a distinct decline in stewardship and public safety in the so-called Fort Circle Parks since the original publication of this volume. Today, twenty-two historic fort sites are under the jurisdiction of the National Park Service, including the inadequate visitor experience at Fort Stevens and Battle Ground National Cemetery in northwestern Washington. Visitors to this National Park Service site will search in vain for any adequate interpretation of the nationally significant events that took place there. It remains to be seen if the base-reduction actions by the Department of Defense scheduled to close nearby Walter Reed Army

Medical Center by 2011 will result in public access to the site and the opportunity to finally interpret the last remnants of the Fort Stevens battlefield of 1864—D.C.'s sole Civil War battle site.

The public, the nation, and posterity warrant a better definition of this famous battle with a modern interpretive center devoted to the people and events memorialized there. At this site, an American president stood under enemy fire while in office, the only instance in our country's history. The dead of that fight can be found in a small cemetery with only their regimental markers signifying their sacrifice. At this battle, an American soldier won the Medal of Honor.

Visitors will find limited but better interpretation at other National Park Service fort sites. Among these are Fort Marcy on the Potomac Palisades in Virginia and Fort Foote and Fort Washington guarding the Potomac River in southern Maryland. Fort Foote features authentic Rodman guns original to the site.

Currently, there is collaboration between citizens' groups, the National Park Service, and the D.C. government to evaluate hiking and biking trail connectors between forts and approved funding for fort signage.

Only Alexandria, Virginia, continues to operate the "flagship" site that interprets Fort Ward and the fort's restored Northwest bastion. The small full-service museum at Fort Ward Park and Historic Site stands in stark contrast to other interpretation found at other sites in the system. However, it too suffers from a 1960s aging infrastructure. The museum needs to be updated and expanded to create an attractive venue that encourages the profitable business of heritage tourism.

Several key organizations have been instrumental in promoting fort preservation. The Friends of Fort Ward in Alexandria annually sponsors the John G. Barnard Preservation Award and hosts major events to promote the Defenses of Washington. Another group, the Arlington Heritage Alliance, has formed a subgroup called the Friends of Fort Ethan Allen and the Arlington Line and has been active promoting heritage tourism, Fort Ethan Allen, and the Arlington line of forts. A recently formed support group, the Alliance for Preservation of the Civil War Defenses of Washington, also seeks to publicize and coordinate public awareness of the plight of this part of our national heritage. However, this organization has limited its scope to include only Washington, D.C., sites.

One of the goals for the first edition was to highlight the fort history hidden in our neighborhoods that would bring attention to the preservation concerns that exist at many of the fort sites. Sadly, that goal has not been completely realized.

The plight of the Defenses of Washington led the Civil War Preservation Trust to place the Civil War Defenses of Washington on its 2006 list of most endangered sites. President Jim Lighthizer of the trust said that "what remains of the forts is dying because of neglect and lack of coordination for maintenance and interpretation." The single largest threat to the forts is unknowledgeable administrators and frontline park staff who have no background in fortification preservation practices and have not been trained to care for the resources under their control. Many recreation and park departments leave themselves open to criticism by seeming to view these cultural resources with disdain by not hiring professional staff with the proper preservation backgrounds to understand or care for the forts.

What might be needed to meet the challenges of preserving the Defenses of Washington is a single collaborative organization—one with a comprehensive mission to represent the entire system of forts with a strong focus on stewardship education, an organization that can work with the myriad local governments, jurisdictional agencies, and the National Park Service. By working together, the stewards of the Defenses of Washington could promote collaborative cost savings, integrated interpretation and marketing, and shared knowledge and resources.

The story of Washington's Civil War forts remains an unsung chapter in the history of the nation's capital. Cannon and forts, marvels of engineering design for their time, and the personnel who defended them provided the backdrop for the din of battle and the heroism of sacrifice. Above all, the story is concerned with humanity and the humor and pathos of service in wartime. These fortifications of the past now provide parkland and "green space" for recreation, economic stimulus in the form of heritage tourism, and outdoor classrooms to learn about natural and cultural resources. Their story is timeless. The fate of the Defenses of Washington is in each of our hands; only we can accept the challenge to preserve them.

Readers desiring more information about these activities and how to join the Friends of Fort Ward should contact the Fort Ward Museum. Those readers concerned about the future preservation and interpretation of the forts throughout the area should contact the City of Alexandria, Arlington County, or the National Park Service, National Capital Region. The National Capital Parks and Conservation Association in Washington plays a major role in the work and programs of the National Park Service and seeks public interest in the Department of the Interior custodianship of our national heritage.

DEFENSES OF WASHINGTON SOUTH OF THE POTOMAC RIVER

Forts and Batteries	Perimeter in Yards
1. Battery Rodgers	330
2. Fort Willard	240
*3. Six-gun battery to the right of Fort Willard	
*4. Five-gun battery to the left of Fort Willard	
5. Fort O'Rourke	160
*6. Six-gun battery to the left of Fort O'Rourke	
7. Six-gun battery between Forts O'Rourke and Farnsworth	
8. Fort Farnsworth	255
9. Fort Weed	253
10. Fort Lyon	937
*11. Six-gun battery between Hunting Creek and Fort Lyon	
12. Blockhouse Number 1	
13. Fort near Old Fairfax Road	
*14. Five-gun battery at Old Distillery	
*15. Blockhouse Number 2	
16. Fort Ellsworth	618
*17. Two batteries between Fort Williams and Blockhouse Number 2; fifteen guns	
*18. (Second of two batteries)	
19. Fort Williams	250
*20. Two batteries between Seminary and Fort Ward; eight guns	
*21. (Second of two batteries)	
22. Fort Worth	463
*23. Battery to the left of and auxiliary to Fort Worth; four guns	
*24. Three batteries between Forts Worth and Ward; twenty-four guns	
*25. (Second of three batteries)	
*26. (Third of three batteries)	
27. Fort Ward	818
*28. Six-gun battery in front of Fort Ward	
29. Blockhouse Number 3	
*30. Six-gun battery to the right of Leesburg Turnpike	
31. Battery Garesche	166
32. Fort Reynolds	360
33. Fort Barnard	250
*34. Six-gun battery to the left of Fort Barnard	
35. Fort Berry	215
*36. Three batteries in rifle pits between Forts Richardson and Fort Barnard; ten guns	
*37. (Second of three batteries)	
*38. (Third of three batteries)	
39. Fort Richardson	316
40. Fort Albany	429
41. Fort Runyon	1,484
42. Fort Jackson	
43. Fort Scott	313
*44. Battery to the right of Fort Scott	
*45. Four Batteries between Forts Craig and Richardson; twenty-two guns	
46. (Second of four batteries)	
*47. (Third of four batteries)	
*48. (Fourth of four batteries)	
49. Fort Craig	324

*Unarmed fortification

Forts and Batteries	Perimeter in Yards
*50. Eight-gun battery in front of Fort Craig	
*51. Two batteries in between Forts Craig and Tillinghast; ten guns	
*52. (Second of two batteries)	
53 Fort Tillinghast	298
54. Fort McPherson—not completed	
*55. Four-gun battery to the left of Fort Whipple	
56. Fort Whipple	640
57. Fort Cass	288
58. Two batteries in rifle pits between Forts Cass and Tillinghast; twelve guns	
*59. (Second of two batteries)	
60. Fort Woodbury	275
61. Fort Morton	250
62. Fort Haggerty	128
63. Blockhouses at Aqueduct Bridge; three guns	
64. Fort Corcoran	576
65. Fort Bennett	146
66. Fort Strong	318
67. Fort C. F. Smith	368
68. Fort Marcy	338
*69. Two batteries to the left of Hawkins' Run; eight guns	
*70. (Second of two batteries)	
*71. Two-gun battery between Forts Marcy and Ethan Allen	
*72. Eight-gun battery in front of Fort Marcy	
73. Fort Ethan Allen	736
74. Two batteries in front of Fort Ethan Allen; four guns	
*75. (Second of two batteries)	
*76. Six-gun battery in front of Fort Ethan Allen	
*77. Six-gun battery in front of Fort Ethan Allen advanced	

Advance forts not counted in the formal defenses of Washington:

Fort Ramsay
Fort Buffalo
Fort Taylor
Fort Munson
Freedom Hill Fort—fortified picket post
Star Fort, Vienna, Virginia

DEFENSES OF WASHINGTON NORTH OF THE POTOMAC RIVER

Forts and Batteries	Perimeter in Yards
78. Two-gun battery at Chain Bridge	
79. Battery Martin Scott	
80. Battery Vermont	
81. Battery Kemble	
82. Battery Parrott	
83. Battery Cameron	
*84. Two-gun battery opposite Fort C. F. Smith, No. 1	
*85. Five-gun battery opposite Fort C. F. Smith, No. 2	
86. Battery Alexander	
87. Fort Sumner	843
88. Battery Benson; five guns	
*89. Battery Bailey; six guns	

Forts and Batteries	Perimeter in Yards
*90. Battery Mansfield; seven guns	
91. Fort Mansfield	220
*92. Battery Simmons; four guns	
93. Fort Simmons	177
*94. Three-gun battery to the right of Fort Simmons	
*95. Two-gun battery to the left of Fort Bayard	
96. Fort Bayard	123
*97. Battery Bayard; three guns	
98. Fort Gaines	171
99. Fort Reno	917
*100. Sixteen guns along the covered way between Fort Reno and Battery Reno	
101. Battery Reno	
102. Battery Rossell	
103. Fort Kearny	320
*104. Battery Terrell; seven guns	
*105. Three-gun battery to the right of Board Branch	
106. Battery Smeade	170
107. Fort DeRussy	190
*108. Battery Kingsbury; nine guns	
*109. Six-gun battery to the left of Rock Creek	
*110. Battery Sill; nine guns	
*111. Battery to the right of Battery Sill	
*112. Three-gun battery to the left of Fort Stevens	
113. Fort Stevens	375
*114. Eight-gun battery to the right of Fort Stevens, No. 1	
*115. Two-gun battery to the right of Fort Stevens, No. 2	
*116. Four-gun battery to the left of Fort Slocum	
117. Fort Slocum	653
*118. Six-gun battery to the right of Fort Slocum	
119. Battery Totten	
120. Fort Totten	272
*121. Two-gun battery to the right of Fort Totten	
*122. Six-gun battery to the left of Fort Slemmer	
123. Fort Slemmer	93
*124. Five-gun battery to the right of Fort Slemmer	
*125. Seven-gun battery to the left of Fort Bunker Hill	
126. Fort Bunker Hill	205
*127. Seven-gun battery in front of Fort Bunker Hill	
*128. Nine-gun battery to the right of Fort Bunker Hill	
*129. Four-gun battery to the left of Fort Saratoga	
130. Fort Saratoga	153
*131. Twelve-gun battery to the right of Fort Saratoga	
132. Battery Morris	
133. Fort Thayer	180
*134. Three-gun battery to the right of Fort Thayer	
*135. Seven-gun battery to the left of the Baltimore & Ohio (B&O) Railroad	
*136. Three-gun battery to the right of the B&O Railroad	
*137. Three-gun battery to the left of the Baltimore Turnpike	
*138. Six-gun battery to the left of Fort Lincoln	
139. Fort Lincoln	466
*140. Seven-gun battery in front of Fort Lincoln	
141. Battery Jameson	80
*142. Five-gun battery to the right of Battery Jameson, No. 1	
*143. Battery to the right of Battery Jameson, No. 2	

DEFENSES OF WASHINGTON EAST OF THE ANACOSTIA RIVER

Forts and Batteries	Perimeter in Yards
144. Fort Mahan	354
*145. Battery Mahan; four guns	
146. Fort Chaplin	
147. Fort of Circular Form	
148. Fort on Kennedys Hill	
149. Fort Meigs	500
150. Battery Rucker	
151. Fort Dupont	200
152. Fort Davis	220
153. Fort Baker	492
154. Fort Wagner	160
155. Fort Ricketts	123
156. Fort Stanton	322
157. Fort Snyder	210
158. Fort Carroll	340
159. Battery Carroll; four guns	
160. Battery to the west of Fort Carroll	
161. Fort Greble	327
162. Battery Greble	
163. Battery to the south of Fort Greble	
164. Fort Foote	472

An Invitation to Help

The authors welcome comments on the new edition of this guide. Many of the quotes offered in the updated volume came from individuals who offered copies of letters, diaries, drawings, and photographs from their ancestors who were stationed in the forts during the war. New information about the forts themselves will always enhance future knowledge and interpretation of this subject. If you have information that you would like to share, consider making copies available to the library at Fort Ward Museum.

How to Visit a Fort and What to Look For

The authors have attempted to provide a reasonably comprehensive and user-friendly guide to Washington's Civil War forts. A good city map, some preparation reading via the suggested bibliography at the back of this guide, sturdy shoes, and a love of fresh air should accompany users of this book. We frankly recommend that the period from late fall through spring offers the best time to visit any Washington fort. The absence of foliage and natural pests makes the task of searching for earthworks, gun platforms, and fields of fire from the parapets infinitely more pleasurable and informative. Research and reading can attend the warmer months.

Typical Unrestored but Preserved Washington Fort Today, Fort Willard, Fairfax County, Virginia. *Authors' Collection*

National Park Service Stone and Plaque Marker. *Photo by Abbie Rowe, courtesy of National Park Service*

BE AWARE THAT SOME WORKS LISTED HEREIN REMAIN ON PRIVATE PROPERTY. ALSO, GOVERNMENTAL JURISDICTIONS HAVE RULES ABOUT PARK USE—NO METAL DETECTORS, PICNICKING IN APPROPRIATE AREAS, AND STRICTURES AGAINST MOTOR VEHICLE OR OTHER CONVEYANCE USE ON THE EARTHWORKS.

On arrival at a site, familiarize yourself with the physical security of the site. Look for interpretive waysides or markers.

Examine the sector maps for each fort to understand the historic landscape and how the modern terrain may have changed. Use the engineer diagram for each fort and try to orient it with earthen remains that exist on the ground. Appendix F features enlarged engineer drawings of selected forts that have significant earthen remains. Walk the site carefully to locate common features that exist at each site, such as the fort entrance or sally port, magazines, bombproofs, the fort well, and gun platforms. Note the dimensions, design, and other features that reflected human, not machine, construction during the Civil War. Visualize the site in its original wartime condition. Imagine the site stripped of vegetation, with whitewashed revetments and sod-covered parapets. Study the visual neighborhood of the fort and what it was designed to accomplish (protection of roads, ravines, and creeks). Examine the quartermaster plan for the fort to understand the location of the fort's barracks and campgrounds. Finally, enjoy the parklike setting and protect the site for posterity.

A Word about Maps

Because of the ever-changing road patterns in the metropolitan Washington area, we have not included modern maps with this guide. We recommend that each reader secure a good Washington and northern Virginia map booklet before embarking on the suggested fort tour. For those visitors interested in using navigation devices, we have included specific street address locations as much as possible. Many sites do not list a street address. Future editions of the guide will include GPS coordinates.

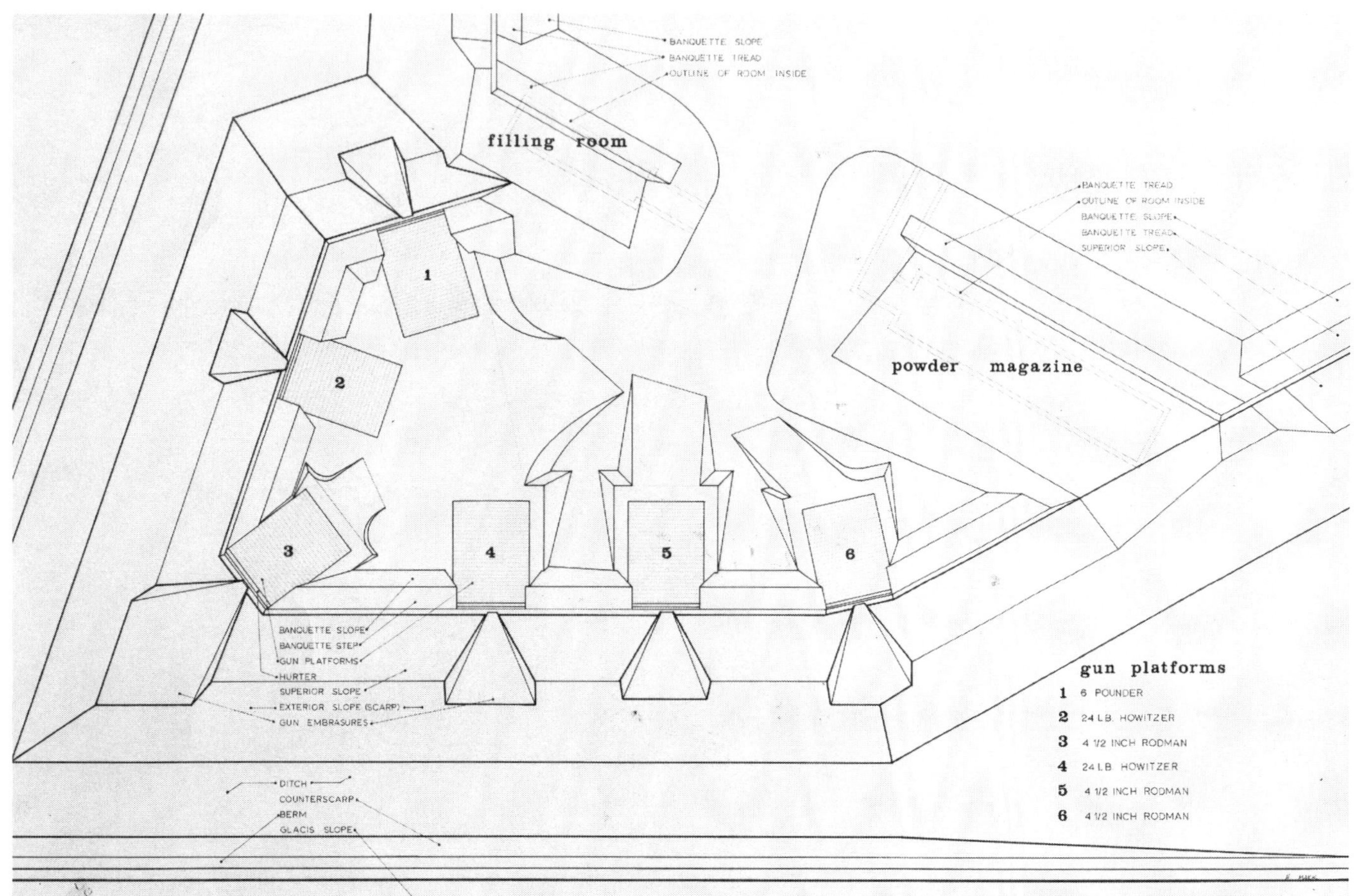

Diagram of Fort Features Northwest Bastion. *Fort Ward Museum Collection*

1

The Most Heavily Fortified City in North America

THE CIVIL WAR DEFENSES OF WASHINGTON

Humans have long sought to protect places of settlement, wealth, and governance. Political centers in particular, the seats of power and government, are often fortified. By the nineteenth century, European cities like Vienna, Berlin, and Madrid had gained fortifications; Paris and London had not, although the French capital certainly employed the latest technology of masonry and ordnance to do so by the latter half of the period. It was in the middle of this same century that Washington, D.C., because of its virulent Civil War, became the most heavily fortified capital and urban area in North America, if not the world. At the start of the war, the city had but one neglected and obsolescent fort. By war's end, Washington's formal system of fortifications comprised 164 forts and batteries; sixty-eight of these were considered to be major fortifications. There were ninety-three unarmed batteries, seven block houses, 807 cannon, more than thirteen miles of connecting rifle trenches, more miles of military communication roads, and a vast infrastructure of logistical support facilities that included everything from headquarter buildings to small supply sheds for ordnance and engineer tools. At the same time, the city itself had gone from a sleepy political backwater to a vast command-and-control, supply, and rehabilitation hub for preservation of the Union. The capture of Washington, like its Confederate counterpart in Richmond, Virginia, became a cardinal objective during the war in the eastern theater. Indeed, Washington's earthen, field fortification system performed admirably in preventing this outcome for four long years.

From the start, the American way of war was offensive, not defensive. Vast field armies of volunteers were raised to fight the war. However, Union and Confederate authorities soon recognized the need for insurance in the form of fortifications to protect their capitals just in case the field armies failed or became stalemated. Field fortifications systems like the Defenses of Washington provided a deterrent. The Army of the Potomac was the sword, and the Defenses of Washington provided the shield to protect the symbol of the Union. Since static defensive systems could not promise the glamour of quick victory that offensive campaigning might, philosophical battles between generals and civil administrators always attended the subject of how best to protect Mr. Lincoln's City. Yet "deterrence" has always held a place of prominence in warfare. It did during the Civil War as it does today. The protection of Washington by aerospace defense and homeland security continues the story into the twenty-first century.

THE NATURE OF THE THREAT—1861

The nation's capital in 1861 was a city filled with rumors, fear, and uncertainty—ingredients that are present to a degree in all wars. As a military post, the city had no natural strength. Sprawled along the low-lying banks of the muddy Potomac, Washington was better known for its architectural anomalies and abominable streets than for qualities of impregnability. Most astute observers thought that the city was accessible to an enemy from all sides. The previous experience of the capture of the nascent capital by the British in August 1814 gave little comfort. Grandiose postwar plans had yielded first Fort Warburton and then Fort Washington at Digges Point across from President George Washington's country home, Mount Vernon. However, most postwar plans remained unrealized. Fort Washington became a magnificent river-protection fortification, a stone masonry edifice with a full garrison and thirty 24-pounder seacoast guns according to ordnance returns for 1850. Three years later, men and guns were removed, and on the eve of secession, one alcoholic ordnance sergeant manned the unarmed ramparts and provided the city's main protection—protecting Washington against water, not land attack.[1]

For all its shortcomings, Washington became both a symbol and a sword in the eyes of the North. The city was the symbol of the Union, resolute against sectional opposition. As a sword, Washington literally became the spearhead of the federal military effort, for here the eastern forces assembled, equipped, trained, and went across the Potomac to fight in Virginia. A "shield" of protection became imperative for this vital area. The system of fortifications provided that shield.

The Lincoln administration's concern for the safety of the nation's capital may be traced to the spring of 1861. Prior to the fall of Fort Sumter, Washington's military defense was much more an illusion than a reality.[2] Unlike other national capitals, the city never had large complements of garrison or parade forces. Washington, early in 1861, could boast of little more than the usual number of clerks and bureau chiefs and a sprinkling of gold-laced officers from the Navy Yard.

Uncompleted Capitol. *National Archives*

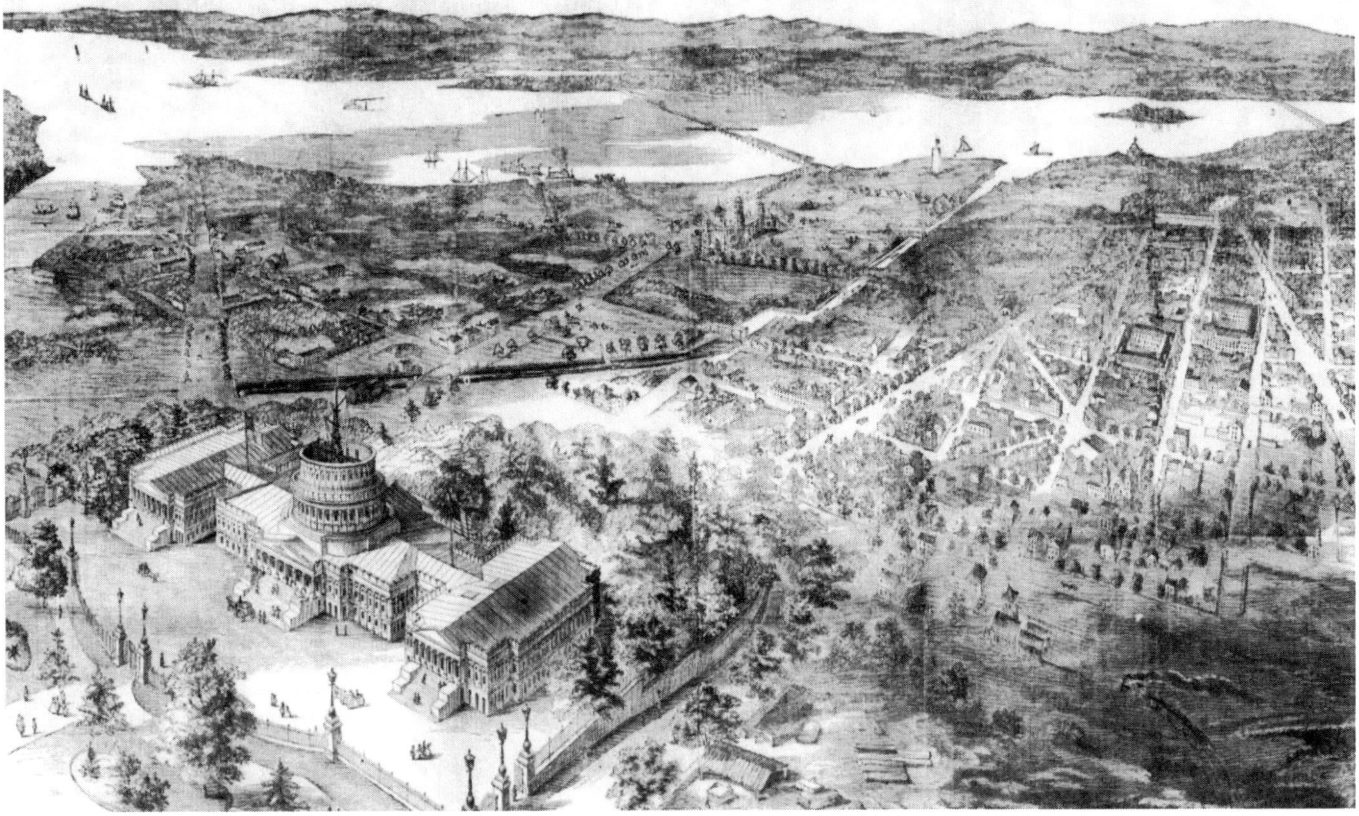

Bird's-Eye View of Washington, 1861. *National Archives*

Lane's Battalion of Volunteers at White House. *National Archives*

U.S. Marines at Marine Barracks, DC—*Harper's Weekly*, September 14, 1861. *National Archives*

Colonel Charles P. Stone, newly appointed inspector general for the city, summarized available forces:

> The only regular troops near the capital of the country were three or four hundred marines at the Marine barracks, and three officers and fifty-three men of ordnance at the Washington Arsenal. The old militia system had been abandoned without being legally abolished, and Congress had passed no law establishing a new one.[3]

In fact, the District of Columbia militia numbered but four innocuous organizations of questionable loyalty.

President Lincoln's call for volunteers on April 15, 1861, fanned the flames of secession even in neighboring Maryland. For a time, Washington was isolated from the North. Telegraph communications were severed and railroad bridges burned north of Baltimore. Visible signs of panic were etched on the faces of many Washingtonians. Business came to a virtual standstill as residents fled from the District.[4] The arrival of such volunteer units as the Seventh New York, Eighth Massachusetts, and First Rhode Island by April 26 provided only limited relief. The seeds of concern for the safety of the capital had been sown in the minds of administration officials. These concerns would remain for four long years.

The First Response

Across the Potomac lay a hostile Virginia. On April 17, 1861, that state had ratified the ordinance of secession. Confederate authorities now could seriously endanger the northern capital by placing fortifications and artillery on Arlington Heights and at Alexandria. Giving first consideration to Washington's safety, as soon as sufficient troops arrived, the Lincoln administration decided to deter such Confederate moves by seizing footholds on Virginia soil.

At 2:00 A.M. on the moonlit night of May 23–24, eight federal regiments under the command of Colonel (later Major General) J. F. K. Mansfield crossed the river and took up positions in Virginia. One column under Major W. H. Wood moved by the Georgetown Aqueduct. Another column under Major (later Major General) Samuel P. Heintzelman crossed over the long Bridge. A third contingent led by Colonel Elmer Ellsworth went by steamers to land at the Alexandria wharves.[5] The morning of May 24 dawned mild and bright. Young blue-clad soldiers sprawled in bivouacs under shade trees near Robert E. Lee's abandoned Arlington house. Engineer officers hastily laid out field fortifications nearby. The Washington *Evening Star* of that date reported,

> At 4 o'clock this morning a large number of government wagons went across the Long Bridge loaded with picks and shovels, and all manner of tools . . . and accompanied with a full corps of carpenters and workmen. The United States forces are now busily throwing up fortifications on the heights on the Virginia shore, commencing at daybreak.[6]

HARPER'S WEEKLY
A JOURNAL OF CIVILIZATION

VOL. V.—No. 226.] NEW YORK, SATURDAY, APRIL 27, 1861. [PRICE FIVE CENTS.

Entered according to Act of Congress, in the Year 1861, by Harper & Brothers, in the Clerk's Office of the District Court for the Southern District of New York.

THE BOMBARDMENT OF FORT SUMTER.

We devote most of our space this week to illustrations of this memorable event. On pages 264 and 265 will be found a general picture of the BOMBARDMENT, SEEN FROM FORT JOHNSON. On page 260 we give a picture of the INTERIOR OF FORT SUMTER during the terrible rain of shot and shell from the Confederate batteries; and on page 261 an accurate MAP OF THE HARBOR OF CHARLESTON, showing the relative position of Sumter and of the batteries by which it was surrounded. We now subjoin, by way of record, a brief account of the transaction.

On 8th April Lieutenant Talbot and Mr. Chew, messengers from the President, informed General Beauregard that the Government would supply Major Anderson with provisions—which were denied him by the South Carolinians—peaceably if they could, forcibly if they must. General Beauregard referred the message to his Government at Montgomery, and was ordered to reduce the fort. He summoned Major Anderson to surrender on 11th. The reply was:

"I have the honor to acknowledge the receipt of your communication, demanding the evacuation of this fort, and to say, in reply thereto, that it is a demand with which I regret that my sense of honor and my obligations to my Government prevent my compliance."

Accordingly at 4.27 A.M. on 12th fire was opened from Fort Moultrie on Fort Sumter. To this Major Anderson replied with three of his barbette guns, after which the batteries on Mount Pleasant, Cummings's Point, and the Floating Battery opened a brisk fire of shot and shell. Major Anderson did not reply, except at long intervals, until between seven and eight o'clock, when he brought into action the two tiers of guns looking toward Fort Moultrie and Stevens's iron battery. The fire continued brisk all day. At 7 P.M. a heavy rain-storm caused a cessation of hostilities till 11 P.M. Major Anderson appears to have employed the interval in repairing damages. At or about 11 P.M. the fire recommenced, and a shell was thrown into Fort Sumter from each battery every twenty minutes during the night. With daybreak the heavy bombardment recommenced from all the batteries; the fire was returned from Fort Sumter with vigor until about 8 A.M., when Fort Sumter was perceived to be on fire. Major Anderson's fighting then slackened, but the fire of the besiegers increased in intensity. At about 10 A.M. Major Anderson lowered his flag to half-mast in token of distress; perhaps as a signal to the United States vessels which were lying at anchor outside the bar, unable to get into the harbor so as to participate in the conflict. About half past ten one or two explosions took place in the fort; it has since been ascertained that these proceeded from the heating of piles of shells. Meanwhile the fire progressed rapidly: the whole roof of the barracks was a sheet of flame, and flames and smoke issued thickly from the casemates. At or about eleven Major Anderson ceased firing, and devoted his whole attention to putting out the fire. At about noon some of his men were noticed on the wharf of the fort handing in buckets of water; the besiegers' fire, which had never slackened, was at once directed upon them. In a few minutes afterward Major Anderson hauled down his flag. A boat then put off, containing ex-Governor Manning, Major D. R. Jones, and Colonel Charles Allston, to arrange the terms of surrender, which were the same as those offered on the 11th. These were official. They stated that all proper facilities would be afforded for the removal of Major Anderson and his command, together with the company arms and property, and all private property, to any post in the United States he might elect. Major Anderson stated that he surrendered his sword to General Beauregard as the representative of the Confederate Government. General Beauregard said he would not receive it from so brave a man.

The correspondent of the Press telegraphs on 14th:

"The last act in the drama of Fort Sumter has been concluded. Major Anderson has evacuated, and, with his command, departed by the steamer *Isabel* from the harbor. He saluted his flag, and the company, then forming on the parade-ground, marched out upon the wharf, with drum and fife playing 'Yankee Doodle.'

"During the salute a pile of cartridges burst in one of the casemates, killing two men and wounding four others. One was buried in the fort with military honors. The other will be buried by the soldiers of South Carolina.

"The scene in the city after the raising of the flag of truce and the surrender is indescribable; the people were perfectly wild. Men on horseback rode through the streets proclaiming the news, amidst the greatest enthusiasm.

"On the arrival of the officers from the fort they were marched through the streets, followed by an immense crowd, hurrahing, shouting, and yelling with excitement.

"The number of soldiers in the fort was about seventy, besides twenty-five workmen, who assisted at the guns. His stock of provisions was almost exhausted, however. He would have been starved out in two more days.

"The entrance to the fort is mined, and the officers were told to be careful, even after the surrender, on account of the heat, lest it should explode.

"Several fire companies were immediately sent down to Fort Sumter to put out the fire, and any amount of assistance was offered.

"The fort is burned into a mere shell; not a particle of wood-work can be found. The guns on one side of the parapet are entirely dismounted, others split, while the gun-carriages are knocked into splinters.

"The flames have destroyed every thing. Both officers and soldiers were obliged to lie on their faces in the casemates to prevent suffocation."

SWEARING IN VOLUNTEERS AT WASHINGTON.

We publish herewith, from a sketch by our special artist in Washington, a picture of the SWEARING IN OF THE VOLUNTEERS called out by the President for the defense of the Federal Capital. The Washington *Star* describes the scene thus:

"As we went to press yesterday the volunteer companies were responding to the call of the War Department for volunteers to defend the city of Washington from assault. In the case of some of the companies a portion of the members declined to take the oath required by the Department of all soldiers mustered into the United States service, and the deficit in the ranks of said companies thereby brought them below the standard requirement as to numbers, and they were not received by the Government.

"The following is the form of the oath administered to the volunteers who were mustered into the service of the United States yesterday. It is nothing more than the usual army oath. It was administered by General Thomas, of the District of Columbia Militia:

"'I, ——— ———, do solemnly swear that I will bear true allegiance to the United States of America; that I will serve them honestly and faithfully against all enemies or

GENERAL THOMAS SWEARING IN THE VOLUNTEERS CALLED INTO THE SERVICE OF THE UNITED STATES AT WASHINGTON, D. C.

D.C. Militia Taking Oath to United States Government—*Harper's Weekly*, April 27, 1861. *National Archives*

71st New York Drilling at Washington Navy Yard. *Library of Congress*

Aqueduct Bridge at Georgetown, D.C. *Library of Congress*

These first isolated works bore little resemblance to a defense system, but they did provide a foundation for future development. Situated for the most part on low ground, they were intended only as footholds in Virginia. Forts Corcoran, Haggerty, Bennett, Runyon, Jackson, and Ellsworth were the first forts that were constructed that would become the Defenses of Washington. Over the next seven weeks, all efforts were made to complete this initial formal defense of the southern approach to the capital. Little thought or attention was given to more general studies or the reconnaissance necessary for planning a circumferential defense system.[7] Even Colonel Mansfield, now commanding the Department of Washington, espoused complacency when he announced that northern approaches to Washington could be "readily fortified at any time by a system of redoubts encircling the city." The army engineers, preoccupied with the Virginia forts, also failed to appreciate any more comprehensive need.

The state of the capital's defensive fortifications did not escape the notice of the southern forces. In a letter sent from Washington City on June 29, 1861, by the spy D. L. Dalton to Confederate president Jefferson Davis, Dalton told how Federals under Colonel Charles P. Stone had set up "a kind of picket line from the Chain Bridge to the Point of Rocks, on the Maryland side" of the Potomac upstream from the city. Thus, some 4,000 men screened any flank approach to the capital. Similarly, troop encampments just north of the city on "Calorama" or "Meridian Hill" as well as a regiment at the arsenal, about 2,500 men at the Navy Yard, and a regiment at "Beals Bridge on the Eastern Branch" protected north and east of Washington. "There are no field works constructed on the Potomac below Georgetown, or North or East of the city," he wrote. South of the city across the Potomac River lay the army buildup and defensive works. Noted the spy, "I have not been over to see them, but from what I have heard of them they are quite formidable, and extend from about the 'three Sisters' above Georgetown to Alexandria, having been constructed under the direction of skilful [*sic*] engineers." He particularly debunked the militia volunteers as "the very dregs of creation, collected from cities" who "can't stand the sun, a brisk march of a mile would leave very many by the wayside, and the offices are general 'Sunday Militia,' ala Col. [Benjamin] Butler." Moreover, he expressed, most of the northerners were Democrats "wholly ignorant of the principles involved in the contest, or the issue between the sections." "They fired on our flag" was about all any of them assigned as the reason for their taking up arms, in Dalton's opinion. "Most of them alleged that they volunteered to defend the Capitol." Dalton offered an interesting view on the role of a "fifth column" of southern-sympathizing informants and spies that was always an internal threat with the southern fabric of Washington's society. "The most alarming feature of the contest," he commented, "has all the time to me, been the apprehension that, though not the formed object of the North—still their purpose was to destroy the institution of Slavery.[8]

Despite the wartime influx of northern soldiery, civilians to work in the city, and the first emancipation in the nation—the freeing of Washington's slave population in April 1861—Dalton's ilk forever remained a seedbed of collaboration with Confederates, operating clandestinely and sometimes openly in the national capital region.

Building a Defense System

Chaos enveloped Washington during the weeks following the rout of Union forces at the First Battle of Bull Run (or Manassas) on July 21, 1861. It became apparent to military authorities that in addition to rebuilding the army, a more elaborate system of formal protection would have to be constructed for Washington. Concentration on fort construction began after Major General George B. McClellan succeeded Brigadier General Irvin McDowell as Union army commander on the Potomac. McClellan realized that one of his most pressing demands involved the city's immediate safety and redeployment of troops for defense.[9] But at the same time, he wanted to free his growing army for offensive field service.

Undaunted by the sizable circumference of the city, the "Little Napoleon" (as McClellan was called) enthusiastically endorsed proposals for a system of forty-eight forts, lunettes, redoubts, and batteries, mounting 300 guns. In August 1861, McClellan placed Major (later Brevet Major General) John Gross Barnard of the Corps of Engineers in charge of the construction project. Thus to this capable officer passed a task that would become increasingly costly, frustrating and to a large extent unappreciated over the course of the war.[10]

At first, attention went to completing and perfecting the Arlington Heights positions. Initially, redoubts and forts were located to protect strategic points and guard roads. Later, as the engineers found time, filler works were constructed, designed to handle weak or relatively unguarded spaces. The development of the network of fortifications was systematic. Once the sites for the forts had been determined, the stern law of military necessity governed possession of the land. Lines of rifle pits, massive earthworks, and military roads cut into cultivated fields, orchards, and even dwellings, and other structures were ripped down.[11] Despite injustices to local property owners, military authorities felt that the interests of national security dictated such harsh action.

Fort Pennsylvania—Camp of the 113th Regiment New York State Volunteers. *Authors' Collection*

Head Quarters,
Military Department of
Washington, June 17, 1861.

Pass H. W. Hubbell
over the Bridges & within the lines

By order of General Mansfield, Commanding:

Drake De Kay
Aide-de-Camp.

TURN OVER

A Famous Drake DeKay Pass for Access to Washington. *Authors' Collection*

The main forts, placed nearly half a mile apart, had parapets twelve to eighteen feet thick on exposed fronts. Engineers and laborers then surrounded each work with an "abatis" of cut trees, entwined and placed with branches pointed away from the line of defense. The engineers meticulously based their work on D. H. Mahan's *A Treatise on Field Fortifications*.[12]

The processes of construction must have been fascinating to behold. One observer from the Seventy-Ninth New York "Highlanders" described the process of felling trees:

> It was an interesting sight to witness the simultaneous falling [*sic*] of a whole hill-side of timber, the choppers would begin at the foot of the hill, the line extending for perhaps a mile, and cut only part way through the tree, and in this way work up to the crest, leaving the top row so that a single blow would bring down the tree—then, when all was ready, the bugle would sound as a signal, and the last stroke of the axe be given, which brought down the top row; these falling on those below would bring them down, and like the billow on the surface of the ocean, the forest would fall with a crash like mighty thunder.[13]

Such a process of deforestation, he added quickly, "was the hardest kind of manual labor; spades were trumps and every man held a full hand."

Proper defense of Alexandria also concerned military authorities. This Virginia port and railroad center was a valuable supply point. Thus, the fortifications south of the Potomac were extended to cover the city. However, no continuous line of rifle pits connected the separate forts, and there were many open intervals in the so-called defense line.

Low water in the Potomac during the late summer and fall of 1861 caused officers charged with the defense construction to reevaluate the urgency of fortifying northern approaches to Washington.[14] As with the early Virginia forts, works north of the Potomac River had been located to command arteries of travel. Fort Pennsylvania (later renamed Fort Reno) was the first work laid out in August. It controlled the turnpike from Rockville leading to Georgetown. Fort Massachusetts (later called Fort Stevens) covered the Seventh Street Road with Forts Slocum and Totten positioned to the east as auxiliary works. Further to the east, Fort Lincoln, on a high elevation above the turnpike to Baltimore, guarded both that artery and a nearby railroad line between the cities. Wide gaps between these works soon filled with supporting fortifications.

Barnard and his small coterie of professionals also built massive fieldworks and auxiliary batteries atop such strategic points as the ridge east of the Anacostia River (or Eastern Branch) and above the

Major John Gross Barnard. *National Archives*

"receiving reservoir" of the Aqueduct, Washington's water supply along the Potomac River. The engineer officers assigned to the task hardly numbered more than a dozen at any given time.[15] Assisted by civilian overseers, they were hard pressed to cope with problems of terrain, weather, temperamental volunteer officers, erratic soldier fatigue units, and hired African American and white civilian laborers. Nonetheless, they could point with some pride to a rather imposing array of statistics concerning the formal defenses of Washington by the end of 1861. Twenty-three forts south of the Potomac, fourteen forts and three batteries between the Potomac and Anacostia rivers, and eleven forts beyond the Anacostia—a total of forty-eight defensive works now encircled the city. Great variety existed in their shapes and sizes. The forts south of the Potomac were generally larger, for they guarded the more dangerous front.

The majority of the forts were enclosed earthworks, although several like Forts Craig, Tillinghast, and Scott (all south of the Potomac) were lunettes with stockaded gorges. At first, armament consisted chiefly of 24- and 32-pounder cannon mounted on seacoast carriages. While this was not satisfactory to Barnard and the engineers, nothing else was readily available early in the war. Later, a limited number of

Railroad Shops at Alexandria, Virginia. *National Archives*

24-pounder siege guns, rifled Parrott cannon, and field guns of lighter caliber were added. Each fort had an ammunition magazine for 100 rounds.[16]

Conceptual Differences

During most of 1861, Washington had some form of organized field army nearby to provide for its safety. This army could act as the primary bulwark against any attacking Confederate force. With the advent of favorable weather in the spring of 1862 and the impatience of the Lincoln administration, Congress, and the northern public, McClellan wanted to move this field army southward against Richmond. Once more, "On to Richmond!" became the battle cry. And so, a crucial test of Washington's ring of forts would come as "Little Mac," as his soldiers called him, led his Army of the Potomac aboard steamboats for a voyage to the Virginia peninsula.

In agreeing to this move, Lincoln had stipulated as early as January 31, 1862, that Washington should be left secure against potential attack.[17] The president relied on McClellan as general in chief and his corps commanders to decide how to make the city secure. On March 13, a council of McClellan's corps commanders declared that from 25,000 to 40,000 men were needed to defend the city.[18] These men would use the fort system as a base for guarding the city. Before his departure on April 1, 1862, McClellan reported that 73,456 men and 109 pieces of light artillery protected Washington. These figures included 35,467 soldiers in the Shenandoah Valley.[19] President Lincoln became alarmed when, on April 2, Brigadier General James

Camp of the 31st Pennsylvania Infantry near Washington. *Library of Congress*

Regimental Officers of 2nd Pennsylvania Heavy Artillery at Fort Lincoln. *Ward,* History of the Second Pennsylvania Heavy Artillery

Checking a Pass at Mason Island Ferry. *Library of Congress*

Wadsworth, in charge of the Military District of Washington, said that he actually had only 19,022 "new and imperfectly disciplined men fit for duty." Secretary of War, Edwin M. Stanton sent officers to verify the facts and it was reported that the city was far from secure.[20] In Mr. Lincoln's mind, the men in the Shenandoah Valley could hardly constitute a reliable defense force for Washington. Too many miles separated them from the city.

Much to McClellan's consternation, on April 3, Lincoln directed,

> The Secretary of War will order that one or the other of the corps of General McDowell and General Sumner, [to] remain in front of Washington until further orders from the War Department, to operate, at or in the direction of Manassas Junction or elsewhere, as occasion may require, that the other corps not so ordered to remain, go forward to General McClellan as soon as possible; that General McClellan commence his forward movements from his new base at once, and that such incidental modifications as the foregoing may render proper be also made.[21]

Lincoln's decision had merit. Elaborate as Washington's ring of fortifications appeared to be, it was hardly impregnable. The Army of the Potomac operating 100 miles distant and auxiliary forces pinned down in the Shenandoah would not and could not be immediately available if the Confederates suddenly advanced directly on the city. Meanwhile, public opinion basked in the glow of Union victories at Forts Henry and Donelson in Tennessee and expected McClellan to end the war in Virginia by quickly capturing Richmond. Congress reflected this opinion, appropriating $150,000 for completing the existing defenses but also stipulating "that no part of the sum hereby appropriated shall be expended on any works hereafter to be commenced."[22] As they saw it, there would be no future need to protect Washington.

The officials responsible for Washington's safety realized that the existing forts hardly constituted a thoroughly integrated line of defense. Rather, they said, such detached works as then existed around the city could provide only "points d'appui" (points of support) assisting a field force defending the city.

Artillery Park at the Washington Arsenal Grounds. *Library of Congress*

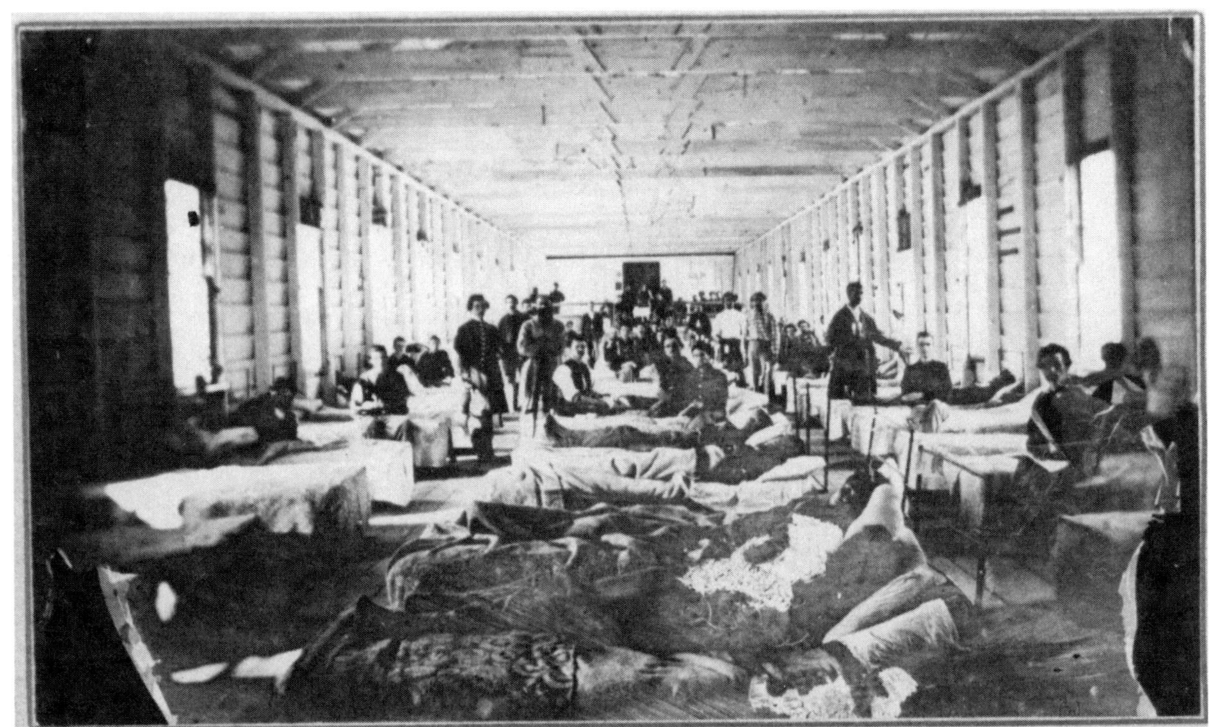

Washington as a Hospital Center. *U.S. Army Military History Institute*

Ward in Armory Square Hospital. *U.S. Army Military History Institute*

That was the whole idea; a garrison alone could hardly defend against any superior Confederate attack. So it was little wonder that the situation had approached crisis proportions by August and September 1862. All that spring, Thomas "Stonewall" Jackson's movements in the valley gave Lincoln and other Washington authorities many sleepless nights. The capital reacted with even greater fear at the end of summer when Lee's whole Army of Northern Virginia came to within one day's march of the capital after defeating John Pope at the Second Battle of Bull Run (or Manassas). The threat engendered by the proximity of Lee's army revealed the inadequacy of the existing defenses. Barnard expressed the need for further improvements, writing on August 28 to Major General Halleck (succeeding McClellan as general-in-chief) "I feel called upon to state that against any serious attack I have no means of holding the line of fortifications from Fort Richardson along the front of Arlington to Fort Corcoran, nor of those of Chain Bridge, nor the line on this [Maryland] side of the Potomac."[23]

Lee's Lost Opportunity

Apparently, garrisons in the forts had been withdrawn the preceding week and sent to reinforce Pope. In fact, contingents of the Army of the Potomac, pulled back from the peninsula, likewise went off to reinforce Pope. Only a token cadre of regiments remained in the forts, a fact that distressed Barnard greatly.[24] As sounds of gunfire echoed from the Manassas plains, he continued to ask for more help and shifted his meager garrisons to cover all points. Actually, two full army corps had landed at Alexandria and could have been put into the southern defense line. And, although defeated, the combined units of Pope and McClellan still provided a perceptible "sword" for Washington. Lee recognized that 73,000 Federals, reorganized under McClellan, in addition to the "shield" provided by the fortifications, posed a barrier to capture the capital.[25] When Stonewall Jackson was rebuffed at Chantilly on September 1, Lee chose to shy away from direct assault on Washington. Bold as the victorious Confederate commander appeared to be after perhaps his greatest success, confrontation with Washington's forts and McClellan's army did not suit him. Lee

Cavalry Depot at Camp Stoneman, Giesboro Point, D.C. *Library of Congress*

Washington as a Supply Base—Army Clothing and Equipment Depot. *U.S. Army Military History Institute*

turned his columns northward into Maryland to feed his soldiers.

Lee left a frightened city in his wake. On September 2, McClellan assumed command of the defenses and all troops charged with the protection of the city. Clerks and government employees were organized for defense. Large details of troops worked vigorously on the forts. Engineer authorities remained pessimistic about the ability of the defensive lines to contain an enemy assault. Nevertheless, many of the troops who did the spadework were somewhat more optimistic. One wrote to his wife that a large force was "within signal call" and that "such is the strength of our fortifications that we can repulse a vastly superior force." He was convinced that "Washington cannot be taken by any force advancing upon it from the west [south of the Potomac]."[26] But the Confederates were now north of the Potomac and northwest of Washington. Four days before the battle of Antietam, Barnard wrote that "an enemy in force, say to the North of us, may make a sudden effort that way and break through the intervals."[27]

Recruiting Poster for the 1st New York Heavy Artillery. *Library of Congress*

The mere presence of the Confederate army less than fifty miles from the city in August and September caused more than the usual official concern about the state of Washington's security. Unmanageable heavy artillery in the forts, wide gaps between individual works, and the need for better river defenses were among the more obvious deficiencies. As the gray tide receded from Antietam, Federal leaders once again called for reevaluation of the defense of Washington. Secretary of War Stanton responded by creating a commission on October 25, 1862, to study the defenses. Its members included Barnard and Brigadier Generals Joseph G. Totten, chief of engineers; W. F. Barry, chief of artillery; Montgomery C. Meigs, quartermaster general; and G. W. Cullum, chief of staff to the general-in-chief.

STUDYING A WAY FORWARD

On due deliberation, the commission pronounced that 25,000 men were required for infantry garrisons. They based this figure on computations of two men per yard of front perimeter and one man per yard of rear perimeter. The board also established a requirement

Gun Drill in an Unidentified Fort. *National Archives*

for 9,000 artillerymen (three reliefs for each gun) and 3,000 cavalry. The infantrymen could camp near the assigned works, maintain rigorous drill schedules, and be available in case of emergency. Cannoneers, however, whose training required more time, were to be stationed in each fort or battery. Once the gunners had learned the technical handling of the guns, range finding, and disposition of the armament, they would remain on permanent assignment in the defenses.

Maintenance of a mobile force appeared as a key element in the commission's report. Such a force, numbering no less than 25,000 men, would maneuver outside the defenses against any enemy attacking column. The commission hastened to add that "against more serious attacks from the main body of the enemy, the Capital must depend upon the concentration of its entire armies in Virginia or Maryland."[28] They should precede or follow any movement of the enemy seriously threatening the capital.

Other commission recommendations included numerous individual additions or changes to existing works and the construction of five or six new forts. The commission also proposed adding a new feature to the defense system by the construction of works to defend the river from naval attack. Fort Washington, the masonry relic downriver from the city, had long since ceased to provide adequate protection in that quarter.

Suggestions of the commission were vigorously pursued during the early part of 1863. No immediate danger threatened the capital as the Army of the Potomac floundered through ill-fated campaigns near Fredericksburg. However, Major General Joseph Hooker's Chancellorsville campaign produced some labor shortages. The work force for the defenses normally relied on troop details, African Americans or "contrabands," and, as a last resort, hired laborers. The withdrawal of potential combat troops left Barnard and his engineers shorthanded. He was forced to employ 1,000 hired civilians to complete work recommended by the commission. Many such workers came from places as far distant as New York City.[29]

This turn of events measurably reduced the $200,000 appropriation of that year, earmarked for improvements to the defenses.

The problem of adequate labor plagued Barnard and his subordinates throughout the war. Whether they tried to use apathetic soldiers, sickly convalescents, or contrabands, the result was usually the same—poor workmanship, shortage of manpower, and ill-kept schedules. Common laborers received from $1.00 to $1.25 per day; Foremen commanded $2.50 per day. Considering that the work usually required 500 to 1,000 men, the fiscal expenditures reached alarming heights.[30]

Still, 1863 saw progress. New works, such as Forts Whipple, Berry, and C. F. Smith (named after Federal officers who had died during the war), were added to the defenses south of the Potomac. Additional field gun emplacements, exemplified by Batteries Terrill and Sill, were built north of the river. The engineers enlarged several forts, including Massachusetts and the group protecting the reservoir above Chain Bridge, renaming those Forts Stevens and Sumner after fallen generals. No wonder that E. G. Jones stationed with the 117th New York infantry at Fort Baker, east of the Anacostia, wrote a friend on January 21, 1863,

> If Washington ever falls into the hands of the enemy he will posess [*sic*] himself of an indefinite number of cannons for every hilltop in a circle of forty miles circumference is covered with them and this number is daily increasing. Washington is situated in a great basin and is completely surrounded by a high ridge of hills. At some points it is invulnerable. It would be the ruin of the most desperate army in the universe to endeavor to approach the city from the direction of Poolsville [*sic*] or Rockville. The chain of defenses on that side of the city from Fort Alexander to Fort De Russey [*sic*] is strong in every element of strength—too much so I think for any attacking force to be successful. If the Rebs ever attempt to cross the plains below and to the north of those fortifications they will have a taste of our Fredericksburg and I can wish them nothing worse.

On the other hand, the Potomac River remained the one gap in Washington's defenses. It bisected the defensive lines at two places: Chain Bridge to the north and Jones Point to the south. A threat of attack by the river existed as long as European powers like Great Britain and France showed a willingness to aid the Confederate cause. Although Fort Washington had been quickly garrisoned in the 1861 emergency, authorities never placed much confidence in its strength. So, until 1863, river defense rested largely with the U.S. Navy.[31]

The small unsung Potomac Flotilla contributed to the war effort by torpedo removal, river patrols, and neutralization of Confederate shore batteries downriver near Quantico in Virginia. Originally organized in April 1861 for service in the Washington and Chesapeake Bay area, the lightly armed steamers of the flotilla provided the only security Washington had on the river for much of the war. Of course, they would have been of little use against European naval squadrons.

In 1863, Battery Rodgers at Alexandria and Fort Foote across the river in southern Maryland were constructed to remedy this situation. The experience gained by the engineer officers during the preceding two years of fort building enabled them to make these positions "model works." Fort Foote was regarded as the most elaborate, in its internal arrangements, of all the defensive works around Washington. Both positions formed water batteries and mounted 200-pounder rifled Parrotts and fifteen-inch Rodmans. Their parapets were from twenty to twenty-five feet in thickness. Positioned on either bank of the Potomac, they could deliver a deadly crossfire against vessels attempting passage in the narrow channel. These works, however, never received the crucial test of combat.

LIFE AND COMPLACENCY IN THE DEFENSES OF WASHINGTON

Soldiers manning Washington's fortifications saw little, if any, actual fighting during the early years of the war. Rumors of battle continually circulated, but the occasional shot exchanged with a bushwhacker or prowling "guerrilla" from Major John Mosby's partisan band largely constituted the extent of combat. Life passed tranquilly enough for those within the defenses, if monotonously at times. "With the exception of drilling, guard mounting, and inspection of knapsacks," recalled one enlisted man, "we had but little to do, and the time passed pleasantly enough, each day shortening our term of service."[32] Heavy artillery units did receive infantry and bayonet instruction in addition to the prescribed drill of their respective service. Any variety in the drill, however, came only from more ingenious officers. Little wonder, then, that veterans of the Army of the Potomac derided duty in Washington's fortifications as "soft assignments."

Life proved just as felicitous for garrison officers. Favored with greater privileges, many of the young men were welcome guests in the homes of local society. Generally, though, the officers shared the tedium of the same drill as their men, broken occasionally by assignments to courts-martial duty in the city. Major George F. Chamberlin of the 11th Vermont wrote from Fort Totten in January 1863, "I am destined to spend the most of my term of service on military courts and boards of some kind."[33] Even the usually indefatigable

Barnard wrote dejectedly to the War Department in January 1864,

> It is proper to state that I had intended on the close of the campaign of 1862 to ask to be assigned to duty with troops believing that after serving two years as an Engineer Officer I was entitled to share with my Juniors the advantages in the way of promotion attending the command of troops and the still more important advantage of instructing myself by actual practice in all the duties of the soldier, convinced that such practice was important to me even for a complete knowledge of my duties as an Engineer.[34]

A degree of complacency prevailed in the city, and government officials became overconfident as the months and years passed with no direct assault on Washington. Barnard and his colleagues voiced more fear of cavalry raids than of any main attack. True, Lee's invasion of Pennsylvania temporarily produced enough concern that mechanics, laborers, and 100 army sutlers offered their services for potential defense of the city.[35] Although Lee passed far to the west of Washington, using the Shenandoah Valley as passage northward, the action was indeed intended to threaten the capital indirectly. The Army of the Potomac, however, imposed itself between the Confederates and Washington. While the withdrawal of troops from the defenses to reinforce this army reduced Washington's garrisons somewhat, these additional troops at the same time enhanced the army's "maneuver" element.[36] Then, all at once, the danger diminished as news of Gettysburg reached the city.

By the end of the year, sixty forts, ninety-three batteries, and 837 guns encircled the city. Twenty-three thousand men were in position to man the defenses. A connected system of fortifications now existed by which every important point, at 800- to 1,000-yard intervals, was occupied by an enclosed fort. A battery of field guns swept every important approach or depression not covered by the forts. Rifle pits, furnishing emplacement for two ranks of men, connected the whole perimeter. As one bloody year followed another, Washington authorities felt that the city was capable of withstanding any threat from the Confederacy.

The Moment of Maximum Danger—Early's Raid

Insufficient garrisons again struck the defenses of Washington in the spring of 1864. The Army of the Potomac, as it moved south accompanied by the new general-in-chief, Lieutenant General Ulysses S. Grant, required all available reinforcements to fill its depleted ranks. Washington's forts yielded its able-bodied men and disciplined infantry. Semi-invalid Veteran Reserves then took their place on guard duty. Even

Confederate Lieutenant General Jubal Early. *National Archives*

Barnard was reassigned to the fighting front. Despite admonitions from the engineers, heavy losses in the Wilderness and around Spotsylvania caused removal of the well-trained heavy artillery regiments from Washington garrisons. Most of these experienced gunners, numbering nearly 18,000 men, were sent to Grant as infantry. Replacing these skilled technicians were state militiamen serving as "100-day soldiers" brought into federal service for 100 days so that regular troops could be sent to the front.

Such were the conditions in the early summer when Confederate forces under Lieutenant General Jubal Early made the most ambitious attempt to capture Washington during the war. It remains a central point in the history of the defenses, the Civil War, and the nation's history. George Perkins of the 6th Massachusetts Independent Battery certainly held no high regard for the city, as he commented in a dispatch to the *Middlesex Journal* on June 12, "Washington is a monstrous humbug" with only the public buildings saving it "from an appearance of poverty." Consisting chiefly of public buildings, hospitals, and government corrals, the residents subsisted mainly "by working for and swindling the government" and especially swindling the soldiery. He continued with the thoughts that half the females in the city were courtesans and that every second house was a barber shop and the remainder restaurants. However, he did note the imposing fortifications girdling the city "which have cost so much labor and expense." Clustering along the ridges with flag and staff signifying the situation of a redoubt, Perkins boasted, "This chain of forts is perfect on both sides of the Potomac."[37]

Confederate leaders in Richmond and particularly Robert E. Lee meant to test Washington's defenses. A demonstration against Washington might profoundly shock the war-weary North. The city might be captured, the northern government dispersed, and Lincoln and others in the administration even captured. Grant might be induced to lift the pressure at Petersburg. The fall elections might be significantly affected. The strategy of relying on northern fear for the safety of Washington to aid Confederate fortunes elsewhere had worked in the past. It could possibly succeed again.

Moving swiftly, Early's raiding force of approximately 12,000 to 15,000 men marched down the Shenandoah Valley late in June. By early July, they had crossed the Potomac unannounced and virtually unopposed and soon occupied Frederick, Maryland, only forty miles from Washington. Early ransomed the town for $200,000; he had already tapped Hagerstown and tiny Middletown in such fashion. At the same time, his legions advanced slowly toward Washington but ran into unexpected opposition just south of Frederick on the Monocacy River. Here, on July 9, Major General Lew Wallace from Baltimore, and the motley force he had assembled at the railroad junction disputed Early's crossing. A bloody afternoon battle ensued that upset Early's timetable and announced to an unbelieving Washington, as well as Grant at Petersburg, that a serious and sizable body of Confederates stood poised to threaten and perhaps take the nation's capital.

A confusing command structure, ill-matched troop units, panicky citizens, and sheer chaos characterized Washington during the ensuing weekend of July 9 and 10, 1864. At that instant, barely 9,000 men manned the line of fortifications. Meager consolation came from the knowledge that Grant was rushing reinforcements from Petersburg. Only President Lincoln appeared calm. To a group of hysterical Baltimore citizens, he suggested, "Let us be vigilant, but keep cool. I hope neither Baltimore nor Washington will be taken."[38]

On the Confederate side, Jubal Early also encountered problems. He had sent much of his cavalry on a raid to sever rail and telegraph lines around Baltimore. This foray, led by Marylander Bradley Johnson, was also supposed to travel the 100 miles to Point Lookout where the Potomac River joined the Chesapeake Bay and free Confederate soldiers imprisoned there. Then they were to return with their swelled ranks to join Early in front of Washington. However, Johnson never got anywhere near Point Lookout, and if he had, he would have discovered that the Federal government had already sent most of the prisoners north to Elmira, New York. And as Early thrust two columns toward Washington, the extreme heat and dusty march wrought havoc with his tired Rebels. Washington may well have been saved by such quirks of fate as the delay at Monocacy, Johnson's folly, and the weather.

When Early did arrive before the works at Forts Slocum, Stevens, and DeRussy near the Seventh Street road, north of the city around noon on July 11, he reasoned that his veterans could break through the militia garrisons. The defenses lacked both veteran garrisons and the "maneuver" element of a protecting army. Moreover, the ramparts of the forts appeared poorly manned. Formation of a Confederate assault, however, proved to be another matter. Early's veterans were not up to the task. They simply wanted shade, water, and a little rest. The battle of Monocacy, the absence of reinforcements from Point Lookout, and the heat and dust of the march to the capital cost Early his objective of capturing the city.

The warm dawn of July 12 found Early studying the Federal lines at Fort Stevens. Veteran reinforcements landed at the Washington wharves, to be greeted by Lincoln himself, and soon the faded blue coats of the veteran units and the president arrived at the northern lines. Lincoln was no stranger to Washington's forts, having visited many of them. But on this day, the chief executive's visit was prompted by the desire to view the battle. So he mounted the parapet and stood in his signature stovepipe hat and a yellow duster covering his dark suit as sharpshooters' bullets whistled around him. For the only recorded instance in American history, a sitting president came under enemy fire.

Fearing for his commander in chief's life, Major General Horatio Wright decided that it was time for Lincoln to seek shelter. Wright also sent a brigade out to deal with Early's sharpshooters and skirmishers. Early realized the precarious position in which he had placed his troops. His army lay far from Lee's support and virtually isolated above the Potomac on the Maryland side of the river. Federal troops were rapidly closing his path of retreat, and the arrival of the veterans from the Army of the Potomac prevented the capture of Washington. Early decided to await covering darkness and withdraw from in front of the fortifications. In large measure, the so-called Battle of Fort Stevens was somewhat of a misnomer. In the two-day action, there was no rolling up of a flank, no piercing of a line, no all-out attack, no real maneuvering, no rout, and no pursuit. But on the afternoon of July 12, just as it had been three days before at Monocacy, there was

Veteran Reserve Corps Troops—Convalescent Soldiers Who Defended Washington in 1864. *Library of Congress*

Treasury Department Officers. *Library of Congress*

an important confrontation, a nasty bloodletting, and a wise decision. There was, in one sense, a victor, but no one was truly vanquished. Dusk ended what fighting there had been, and Early began his retreat to Virginia. The Defenses of Washington had held. Washington's defenders, overjoyed with the accomplishment of saving the city, engaged in no immediate pursuit. For the 100-day soldiers whose terms of service would soon be ending, it was an adventure of a lifetime.

Thus, the Confederate threat to Mr. Lincoln's city ended. Grant continued his relentless pressure at Petersburg. Jubal Early stayed in the lower Shenandoah Valley for the rest of the summer, threatening once more to move north of the Potomac. But Washington and the North had been scared: faith in the Union cause was shaken by the audacity of such a raid and its near success. The *Times* of London of July 25, 1864, concluded, "The Confederacy is more formidable an enemy than ever." One modern observer has concluded, "That so splendid a ruse had been achieved is perhaps the finest tribute to Jubal's raid."[39] Lincoln survived to win reelection in November and enjoy another nine months in the White House. But it had been a close-run thing.

ENDING THE THREAT

Direct threat to the Federal capital decreased sharply after Early's attack. Interest in perfecting the defenses did not—at least not as far as the engineer officers were concerned. Surveys of the fortifications made prior to Early's summer raid had noted many deficiencies and the need for improvements to individual forts. The sodding and repair of parapets, the construction of bombproofs, and the cutting and clearing of undergrowth required many man-hours and occupied several hundred laborers each month once

Temporary U.S. Soldier Graves near Fort Stevens' Barracks. *Courtesy of Gil Barrett*

the Confederates left the area.[40] The engineers even planned to place obstructions in the Potomac, but this project never reached completion. They did manage to establish a series of entrenched camps or picket posts some distance in advance of key points along the lines south of the Potomac. Moreover, an impromptu board of officers familiar with the defenses advised departmental commander Major General Christopher C. Augur (who had witnessed Early's threat at Fort Stevens firsthand) concerning ordnance improvements. Its detailed analysis suggested the need for 167 more guns, "although it is not supposed that all of these guns can now be obtained." Augur told the War Department at the end of July that he would requisition only seventy-five field guns. "As the enemy cannot approach the city in all directions at the same time," he told Henry Halleck, "it is hoped with due watchfulness that we may with the additional field guns now asked for so arm any point of attack as to hold the enemy in check until the city can be re-enforced with the necessary additional troops and batteries." He gratuitously added, "In this conviction I cannot withhold the remark that our works are strong in them selves and strong in their armaments, but forts and cannon, even if Gibraltar, cannot of themselves defend a city against an enemy." In case of enemy attack, "we will also require soldiers."[41]

Then, Lee's surrender at Appomattox put an end to the war in the East. Washington's defense system by that time was impressive and totaled 164 forts and batteries. Barnard cites sixty-eight major enclosed forts that were supported by ninety-three unarmed batteries for field guns. The aggregate perimeters of the forts approached thirteen miles. Some 1,421 gun emplacements had been constructed in the forts and batteries. Eight hundred and seven artillery pieces and ninety-eight mortars had actually been mounted in the emplacements. Twenty miles of rifle pits and thirty miles of military roads also encircled the city. Seven blockhouses added to the aggregate during the war.[42]

On April 29, the chief of engineers directed Lieutenant Colonel Barton S. Alexander, Barnard's successor as chief engineer of the defenses, to suspend operations on field fortifications and collect and preserve engineer equipment "for reducing the expenses of the military establishment."[43] Alexander in turn requested deter-

Grand Review—1865. *Library of Congress*

mination of what was to be done ultimately with the various forts. As he told Brigadier General Richard A. Delafield,

> I have always supposed that it will be the policy of the Government, even after the termination of the rebellion, to maintain the more important works of defense around this city. It seems to me after our experience during this rebellion that a wise foresight will not permit us to allow the seat of government to become again entirely defenseless.[44]

Mindful of the expense of upkeep, however, he recommended that the majority of the works should be dismantled. Alexander felt that twenty forts (ten on either side of the river) must be retained for the foreseeable future.

The chief of engineers and the War Department temporarily accepted Alexander's suggestion. General Order 89, dated June 23, 1865, directed that twenty-five works should be maintained. The rest of the forts would be abandoned and the land restored to the rightful owners.[45] The disposal work progressed through the summer and fall of 1865. The engineers sold used lumber, timber, and tools at public auction, generating more than $15,000 to the U.S. Treasury. Some supplies, such as gates, doors, locks, hinges, and lumber for gun platforms, bombproofs, and magazines, were kept for possible future use.[46]

ASSESSMENT

By November 1865, additional forts had been abandoned, although the Corps of Engineers continued with plans to strengthen the water fortifications and even investigated the idea of building new batteries at Fort Washington. But on July 14, 1866, Lieutenant Colonel Alexander formally closed his books on the vast wartime defenses of Washington.[47] Over subsequent decades, the once-proud earthen works gave way to time, the elements, and development. Other wars brought fear for the safety of the capital, and the construction of modern river batteries and antiaircraft defenses reflected such concerns. But military authorities would never again construct extensive field fortifications to defend Washington. Eventually, remains of some forts would become the nucleus of a city park system—the McMillan Plan and a grand "Fort Circle Drive," which was to link the parks and embrace "a pleasure drive of natural and historical interest" for an expanding cityscape but was never fully realized.[48]

To John Gross Barnard, the fortification system around Washington surpassed anything comparable in Europe at the time, including the lines of Torres Vedras, Lisbon, and Sevastopol. Admittedly, Washington's forts never received a concentrated assault or siege such as suffered by Vicksburg or Richmond-Petersburg.

In the end, the mere existence of the Defenses of Washington during the Civil War gave pause to Confederate intentions to capture the Federal capital. Robert E. Lee remained respectful of the system's strength on at least two occasions; on the third, he nearly accomplished its demise. Jubal Early's raid failed because the system worked as intended—forts, cannon, and maneuver force working together stopped the attackers. The financial expenditures, the long man-hours of construction and upkeep, the dreary garrison life, and the thankless task of the engineers made their contribution. Because of these elements, Washington, the symbol and the sword of the Union, emerged unscathed from the Civil War.

2

Engineer Details of Construction[1]

PROFILES—The works were originally profiled in accordance with the general section given in Mahan's Field Fortifications. The relief varied from 7 to 9 feet; the thickness of parapets between crests from 8 to 12 feet. The exterior slope was 45 degrees, and the interior, or breast-height slope, three upon one, with a plank revetment. A berm of 18 inches was left between the foot of the exterior slope and the edge of the ditch, and to the scarp was given a slope of two upon one. This form of profile is suitable only for temporary fieldworks, and experience taught us that some modifications were necessary to give to the defenses of Washington that degree of durability which their prolonged maintenance demanded. The thickness of the parapets, on exposed fronts, was increased to a minimum of 12 feet, and ranged from 12 to 18 feet. The erosion of the scarps by the action of rain and frost was found to be so great, after a single winter, as to annihilate the berms and undermine the parapets, causing external portions to slide into the ditch. To obviate this issue, the berm was abandoned, and a uniform slope of 45 degrees, extending from the exterior crest to the bottom of the ditch, was adopted. In most cases these exterior slopes were sodded, and those so treated were still in perfect preservation at the close of the war. In some instances the scarps of the older works were revetted, either with plank, after the plan given in Mahan's Field Fortifications, or with vertical posts, as hereafter to be described.

The width given to ditches depended, of course, on that assigned to the parapets. The depth was usually about six feet. At a distance of a few feet from the counterscarp a glacis was thrown up, so as to bring the ground in front of the works within the plane of musketry fire from the parapets. On the glacis a strong abattis was laid and secured, extending entirely around each fort.

REVETMENTS—The ordinary board revetment for interior earth slopes, adopted in the earlier works, was found to be incapable of resisting, for any length of time, the action of rain and frost, and to be, moreover, very perishable. Hence it became necessary, out of the materials at hand, to devise a more durable construction. When suitable timber, in sufficient quantities, could be obtained, a revetment of *vertical posts* was generally adopted. This consisted of posts from 4 to 6 inches in diameter, of oak, chestnut, or cedar, cut into lengths of 5½ Feet, and set with a slope of six upon one in close contact in a trench, at the foot of the breast-height, 2 feet in depth.

These were sawed off 16 inches below the crest and shaped to receive a horizontal capping piece of six-inch timber, hewed, or sawed, to a half round, as shown in the following sketch (Graphic 1, p. 26). Anchor ties were dovetailed into the capping piece A and anchor log B.

This kind of revetment, having sufficient durability for the purpose required, possesses this advantage over any other, that a shot perforating the parapet, while it may knock out one or even two posts, causes them to rotate in a vertical plane, whereas the timbers or splinters of a horizontally laid revetment arc, under the same circumstances, rotated horizontally, to the endangering of a much greater number of the defenders.

The vertical post revetment was also sometimes applied to scarps, and was frequently used to curtail the slopes of magazines, traverses, and bombproofs, when the full earth slope would occupy too much of the terre-plein. In these cases the top was placed below the level at which an enemy shot could strike the interior works.

When suitable timber could not be obtained, a sod revetment was used, which, though more expensive in original construction, is probably superior to any other, on account of its yielding no splinters and of its

United States Volunteers Erecting Earthworks on Arlington Heights. *Library of Congress*

durability when properly laid and carefully attended to. The sods were cut to a thickness of 4 inches, in lengths of 18 inches, and widths of 12 inches. These were laid (grass downward) so as to form a *sod-wall* of about 12 inches in thickness, built on a slope of three upon one the earth of the parapet being carried up behind the revetment, and thoroughly rammed, simultaneously with the laying of the sod-wall. At vertical intervals of about one foot, a course of sods was laid transversely so as to bind into the parapet. Small pegs ¾ inch in diameter and 9 inches long were driven through each alternate course into the layers beneath. The revetment thus laid at Fort Whipple in the spring of 1863 was in perfect preservation at the close of the war, notwithstanding a prolonged drought which, in the summer of 1863, killed the grass roots and rendered it, for a time, a wall of dead turf. The grass was thoroughly restored by applying horizontally an iron-toothed rake to the face of the breast-heights, and by sprinkling grass seed on the abraded surface.

The interior slopes of some of the older works, previously revetted with plank, were *repaired* by cutting away the breast-heights to a slope of two upon one and covering the slope with sods laid on *superficially*, using, however, the post revetment in front of gun platforms. This slope was found to stand very well in clayey soils, and where the parapets had become thoroughly compacted by long standing; but would not answer in the construction of new works.

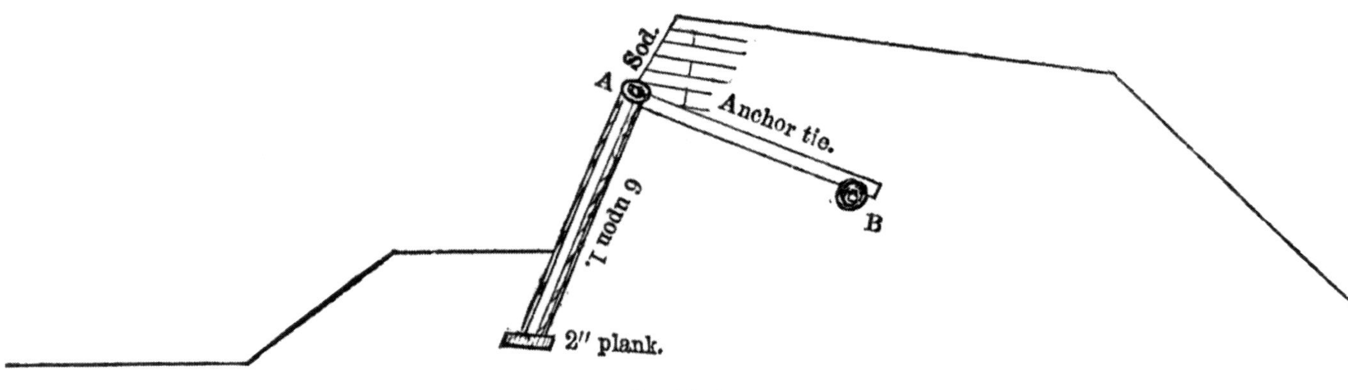

Graphic 1

The cheeks of embrasures, and in some cases the slopes of magazines and traverses, were revetted with gabions. For filling the gabions it was found that turf (usually the trimmings of sod revetments), thoroughly rammed, was the best material, as the grass soon enveloped the basket work and formed a durable revetment even after the gabions themselves had decayed. The turf-filled gabions were not affected by the blast from the guns, whereas sand or earth was blown from them by a few discharges.

MAGAZINES, BOMB-PROOFS—The interior structures, magazines, bomb-proofs, etc., as at first built, partook of the temporary character of the works themselves. They were in accordance (with some variation in details) with the plans given in Mahan's Field Fortification. Though answering very well the temporary purposes which field works generally subserve, their mode of construction was quite inadequate to the securing against moisture and the prolonged preservation of the large stores of ammunition maintained in the "forts," and indeed the light frame-work of the interior was incapable of sustaining for long periods the superincumbent earth. Hence, after the first year's experience, when extensive repairs of the original works and the construction of new ones was undertaken, increased strength and durability, combined with more perfect security from moisture and thorough ventilation, were sought for. Cross sections of such modified structures are exhibited . . . on plans of Forts Slocum and Ward. The first was generally applied to works north of the Potomac, where timber was found in great abundance; the other, [as at], Fort Ward, to the works south of the Potomac, where timber had become scarce.[2] The essential difference in these plans consisted in this, that the walls of the former were built of round timber posts placed in close contact, vertically, while in the latter the walls were of hewn timber bents, consisting of plate and sill and posts, placed at intervals of four feet. [As found at], Fort Slocum, may be thus described: For the walls, timber posts of oak or chestnut, nine feet long and not less than one foot in diameter, were placed in close contact, vertically, upon a 2-inch plank two feet below the level of the floor. The tops of these posts were capped with a 2-inch plank spiked to each, and a narrow strip of 2-inch plank extended down the inside of the walls about four inches, the upper edge of which was flush with its capping plank. This arrangement afforded a uniform bearing to the roof-logs. The width of the chamber was generally 12 feet (this width being adapted to the storage of powder barrels in thee ranges), and of lengths according to the required capacity of the magazine. The roof-logs, not less than twelve inches in diameter, spanned the interval between the walls, and projected about six inches beyond them. They were *notched* at each end about three inches in depth, so as to saddle on to the capping of the side walls, with an interior square shoulder at each side, to resist the pressure caused by the superincumbent earth. The roof-logs were hewed so as to lie in sufficiently close contact to retain the earth covering. The ends were sawed off obliquely, . . . and against these projecting ends were placed, at intervals of three feet, inclined posts, six to eight inches in diameter, resting at the base, upon a log hewed to a half round. Behind these inclined supports, a revetment of small poles, two to four inches in diameter, or

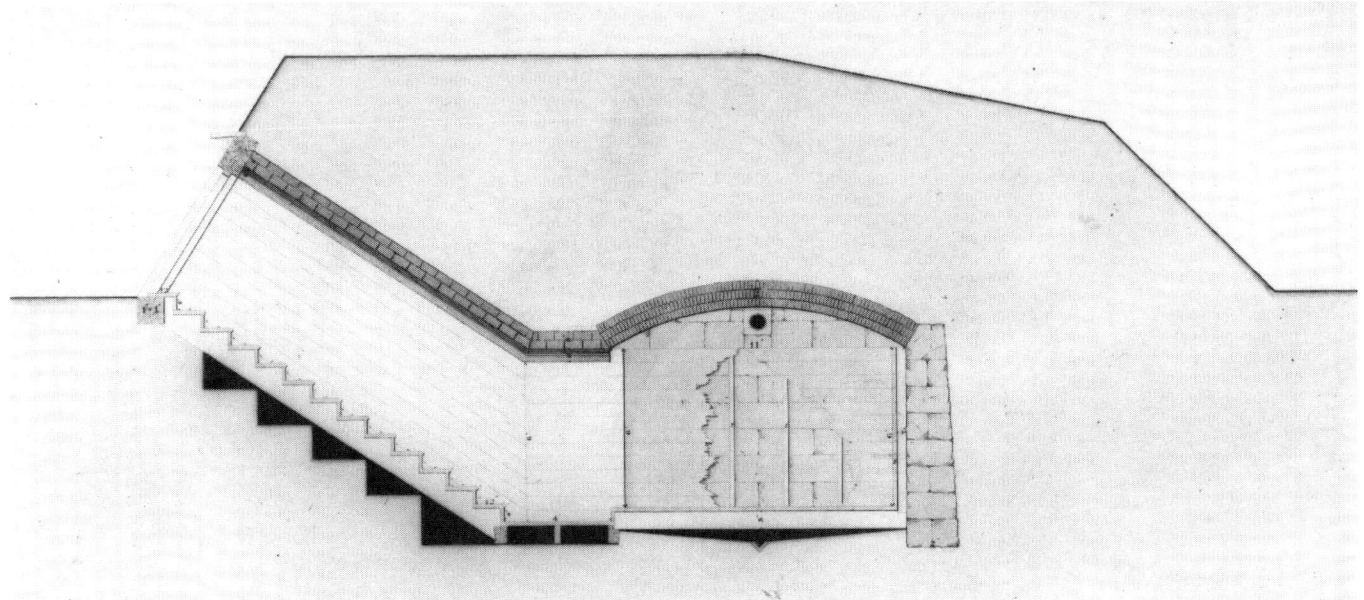

Engineer Design for Magazine at Fort Ethan Allen. *National Archives*

of larger ones split in two, were placed horizontally, and carried up uniformly as the earth was replaced externally. This arrangement afforded an air chamber around the magazine, which, in connection with the ventilating popes, secured a very thorough ventilation. The floors were laid on sleepers transversely and so as to allow seven feet clear head-room.

The framed magazine [at] Fort Ward consisted of two longitudinal bents with sill plates and posts all hewn from round timber. The sill was hewn on the upper and lower side only, to a thickness of twelve inches. The posts were hewn on the inside only, so as to afford a plane surface on which to nail the magazine lining of 1½-inch plank. The posts were cut to lengths of 6 feet 9 inches, with a *tenon* at each end of 3 inches in length and 4 inches by 2½ inches in section (leaving a length between shoulders of 6 feet 3 inches), and fitting into corresponding mortises, 4 feet apart from center to center, in plate and sill. The plate was hewn to 12 inches square. When these framed side walls were placed in position the further construction of the magazine was identical with that shown in . . . Fort Slocum, heretofore described.

To prepare a roofing which should be impervious to the percolation of water, the following process was adopted and applied, not only to magazines, but to bomb-proofs, implement-rooms, guard-houses, and all other structures requiring an earth covering. Above the roof-logs was placed, along the longitudinal center of the structure, a log not less than 12 inches in diameter, and parallel with it smaller logs 2½ feet from center to center. These were so hewn as to correspond to superior face or slope, having an inclination of one upon four. The earth was then thrown on and rammed compactly, flush with the upper surface of these hewn purlines. Upon these were nailed, first a course of 1-inch plank, tongued and grooved, and *painted* on the under side with a composition, applied while hot, of coal tar and resin boiled together. A heavier composition of coal tar, resin, and sand was used to flush the joints as they were driven home. The upper side of this roofing course was then painted thickly with the composition, after which was applied another course of 1-inch pine boards nailed to the previous course of oak plank. Great care was necessary in the laying of this roofing, so as to leave no opening through which water might penetrate. The second course of boards was laid simultaneously with the application of the hot composition to the upper side of the oak boards. A strip of the oak roofing, not more than one foot in width, was covered with the hot composition applied with a *swab* or *mop* of old canvas, and a board of the second course immediately followed, being pressed and worked into the composition by two or three longitudinal motions of each piece under pressure of the hands of the workmen. After the second course was nailed down another coating of the tar was applied, covering every portion of the surface and flushing the joints. Two or three inches of fine, clean sand was then thrown on, followed by about 2 feet of clay applied in layers of 6 to 8 inches, very thoroughly rammed. The remainder of the earth covering was then thrown on and compacted sufficiently to preserve the proper slopes, the whole being covered with sod laid on superficially where the angle of the slope would admit of it.

No fixed rule could be adopted as to the level of the floor of magazines below the terre-plein. It was desirable to place them as low as practicable, and yet preserve good drainage (generally into the ditch). But magazines were frequently made to serve the purpose of traverses, in which case a higher level for the floor was adopted. As to the amount of earth covering, the rule was, however, inflexible. A minimum depth of 10 feet from the ends of the roof-logs, measured on a line rising therefrom with an angle of 30 degrees, was required on all exposed sides of the magazines; from a point so determined a slope of one on one and one-half down to the grade of the terre-plein, and superior slopes of one on four, gave sufficient protection in the vertical as well as in all other directions. This rule was deduced from experiments made on the penetration of rifled, field, and siege artillery, at probable distances for enemy's guns, into the earth in which these works were built; and it was intended not only that shells should not reach the wood-work, but that they should not approach near enough to inject fire by their explosion. With this rule applied, the shell thrown by direct fire and striking the interior slopes must really penetrate fifteen or twenty feet before it could reach the timber even if pursuing its course, from which, however, it would be deflected up ward by the external slope of the earth.

BOMB-PROOFS—Of the bomb-proofs constructed there were two general plans, sections [at] Fort Ward, applicable to the works south of the Potomac, and [at] Fort Slocum, to those north of the Potomac. The essential difference in these plans consisted in the walls, of which the former were of timber framework, and the latter of vertical posts placed in close contact. Sections [at] Fort Ward, may be thus described. The plates and sills were hewn to 12 inches square and mortized, to receive the post tenons, at points 4 feet apart from center to center. The rear posts were hewn on the opposite side to a thickness of 12 inches, and cut in lengths of 9 feet from shoulder to shoulder; the front posts were hewn on the inside only, and cut to lengths of 7 feet between shoulders. These longitudinal bents were placed 12 feet apart, from inside to inside of the posts, and, when secured in position, the roof-logs were applied as in the magazines heretofore described; The

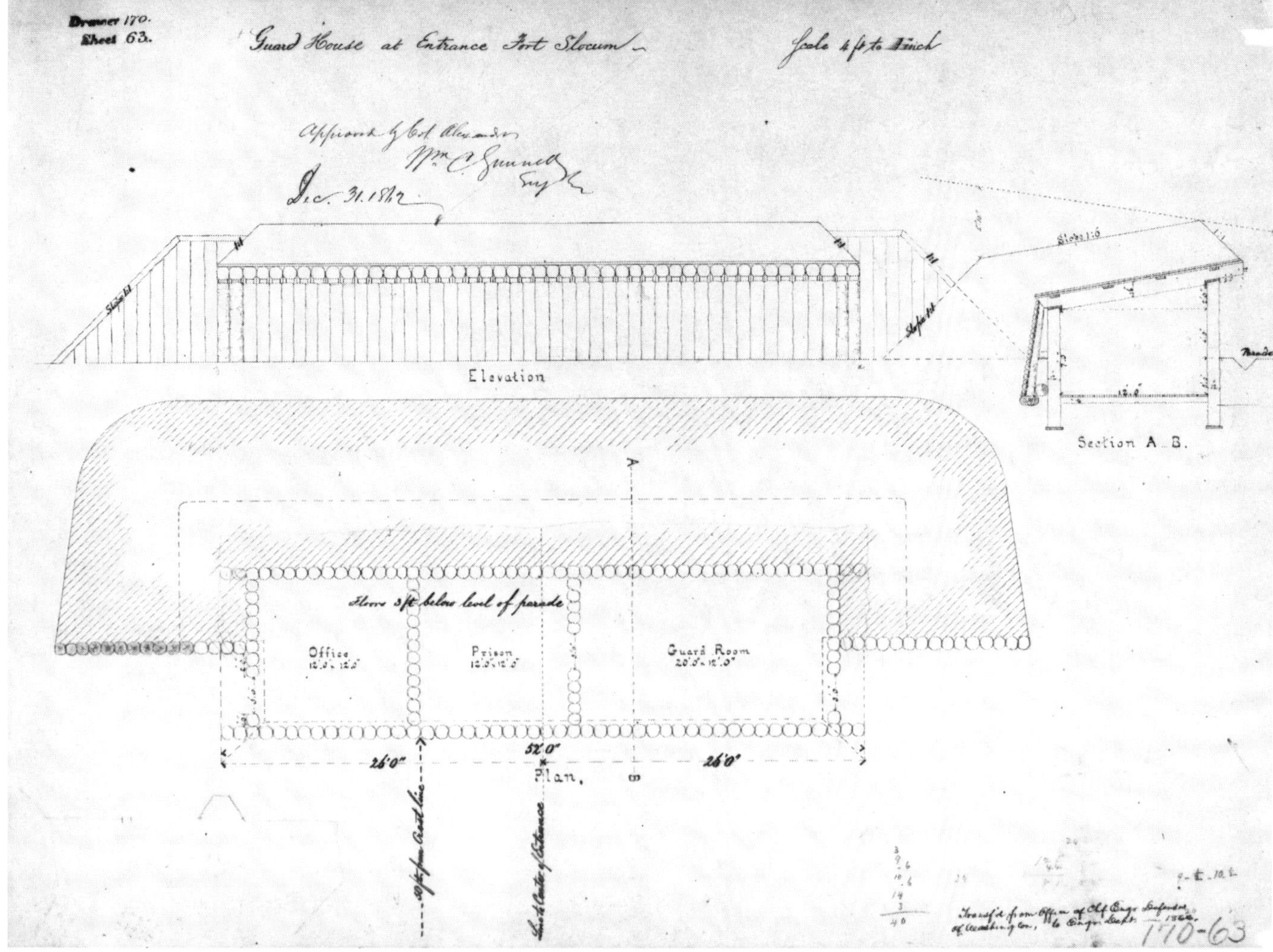

Engineer Design for Guard House at Fort Slocum. *National Archives*

roof-logs were not less than 12 inches in diameter and cut to lengths of 17½ feet, projecting over the rear plate 3 feet; This projection formed a base for a banquette, from which a musketry fire could be delivered over the superior slope of the bomb-proof.

The water-proof roofing was similar to that heretofore described in the case of magazine construction, as was also the air chamber on the sides brought in contact with the earth covering. The interior was lined with inch boards, and the rear wall was faced on the outside with ordinary clap-boarding. The floors were sunk from 3 to 4 feet below the general level of the terre-plein; and an area was excavated in the rear, on the level with the floor from 4 to 6 feet in width, with slopes of one and one-half on one up to the terre-plein. This excavation not only rendered the bomb-proof quarters more habitable by exposing the whole rear wall to light and air, but it also formed an additional space nearly as safe from an enemy's fire as the bomb-proof itself; The slopes of this area were sodded, the bottom gravelled and connected with the drainage system of the fort.

The earth covering on the bomb-proofs was required to be not less than 8 feet through, measured from the ends of the roof-logs, on a line rising there from with a vertical angle of 30 degrees. The superior slope was $1/6$ and the lateral slope varied from $1/1$ to $2/3$. To resist the pressure of this mass of earth, on one side of the structure, tending to push it over to the rear, one in every two of the roof logs was cut to a sufficient length to extend about eight feet beyond the front wall and was securely anchored to a longitudinal log held in position by vertical posts—the anchor log being sufficiently covered with earth to protect it from injury by an enemy's shot.

Reference having already been made to the only essential difference in the plans of bomb-proofs north and south of the Potomac (viz, that, in the former, the walls were of vertical logs), further description of them is deemed unnecessary.

Care was taken in the location of all these interior structures to make them subserve other purposes than that of mere rooms for the safe storage of ammunition or implements. Thus, at Fort Ward, all of these structures are also traverses, defilading the faces of the work, and are arranged with banquette and breast-height for infantry fire. The bastions and salient angles of the fort are isolated from the main work by these structures, and would with difficulty be held, if carried by an enemy, against the infantry fire which could be delivered into them from the banquettes of these interior works. The plans of Fort Whipple and Fort Ethan Allen afford further illustrations of the application of this principle. Its importance may be appreciated by recalling to mind the obstinate resistance made by the garrison of Fort Fisher[3] in renewing the contest from traverse to traverse after the work had been entered by our own troops.

Bomb-proofs were often built (especially in the works north of the Potomac) on the gorge line, in which case the rear wall of vertical logs was provided with loopholes, and a V ditch was cut in front of this loopholed wall. The plans of Fort Weed illustrate this arrangement.

The magazines, and indeed all interior structures, as bomb-proofs, guardhouses, implement and filling-rooms, were thoroughly whitewashed in the interior. The advantage of this application, renewed from time to time, consisted in lighting up the otherwise dark underground structures, and in purifying the air within. The timber walls of bomb-proofs and the stockades were coated with a wash of lime, to which was added lamp-black, a dark lead color resulting therefrom.

GUN PLATFORMS—Gun platforms for field and siege guns were constructed as follows: a foundation of earth was prepared, by thorough ramming, at such a level that the platform surface should be nor less than 7½ feet below the crest. The planking was laid on sleepers bedded into the earth parallel with the axis of the embrasure, placed 2 feet apart from center to center. The sleepers were of round timber not less than 9 inches in diameter and 18 feet in length, hewn on the upper side. On these were spiked 3-inch plank, 14 feet in length, laid transversely. They were arranged with an ascent to the rear of 6 inches, to check the recoil and to cause the gun to return easily into battery. A *hurter* of 6-inch timber was placed at the forward end of the platform at a distance from the parapet just sufficient to keep the wheels of the carriage clear of the revetment. Behind the hurter 2-inch holes were bored through the plank, to allow the water to pass off into drains underneath. An improved gun-platform was constructed in the later works, when suitable timber could be obtained. This was of hewn timber, 6 inches thick by 10 to 14 inches wide. The advantage of this hewn timber flooring over plank consisted in greater firmness and durability; it having been found that the smaller field guns, such as 10-pounder Parrotts, and 12-pounder howitzers, after much practice, cut through the 3-inch plank. If the logs used are clear and straight-grained the timbers may be split out and hewn to an even surface, or they may be cut with a whip-saw.

The sections of the banquettes adjacent to the platforms were revetted either by short posts or by 2-inch plank, a bridge of such plank 2 feet in width being kept at each platform ready to be thrown across the gap, and thus restore the banquette for the use of infantry, should it be desirable. A distance of 23 feet from center to center of platforms was adopted as the minimum. This distance gave the greatest practicable amount of artillery fire in a given length of face consistent with the convenient working of the guns. This minimum distance between guns was exceeded whenever the length of face would permit. A distance of 30 feet between guns will admit of an intermediate traverse 12 feet thick, if the earth slopes are cut off below the level of the crest by a post revetment.

EMBRASURES—It was generally important to give to the guns the greatest possible field of fire; hence the embrasures were cut to a splay of 48 degrees (except in special cases), that being the maximum consistent with adequate strength and cover at the throat, They were generally revetted with gabions; in several works, however, wall-sodding was used for the purpose. The latter was found to be very durable, if properly cared for and occasionally watered in times of drought.

Whenever the gun has a particular object, of limited extent, for its fire, it is desirable that the splay of the embrasure should be a minimum, not only because its opening, with increased size, offers an increased object to the enemy's fire, but because the covering angles at the throat are weakened. With a view of adapting the embrasures to particular circumstances the following sketch and table were prepared (Graphic 2, p. 31).

BATTERIES—The same section of parapet was given to batteries, whether open or inclosed, as to the forts. Many of them were provided with magazines, and all of them with traverses when necessary. The arrangements of embrasures and platforms, and their manner of construction was precisely the same as described for the forts, and the revetment generally of vertical posts was of an equally substantial and durable characters. In the construction of open batteries, generally, no ditch was excavated, but the material for the parapet was obtained by excavating in the rear to such an extent and depth as to give a convenient area of terre-plein, with a cover of 7½ to 8 feet. The most perfect and complete batteries of this form (open works) were Batteries Parrott and Kemble, armed

Angle of fire of siege guns in embrasure, parapet 15 feet thick. Throat of embrasure 20 inches.

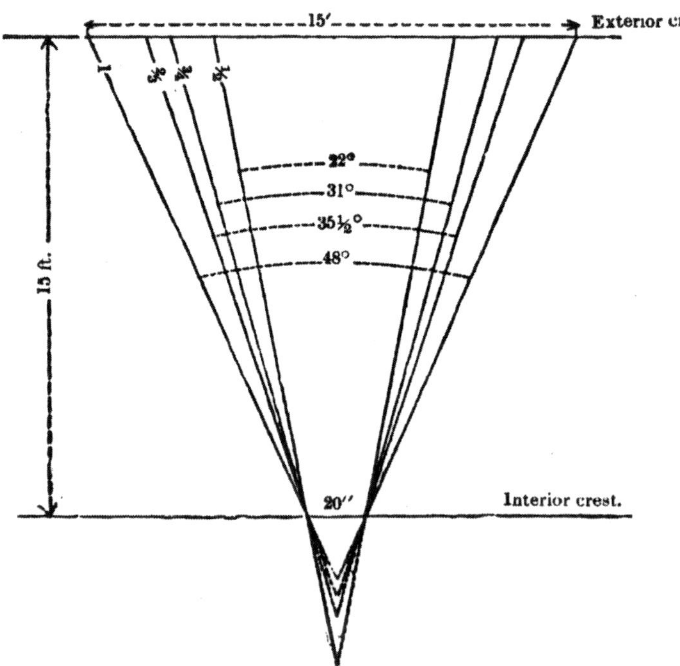

TABLE, (FROM CALCULATION.)

Proportionate width of embrasure and thickness of parapet.	Width of embrasure at exterior crest.	Angle of fire.
	Feet.	*Degree.*
1	15	48
	14	44½
	13	41½
	12	36
¾	11.25	35½
	11	34½
⅔	10	31
	9	27½
	8	24½
½	7½	22

Graphic 2

with 100-pounder rifles, and Battery Rodgers, at Alexandria, armed with five 200-pounder Parrott rifles and one 15-inch gun; but the purpose of these was peculiar, and differed very much from that of batteries for field or siege guns, armed or unarmed, of which so many were arranged along the lines of defense.

WELLS.—Nearly all of the more important works and especially those which, from their position, might be exposed to a siege or cut-off from water supplies in the rear, were provided with wells, These were sunk in some instances to very great depths, as at Fort Stanton, 212 feet and at Fort Lyon, 175 feet, in order to obtain the necessary supply of water; though generally it was found within the more reasonable depth of 30 to 60 feet. The wells, after being curbed with brick, stone, or wood (the latter used in one or two cases only), were from 8 to 10 feet in diameter.

TRENCHES AND COVERED WAYS—The three sections on page 32 represent different kinds of trenches used in connecting the works and forming the line of defense, or for furnishing a covered fire upon ground in contiguity to, but unseen from, the forts. The connecting lines, destitute of interior revetments, had, in place thereof, earth slopes of about 45 degrees. The earth was thrown up from an inside excavation, which was carried to sufficient depth (usually 3 feet) to afford, in conjunction with the embankment, a cover of 7½ feet. The banquette was made on the natural surface of the ground. To facilitate access from the trench an intermediate step, 2 feet in width, broke the continuity of the earth slope. The bottom of the trench was graded to throw the drainage to the rear, and outlets for it were provided at suitable localities. For the uses of infantry alone a width of 5 feet was given to the bottom of the trench, from which resulted a thickness, between crests, of parapet of 4 feet. Whenever it was considered desirable to provide for the passage of guns these dimensions were increased to 8 feet for both trench and parapet. Sometimes such trenches were adapted to the service of guns, in which cases platforms of well-compacted earth were made, and on each side of the embrasure the parapet was revetted, either with wall-sodding or posts. The embrasures were revetted either with gabions or with sods. The full width of trench was cut to the rear of the platforms, with easy ramps for crossing them and for running the guns into position. When the second form of trench was used to connect a fort with a contiguous battery the interior slope was usually revetted with posts, instead of being of earth at its natural slope.

SURFACE GEOLOGY—The nature of the material in which the "Defenses" were constructed will be best understood in connection with its geological characteristics, for an account of which I am indebted to Professor George C. Schaeffer, of Washington.

Washington, or rather Georgetown, the older city, had been placed, in common with many others of our Atlantic States, at the head of tide-water, and where, in ascending the rivers, the vertically-stratified metamorphic rocks were first met. These, varying in

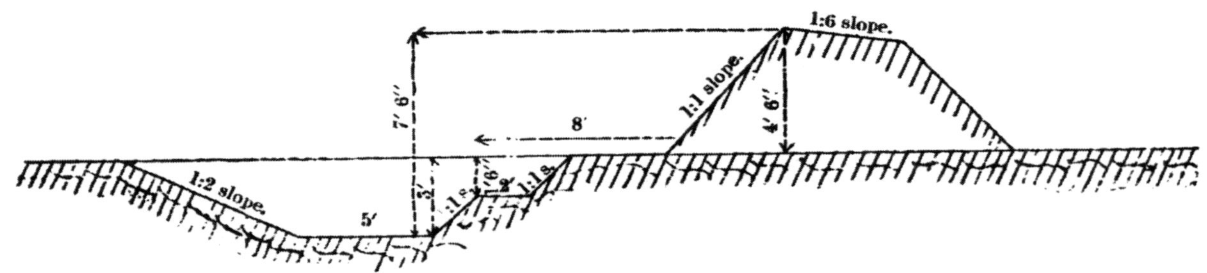

COVERED WAY FOR INFANTRY.

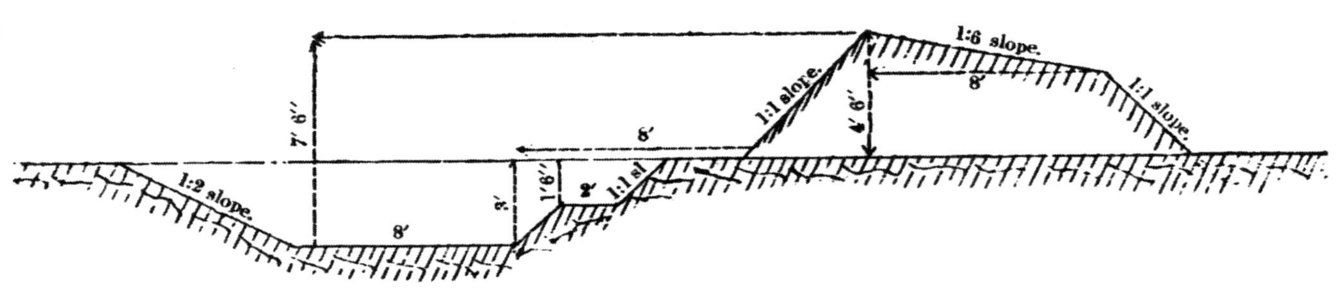

COVERED WAY FOR ARTILLERY.

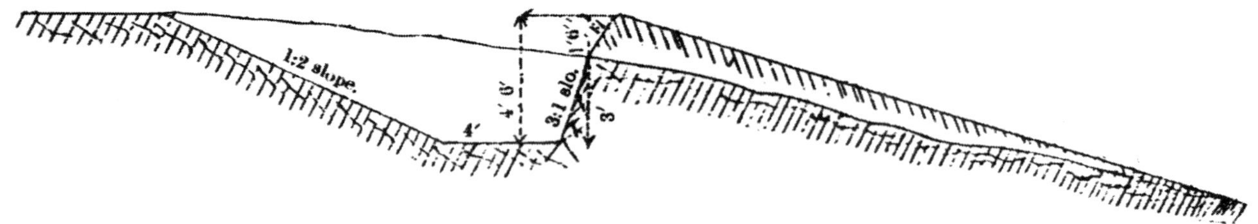

RIFLE TRENCHES AROUND FORTS.

Graphic 3

composition, from hard gneiss to soft mica slate, yield unequally to degrading action, and thus produce the bold headlands arid deeply excavated valley in which the land terminates at the margins of the Potomac. Overlying these rocks is a series of nearly horizontal beds, which form the various distinctive earth masses around the cities of Washington, Georgetown, and Alexandria. These peculiar sands and clays, with their fossil woods, belong to an older part of the cretaceous formation which borders on Atlantic. Possibly the tertiary may come into view to the south, as at Rozier's Bluff; but this is quite doubtful.

On the northwest the line of defenses may cross a peculiar and local deposit, formed of material evidently eroded from the red sandstone at Seneca, when the river flowed at a vastly higher level (say 400 feet)

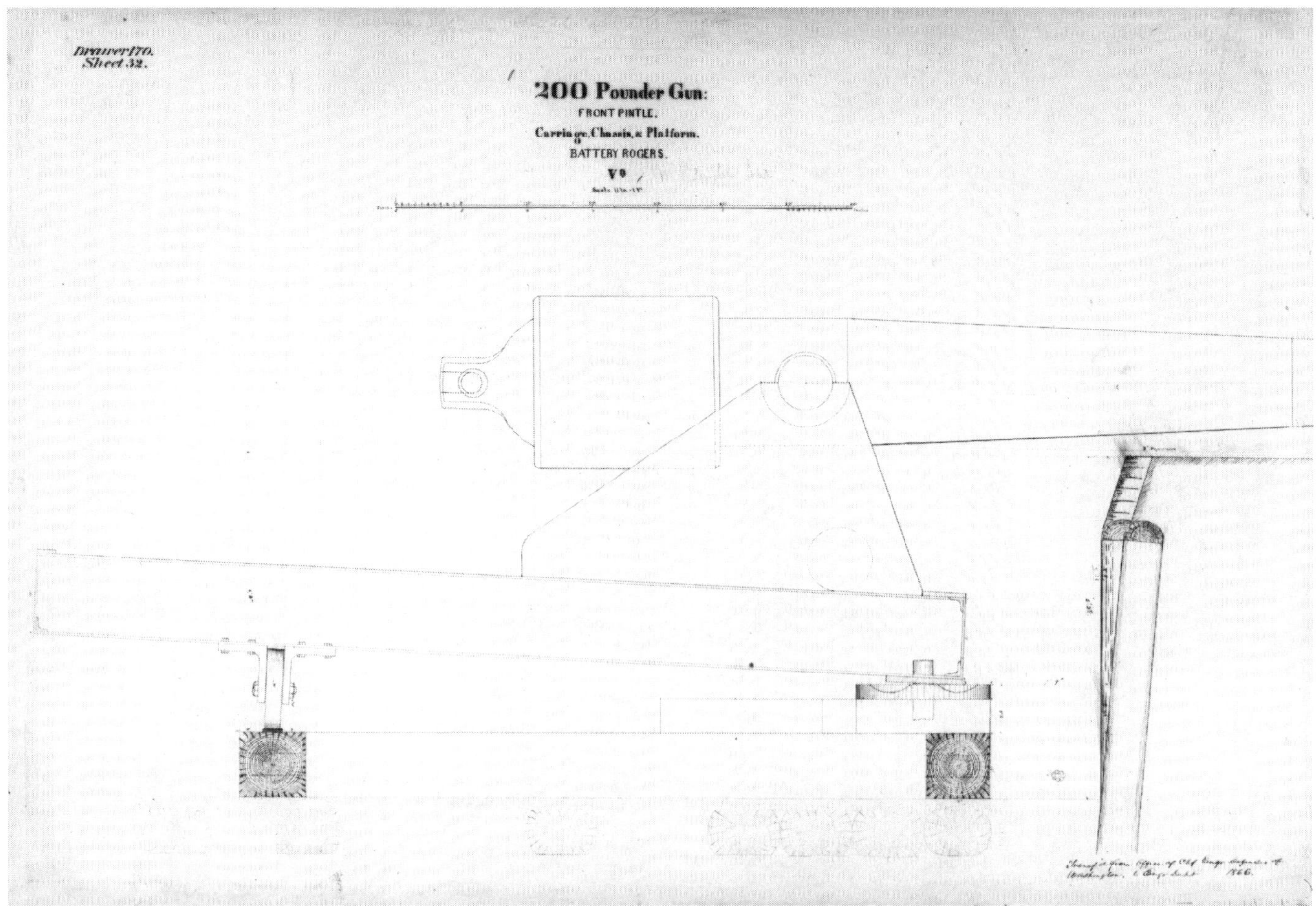

Engineer Design for 200-Pounder Parrott Rifle, Front Pintle for Battery Rodgers. *National Archives*

than at present. With the exception of Fort Runyon and one or two other works on the immediate margin of the Potomac, the defenses of Washington are made in these cretaceous beds, with all the peculiar advantages and disadvantages of this formation; the former being the mere facility of excavation; the latter the difficulty of maintaining the earthen slopes when made, and its unfitness for road surface.

The underlying metamorphic rocks are not exposed along the Anacostia or its tributaries. Rock Creek has excavated its channel through them and owes its name to the exposed rocks which almost everywhere forms its bed. Appearing first on the Potomac, at Georgetown, they are seen almost continuously along the left bank above that place, and show the first sign of crossing to the other side at the rocks called the Three Sisters above the aqueduct. In the highest part of Georgetown the clay is nothing more than the decomposed rock, showing its undisturbed stratification.

The horizontal beds first mentioned extend across Maryland, Delaware, and New Jersey, and are traced on the south side of Staten Island. They consist of beds of clay, and clay and sand curiously mixed. In some cases a peculiar small gravel is present, and where this occurs it is frequently cemented into rock-like masses by oxide of iron, which substance is also found in such quantities that it furnishes ore for furnaces, one of which, not far from Washington, is one of the oldest in the country. It is a peculiarity of these soils that the surface, on drying, allows the sand to blow out from the clay. Banks are sometimes seen, especially in Maryland, with clay enough to keep them almost vertical to a height of from 15 to 20 feet; and yet, in every furrow in these steep slopes, the pure sand is constantly running down to the base.

BLOCK-HOUSES—The wide interval between Fort Lyon and its redoubts on the south, and Forts Worth, Williams, and Ellsworth on the north side of the valley of Hunting Creek, gave rise in the summer of 1864 to apprehensions of cavalry raids by night into the city of Alexandria, accompanied by the destruction of the immense military depots at that place. To guard against this danger a battery was constructed in the valley near the "old distillery," and block-houses were erected—one at the Little River Turnpike on the north side of the valley, one near the bridge over Hunting

Creek on the telegraph road, and one on the Leesburg turnpike where it entered our lines near Fort Ward. The ground plan of these structures had the form of a Greek cross. The walls were built of large logs from 16 to 18 inches in diameter, hewed on two sides and placed vertically in close contact. They were made 10½ feet in height in the clear from the floor. The roof was made of logs extending over the walls one foot on all sides. On these logs was thrown an earth-covering four feet thick at the crown and sloping down to a depth of six inches at the ends of the logs. This was thoroughly rammed, and in it were bedded purlines, upon which was constructed a shingle roofing. Loop-holes for musketry fire were cut through the walls at a height of 8 feet above the floor, their splay being on the *inside*. A banquette of plank, 3½ feet above the floor and 6½ feet in width, was carried around the interior; this served also as a substitute for bunks. The floors were of 2½-inch plank. Embrasures for a 12-pounder howitzer were arranged on every face of the block-houses, in each of which buildings there were two such guns. The throats or the embrasures were closed, when not in use, by heavy timber doors, barred on the inside, and the banquette was made in movable sections behind each embrasure. Around the outside was dug a deep V ditch, the earth being thrown up on a slope of forty-five degrees, as high as the soles of the loop-holes. The cheeks or the embrasures were of hewn timber, and a roof of the same was thrown across to sustain the earth slope just mentioned. Each block-house was provided with a small magazine below the floors. These structures, though not entirely *bomb-proof*, were so buried in earth as to be pretty secure against any artillery accompanying cavalry raids. Their garrisons consisted of sixty men each. These buildings were erected by the Quartermaster's Department, under the direction of the engineer of the Defenses at the time (Col. B. S. Alexander).

MILITARY ROADS—The line of defensive works was readily reached by the several county roads radiating from the cities of Washington, Georgetown, and Alexandria; but there existed, at first, no adequate means of communication along any portion of the line, and none at all along some portions of it. The necessity for such communicating roads became apparent as soon as the general line of works was established. The conditions governing their location and construction were, that they should not be seen from any ground that an enemy might be able to occupy in front, that they should be as direct as practicable consistently with easy grades, and that they should have sufficient width for the movement over them of field batteries or army trains.

The first road of this character was constructed in the autumn of 1861 for the purpose of connecting the isolated works at the Chain Bridge with the right of the Arlington lines at Fort DeKalb (Strong). This road, about three miles in length, was laid out by Captain B.S. Alexander, mainly through a broken and densely wooded country. It was completed by details of troops, working under that officer's direction, in two or three days.

The occupation by the army of the Potomac, during the winter of 1861 of the territory from Arlington Heights to and beyond Fort Lyon, caused it to be traversed by innumerable rough wagon roads, and communication along the lines soon became practicable, though, in wet weather, exceedingly difficult. At a later period a route was selected conforming to the requisite condition as far as possible; and partly by details of troops and partly by hired labor a good road was constructed, passing to the rear of and com-

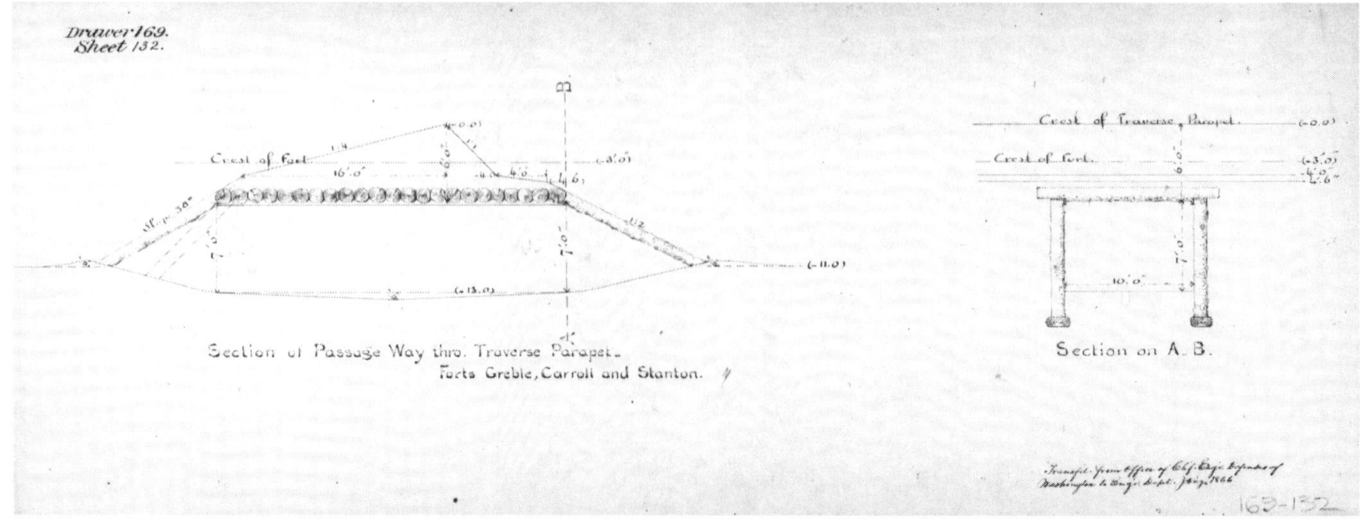

Engineer Design for Section of Passageway through Traverse Parapet at Battery Kemble and Forts Carroll and Stanton. *National Archives*

municating with all the works from Fort DeKalb to Fort Lyon. In the autumn of 1862 the wide interval previously existing between Fort Sumner and Fort Reno, north of the Potomac, was filled up by the construction of intervening works. In September of that year, as these works progressed toward completion, a military road was located, and constructed in a few weeks, from Fort Sumner, near the Potomac, to Fort Stevens, east of Rock Creek, a distance of about 5½ miles, exclusive of the branches to the several forts. Nearly the entire length of this route was through a densely wooded and very broken country. A very excellent road, thoroughly drained by side ditches and with substantial bridges and culverts, was made, to which was given a width of 45 feet and a full, rounded surface. It was subsequently extended to Fort Lincoln, near the Eastern Branch. Others were made from the Aqueduct Bridge to Forts C. F. Smith and Strong, (DeKalb;) from the same point to Fort Whipple, and thence to Fort Albany. The aggregate length of military roads constructed about 32 miles. Providing, as they did, the means of rapidly moving troops or guns, unobserved by the enemy to reinforce any part or the line that might be attacked, their importance as adding to the strength of the defensive system can scarcely be over-estimated.

I take the liberty of quoting in this connection, a passage from a letter of Professor George C. Schaeffer: "One of the important parts of the 'defenses' was the construction, or the improvement, of the roads uniting them, which never before had been properly laid out. Good roads are in our country rare, but on such soils they require skill; and I think that when all the 'defenses' are swept away the roads may remain as a lasting benefit. They certainly have afforded models which have been, although imperfectly, imitated."

BRIDGES—The circuit of defenses (37 miles in development), as it has been described in the preceding pages, is thrice broken—twice by the Potomac and once by the Anacostia or Eastern Branch. The existing bridges (the Navy Yard and Benning's) were quite sufficient for communication with that portion of the works over the Anacostia. They were both pile bridges with "draws." It was necessary to strengthen these latter to capacitate them for bearing the passage of heavy guns, and indeed, the Navy Yard bridge was almost entirely rebuilt before the close of the war. Tetes-de-pont to these bridges were formed by intrenchments at their immediate termini.

The Potomac was spanned, 1st, by the Long Bridge from the foot of Fourteenth street; 2d, by the aqueduct of the Chesapeake and Ohio Canal, at Georgetown; 3d, by the Chain Bridge, three miles above Georgetown.

The first formed, for land travel, the main link of communication with Alexandria and the principal southern routes. It is one mile in length; nearly two-thirds of which, over the wide shoals of the Potomac, is solid causeway, and the rest on piles. There are two "draws," one near either shore. The immense transportation for the Army over this bridge imposed the speedy necessity of a entire rebuilding of the wooden structure and draws. This was done in the fall of 1861 by the Quartermaster's Department. Subsequently it was judged necessary to connect the great railroad route from the North with those from the South terminating at Alexandria, and in 1864 an entire new railroad bridge was constructed on piles parallel to the one just described. After reaching the Virginia shore the latter is prolonged by a causeway over a flat and marsh until it reaches the more elevated ground at Fort Runyon, where our first tete-de-pont was established. A more contiguous protection was deemed necessary, and Fort Jackson, an earthwork with wet ditches was thrown up in the fall of 1861, just at the end of the bridge. Never armed, it was suffered to fall into decay. In 1864 the gates or barriers were restored as a precaution against raids, but the fort in the meantime had been cut through by the railroad and was much dilapidated. The guard for the bridge consisted at that time of an officer of the Veteran Reserves and sixty or seventy men stationed on the Washington side, but maintaining a picket at Fort Jackson.

The Chesapeake and Ohio Canal follows the descending course of the Potomac to Georgetown, where it crosses the river and is prolonged to a secondary terminus at Alexandria, The stone piers of the aqueduct are works of the highest class of engineering, the bed rock on which they rest being from 20 to 30 feet below the surface of the river and covered to half the depth by mud. The *superstructure* was of wood, much out of repair but still subserving its purposes.

The main object of the continuation of the canal to Alexandria was the delivery of Cumberland coal for shipment at that port. All commercial uses ceased, of course, with the commencement of the war, (Georgetown answering nearly as well as a shipping port,) and, though a certain service could have been rendered by the canal in the transportation of military supplies to Alexandria. This utility was insignificant weighed against the importance of having a second permanent and secure bridge connecting Washington with the Virginia shore.[4] Two bridges were necessary, even if the liabilities to destruction of *one* by accident or the incendiary had not been, in itself, a decisive motive. The tow-path of the aqueduct did indeed furnish a narrow passageway to horsemen and footmen; but this was far from adequate to the military exigencies. Accordingly, early in the winter of 1861–'62, the water was shut off from the aqueduct and its trough converted into a double-track wagon road, the floor being overlaid with 4-inch planks and long inclines, on trestles, forming connections with the roads on either side.

Fort Corcoran, with the small forts Haggerty and Bennett, formed the principal defense to this debouche; but, to give a more immediate defense, a kind of interior tete-de-pont was created by the construction of three wooden block-houses, and by taking advantage of excavation made in building the aqueduct, to form a musketry trench around the end of the bridge. The block-houses were found to be located too far off, and better security against cavalry raids becoming desirable, the head of the bridge was inclosed by a stockade, provided with a gate or barrier. It was also contemplated to establish on the Georgetown shore a battery to sweep the length of the aqueduct. This was never done. The usual guard was an officer and about thirty men at each end of the bridge, both under a single command.

Thus modified the aqueduct served perfectly, throughout the entire period of the war, its new destination, and was recognized as an important and essential adjunct to the "Defenses of Washington" and to the great military operations in Virginia.

The "Chain Bridge" owed its name to a former suspension structure, long since carried away by floods. It had been replaced by a fine timber trussed bridge of over four hundred yards in length, resting on masonry abutments and seven masonry piers. At ordinary stages the river, rapid and unfordable, flowed beneath the single span next the Virginia shore; the rest of the bed being dry and strewn with fragments of rocks of large size. At high stages the whole width spanned was swept over by a furious flood. This was the sole existing bridge between Washington and Harper's Ferry at the breaking out of the war, one formerly existing at Berlin having been destroyed by fire. It connected Washington with the Leesburg Turnpike and neighboring parts of Virginia. Its ordinary uses ceased with the outbreak of war, but it immediately acquired a high military importance. Though not strictly necessary to a mere passive defense of Washington, it had, nevertheless, a high incidental utility as a means of maintaining communication with the Virginia theatre of war, and of throwing forces on the flank of an enemy menacing the lines of Arlington. To hold this debouche for our own purposes and to defend the bridge against the passage of an enemy formed distinct but connected problems. The system of works elsewhere described is mainly for the first named object. For the immediate defense Battery Martin Scott and another for mountain howitzers at the very extremity (Maryland side) swept the roadway. A musket-proof loopholed barrier was thrown across the bridge over the pier next to the Virginia shore, and means of escape to the river bed below were provided for the defenders if overpowered, so that the track might be laid open to the artillery fire. The floor planks of the span between the barrier and shore were loosened and a portion of them taken up every night. There was a permanent guard, consisting of an officer and about sixty men, at the Virginia end of the bridge. A sergeant and a few men had charge of the guns at the other end. The engineering arrangements for the defense were sufficient, but there never was proper discipline and regulation established as to the duties of the guard, nor were the precautions against fire here or elsewhere such as they should have been.

ADMINISTRATION AND ORGANIZATION OF LABOR—The defenses were commenced under circumstances which precluded the possibility of any thoroughly organized system of labor. Nor was the necessity of such an organization immediately apparent. With the occupation of the Virginia shore, a few fieldworks (as has been elsewhere mentioned) were hastily laid out, and constructed by details of troops working under the direction of engineer officers. But when, to these, fort after fort was added, and the whole gradually expanded into a fortified line encompassing on the two sides of the Potomac the cities of Washington, Georgetown, and Alexandria, more supervision was required than the limited number of engineer officers available for the duty could supply, and recourse was had to the employment of civil engineers and overseers to assist in directing the labors of the troops. In the autumn of 1861, after the line had become permanently established, details of troops were almost entirely withdrawn, (in consequence of the paramount necessity of drilling and organizing the mass of raw volunteers,) and a large force of hired laborers and mechanics was placed upon the work. As it was not then supposed that it would continue for a long time, the organization of labor was of a transient and imperfect character. During the ensuing winter this hired force was reduced to a comparatively small number and the work nearly suspended, the action of Congress forbidding its further expansion. Upon the termination of the disastrous Virginia campaigns of the spring and summer of 1862, the necessity of giving increased strength and durability to the defenses was fully recognized, and a permanent organization of supervision and labor was at once effected and maintained until the close of the war. The works were divided into two subordinate departments, consisting respectively of the Defenses north and the Defenses south of the Potomac, and the immediate direction was placed in charge of two civil engineers, one to each of the above-named divisions; the demand for the service in the field being such as to preclude the possibility of obtaining engineer officers for this duty.

The civil engineers, William C. Gunnell on the north, and Edward Frost (subsequently A. Grant Childs) on the south, had been, prior to the war engaged on the Washington aqueduct. They exhibited great zeal and intelligence, and soon mastered all those branches of military engineering which concerned their duties of construction. They were required to execute the plans prepared in the office of the chief engineer, to exercise a close supervision over their respective divisions, and generally to act as administrative officers in the details of the work. The subordinate organizations of each of the civil engineers in charge of divisions consisted as follows:

A draughtsman to prepare plans, maps, etc.

An assistant engineer to assist in laying out the work from plans and to make the necessary field surveying for maps.

A clerk to consolidate the daily reports of working force; to make out the monthly pay-rolls, keep accounts of purchases, and to prepare vouchers for payment; and to keep account of property drawn on requisition upon the quartermaster's and other departments.

Two or more superintendents were employed on each division, to whom were apportioned subdivisions of the line. Their duties were to control and direct, through their foreman, the laboring force; to keep the time-books, make daily reports of the occupation of every person under them, as well as of the military details; to supervise the camps and depots or material; to make requisition on the engineers in charge (who were the purchasing agents) for materials; and, generally, to aid the civil engineers by giving a closer and more constant oversight to all the operations on each subdivision than they could themselves exercise.

The laboring force was variable (according to the necessities of the work), reaching its maximum probably in the spring and summer of 1863, when, for the purpose of carrying out the recommendations of the "Commission," the hired force was increased to about 1,500 men.

The laborers were arranged in squads of from thirty to fifty men working under one foreman, who was required to exact from each man a fair day's work, to keep a record of the time made, reporting it to the superintendent each night, and to control them in all police arrangements of their portion of the camp.

On each side of the Potomac was also employed a force of twenty-five to forty carpenters, distributed along the line, and working under the direction of a master-carpenter to each sub-division. By these were made the timber constructions used in the forts, and the repairs of wagons, barrows, and tools, etc.

For hauling logs and for distributing materials, wagon trains of from twenty-five to forty four-horse teams, obtained from the Quartermaster's Department, and permanently assigned to the work, were stationed on each subdivision of the line. When extra transportation was required, additional wagon trains were temporarily detailed from the Quartermaster's Department for the purpose.

As all the field employees had to be quartered and subsisted on the work, camps and depots of materials were established at convenient points. These establishments consisted of a superintendent's office, store-house, cook-house, mess-room, carpenter's shop, blacksmith's shop, stables, etc. The men were generally quartered in tents. The attachés of the camp were one "clerk and commissary," whose duty was to assist the superintendent in keeping the time-books and making daily reports; to attend to the drawing and issuing of rations for the men, and to supervise all the arrangements of the cook-house and mess-room. A "quartermaster" or "property clerk" had general charge of the trains and other property of the Quartermaster's Department, together with the tools and purchased materials. He also kept the time-books of teamsters, blacksmiths, and stable men. A blacksmith and one to three helpers were constantly employed at each camp. A messenger, a sufficient force of cooks and teamsters, and a few stable boys complete the list of camp employees.[5]

Details of troops were used whenever (and to the fullest extent) practicable; but this force was variable and uncertain, generally furnished with reluctance by the commanding officers, and comparatively inefficient when furnished. In the autumn of 1862 a force, numbering several thousand troops, was employed for a few weeks in constructing military roads and rifle-trenches, in felling timber and in strengthening the old and building new works. During the year 1863 large details were drawn from the convalescent, stragglers, and deserters' camps south of the Potomac, and made up in numbers what they lacked in individual efficiency. But it was at all times necessary to keep up at least a small force of hired laborers and mechanics as a dependence under emergencies, as also a considerable number of experienced foremen to direct the labors of the troops.

Having referred to the difficulty of obtaining such details of troops as the works required, and to their general inefficiency as working parties, it may be proper to state that this was in a great measure owing to the constantly recurring changes in the garrison, and perhaps to a lack of interest on the part of subordinate officers in the completion and repairs of forts to which they considered themselves only temporarily assigned. Much better results were obtained from such commands as were for any considerable length of time assigned to work on the Defenses.

OCCUPATION OF LANDS—The sites of the several works being determined upon, possession was at once taken, with little or no reference to the rights of the owners or the occupants of he lands—the stern law of "Military necessity" and the magnitude of the public interests involved in the security of the nation's capital being paramount to every other consideration, in one case a church, and in several instances dwellings and other buildings were demolished, that the sites might be occupied by forts. Long lines of rifle-trenches and military roads were located and constructed where the principles of defense or the convenience of communication required them, without regard to the cultivated fields or orchards through which they might pass. In addition to the ground immediately occupied by the defensive works, the lands in front for a distance of two miles were cleared of standing timber. At this work alone there were employed in the autumn of 1862 details of troops numbering from 2,000 to 3,000 men for a period of several weeks. The timber so cut down was used, so far as it was found to be suitable, in the construction of the forts, or for abattis.

The injuries thus inflicted upon the citizens living along the lines, in the destruction and use of private property, were in the aggregate very considerable, and there were probably individual cases of extreme hardship; but, however much these evils might be deplored, they could not he avoided. No compensation for such damages or occupation of lands was made or promised, nor was it even practicable to make an estimate of their pecuniary amount. In some instances a statement of the number of acres denuded of timber, and a general description of its kind and quality, and in others of the number and kind of trees cut down, was given to the owners, upon request being made therefore, as a supposed basis for future in indemnity by the Government; but no general system of estimating damages was attempted.

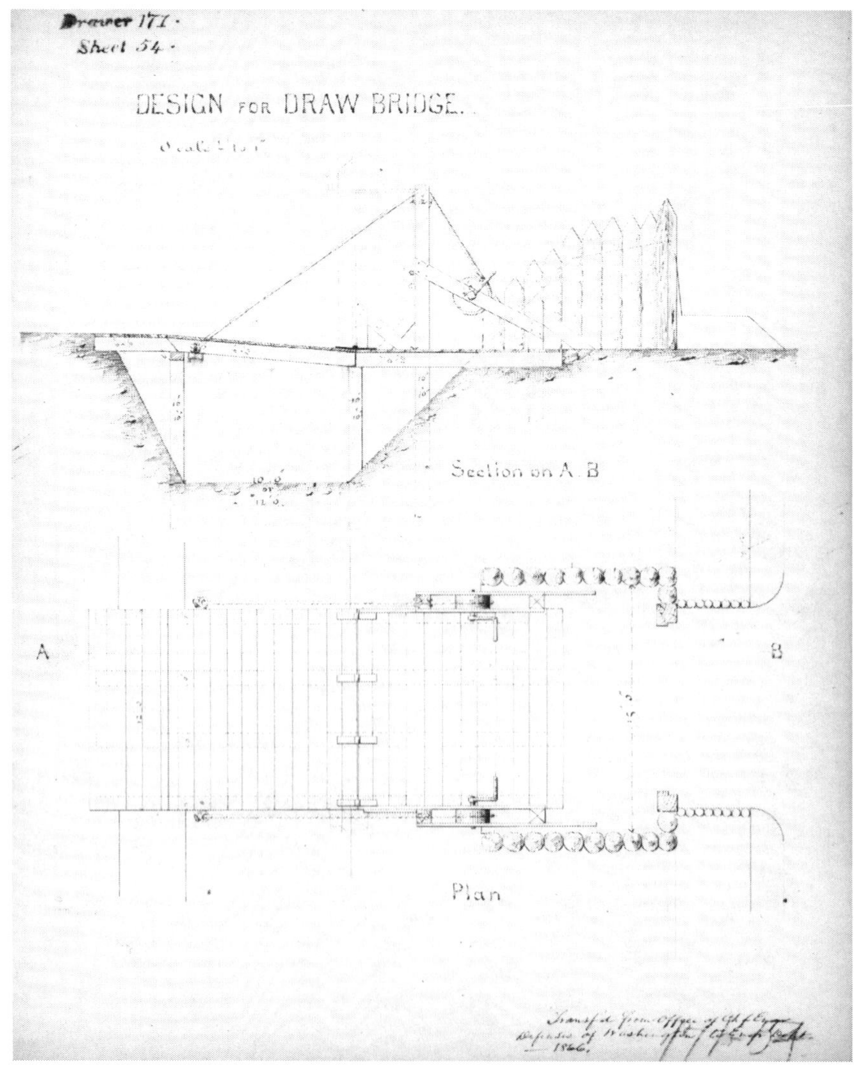

Engineer Design for a Fort Drawbridge. *National Archives*

3

Touring the Forts South of the Potomac

The Defenses of Washington south of the Potomac River encompassed a line of earthworks starting with Battery Rodgers at Alexandria, Virginia, and ending with Fort Marcy above Chain Bridge. By 1865, the defenses were impressive, containing thirty-three named fortifications, twenty-five batteries, and seven blockhouses. Fieldworks were established at intervals of 800 to 1,000 yards, with intersecting fields of fire commanding every important approach to the city. In General Barnard's report, the "Table of Armament of Works South of the Potomac River" lists 256 smoothbore cannon, 170 rifled cannon, and sixty mortars. Many of the forts were connected by rifle pits, and military roads were constructed to each fort for avenues of supply and reinforcement.

For ease of understanding, the Defenses south of the Potomac River can he divided into three major groups:

1. *Forts Protecting the City of Alexandria.* Starting with Battery Rodgers and terminating with Fort Reynolds near Four Mile Run, this line of fortifications protected the valuable supply center and port of Alexandria. This line of works can be subdivided into two groups: the forts south of Alexandria, starting with Fort Willard and ending with Fort Lyon, and the forts running from Shuters Hill to Seminary Ridge, starting with Fort Ellsworth and ending at Fort Reynolds.
2. *Forts Protecting the Arlington Line.* The fortifications of the Arlington Line form two groups: the "Proper Defenses of Washington," or those sites from which the Union capital could be shelled if commanded by Confederate forces, and the forts that form the outer perimeter defenses. The forts of the "Proper Defenses of Washington" on the Virginia shore started with Fort Scott and ended with Fort Bennett across from Georgetown. The outer perimeter defenses of the Arlington Line formed a line of works to the west of the "Proper Defenses of Washington" and started with Fort Barnard and ended with Fort C. F. Smith.
3. *Forts Protecting Chain Bridge.* Forts Ethan Allen and Marcy were constructed in September 1861 and form a separate defense sector. These two forts were supported by powerful batteries north of the Potomac River.

Hidden in the urban congestion of our neighborhoods are the earthen remains of a fascinating drama that literally changed the landscape in the name of national survival. Although many of the forts south of the Potomac River have been destroyed by time and modern development, the visitor will find several of the best-preserved and best-interpreted forts in the system.

TOURING THE FORTS SOUTH OF THE POTOMAC: START OF FORTS TOUR

Fort Ward—Guarding the Roads from Leesburg

Location

4301 West Braddock Road, Alexandria, Virginia. From 395 Exit, take Seminary Road East to North Howard Street. Turn left on North Howard Street to West Braddock Road. Turn right on West Braddock Road to the entrance of Fort Ward Park on the left. Visitor parking is located behind the nineteenth-century–style building that houses the museum at the front of the park.

Reconstructed Gate at Fort Ward. *Fort Ward Museum Collection*

Visible Remains

Fort Ward Museum & Historic Site, owned and operated by the City of Alexandria, offers an excellent orientation to the Civil War Defenses of Washington. The historic site, about 95 percent extant, features an accurate reconstruction of the northwest bastion and 1865 gate of Fort Ward. The museum was opened to the public on Memorial Day 1964 and is accredited by the American Association of Museums. A small professional staff curates a diverse 4,000-object military collection that can be seen in the changing exhibits program. The museum contains a small research library on the second floor and sponsors a variety of public programs, including lectures, living-history interpretations with soldiers and civilians in period dress, and an award-winning school education program. The museum, officers' hut, and the adjacent restroom facility were designed from Civil War photographs of buildings that existed as part of the Defenses of Washington. The museum's exterior is patterned after the headquarters building at Fort Sumner, and the restroom facility adjacent to the parking area is a copy of the headquarters building at the second Camp Convalescent, which stood in modern-day Arlington, Virginia, near the Army Navy Country Club.

Description

The fort was named for Commander James Harmon Ward, a native of Hartford, Connecticut, who was killed by gunfire from a Confederate shore battery at Mathias Point on the Potomac River on June 27, 1861. Ward was the first Union naval officer killed in the war.

Fort Ward was built on the land of Phillip Hooff, who owned the property until after the Civil War (Fairfax Deed Book H3:173). The fort is representative of the development and problems of the Defenses of Washington as a whole. It is a good example of a first-generation fort that began as a hastily constructed fort in the wave of panic after the First Battle of Bull Run (Manassas) and developed into a model field fortification that utilized many of the technological improvements learned during the war. General Barnard noted, "Fort Ward, by its location and commanding site [is] one of most important of the defenses of Alexandria." It defended the Leesburg and Alexandria Turnpike (modern Route 7) and overlooked the country to the north and west toward Bailey's and Balls Cross roads. Construction on the fort started about September 1, 1861, simultaneously with the appearance of the rebel forces on Munson's Hill. The engineers found most of the site covered with a second growth of young trees and bushes that prevented a complete survey of the topography. As a result, the design of the fort was built with a defective trace; the guns of the fort did not cover a ravine where the enemy might mass for attack.[1]

The original perimeter of the fort was 540 yards with emplacements for twenty-four guns. The armament in this early period consisted of five 32-pounder guns, six 24-pounder guns, and seven 10-pounder Parrott rifles. By December 1862, preparations had been made to strengthen the fort by adding a two-gun battery in advance of the fort and the installation of a 100-pounder Parrot rifle in the southwest corner or the fort. (A historic sign marks the improved 1864 site of the cannon.) The extensive range of the 100-pounder Parrott rifles at Forts Ward, Worth, Ellsworth, and Richardson dominated the line from Munson's Hill and the entire range of heights south of Hunting Creek that controlled Little River Turnpike (Duke Street) and the Orange and Alexandria Railroad. Even with these added improvements to the fort, the heavier projectiles of the Civil War made the old design for parapets and magazines obsolete. By May 1863, Barnard warned the commander of the fort,

> When I can spare a force I will overhaul the Fort Ward magazines thoroughly—but in the meantime, if the pinch should come, you must be prepared to throw up earth from the Terre-plein immediately in front, which can be done very quickly.[2]

The development and construction of other forts and batteries along the Virginia front produced a continual change of armament in the forts. The pirating of armament from Fort Ward angered the commander but showed Barnard's concern with the defenses as an integrated system intended to establish crossfire on any enemy position. Rifle pits were constructed connecting

Fort Ward Museum. *Fort Ward Museum Collection*

Fort Ward to adjacent fieldworks. (A marker interprets a segment of the line near the North Bastion.)

Through the spring and summer of 1863, improvements to the fort progressed very slowly because of the short supply of labor and the reassignment of soldier fatigue details. By January 1864, with an appropriation from Congress, Barnard was finally able to direct a major effort to correct the defective trace of Fort Ward. Laborers and soldiers began to rebuild the fort, increasing the perimeter from 540 to 818 yards and the number of emplacements for guns from twenty-four to thirty-six. All the interior structures were replaced and reconstructed with banquette and breast height to serve as secondary lines of defense. Within the new fort, there were 400 lineal feet of bombproofs, twelve and a half feet wide; 150 feet of magazines, ten feet wide; and forty-five feet of filling or service magazines. The fort was thoroughly flanked (able to protect itself on all sides) and contained a brick-curbed well and flagstaff. Three barracks (ninety by eighteen feet) were located near the fort gate (site of the museum), and officers' quarters were located along Braddock Lane (site of the modern park road in front of the museum). Other buildings included a mess house and stables and a privy. The enlargement and remodeling of the fort demanded changes in armament. General Barnard's report noted that Fort Ward's armament consisted of twenty-nine guns. Included in this total were five 32-pounder guns, six 24-pounder guns, six 12-pounder guns, five 6-pounder guns, one 100-pounder Parrott rifle, five four-and-a-half-inch Rodman guns, one 10-pounder Parrott, seven eight-inch siege mortars, and one 24-pounder Coehorn mortar. On February 17, 1865, a request was sent to the chief of ordnance asking for six 6-pounder howitzers, four 12-pounder howitzers, and six four-and-a-half-inch

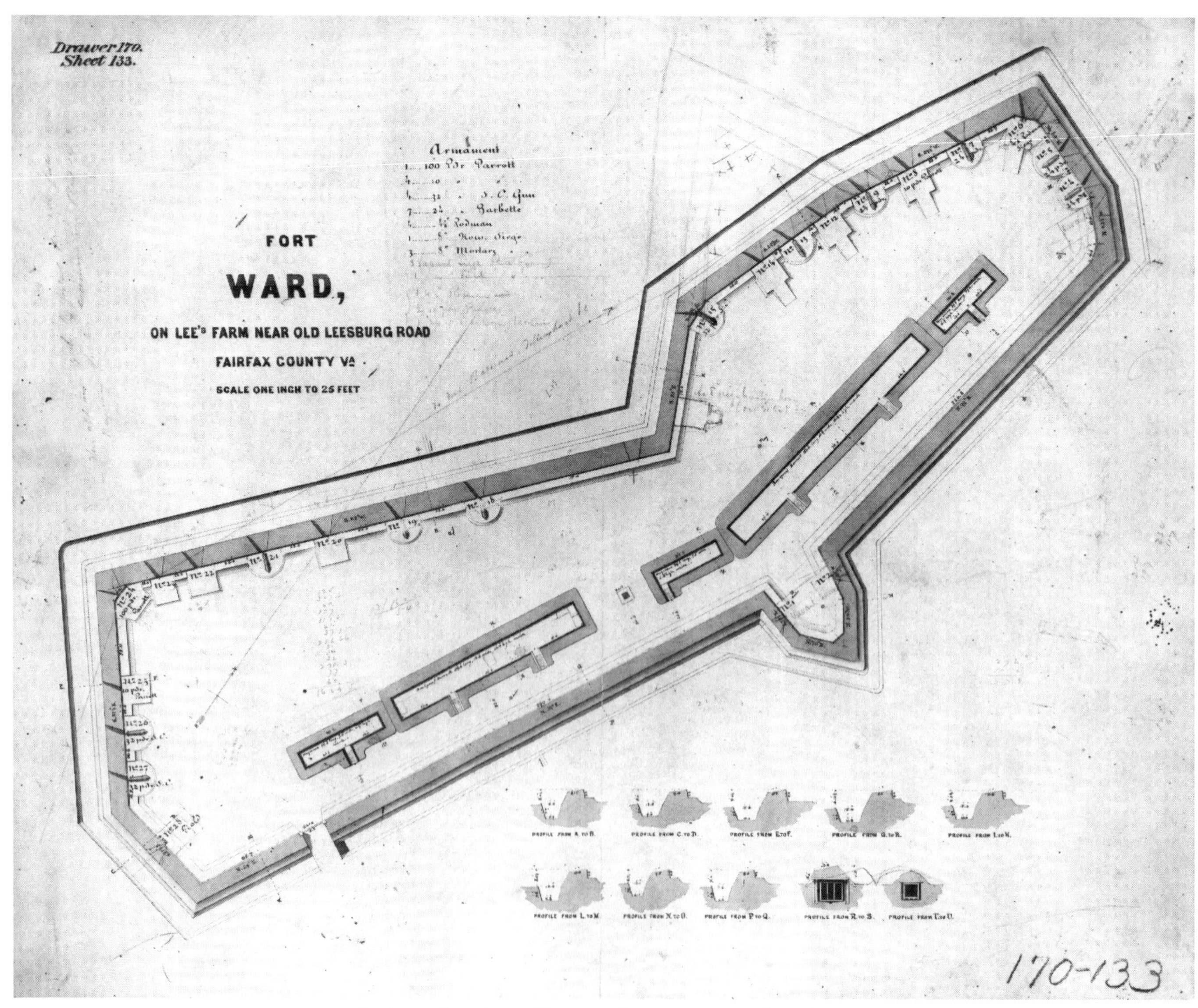

Engineer Drawing of Fort Ward, 1862. *National Archives*

First Battalion, Companies C, E, and L, 1st Connecticut Heavy Artillery, Fort Ward. *National Archives*

ordnance rifles.[3] The monthly report made three days before the surrender at Appomattox shows that construction was nearly completed; "ventilator hoods put up on bombproofs; platforms at the doorways of magazine laid; steps to the breast-height on the magazines and bombproofs; Facia, balustrading and framing of gateway in progress."[4] In May 1865, the ceremonial gate crowned by a turreted castle, the symbol of the army engineers, was completed, and Fort Ward stood as one of the most formidable forts in the Defenses of Washington. It was the fifth-largest fort and a model of nineteenth-century military engineering. Ranking third in order of importance for works south of the Potomac River, guards were stationed at Fort Ward to protect government property through the end of November. On December 6, 1865, Colonel Alexander sent the chief engineer, General Delafield, "An Account of Auction sales of property of Defenses of Washington for week ending Dec. 2, 1865." Included in the list of sales for November 30 were the following:

Abattis	Ft. Ward—E.C. Morrison	$101
Pole revetment of parapet	Ft. Ward—E.C. Morrison	$72
Timber, Lumber inside of parapet	Ft. Ward—Bodfish, Mills & Co.	$815

Fort Ward was salvaged for $988. The fort was dismantled for the value of its cut lumber and wood, which had been so plentiful in the area before 1861 but had become a scarce commodity during the occupation.[5]

Note/Anecdote

A few days after Jubal Early's raid on Washington, Private Charles Fanning Lee wrote home to his mother on July 14, 1864, to share the news from his post at Fort Ward. "Charlie" served in company B, 166th Ohio Volunteer Infantry. A former clerk turned 100-day soldier, Lee was twenty years old and stood five feet four and a half inches tall with hazel eyes, dark hair, and fair complexion. He writes,

> Dear Mother,
>
> . . . We are having exciting times here now. Almost every day we hear firing, sometimes pretty near us, although as yet we have had no attack at this fort. The most of the fighting being on the other side of the river—the rebels took Falls Church Village about 5 miles from here and our cavalry pickets who were there. We were called into the fort and stood at the guns all day expecting an attack but were beginning to think we were to be disappointed when at about half past six o'clock we saw a large cloud of dust in the direction we

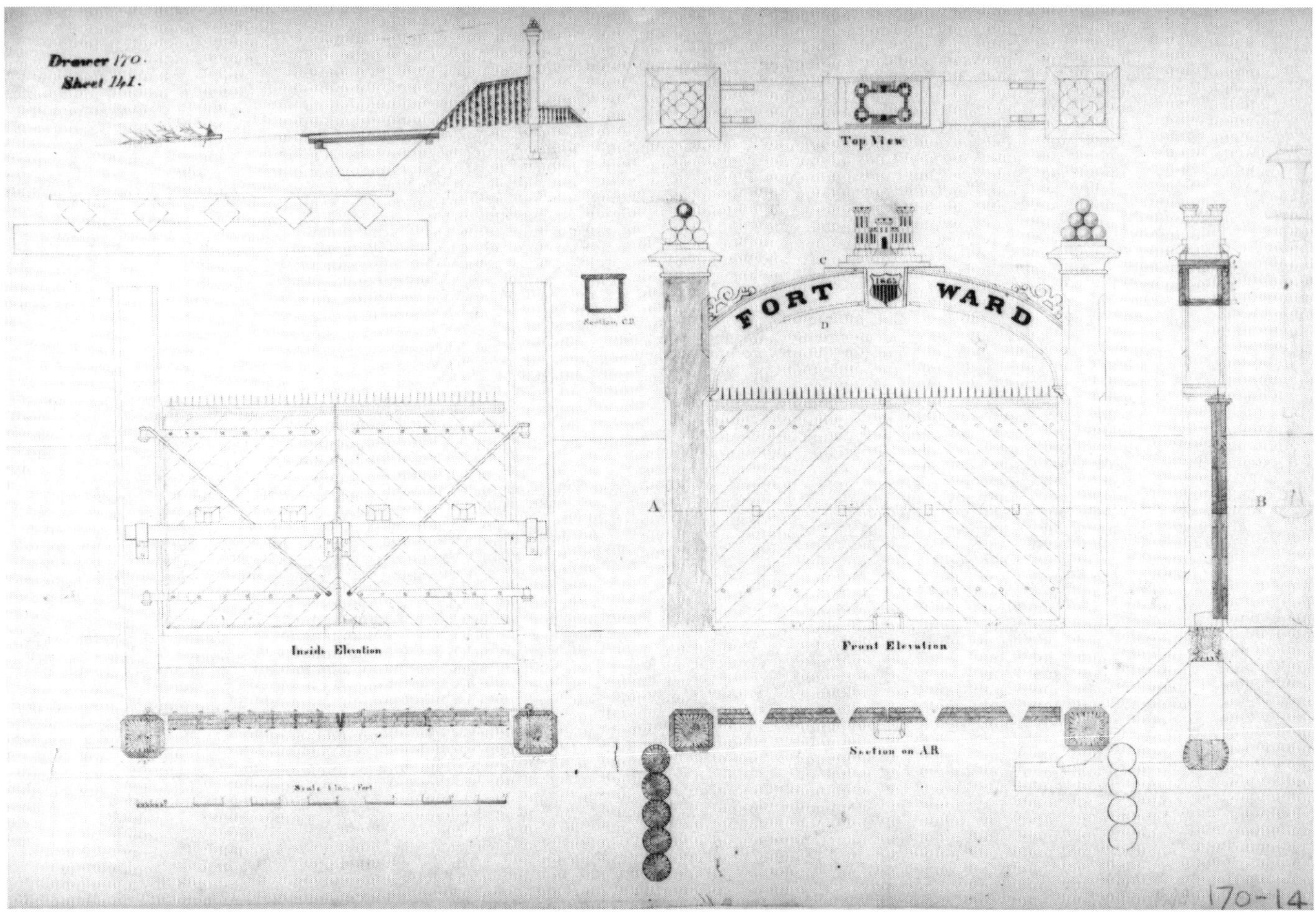

Fort Ward—Engineer Drawing of Gate, 1865. *National Archives*

> were expecting them. The men were called to attention and everything got in readiness but they did not come within range, so I had no chance to see how well I could aim a cannon. About this time a heavy firing commenced at one of the forts on the other side of the river. We could see the smoke from the guns and the shells as they burst in the air. . . . There are quite a number sick now, the principal disease is fever. One man died in our company last night.[6]

When Private Charles Lee mustered out on September 9, 1864, his unit had lost thirty-nine men to disease, and he had experienced an adventure of a lifetime.

An illustration of the problems of fort construction using army fatigue details after the surrender at Appomattox is the incident of a "mutiny" that occurred at Fort Ward on June 3, 1865. Work parties were made up of detachments from different regiments. The engineer officers often had little control over the number of troops they supervised or the length of time the soldiers would work. Colonel Alexander described the incident this way:

> Yesterday a mutiny occurred at Fort Ward in consequence of [a] disagreement as to working hours. Lieut. Falkerson in charge of the detail from Ft. Worth, refused to work his men after 4 p.m. on the plea that *he could not control them.* They quit at 4 and refused to work longer. . . . The lieut, succeeded[ed] in coaxing his men to work until 5 p.m. at which hour he told his men "not to mind a D-m about the tools and to leave them in the ditch."[7]

An often-overlooked source of detail about objects in the forts is the Quarterly Return of Ordnance Stores. Selected items from the September 31, 1864, return (to be filled out in triplicate) for Fort Ward shows that the fort had on hand the following:[8]

30 sponge buckets
22 Budge Barrels
29 Cannon spikes
121 Lanyards
58 Priming wires
18 Pass boxes

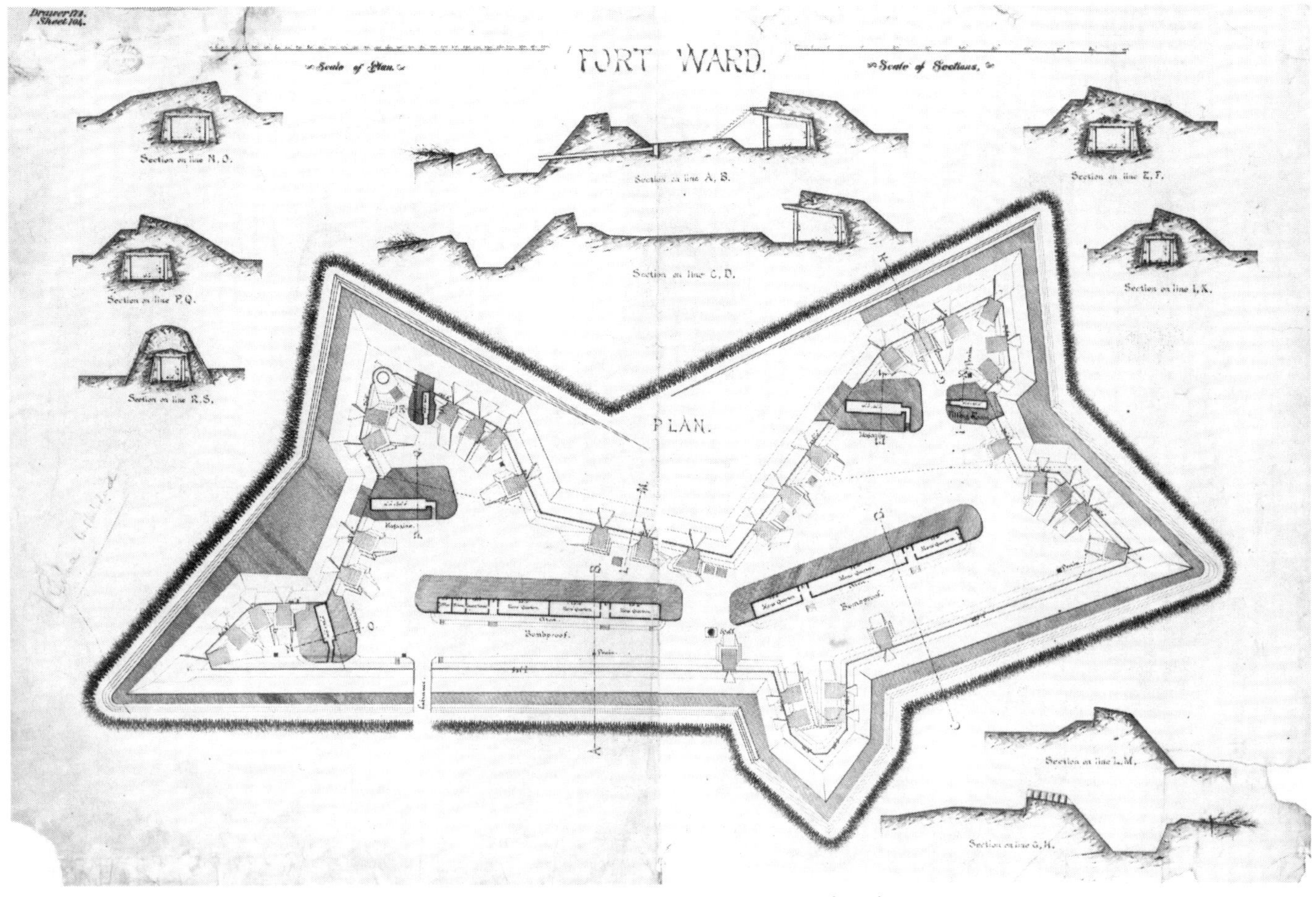

Fort Ward Engineer Drawing, 1864. *National Archives*

61 Thumbstalls
36 Vent Covers
2 Balls of lampwicking
149 24-pdr. shot
684 8-inch Siege mortar shells
150 4.5-inch canister
17,500 elongated .58 cal. ball
9,400 Percussion caps
23 lbs. of green paint
6 lbs. of yellow paint
8 Gals. of lacquer
2 Gals. of paint drier
40 lbs. of wheel grease
4 Corn brooms
1 Copy of Heavy Artillery Tactics
1 Copy of Field Artillery Tactics
1 Copy of Revised Army Regulations
121 32-pdr. shot
300 1-pdr. Hand grenades
174 3-pdr. Hand grenades
1000 lbs. of Cannon powder
850 lbs. of Rifle/Musket powder

The garrison of the fort included the following:

38th New York Infantry, Regiment, September 1861—fort construction
40th New York Infantry, Regiment, September 1861—fort construction
15th New York Engineers, September 1861—fort construction
18th New York Infantry, September 1861—fort construction
31st New York Infantry—fort construction
32d New York Infantry—fort construction
2d New York Heavy Artillery, Co. K, December 1861
2d New York Heavy Artillery, Cos. A, H, December 31, 1861–June 1862
2d New York Heavy Artillery, Co. C, December 31, 1861–June 30, 1862
2d New York Heavy Artillery, Co. H, December 31, 1861–February 1862
2d New York Heavy Artillery, Co. M, December 31, 1861–June 30, 1862

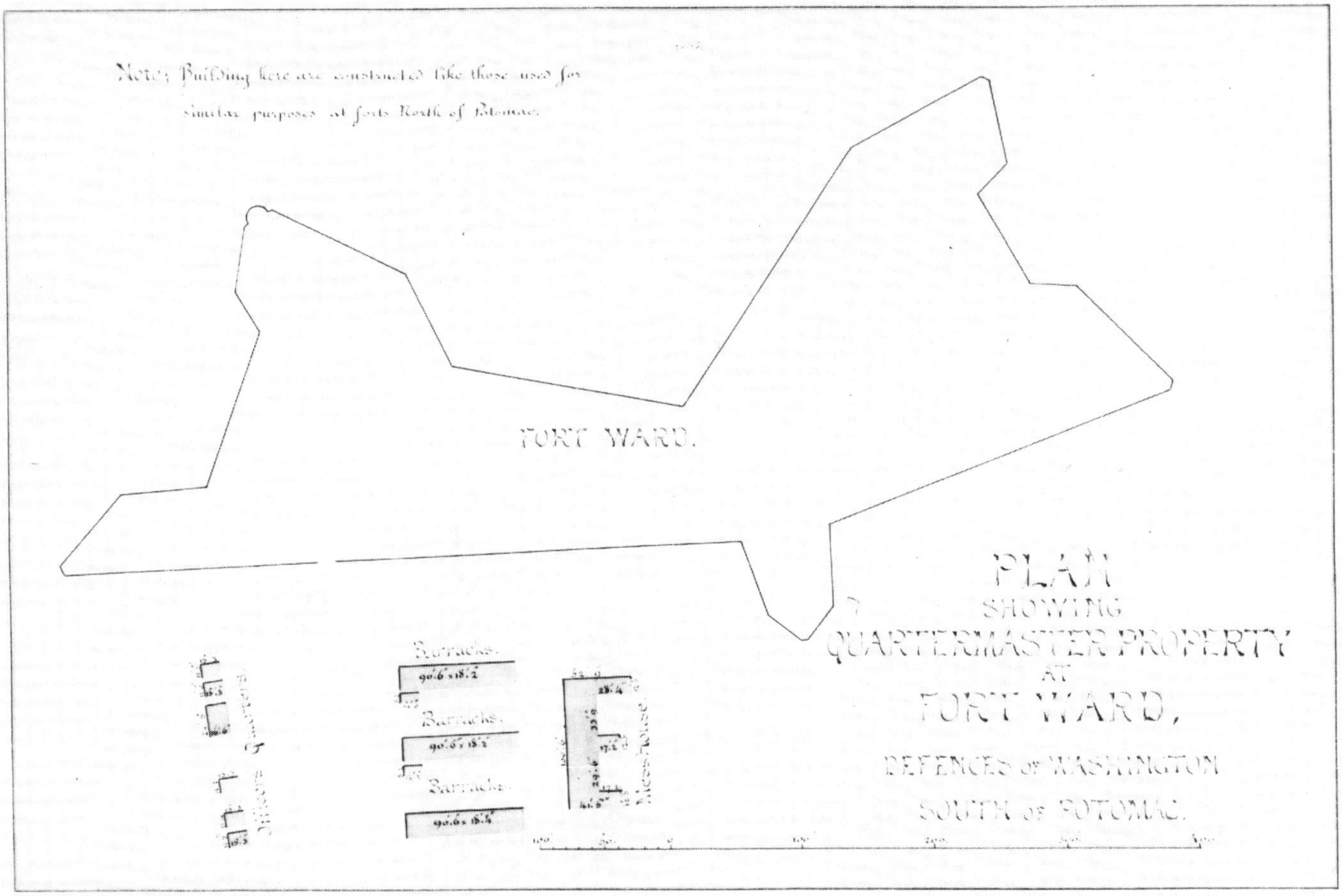

Note; Building here are constructed like those used for similar purposes at forts North of Potomac.

FORT WARD.

PLAN
SHOWING
QUARTERMASTER PROPERTY
AT
FORT WARD,
DEFENCES OF WASHINGTON
SOUTH OF POTOMAC.

Barracks. 90.6 x 18.2

Barracks. 90.6 x 18.2

Barracks. 90.6 x 18.4

Mess House

Plan of Quartermaster Property—Fort Ward. *National Archives*

Fort Ward's Reconstructed Northwest Bastion. *Fort Ward Museum Collection*

2d New York Heavy Artillery, Co. D, January 1862–February 1862
2d New York Heavy Artillery, Co. I, January 1862–April 1862
1st Connecticut Heavy Artillery, Co. C, July 1862
3d Battalion New York Heavy Artillery, August 23–29, 1862
1st Connecticut Heavy Artillery, Co. M, August 14, 1862–December 5, 1862
1st Connecticut Heavy Artillery, Co. L, November 1862
2d New York Heavy Artillery, Co. C, April 10, 1863
1st Connecticut Heavy Artillery, Co. M, March 1864–April 1864
9th New York Heavy Artillery, Cos. C, D, G, May 1864
166th Ohio National Guard, Cos. B, C, May 15, 1864–July 1864
Hampton's Independent Battery F, Pennsylvania Light Artillery, May 26, 1864–July 4, 1864
3d Regiment Veteran Reserve Corps, Cos. C, E, G, I, July 1864–July 31, 1864
1st West Virginia Light Artillery, Battery C, September 1864–November 1864
1st New Hampshire Heavy Artillery, Co. H, November 11, 1864–November 15, 1864
6th Pennsylvania Heavy Artillery, Co. C, November 1864–April 1865
6th Pennsylvania Heavy Artillery, Co. M, November 1864–February 1865
4th Massachusetts Heavy Artillery, Co. M, December 30, 1864–February 8, 1865
4th Massachusetts Heavy Artillery, Co. F, January 1865–April 1865
4th New York Heavy Artillery, Co. C, May 1865–June 1865
4th New York Heavy Artillery, Co. M, May 1865–June 1865

Fort Ellsworth—Alexandria's Rear-Echelon Fort

Location

From Fort Ward, turn left on West Braddock Road to King Street, continue on King Street, turn right on Callahan Drive, turn right into the entrance for the George Washington Masonic National Memorial, and drive up the hill past the Memorial steps and around to the parking area. Park at the far end (north corner) of the parking lot and walk up the back road (Carlisle Drive) about fifty yards and face west. The site of Fort Ellsworth is in front of you on the crest of the knoll. You will be approaching the fort from the eastern side. If you look to your left, you will see the heights south of Hunting Creek where Fort Lyon was located (near the Huntington Metro Station on North Kings Highway).

Visible Remains

Faint tracings of the parapet and ditch are visible along the middle of the north wall and southeast bastion of the fort. The outline of the northeast bastion, east wall, and east bastion can be seen by following the dark green grass of the filled-in ditch. The fort proper sits on three parcels of land divided by fences, the northeast and east bastions sit on the Mason's property, the southeast bastion and part of the gorge are located on the Virginia American Water Company property, and the western perimeter of the fort is occupied by the Ellsworth Condominium Association. The northwest bastion trace can still be seen in the topography of the hill. David V. Miller, in his book *The Defenses of Washington during the Civil War*, stated that in 1962 the location of the northwest magazine was occupied by the home of A. E. Umholtz and that very little digging had been necessary for their basement.[9] The tennis court marks the site where the home once stood. If you have time to do the George Washington Masonic Memorial tour, the angles of Fort Ellsworth's bastions can be seen clearly from the observation deck at the top of the memorial.

Description

The fort was named in honor of Colonel Elmer E. Ellsworth, 11th New York "Fire" Zouaves. Ellsworth, a personal friend of Lincoln and a northern martyr, was killed at the Marshall House in Alexandria on the morning of May 24, 1861, during the occupation of the city. He was also largely responsible for promoting the Zouave movement in the United States. Fort Ellsworth was built on land owned by the Henry Dulany and was considered a "work of large dimension." In 1861, it was an isolated field fort commanding Alexandria's strategically important river port and railroad depot. Barnard noted that as an isolated work, "it might affect an influence over the inimical population of the city of Alexandria; it might help to defend the place against small expeditions, but in relation to operations it could neither offer much aid to the defense nor materially deter attack." The site was selected by Captain H. G. Wright (later a major general who commanded troops at the Battle of Fort Stevens), and the trace of the fort was laid out on May 25, 1861. After the construction of Forts Worth, Williams, and Ward on Seminary Heights and Fort Lyon on the heights south of Hunting Creek, Fort Ellsworth served as a secondary line of defense. Together with two blockhouses and a battery located in the Hunting Creek Valley, the fort closed the gap between Forts Lyon and Williams and helped prevent the enemy from establishing batteries on the more elevated heights across the valley. The fort's perimeter was 618 yards with emplacements

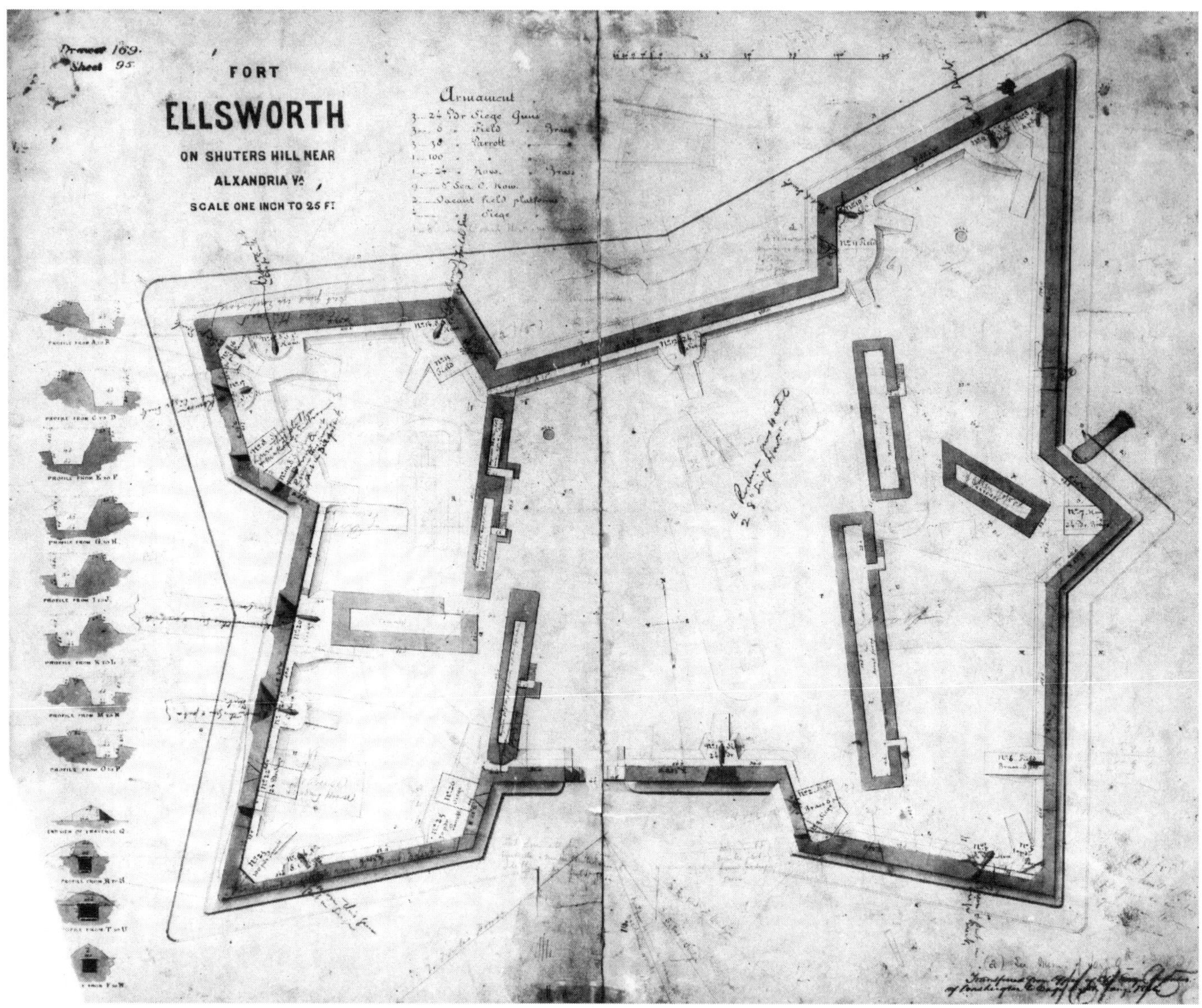

Fort Ellsworth—Engineer Drawing. *National Archives*

for twenty-nine guns. The armament included nine eight-inch seacoast howitzers, three 24-pounder guns, four 6-pounder field guns, one 100-pounder Parrott, and two 24-pounder Coehorn mortars. Within the fort were extensive bombproofs, magazines, a flagstaff, and two wells.[10] One inspection report of the fort's wells stated that "both want cleaning out . . . [as] one has dead rats in it." Soldiers' barracks stood on the east side of the fort, and a large brick house owned by the Dulany family was commandeered for use as a headquarters, regimental hospital, and barracks.

Notes/Anecdotes

Soldiers who passed through the city often commented on Fort Ellsworth in their letters and diaries. One such account, written in November 1861 by Colonel J. Howard Kitching, 2d New York Artillery, described the fort this way:

> Fort Ellsworth, you remember, was built by the Ellsworth's Zouaves when they first entered Virginia. It is a very fine piece of work on a splendid commanding position, overlooking Washington, Alexandria, and all the surrounding country for fifteen or twenty miles. When we came here . . . it was occupied by four hundred "man-of-war's men"; in fact, a complete frigate's crew,—and they have been spending the past two months in putting the fort in complete order, just as sailors do, sodding and whitewashing everything, and planting evergreens until the work is a picture of neatness.[11]

One charming tale of folklore explains why the shade of grass is darker in the "old fort" ditch. During

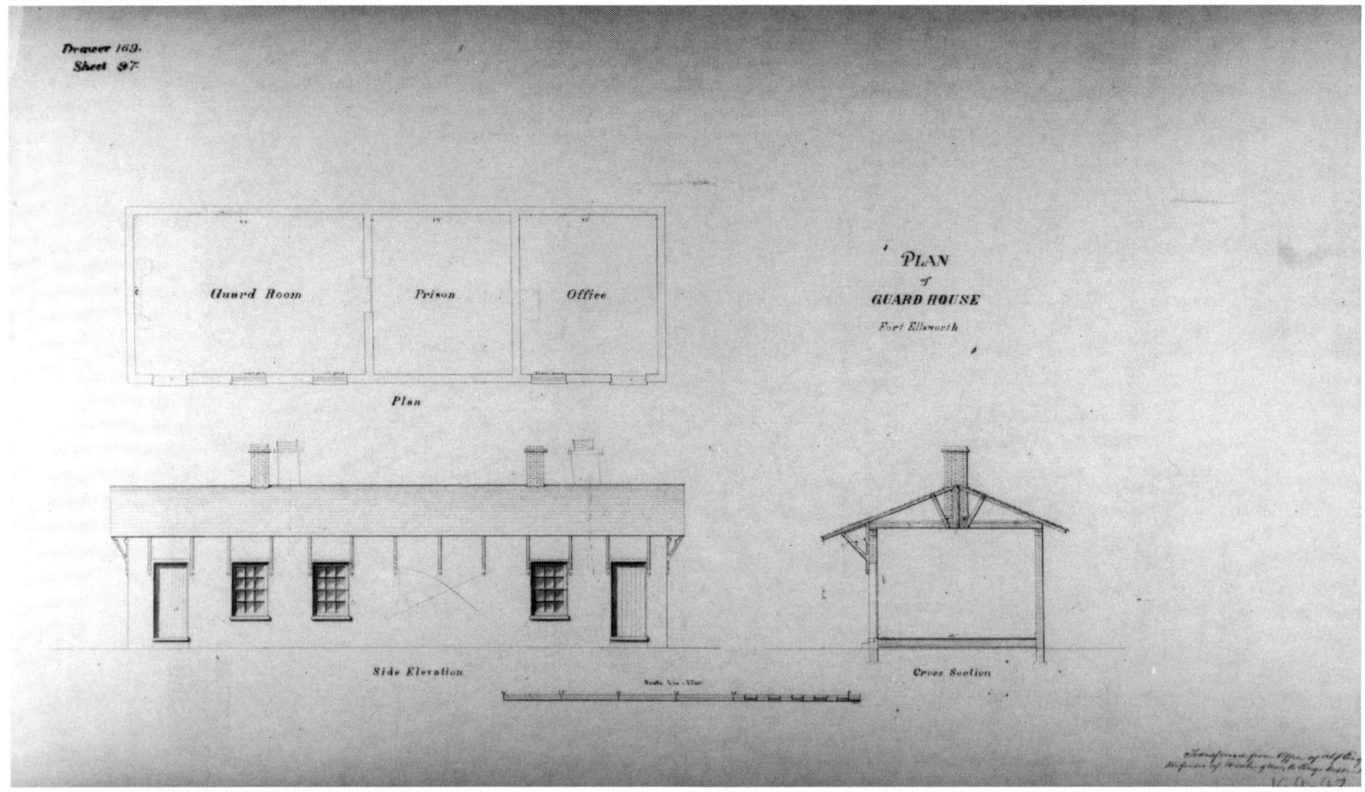

Plan of Guard House—Fort Ellsworth. *National Archives*

PLAN
SHOWING
QUARTERMASTER PROPERTY
AT
FORT ELLSWORTH,
DEFENCES of WASHINGTON
SOUTH of POTOMAC.

Officers' Quarters.

Barracks.

Barracks.

Mess & Cook House

FORT ELLSWORTH.

Note; Buildings here are constructed like those used for similar purposes at forts North of Potomac.

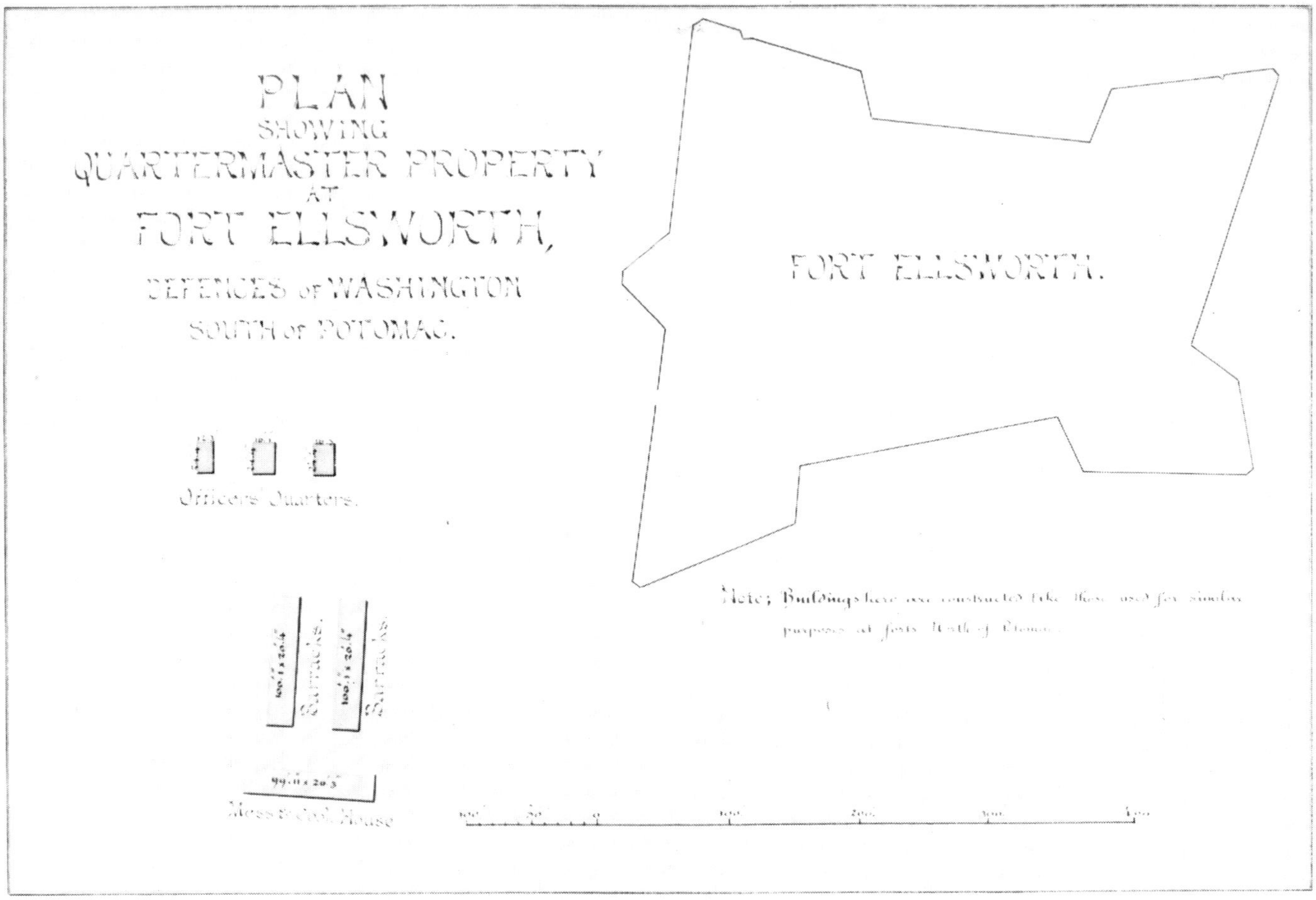

Plan of Quartermaster Property—Fort Ellsworth. *National Archives*

Outline of Fort Ellsworth's Ditch. *Authors' Collection*

the war, bags of gunpowder in the hands of the untrained volunteers were continually spilling into the ditch. Each blast from the cannons scattered more powder along the ditch until it was saturated with powder. Well over 100 years have passed since the Civil War, but the nitrogen from the gunpowder has kept the grass a darker shade of green.[12] The real reason? Destruction of the sub soil in the ditch caused the shade variation.

An additional earthwork constructed on Shuter's Hill to the northeast of Fort Ellsworth was called Fort Dahlgren. This early war fortification guarded the Leesburg Turnpike (modern-day King Street, Route 7). In August 1861, it was manned by the marines of the USS *Pawnee* and sailors from the USS *Perry*. Adjacent to Fort Ellsworth extending down the hill onto lower ground is the site of the first Camp Convalescent, or "Camp Misery." In the winter of 1862, 10,000 to 15,000 soldiers were gathered in this camp.[13] Many of the soldiers were sick and destitute without blankets, clothing, or overcoats. After Union soldiers froze to death, a congressional investigation closed the camp and established a new Camp Convalescent near Fort Richardson in what is now modern-day Arlington.

In the aftermath of the turmoil caused by Jubal Early's raid on Washington, Corporal William A. Smith, Company D, 1st Battalion, 3d Regiment, Veteran Reserve Corps, wrote to his mother, father and sisters,

> We have gone into Fort Ellsworth. There is four companies here. The other five companies have gone to Fort Ward and it is about two miles from here. We will have a pretty hard time of it for a while. We will have to learn to drill on heavy artillery. Some 24-pdrs. and 64-pdrs. and one 100-pdr. guns—these are a little heavier than we have been using—for it is very hot here now and the darn barracks in the fort is alive with bed bugs. They bite so hard that a body can't sleep at all. They have a regular dress parade on a body and then form a line and go out in a line of skirmishers and then give us fits.[14]

The following regiments include garrison and construction units named in regimental histories and official records:

1st Michigan Infantry—construction
11th New York "Fire" Zouaves—construction
1st New Jersey Infantry—construction

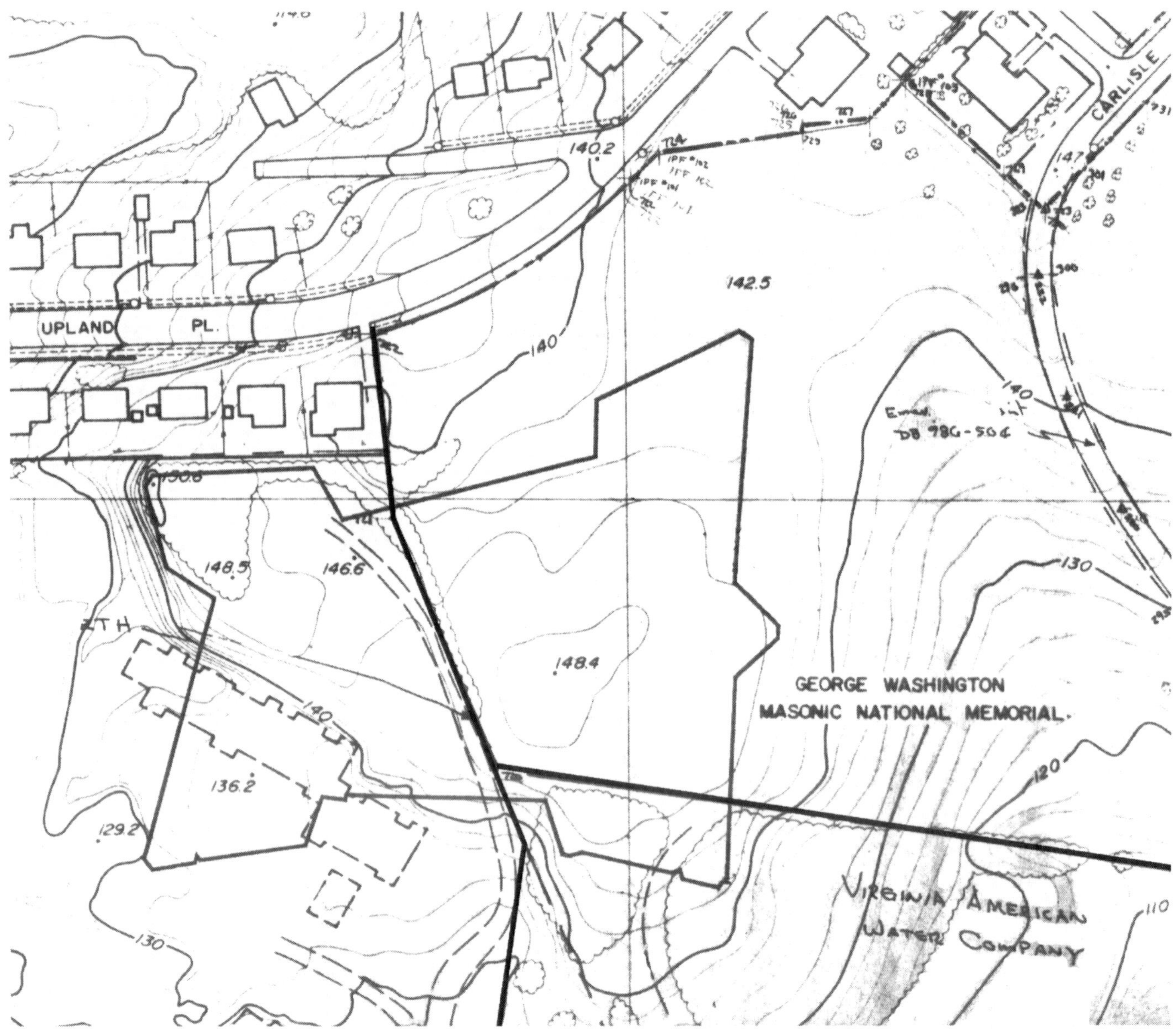

June 1978 Survey Outline of Fort Ellsworth. *Fort Ward Museum*

A detachment of sailors from the Washington Navy Yard
4th Pennsylvania Infantry—construction
5th Pennsylvania Infantry—construction
17th New York Infantry, Co. C, May 20, 1861—August 31, 1861
17th New York Infantry, Cos. B, E, July 1861—August 1861
11th Massachusetts—August 1861
11th New Jersey Infantry, Co. K, September 1861
88th Pennsylvania Infantry, Cos. B, F, August 1861–February 1862
26th New York Infantry, Cos. B, G, November 1861–December 1861
11th Independent Battery, New York Light Artillery, Battery, February 28, 1862–June 30, 1862
12th Independent Battery New York Light Artillery, February 2, 1862–June 7, 1862
15th New York Heavy Artillery, Co. E (part), July 1862–September 15, 1862
2d New York Heavy Artillery, Co. D, September 1862–November 27, 1862
2d New York Heavy Artillery, Co. G, September 1862–October 1862
1st Wisconsin Heavy Artillery, Co. A, November 1862–August 1863
2nd Connecticut Heavy Artillery, Cos. B, F, G, May 1863
2d Connecticut Heavy Artillery, Cos. C, H, September 1863–April 1864
2d Connecticut Heavy Artillery, Co. L, February 29, 1864–April 1864

136th Ohio National Guard, Cos. B, H, May 2, 1864–June 30, 1864
3d Regiment Veteran Reserve Corps, Cos. B, D, H, K, July 1864
James Thompson's Independent Battery C, Pennsylvania Light Artillery, July 1864–July 12, 1864
3d Regiment Veteran Reserve Corps, Cos. B, G, I, August 1864–September 30, 1864
1st Wisconsin Heavy Artillery, Cos. F, G, April–May 1865
15th New York Heavy Artillery, Cos. K, L, M, May 1865–June 1865

1864 Alexandria Panoramic Photograph

Location

Drive to the parking area closer to the front of the George Washington Masonic National Memorial and park. Walk to the front of the building.

Description

Located near the base of the main steps is the marker that shows the "Model Camp" of the 44th New York Infantry. The series of photographs create a panoramic view of Alexandria during 1864 and were taken near the site of the marker that gives a vivid portrait of the city landscape during the Union occupation. Notice the Hunting Creek Bridge in the right panel. The tour will lead you over the approximate location of the bridge after you visit the site of Battery Rodgers. If you have time, the George Washington Masonic National Memorial is opened from 9:00 A.M. to 4:00 P.M. and has scheduled guided tower tours daily. The building is closed on major holidays.

Officers of the 44th New York Infantry. *National Archives*

ALEXANDRIA'S CONTRIBUTION TO RIVER DEFENSE

Battery Rodgers

Location

From the Masonic Memorial, follow the drive down the hill and make a right turn on Callahan Drive. Proceed on Callahan Drive to the light and turn left on Duke Street. Continue on Duke Street, past Washington Street until you reach South Lee Street. Turn right on South Lee Street and continue to Jefferson Street. Battery Rodgers was located where the townhouses sit (800 block) on the east side of South Lee Street.

Visible Remains

No remains of the battery exist.

Description

The fort was named for Navy Captain George W. Rodgers, who was killed on August 17, 1863, during the attack on Fort Wagner, Charleston Harbor, South Carolina. Rodgers commanded the ironclad USS *Catskill* and was instantly killed by pieces of bolts that fractured when a solid shot struck the pilothouse. Constructed in 1863 and situated nearly half a mile below the city wharves and populated areas, Battery Rodgers was located on a bluff about twenty-eight feet above high water. Barnard noted that it was arranged to throw its principal fire on any vessel attempting to pass up the river at a range of 600 yards, that being the distance to midchannel, half a mile. It also commanded, with an enfilading fire, the entire river channel from shore to shore. The main face of the work was 185 feet long, the flanks sixty and eighty feet. The parapets were twenty-five feet thick, and the breast height was formed with vertical post revetment. The battery had two magazines that were protected by seventeen and a half feet of earth.

Drawer 170.
Sheet 39.

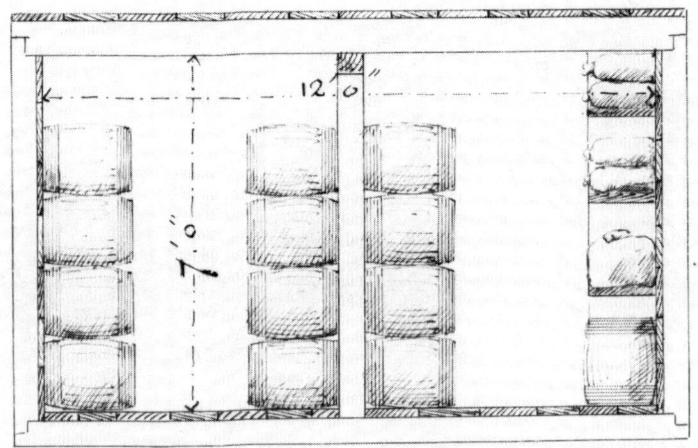

Transverse Section.

MAGAZINE AT BATTERY RODGERS

Scale 1/2 an in. [illegible] ft.

Transfd. from Office of Chf. Engr. Defenses of Washington to Engr. Dept. Jany. 1866.

Section of Powder Magazine—Battery Rodgers. *National Archives*

Airing the Powder Magazine—Battery Rodgers. *National Archives*

The work was designed for an armament of five 200-pounder Parrott rifles and one fifteen-inch Rodman gun. The guns were protected by two large traverses that served as bombproof filling rooms or service magazines. Quartermaster buildings included a hospital, two barracks (twenty-four by sixty five feet), a prison, and a mess hall. Battery Rodgers worked together with Fort Foote to guard the Potomac River approaches to Washington. The battery also commanded the southern approaches to Alexandria by covering the Accotink Road (modern Fort Hunt Road). The battery was garrisoned after the war, and the post was finally abandoned, the quartermaster buildings being sold at public auction in the spring of 1869.[15]

Notes/Anecdotes

One of the most unusual and comical photographs taken of the Defenses of Washington is the picture of a man's face peering out of the muzzle of the fifteen-inch Rodman gun at Battery Rodgers. A large owl sits on top of the gun tube. The photographic event must have been attended by a gathering of sightseers because several different soldiers mention the occasion in letters home. There is speculation that the man in the gun may be a visiting Russian sailor whose ship docked at Alexandria in early December 1863. The garrison of Battery Rodgers during the Civil War consisted of companies from the 1st Wisconsin Heavy Artillery and the 2d Connecticut Heavy Artillery.

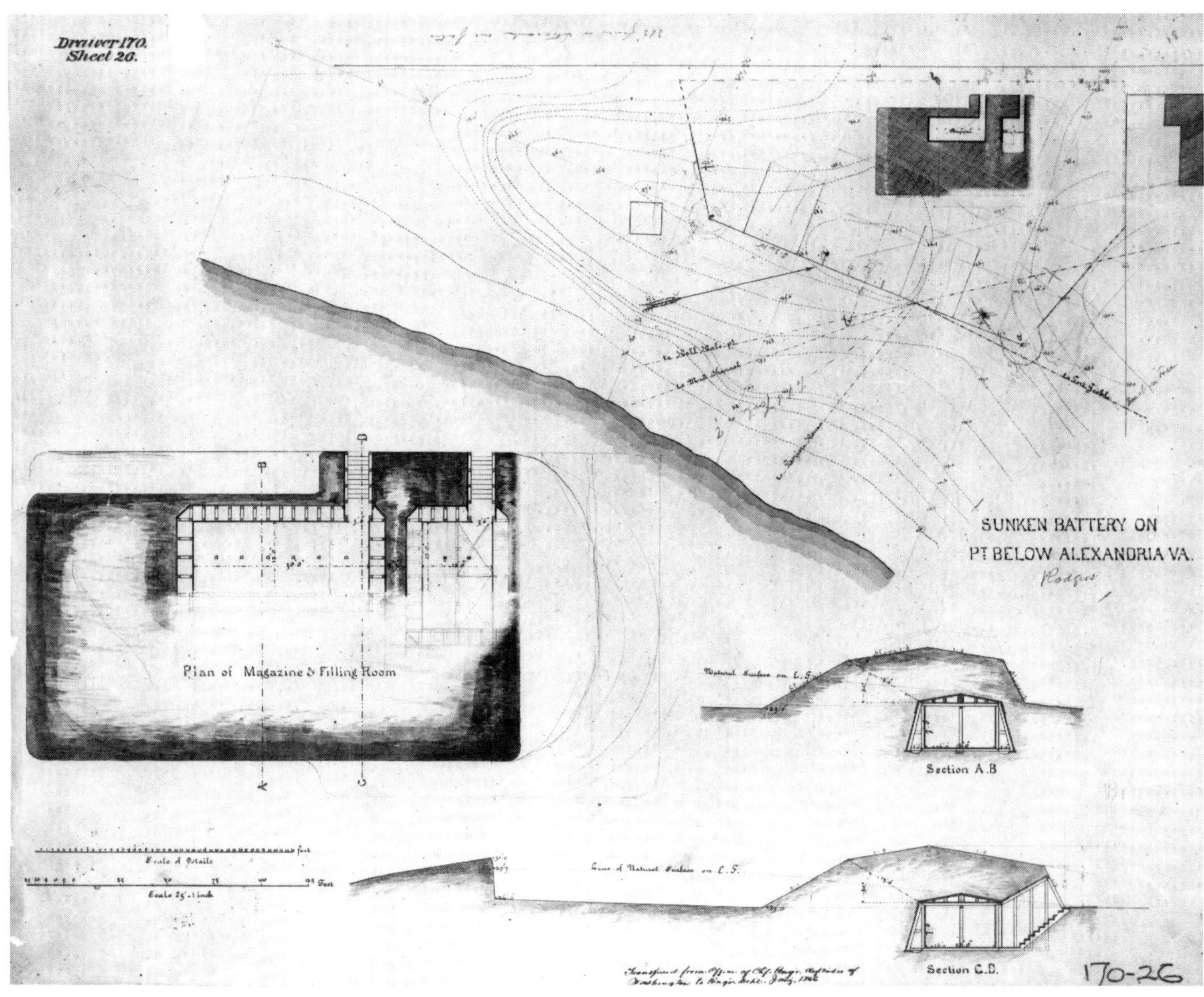

Plan of Magazine and Filling Room—Battery Rodgers. *National Archives*

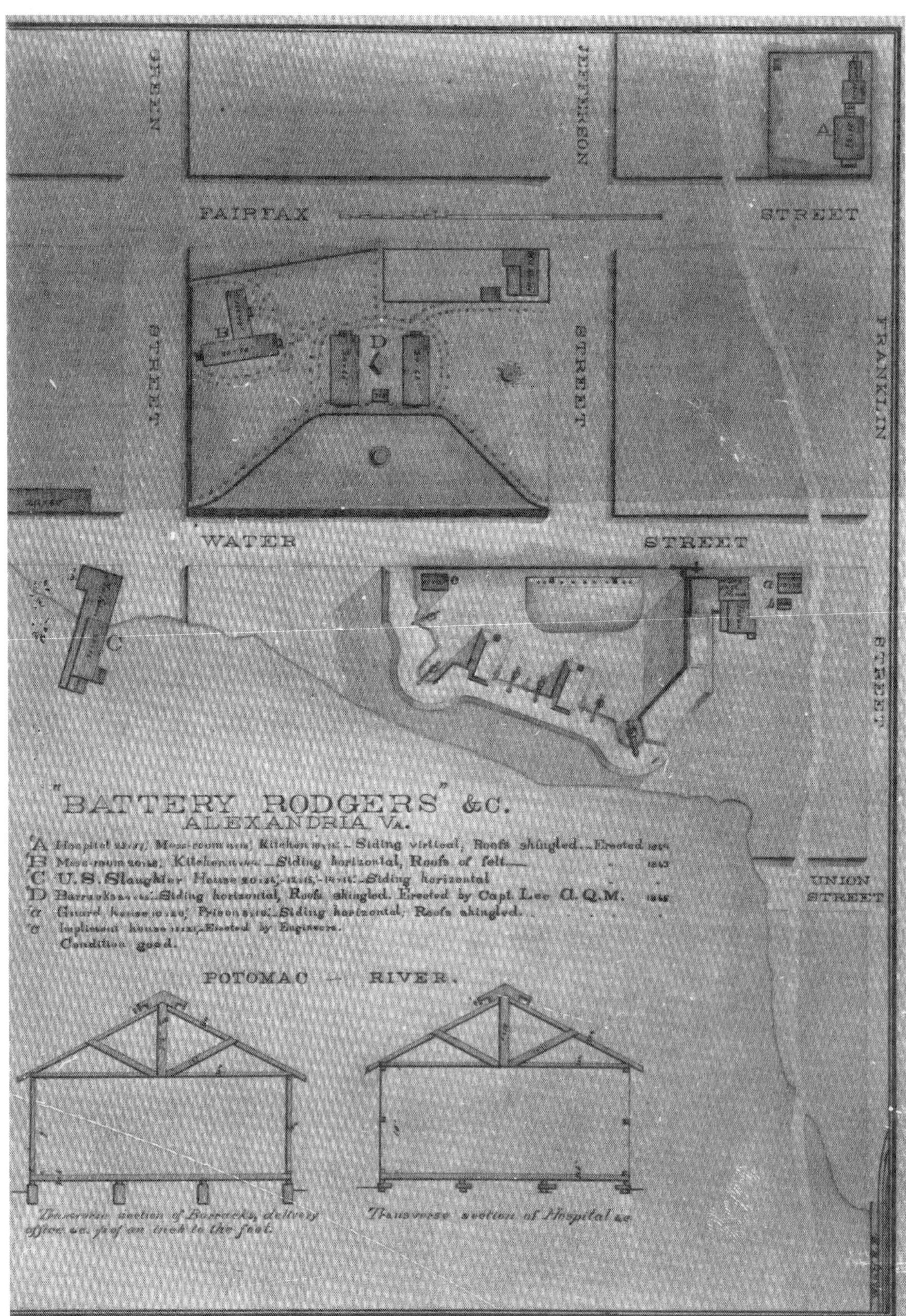

Plan of Quartermaster Property—Battery Rodgers. *National Archives*

Posing in the Fifteen-Inch Rodman Gun—Battery Rodgers. *National Archives*

Fifteen-Inch Rodman Gun—Battery Rodgers. *Library of Congress*

THE DEFENSES SOUTH OF ALEXANDRIA

Five forts were constructed during the war to hold the heights south of Hunting Creek. These works formed the extreme left flank of the Defenses of Washington and protected Alexandria's southern approaches. The first fort constructed in this sector was Fort Lyon (parapet trace exists along the south side of James Drive). Its isolated position demanded that it be large and well flanked. During an evaluation of the area that took place in 1862, it was decided to construct three additional works in front of Fort Lyon. These three forts were named Fort Weed, Fort Farnsworth, and Fort O'Rourke (no visible remains of these forts exist). General Barnard remarked in his report that "these works, connected with each other and with Fort Lyon by a rifle-trench containing powerful auxiliary 'batteries,' constituted a position of much strength from which the very broken ground of the site was pretty thoroughly seen." A fifth work, Fort Willard (located at Fort Willard Circle), was built on a separate ridge that commands the Accotink Road (modern Fort Hunt Road) and the flat ground next to the river. A military road united Fort Willard with the other works in the system. Hunting Creek Bridge connected the city of Alexandria with Mount Vernon Road over which supplies were taken to the forts. The bridge was constructed with a blockhouse and stockade.[16]

Fort Willard—Guarding the Accotink Turnpike and King's Highway

Location

From South Lee Street, drive to Green Street. Turn right on Green Street traveling to South Washington Street. Turn right on South Washington and proceed north to Gibbon Street. Turn left on Gibbon Street to South Patrick Street (Route 1). Turn left on South Patrick Street, which will take you to the Richmond Highway: Route 1, South. Follow this to Fort Hunt Road. Watch for a sign indicating the Fort Hunt Road to your right. Proceed on Fort Hunt Road (Old Accotink Road) to Belle Haven Road. Turn right on Belle Haven Road

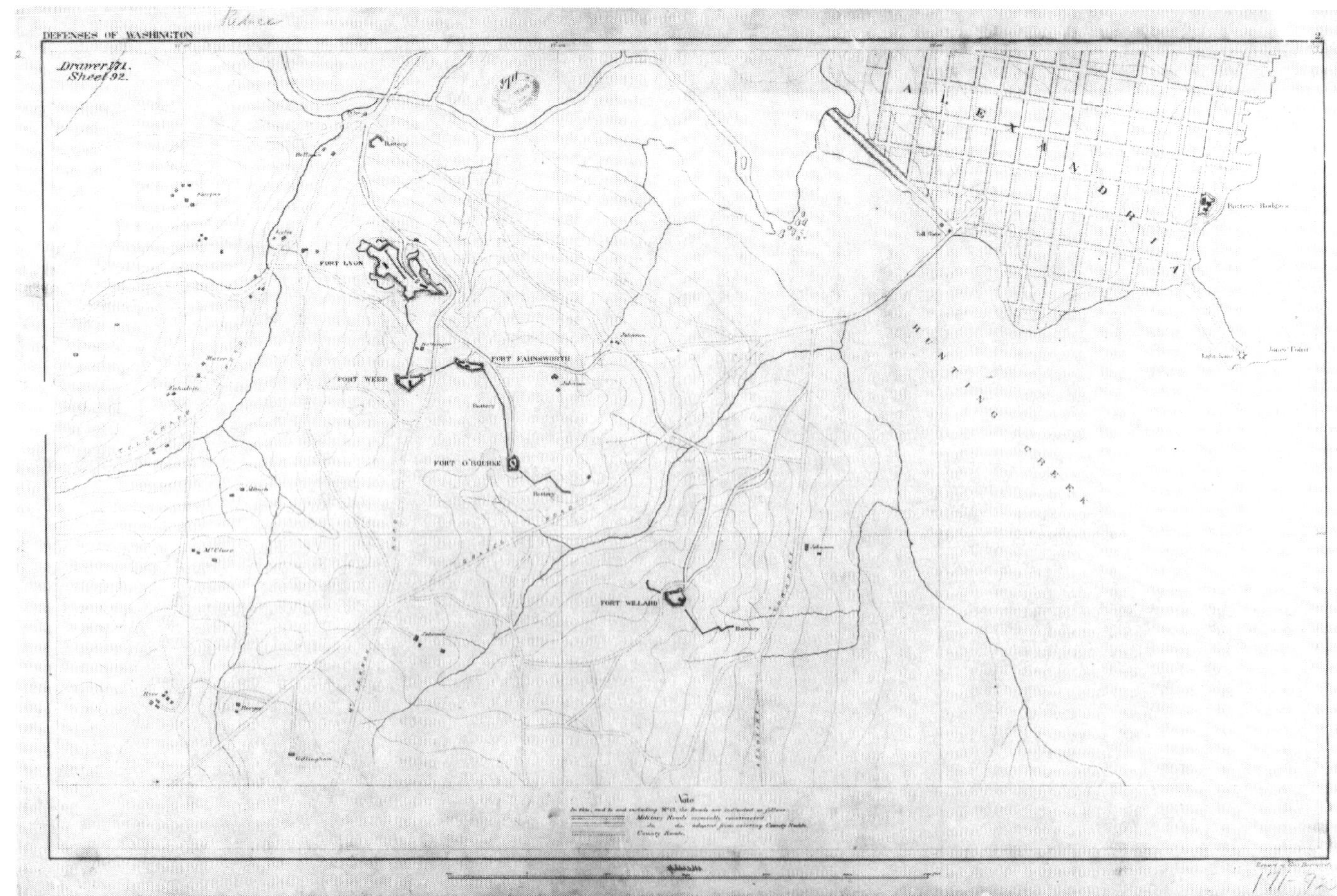

Sector Map from Fort Willard to Fort Lyon. *National Archives*

Hunting Creek Bridge Blockhouse. *National Archives*

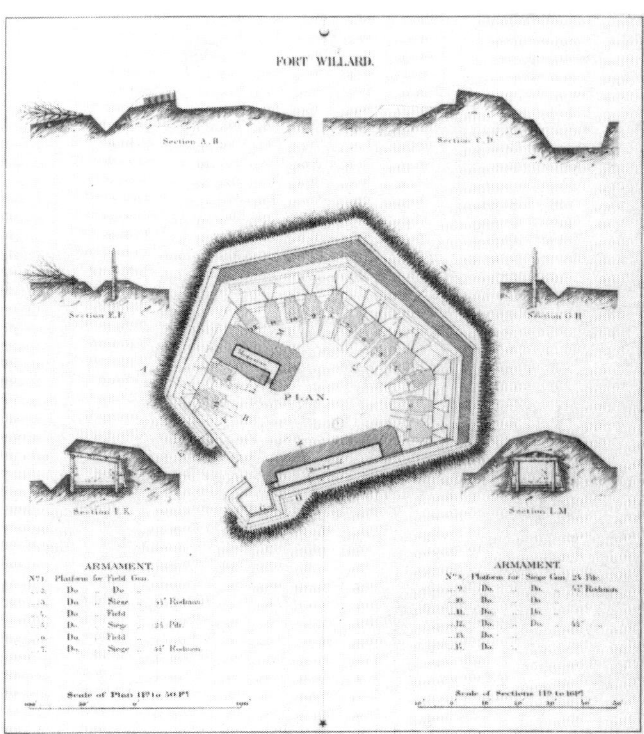

Fort Willard—Engineer Drawing. *National Archives*

driving up a steep hill to Radcliff Road. Turn right on Radcliff Road and then turn left on Fort Drive to Fort Willard Circle. Fort Willard is owned, operated, and maintained by the Fairfax County Park Authority.

Visible Remains

The fort is in a fair state of preservation. The ditch, parapets, magazine, and several platforms are well defined. The north wall is not as defined as a result of the removal of the wood from the fort's bombproof when the fort was abandoned. The parapets appear scalloped, showing the sites where embrasures were located. The land was donated to Fairfax County by the Eugene Olmi family.

Description

The fort was first called Redoubt "D" of Fort Lyon but was named in honor of Colonel George L. Willard, who was killed at Gettysburg on July 2, 1863. The fort was built on the land of Samuel R. Johnson in the fall of 1862 by detachments of the 34th Massachusetts Infantry.[17] Fort Willard was a small, unflanked,

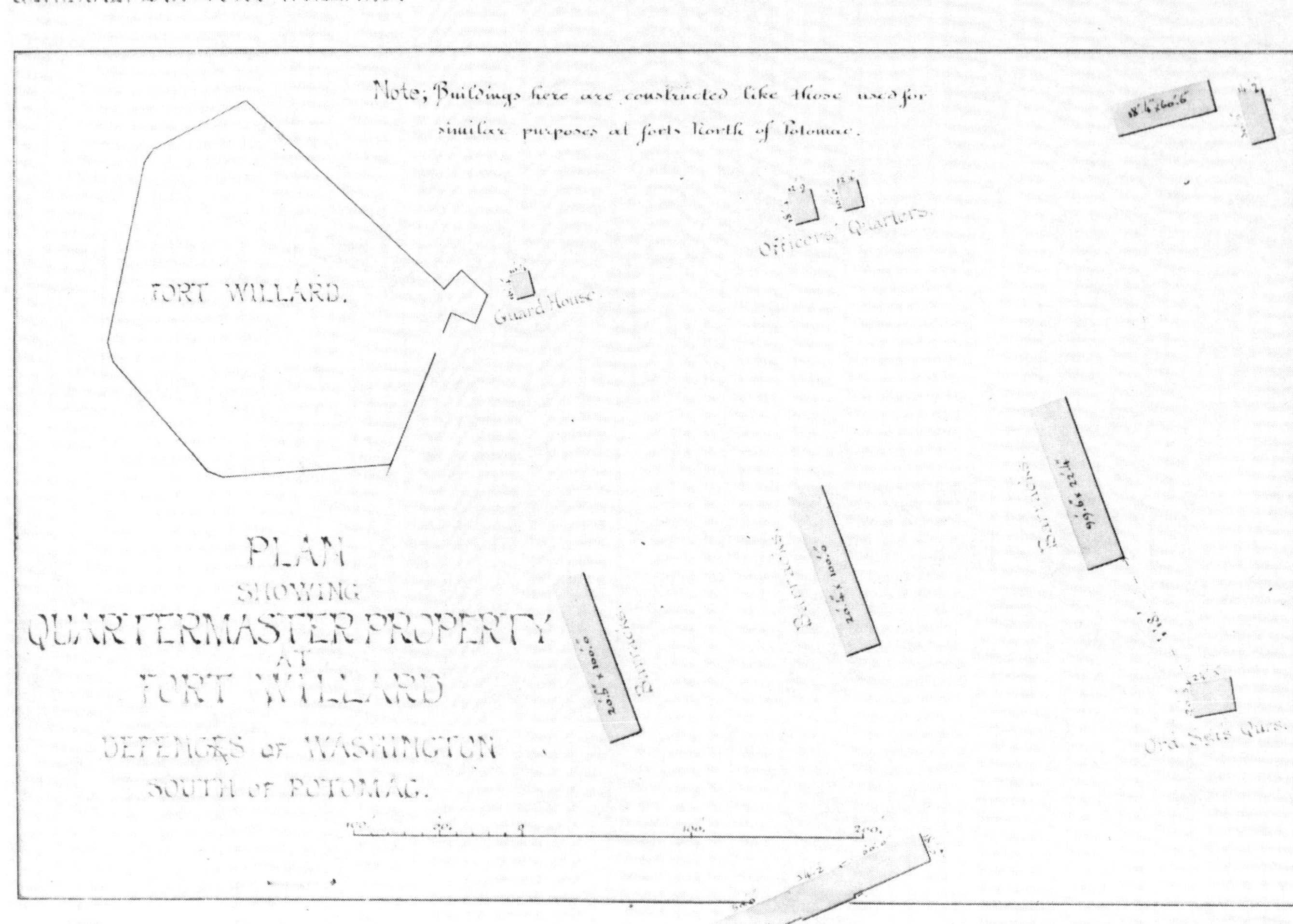

Plan of Quartermaster Property—Fort Willard. *National Archives*

enclosed work with a bombproof on the north wall of the fort and one magazine. The perimeter is 240 yards. The fort had emplacements for fourteen guns, and its armament consisted of two 24-pounder siege guns, two 12-pounder howitzers, four four-and-a-half-inch ordnance rifles, four 6-pounder guns, two ten-inch siege mortars, and two 24-pounder Coehorn mortars. Quartermaster property consisted of three barracks (twenty by 100 feet), a guardhouse, officers' quarters, a cook house, and ordnance sergeant's quarters. The fort commanded the Accotink Road, the flats next to the Potomac, and the Hunting Creek Bridge. Two detached batteries supported the fort. The battery to the right of Fort Willard was located at the end of Wakefield Court, and a battery to the left was located on the corner of Radcliff Road and Fort Drive extending east on Fort Drive.[18]

Anecdotes

In a letter written on Wednesday, December 28, 1864, Private Leroy Stafford, a soldier serving in the 1st Wisconsin Heavy Artillery, thanked his wife, Lydia, for the Christmas box of "delicacies" he received at Fort Willard:

> Well Lydia, the box has got along at last. It was delayed at Washington on account of the river being froze so that boats could not run for several days. I got it yesterday afternoon. Everything came in the best shape. Not a single thing was injured in the least—nor jarred. Even those cakes & cookies was all whole & nice as though just taken from the pantry. The bottle of wine was safe. Did not leak a bit & how nice it is. All the more so because mother helped to make it as you told me. . . . The cheese is very nice and good one. Quite different from

> what we get here. The butter is so sweet and good. Lydia, for breakfast this morn we fried some of that sausage, had some of that nice white bread of yours & butter & a pickle . . . for such delicacies are rare things in the army.[19]

Another soldier serving in the 10th New York Heavy Artillery, in a letter to his wife, expressed his extreme displeasure at the distance he had traveled to reach his new post. "After a march of about 5 miles with every amount of sore toes and lame legs and bucks—we find ourselves at Fort Willard, situated on the opposite side of the River from Fort Carroll. . . . It was the hardest gant I ever had in my life."[20]

Regiments that were garrisoned at the fort included the following:

Constructed by detachments of 34th Massachusetts Infantry
2d Connecticut Heavy Artillery, Co. I, May 1863–June 1863
2d Connecticut Heavy Artillery, Co. E, May 1863–August 1863
15th New York Heavy Artillery, Cos. F, H, September 1863–February 1864
15th New York Heavy Artillery, Co. E, November 1863–February 1864
10th New York Heavy Artillery, Cos. B, E, H, March 1864–April 1864
142d Ohio National Guard, Co. D, May 21, 1864–June 6, 1864
12th Regiment Veteran Reserve Corps, Co. B, July 1864–August 1864
12th Regiment Veteran Reserve Corps, Co. B (part), September 1864–October 1864
1st Maryland Light Artillery, Battery D, September 17, 1864–September 22, 1864
1st Wisconsin Heavy Artillery, Co. L, October 4, 1864–April 1865
1st Wisconsin Heavy Artillery, Co. F, November 1864–April 1865
15th New York Heavy Artillery, Cos. G, H, May 1865–June 1865

Fort O'Rourke—Guarding Mount Vernon Road and King's Highway

Location

From Fort Willard Circle, take Fort Drive back to Belle Haven Road. Turn left onto Fort Hunt Road and

Soldiers of the 34th Massachusetts Infantry Drill at Fort O'Rourke. *U.S. Army Military History Institute*

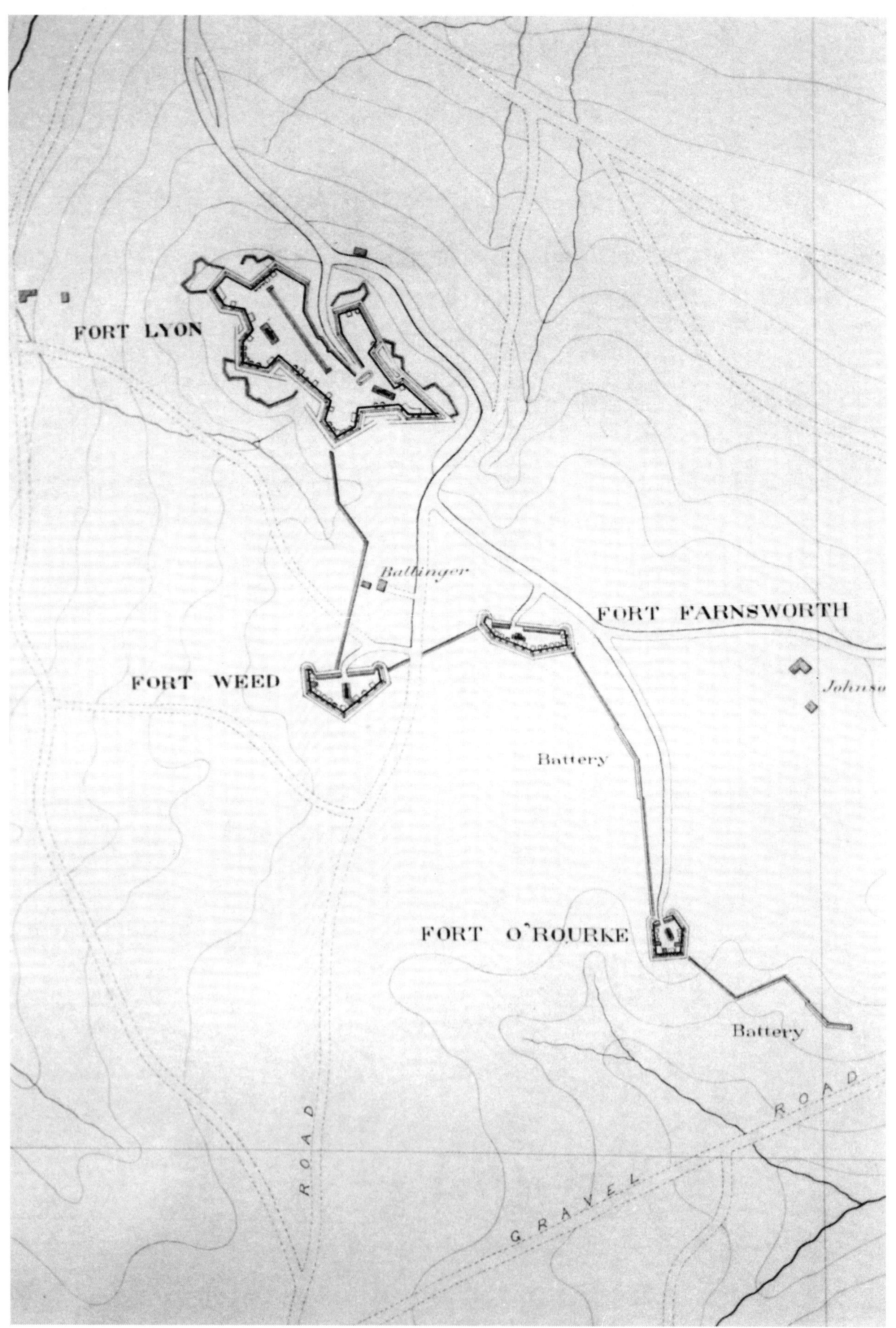

Sector Map—Fort O'Rourke to Fort Lyon Showing Batteries. *National Archives*

drive to Huntington Avenue. Turn left and drive to Richmond Highway. Turn left onto Richmond Highway and proceed to Fairhaven Avenue. Turn right on Fairhaven Avenue and make a right turn on Rixey Drive. From Rixey Drive, turn right on Fort Drive to its intersection with Park Place. The site of Fort O'Rourke was located on the southeast corner of Fort Drive and Park Place.

Visible Remains

No visible remains of the fort exist. The fort stood on the grounds of the small community center that is enclosed by a fence.

Description

The fort was named for Colonel Patrick Henry O'Rourke of the 140th New York Infantry, who was killed at Gettysburg on July 2, 1863. Initially called Redoubt "C" of Fort Lyon, Fort O'Rourke was a small fort with a perimeter of 160 yards and emplacements for sixteen guns. The fort was completed by detachments of the 34th Massachusetts Infantry. The armament of the fort included two eight-inch seacoast howitzers, one 24-pounder gun, two 12-pounder howitzers, and six 20-pounder Parrott rifles. The battery to the left of Fort O'Rourke was located to the rear of 23–25 Fort Drive.

Notes/Anecdotes

The guardhouse at Fort O'Rourke was destroyed long ago, but Special Order Number 4, issued from Battalion Headquarters, 1st Wisconsin Heavy Artillery, Fort Willard, preserves the site in official records:

> Private John Williams of "E" Co., 1st Regt. Wisconsin Volunteer Artillery is hereby ordered to be confined in the guard house at Ft. O'Rourke for twenty days with a 24 pound Ball and Chain attached to his right leg for permitting the field officer of the day to ride up the picket post No. 3 at 12:30 am., March 13th [1865], unchallenged, the said John Williams being on duty at that site as a sentinel. The commanding officer at Ft. O'Rourke will see that this order is carried out immediately.[21]

The garrison of the fort included the following:

Constructed by detachments of 34th Massachusetts Infantry
15th New York Heavy Artillery, Co. G, September 1863–February 1864
1st West Virginia Light Artillery, Battery C, May 1864–June 1864
136th Ohio National Guard, Co. D, May 13, 1864–June 30, 1864
12th Regiment Veteran Reserve Corps, Co. A, July 1864–August 1864
12th Regiment Veteran Reserve Corps, Co. B (part), September 1864–October 1864
1st Wisconsin Heavy Artillery, Co. E, September 23, 1864–April 30, 1865
15th New York Heavy Artillery, Co. C, May 1865–June 1865
2d Connecticut Heavy Artillery, Co. C, H, K, May 1863–August 1863

DEFENDERS OF THE ROADS TO ALEXANDRIA—KING'S HIGHWAY, MOUNT VERNON ROAD, AND TELEGRAPH ROAD

Battery between Fort O'Rourke and Fort Farnsworth

Location

Continue on Fort Drive and turn right on Grand Pavilion Way. This route will take you into a new townhouse community called "Pavilions at Huntington." Turn right on Huntington Park Drive and follow it around to the parking area and access road to Mt. Eagle Park, where you can park your car. The area is undergoing redevelopment that is part of the Huntington Metro Station and road changes may occur in the future. Access to Mt. Eagle Park used to be obtained from Fort Drive.

Visible Remains

Tracing of parapet and gun platforms for field guns can be seen in the tree line of the park.

Description

Earthen parapet originally designed for six field guns. In 1988, this site was a pristine excellent example of an "unmanned" battery. Today, it is an excellent example of what can happen to a historic site without proper preservation planning. In an "unmanned" battery, the platforms were left vacant unless the defenses south of Alexandria were threatened. The battery closed the gap between Forts Farnsworth and O'Rourke. It was arranged so that its face was nearly perpendicular to Forts Weed and Farnsworth and served to provide crossfire that would strike the enemy in the flank if they approached the forts.

Before leaving the park, see the section on Fort Farnsworth.

A Gun Platform in Mt. Eagle Park.

Fort Farnsworth

Location

By walking to the northern end of the battery, you can observe the site of Fort Farnsworth.

Visible Remains

No visible remains of the fort exist. The site of the fort was located toward the eastern side of the Washington Metropolitan Transit Authority parking lot, about 133 yards north-northwest of the battery.

Description

The fort was named in honor of Brigadier General Elon J. Farnsworth, 8th Illinois Cavalry, who was killed at Gettysburg on July 3, 1863. The fort was completed by detachments of the 34th Massachusetts Infantry under the supervision of Captain William Bacon. Originally called Redoubt "B" of Fort Lyon, Fort Farnsworth was a lunette with a stockade gorge. The fort had a perimeter of 255 yards and emplacements for thirteen guns. The armament included four 24-pounder guns,

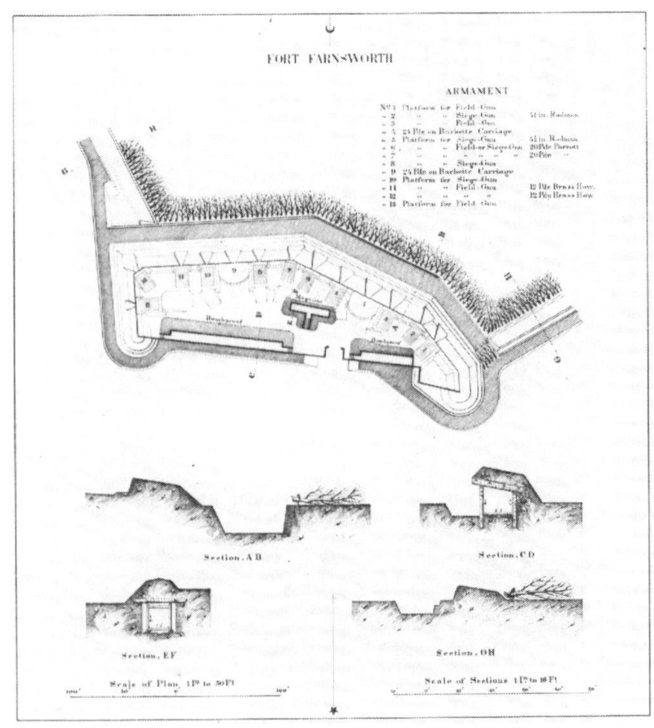

Fort Farnsworth—Engineer Drawing *National Archives*

two 12-pounder howitzers, and four four-and-a-half-inch ordnance rifles. The fort had one magazine and bombproof barracks along the north wall. Along with Forts Weed and O'Rourke, it occupied the plateau in front of Fort Lyon and commanded the Mount Vernon Road approaches to Alexandria.[22] The fort was destroyed for the construction of the Huntington Metro Station and adjacent parking facilities.

Notes/Anecdotes

Near the Union Lines stood the estate of Spring Bank, the stately home of George Mason. Mason was a grandson of the famous Virginia patriot. The trees on his property obstructed the fields of fire of the cannon in the forts. It was said that his heart was nearly broken when the pioneer corps began to fell his magnificent oaks. An officer from the 16th New York Infantry recorded these impressions of the sixty-four-year-old gentleman who lived near the forts and suffered under the stern law of military necessity:

> One of the most interesting characters in that part of Virginia was George Mason; he was a typical representative of an old and distinguished family. . . . He was of the old school, a man of culture . . . and frigid dignity. . . . I was in charge of a picket post near his house, when one of his servants brought me a letter. . . . It was a request that I should call at his house, that he might acquaint me with certain trespasses committed by the soldiers. . . . I was shown into his library. . . . Desiring to get a clue to his character, I asked if I might look at his library, for, if one lacks opportunity of personal contact, there is no better guide to the understanding of a man than the books he reads. . . . Here I found the best private library which I saw in Virginia. Although encamped, in the winter of 1862–3, near enough to see his place in going to Alexandria, I did not have the heart to call upon him, for I saw his house standing in a great waste.[23]

(Spring Bank stood until the early 1970s and was about half a mile from Fort Farnsworth.)

Garrison troops at Fort Farnsworth included the following:

- Construction by detachments of the 34th Massachusetts Infantry
- 2d Connecticut Heavy Artillery, Co. D, May 1863–August 1863
- 10th New York Heavy Artillery, Co. A, March 1863–May 27, 1864
- 15th New York Heavy Artillery, Co. K, October 31, 1863–February 29, 1864
- 14th Regiment Veteran Reserve Corps, Cos. G, I, July 15, 1863–July 16, 1864
- 1st West Virginia Light Artillery, Battery C, July 1864–August 1864
- 12th Regiment Veteran Reserve Corps, Co. H, September 1864–October 1864
- 1st Wisconsin Heavy Artillery, Co. M (part), October 10, 1864
- 1st Wisconsin Heavy Artillery, Co. I, April 1865
- 15th New York Heavy Artillery, Co. B, May 1865–June 1865
- 142d Ohio National Guard, May 1864

Fort Weed

Location

From Mt. Eagle Park, drive back to the intersection with Fort Drive. Turn right and continue on Fort Drive across North Kings Highway to the intersection of Fort Drive and Monticello Road. Fort Weed was located on and to the south of Fort Drive and west of Williamsburg Road and north of Albemarle Street. Monticello Road cuts the fort nearly in half, with the entrance located near the intersection at Fort Drive.

Visible Remains

No visible remains of the fort exist.

Description

The fort was named for Brigadier General Stephen Hinsdale Weed, 5th U.S. Artillery, who was killed at Gettysburg on July 2, 1863. The fort was built by detachments of the 34th Massachusetts Infantry under the supervision of Captain Andrew Potter. Fort Weed was originally called Redoubt "A" of Fort Lyon. It is a lunette with a stockade gorge. The fort perimeter was 253 yards with emplacements for twelve guns. The fort armament consisted of three 24-pounder guns, two 12-pounder howitzers, and six 30-pounder Parrott rifles. It contained one magazine, and bombproof barracks were constructed along the north wall of the fort. A rifle pit connected Fort Weed with Fort Lyon. Fort Weed worked together with Forts Farnsworth and O'Rourke to command the Mount Vernon Road approaches to Alexandria.[24]

Notes/Anecdotes

A soldier from the 2d Connecticut Heavy Artillery wrote home to his father in July 1863 and commented on the rats at Fort Weed. While on guard duty one night, he heard a loud noise coming from the captain's quarters. The next morning, he asked the captain if he had been putting the rats through battalion drill. The

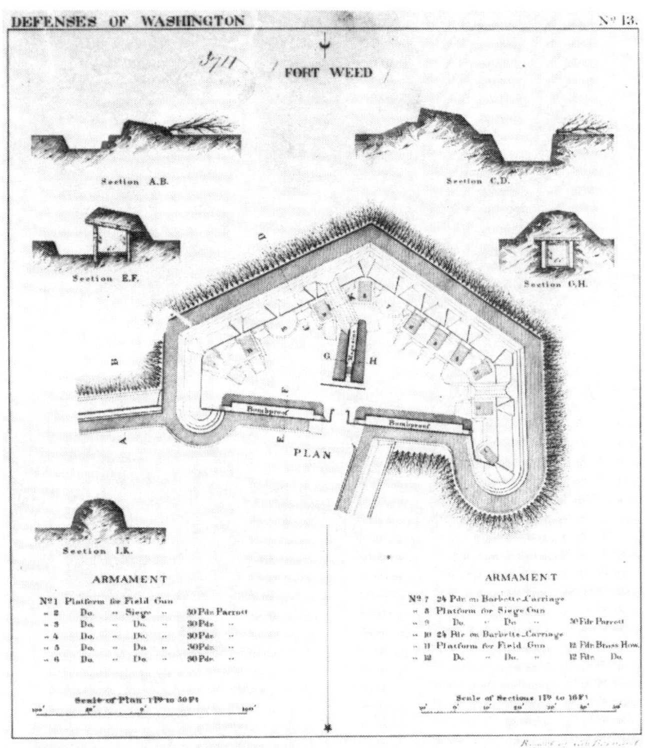

Fort Weed—Engineer Drawing. *National Archives*

captain responded that he had gone to bed but that the rats had taken the "liberty" of running over him while he was trying to sleep. He had ordered them to leave, but they had disobeyed. He then got up both lieutenants and a private and "went at them." That same evening when the soldier had finished his beat and returned to the writing table in the bombproof, "Mr. Rat" made his appearance on the table and took hold of the soldier's candle. The soldier ended his description of the episode by declaring, "I finished his exploits with my bayonet."[25]

Some of the regiments that garrisoned the fort included the following:

2d Connecticut Heavy Artillery, Cos. A–K, May–August 1863
15th New York Heavy Artillery, Co. D, September 1863–October 1863
17th Independent Battery, New York Light Artillery, May 25, 1864–June 2, 1864
15th New York Heavy Artillery, Co. L, December 31, 1863–February 1864
10th New York Heavy Artillery, Co. L, March 1864–April 1864

View of Fort Weed from the Back of the Fort. *The Civil War Letters of Lewis Bissell*

Interior View of Fort Weed. *U.S. Army Military History Institute*

A Field Battery Drills in the Rear of Fort Weed's Bombproof. *U.S. Army Military History Institute*

16th Independent Battery, Massachusetts Light Artillery, June 1, 1864–July 10, 1864
12th Regiment Veteran Reserve Corps, Cos. C–E, G, July 1864–October 31, 1864
1st Wisconsin Heavy Artillery, Co. M (part), October 31, 1864
1st Wisconsin Heavy Artillery, Co. M, November 1864–April 1865
15th New York Heavy Artillery, Co. D, May 1865–June 1865

COVERING TELEGRAPH ROAD

Fort Lyon: Stop Number 1

Location

Backtrack on Fort Drive to North Kings Highway. Turn left on North Kings Highway and travel one block to the entrance of the Metro Station. Turn right into the temporary parking area (Kiss & Ride Stop). Park and walk over to the scenic overlook that features a vista of Alexandria and Washington.

Visible Remains

No visible remains of the fort exist. You are standing near the site of the southeast bastion of Fort Lyon. From this point, the strategic location of the fort can be appreciated. The main camp was located behind the fort on the slope now occupied by apartment buildings. When Colonel Wells of the 34th Massachusetts Infantry moved his troops to this site, he called it "a camp of magnificent distances."[26]

Description

The fort was named in honor of Brigadier General Nathaniel Lyon, who was killed at Wilson's Creek, Missouri, on August 10, 1861. Fort Lyon formed the main work on the left flank of the Defenses of Washington. Its function was to hold the heights south of Hunting Creek, from which Alexandria could be shelled if controlled by Confederate artillery. The trace was laid out on the ground on September 6, 1861, by Major John Newton of the army engineers. Fort Lyon was the second-largest work in the system and covered an area of nine acres with a perimeter of 937 yards. Four of its faces were bastioned in trace, and the rest of the fort was built to conform to the topography of the ground. The site of the fort was placed on the spur of a plateau and arranged to command the broad valley of Hunting Creek and Telegraph Road. Below in the valley, the fort protected the railroad depot, Little River Turnpike, and the city of Alexandria. In the fall of 1862, the fort was strengthened by three additional

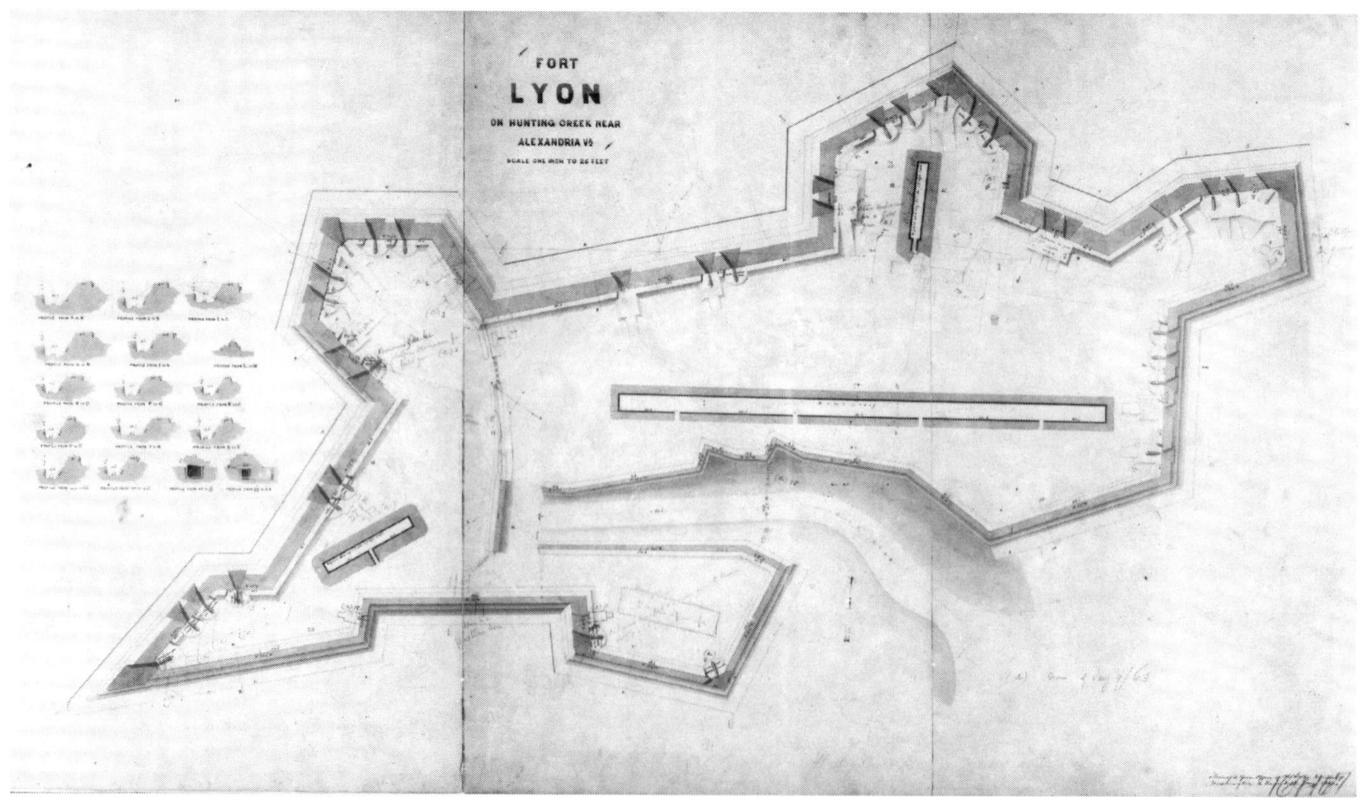

Fort Lyon—Engineer Drawing. *National Archives*

34th Massachusetts Infantry at Camp Worcester, Fort Lyon. *U.S. Army Military History Institute*

works constructed on the slightly higher plateau to the south.[27]

Notes/Anecdotes

In September 1861, the 27th New York Volunteer Infantry was ordered to the site of Fort Lyon to begin construction of the fort. One member of the regiment left a vivid impression of the view:

> Fort Lyon was the grandest camping ground the regiment ever occupied. Standing on the entrenchments, and looking to the right, across the Potomac, could be seen the City of Washington, with the dome of the Capitol rising proudly towards the sky. Vessels were plying to and fro in the river, while Alexandria lay beneath us, like a sullen child—its Confederate sympathizers cowed into silence by the presence of troops and the frowning cannon. In front stretched the green valley of Hunting Creek . . . an artistic view, worthy of a painter's skill.[28]

Fort Lyon: Stop Number 2

Location

From the metro area, drive diagonally to the right across the street to James Drive.

Visible Remains

On the south side of James Drive is a trace of Fort Lyon's southern parapet. The house on the corner of James Drive and North Kings Highway sits near the site of gun platform number 1. The northeast trace of the fort can be seen in the outline of the hill as you travel down North Kings Highway toward Telegraph Road. North Kings Highway follows the same path as the Civil War road into the fort, but the modern road is built on a much lower elevation. In 1988, only one property owner had removed a section of the old fort wall behind their house to gain access to their backyard from James Drive. Today, you will see that several property owners have copied the practice, thereby destroying the earthwork that was built to protect Alexandria and Washington.

Description

As late as 1931, Fort Lyon was one of the best-preserved forts in the chain of defenses. By 1948, local post–World War II development had obliterated what nature could not destroy, leaving only one section of fort wall. The fort contained a bombproof that was about 420 feet long and fourteen feet wide. Other interior structures included two magazines, a well, and a traverse that was constructed to defend the fort entrance gate.

The fort had emplacements for forty guns, and the armament consisted of ten 32-pounder guns, ten 24-pounder guns, seven 6-pounder guns, two eight-inch mortars, and four 24-pounder Coehorn mortars.

Notes/Anecdotes

By June 1863, soldier life in the defenses had become a monotonous vigil of drilling and inspections. Fort Lyon was garrisoned by German immigrant soldiers of the 3d Battalion New York Artillery. The battalion was known for its singing, lager beer, and numerous pet dogs. "If you wish any dogs," one soldier remarked, "there are plenty of them in Fort Lyon as the Dutchmen have three dogs to every man and peck of fleas in the bargain." On Tuesday, June 9, 1863, a catastrophic explosion destroyed the north magazine and a portion of the fort. The force of the blast shattered glass in homes as far away as Alexandria. Newspapers reported twenty-one men killed instantly and ten men wounded, The accident occurred when a detail of twenty-six men under the command of Lieutenant L. Kuhne were engaged in examining, airing, and refilling shells near the magazine door. Some of the soldiers had been given wooden spoons to remove caked powder from inside the shells that had absorbed moisture in the magazine. The lieutenant, dissatisfied with the slow progress of the detail, then handed out priming wires to aid in the removal of the damp powder. Friction on the powder in one of the shells set off the explosion, which ignited eight tons of powder and several thousand rounds of fixed ammunition in the magazine. The blast shook the ground like an earthquake. Debris, dirt, screaming shells, and bodies were hurled over a half mile away from the fort.[29] The *New York Times* printed the fantastic accounts of two sentinels:

> Private Musser, while pacing his beat on the parapet, was hurled through the air one hundred yards from beyond the fort into a clump of bushes, with his musket in his hands. It is a positive fact that he sustained no serious injuries, and in ten minutes afterward he was back again upon his path, walking with his piece at his shoulder. Another sentinel was thrown fifty yards out of the fort into the ditch, with his musket in his grasp. Some officers happening to pass, he gathered himself up, face and hands begrimed with powder, and his clothes in shreds, and, with soldierly habit, presented arms.[30]

The next day, President Lincoln and Secretary of War Stanton visited the fort to see the extent of the damage. Years after the war had ended, the *Washington Post* featured a small article on the incident in the September 9, 1883, issue. An eyewitness to the explosion, Mr. James McWilliams of Alexandria, reported that he saw the air filled with mutilated bodies, and special care was taken to conceal the disaster because it was believed that Confederate Partisan Ranger Colonel John S. Mosby was in the neighborhood.[31] Many of the soldiers who died in the explosion were interred in Alexandria National Cemetery.

Regiments that garrisoned Fort Lyon included the following:

38th New York Infantry, November–December 1861
16th New York Volunteer Infantry, September 1861
27th New York Infantry, September–October 1861
2d Michigan Infantry, Cos. A, B, K, September 1861–October 1861
3d Michigan Infantry, Cos. A, D, F, H, October 1861–November 1861
Battery B (Second) New Jersey Light Artillery, November 1861–February 1862
26th New York Infantry, Cos. F, H, I, November 1861–April 1862
26th New York Infantry, Co. D, December 31, 1861–April 30, 1862
26th New York Infantry, Cos. B, C, E, G, K, December 31, 1861–April 30, 1862
1st Rhode Island Light Artillery, Battery E, February 28, 1862–March 1862
26th New York Infantry, Co. C, April 1862–June 1862
101st New York Infantry, May 12, 1862–June 6, 1862
12th Independent Battery, New York Light Artillery, June 7, 1862–June 30, 1862
74th New York Infantry, Co. D, July 1862–August 1862

The Last Trace of Fort Lyon's Parapet, 1988, Looking East on James Drive. *Fort Ward Museum Collection*

15th New York Heavy Artillery, Co. E (part), July–October 1862
69th New York State Militia, Cos. G, I, July 1862
34th Massachusetts Infantry, September 1862–April 1863
11th New York Cavalry, Co. L, May 1863–June 1863
15th New York Heavy Artillery, August 1863–February 1864
10th New York Heavy Artillery, Cos. D, G, I, K, L, March 1864–April 1864
136th Ohio National Guard, Cos. A, K, May 1864–June 1864
142d Ohio National Guard, May 1864–June 1864
17th Independent Battery, New York Light Artillery, May 1864–June 1864
16th Independent Battery, Massachusetts Light Artillery, June 1864–July 10, 1864
1st West Virginia Light Artillery, Battery C, July 1864
12th Regiment Veteran Reserve Corps, Co. K, July 1864–August 1864
1st Wisconsin Heavy Artillery, Cos. F, H, K, October 1864
1st Wisconsin Heavy Artillery, Co. K, April 1865
15th New York Heavy Artillery, Cos. A, E, F, I, May 1865–June 1865

ALEXANDRIA'S WESTERN DEFENSES

Fort Williams and Blockhouses 1 and 2

Location

From James Drive, turn left on North Kings Highway and drive down the hill to Telegraph Road. Turn right on Telegraph Road, driving through the valley where Blockhouse Number 1 and two batteries were located. Follow the traffic signs to Duke Street (Route 236 West). Driving west on Duke Street will bring you to the general location of Blockhouse Number 2, which was constructed to defend the Orange and Alexandria Railroad south of Duke Street near 2922 Duke Street. Move to the right lane and turn right on North Quaker Lane. Proceed up the steep hill to the vicinity of 212 North Quaker Lane. The site of Fort Williams is located on private property in the area bounded by a brick wall in the 200–300 block of

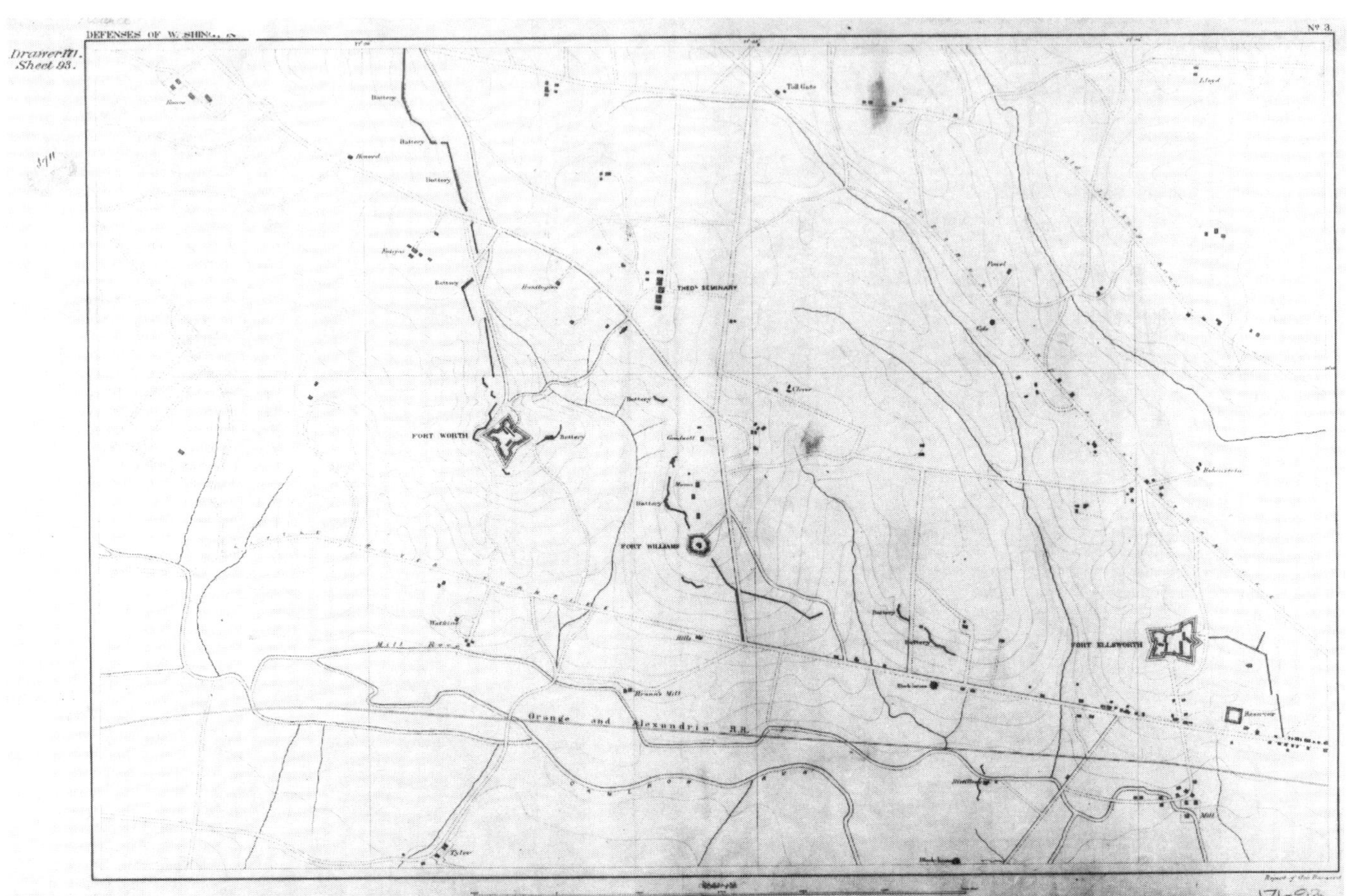

Sector Map from Fort Ellsworth to Fort Worth. *National Archives*

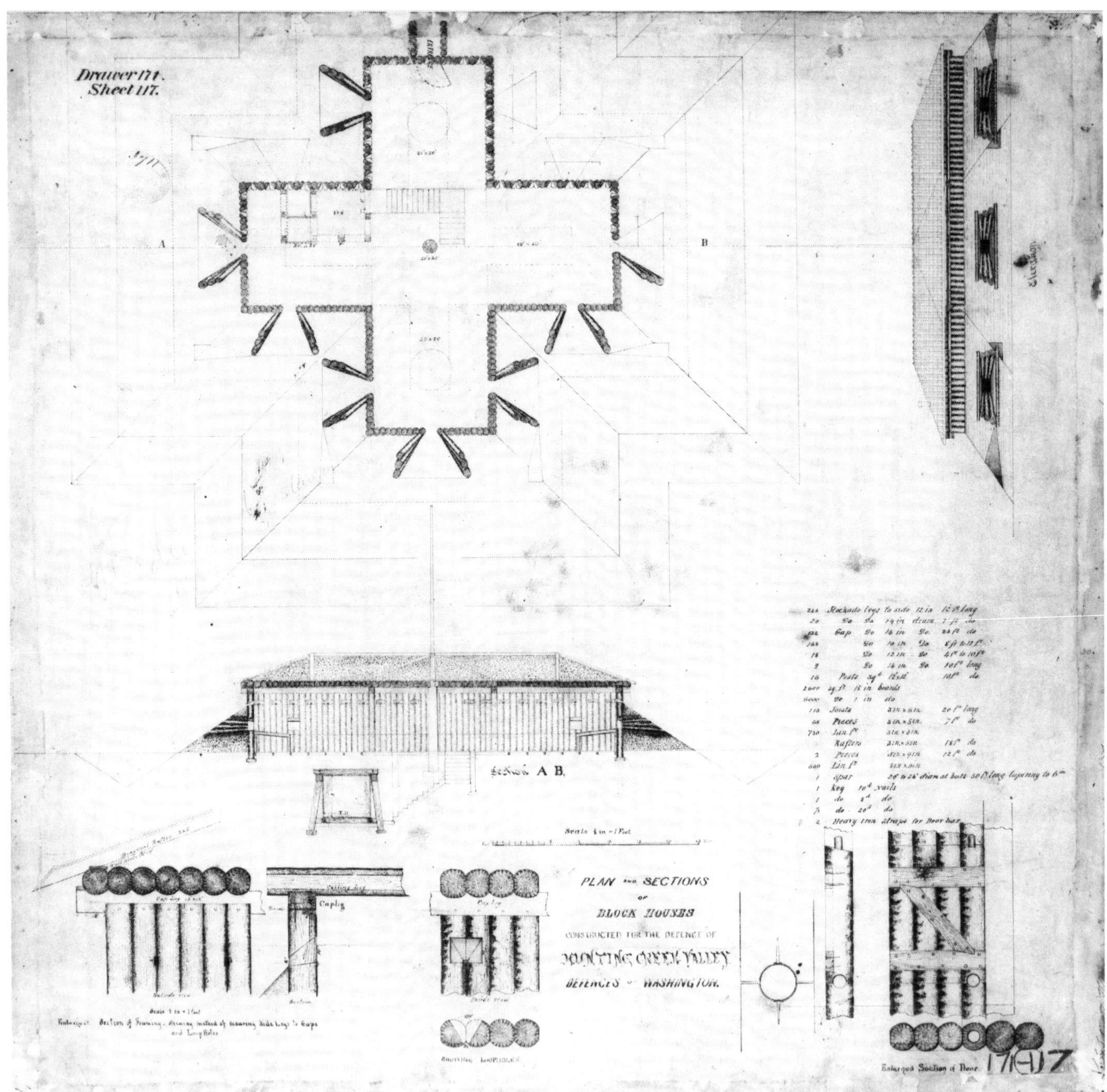

Plan and Sections of Blockhouse for Defense of Orange and Alexandria Railroad. *National Archives*

North Quaker Lane. Access to the site is restricted, and no trespassing is allowed.

Visible Remains

To the rear of the house at 212 North Quaker Lane, there exists the complete brick powder magazine and faint traces of the parapet and gorge of Fort Williams. The site of the fort sits up and back from the road and cannot be seen from the street.

Description

The fort was named in honor of Brigadier General Thomas Williams, who was killed at Baton Rouge, Louisiana, on August 5, 1862. The fort was constructed by detachments of the 2d Connecticut Heavy Artillery in 1863. General Samuel Cooper, adjutant general of the U.S. Army, owned the hill and a house that was called Cameron. On the eve of the war, General Cooper resigned from Federal service and joined the Confederacy. Union soldiers who

Blockhouse Number 2, Defending the Orange & Alexandria Railroad. *U.S. Army Military History Institute*

later occupied the site called it "Traitor's Hill." Cameron was destroyed when construction began on Fort Williams, and it is said that the existing magazine was built of bricks from General Cooper's home. Fort Williams was a small, unflanked, enclosed work with a perimeter of 250 yards and emplacements for thirteen guns. The armament consisted of one eight-inch howitzer, two 24-pounder brass field howitzers, six four-and-a-half-inch Rodmans, four 20-pounder Parrotts, and two 24-pounder Coehorn mortars. The fort commanded a deep ravine that enveloped the rear of Fort Worth, the heights south of Hunting Creek, and Little River Turnpike (Duke Street). The fort contained one magazine, and quartermaster buildings were constructed to the east of the fort on the property extending down the hill into modern-day North Quaker Lane. The quartermaster buildings included two barracks, two mess halls, and officers' quarters.[32]

Notes/Anecdotes

Construction superintendent Bennett, writing with frustration and asking for additional guards at the

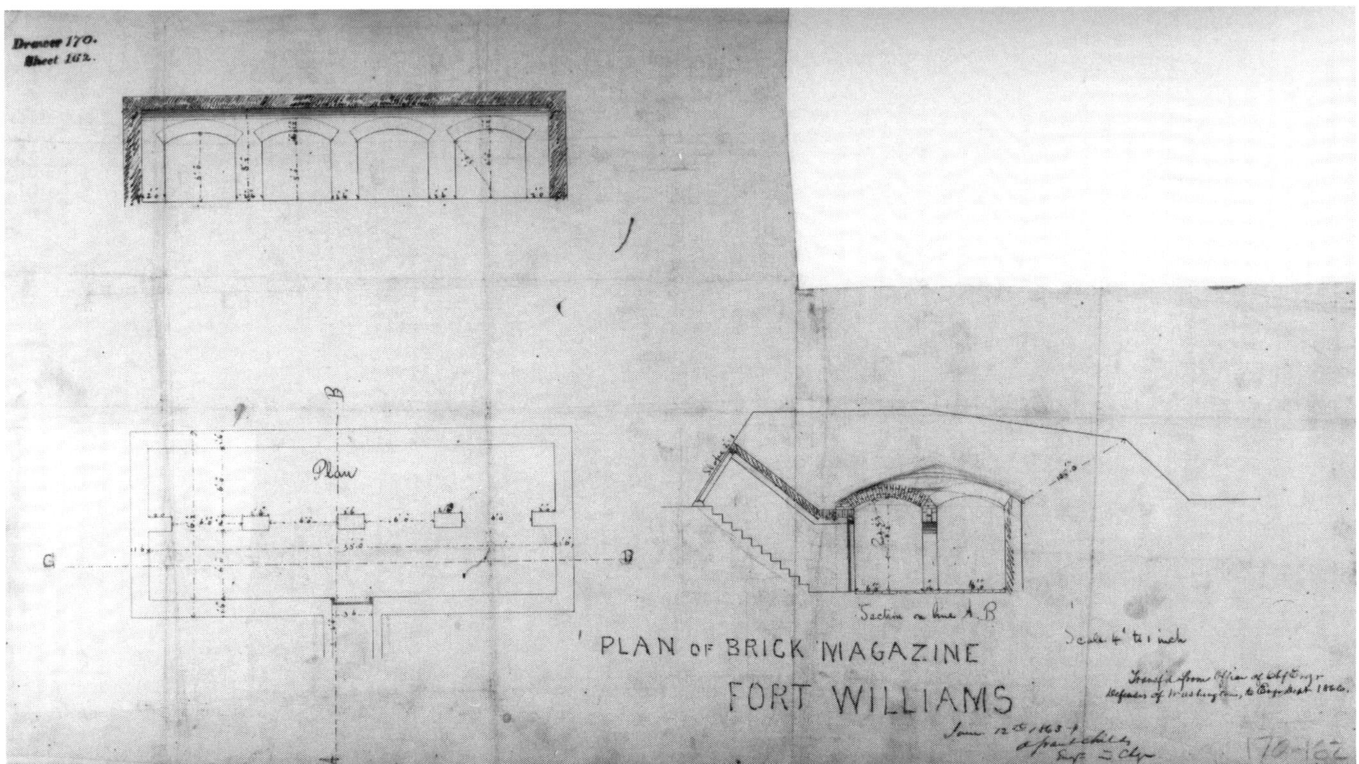

Plan of Brick Magazine—Fort Williams. *National Archives*

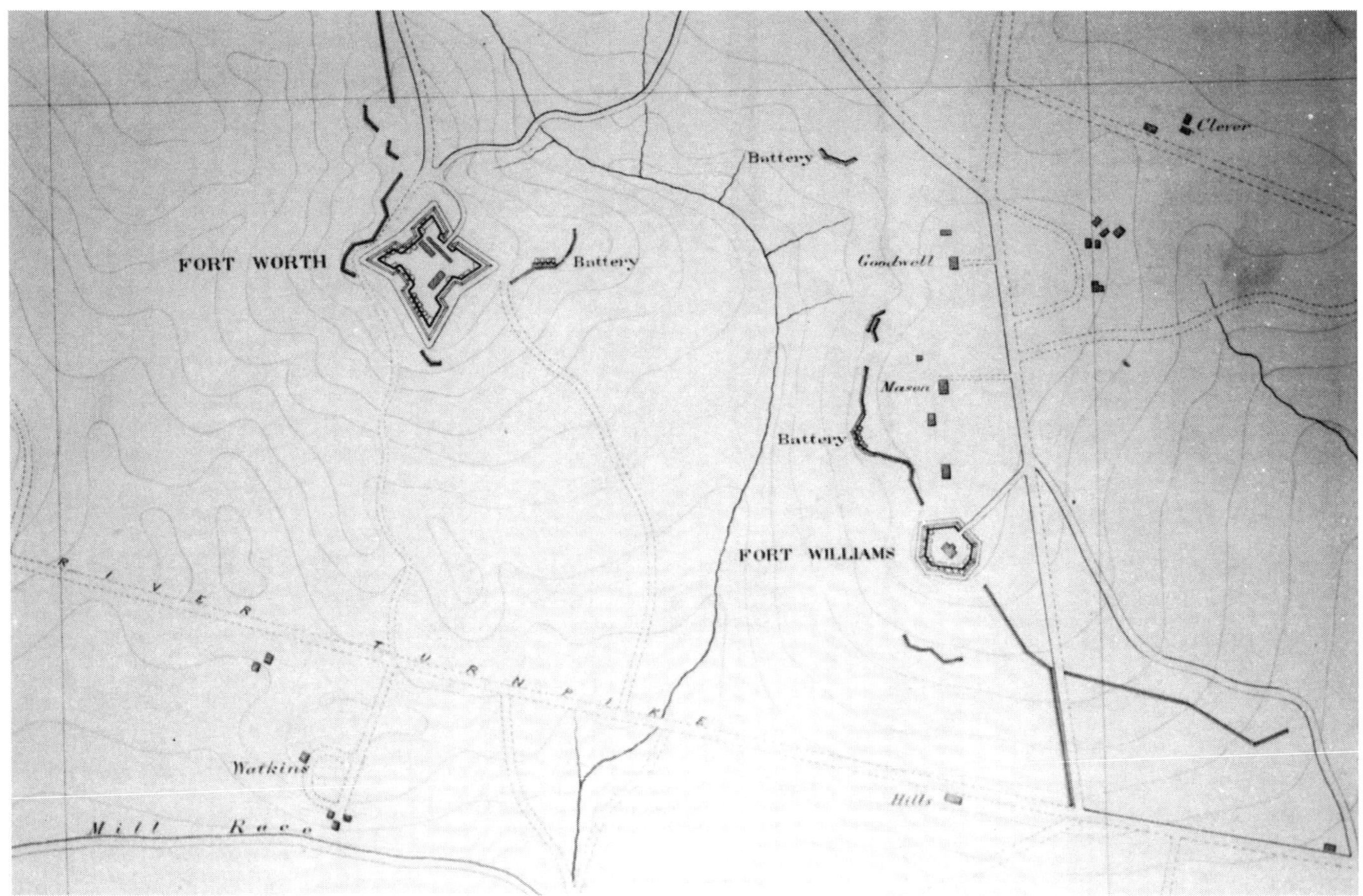

Sector Map—Forts Williams and Worth. *National Archives*

construction camp at Fort Williams, penned this request on April 20, 1863:

> Camp on Traitors Hill, Va. to Engineer-in-Charge, A.G. Childs
>
> I have one soldier—sixty-two years old—just a convalescent—as a guard for this camp. Please make application for a guard consisting of one commissioned officer and at least twenty-five men. Or else allow me to direct this old man to return to his regiment. The first night he reported for duty he stayed in camp alone and was nearly frightened to death by the rats. Since that time five carpenters stayed here and protected him. He may possibly be of some service to General Tyler but he is not of the slightest use here—only in our way.[33]

On January 12, 1863, Private Edward C. "Ned" Hopson, a soldier serving in the 2d Connecticut Heavy Artillery stationed at Fort Williams, reported home how he and his fellow soldiers used the steep hill where the fort was located:

> We had quite a snow storm a few days since. It froze hard afterward, and for the first time since we come out, I enjoyed the luxury of sliding down hill. The boys made all sorts of temporary sleds, mounting boxes on barrel staves, and making other similar arrangements, and we had lots of fun for a while.[34]

On May 4, 1864, Private Joseph Laycox, a 100-day soldier from Ohio stationed at Fort Williams, sent his wife a letter that included a short poem. "Libbie, I am going to send you this sublime poetry," wrote the private. "I think it is the nicest thing I ever saw for this occasion." What Private Laycox copied is a typical example of soldier poetry. A poem would be written or discovered by a creative soldier and then passed on through the company or regiment and sent to all the wives and ladies back home:

To My Wife

Dearest wife I still remember
With a husband's aching heart
How it filled my soul with sorrow
When we two were called to part.
Though I'm but a private Soldier
Gone to fill my country's call
All my trust is in the savior
Let me stand or let me fall.
When I get your welcome letters
As in Dixie land I roam

And you speak of our dear children
How it makes me sigh of home.
Then if we are only faithful
To the lord our truest friend
Safe we'll rise to realms of glory
Where our bliss will never end.

Like many of the soldiers who served at the Defenses of Washington, Joseph Laycox never experienced battle. He died in the hospital at Fort Williams of a camp disease, fifty-one days after the poem was written to his wife.[35]

Garrison troops at Fort Williams included the following:

2d Connecticut Heavy Artillery, Co. I, July 1863–April 1864
2d Connecticut Heavy Artillery, Co. F, August 22, 1863–April 1864
2d Connecticut Heavy Artillery, Co. D, September, 1863–April 1864
2d Connecticut Heavy Artillery, Co. M, February 29, 1863–April 1864
James Thompson's Independent Battery C Pennsylvania Light Artillery, May–July 1864
136th Ohio National Guard, Cos. F, G, May 13, 1864–June 1864
3d Regiment Veteran Reserve Corps, Cos. A, C, E, H, September 1864–September 30, 1864
3d Regiment Veteran Reserve Corps, Co. C, October 1864
1st New Hampshire Heavy Artillery, Co. C, October 20, 1864–November 4, 1864
4th Massachusetts Heavy Artillery, Co. I, October 20m 1864–November 14, 1864
Robert Nevin's Independent Battery I, Pennsylvania Light Artillery, November–December 1864

A Special Tour Visiting the Magazine at Fort Williams. *Photograph by James Dacey*

Post Hospital Near Fort Williams. *U.S. Army Chaplain Museum*

4th Massachusetts Heavy Artillery, Co. M, February 8, 1865–April 1865
4th Massachusetts Heavy Artillery, Cos. G, I, May 1865–June 1865

Fort Worth

Location

Continue north on North Quaker Lane and turn left on Trinity Drive. Drive down the hill to Fort Williams Parkway. Turn right on Fort Williams Parkway and drive to Fort Worth Avenue. Turn left on Fort Worth Avenue and proceed to Garland Street. Turn right on Garland Street and drive to St. Stephens Road. Turn left on St. Stephens Road and then left onto Harris Place. Fort Worth stood on and to the east of the cul-de-sac at the end of the street.

Visible Remains

No visible remains of the earthen fort exist. The large frame house at 4010 Harris Place is built on the south magazine of the fort. Much of the fort was in an excellent state of preservation until the site was destroyed for development in 1970.

Description

This fort was named in honor of Brigadier General William Jenkins Worth, who was a distinguished soldier in the Mexican War. Construction on Fort Worth began about September 1, 1861. In his report, General Barnard noted, "Fort Worth occupies a very commanding position. A larger work would have been desirable, but the site would not have permitted it." The perimeter of the fort was 463 yards, and the interior provided space for twenty-five gun emplacements. The armament of the fort included eight 24-pounder guns, five 12-pounder howitzers, five four-and-a-half-inch Rodmans, two 20-pounder Parrott rifles, two 12-pounder Whitworth rifles, four ten-inch mortars, and two 24-pounder Coehorn mortars. A 100-pounder Parrott rifle was mounted in the corner of the south bastion that could sweep the sector from Fort Lyon around to Fort Ward.[36] The fort was built on property owned by William Silvey, and after the war, Colonel Arthur Herbert, C.S.A., built his home on the hill that he called Muckross. Legendary fact says that Colonel Herbert used the solid masonry walls of the south powder magazine, which served as a "fine cellar for his new home."[37]

Notes/Anecdotes

In 1868, Theodore Vaill, first lieutenant and adjutant of the 2nd Connecticut Heavy Artillery (formerly the 19th Connecticut Infantry), wrote a history of the unit's term of service in the war. His description of Fort Worth is only one of many that have been written:

> Fort Worth was a neat little earth work, situated above a quarter of a mile in the rear of Fairfax Seminary, overlooking the broad valley of Hunting Creek, and the Orange and Alexandria Railway, and mounting some twenty-four guns of all kinds—Rodman, Parrott, Whitworth, 8-inch Howitzers, and Coehorn mortars. Here began our artillery service; and for many months the Nineteenth, although an infantry regiment, performed garrison duty in this and half dozen other forts and redoubts in the vicinity—thereby attaining a proficiency in artillery that eventually won the "red," and would doubtless have been effective at the front if such service had ever been required of us. But it was not to be. The only foes that ever drew the fire of guns manned by the regiment were harmless targets, planted on the hillside a couple of miles away. . . . It was pleasant to witness the prompt execution of such commands as "From Battery! Load by Detail! Load!—In Battery! Point! Fire!" and then to hear a 24-pounder shot "sprang" and sque-e-eal away over the intervening valley, and to see it announce its arrival by knocking a hole in the bull's eye, or striking the ground and throwing a considerable portion of some rebel gentlemen's farm into the air. . . . Many excellent shots were made but the painted enemy never returned the fire.[37]

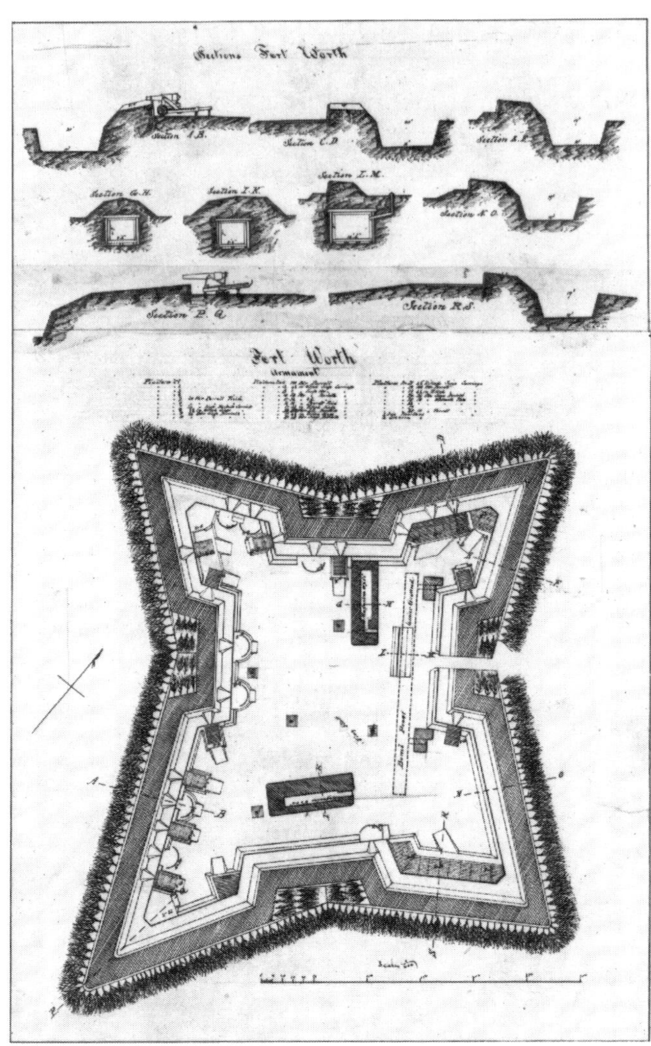

Fort Worth—Engineer Drawing

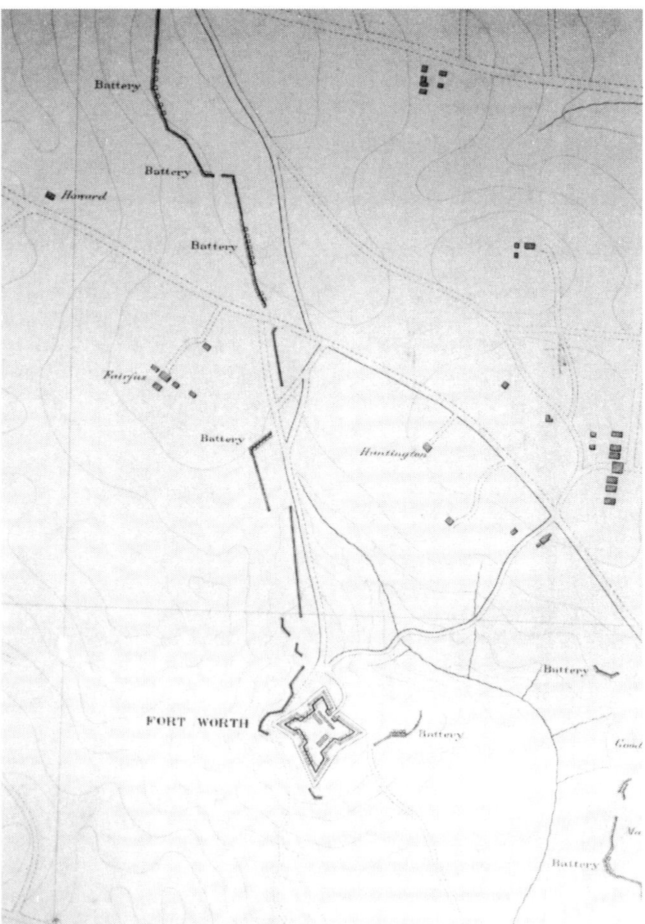

Sector Map—The Line between Forts Worth and Ward. *National Archives*

Twenty-five years after the war ended, a group of aging veterans visited Fort Worth to reawaken memories of the past. One veteran experienced the fort as a thirteen-year-old drummer boy and left a pensive account of the visit:

> The owner of the land on which the fort was built, and who served as a colonel in the Confederate army, then had a beautiful home on the site and utilized the old bombproof for an outside cellar. Near his barn was a little of the old parapet remaining and our party stood on the earthwork while our old regimental bugler, a man bent with the weight of more than three score years, sounded reveille, tattoo, and lights out. There were no dry eyes in the party when the last bugle notes echoed and re-echoed through the charming Virginia valley. . . . It is hardly necessary to say that we did some pretty deep thinking as we met that day on the old camp ground. Our comrades stood before us again—boys who had been schoolmates, the companions of our youth. . . . The thoughts brought keen pangs of sorrow to us, yet withal there were many pleasant recollections revived.[39]

The garrison of Fort Worth included the following:

3d New Jersey Infantry, Cos. H, K, November 1861
2d New York Heavy Artillery, E, November 1861–August 23, 1862
3d New Jersey Infantry, Cos. A–C, F, G, I, January 1862–February 1862
2d Connecticut Heavy Artillery, Co. C, January 1862–April 1863
2d New York Heavy Artillery, Co. K, January 1862–June 1862
2d New York Heavy Artillery, Cos. F, H, March 1862–June 1862
2d New York Heavy Artillery, Co. I, May 1862–August 1862
1st Connecticut Heavy Artillery, Cos. F, K, July 1862–December 1862
1st Connecticut Heavy Artillery, Co. L, July 1862–October 1862
15th New York Heavy Artillery, Co. D, August 22, 1862–August 28, 1862
2d Connecticut Heavy Artillery, Cos. B, D–I, K, January 1863–April 1863
2d Connecticut Heavy Artillery, Co. A, March 1863–April 1863
2d Connecticut Heavy Artillery, Cos. B, E, K, September 1863–April 1864
2d Connecticut Heavy Artillery, Co. A, October 1863–April 1864
9th New York Heavy Artillery, Cos. B, L, May 1864
136th Ohio National Guard, Cos. C, E, I, May 13, 1864–June 1864
Robert Nevin's Independent Battery I, Pennsylvania Light Artillery, May 1864–November 15, 1864
3d Regiment Veteran Reserve Corps, Cos. C, E, August 1864–August 31, 1864
3d Regiment Veteran Reserve Corps, Co. K, September 1864
12th Regiment Veteran Reserve Corps, Co. B (part), September 1864–October 1864
4th Massachusetts Heavy Artillery, Co. L, November 1864–April 1865
4th New York Heavy Artillery, Co. D, May 1865–June 1865

GUARDIANS OF THE LEESBURG AND ALEXANDRIA TURNPIKE— FORT WARD, BLOCKHOUSE NUMBER 3, AND BATTERY GARESCHÉ

Battery Garesché

Location

From Harris Place, turn left onto St. Stephens Road and drive to Seminary Road. Turn right on Seminary Road and drive down the hill to North Quaker Lane. Turn left on North Quaker Lane and travel to the large crossroad intersection. Turn left on King Street (Route 7 West). Cross over Interstate 395 and turn right on 30th Street. Continue on 30th Street going around the circle. Turn right on South Abingdon Street and travel to the intersection of South Abingdon Street and 30th Road. Battery Garesché was located on the east corner of 30th Road.

Visible Remains

No visible remains of the earthwork exist. A historical marker cites the general location of the fort.

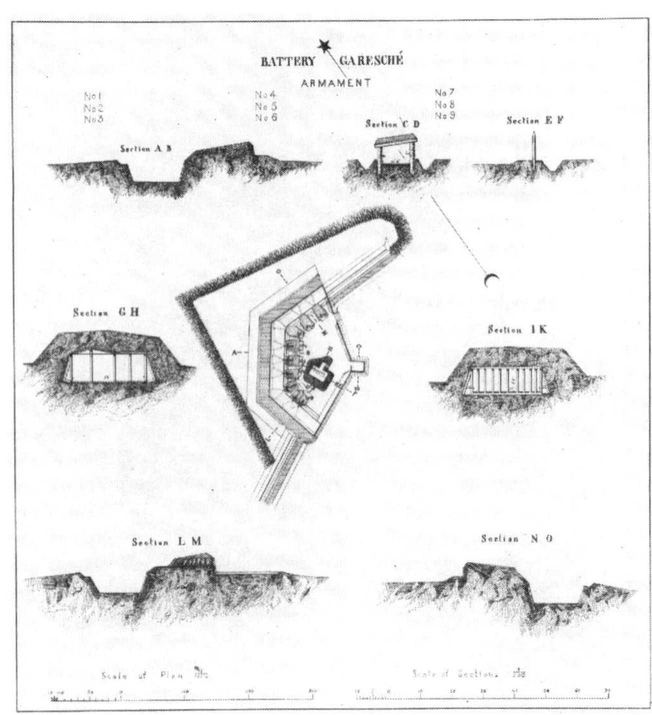

Battery Garesché—Engineer Drawing. *National Archives*

Description

The fort was named in honor of Colonel Julius Peter Garesché, who was killed by a cannonball at the Battle of Stones River (Murfreesboro), Tennessee, on December 31, 1862. Blockhouse Number 3 (located about 3033 South Columbus Street; no remains exist) and Battery Garesché were built on the land of Margaret Dangerfield and were designed to remedy the defective trace of Fort Reynolds, which stood on lower ground about 200 yards to the east of the battery. Battery Garesché was a lunette with a stockade gorge that had a perimeter of 166 yards. The earthwork had emplacements for nine guns, and the armament included two eight-inch howitzers, two 32-pounder brass howitzers, and four 20-pounder Parrot rifles. The battery had one magazine (twenty-two inches by ten feet). The guns were arranged to command the Leesburg and Alexandria Turnpike, which could not be seen by the troops at Fort Reynolds.[40]

Garrison troops included the following:

1st Connecticut Heavy Artillery, Co. E, May 1863–April 1864
9th New York Heavy Artillery, Co. H, May 1864
166th Ohio National Guard, Co. I, May 1864–July 1864
103d New York Infantry, Co. G, August 1864
4th Massachusetts Heavy Artillery, Co. H, November 1864–April 1865

COVERING FOUR MILE RUN—FORTS REYNOLDS AND BARNARD

Fort Reynolds

Location

Continue east on South Abingdon Street. Turn left on 31st Street and drive to the 4500 block. Fort Reynolds was located on and to the north side of 31st Street.

Visible Remains

No visible remains of the earthwork exist. A historical marker cites the general location of the fort and the "Fort Reynolds Park" sign memorializes the location.

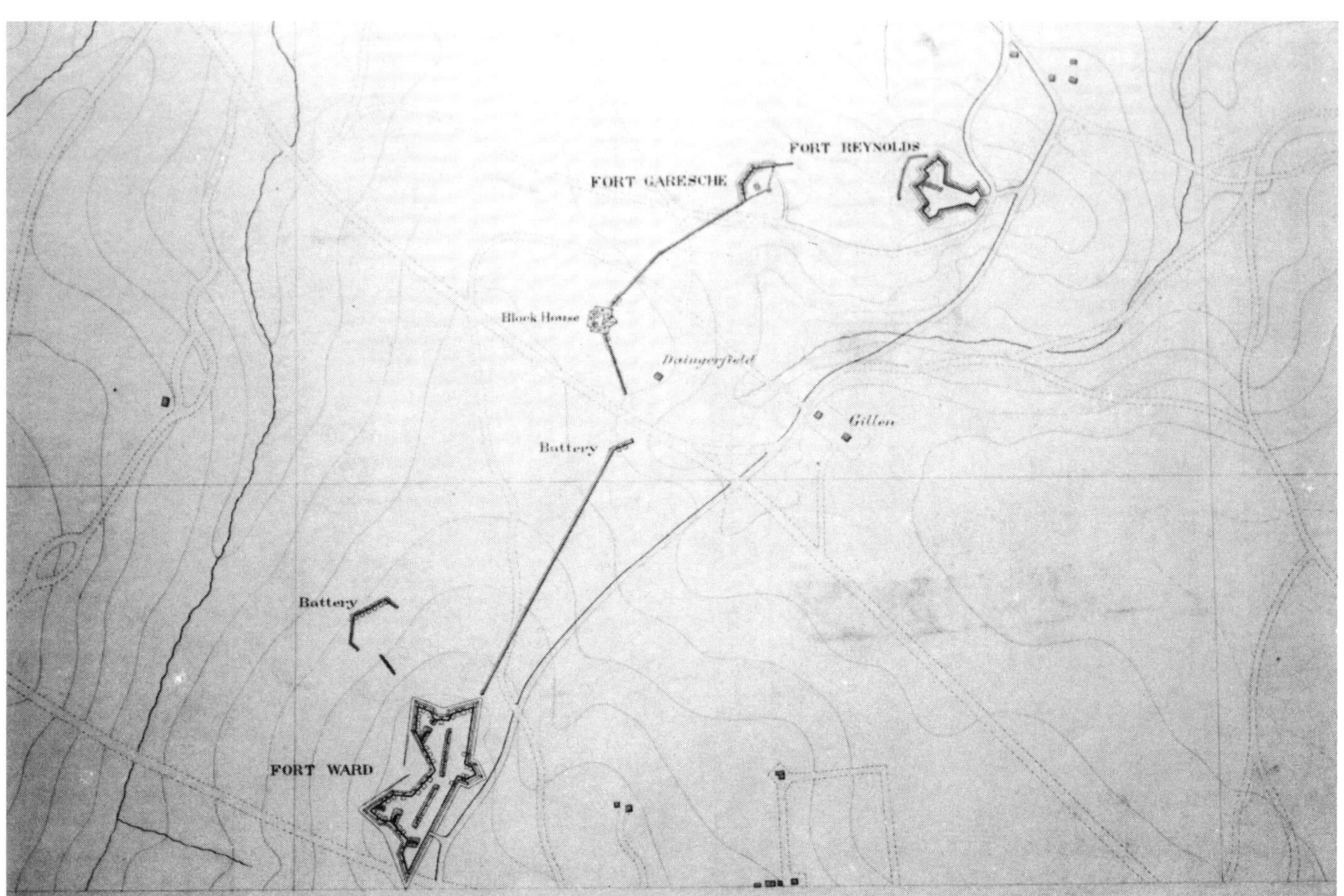

Sector Map from Fort Ward to Fort Reynolds. *National Archives*

Description

The fort was named for Major General John Fulton Reynolds, who was killed on July 1, 1863, by a Confederate sharpshooter during the opening engagement of the Battle of Gettysburg. The fort was originally called Fort Blenker in honor of Brigadier General Louis (Ludwig) Blenker, whose division of German soldiers constructed the fort in the fall of 1861. The site was selected for its commanding position over the broad valley of Four Mile Run. In the commission's report, it noted that Fort Blenker "is defective in trace and in having no view of the approaches from the west, the ground rising in that direction. The latter is being remedied by construction of a seven-gun battery. . . . The work being in a re-entrant, and its approaches under powerful fire from Forts Ward, and Barnard." Bombproof structures were not recommended because the ravine in the rear of the fort could protect the garrison against an enemy artillery attack. Below in the valley of Four Mile Run, "wide slashings" of cut trees were placed to obstruct the approaches. Rifle pits were dug across the valley, and emplacements for field guns were built to enfilade the area. Fort Reynolds had a perimeter of 360 yards and emplacements for twelve guns. The armament included four 32-pounder guns, four 12-pounder howitzers, three 30-pounder Parrott rifles, one ten-inch mortar, and two 24-pounder Coehorn mortars.[41]

Notes/Anecdotes

The constant concern of the Army Corps of Engineers with improving and strengthening the Defenses of

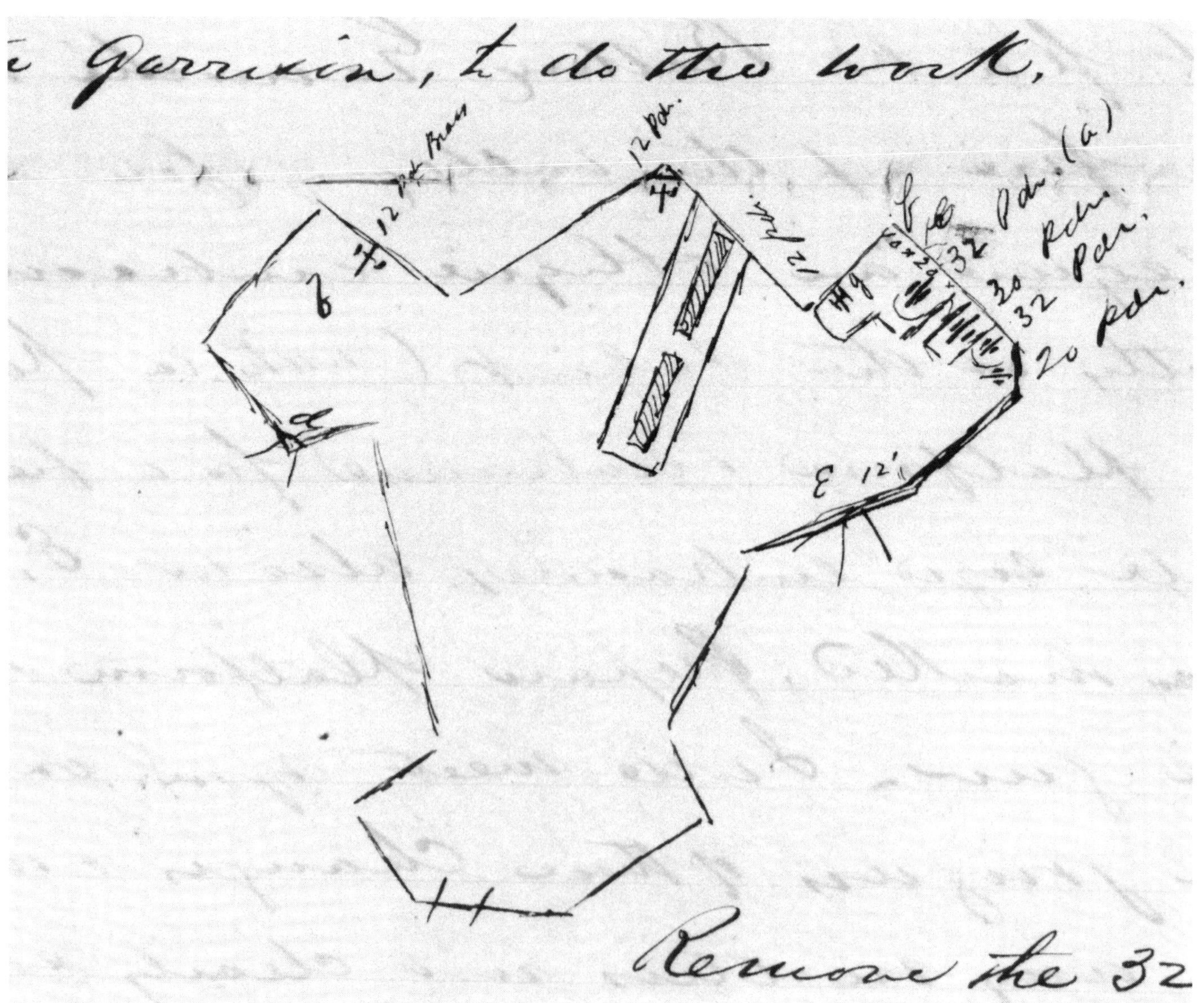

Engineer-in-Charge, A. G. Child's Sketch of Armament Changes at Fort Blenker. *Author's Collection*

Company A, 1st Connecticut Heavy Artillery, Captain Edward A. Gillette, Commanding at Fort Reynolds. *National Archives*

Washington can be seen in the hand-drawn sketch and instructions done by civilian engineer in charge, Defenses South of the Potomac River, A. G. Child, for armament improvements at Fort Blenker. "Field improvements" made during the war are often not reflected on the original engineer drawings and can be a source of confusion to archaeologists and those studying the extant remains of the forts:

> Washington, May 4, 1863
> Mr. Bennett, Supt. Sir,
> The following changes in the armament of Fort Blenker may be commenced immediately. I have written today to Col. Abbott, to request a detail from the garrison, to do the work. Remove the 32 pdr. at (a) to the position (b) now occupied by the 12 pdr. brass howitzer (at the left of the fort). At (a) 30 ft. to right of the angle (f) prepare a platform and embrasure for a 30 pdr. (siege) and also at (c) 10 ft. to the right of the angel (f). One continuous platform may be made for these two guns, and if we find it practical to extend it so as to include the platform for 12 pdr. brass howitzer at (g) thereby enabling us to get another embrasure or a pan coupe in the angle (f) we will do so. . . . If space can not be had for a good intermediate merlon at (c) then the embrasure at (c) must be so arranged as to flank Battery Garesché and also get a good fire up the valley of four mile run. This may require an oblique embrasure.[42]

In 1892, the Engineering Platoon of the Corps of Engineers, District of Columbia National Guard, created an early guide to the Civil War fortifications of Washington. When they visited Fort Reynolds, the profile of the fort was as sharp as when it was occupied, "the slopes having been perfectly preserved by thick growth of blue grass and bushes."[43] In 1954, Arlington County citizens unsuccessfully tried to preserve the fort from development. An apartment building stands on part of the site today.

Officers' Huts at Fort Reynolds. *U.S. Army Military History Institute*

Units stationed at Fort Reynolds included the following:

- 15th New York Heavy Artillery, Co. A, October 1861
- 74th Pennsylvania Infantry, January 16, 1862–February 1862
- 16th Battery, Indiana Light Artillery, May 1862
- 2d New York Heavy Artillery, Co. B, January 1862–June 1862
- 1st Connecticut Heavy Artillery, Co. A, August 1862
- 124th Pennsylvania Volunteer Infantry, August 1862
- 15th New York Heavy Artillery, Co. C (part), August 1862
- 16th Battery, Indiana Light Artillery, September 1863–December 1863
- 9th New York Heavy Artillery, Co. E, May 1864
- 166th Ohio National Guard, Co. G, May 1864–July 1864
- 103d New York Infantry, Cos. H, I (part), August 1864
- 12th Regiment Veteran Reserve Corps, Co. K, September 1864
- 1st New Hampshire Heavy Artillery, Co. D, October–November 1864
- 4th Massachusetts Heavy Artillery, Co. G, November 1864–April 1865
- 4th New York Heavy Artillery, Co. L, May 1865–June 1865

THE ARLINGTON LINES

The forts that covered the Aqueduct and Long Bridges and the intermediate heights of Arlington were part of what was called "The Arlington Lines." In May 1861, when Federal troops seized Arlington Heights, they began construction of a series of detached earthworks to protect the bridgeheads and establish points of support for the Union army in the field. These works included Forts Runyon, Scott, Albany, Corcoran, Haggerty, and Bennett. This early phase of construction formed the "Proper Defenses of Washington" south of the Potomac River because the forts occupied sites from which the capital could be shelled if commanded by Confederate forces.

After the Union disaster at the First Battle of Bull Run (Manassas) in late July 1861, work was begun on a line of breastworks and lunettes to the west of the Proper Defenses of Washington. These works included Forts Barnard, Berry, Craig, Tillinghast, Cass, Woodbury, and DeKalb (Strong). Additional rifle pits and batteries were constructed to fill in gaps or strengthen the line. By 1865, the army engineers could survey this area with pride and see a line of mutually supporting earthworks composed of two lines of defense that could protect the Virginia approach to the capital and stand independent of the defenses of Alexandria.

Fort Barnard

Location

Backtrack on 31st Street and proceed to Columbus Street. Turn right on Columbus Street passing the site of the Blockhouse Number 3 at 3033 Columbus Street and continue around the circle to King Street (Route 7 West). Turn right and drive to Walter Reed Drive. Turn right on Walter Reed Drive and continue crossing the valley of Four Mile Run and up the steep hill to Fort Barnard. Fort Barnard Park is located on the right at South Pollard Street and Walter Reed Drive.

Visible Remains

No remains of the fort exist. A historical marker notes the general location of the fort. The fort proper was located on the southeast section of the park near the end of South Oxford Street, where a playground and basketball court now stand. In 1976, a small section of the fort existed near South Oxford Street, but the remnant was destroyed by park landscaping. A short side trip to the end of South Pollard Street will lead to the remains of the battery to the left of Fort Barnard. The position overlooks Four Mile Run valley and has a magnificent view. Sections of a rifle pit are visible to the rear of 3816 22nd Street.

Description

The fort was named for Major General John Gross Barnard of the army engineers and "Father of the Defenses of Washington" (see Appendix A). The site of the fort held a naturally strong commanding position on the ridge. Constructed during the fall of 1861, Fort Barnard was a small enclosed work with a perimeter of 250 yards. It has emplacements for twenty guns, and the armament consisted of three eight-inch howitzers, five 32-pounder guns, three 24-pounder guns, three 24-pounder field howitzers, three 30-pounder Parrott rifles, one eight-inch mortar, and one 24-pounder Coehorn mortar. The fort covers the head of ravines that could be used to assemble and conceal large bodies of Union troops in preparation for a flank attack against an enemy line.[44]

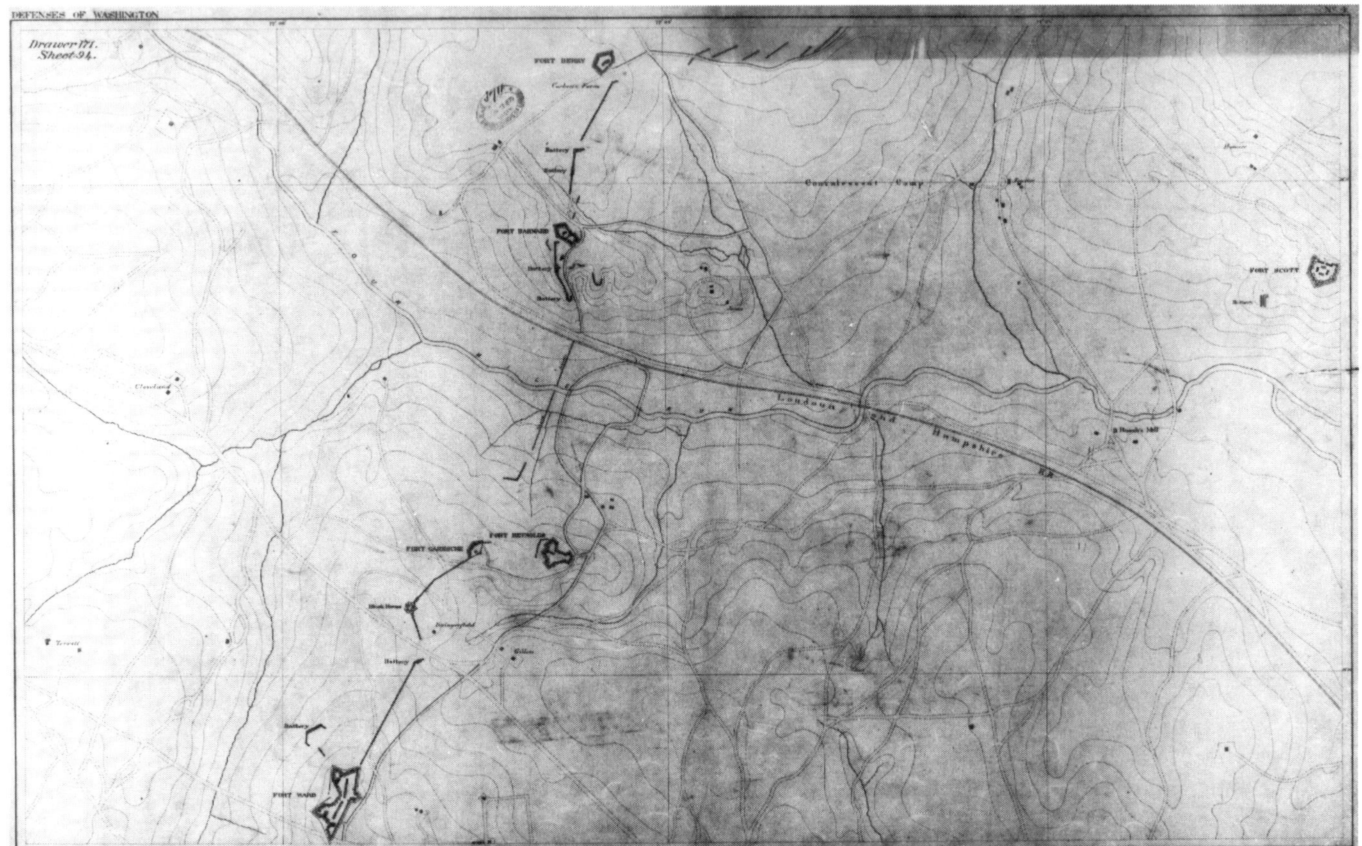

Sector Map from Fort Ward to Fort Scott. *National Archives*

Notes/Anecdotes

The soldiers of the Defenses of Washington fared much better than soldiers in the field when it came to "culinary delights." One soldier from the 9th New York Heavy Artillery remarked, "Captain Lyons ordered ten gallons of oysters and twelve dollars' worth of poultry. Henry Porter . . . and J. J. Vickery went out with guns and dogs and secured a buck deer weighing 200 pounds, all of which served to brighten the surroundings not a little."[45] Other soldiers found extra rations in orchards, as the following story suggests:

> One day after we had been at the forts some time, an old citizen from near Fort Barnard came to Colonel Tyler, stating that the Colonel's men were stealing his peaches. "They are?" says the Colonel, "I don't allow my men to steal sir, if you catch any of them at it bring them to me and I will punish them sir." The farmer succeeded one day in catching three men from one of our companies, and brought them to the Colonel saying: "Here are some of your men who have just been over stealing my peaches." "My men are they," asked the Colonel, and then turning to the parties caught, demands, "What regiment do you belong sir." "To Co.—— of the 1st Massachussir," was the reply. "There, you see, sir, these are not my men," says the Colonel, and turning to the men again, "You sirs, go to your regiment and don't let me catch you around my camp again." "Now, sir," to the farmer, "You can go home, I told you my men would not steal, sir, I do not allow it."[46]

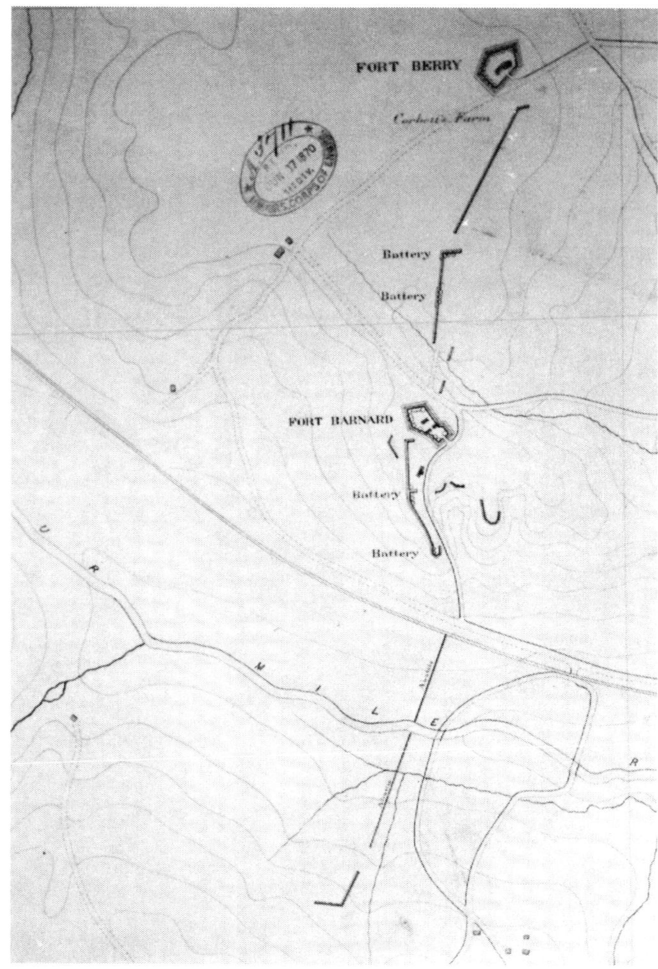

Sector Map from Fort Barnard to Fort Berry. *National Archives*

Garrison troops at Fort Barnard included detachments from the following:

- 1st Connecticut Heavy Artillery, Co. E, October 29, 1861–February 1862
- 74th Pennsylvania Infantry, January–February 1862
- 1st Connecticut Heavy Artillery, Co. B, February 1862
- 1st Massachusetts Heavy Artillery, Cos. A, B, March 1862
- 1st Massachusetts Heavy Artillery, Cos. I, L, May 1862–June 1862
- 125th Pennsylvania Infantry, Cos. A–K, August 1862
- 1st Connecticut Heavy Artillery, Co. G, November 1862–June 1863
- 1st Connecticut Heavy Artillery, Co. H, August 1862
- 9th New York Heavy Artillery, Cos. B, I, May 1864
- 1st Connecticut Heavy Artillery, Co. B, April 1864
- 166th Ohio National Guard, Co. A, May 1864–June 1864
- 1st New York Light Artillery, Battery F, May 1864–October 1864
- 1st Connecticut Heavy Artillery, Co. G, September 1864
- 166th Ohio National Guard, Cos. A, K, June 1864–July 1864
- 103d New York Infantry, Cos. D, F, I (part), August 1864
- 4th Massachusetts Heavy Artillery, Co. A, November–December 1864
- 1st New Hampshire Heavy Artillery, Co. H, November 1864
- 1st Maryland Light Artillery, Battery D, November 1864
- 29th Unattached Co. Massachusetts Heavy Artillery, December 1864
- 4th New York Heavy Artillery, Cos. E, H, May 1865–June 1865
- 4th Massachusetts Heavy Artillery, Co. K, November 1864–April 1865

FILLER FORTS— FORTS BERRY AND RICHARDSON

Fort Berry

Location

From Fort Barnard, turn around and continue on Pollard Street across Walter Reed Drive to 16th Street. Turn right on 16th Street and drive to the intersection of 16th and Monroe streets. Fort Berry was located on the site of the intersection extending into the four adjacent yards.

Visible Remains

No visible remains of the fort exist. David Miller noted that the home at 3225 17th Street occupies the site of the officers' quarters. The historical marker for the fort is located at Glebe Road and 17th Street.[47]

Description

This fort was named in honor of Major General Hiram George Berry of the 4th Maine Infantry, who was killed at Chancellorsville, Virginia, on May 2, 1863. Fort Berry was constructed in 1863 as an intermediate point between Forts Barnard and Richardson. General Barnard's report describes the fort as an enclosed "unflanked work of moderate dimensions and . . . a prominent point for attack." Recognizing the weakness of the position as a salient angle in the line, guns at Fort Barnard and Richardson were arranged to sweep the plateau in front of Fort Berry with supporting fire. The fort's perimeter was 215 yards with emplacements for ten guns. The armament included two eight-inch howitzers and two four-and-a-half-inch Rodman guns. Quartermaster buildings were located outside the fort near the gorge.[48]

Garrison troops included the following:

1st Connecticut Heavy Artillery, Co. G, July 1863–May 9, 1864
3rd Massachusetts Heavy Artillery, Co. A, May 1864–August 1864
9th New York Heavy Artillery, Co. K, May 1864
1st New Hampshire Heavy Artillery, Co. I, October 20, 1864–November 1864
30th Unattached Company Massachusetts Heavy Artillery, December 1864
4th Massachusetts Heavy Artillery, Co. E, December 1864–March 10, 1865
4th New York Heavy Artillery, Co. F, May 1865–June 1865

Fort Richardson

Location

Continue on 16th Street to Glebe Road. Turn right on Glebe Road and drive to 17th Road following the signs to the Army Navy Country Club. Turn left on 17th Road veering right onto 18th Street and the private road leading to the Army Navy Country Club. Follow the private road around to the second parking area opposite the tennis courts near the ninth green of the golf course. The ninth green is located in the center of Fort Richardson.

Visible Remains

The fort's south walls and ditches are well preserved. A historical marker is located to the left of the private road near the fort parapet. In the fall, the vista toward the Capitol is worth a special visit to the site.

Description

The fort was named in honor of Brigadier General Israel B. Richardson of the 2d Michigan Infantry, who died on November 3, 1862, of wounds received at the Battle of Antietam. Fort Richardson was constructed in the fall of 1861 and had a perimeter of 316 yards. It was well armed and contained six 24-pounder guns, two 24-pounder field howitzers, three 30-pounder Parrott rifles, one ten-inch mortar, one 24-pounder Coehorn mortar, and one 100-pounder Parrott rifle that could sweep the sector from Fort Ellsworth to Fort DeKalb (Fort Strong). Internal fort structures included two magazines and a bombproof.[49]

The second Camp Convalescent was located south of Fort Richardson in the valley (modern-day slopes of the golf course and valley where Interstate 395 sits). The camp replaced the infamous "Camp Misery," which was located on the slopes of Shuters Hill northeast of Fort Ellsworth near Alexandria. The camp was moved to this site and constructed in 1863.

Notes/Anecdotes

On the first anniversary of the regiment's enlistment, Chaplain Edward Walker, 1st Connecticut Heavy Artillery, wrote a reflective portrait of soldier life at the fort during the winter of 1861–1862:

> Looking back over the five months spent at Fort Richardson, the mind is confused with details that struggle for expression. We see them as in kaleidoscopic vision. Long lines of snow-white gloves, of glistening bayonets, of polished brass, and spotless uniforms, mixed

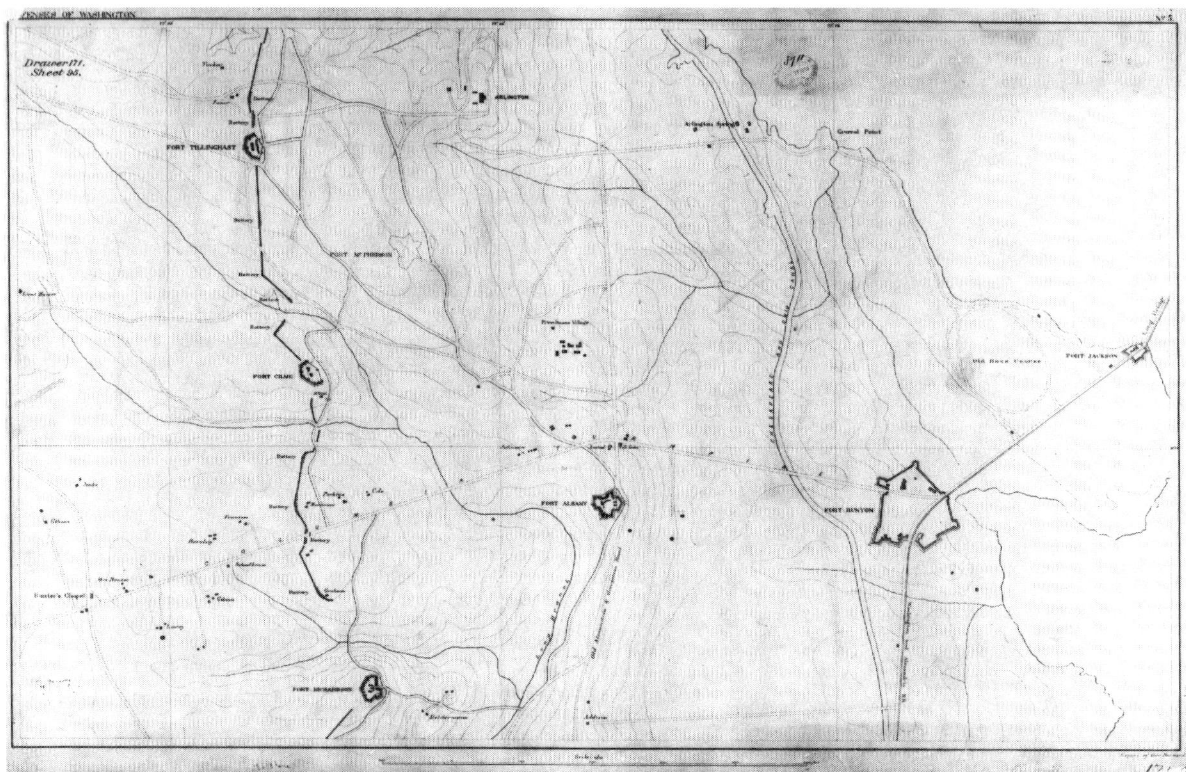

Sector Map from Fort Richardson to Fort Jackson. *National Archives*

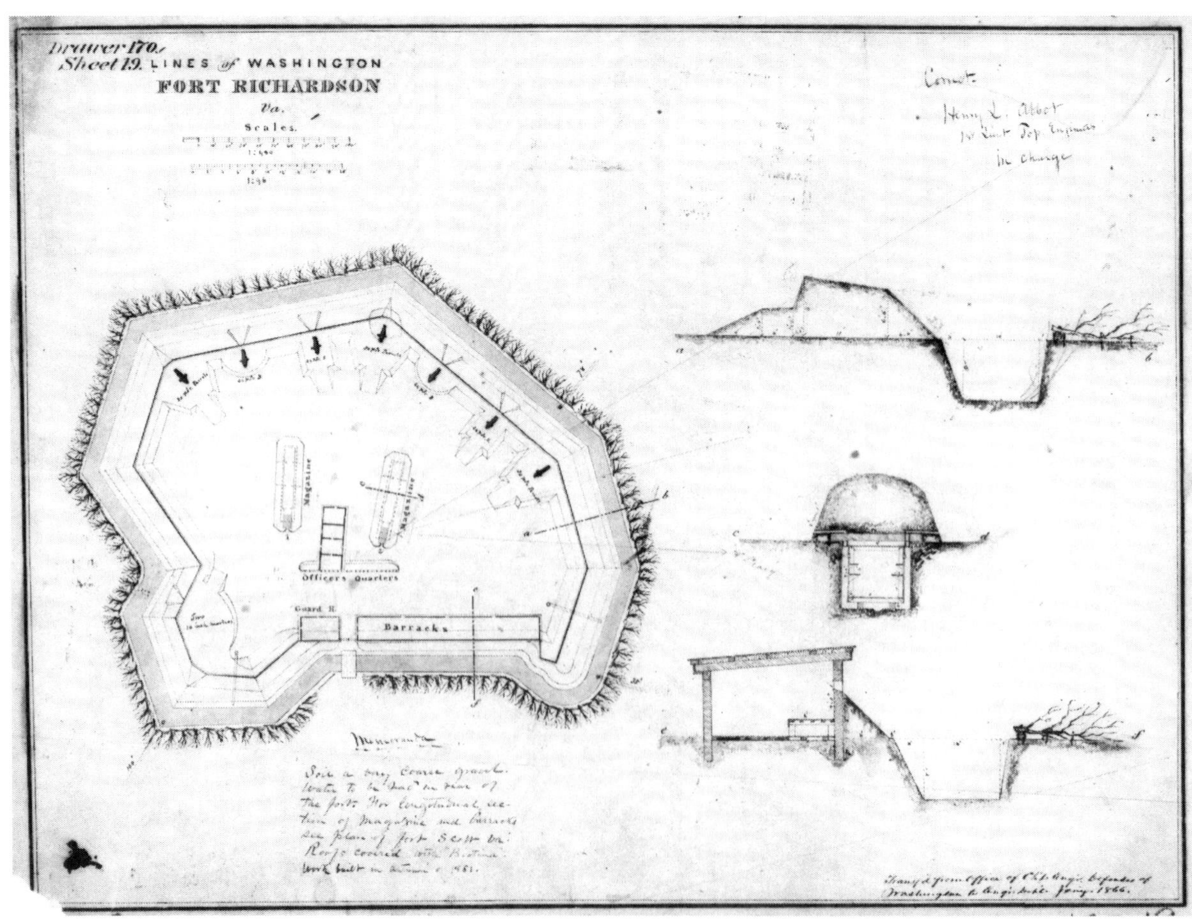

Fort Richardson—Engineer Drawing. *National Archives*

The 1st Connecticut Heavy Artillery at Drill, Fort Richardson. *Library of Congress*

Camp Ingalls, 1st Connecticut Heavy Artillery, Taken from Fort Richardson. *National Archives*

Army and Navy County Club 8th Green Surrounded by Fort Richardson's Parapets Today. *Fort Ward Museum Collection*

GENERAL PLAN - FORT RICHARDSON

Note; Buildings here are constructed like those used for similar purposes at forts North of Potomac.

Mess House

Barracks.

Officers' Qrs.

Barracks.

Barracks.

FORT RICHARDSON.

PLAN
SHOWING
QUARTERMASTER PROPERTY
AT
FORT RICHARDSON,
DEFENCES OF WASHINGTON
SOUTH OF POTOMAC.

Quarters

DEFENCES SOUTH of POTOMAC,
OCTOBER 7th 1865.

Plan of Quartermaster Property—Fort Richardson. *National Archives*

View of Camp Ingalls and Fort Richardson Looking West. *Library of Congress*

> up carriage-loads of ladies, officers on horseback, flags and cannon-smoke; and with these, soberer bits of glass in the shape of sling carts, statuary, spread eagles; and again, stumps, picks, shovels, and the like, set off by mud and cold and wind; and these again relieved by gorgeous sunrises and sunsets, lovely days and nights, and ever changing, ever charming views from the summit of the hill. Turn the glass, and again we have the same things in different combinations. But in every scene may be detected the vigilant eye of our commander scrutinizing everything, approving every soldierly act or trait, and punishing with rigor each minute offense against perfect military discipline.[50]

What the chaplain described may have been more relevant to the officers than the enlisted men.

When the companies from the 9th New York Heavy Artillery replaced the 1st Connecticut Heavy Artillery at Fort Richardson in May 1864, the New York troops found a wood sign over the main entrance left by the soldiers of the "Wooden Nutmeg State." In Latin on the sign was the motto written in large letters, "Qui transtulit sustinet," which some of the boys just from school were able to render for their fellows as "Who brought us, will sustain."[51]

Garrison troops stationed at Fort Richardson included the following:

- 37th New York Infantry, September 1861
- 1st Connecticut Heavy Artillery, Co. A, May 31, 1861–October 1861
- 1st Connecticut Heavy Artillery, Cos. B, D, F, H, K, September 1861–February 1862
- 1st Massachusetts Heavy Artillery, Co. H, March 1862–June 1862
- 1st Massachusetts Heavy Artillery, Co. C, May 1862–June 1862
- 1st Connecticut Heavy Artillery, Co. C, May 1862–June 1862
- 1st Connecticut Heavy Artillery, Co. E, July 1862–April 1863
- 15th New York Heavy Artillery, Co. C (part), August 1862
- 1st Connecticut Heavy Artillery, Co. B, August 1862–December 1862
- 10th New York Heavy Artillery, Co. D, October 1862–April 1863
- 1st Connecticut Heavy Artillery, Cos. F, K, January 1863–April 1864

9th New York Heavy Artillery, Cos. A, F, M, May 1864
166th Ohio National Guard, Cos. D–F, H, May 1864–July 1864
1st Rhode Island Light Artillery, Battery H, June 1864–July 1864
1st Maryland Light Artillery, Battery D, August 1864–October 1864
103d New York Infantry, Cos. A, B, E, I (part), K, August 1864
1st Pennsylvania Light Artillery, Battery C, I, November 1864
1st New Hampshire Heavy Artillery, Co. C, November 1864
4th Massachusetts Heavy Artillery, Cos. C, D, November, 1864–April 1865
4th New York Heavy Artillery, Cos. A, K, May 1865–June 1865

DEFENSE POSTS FOR THE LONG BRIDGE—FORTS ALBANY, RUNYON, AND JACKSON

Fort Albany

Location

From Fort Richardson, drive down the hill toward Army Navy Drive and turn left onto Army Navy Drive. Continue and veer to the right onto Nash Street. Drive up the hill to Prospect Hill Park, 1025 South Arlington Ridge Road, and stop at the small overlook park at Nash Street and Arlington Ridge Road.

Visible Remains

No visible remains of the fort exist. The ground on which the fort stood was cut away during the construction of Henry C. Shirley Memorial Highway (Interstate 395). A historical marker cites the general location of the fort. Nearby is the marker for the estate of Prospect Hill.

Description

Fort Albany was constructed by New York troops who named it to honor the capital of their state. The fort was built on the land owned by James Roach, and work was begun on the fort during the end of May 1861. Construction was supervised by Captain Barton S. Alexander of the Army Corps of Engineers, and the fort was completed in about seven weeks. Barnard's report notes that it "is a work partly bastioned, well built, and in admirable condition; the parapets being turfed and the scarps revetted with boards." Fort Albany commanded Long Bridge (located south and near the present-day site of the 14th Street Railroad Bridge) and provided supporting fire for Forts Richardson, Craig, and Tillinghast. The fort's guns also controlled the Columbia Turnpike access route to Long Bridge and the ravine between Forts Richardson and Scott. The perimeter of Fort Albany was 429 yards with emplacements for twelve guns. It was well provided with magazines, embrasures, and bombproofs. The armament included four 24-pounder siege guns, two 24-pounder field howitzers, two 30-pounder Parrott rifles, and four vacant platforms.[52]

Notes/Anecdotes

Major Abner Small, writing of his war experiences building earthworks along the Arlington line, suggested that army fatigue duty was not so bad; it was only a matter of comparison:

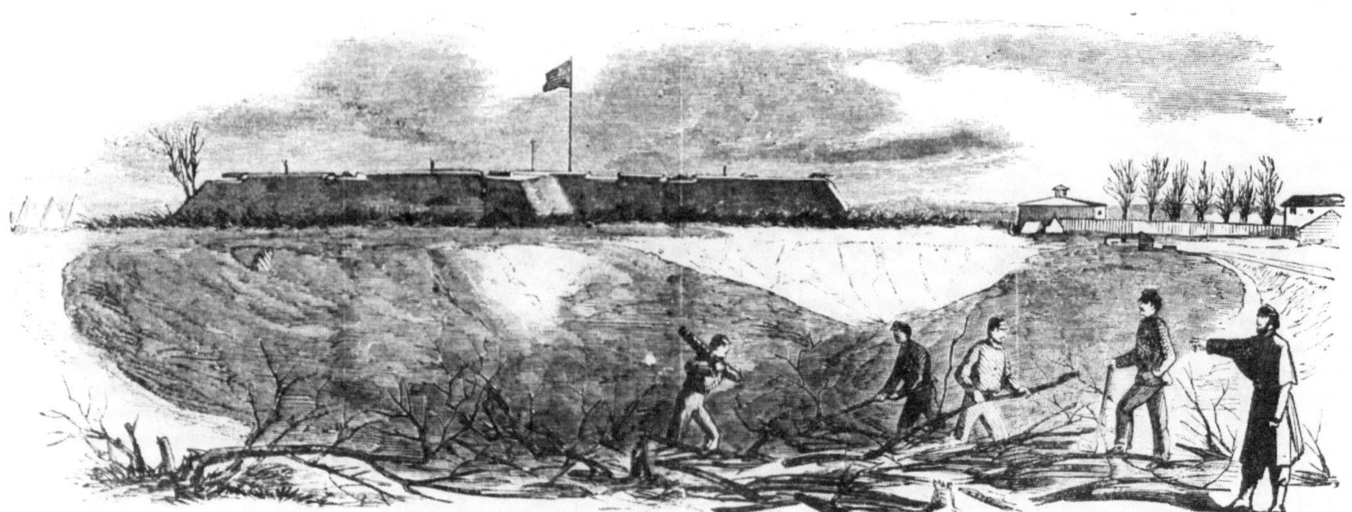

Fort Albany—*Harper's Weekly*, November 30, 1861

Details were made daily to work on a line of breast-works connecting the forts. The boys went at it with a will. Many of them, reared on farms, had natural propensity for digging holes and shoveling dirt, which had not been fully satisfied by details to dig "sinks" and tent drains. They had read about the breast-works and redoubts of George Washington's day, and were glad of a chance to exhibit their artistic qualities on something less degrading than a camp sink. They were not at first impressed with the fact that the army sinks are a government institution. . . . Men questioned how digging a hole in Virginia mud would rebound to their credit, and add to the laurels of a soldier. . . . Army correspondents, safely seated behind a redoubt, with a pipe and some rum, will write all about the forts, the long line of breast-works, how strong they are, how many bastions and angles, how much repelling power, and charmingly congratulate some pioneer corps on the splendid engineering qualities of—their general. But they never dilate on a line of army sinks, or compliment a regiment for the . . . discharge of an irksome duty required by all good soldiers in camp.[53]

At least one special artist, D. H. Grover, was arrested in April 1863 at Fort Albany and had his drawing confiscated by the officer of the day for sketching the fort in too much detail. Fort commander Colonel Thomas R. Tannatt, 1st Massachusetts Heavy Artillery, wrote that he did not believe it was intended as merely a drawing because the guns in embrasures and barbette are closely shown, abatis and contours of the ground were illustrated, and the artist attempted to "secrete" his drawing. The incident was referred to Colonel Cogswell commanding the brigade.[54]

Garrison and construction units stationed at Fort Albany were the following:

7th Regiment New York State Militia Infantry—construction
12th Regiment Infantry (three months)—May 1861—construction
25th Regiment Infantry (three months)—May 1861—construction

A Soldier's Drawing of Fort Albany, 1863. *U.S. Army Military History Institute*

- 25th New York National Guard, May 1861–August 1861
- 37th New York Infantry, Cos. A–G, K, July 1861–August 1861
- 1st Massachusetts Heavy Artillery, Cos. A–K, July 1861–October 1861
- 1st Massachusetts Heavy Artillery, Cos. A, B, E, H, I, G, February 1862
- 11th Independent Battery, New York Light Artillery, December 1861
- 12th Independent Battery, New York Light Artillery, January 1862
- 56th Pennsylvania Infantry, Co. I, February–March 1862
- 1st Massachusetts Heavy Artillery, Cos. L, M, April 1862
- 1st Massachusetts Heavy Artillery, Cos. D, May–June 1862
- 1st Massachusetts Heavy Artillery, Cos. I, L, July 1862
- 16th Maine Infantry, two companies, September 1862
- 15th New York Engineers, Cos. C, K, September 1862–October 1862
- 1st Massachusetts Heavy Artillery, Co. L, July 1862–April 1863
- 1st Massachusetts Heavy Artillery, Co. G, November 1863–April 1864
- 145th Ohio National Guard, Co. A, May 1864–June 1864
- 138th Ohio National Guard, Cos. B, C, G, June 1864
- 10th New York Heavy Artillery, Co. A, July–August 1864
- 4th Massachusetts Heavy Artillery, Co. K, October–November 1864
- 6th Pennsylvania Heavy Artillery, Co. E, December 1864–April 1865
- 2d New York Heavy Artillery, Co. I, May 1865–June 1865

Fort Runyon and Fort Jackson

Location

From the overlook site of Fort Albany, proceed down Arlington Ridge Road, making a hard left turn onto Lynn Street. Continue on Lynn Street to Army Navy Drive. Turn right on Army Navy Drive to Eads Street. Turn right on Eads Street and travel to 12th Street. Turn left on 12th Street and continue straight, driving to South Clark Street and Old Jefferson Davis Highway. Turn left onto South Clark Street and continue straight to Old Jefferson Davis Highway, driving to the end where the road meets Boundary Channel Drive. Expect road changes in this area because of future development.

Visible Remains

No visible remains of the forts exist. In 1988, a historical marker cited the general location of Fort Jackson and Fort Runyon, but the marker has been removed. The area where the forts were located is currently undergoing master planning for Arlington County's "Long Bridge Park" and mixed commercial development.

Description

This fort was named in honor of Brigadier General Theodore Runyon, whose New Jersey Brigade helped build the forts. Fort Runyon was the largest fort in the Defenses of Washington, covering twelve acres of land with a perimeter of 1,484 yards. It was built on the land of James Roach. Construction of the fort began on the morning of May 24, 1861, under the supervision of Captain Barton S. Alexander and was completed in about seven weeks. Fort Runyon guarded Long Bridge and the important junction of the Washington-Alexandria and Columbia turnpikes. The fort served as a point of support for Union troops on the Virginia shore and was built on the low bottom land along the Potomac River. The location was vulnerable to attack from the heights above, and within a week after construction began on Fort Runyon, the trace was laid out on the heights above for Fort Albany. After construction of the Arlington Line two miles to the west, many of Fort Runyon's guns were removed, and the fort was used as a supply depot and, on one occasion, as a corral for livestock. By the fall of 1862, the commission's report stated, "Though this work has not the importance it first had, it should not have been permitted to fall to decay nor to be disarmed. As a tete-du-pont it should be rearmed and kept in perfect condition in every respect." When the report was written, Fort Runyon had only two guns mounted: one eight-inch seacoast howitzer and one 32-pounder Located to the northeast of Fort Runyon at the Virginia end of Long Bridge was the site of Fort Jackson. This work defended the bridge and was used as a control point for bridge traffic. Fort Jackson probably took its name from the area where the fort stood. In 1835, speculators tried to develop a community at the Virginia end of Long Bridge. The cornerstone of the town was laid on January 11, 1836, in the presence of President Andrew Jackson, for whom the village was named. The Jackson City venture failed, and in 1851

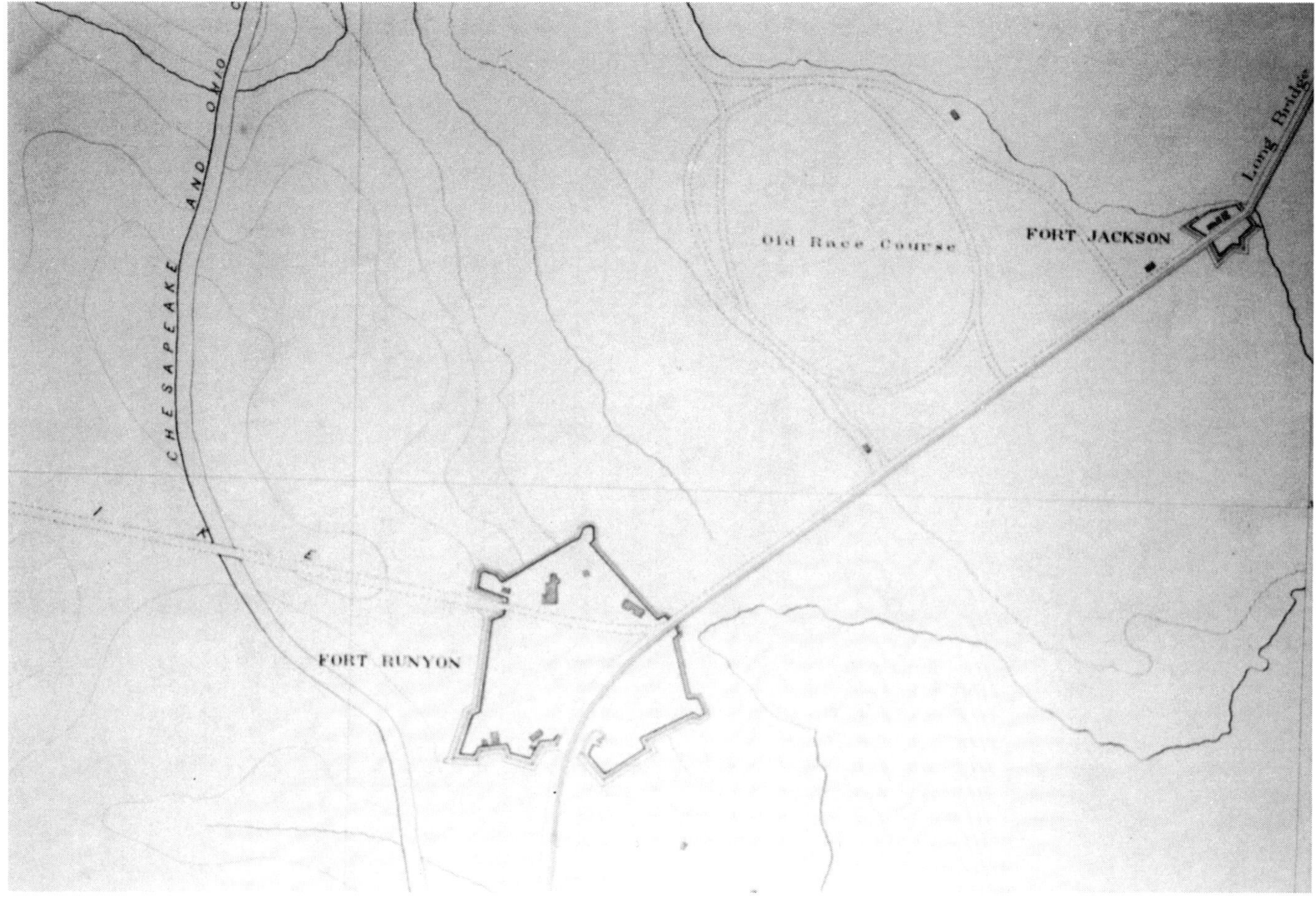

Sector Map, Fort Runyon to Fort Jackson. *National Archives*

the property was sold at auction. The location of this fort was about fifty yards south of the intersection of the present-day 14th Street Railroad Bridge and the Virginia shore.[55]

Notes/Anecdotes

The historian for the 7th New York State Militia recorded these impressions of the construction of Fort Runyon when war was still seen as an adventure:

> Early on the following morning, Saturday, May 25th, a detail of men with axes was marched by Captain Viele, the engineer officer of the Regiment, to the place afterwards known as "Fort Runyon," and proceeded to level to the ground a fine peach orchard of three hundred trees. The fortification commanded Long Bridge and . . . had already been laid out, the New Jersey Brigade had commenced with pick and spade the construction of its southeast angle. . . . On Sunday, the 26th, the labor on the fortifications was not suspended; and so important and urgent was the work that Chaplain Weston, after divine service, sanctified the duty by his example, marched at the head of a detachment, and labored for two hours. . . . The detachment, when relieved from the work by new details, were allowed an hour to bathe in the neighboring canal, and as the adjoining fields abounded with strawberries, the men embraced the opportunity to add luxury to their hard fare.[56]

Captain White of the 15th Connecticut Volunteer Infantry noted that if guarding Long Bridge was disagreeable, it had the element of activity in it and "meant business." It was also an "eye opener to the wiles of human nature." Captain White wrote,

> Long Bridge was the only route for travel leading directly out of Washington into the Southern Confederacy. As a school for the study of human nature, the station at . . . the end of the Bridge might, in '62, have justly been styled a university. What could not be seen anywhere else in the way of subterfuge, double dealing and duplicity could be found there. The first time the 15th C.V. ever saw quinine put up in the form of a bologna sausage, was there. The first time it ever saw a veritable wooden coffin, ostensibly designed for a

Fort Jackson and Fort Runyon—Historic Map Overlay on Modern Aerial Image Showing the Location of the Forts and Pentagon. *Courtesy of the National Park Service*

Dutch colonel—*dead* but in reality filled with bottled Rhine wine and lager for a Dutch sutler—*living*, was there. And there, it will be remembered, as company after company occupied the sumptuous quarters provided at the sacred end of bridge, the regiment was first initiated into the never-to-be-forgotten luxury of "scratching itself to sleep."[57]

Garrison troops at Fort Runyon included the following:

7th Regiment New York Militia Infantry, May 1861—construction
2d New Jersey Infantry (three months), May 1861
3d New Jersey Infantry (three months), May 1861
21st New York Infantry, May–August 1861—construction
25th New York National Guard, August 1861
1st Massachusetts Heavy Artillery, Cos. C, F, November 1861
1st Massachusetts Heavy Artillery, Co. C, February 1862–April 1862
2d New York Heavy Artillery, Co. E, September 1863

Units listed that were assigned to Fort Jackson were the following:

21st New York Infantry, Co. D, August–September 1861—construction
1st Massachusetts Heavy Artillery, Co. D, September 1861–April 1862

Fort Runyon—*Frank Leslie's Famous Leaders and Battle Scenes, 1861–1865. Fort Ward Museum Collection*

Fort Scott—A Rear-Echelon Flank Fort

Location

From the site of Fort Runyon, backtrack on Old Jefferson Davis Highway to 12th Street South. Turn right on 12th Street South and drive to Eads Street. Turn left on Eads Street and travel to Fort Scott Drive. Turn right on Fort Scott Drive and drive up the hill until you reach Fort Scott Park on your left. Park in the parking lot. As you face the park, walk to the right side of the

Long Bridge. *National Archives*

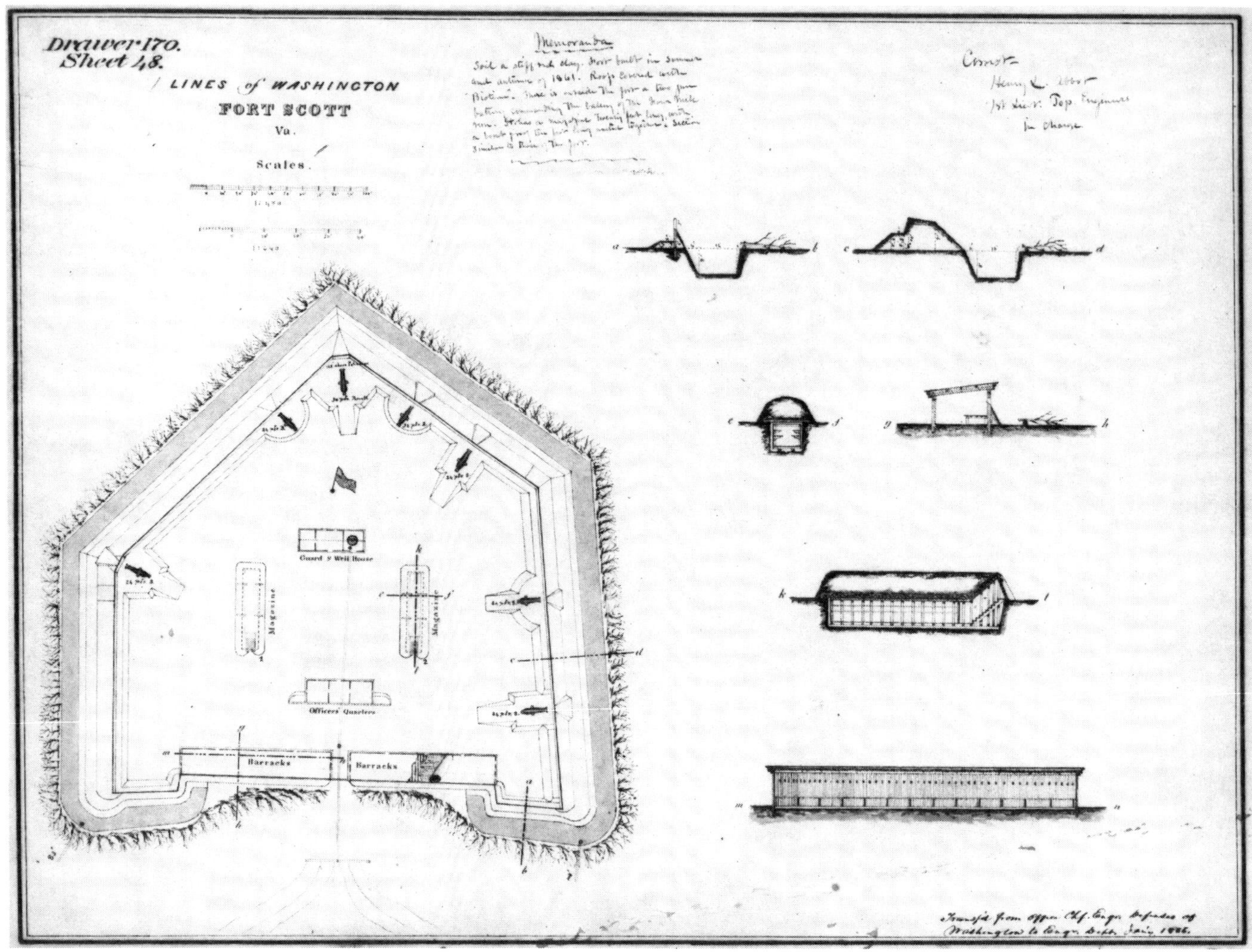

Fort Scott—Engineer Drawing. *National Archives*

property line and to the back of the park. The limited extant remains of the fort can be seen in this area of the park.

Visible Remains

Approximately 190 feet of the fort parapet exist on private and park properties. Arlington County acquired the area of land encompassing the apex of the fort. The parapet is poorly preserved, but the faint traces of a gun platform can still he seen. A historical marker for the site is located near Fort Scott Drive.

Description

The fort was named in honor of Lieutenant General Winfield Scott, who commanded the Union army in the early months of the rebellion. Fort Scott was a large lunette occupying the left of the Proper Defenses of Washington. The fort was constructed on the site of a wooded ridge north of and parallel to Four Mile Run, and the land was owned by L. E. Chrittenden and the Hunter family. About 200 acres of forest were cleared on the ridge so that the fort trace could be laid out.[58] The fort dominated the Four Mile Run valley, but the extension of the line westward to embrace the ridges west of Alexandria placed Forts Scott and Albany in a second line of defense. However, as General Barnard noted, Fort Scott, "taken in connection with Forts Richardson, Craig, and others, completed a defensive line for Washington independent of the extension to Alexandria." Fort Scott had a perimeter of 313 yards and emplacements for eight guns. The armament of the fort consisted of one eight-inch howitzer, five 24-pounder guns, one 20-pounder Parrott rifle, one 6-pounder gun, and two ten-inch mortars.[59] Inside the fort were two magazines, a guard and well house, and bombproof barracks. In October 1863, Fort Scott was the site of experiments with spherical case using ten-inch mortars shells. Standard ten-inch mortar shells were filled with twenty-seven 12-pounder, iron canister balls and loaded with a bursting charge of two and a half pounds of powder. The complete round weighed 104 pounds. Firing the projectile with one pound, six ounces of powder from a Model 1861, ten-inch siege mortar sent the projectile 800 yards and used a thirteen-second time fuse. The shell burst, scattering the balls and allowing them to fall within a circle roughly equal in diameter to the height of the burst above the ground, and struck the ground with sufficient force to kill. The experiments provided valuable knowledge to the artillerymen. The typical mortar shell did not contain lead balls and used a heavier bursting charge. Unless the projectile was a direct hit, high-air bursts did limited damaged to troops on the ground because the fragments were dispersed over a large area.[60]

Notes/Anecdotes

Private G. W. Vail, Company I, 1st Connecticut Heavy Artillery, wrote his sister Mary from Fort Scott on November 30, 1862. "I must confess, I don't feel much like writing tonight," wrote the private, "for it is Sunday." The "spirit" must have been with the private because not only did he write a long letter but he also addressed a complex moral issue: the Christian character of soldiers in the ranks:

> You say that you think that the Sabbath School scholars make the best soldiers and are to be trusted rather than some others, and ask if I think so. I confess I

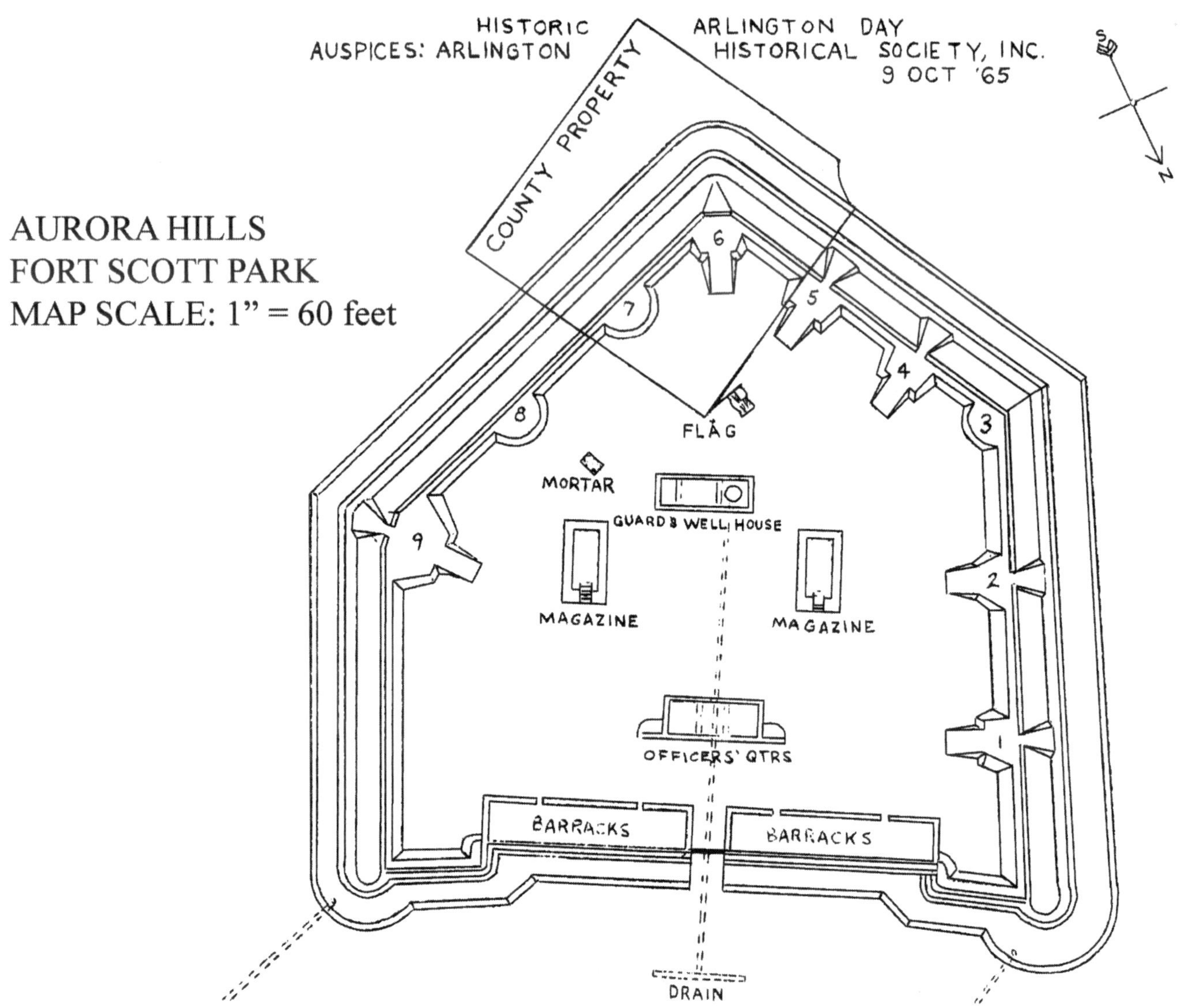

Roy C. Brewer's Drawing of Fort Scott. *Arlington County Library*

FLAGPOLE BASE (BRICK)
SCALE: 1" = 40"

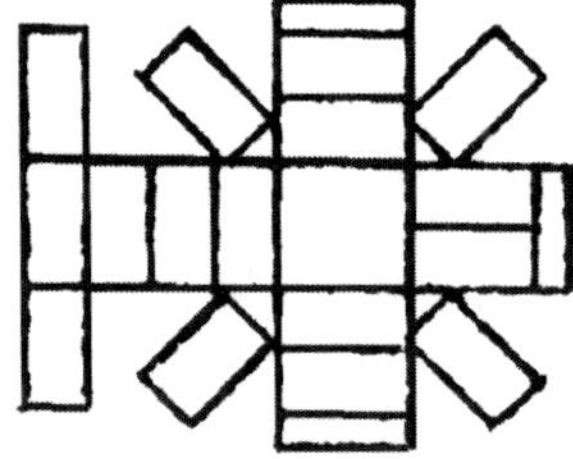

Fort Scott's Flagstaff Base Design Drawn by Roy Brewer. *Arlington County Library*

> cannot agree with you on that subject, although I admit you may be right and I wrong. But as for any observation extends in this regiment, I must confess I think that the young men who were reputed hard cases at home exhibit more honor now here than those who were professing Christians and thought to be the best of men at home. At least I would sooner trust the former class. Now I will tell you my reasons for thinking so. My observations on this subject are these. A man's moral character is never at a standstill. He daily grows better or worse. At least I think so. And I find that young men who came out with me who were professing Christians and were members of the church held out strong and firm for a short-time and guarded themselves, but after a while they gradually ceased their watchfulness over themselves and began to fall from Grace if you like the term, until they have lost all of their religion and are now gradually losing their character for good morals, and in eighteen months or longer—bid fair to be the hardest characters we have in the regiment.[61]

In 1965, Roy C. Brewer lived adjacent to Fort Scott and became interested in the fort's history. Gaining permission from the county's Department of Recreation and Parks, Brewer, along with several neighbors, began an excavation to locate the site of the flagstaff at Fort Scott. After several weeks of digging, the amateur archaeologists found the remains of a decorative brick walkway that surrounded the flagstaff. Today, Roy Brewer's work on behalf of the Defenses of Washington lives on in two detailed drawings that he did of Fort Scott and Fort Ethan Allen that can be found in the special collections branch of the Arlington County library. However, the extant remains of Fort Scott are not protected as an Arlington County "historic district," and the remains of the fort are left neglected by the parks department.[63]

Garrison troops stationed at Fort Scott included the following:

- 1st Connecticut Heavy Artillery, Co. A, October 10, 1861
- 1st Connecticut Heavy Artillery, Co. A, January 1861–February 1862
- 1st Massachusetts Heavy Artillery, Cos. F, G, March 1862–April 1862
- 1st Connecticut Heavy Artillery, Co. I, July 1862–April 1864
- 9th New York Heavy Artillery, Co. L, May 1864
- 1st New York Light Artillery, May 1864–June 1864
- 3d Massachusetts Heavy Artillery, Co. L, June 1864–August 1864
- 3d Regiment Veteran Reserve Corps, Co. D, September 1864
- 1st New Hampshire Heavy Artillery, Co. G, September 1864–April 1865
- 4th Massachusetts Heavy Artillery, Co. B, December 19, 1864–April 1865
- 4th New York Heavy Artillery, Co. B, May–June 1865

THE UPPER ARLINGTON LINES—FORTS CRAIG, MCPHERSON, WHIPPLE, CASS, TILLINGHAST, WOODBURY, AND MORTON

Fort Craig

Location

From Fort Scott, turn right from the parking area and drive down the hill to South Eads Street. Turn right on South Eads Street and proceed to South Glebe Road. Turn right on South Glebe Road and continue to Walter Reed Drive. Veer right on Walter Reed Drive and travel to Columbia Pike. Turn right on Columbia Pike and drive to South Court House Road. Turn left on South Court House Road and drive to the intersection with 4th Street South. The fort stood on the site of the intersection.

Visible Remains

No visible remains of the fort exist. A historical marker notes the general location of the fort.

Description

The fort was named in honor of Lieutenant Presley Craig of Massachusetts, who was killed at the First Battle of Bull Run (Manassas) on July 21, 1861. Fort Craig, a lunette with a stockade gorge, was constructed in August 1861 on the land owned by Septimus Brown. The fort's perimeter was 324 yards and had emplacements for eleven guns. The armament consisted of four 24-pounder guns, one 24-pounder field howitzer,

Captain Pope's Quarters, Fort Craig. *U.S. Army Military History Institute*

five 30-pounder Parrotts, one ten-inch mortar, and one 24-pounder Coehorn mortar. The fort had two magazines, and quartermaster buildings stood outside the fort near the gorge.[63] Behind the fort, about a mile to the east near the Old Alexandria and Georgetown Road, stood the famous Freedman's Village for refugee African Americans and former slaves.

Regiments that were garrisoned at the fort included the following:

- 12th New York Infantry, Cos. G, H, December 1861–January 1862
- 19th Indiana Infantry, Cos. A–K, January 1862–February 1862
- 12th New York Infantry, Co. G, February 1862–March 1862
- 1st Massachusetts Heavy Artillery, Co. I, March 1862–April 1862
- 1st Massachusetts Heavy Artillery, Co. A, May 1862–June 1862
- 4th New York Heavy Artillery, Co. E, July 1862–August 1862
- 16th Maine Infantry, one company, September 1862
- 1st Massachusetts Heavy Artillery, Cos. B, G, September 1862–April 1863
- 1st Massachusetts Heavy Artillery, Co. D, January 1863–February 1863
- 22d Connecticut Infantry, February 1863–March 1863
- 1st Massachusetts Heavy Artillery, Co. D, May 1863–October 1863
- 1st Massachusetts Heavy Artillery, Co. G, July 1863–October 1863
- 1st Massachusetts Heavy Artillery, Cos. F, K, November 1863–April 1864
- 1st Massachusetts Heavy Artillery, Co. C, March 1864–April 1864
- 5th Independent Battery New York Light Artillery, March 1864–April 1864
- 6th Pennsylvania Heavy Artillery, Co. H, March 1864–April 1865
- 145th Ohio National Guard, Co. F, May 18, 1864–May 23, 1864
- 138th Ohio National Guard, Cos. E, H, K, June 6, 1864–June 14, 1864
- 10th New York Heavy Artillery, Cos. F, K, July 1864–August 1864
- 4th New York Heavy Artillery, Co. H, August 8, 1864–October 1864
- 1st New Hampshire Heavy Artillery, Co. I, September 1864–October 1864
- 1st West Virginia Light Artillery, Battery C, November 1864–April 1865
- 2d New York Heavy Artillery, Cos. D, K, May 1865–June 1865

Fort McPherson—An Uncompleted Work

Special Note

From the site of Fort Craig, the tour directions will lead you onto the grounds of Fort Myer. Fort Myer is a military base, and access to the areas where Fort Whipple, Fort Cass, and Fort McPherson were located may be restricted. Be prepared to have your car inspected and have valid identification with you. If you choose not to visit the forts located on the grounds of Fort Myer, proceed to the location of Fort Tillinghast and follow the tour using the section marked "Alternate Directions."

Location

From the site of Fort Craig, continue on South Court House Road to 2nd Street. Turn right on 2nd Street and drive through Hatfield Gate within the boundaries of Fort Myer. Continue straight and turn left onto McNair Road. To the right on the grounds of Arlington Cemetery beyond the cemetery wall is the site of Fort McPherson. The fort was located on what is now a Civil War veterans' portion of the cemetery. The site of the fort is west of McPherson Avenue opposite the Rough Riders Memorial, just south of Jackson Circle.

Visible Remains

No visible remains of the fort exist.

Description

The fort was named in honor of Major General James Birdseye McPherson, who was killed near Atlanta,

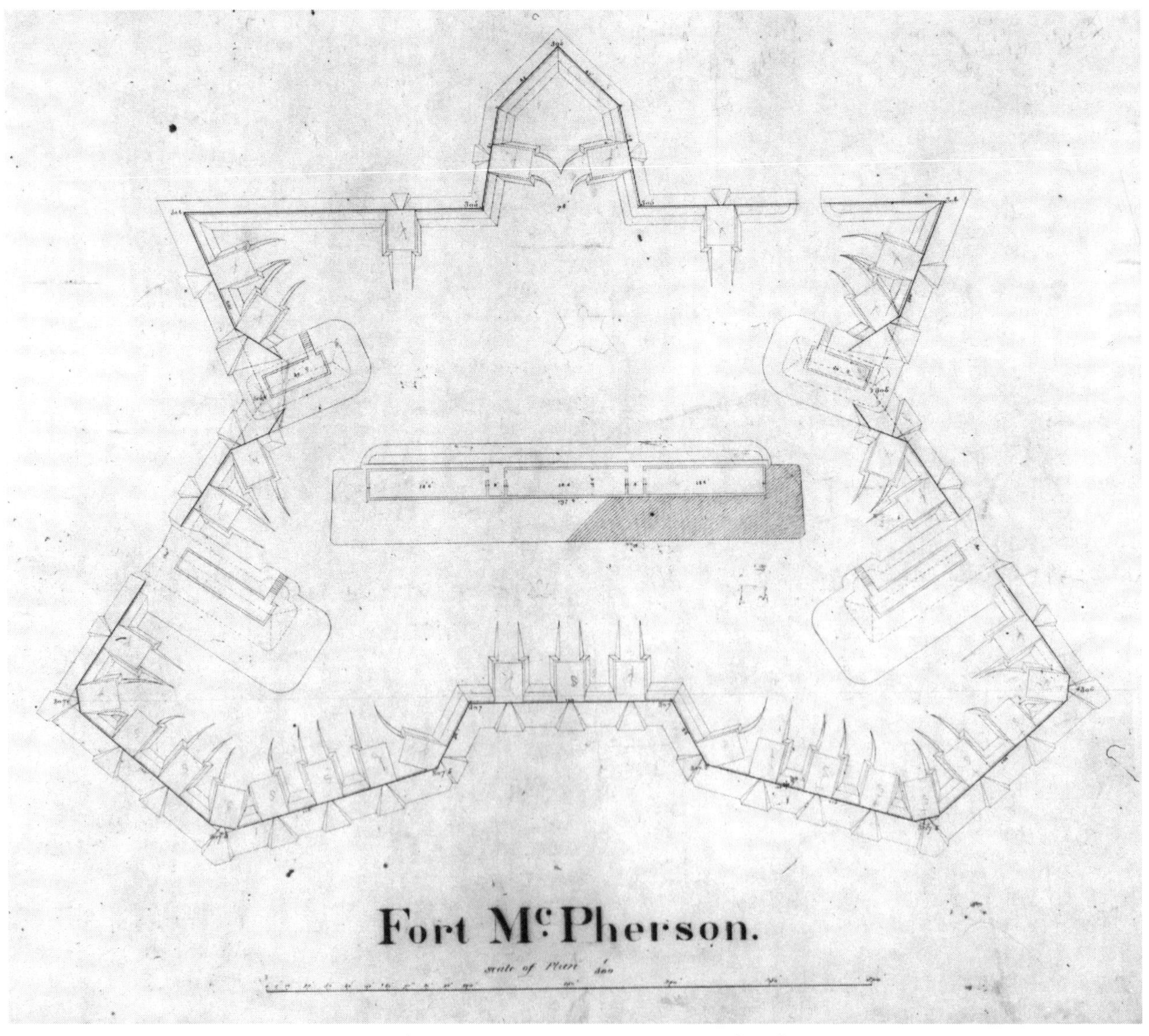

Fort McPherson—Engineer Drawing. *National Archives*

Part of Arlington Cemetery; Fort McPherson Was Destroyed in 1947. *Virginia State Library*

Georgia, on July 22, 1864. Construction began on the fort in 1864 but was never completed. It was a large enclosed bastion work that was designed to support Fort Craig and fill the gap in the second line between Forts Whipple and Albany. The fort was destroyed in 1947 to make room for more gravesites. The 45th United States Colored Troops, Co. D, were part of the construction troops in September–October 1864.[64]

Fort Whipple—Forerunner to a Modern Fort

Location

Continue on McNair Road driving to Lee Avenue. Turn right and make a sharp left turn onto McNair Road at the "Old Post Chapel." Drive down the long hill until you reach the junction with Marshall Drive. Turn left onto Marshall Drive and proceed up the hill.

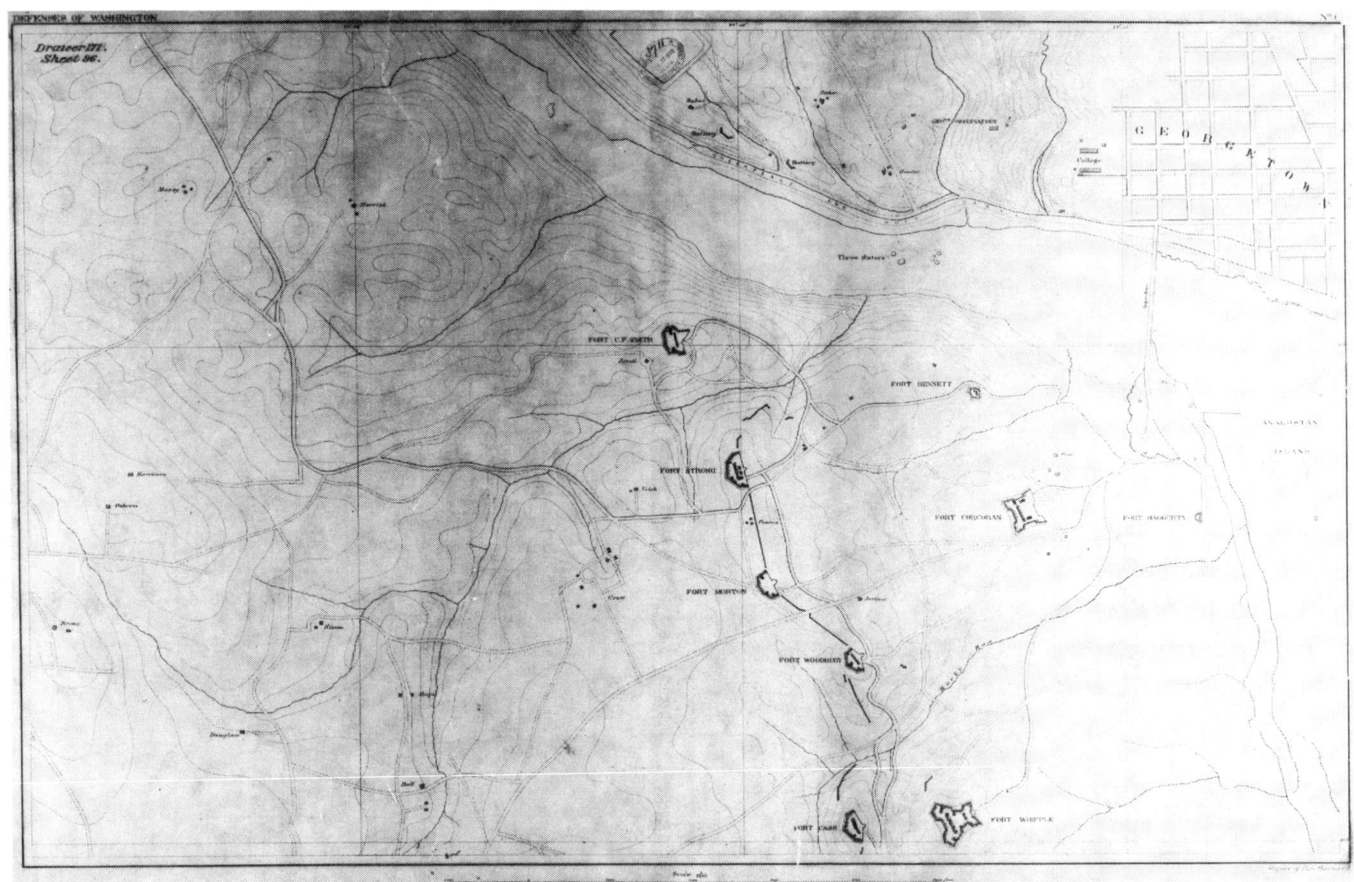

Sector Map from Fort Whipple to Fort C. F. Smith. *National Archives*

The large field to your immediate right was the location of Fort Whipple. The fort occupied nearly half the block on Grant Avenue and Jackson Lane. Note: At times, this area may have restricted access.

Visible Remains

No visible remains of the fort exist. The historical marker for the fort is located at Arlington Boulevard and Pershing Drive. The site is encompassed by Fort Myer, a modern army post.

Description

This fort was named in honor of Major General Amiel Weeks Whipple, who died in Washington, D.C., on May 7, 1863, of wounds he received at Chancellorsville, Virginia. Fort Whipple was a large detached "bastioned quadrelateral work" designed to support the line of lunettes along Arlington Heights. The perimeter of the fort was 658 and two-thirds yards and had emplacements for forty-three guns. The description of Fort Whipple in General Barnard's report is nearly two pages long. For the sake of brevity, it could be said he described one of the finest field fortifications constructed in the Defenses of Washington. The fort had two large magazines, two filling rooms, and extensive bombproofs. The armament of the fort included four 12-pounder howitzers, six 12-pounder Napoleons, eleven forty-five-inch Rodmans, and eight 12-pounder guns. Quartermaster buildings were erected adjacent to the fort.[65]

Notes/Anecdotes

Defending Washington during the war did not always involve gun drills or fatigue duty. Colonel Thomas R. Tannatt of the 1st Massachusetts Heavy Artillery left behind a legacy of his work on the Defenses of Washington:

> General: Your request for data to embody in your Annual Report, had been deferred in order to obtain a correct account of the nature of service performed by the battalion. . . . The regiment has performed a vast amount of labor during the year, having erected

Fort Whipple—Engineer Drawing of Gate. *National Archives*

> fine quarters for officers and men; completed and occupied a forty-three-gun fort, besides erecting three large bomb-proof barracks, capable of quartering the men. . . . In no case has political or social influence been allowed to govern the position, promotion, or conduct of an officer or soldier, but a clear and conscientious consideration has greatly assisted me in my feeble efforts to make the regiment capable of maintaining an honorable place among the troops sent from Massachusetts.[66]

Garrison troops at Fort Whipple included the following:

- 1st Massachusetts Heavy Artillery, Co. A, May 1863–April 1863
- 1st Massachusetts Heavy Artillery, Co. F, May 1863–October 1863
- 1st Massachusetts Heavy Artillery, Co. E, June 21, 1863–October 1863
- 1st Massachusetts Heavy Artillery, Co. B, November 1863–February 1864
- 1st Massachusetts Heavy Artillery, Co. D, November 1863–April 1864
- 1st Massachusetts Heavy Artillery, Co. H, March 1864–April 1864
- 145th Ohio National Guard, Cos. B, E, May 18, 1864–June 1864
- 145th Ohio National Guard, Co. H, June 1864
- 10th New York Heavy Artillery, Cos. B, E, H, July 1864–August 1864
- 1st Pennsylvania Light Artillery, Battery H, August 10, 1864–September 1864
- 4th Massachusetts Heavy Artillery, Co. A, August 18, 1864–October 1864
- 3d Massachusetts Heavy Artillery, Co. A, L, September 1864–October 1864
- 1st Massachusetts Heavy Artillery, Co. E, September 1864–October 1864
- 1st Massachusetts Heavy Artillery, Cos. A, D, M, November 1864–December 1864
- 1st Maryland Light Artillery, Battery D, December 17, 1864–May 1865
- Robert Nevin's Independent Battery H, Pennsylvania Light Artillery, December 1864–April 1865
- 2d New York Heavy Artillery, Cos. G, L, M, May 1865–June 1865
- 2d New York Heavy Artillery, Co. E, June 1865

Brigadier General Albert Myer Monument on the original site of Fort Whipple. *Fort Ward Museum Collection*

Gun Drill at Fort Whipple. *U.S. Army Military History Institute*

Fort Cass

Location

From the site of Fort Whipple, continue on Jackson Avenue to Sheridan Avenue. The site of Fort Cass was located to your right within the area of Forest Circle.

Visible Remains

No visible remains of the fort exist. A historical marker for the site is located outside Fort Myer on 10th Street North at Wayne Street.

Description

This fort was named in honor of Colonel Thomas Cass, 9th Massachusetts, whose regiment constructed the fort and who was mortally wounded during the Seven Days Campaign. Fort Cass was constructed in August 1861 under the supervision of Captain Alexander of the Corps of Engineers. The fort was first named Fort Ramsay and was designed as a lunette with a stockade gorge. The fort's perimeter was 288 yards and had emplacements for twelve guns. The armament included four 24-pounder guns, three 6-pounder guns, five 20-pounder Parrott rifles, and one 24-pounder Coehorn mortar. Fort Cass worked together with Forts Craig, Tillinghast, Woodbury, Morton, and DeKalb (Strong) to extend the line from Forts Richardson and Albany to the Potomac River across from Georgetown and to provide an outer defense line for the Aqueduct Bridge.[67]

Notes/Anecdotes

Captain Macnamara of the 9th Massachusetts Infantry arrived at Arlington Heights during the summer of 1861. "About this time picket duty was becoming a serious affair," recorded the captain, "the Rebels being in force about two or three miles on our front." His regiment was assigned the task of felling rows of trees with their branches sharpened to form an abatis to obstruct the passage of the rebel cavalry, but what impressed the captain was his unit's work on the fort. Captain Macnamara wrote,

> It took but a short time to complete the abatis upon our front and flank; and when this was done, a new and more stupendous work presented itself, which was no less than the erection of a large fort on our left, constructed to mount five guns. To green troops this was no ordinary undertaking; but the officers and men entered into work with great spirit; space for a magazine was cleared, the breast works gradually arose; the embrasures speedily appeared; then quarters for officers and men; till, in the space of two months, that noble work now known as "Fort Cass," . . . arose in frowning defiance.[68]

Garrison troops at Fort Cass included the following:

- 1st Wisconsin Heavy Artillery, Co. A, November 1861
- 9th Massachusetts Infantry, construction, August 1861–October 1861
- 1st Massachusetts Heavy Artillery, Co. D, September 1862–December 1862
- 16th Maine Infantry, one company, September 1862
- 2d New York Heavy Artillery, Cos. D, G, November 1862–October 1863
- 1st Massachusetts Heavy Artillery, Co. E, November 1863–April 1864
- 1st Massachusetts Heavy Artillery, Co. I, December 1863–April 1864
- 145th Ohio National Guard, Cos. F, H, I, May 1864–June 1864
- 10th New York Heavy Artillery, Co. I, July 1864–August 1864
- 3d Massachusetts Heavy Artillery, Co. M, September 1864–November 1864
- 1st Pennsylvania Light Artillery, Battery I, February 1865–April 1865
- 2d New York Heavy Artillery, Co. H, May 1865–June 1865

Fort Tillinghast

Location

From Jackson Avenue, turn left onto Sheridan Avenue and continue to Pershing Drive. Turn left on Pershing Drive and proceed to McNair Road. Make a right turn on McNair Road and continue to 2nd Street South. Turn right on 2nd Street South and drive out Fort Myer Gate. Keep right turning onto the access road to Washington Boulevard traveling toward Wilson Boulevard and Clarendon. Continue on Washington Boulevard and turn right onto North Wayne Street. Follow North Wayne Street around, past the circle, stopping in front of 205 North Wayne Street. Fort Tillinghast was located on the site of the apartment building at 205 Wayne Street.

Alternate Directions: From Fort Craig to Fort Tillinghast

From the site of Fort Craig, continue on South Court House Road to 2nd Street South. Turn right on 2nd Street South and move to the center lane. When you reach the overpass, follow the left-turn-only lane that will lead to down to Washington Boulevard traveling toward Wilson Boulevard and Clarendon. Continue on Washington Boulevard and turn right onto North Wayne Street. Follow North Wayne Street around, past the circle, stopping in front of 205 North Wayne Street. Fort Tillinghast was located on the site of the apartment building at 205 Wayne Street.

Visible Remains

No visible remains of the fort exist. A historical marker citing the general location of the fort stands at Arlington Boulevard and 2nd Street North.

Description

This fort was named in honor of Captain Ottis H. Tillinghast, chief quartermaster of General McDowell's army. Captain Tillinghast was mortally wounded on July 21, 1861, at the First Battle of Bull Run (Manassas) while attempting to rally Union volunteers who were fleeing the field. The fort was built on land owned by Columbus Alexander. General Barnard's report noted, "The plan of Fort Tillinghast . . . may be regarded as typical of the lunettes with stockaded gorges, which were so numerous along the Arlington lines and

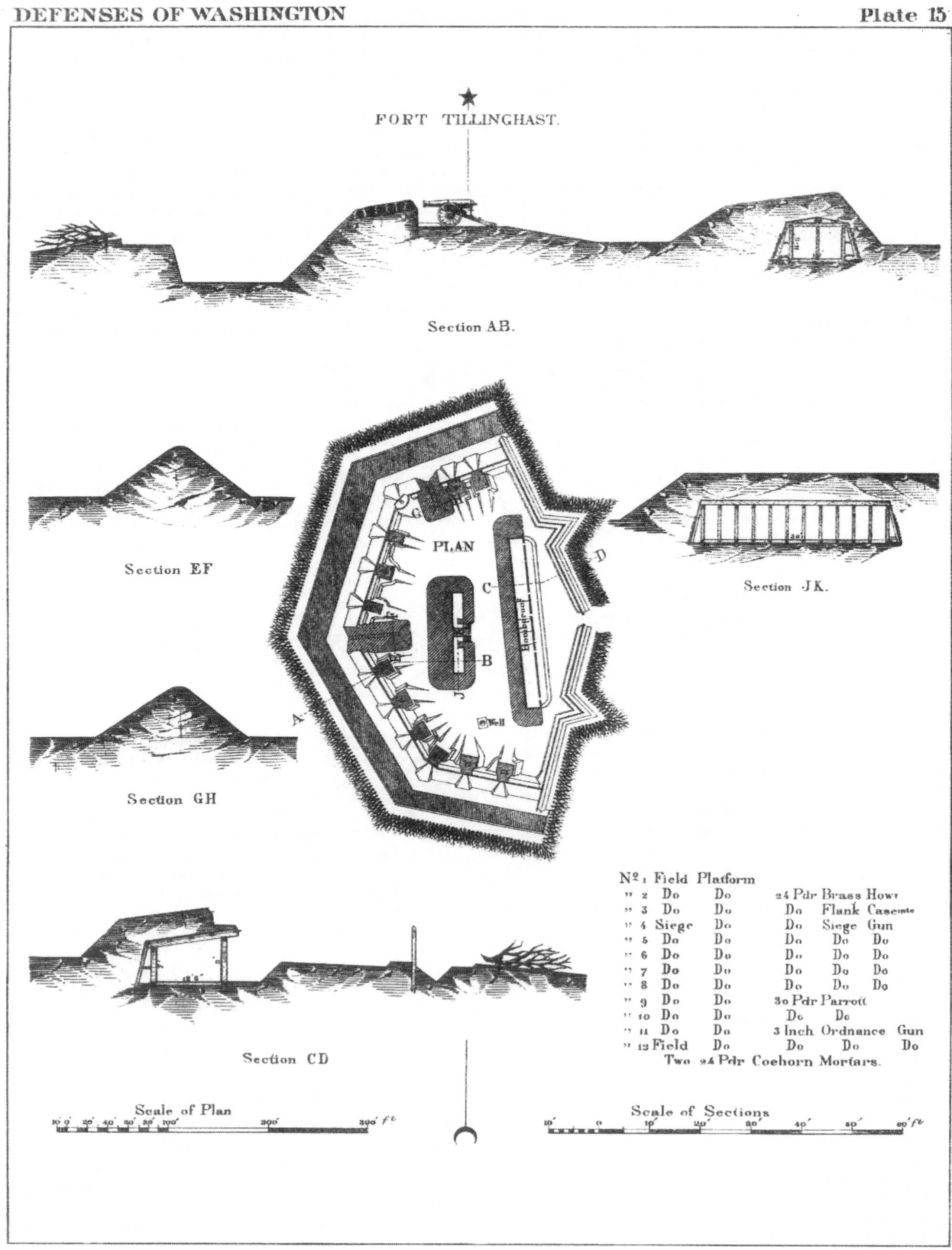

Fort Tillinghast—Engineer Drawing. *Barnard's* Report

A Soldier's Drawing of Fort Tillinghast. *U.S. Army Military History Institute*

occur frequently elsewhere." The fort's perimeter was 298 yards and had emplacements for twelve guns. The armament included four 24-pounder guns, one 24-pounder field howitzer, four 30-pounder Parrott rifles, two 20-pounder Parrott rifles, and two 24-pounder Coehorn mortars. The fort contained two magazines and bombproof barracks with a breast height for infantry along the top that could be used as a second line of defense. The fort also contained a well.[69]

Garrison troops stationed at Fort Tillinghast consisted of detachments from the following:

12th New York Infantry, Cos. B, I, November 1861–January 1862
2d Wisconsin Infantry, Cos. E, G, December 1861–February 1862
12th New York Infantry, Co. I, February 1862–March 21, 1862
16th Maine Infantry, one company, September 1862
1st Massachusetts Heavy Artillery, Co. M, September 1862
1st Massachusetts Heavy Artillery, Co. E, March 1863–April 1863
22d Connecticut Infantry, June 1863—construction on rifle pits
1st Massachusetts Heavy Artillery, Co. L, May 1863–October 1863
1st Massachusetts Heavy Artillery, Co, C, November 1863–February 1864
1st Massachusetts Heavy Artillery, Co. K, March 1864–April 1864
5th Independent Battery, New York Light Artillery, May 1864–July 1864
145th Ohio National Guard, Co. K, May 11, 1864–June 1864
145th Ohio National Guard, Co. I, June 1864
138th Ohio National Guard, Cos. A, D, F, I, June 1864
1st Maryland Light Artillery, Battery D, June 7, 1864–August 15, 1864
10th New York Heavy Artillery, Co. C, July 1864–August 1864
4th New York Heavy Artillery, Cos. C, D, October 1864–November 1864
1st New York Light Artillery, Battery F, November 1864–May 1865
2d New York Heavy Artillery, Cos. B, C, May 1865–June 1865

Fort Woodbury

Location

From the site of Fort Tillinghast, follow North Wayne Street around and make a right turn out of the apartment complex parking onto North Wayne Street and drive to North Pershing Drive. Turn right on North Pershing Drive and then left on Arlington Boulevard. Continue on Arlington Boulevard staying in the left lane. Take the exit to Court House Road and follow it to 13th Street North. Turn right on 13th Street North and then left on Troy Street North driving up the hill to the intersection of Troy Street North and 14th Street North. Fort Woodbury was located on the site of the intersection.

Visible Remains

No visible remains of the fort exist. A historical marker citing the general location of the fort stands at the corner of 14th Street and Court House Road.

Description

The fort was named in honor of Brigadier General Daniel Phineas Woodbury, who died of yellow fever on August 15, 1864, at Key West, Florida. Fort Woodbury was built on land owned by John Lambden and was a lunette with a stockade gorge. The fort's perimeter was 275 yards and had emplacements for thirteen guns. The armament consisted of five 24-pounder guns, three 30-pounder Parrott rifles, four 6-pounder guns, and one 24-pounder Coehorn mortar. The fort contained two magazines and bombproof barracks.[70]

Notes/Anecdotes

The 4th New York Heavy Artillery garrisoned the line of lunettes on Arlington Heights. Lieutenant Hyland Kirk tells the short story of how General Whipple taught one soldier the proper way to perform his duties as a sentry:

> One visit of General Whipple will never be forgotten—probably—by the sentinel who was on guard at the entrance to the fort that day. The soldier had just joined the command, but had been instructed to halt and present arms to a general officer, should one appear. When he saw General Whipple approaching on foot his musket was at a "right soldier shift." Halting and facing to the front, he immediately brought the gun from that position to a "present." The General smiled and said: "Let me see you do that again, sir." The guard repeated the movement with great precision. After asking a number of questions about the movement, the General said, suavely: "Let me take your piece, sir." The confiding sentinel promptly handed over his gun. "Now, Sir, what kind of a guard are you? Here Corporal, take this man to the guardhouse!" At the conclusion of his visit the General had the unfortunate sentry released, after giving him some suggestions. A sentry from the same Company pursued quite a different course with General Banks, on one occasion. . . . He would not allow the General to go on to the parapet. As he was acting under orders, the General complimented him highly.[71]

Posing before the Big Guns at Fort Woodbury. *U.S. Army Military History Institute*

In a letter home, dated April 23, 1865, G. J. Clark, a soldier serving at Fort Woodbury writes,

> Lena, I cannot but think that this War is nearly at an end . . . they have begun to dismount the guns in the forts, there is two forts between us & the river that the guns have been taken out & turned into the Arsenal. There are twenty forts on the line to be dismounted soon. . . . Since I wrote you last, one of our boys has been shot—this is a hard thing, he had been down to the fort below here, it was about 8 in the evening. He had to pass the sentinel post, he was challenged three times, but did not stop nor speak. The sentinel fired—the ball went through his right wrist, entered his body just above the right hip and passed out above the left hip. He lived until the next day—and in the afternoon he died. The company has raised a fund & sent him home to his Mother who is a widow. He was I am sorry to say under the effects of liquor at the time he was shot. How can men after seeing such a thing help but keep himself from under the influence of this life destroyer.[72]

Units stationed at Fort Woodbury included detachments from the following:

1st Massachusetts Heavy Artillery, Co. C, July 1861–August 1862
4th Michigan Infantry, September 1861
88th Pennsylvania Infantry, February 1862
4th New York Heavy Artillery, Co. A, April 1862–August 1862
4th New York Heavy Artillery, Co. E, April 1862–May 1862

16th Maine Infantry, one company, September 1862.
128th Pennsylvania Infantry, Cos. B–K, August 1862
2d New York Heavy Artillery, Co. C, September 1862–February 1863
2d New York Heavy Artillery, Co. H, September 1862–October 1862
2d New York Heavy Artillery, Co. I, November 1862–October 1863
2d New York Heavy Artillery, Co. B, March 1863–October 1863
2d New York Heavy Artillery, Co. C, May 1863–October 1863
1st Massachusetts Heavy Artillery, Co. H, November 1863–February 1864
1st Massachusetts Heavy Artillery, Co. L, November 1863–April 1864
1st Massachusetts Heavy Artillery, Co. B, March 1864–April 1864
1st Maryland Light Artillery, Battery A, May 1864–June 1864
164th Ohio National Guard, Cos. D, H, May 11, 1864–June 1864
145th Ohio National Guard, Co. I, May 1864
1st New York Light Artillery, Battery K, September 1864–February 1865
1st New Hampshire Heavy Artillery, Co. I, October 1864
4th Massachusetts Heavy Artillery, Co. B, November 1864–December 19, 1864
1st New York Light Artillery, March 1865–May 1865
2d New York Heavy Artillery, Co. A, May 1865–June 1865

Fort Morton

Location

From the site of Fort Woodbury, turn left on 14th Street to Court House Road. Turn right on Court House Road and proceed to Wilson Boulevard. Turn left on Wilson Boulevard and then turn right onto North Veitch Street. Fort Morton was located on the grounds of Key Elementary School near the area bordering 16th Street and North Custis Road.

Visible Remains

No visible remains of the fort exist.

Description

This fort was probably named in honor of Brigadier General St. Clair Morton, a talented engineer officer, killed at Petersburg on June 17, 1864. Fort Morton was first constructed as an open battery and was not mentioned in the 1862 commission report. The site of the battery occupied an important point, filling the interval between Forts Woodbury and DeKalb (Strong). It was converted into an enclosed work with a stockade gorge in 1863 and served to strengthen the Arlington Line. The fort had a perimeter of 250 yards and emplacements for seventeen guns. The armament listed in Barnard's report shows that the fort had only six 12-pounder Napoleon guns in place. In 1976, David Miller reported that a small remnant of the fort existed behind 2311 North Custis Road. No remains exist today.[73]

Notes/Anecdotes

Little is known concerning the units that were stationed at Fort Morton. Since many of the forts along the Arlington Line were small, companies or detachments from one regiment would be responsible for a sector of forts. Battery H, 1st Pennsylvania Light Artillery, was one of the units stationed at the fort in May 1865. It is quite probable that regiments listed for Forts Woodbury and DeKalb (Strong) also garrisoned at Fort Morton.[74]

PROTECTING THE AQUEDUCT BRIDGE: FORTS HAGGERTY, CORCORAN, AND BENNETT

Fort Haggerty

Location

From the site of Fort Morton, continue on North Veitch Street to Lee Highway (Route 29). Turn right on Lee Highway driving to North Nash Street. Turn right on North Nash Street driving up the hill to Key Boulevard. Turn left on Key Boulevard and another left turn following the road to 19th Street North. Continue on 19th Street North to Arlington Ridge Road. At the intersection of Arlington Ridge Road and Wilson Boulevard stands the historical marker for Fort Haggerty. Stay to the right and follow the access road to Wilson Boulevard, which will lead to Fort Corcoran.

Visible Remains

No visible remains of the fort exist. A historical marker cites the general location of the fort.

Description

This fort was named in honor of Lieutenant Colonel James Haggerty of the 69th New York State Militia,

Fort Haggerty and Garrison Barracks. *Authors' Collection*

who died of wounds received at the First Battle of Bull Run (Manassas). Fort Haggerty was constructed in May 1861 on the land owned by Owen and Mary Murray. The fort was a small enclosed work designed to protect the Aqueduct Bridge and sweep the slope south of Fort Corcoran with cannon fire. The fort's perimeter was 128 yards with emplacements for four 24-pounder guns. The Aqueduct Bridge was part of the Chesapeake and Ohio Canal that served as a means of transportation for goods, especially Cumberland coal, to the port of Alexandria. When the war began, Union authorities shut off the water to the aqueduct and converted its trough into a double-track wagon road by overlaying the floor with four-inch planks. Three small blockhouses and rifle pits were built on the Virginia end of the bridge to defend against cavalry attacks.[75]

Notes/Anecdotes

By April 6, 1865, Lieutenant Colonel Barton S. Alexandria wrote, "An examination of Forts Haggerty and Bennett shows them to be in very dilapidated condition, requiring extensive repairs if the forts are to be maintained." He explained that the small forts guarding Aqueduct Bridge were intended to hold the bridge providing for a contingency of defeat until "our retreating troops" could pass over the bridge. The forts were armed with old-style guns on barbette carriages and could not protect the fort if an enemy held the heights and attacked the forts with long-range rifle cannon. Alexander recommended the removal of the barbette carriages and platforms and replacing them with gun embrasures for field batteries and that the garrison be removed from Fort Haggerty because of the unhealthy conditions. The secretary of war approved the recommendation, and Henry Halleck, U.S. chief of staff, sent an order forward on April 10, 1865.[76]

Fort Haggerty was garrisoned by detachments from the following:

69th New York State Militia
2d New York Heavy Artillery, Co. I, September 1862–October 1862
2d New York Heavy Artillery, Co. H, November 1862–April 1864
164th Ohio National Guard, Co. B, May 1864–June 1864

Fort Corcoran

Location

From the site of Fort Haggerty, drive up Wilson Boulevard to North Quinn Street. Turn right on North Quinn Street and stop near 18th Street. Fort Corcoran stood

Blockhouse Guarding Aqueduct Bridge. *Library of Congress*

about 100 yards from North Quinn Street, encompassing the area between 18th Street and Key Boulevard. A historical marker cites the general location of the fort and is located at Key Boulevard and North Ode Street.

Visible Remains

No visible remains of the fort exist.

Description

This fort was named for Colonel Michael Corcoran of the 69th New York State Militia, whose soldiers constructed the fort in May 1861. Fort Corcoran, with its auxiliary works Forts Bennett and Haggerty, was established to secure the Virginia end of the Aqueduct Bridge and to provide points of support for the Union army. The fort was bastioned in trace with a stockade gorge. The perimeter was 576 yards with emplacements for ten guns. The armament consisted of two eight-inch howitzers and three 20-pounder Parrott rifles.[77]

Notes/Anecdotes

Father Thomas Mooney, the Roman Catholic chaplain assigned to the 69th New York State Militia, found his term of service to be of a short duration. He was recalled by the Church for certain unconventional acts, particularly the baptizing of one of the big guns mounted at Fort Corcoran, which he named and christened with holy water. The following are excerpted remarks from the occasion:

> In kind providence of God, it has been for me as a priest, during the last nine years, to baptize many a fine blue-eyed babe; but never had I brought before me such

Sally Port at Fort Corcoran. *U.S. Army Military History Institute*

> a large, quiet, healthy, and promising fellow as the one now before me. Indeed, I may remark, it has often occurred, when pouring the baptismal water on the child's head, he opened his little eyes, and got a little more of the baptismal water than he wished; but on this occasion, this noble son . . . has his mouth open, evidently indicating that he is ready to speak . . . in a thundering voice. Now parents anxiously listen to the first lispings of the infant's lips, and the mother's heart swells with joy when she catches the first utterance of her cherished babe, in the words "mamma, mamma!" But here I shall guarantee to you that this promising boy will speak for the first time, in loud, clear accents, those endearing words—Papa, Papa, Papa . . . and thus may he . . . speak to the glory of the Stars and Stripes.[78]

President Lincoln visited Fort Corcoran on several occasions. The historian for the 4th New York Heavy Artillery recorded one such visit:

> President Lincoln inspected the command and several times. On one occasion, while engaged in artillery prac-

107th U.S. Colored Infantry in Front of the Guard House at Fort Corcoran. *U.S. Army Military History Institute*

Signal Station at Fort Corcoran. *Brown,* The Signal Corps, USA in the War of the Rebellion

tice, the companies of the fort were surprised by a visit from the President accompanied by his son "Tad.". . . The gun they stopped at, a rifled piece, was being fired at a range of two thousand yards. The gunner made an indifferent shot. . . . The President who was holding Tad up in his arms to see the result, without a word moved on to the next gun, which was a smoothbore casemate howitzer used for clearing the ditch, and being fired . . . at a short range. . . . The target was a wall tent fly suspended between two poles by wires. The gunner took careful aim, and as the smoke cleared the central portion of the fly had disappeared. President Lincoln throwing up his right-hand, slapped his leg in seeming delight, as he cried out: "Give me the old shotgun yet." The piece was afterwards known as Uncle Abram's shotgun.[79]

The following garrison troops were stationed at Fort Corcoran:

69th New York State Militia (three months), June 1861–July 1861

2d Maine Infantry, July 1861–August 1861

2d Wisconsin Infantry, Co. K, July 1861–August 26, 1861

13th New York Infantry, September 1861–March 10, 1862

9th Independent Battery, New York Light Artillery, September 1861–October 1861

3d New York Light Artillery, February 1861–March 1862

97th New York Infantry, March 1862

79th New York Infantry, March 1862–April 1862

4th New York Heavy Artillery, Cos. D, H, April 7, 1862–June 1862

4th New York Heavy Artillery, Co. C, May 1862–June 1862

1st Massachusetts Heavy Artillery, Cos. B, D, M, July 1862–August 1862

2d New York Heavy Artillery, Cos. A, B, K, M, September 1862–April 1863

5th Independent Massachusetts Light Artillery, September 1862–October 1862

Soldiers from the 4th New York Heavy Artillery Pose for a Photograph at Fort Corcoran, 1862. *Library of Congress*

- 16th Maine Infantry, Co. F, September 1862
- 2d New York Heavy Artillery, Co. L, February 1864
- 2d New York Heavy Artillery, Co. K, March 1864–April 1864
- 1st Pennsylvania Light Artillery, Battery G, May 1864–July 3, 1864
- 2d New York Heavy Artillery, Co. F, May 1864
- 164th Ohio National Guard, Cos. C, F, May 11, 1864–June 1864
- 1st Pennsylvania Light Artillery, Battery H, September 1864–October 1864
- 1st New Hampshire Heavy Artillery, Cos. D, I, September 1864
- 1st New Hampshire Heavy Artillery, Cos. C, H, October 10, 1864
- 4th Massachusetts Heavy Artillery, Co. E, October 21, 1864–December 17, 1864
- 16th Battery, Indiana Light Artillery, December 1865–May 1865
- 2d New York Heavy Artillery, Co. F, May 1865–June 1865

Fort Bennett

Location

From Fort Corcoran, continue on North Quinn Street down the hill to Lee Highway (Route 29). Turn right and proceed in the left lane to North Nash Street. Turn left at the light onto North Nash Street crossing over Interstate Route 66. Turn left onto Lee Highway and then turn right onto North Oak Street. Follow North Oak Street around to the 1600 block of 22nd Street, where the historic marker stands in front of the Park Georgetown Apartments.

Visible Remains

No visible remains of the fort exist. A historical marker cites the general location of the fort. In 1988, the apartment complex was named "Fort Bennett Apartments," memorializing the rich local history of the site.

Description

The fort was named in honor of Captain Michael P. Bennett, 28th New York Infantry, who supervised the fort's construction. Fort Bennett was a small enclosed work with a perimeter of 146 yards and emplacements for five guns. The fort was constructed during May 1861 and served to support Fort Corcoran and protect the Virginia end of the Aqueduct Bridge. The armament consisted of two eight-inch howitzers and three 24-pounder guns.[80]

Notes/Anecdotes

An unidentified soldier from Company E, 2d New York Heavy Artillery stationed at Fort Bennett, took pen in hand and "pale ink" to write to Miss Anna N. White, Butternuts, Otsego County, New York, on January 7, 1863:

> I have one thing to console me and that is I have not got to stay here but twenty-two months more. Then my time will be out and then good bye to the Army of the Potomac. I have often thought when I have sat down to dinner of Salt Horse and dry bread or to supper of dry bread and coffee that when I get home I shall never complain again of hard fair. I think that it has been a good thing for me for I have never been so healthy as I am now. I must now conclude for the bugle is sounding for us to fall out for drill.[81]

Fort Bennett was garrisoned by detachments from the following:

- 28th Regiment New York State Militia, May 1861–June 1861
- 13th New York Infantry, Cos. A, C, H, June 1861–August 1861
- 3d New York Cavalry, Co. K, June 1861–August 1861
- 13th New York Infantry, Cos. B, D, E, F, I, K, June 1861–August 1862
- 4th New York Heavy Artillery, Co. F, May 1862–June 1862
- 2d New York Heavy Artillery, Co. E, September 6, 1863–April 1864

164th Ohio National Guard, Co. K, May 11, 1864–June 1864
10th New York Heavy Artillery, Co. M, July 1864–August 1864
4th New York Heavy Artillery, Co. L, September 1864–October 1864
6th Pennsylvania Heavy Artillery, Co. H, November 1864–February 1865

PROTECTING THE NORTHERN FLANK OF THE ARLINGTON LINES—FORTS STRONG AND C. F. SMITH

Fort Strong

Location

From Fort Bennett, backtrack on 22nd Street to North Oak Street. Turn right onto Lee Highway traveling to the historical marker located on Lee Highway and North Adams Street. There is a bus service lane where you can stop. The fort stood between North Adams and North Vance streets.

Visible Remains

No visible remains of the Fort exist. A historical marker cites the general location of the fort.

Description

Originally called Fort DeKalb, the name was changed to honor Major General George Crockett Strong, who was wounded in the thigh during the assault on Fort Wagner, South Carolina, on July 18, 1863. General Strong died of lockjaw twelve days later in New York City, where he had been taken for treatment. Fort Strong was constructed in August 1861 and designed as a lunette. The fort's perimeter was 318 yards and has emplacements for fifteen guns. Fort Strong held the extreme right of the Arlington Line until Fort C. F. Smith was constructed. The armament in the fort included seven 24-pounder guns, one 24-pounder field howitzer, four 30-pounder Parrott rifles, one 6-pounder gun, and two ten-inch mortars.[82] Local historian Eleanor Lee Templeman reported that as late as 1959, remains of the Fort Strong could be seen in the landscaping on the grounds of the grand estate home known as "Altha Hall" that was built on the site of the fort.[83]

Notes/Anecdotes

Captain Charles Morrison, the first captain of Company B, 4th New York Heavy Artillery, had been a militia officer before the war and was said to be very rigid in his ideas of discipline and military protocol. The unit historian recalls on one occasion when the captain became too excited:

> At Fort DeKalb . . . when the command was inspected by President Lincoln, Captain Morrison was in a state of great trepidation. James L. Bailey, known as "Buck Bailey" was the member of the squad whose duty it was to pull the lanyard after the gun was sighted. Captain Morrison was so excited that, instead of giving the proper command, "Gun squad No. 2, fire!" he yelled. "Buck Bailey No. 2, fire!" to the great amusement of the boys. This became a catch-phrase among the men for some time afterward.[84]

Regiments assigned to Fort Strong included the following:

1st Massachusetts Heavy Artillery, Co. A, April 1862
16th Maine Infantry, one company, September 1862
2d New York Heavy Artillery, Co. A, May 1863–October 1863
2d New York Heavy Artillery, Cos. A, C, M, November 1863–April 1864
164th Ohio National Guard, Cos. E, I, May 11, 1864–June 1864
145th Ohio National Guard, Co. F, May 1864
1st Battery, 1st Battalion, Maine Light Artillery, May 26, 1864–July 4, 1864
10th New York Heavy Artillery, Co. G, July 1864–August 1864
1st Massachusetts Heavy Artillery, Cos. A, C, E, May 1865–June 1865
2d New York Heavy Artillery, July 1865–September 1865
3d United States Infantry, October 1865

Fort C. F. Smith

Location

From the site of Fort Strong, continue on Lee Highway (Route 29) to the intersection of North Kirkwood Road (East Route 124) and Spout Run Parkway. Turn right onto the Spout Run Parkway and move to the left lane and take the exit for Lorcom Lane. Drive up the hill, making a right turn near the crest on North Edgewood Street. Proceed to 24th Street North. Turn right on 24th Street North and drive to the Fort C. F. Smith parking area.

Visible Remains

Traces of the gun platforms, magazine, well, gorge, and parapets and a segment of the bombproof are eas-

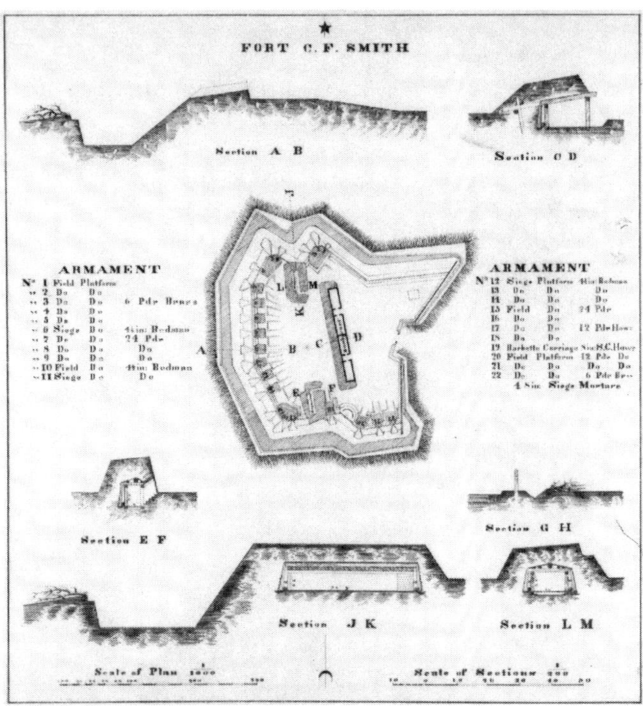

Fort C. F. Smith—Engineer Drawing. *National Archives*

ily identified with the engineer drawings. The western one-third of the fort has been destroyed by modern development of 24th Street, but the fort is in an excellent state of natural preservation.

Description

The fort was named in honor of Major General Charles Ferguson Smith, who died of a leg infection aggravated by dysentery on April 25, 1862, at Savannah, Tennessee. Fort C. F. Smith was constructed in 1863 on a recommendation made by the 1862 commission. The fort extended the "Arlington Line" to the Potomac River and commanded a ravine not covered by the guns of Fort Strong fort. It was built on land owned by Thomas Jewell, and the fort destroyed his red painted house that was dismantled because it interfered with the location of the fort ditch. In some early reports, the fort is referred to as "Fort at Red House" or "Fort McDowell." General Barnard noted in his report that "Fort C.F. Smith was carefully planned and constructed after our latest models." The work was unflanked, and the design of the trace was

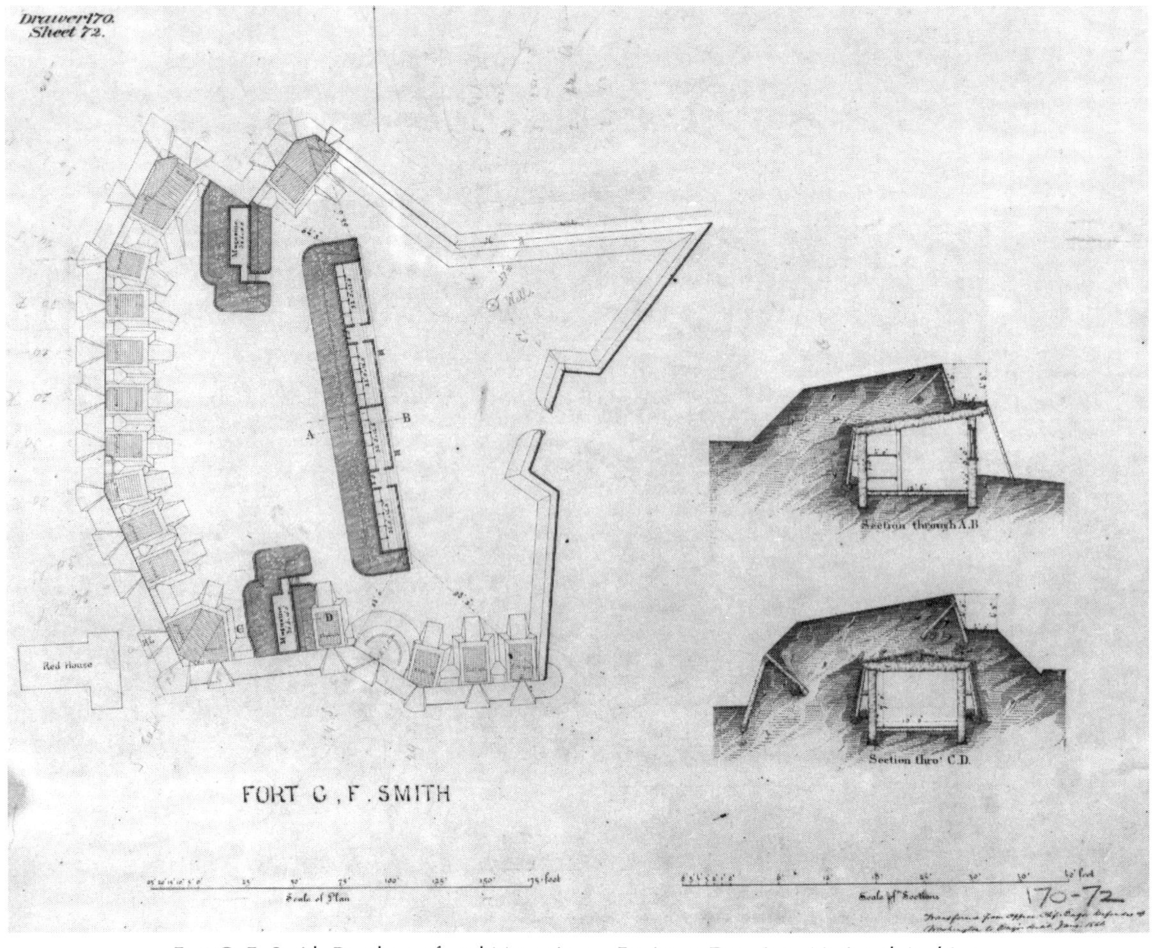

Fort C. F. Smith Bombproof and Magazines—Engineer Drawing. *National Archives*

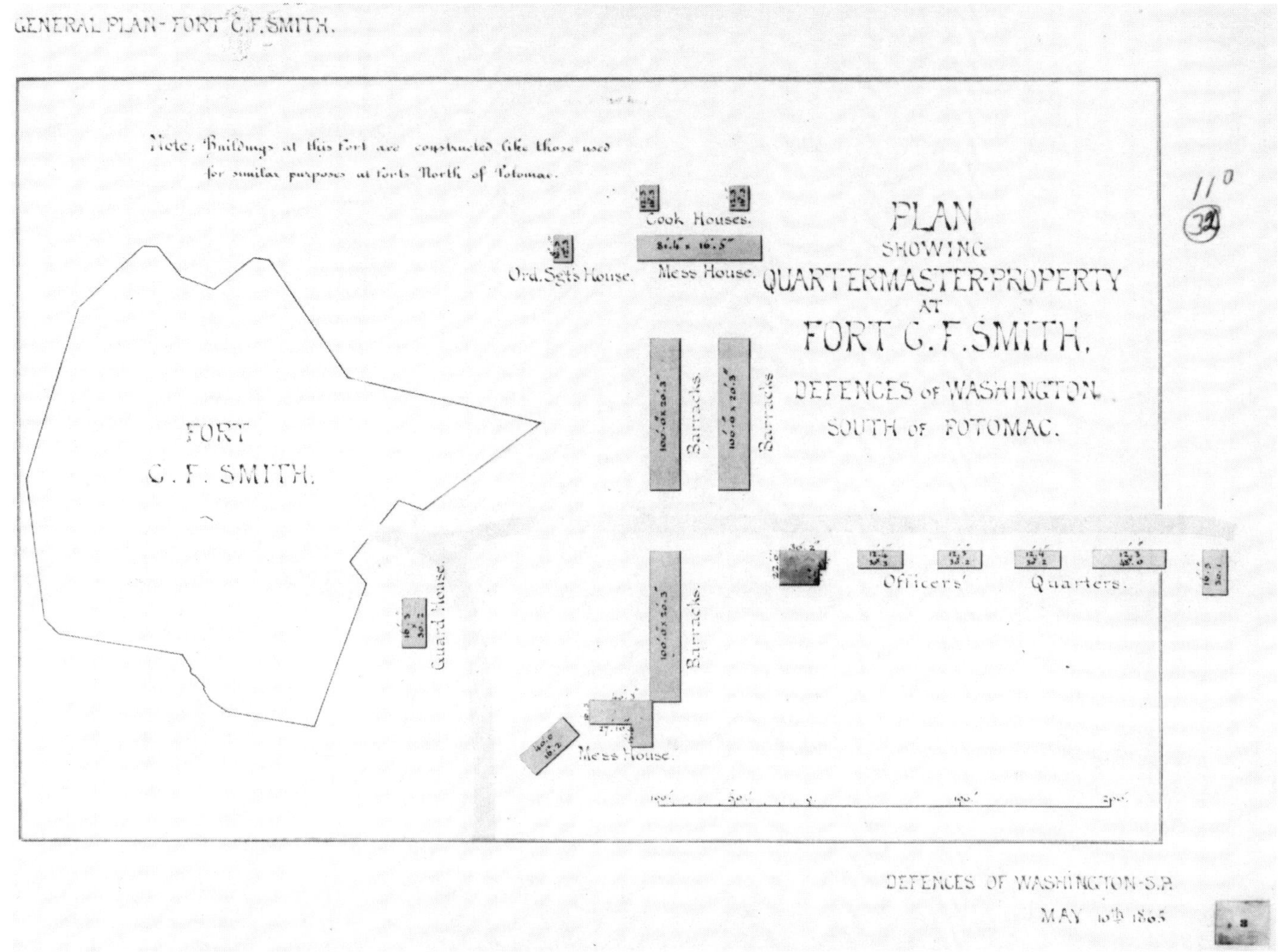

Plan of Quartermaster Property—Fort C. F. Smith. *National Archives*

governed by the topography and required direction of fire. The fort's armament included one eight-inch seacoast howitzer, four 24-pounder siege guns, three 12-pounder field howitzers, six four-and-a-half-inch Rodman rifles, two 6-pounder guns, three eight-inch siege mortars, and six vacant platforms. The perimeter of Fort C. F. Smith totaled 368 yards. Quartermaster property consisted of barracks, a guardhouse, officers' quarters, a cookhouse, and other outbuildings. The front of the officers' quarters faced east with a view of the Potomac River.[85]

Notes/Anecdotes

Loyal landowners could be compensated for military use and destruction of their property during the war. Sometimes, loyal landowners were compensated by agreement with the Quartermaster Department and able to obtain the salvage rights to military buildings, wood, and hardware that were in a fort. Cut lumber, plank, and pole revetment were valuable commodities at the end of the war in a region where hundreds of acres of trees had been sacrificed to clear the fields of fire for artillery and provide wood for fuel and shelter. Many loyal landowners who were not satisfied with salvage compensation would pursue their claims in the 1870s when Congress established the Southern Claims Commission.

In testimony given in 1877, Claim Number 20709, Thomas Jewell, a U.S. Quartermaster employee during the war, and son of William Jewell, explained what happened to the family property:

> My father was William Jewell—he died in January 1854. In 1861, [1863] they took our land for Fort C.F. Smith for guard and mess houses; in 1864, the barn was pulled down and moved to Fort Albany; the farm tools were taken; the barn was of wood with a stone basement, 70 feet long, 40 feet wide, it was 75 yards from the fort; it stood in a deep ravine below the line of the fort—the dwelling house stood on the ground now occupied by

Lieutenant J. C. Abbot's Signal Station at Fort C. F. Smith. *Brown,* The Signal Corps, USA in the War of the Rebellion

Company K, 2nd New York Heavy Artillery in Front of Bombproof at Fort C. F. Smith, August, 1865. *U.S. Army Military History Institute*

Company F, 2nd New York Heavy Artillery at Fort C. F. Smith, August 1865. *Library of Congress*

Company L, 2nd New York Heavy Artillery at Fort C. F. Smith, August 1865. *Library of Congress*

Officers' Quarters, 2nd New York Heavy Artillery at Fort C. F. Smith. *Roe,* The Ninth New York Heavy Artillery

> the fort—it was torn down by the government. . . . After the war, I bought the fort and 5 or 6 houses for which I paid [the government]. Our house that was destroyed was 40 by 16 feet deep with a back building 38 by 14 feet—it was 2 ½ stories high, stone and brick basement with wooden superstructure. The house was built 2 years before the war and completely finished. Other buildings were also destroyed. The soldiers robbed my house and ordered me off—I lost a child trying to stay there.

All together, five people testified including George Beall, a Georgetown neighbor that knew the Jewell family well and said that they lived in Georgetown and did not occupy the premises. Alexander Jones, a former soldier said, "I worked on the fort; the house was in the middle when we staked out the fort, so we tore it down; we used it for a headquarters while we built the fort and removed it in 1863." William Jewell's claim was for $17,123.05 of which $4,887.34 was allowed by the commission.[86]

No purchase inventory has been found that list what buildings were purchased by the Jewell family. However, it probably was not the barracks. On July 29, 1865, a summer storm hit the Washington area with "cyclone winds" and hail that was the size of "robin eggs." The storm injured some soldiers in the forts, tore the roofs off buildings, and collapsed the barracks at Fort C. F. Smith and Fort Strong. Clearing away the debris, the soldiers set up tents on the wood platforms that were once part of their former barracks.[87]

Regiments stationed at Fort C. F. Smith included the following:

- 2d New York Heavy Artillery, Cos. B, D, G, I, November 1863–April 1864
- 164th Ohio National Guard, Cos. A, G, May 11, 1864–June 1864
- 1st Battery, 1st Battalion Maine Light Artillery, May 26 1864–July 4, 1864
- 1st Rhode Island Light Artillery, Battery H, July 5, 1864–October 16, 1864
- 10th New York Heavy Artillery, Co. D, August 1864–September 1864

30th Unattached Company, Massachusetts Heavy Artillery, September 26, 1864–December 2, 1864
1st New Hampshire Heavy Artillery, Co. C, September 1864
29th Unattached Company, Massachusetts Heavy Artillery, October 15, 1864–December 12, 1864
4th Massachusetts Heavy Artillery, Co. M, November 1864
1st Maryland Light Artillery, Battery D, December 12, 1864–December 17, 1864
30th Unattached Company, Massachusetts Heavy Artillery, December 17, 1864–April 1865
29th Unattached Company, Massachusetts Heavy Artillery, December 18, 1865–April 1865
1st Massachusetts Heavy Artillery, Cos. B, D, F–M, May 1865–June 1865
2d New York Heavy Artillery, July 1865–September 1865

A SIDE TRIP TO THE EARLY WARNING LINE

Much of the northern Virginia countryside was dotted with small picket posts, camps, and other strong points designed to offer an early warning net for the Defenses of Washington. As the Federal troops fanned out from the bridgeheads across the Potomac from the capital, they quickly occupied former Confederate outposts. Thus, a particular concentration of Union forces took place in what is today the Seven Corners section of Falls Church and in lesser places in the vicinity of modern McLean.

Seven Corners Concentration

Location

Drive west on Arlington Boulevard or Route 50 to the Seven Corners section of Falls Church. Located in the vicinity were the following:

Fort Ramsay—1100 block of John Marshall Drive
Fort Buffalo—Between Sleepy Hollow Road and Arlington Boulevard
Fort Taylor—Southeast corner of Broad and Roosevelt streets
Fort Munson—Left off Arlington Boulevard at Munson Drive to Apex Circle Drive

Fort Ramsay on Upton's Hill. *Authors' Collection*

Interior View of Fort Ramsay with Camp in Distance. *Authors' Collection*

Field and Siege Carriage Artillery in Fort Ramsay. *Authors' Collection*

Visible Remains

None.

Notes/Anecdotes

Fort Ramsay sat atop Upton's Hill and was known originally as Fort Upton, named for the local property owner and mansion nearby. It was renamed on November 6, 1861, for the chief of ordnance and Virginia native Brigadier General George Douglass Ramsay. In 1863, the 9th and 11th Companies, Massachusetts Heavy Artillery, occupied this position.[88]

Fort Buffalo was built by the 21st New York Infantry and named for its hometown, Buffalo, New York. First occupied by McDowell's army during the First Battle of Bull Run (Manassas) campaign, it changed hands during Confederate occupation of the region following that Federal defeat. McClellan's army reoccupied the position in the fall of 1861. A marker is located at Sleepy Hollow Road (County Route 613) south of Leesburg Pike (Virginia Route 7) at the Seven Corners Fire Station.[89]

Fort Taylor was a small six-gun field battery, also built by the 21st New York Infantry, on the land of nearby tavern owner L. William Taylor. A Virginia Civil War Trails Marker is located at Roosevelt Street at a pull off just short of the entrance to Oakwood Cemetery.[90]

Fort Munson was erected on ground owned by Daniel O. Munson, a Virginia Unionist, whose property suffered from the depredations of both armies during the war and several early war skirmishes. The area east of this work was the scene of the famous "Grand Review" of McClellan's army on November 20, 1861, witnessed by Lincoln and his cabinet. The entire area from the Leesburg and Alexandria Turnpike toward the main Defenses of Washington became a favorite camping ground for Union armies throughout the war.[91]

Random rifle pits were located west of the turnpike on Perkins Hill before it reaches Seven Corners.

Freedom Hill Fort

Location

Drive out Route 7 West to Tysons Corner. Freedom Hill Fort Park is located at 8531 Old Courthouse Road near the intersection of Old Court House Road and Route 123 in the Westbriar area of Tysons Corner.

Visible Remains

Interpretive signs and an earthwork mark this apparent fortified picket post and signal station near the plantation of Peach Grove. The 5th Pennsylvania Heavy Artillery is affiliated with the site.

DEFENDING VIRGINIA APPROACHES TO CHAIN BRIDGE

Fort Marcy

Location

From Fort C. F. Smith, backtrack on 24th Street, north to North Edgewood Street. Turn left on North Edgewood Street and drive to Lorcom Lane. Turn left on Lorcom Lane and travel down the hill to Spout Run Parkway. Turn right on Spout Run Parkway and follow it to the intersection of North Kirkwood Road and Lee Highway (Route 29). Turn left onto Lee Highway and drive to North Lynn Street near the Virginia end of Francis Scott Key Bridge. Turn left onto North Lynn Street and then turn left onto the access road to the George Washington Memorial Parkway and drive to the Fort Marcy exit on your right.

Visible Remains

The fort is well preserved. The parapets, bombproof, gun platforms, gorge, well, and rifle pits are easily identified with an engineer drawing. Interpretive markers explain features of the fort. When approaching the fort from the parking area, you will enter the fort through one of the parapets and not the fort gate.

Description

This fort was named in honor of Brigadier General Randolph Barnes Marcy, father-in-law and chief of staff to General McClellan. The land was owned by Gilbert Vanderwerken, and construction began about September 24, 1861, under the supervision of Major D. P. Woodbury of the army engineers. The fort was first called "Fort Baldy Smith" in honor of Major General W. F. Smith, whose brigade helped build the earthworks. The fort's perimeter is 338 yards with emplacements for eighteen guns. The armament consisted of three 24-pounder guns, two 12-pounder howitzers, six 30-pounder Parrott rifles, three 20-pounder Parrott rifles, three 10-pounder Parrott rifles, one ten-inch mortar, and two 24-pounder Coehorn mortars. Fort Marcy worked with Fort Ethan Allen and the batteries on the northern bank of the Potomac to cover the approaches to Chain Bridge. The Leesburg and Georgetown Turnpike crossed the Potomac River at Chain Bridge and was one of the major avenues of approach to Washington. A strong stockade with large gates was placed across the turnpike to the right of the fort

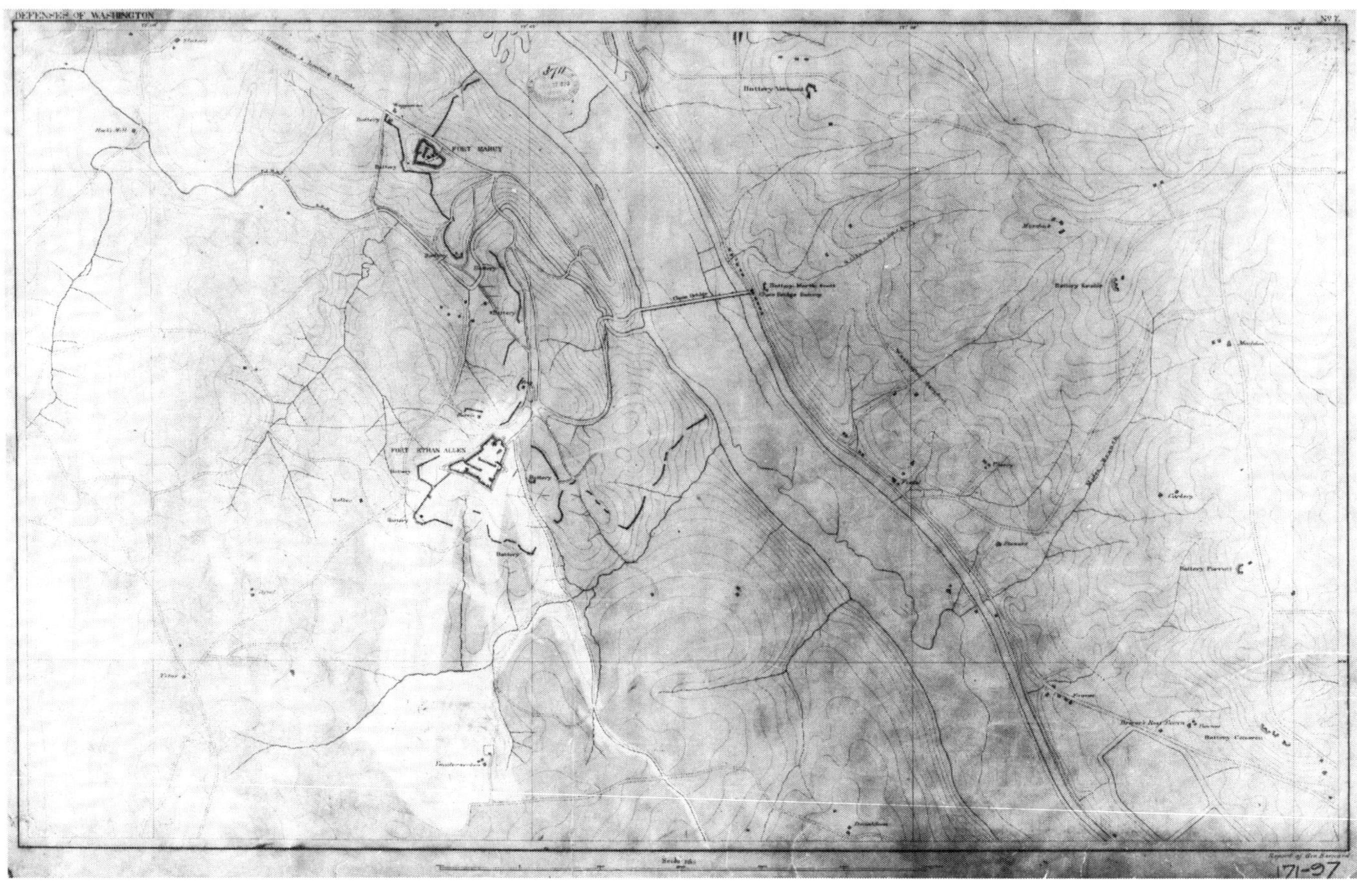

Sector Map—Defenses of Chain Bridge. *National Archives*

to prevent access to the bridge by a sudden dash by Confederate cavalry.[92]

Anna DeLashmutt deeded the land to the Federal government on May 7, 1859, and Fort Marcy Park was opened to the public in 1963. The park is known in recent history for being the place where the body of former deputy White House Counsel Vince Foster was found following his death on July 20, 1993. Several official investigations ruled Foster's death a suicide even though some have argued that his death was a politically motivated murder. From a historic site administrator's point of view, the event is an interesting study in what happens to a Civil War site when it becomes a high-profile crime scene.

Notes/Anecdotes

Soldiers amused themselves in a variety of ways to pass their term of service in the Defenses of Washington. Regimental histories abound with stories of pranks and practical jokes. Members of the 4th New York Heavy Artillery perpetuated one that occurred at Fort Marcy:

Whenever any disturbance occurred among the men, especially anything not in accordance with his wishes, the Captain was wont to use the expression, "Mutiny! There's mutiny in camp!"

At Fort Marcy, on one occasion, some of the boys had put up a job on another member of the command, and arranged that when he entered the barrack's door, a half-bushel of potatoes poised above the door should come down upon his head. This trick was arranged to be executed while the company were on parade. One of the men was up over the door, and another, who was to give him the signal for letting the potatoes go, was sitting in his bunk opposite the door, it being understood that the latter was to lean backward when the potatoes were to drop.

Captain Morrison noticed the absence of the latter soldier from parade after the company had been formed, and rushing to the barrack's door, looked up at the bunk, The man, to avoid being seen, leaned back, and the other chap overhead, taking the movement for the signal, let go the half bushel of potatoes, which came rattling down around the old Captain. He ran out of the barracks, yelling at the top of his voice: "Damn my soul, there's mutiny in camp!" The result was that both of these men were put in the guardhouse.[93]

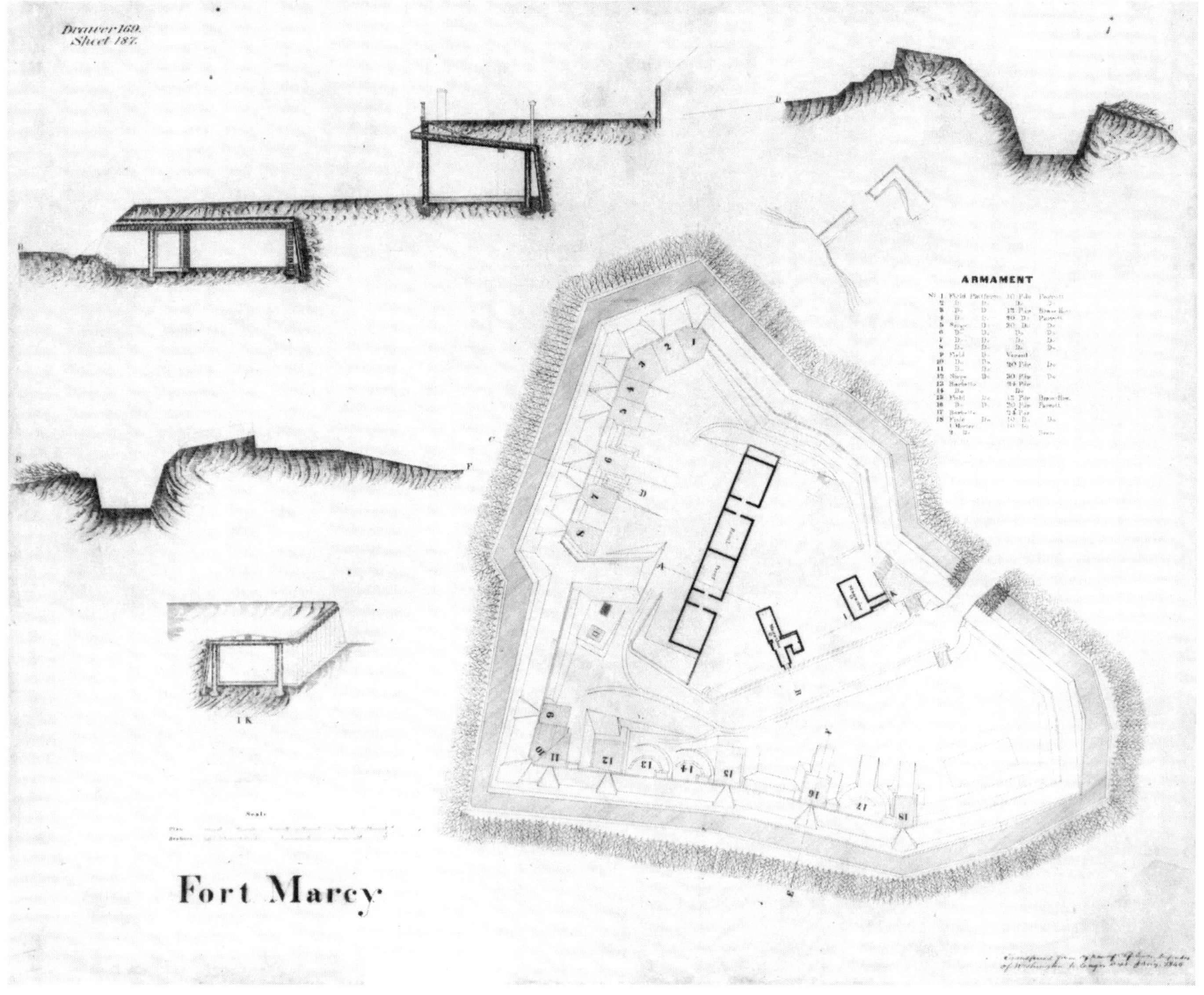

Fort Marcy—Engineer Drawing. *National Archives*

Captain Augustus Brown, Company B, 4th New York Heavy Artillery, left this account of his officer quarters at Fort Marcy:

> The house itself was a model of architectural beauty considering the purposes for which it was created. . . . [It] was painted a light drab color, with dark cornices and trimmings, while the white window frames and veranda posts and railing, and three tiny red chimneys surmounting the black, steep roofs, improved the general effect, and rendered the whole structure one of the prettiest little edifices for officers' quarters that it has been my good fortune to see. The interior was no less neat and appropriate. Each apartment, separate and distinct from the others, was divided into two rooms, the floors of which were laid with narrow matched pine highly polished and the walls and ceilings were done in the best style of hard plaster. In short the officers' quarters of Fort Marcy were universally acknowledged to be the most attractive of anything of the kind in the "Defenses of Washington."[94]

Mrs. Susannah Krips, wife of William H. Krips, Battery B, 2d Pennsylvania Heavy Artillery, served as a company laundress while the regiment was stationed in the fortifications around Washington. In 1902, she wrote,

> Shortly after the regiment went to Fort Ethan Allen and Fort Marcy, across the Chain Bridge. . . . I went in a government wagon, and the boys secured for me a nice log cabin, just outside the fort, on top of a hill and about half a mile from the Potomac River, on the Leesburg Turnpike. Batteries B, C and M occupied Fort Marcy, under command of Major Anderson. I had charge of the officer's table for about two months, when Mrs.

Fort Marcy's Bombproof and Sally Port as Seen from the Camp. *Fort Ward Museum Collection*

Baker, wife of Corporal Baker, and their daughter, took charge of the mess. I then had the clothes of 94 men to look after.

Mr. Krips was detailed as detective in General Augur's department. During his absence a colored woman came to my cabin one night and said she saw "Massa Mosby riding up the creek on his horse," and on investigation it was found to be true that he was reconnoitering. Pickets were stationed at the creek thereafter. A short time later one of Battery C's men was shot in the big toe by one of Mosby's men. He was the first man in the regiment shot by the enemy. One morning in April [1864], when the pickets returned to the fort and fired their rifles off at a target, as was their custom, Corporal

Drawing Water from Fort Marcy's Well. *Fort Ward Museum Collection*

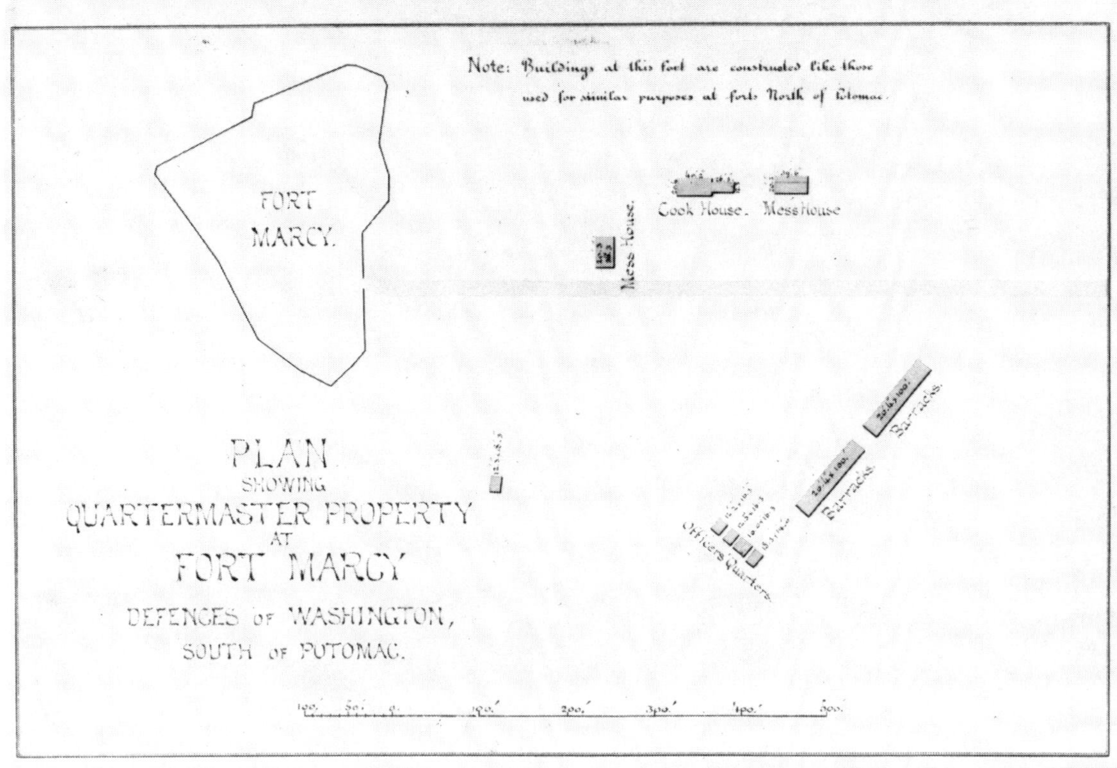

Plan of Quartermaster Property—Fort Marcy. *National Archives*

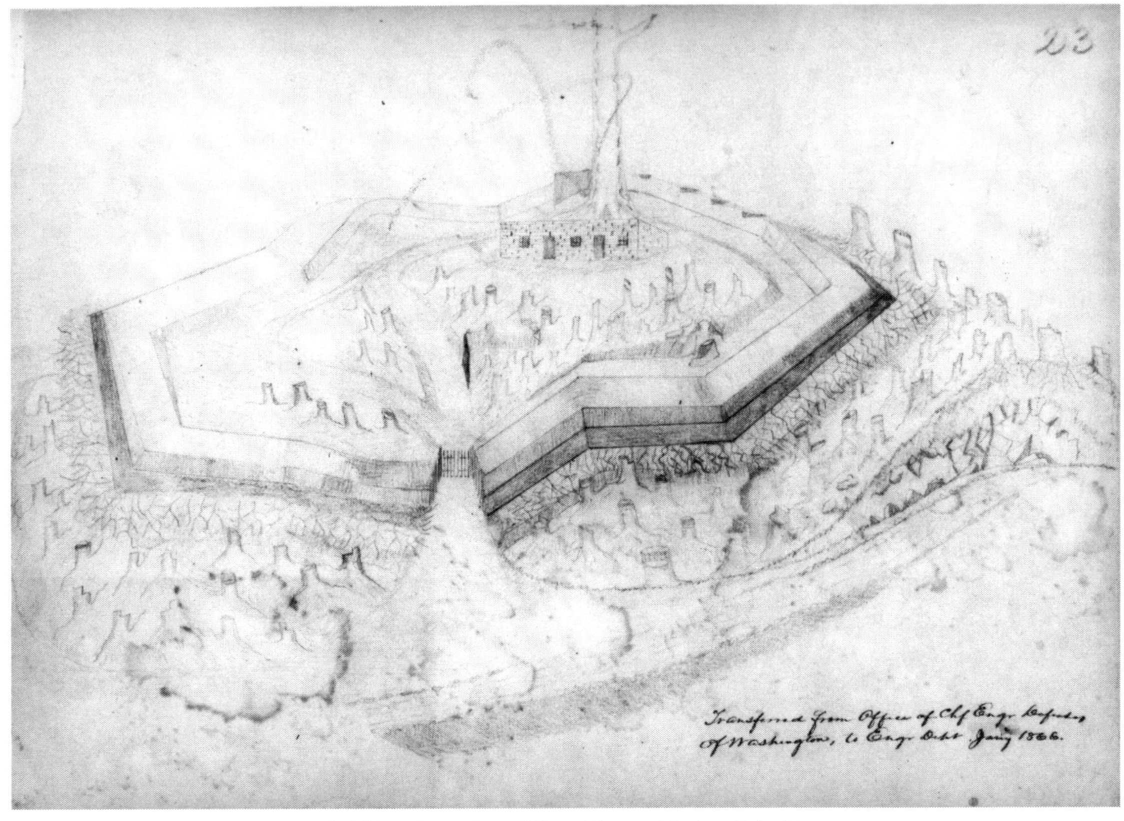

A Soldier's Drawing of Fort Marcy. *National Archives*

Hill permitted me to fire his musket. The target was an old tin coffee pot placed on a stump one hundred yards distant. I hit it square in the centre, and the boys cheered me as an "Amazonian."[95]

On May 27, 1864, when the 2d Pennsylvania Heavy Artillery left the Defenses of Washington for the front, Mrs. Krips continued her service as a hospital nurse.

Regiments stationed at Fort Marcy included the following:

- 2d Vermont Infantry, July 1861–August 1861
- 33d New York, Infantry August 6, 1861–October 11, 1861
- 3d Independent Battery, New York Light Artillery, September 1861–October 1861
- 4th Vermont Infantry, Co. C, September 28, 1861–October 9, 1861
- 15th New York Heavy Artillery, Co. D, December 1861–August 1862
- 4th New York Heavy Artillery, Co. B, July 1862–December 1862
- 11th New Jersey Infantry, Cos. H, G, August 1862
- 113th Pennsylvania Infantry, Cos. A–K, August 1862
- 152d New York Infantry, Cos. A, C, E–K, October 1862
- 4th New York Heavy Artillery, Co. H, November 1862–February 1864
- 152d New York Infantry, November 1862
- 4th New York Heavy Artillery, Co. A, January 1863–February 1864
- 16th New York Cavalry, Co. D, November 1863–December 1863
- 4th New York Heavy Artillery, Co. I, November 1863–February 1864
- 2d Pennsylvania Heavy Artillery, Cos. B, C, M, March 1864–April 1864
- 1st New York Light Artillery, Battery K, May 1864–August 1864
- 147th Ohio National Guard, Cos. B, G, H, K, May 1864–June 1864
- 74th Pennsylvania Infantry, Cos. A, B, D, August 22, 1864–September 1864
- 4th Massachusetts Heavy Artillery, Co. M, September 29, 1864–October 10, 1864
- 6th Pennsylvania Heavy Artillery, Co. A, November 1864–April 1865
- 1st Pennsylvania Light Artillery, Detachment One, November 1864–April 1865
- 6th Pennsylvania Heavy Artillery, Co. F, November 1864–February 1865
- 2d Connecticut Heavy Artillery, Cos. E, I, M, May 1865–June 1865

Fort Ethan Allen

Location

From Fort Marcy, continue on the George Washington Memorial Parkway to the Chain Bridge Road exit. Take the exit and turn left onto Chain Bridge Road following the road until you reach the stop sign at Chain Bridge. Turn right and follow the road around to the exit for Military Road. The exit will lead to Old Glebe Road. Turn left onto Old Glebe Road past the site of

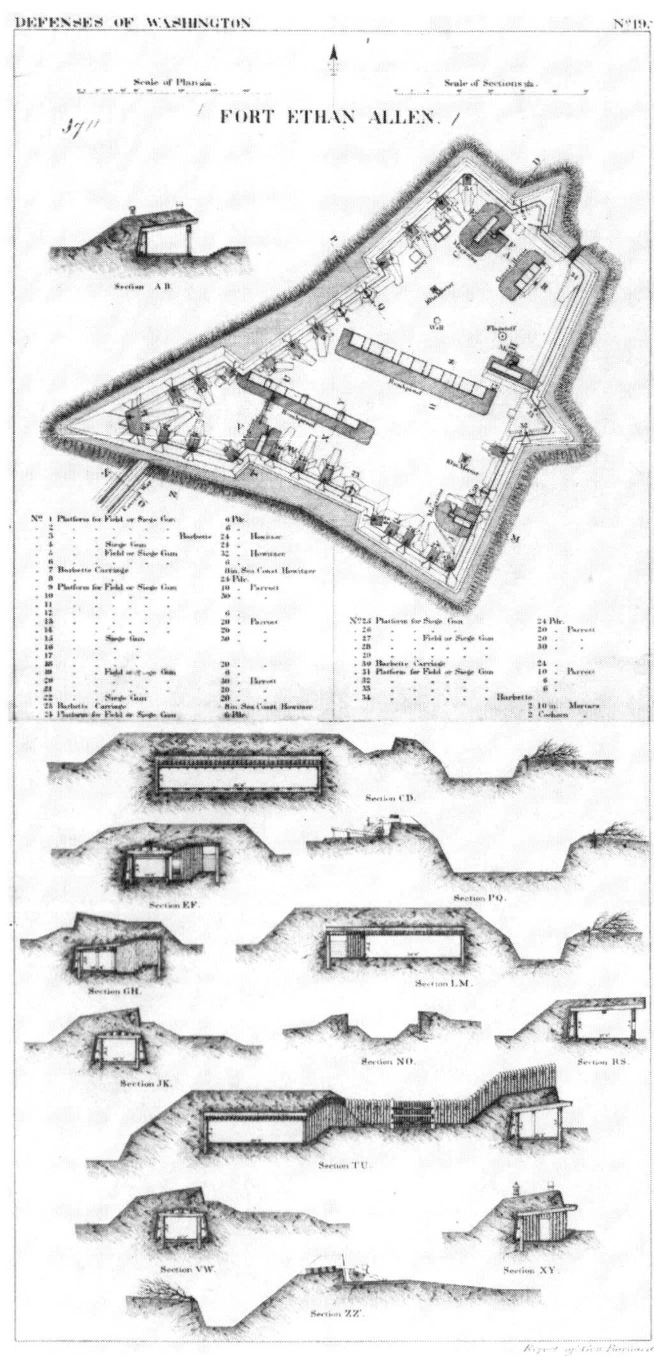

Fort Ethan Allen—Engineer Drawing. *National Archives*

Battery M, 2nd New York Heavy Artillery, August 1865—Fort Ethan Allen. *National Archives*

Fort Ethan Allen and park in the lot of the Madison Community Center. The historical marker for the site stands near Old Glebe Road by the entrance to the parking area.

Visible Remains

Although much of the fort has been destroyed, portions of the fort can easily be identified with an engineer drawing. Segments of the south face, gun platforms, one bombproof, traces of two magazines, and the guardhouse can be seen on the grounds of the old school. Old Glebe Road passes through the western portion of the fort, which extended out to the edge of the hill west of Old Glebe Road. The house at 4348 Old Glebe Road sits on the site of the southwest bastion.

Description

Vermont troops constructing the fort named it in honor of Ethan Allen, the famous commander of the Green Mountain Boys who at the outbreak of the Revolutionary War supported the patriot cause and played a prominent part in the capture of Fort Ticonderoga in 1775. The fort was also called Fort Baker by some of the construction troops in honor of Colonel Edward Baker, who was later killed at the Battle of Ball's Bluff on October 21, 1861. Fort Ethan Allen was a large fort that was garrisoned at times by as many as 1,000 men. The fort's perimeter was 736 yards and contained emplacements for thirty-six guns. The armament of the fort included two eight-inch howitzers, three 32-pounder guns, three 32-pounder howitzers, four 24-pounder guns, six 12-pounder Napoleon guns, three 6-pounder guns, eleven 30-pounder Parrott rifles, three 10-pounder Parrott rifles, four ten-inch mortars, and two 24-pounder Coehorn mortars. The fort formed a part of the defenses of Chain Bridge and commanded the approaches south of Pimmit Run. From the start of the war, securing the approaches to Chain Bridge was a major priority for military commanders. The importance of Fort Ethan Allen can be seen in the extensive infrastructure of quartermaster buildings constructed at the fort during the war, the large number of garrison troops assigned to the fort, and its importance as a signal tower location.[96]

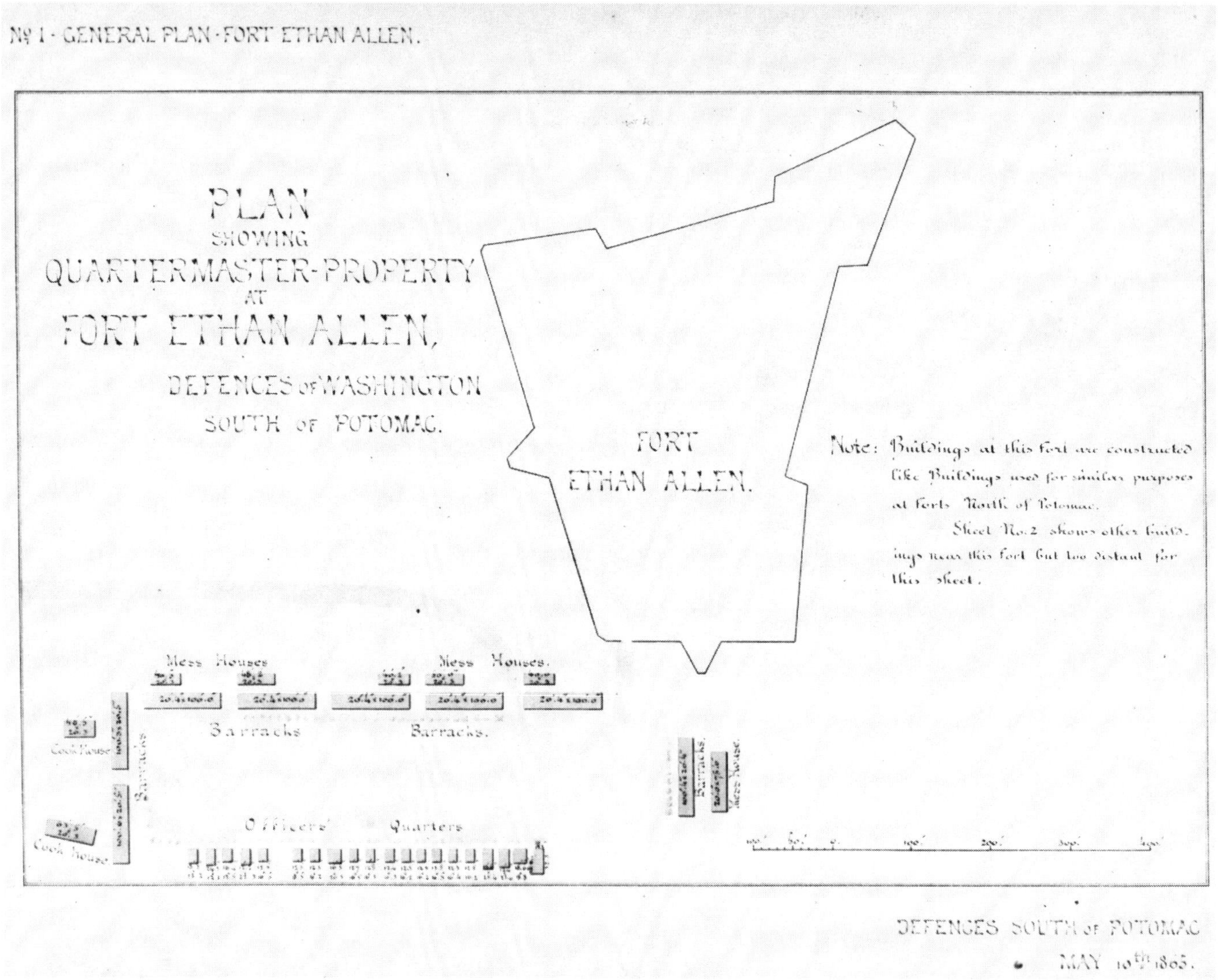

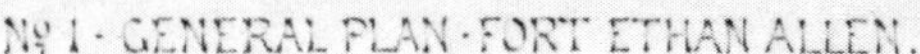

Number 1 Plan of Quartermaster Property—Fort Ethan Allen. *National Archives*

Notes/Anecdotes

Charles Banes, author of the History of the Philadelphia Brigade, wrote an account of an American military "first" that occurred at Fort Ethan Allen when Professor Thaddeus S. C. Lowe, the famous aeronaut, performed the first use of "lateral observation of fire" as an air observer from his balloon:

> While at work in the trenches, on September 24th, [1861] the troops had an opportunity of witnessing one of the uses of balloons in modern warfare. Four miles distant from Fort Ethan Allen, at a station called Falls Church, the Confederates had a considerable body of men. The United States forces at Arlington Heights sent up a captive balloon, and by means of signals directed the battery at Fort Allen how to range its rifle cannon on the camp of the enemy. After a few trial shells were thrown with precision, the Confederates were discomfited by an unexpected foe.[97]

Every fort had an assigned signal station located in the fort (see Appendix D). Fort Ethan Allen's signal station was quite unique because it was built in a large chestnut tree that had a circumference of twenty-one feet and sixteen feet from fork to fork. It acted as a "repeating station" that transmitted messages back and forth along the communication line to other stations. The log house at the base of the tree was first used by the commanding officer of Fort Ethan Allen, whose shelter was under the shade of the grand tree. The superior signal officer moved into the log house (and in one case shared it with his wife), and the tree was later used as a signal station. The station featured an enclosed signal platform that was forty feet high above the ground. The messages were transmitted by signal flag, and the pole with two balls on it was used for telling time, the balls beings raised or lowered at certain times of the day, thus signaling

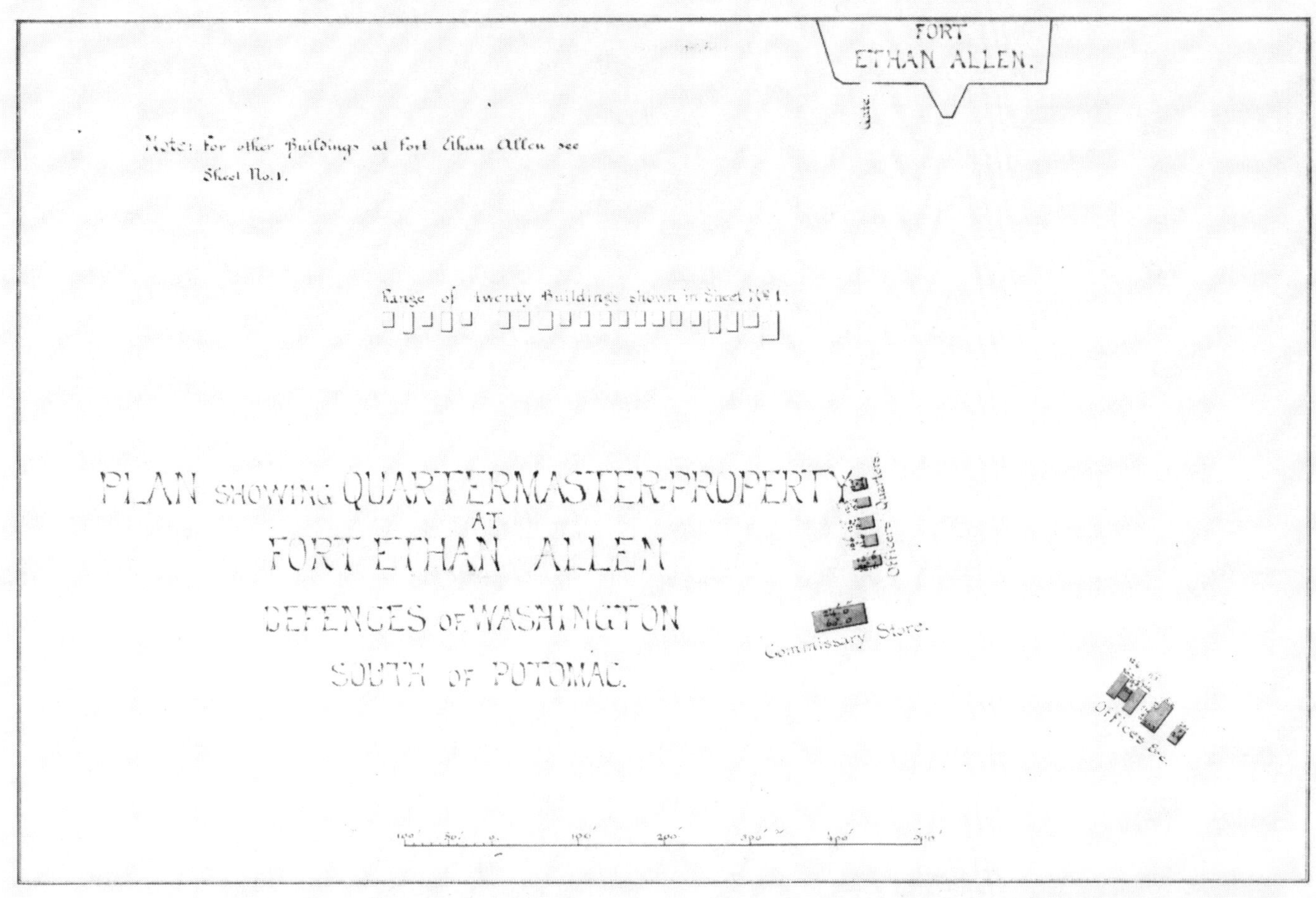

Number 2 Plan of Quartermaster Property—Fort Ethan Allen. *National Archives*

the time to other stations.[98] The station also served as a platform for Pennsylvania photographer William Kunstman, who photographed the barracks at Fort Ethan Allen. He also took images at Fort Marcy and Chain Bridge.[99]

On November 2, 1862, Private John Carpenter, a soldier serving in the 4th New York Heavy Artillery, wrote a letter home to his mother telling her how he spent "Halloween" at Fort Ethan Allen:

> Friday night in camp was a jolly time being Hallow Eve. We had a giant company—a giant being two men, one on the shoulders of the other, with a blanket over the top man's shoulders which in drawn closely around the lower man to make them both appear as one man. We formed a guard to receive the captain who was away from camp. I was mounted on top of the blacksmith's shoulders with my violin, and as the captain passed played the "Star Spangled Banner." The captain enjoyed the joke and made us a short speech. We afterwards had a cotillion by moonlight—I being the chief musician. I was guard that night till 2 o'clock—the night was beautiful and moonlit, not requiring a lantern.[100]

Dancing by moonlight is quite a contrast to the information that appeared as a footnote in Alfred Roe's *The Ninth New York Heavy Artillery*. He reminds us of the cost of war when Union soldiers garrisoned the forts. "When the 169th Ohio National Guard spent its 100 days at Fort Ethan Allen during the summer of 1864, 200 men were permanently disabled through disease alone, and more than 50 died."[101]

George W. Ward, historian and author of the *History of the Second Pennsylvania Veteran Heavy Artillery*, recalls an attack on the picket lines in front of Fort Ethan Allen and Fort Marcy that was attributed to

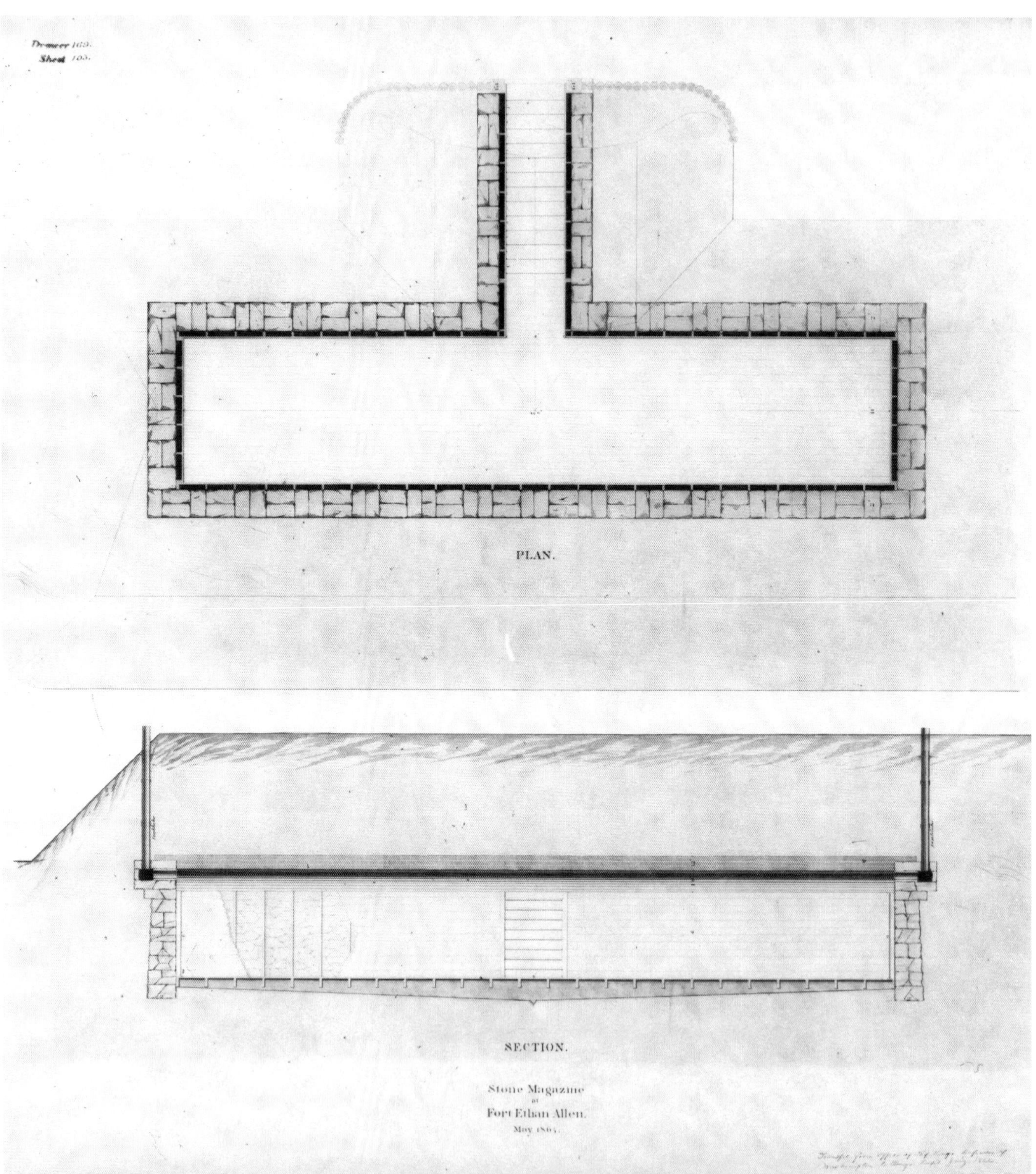

Plan and Section of Stone Magazine—Fort Ethan Allen. *National Archives*

Fort Ethan Allen Camp Stationery Used by the 4th New York Heavy Artillery. *Authors' Collection*

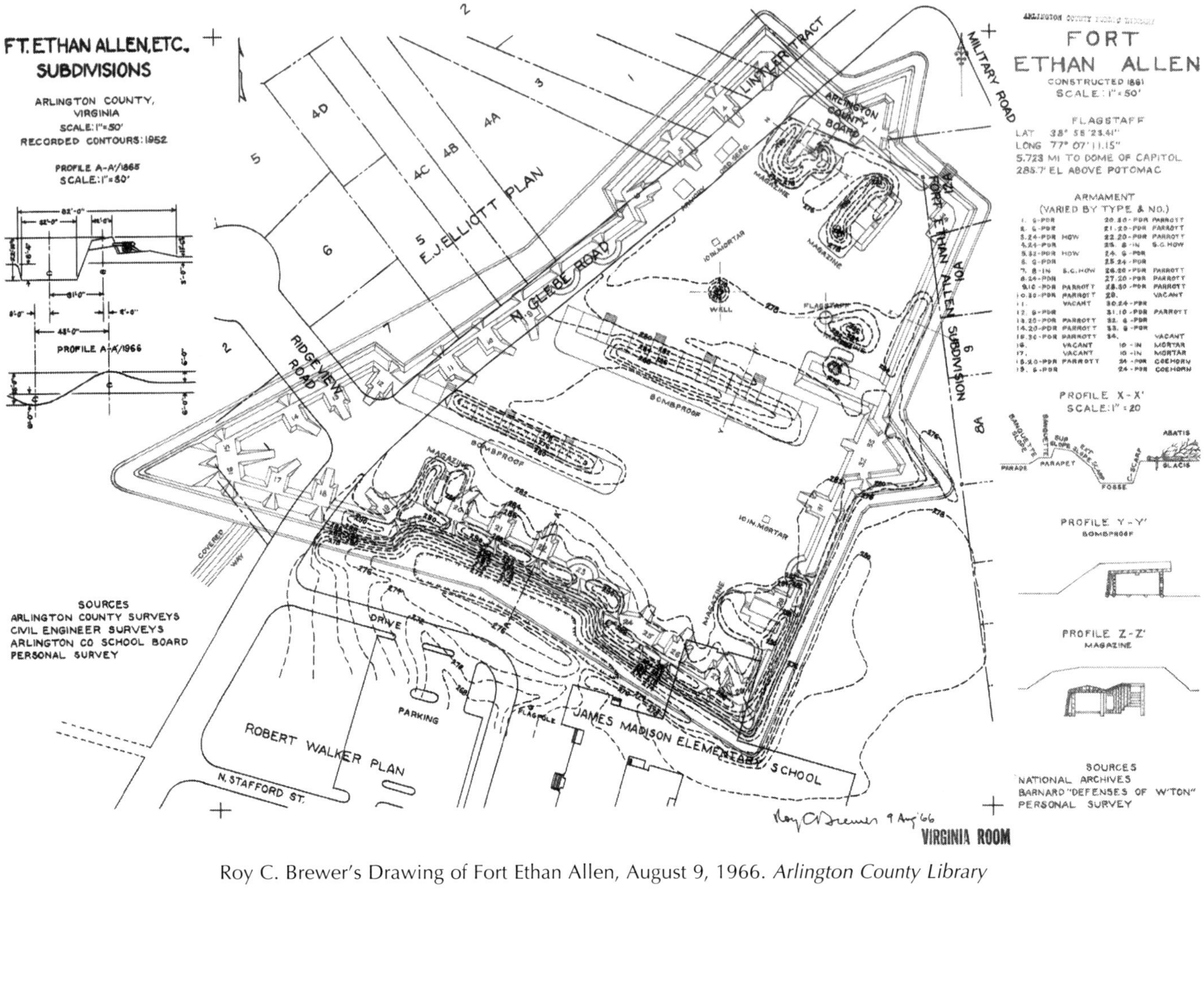

Roy C. Brewer's Drawing of Fort Ethan Allen, August 9, 1966. *Arlington County Library*

Lieutenant Jacob Lowry's Signal Station at Fort Ethan Allen. *Pennsylvania State University Libraries*

Mosby's Rangers and Elijah White's Loudoun County Cavalry:

> While at these forts, many incidents occurred, among which was an attempted midnight attack on May 3, [1864]. . . . The picket firing commenced about twelve o'clock and the bugles sounded "Fall in" shortly after. In five minutes. . . . Batteries G and D were inside Fort Ethan Allen and C at Fort Marcy, ready to man the guns. . . . It was true that many entered the fort half dressed, the writer himself carrying his blouse, shoes, and stockings in his hands.[102]

After daylight, a detail of 100 men were sent out from the fort to "scour" the countryside and returned with two men and a woman under guard and the bodies of two men who had been killed by picket fire the night before. All the men were found to be wearing three suits of clothing—a farmer, Confederate and U.S. Navy. They were sent under guard to Washington.

Garrison troops at Fort Ethan Allen included the following:

2d Vermont Infantry, July 1861–August 1861
2d Wisconsin Infantry, September 1861
5th Wisconsin Infantry, September 1861
19th Indiana Infantry, September 1861
3d Vermont Infantry, August 1861–September 1861
69th Pennsylvania Infantry, September 1861
71st Pennsylvania Infantry, September 1861

William Kunstman's Photograph of the Barracks at Fort Ethan Allen Taken from the Signal Tree. *Authors' Collection*

72d Pennsylvania Infantry, September 1861
79th New York Infantry, September 1861
106th Pennsylvania, September 1861
11th Rhode Island Infantry, September 1861
33d New York Infantry, September 1861–October 1861
15th New York Heavy Artillery, Cos. A–C, E, December 1861–June 1862
47th Pennsylvania Infantry, September
12th Independent Battery Ohio Light Artillery, July 1862–August 1862
4th New York Heavy Artillery, Co. D, July 1862–December 9, 1862
127th Pennsylvania Infantry, Cos. B–E, G–I, K, September 1862
15th New York Heavy Artillery, Co. D, August 1862
14th Connecticut Infantry, Cos. A–K, August 1862–September 7, 1862
40th Massachusetts Infantry, Co. E, October 1862
22d Connecticut Infantry, Co. C, October 15, 1862
169th New York Volunteer Infantry, October 1862
4th New York Heavy Artillery, Cos. C, E, September 1862–February 1864
22d Connecticut Infantry, Co. C, October 1862
27th Connecticut Infantry, Cos. A–K, October 1862
4th New York Heavy Artillery, Cos. A, November 1862–December 1862
4th New York Heavy Artillery, Co. F, November 1862–February 1864
11th Rhode Island Infantry, January 1863
4th New York Heavy Artillery, Co. B, January 1863–February 1864
4th New York Heavy Artillery, Co. G, January 1863–June 22, 1863
4th New York Heavy Artillery, Co. D, March 1863–February 1864
11th New York Cavalry, Co. K, May 1863–June 1863
2d Massachusetts Cavalry, Cos. B, E, I, K, July 1863–August 1863
16th New York Cavalry, Co. D, September 1863–October 1863
4th New York Heavy Artillery, Co. G, September 1863–February 1864
4th New York Heavy Artillery, Co. I, October 12, 1863–November 1863

Battery M, 2nd New York Heavy Artillery, August 1865. *Fort Ethan Allen National Archives*

4th New York Heavy Artillery, Cos. K–M, October 1863–February 1864
13th New York Cavalry, Co. E, January 1864–May 1864
2d Pennsylvania Heavy Artillery, March 1864–April 1864
6th Pennsylvania Heavy Artillery, Co. F, March 1864–April 1864
2d Provisional Second Pennsylvania Heavy Artillery, April 20, 1864–April 26, 1864
169th Ohio National Guard, Cos. A–K, May 22, 1864–June 1864
147th Ohio National Guard, Cos. A, C–F, K, I, May 23, 1864–June 1864
13th New York Cavalry, Co. C, June 1864–September 1864
74th Pennsylvania Infantry, Cos. C, E, F, H, I, K, August 22, 1864–September 1864
6th Pennsylvania Heavy Artillery, Cos. G, M, September 1864
4th Massachusetts Heavy Artillery, Co. B, September 1864–November 15, 1864
1st New Hampshire Heavy Artillery, Cos. C, D, H, September 1864–October 1864
4th Massachusetts Heavy Artillery, Co. I, September 1864–October 1864
1st Pennsylvania Light Artillery, Battery C, D, I, October 1864
4th Massachusetts Heavy Artillery, Cos. F, G, M, October 1864–November 1864
6th Pennsylvania Heavy Artillery, Cos. B, D, G, K, L, November 1864–April 1865
2d Connecticut Heavy Artillery, Cos. C, D, G, H, K, L, May 1865–June 1865
2d New York Heavy Artillery, Co. M, June 27, 1865–September 29, 1865

4

Touring the Forts North of the Potomac

THE CHAIN BRIDGE BATTERIES COMPLEX

Directions

From Fort Ethan Allen, return to Old Glebe Road; turn right onto Military Road and turn left onto North Glebe Road, which will lead you down the hill to Chain Bridge and into District of Columbia.

Five or six powerful auxiliary batteries and several field gun positions swept the Virginia shoreline between the Arlington line and Chain Bridge. They provided long-range coordinated fire with Forts Strong, C. F. Smith, Ethan Allen, and Marcy on the Virginia side and Fort Sumner on the Maryland side of the Potomac. The batteries of importance (in sequence upriver) were Battery Cameron (position trace visible at 1900 Foxhall Road NW), Battery Parrott (parapet extant on private property near 2300 Foxhall Road NW), Battery Kemble (parapet preserved in park on Chain Bridge Road NW), Battery Martin Scott (trace in 5600 block of Potomac Avenue NW), and Battery Vermont (site occupied by Sibley Memorial Hospital complex at Loughboro Road and MacArthur Boulevard NW).

Chain Bridge itself was protected immediately by Battery Martin Scott and an unfortified field gun battery at its northern end as well as by guards. As one member of the 10th Rhode Island also noted, "Near the centre of the bridge are two large, heavy gates, which completely divide the bridge. The gates are plated with iron, with slits for skirmishers and pickets to fire through, which were dented in several places by bullet and rifle-balls fired by secession pickets." Major General John G. Barnard, chief engineer of the defenses, remarked in his report, "The possession of the Chain Bridge communication with the opposite shore of the Potomac, incidentally important in a defensive point of view, was essential to the operations of our forces in Virginia and to the prestige of our arms." For this reason a strong garrison were posted there during the war, including the following:

- 4th New York Heavy Artillery, Co. D, December 9, 1862–February 1863
- 74th Pennsylvania Infantry, Co. G, August 22, 1864–September 1864
- 6th Pennsylvania Heavy Artillery (212th Volunteers), Co. I, March–April 1865
- 2d Connecticut Heavy Artillery, Co. B, May–June 1865[1]

Chain Bridge from the Virginia Side. *U.S. Army Military History Institute*

Interior of Lower Battery at Chain Bridge. *Library of Congress*

Battery Cameron

Location

Turn right from Chain Bridge on Canal Road to Arizona Avenue NW (traffic light). Turn left on Arizona Avenue to MacArthur Boulevard (traffic light). Turn right and go to Reservoir Road. Turn left on Reservoir Road to Foxhall Road (traffic light). Turn left on Foxhall Road to the 1900 block. The battery was located on the left (west) side of Foxhall Road, now the property of the German embassy.

Visible Remains

Slight profile of earthworks are discernible on high ground.

Description

The work was named for Colonel James Cameron, 79th New York (Highlanders), who was killed at the First Battle of Bull Run (Manassas) on July 21, 1861. An earthen parapet, the battery mounted two 100-pounder Parrott guns firing en barbette toward Virginia.

Notes/Anecdotes

Garrisons included the following:

- 4th New York Heavy Artillery, Co. G (part), June 1, 1862–September 1, 1862
- 4th New York Heavy Artillery, Co. F (part), September 22, 1862–October 1862
- 1st New Hampshire Heavy Artillery, Co. A, (part) May–June 1864
- 1st New Hampshire Heavy Artillery, Co. D (part), November 11, 1862–January 1865
- 1st New Hampshire Heavy Artillery, Co. D, January–April 1865
- 1st Maine Heavy Artillery, Co. K, August 26, 1862–May 15, 1864
- 10th Rhode Island Infantry, Co. H

Battery Parrott

Location

Continue north on Foxhall Road NW to the vicinity of the 2300 block. The battery was located on the left (west) side of street, now private property.

Visible Remains

Clearly traceable parapet gun positions exist. The positions mirror what can be found at Battery Kemble.

Description

An earthen parapet, it mounted two 100-pounder Parrott rifles firing en barbette toward Virginia. It was named either for Captain Robert Parrott, Ordnance Corps, who as superintendent of the West Point Foundry developed the ordnance bearing his name, or Rear Admiral Enoch Greenleaf Parrott, U.S. Navy, a native of New Hampshire.

Notes/Anecdotes

Garrisons included elements of the following:

- 1st Maine Heavy Artillery, Co. K, August 26, 1862–May 15, 1861
- 1st New Hampshire Heavy Artillery, Co. A (part), May–June 1864
- 1st New Hampshire Heavy Artillery, Co. D (part), November 11, 1862–January 1865
- 9th New York Heavy Artillery, Co. G, late 1864–early 1865

Battery Kemble

Location

From the Battery Parrott site, continue north on Foxhall Road NW to the intersection with Loughboro Road (traffic light). Turn left on Loughboro Road one block and left again on Chain Bridge Road. The battery is shortly thereafter on the left in a park; continue

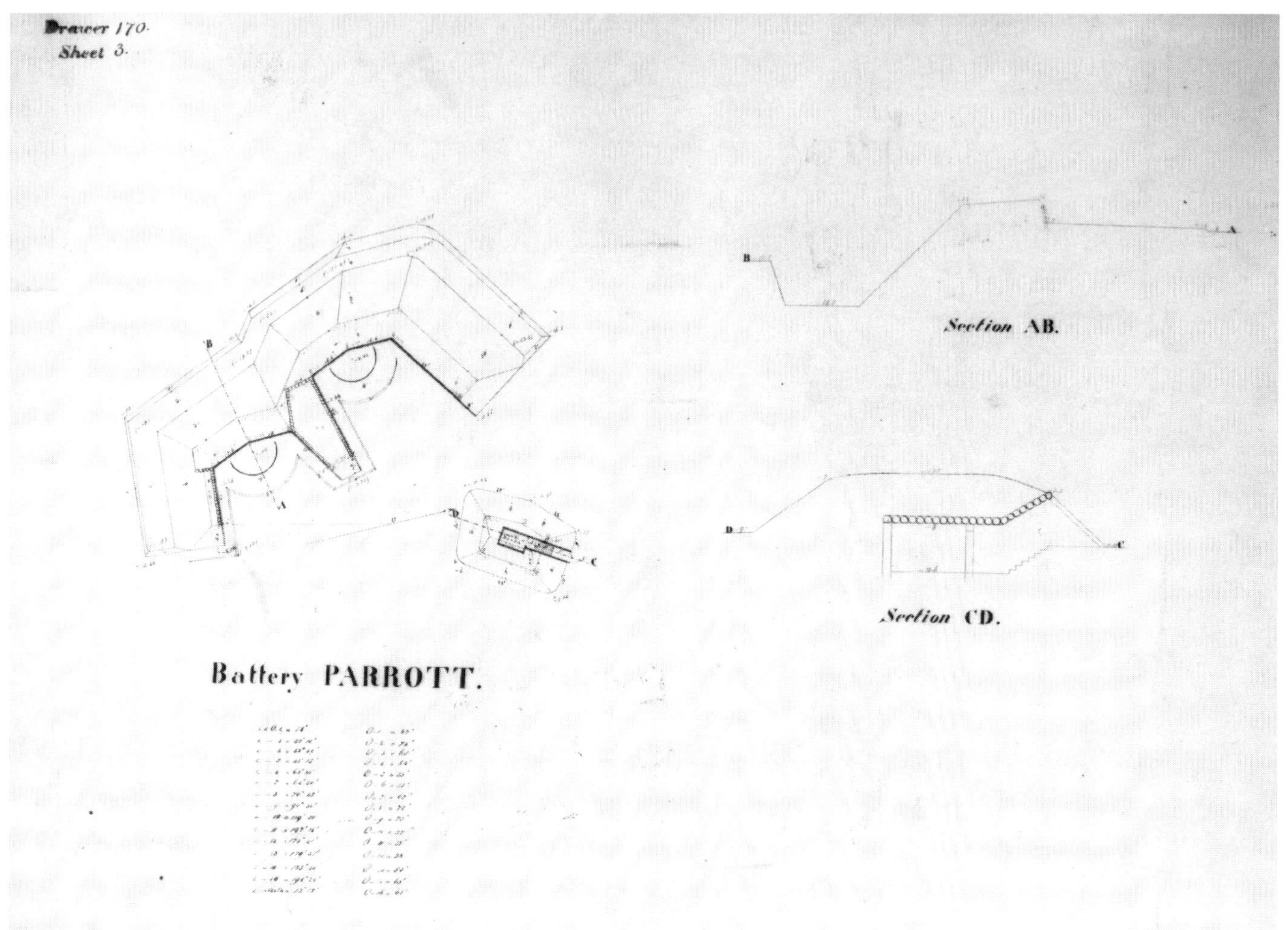

Battery Parrott—Engineering Drawing. *National Archives*

GENERAL PLAN- BATTERY PARROTT.

Implement House.

Ordnance Sgts Qrs.

Lieuts Qrs.

BATTERY PARROTT.

PLAN SHOWING QUARTERMASTER PROPERTY AT
BATTERY PARROTT
D.C.

ROAD

Barracks.

Mess House.

Note: These buildings are constructed like buildings used for similar purposes at Fort Mansfield, D.C.

DISTRICT OF COLUMBIA
JANUARY 27th 1865

General Plan for Quartermaster Property at Battery Parrott. *National Archives*

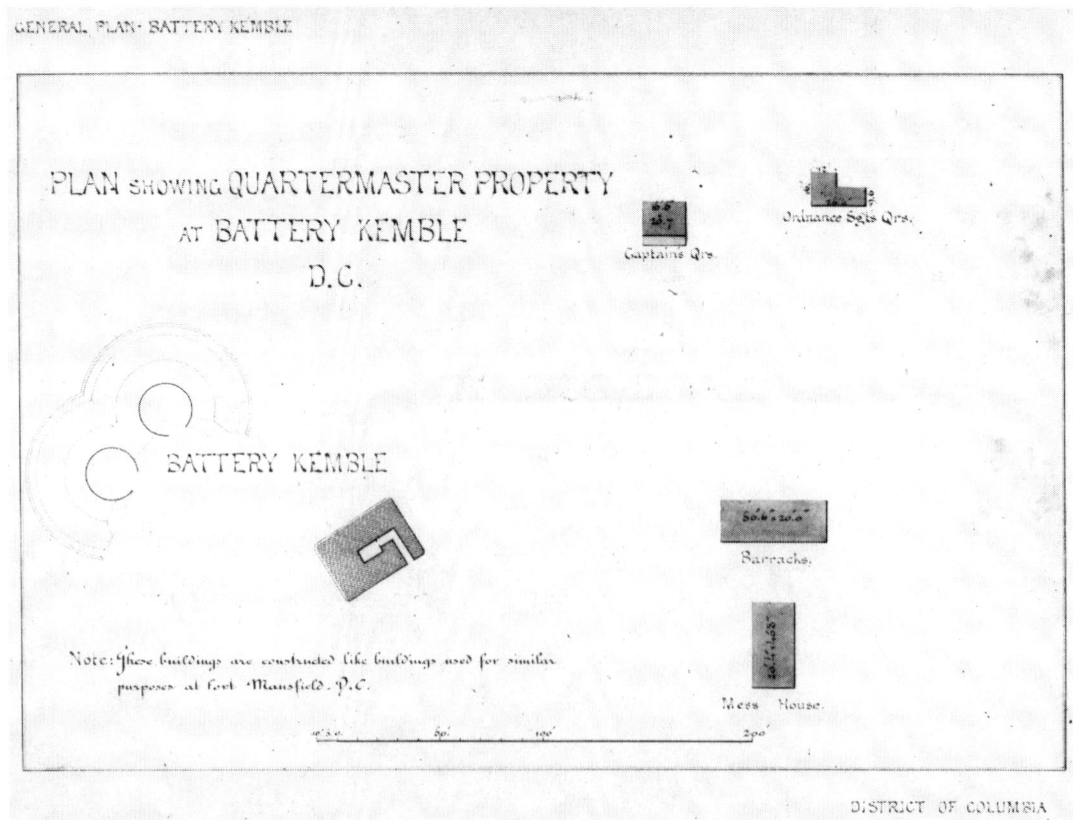

General Plan for Quartermaster Property, Battery Kemble, 1865. *National Archives*

Battery Kemble. *Barnard,* Defenses of Washington during the Civil War

midway down the hill to the park entrance and proceed to the bottom parking lot; walk straight up the hill to the overgrown battery earthwork. Picnic facilities are available.

Visible Remains

The site is well preserved and unrestored and contains overgrown remnants of earthworks and gun positions maintained by the National Park Service. A small centennial interpretive plaque can be seen.

Description

The work is named for Gouveneur Kemble of Cold Spring, New York, who was the prewar superintendent of the West Point Foundry, which supplied heavy ordnance to the government. The earthen parapet protected two 100-pounder Parrott rifles firing en barbette toward Virginia.

Notes/Anecdotes

The battery was erected on land owned by Captain William A. T. Maddox and his twenty-eight-year-old wife Sarah along with ground farther east on which Fort Gaines was partially built. He valued this real estate in 1850 as worth $20,000 and in 1863 was stationed in Philadelphia, Pennsylvania, as an assistant quartermaster.

Garrisons included elements of the following:

2d U.S. Artillery
9th New York Heavy Artillery, Cos. A, L
1st New Hampshire Heavy Artillery, Co. E, August 26, 1862–May 15, 1864[2]

Battery Martin Scott

Location

From Battery Kemble Park, return to Chain Bridge Road. Turn left on Chain Bridge Road to MacArthur Boulevard NW. Turn right on MacArthur Boulevard to Macomb Street. Turn left on Macomb Street to Potomac Avenue, the turn right and drive to 5618 Potomac Avenue. The battery site is on the left (river) side of street.

Visible Remains

A tracing of the parapet is faintly visible along what is termed the Potomac Palisades.

Battery Martin Scott, *Harper's Weekly*, August 24, 1861

Description

This work was named, presumably, for Major (later Lieutenant Colonel) Martin Scott, 5th U.S. Infantry, who was killed on September 8, 1847, in the Battle of Molino del Roy during the Mexican War. He was a native of Bennington, Vermont.

The earthen parapet was designed to contain one eight-inch seacoast howitzer and two 32-pounder cannon, but Barnard listed only two 6-pounder James rifled cannon in his report. This work functioned in coordination with the temporary field gun position for two 12-pounder mountain howitzers, located at the District side of the Chain Bridge. Battery Martin Scott stood fifty feet above and 200 feet behind the bridge itself. Infantry guards patrolled the span.

Notes/Anecdotes

Relatively little is known about this work. It was constructed by Vermont and Maine units, and this may account for its name.

One charming story was recounted by Lieutenant Winthrop DeWolf of the 10th Rhode Island, which sent a detachment to man the battery at one point:

> Here we remained three days, seemingly forgotten by the world, for no familiar face presented itself; no army wagon with rations crept down the long, steep hill; no newspapers, no mail, nobody came to see if we were dead or alive. Yet do not grieve for us. We lived on the fat of the land—and the water too. From the Potomac we had shad, herring, and catfish; by energetic foraging in the neighborhood we obtained milk, butter, eggs, chickens, corn-bread, sugar and coffee, and a dilapidated stove found nearby sufficed to cook them.

No wonder DeWolf and his comrades "on the whole were rather sorry" when orders came to rejoin Company D, then garrisoning Fort DeRussy, farther east near Rock Creek.

An undated, unidentified, inspection report in Corps of Engineer records noted a Lieutenant Fullison of the Invalid Corps commanding forty-four men in the area, including twenty-eight at Battery Martin Scott, drawn from the 4th and 9th New York Heavy Artillery companies. These men spent their tour repairing gabions on the left flank of the parapet.

Garrisons included elements of the following:

4th New York Heavy Artillery, Co. G, June–August 1863

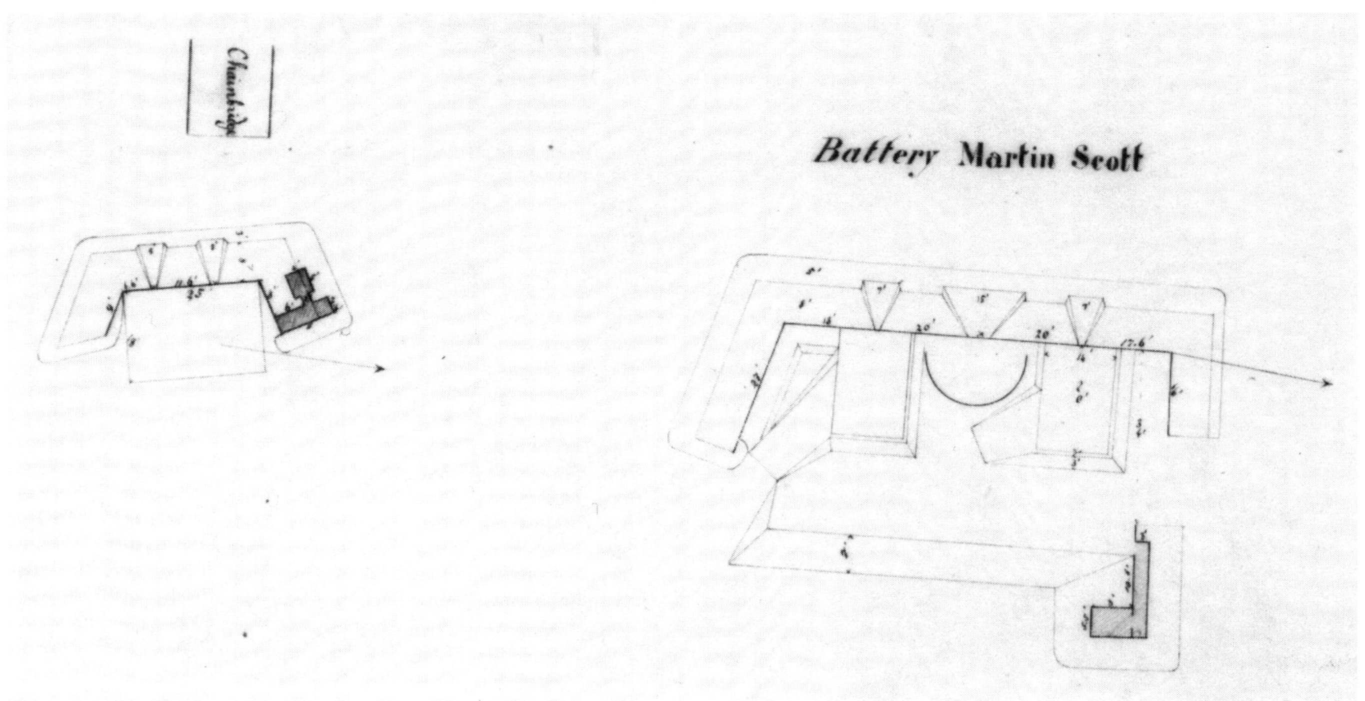

Chain Bridge Batteries—Field Gun Battery—Battery Martin Scott—Engineer Drawing. *National Archives*

3d Massachusetts Heavy Artillery, Battery K, September–October 1864
6th Pennsylvania Heavy Artillery (212th Volunteers), Co. I, November 1864–February 1865[3]
10th Rhode Island Infantry, Co. H

Battery Vermont

Location

From Battery Martin Scott, continue to the end of Potomac Avenue at the reservoir. Turn right back to MacArthur Boulevard NW to the traffic light at the Loughboro Road intersection. Turn left onto MacArthur Boulevard. Battery Vermont was situated on the right side behind present Sibley Memorial Hospital between MacArthur Boulevard, Loughboro Road, and Little Falls Road.

Visible Remains

None.

Description

The work was named for the Green Mountain State by Vermont troops who constructed it. A simple earthen parapet similar to other batteries along the line contained three 32-pounder seacoast cannon firing en barbette like Batteries Cameron, Parrott, and Kemble. The work coordinated with Fort Sumner north of the river and Fort Marcy across the Potomac to sweep the reservoir and Virginia shoreline.

Notes/Anecdotes

Garrisons included elements of the following:

1st New Hampshire, November 1864–February 1865
4th New York Heavy Artillery, Cos. F, G, H, August–November 1862
10th (1st) New York Heavy Artillery
2d Vermont Infantry
10th Rhode Island Infantry, Co. C
170th Ohio National Guard

Transplanted Englishman Thomas A. Bayley of the 4th New York "Heavies" noted in mid-October 1862 how the regiment was divided between Arlington line forts on the Virginia side of the Potomac and those north of the Potomac. Batteries Cameron and Vermont as well as Fort Gaines found the New Yorkers in garrison. Apparently, Bayley and his company at Battery Vermont barracked in an old barn (as their tents arrived later), were constantly aroused for night duty, and kept the battery's guns loaded with grapeshot: "3 detachment reliefs to each gun, all ready for action." This, of course, was the time when Robert E. Lee's army threatened in western Maryland, hence the

Soldier Art—Mess Pan Painting of Battery Vermont Headquarters, 10th Rhode Island Volunteers by Sergeant Charles P. Gay. *Spicer,* History of the Ninth and Tenth Rhode Island and Tenth Rhode Island Battery

alarm. Still, that alarm period found at Battery Vermont that "the boys had got in the way of living on the enemy, digging potatoes, taking tomatoes, cabbage, milking cows, robbing hen rosts [*sic*], pulling corn, apples, peaches and pecans and lived like fighting cocks." When they arrived in the area, he said, "You could hear nothing but the cakling of hens, ducks and geese but now you cannot hear a cackle within an area of 10 miles." With a loaded gun, they "held in check" a black farmer's helper while twenty of the soldiery milked cows while repetition led to "the strictest orders having been issued on the subject which keeps the men in check."[4]

ANCHORING THE LEFT FLANK OF THE NORTHERN LINE

Fort Sumner and Battery Alexander—Protectors of the Reservoir

Location

From Battery Vermont site, continue on MacArthur Boulevard into Maryland. Turn right at Sangamore Road (second traffic light) and continue right past the National Geospatial Intelligence Agency complex on left to the intersection of Sangamore Road and Westpath Way (note the neighborhood marking and the Montgomery County Historical Marker noting "Fort Sumner" area). Turn left on Westpath Way one block to Wapakoneta Road (approximate high-ground site of Redoubt Kirby or Fort Franklin). Continue on Westpath Way to the 5309–5325 addresses (approximate site of Redoubt Davis or Fort Alexander). Continue on Westpath Way/Terrace to Wyandot Court (approximate site of Redoubt Cross or Fort Ripley). These three works were linked by trenches to become Fort Sumner. A separate Battery Alexander site lies closer to the river and at one time was approachable through a private lane from MacArthur Boulevard.

Visible Remains

Virtually all traces of the prominent fort were obliterated during the construction of suburbs in the 1950s and 1960s. An innocuous marker at the intersection of Sangamore Road and Westpath serves as a token gesture toward the earthworks, as do titles of the subdivision-styled "Fort Sumner Hills" and "Sumner Village."

Description

Separate redoubts bore the names of Brigadier General James W. Ripley, then chief of ordnance; Major General William B. Franklin, prominent brigade and later division and corps commander in the Army of the Potomac and Army of the Gulf; and Captain (later Lieutenant Colonel) Barton S. Alexander, construction engineer for the redoubts and John G. Barnard's successor as chief engineer of the defenses. The combined fortification was renamed for Major General Edwin Vose Sumner, corps commander, who died on March 21, 1863, at Syracuse, New York, of wounds suffered at Antietam.

Army engineers designed the works to protect the city's water-receiving reservoir (as conveyed by the aqueduct) as well as the river shoreline. In sum, Fort Sumner was an exceedingly strong fort with a significant concentration of troops encamped nearby.

As finally consolidated, the works of Fort Sumner and Battery Alexander encompassed 843 perimeter yards, one of the larger complexes in the defenses. Ordnance included three eight-inch siege howitzers (en embrasure), two (en embrasure) and six (en barbette) 32-pounder seacoast guns, four 24-pounder seacoast guns (en barbette), one 100-pounder Parrott (en barbette), and four (en embrasure) and two (en barbette) four-and-a-half-inch rifles. A light battery of six 6-pounder James rifled guns as well as two 24-pounder Coehorn mortars and thirteen vacant platforms could also be found in the complex.

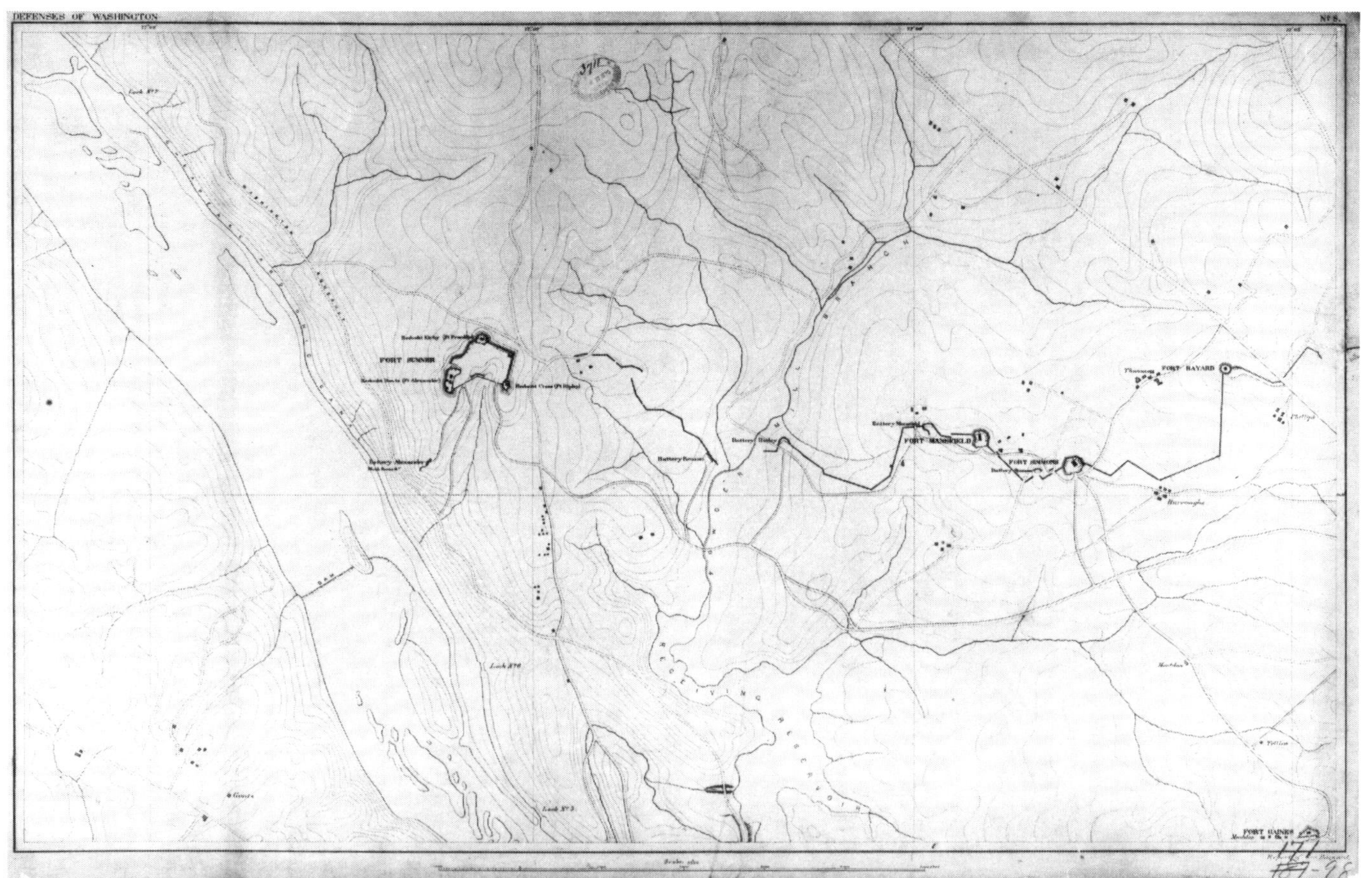

Sector Map—Forts Sumner to Bayard. *National Archives*

Notes/Anecdotes

The 117th New York Volunteers principally constructed the earthworks on the property of Albert Lodge. In late January 1863, members of the unit complained about the fact that the regiment had been divided between Fort Ripley and Fort Baker east of the Anacostia River to the east of the city. A battalion of five companies of the New Yorkers was stationed at Fort Ripley seeking reunification with the rest of the regiment.

Among those units subsequently associated with the position were the following:

4th and 59th New York Infantry, 9th New York Independent Battery, Cos. A, G, E, November 1864–April 1865
1st New Hampshire Heavy Artillery, Co. G
3d Massachusetts Heavy Artillery, Co. G, September–October 1864
1st Maine Heavy Artillery
1st Ohio Light Artillery
150th Ohio National Guard
10th Rhode Island Infantry, Cos. A, E, F, I

Companies A, C, E, F, H, K, L, and M, 9th New York Heavy Artillery, closed out their wartime service there in May and June 1865 before consolidating with the 2d New York Heavy Artillery. Company A, 4th New York Heavy Artillery, specifically garrisoned Redoubt or Fort Alexander of the works from August to October 1862, as did Companies E and I, 10th Rhode Island, in July and August 1862.

The soldiers stationed at Fort Sumner enjoyed the magnificent vistas stretching north and south from their camps. J. A. Mowris of the 117th New York recalled, "The Potomac with its ceaseless murmur, and the canal winding along its bank lay far below, and as the river extended off into the gorge toward the south-east, we could see where, two miles distant, it was spanned by Chain Bridge." Sugar Loaf Mountain in the blue distance vied with hilltops "crowned with forts, and over each floated the glorious old banner of our country," waxed Mowris. Reveille and taps echoed from those hilltops, but T. Chace of the 10th Rhode Island thought that the Potomac looked more like a frog pond than a river at this point. Still, he admired the scene at sunset, when, "after a smoky, hot day, the sun goes down like a ball of fire; and when we have retired to our tents and our blankets, the noise of its waters as they rush over the rocks which obstruct its channel, sounds not unpleasantly." Chace also sug-

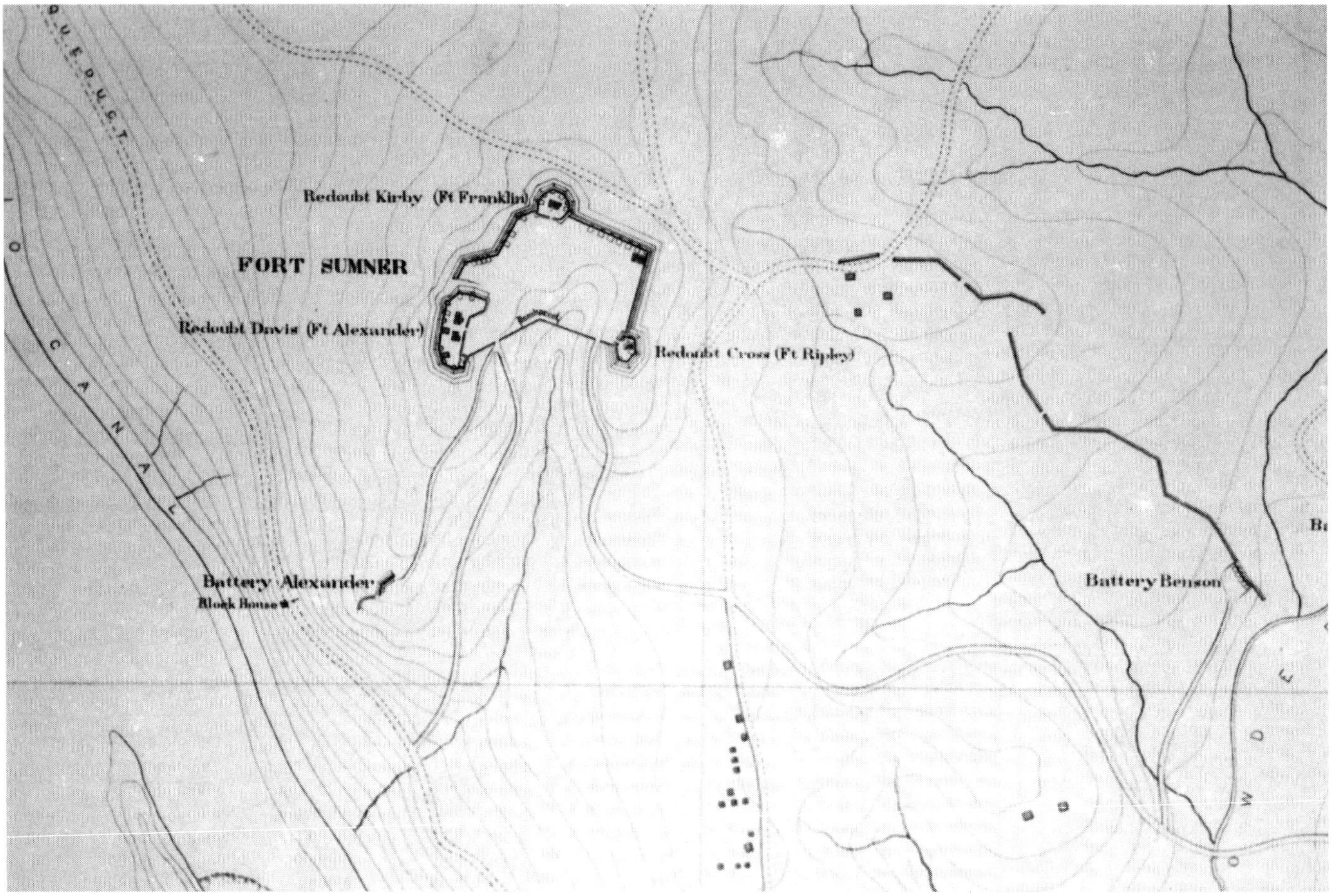

Sector Map—Fort Sumner and Environs. *National Archives*

Interior of Fort Sumner. *Fort Ward Museum Collections*

FORT ALEXANDER.
Headquarters Companies E and I, Tenth Rhode Island Volunteers, July and August, 1862.

Soldier's Sketch of Fort Sumner, Headquarters, Companies E and I, 10th Rhode Island, July and August 1862. *Spicer,* History of the Ninth and Tenth Regiments Rhode Island Volunteers and the Tenth Rhode Island Battery

Post Headquarters (note style used for modern Fort Ward Museum in Alexandria) and Barracks for Officers and Soldiers. *Library of Congress*

Band of the First Maine Heavy Artillery, Brooke Mansion. C. R. Lavalley, A. Goodwin, S. P. Jones, G. P. Smith, C. F. Davis, G. McPheters, L. Palmer, M. A. Colburn, N. R. Witham, F. A. Edwards, A. M. Bragg, F. Swett, A. C. Sawyer, A. Condon, N. S. Grout, W. C. Shaw, W. McFarland, C. W. Beal, E. S. Lawrence, E. L. Hall. *Shaw and House*, The First Maine Heavy Artillery 1862–1865

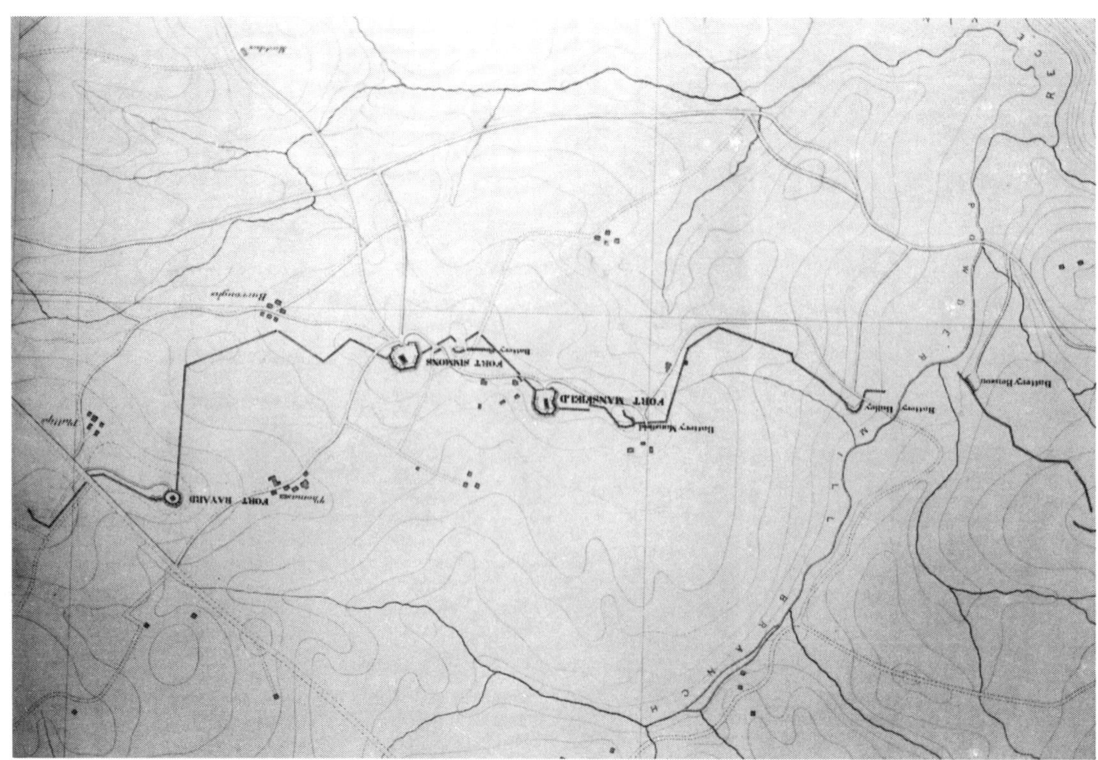

Sector Map—Battery Benson to Fort Bayard. *National Archives*

gested that "we are pleased with our location and its duties—pure air, spring water, wood, cut and dried; excellent drainage, good bathing facilities, little policing, hardly more guarding, and a drill which offers a pleasant change." He cited rifle drill in the morning and heavy artillery in the afternoon.

In the aftermath of Confederate general Jubal Early's 1864 raid on Washington, Major General Christopher C. Augur, commanding the Department of Washington/XXII Army Corps, told Chief of Staff Henry W. Halleck that Fort Sumner should have additional field pieces: two for Fort Sumner, two in Battery Benson on Power Mill Branch, and two more emplaced in Fort Sumner or Battery Alexander (one the fort's principal redoubts) "as may be required." It remains unclear that anything was done.

Regimental historians Horace H. Shaw and Charles J. House noted the infatuation of their 1st Maine Heavy Artillery with the fair daughters of local scion of "Oak Hill," Edmund H. Brooke. Brooke, chief clerk in the office of the paymaster general, was a widower, attended to by daughters Maria and Anne Brooke, headstrong young southern girls "who, at first, had little use or respect for Northern Yankees." But they eventually were won over by the "Down Easters," perhaps by the serenades of the regimental band. In any case, local citizens like the Brooke and Lodge families kept the Fort Sumner garrisons well supplied with milk and produce.[5]

Batteries Benson and Bailey

Location

From the Fort Sumner area, return to Sangamore Road. Turn left on Sangamore Road to Massachusetts Avenue (traffic light). Turn right and go approximately half a mile to Fort Sumner Drive (traffic light). Turn right on Fort Sumner Drive to the vicinity of 4800–4813 Fort Sumner Drive for the site of Battery Benson on private property. Return to Massachusetts Avenue, turn right, and go approximately three-fourths of a mile to Jamestown Drive. Turn right on Jamestown Drive to the bottom of hill, turn right on Elliott Road, and drive straight to Little Falls Park. Battery Bailey's remains are located in this recreational area maintained by the Maryland-National Capital Park and Planning Commission.

Visible Remains

Few discernible remains of Battery Benson exist. However, the horseshoe earthen parapet of Battery Bailey is preserved in a public park. Adequate interpretive markers and preservation efforts mark this well-defined unarmed field gun battery position.

Description

Battery Benson was named for Captain Henry Benson, 2d U.S. Artillery, who died on August 11, 1862, of wounds received "at the second engagement at Malvern Hill." Battery Bailey bore the name of Captain Guilford D. Bailey, commissary of subsistence and 1st lieutenant, 2d U.S. Artillery, who was killed on May 31, 1862, at Fair Oaks (Seven Pines), Virginia.

Both Batteries commanded the Powder Mill Branch valley. Battery Benson contained three vacant field/siege gun platforms, although post–Early's raid analysis suggested the addition of two field guns on a permanent basis.

Battery Bailey numbered six such platforms and received a similar recommendation for adding two field guns in post–Early's raid analysis. It remains unclear that such recommendations were implemented for either battery.

Fort Mansfield and Fort Simmons—Vanished Connector Forts

Location

Return via Elliott Road and Jamestown Drive to Massachusetts Avenue. Turn left to the vicinity of the 5200 block of Massachusetts Avenue (Battery Mansfield lies approximately 100 yards to the left [west] of this spot). Turn around and return to Jamestown Drive, this time turning left. Turn left again at Worthington to the knoll area at approximately 5110 (site of Fort Mansfield), turn around, and return to Jamestown Drive. Turn left and drive one block to Allan Road, turn right to the knoll at the Bayard Street intersection (site of Battery Simmons), turn left on Bayard Street to Berkley Street, and then turn right to the knoll intersection at Crescent Street (site of Fort Simmons).

Visible Remains

None; no interpretive markers exist.

Description

Battery and Fort Mansfield were named for Major General Joseph K. F. Mansfield, who was mortally wounded at Antietam. The positions were garrisoned during the war at various times by Company B, Maine Coast Guard, and detachments of the 151st and 170th Ohio National Guard. Battery and Fort Simmons were named for Colonel Seneca Simmons, 5th Pennsylvania Reserves (a unit that helped construct forts in this sector), who was killed on June 30, 1862, at Glendale (Frazier's Farm), Virginia.

Home of Colonel Joseph Welling, 138th New York (9th New York Heavy Artillery) at Fort Simmons. *Roe*, History of the Ninth New York Heavy Artillery, 1862–1865

Battery Mansfield was an unarmed field gun battery apparently recommended for actual placement of two field guns in the wake of Jubal Early's 1864 raid on Washington. Fort Mansfield's perimeter encompassed 220 yards, and it mounted one eight-inch siege howitzer, four four-and-a-half-inch rifles, two 12-pounder howitzers, and four 12-pounder James rifles with two vacant platforms.

Battery Simmons was an unarmed field gun battery also considered for actual placement of two field guns in the wake of Early's 1864 raid on Washington. Fort Simmons's perimeter encompassed 177 yards, and it mounted one eight-inch siege howitzer, two 12-pounder howitzers, and five 30-pounder Parrott rifles with three vacant platforms.

Notes/Anecdotes

Forts Simmons and Mansfield and Battery Bailey were all erected on land belonging to the Schoemaker family—brothers Isaac, Joseph, and Jesse. Valuing his real estate at $2,800, the latter brother claimed that he lost twenty-three acres, including seven acres of potatoes, five acres of corn, four acres of clover, a fourth of an acre of asparagus, and at least forty-eight apple trees, fifty-one peach trees, forty-six quince trees, twenty-three cherry trees, and two large persimmon trees to the army's takeover of his land for camps and fortifications.

These positions formed an advance line also protecting the receiving reservoir in conjunction with Fort Sumner. They also connected with other works of the northern defense line to the east.

Units associated with Fort Simmons included the following:

9th New York Heavy Artillery
Co. A, March 1863–February 1864
Co. D, March 1863–June 23, 1863
Co. F, March 1863–April 1863
Co. I, March 1863–March 26, 1863
Co. L, December 31, 1863–February 29 and May–August 1864
Co. M, May 1863–February 1864
1st New Hampshire Heavy Artillery, Co. F, November 27, 1864–April 1865

Units associated with Fort Mansfield included the following:

9th New York Heavy Artillery
Co. A, October 18–December 31, 1862
Co. B, October 17, 1862–June 1863
Co. C, October 18, 1862–November 1862
Co. D (part), October 18–December 1862
Co. E, October 17, 1862–June 1863
Co. G, January 1–April 1863

Company A Street and Huts, 138th New York (9th New York Heavy Artillery) at Fort Simmons. *Roe,* History of the Ninth New York Heavy Artillery, 1862–1865

Print of Camp Morris, 138th New York (9th New York Heavy Artillery). *Fort Ward Museum Collections*

Co. H, October 18, 1862–February 1864
Co. K, October 18–31, 1862 and July 1863–February 1864
Co. D, 3d Massachusetts Heavy Artillery, September 28–October 1864
Co. B, 1st New Hampshire Heavy Artillery, November 1864–February 1865

In the late fall of 1862, the 117th New York (Fourth Oneida Regiment) encamped near Fort Simmons in a locale that they promptly dubbed "Camp Mud." Impossible now to locate, soldiers remembered Camp Mud only for the poor ground conditions but also for misdirected practice shots from nearby forts. More amicable were contacts with local Unionist families, such as the Shoemakers, on whose farm Fort Simmons was constructed, as well as the Thomas Dean family, who owned the Fort Mansfield land.

At the time of Jubal Early's raid in the summer of 1864, Benjamin Marshall of the 1st New Hampshire Heavy Artillery wrote his mother on July 17 how "about 12,000" Confederates "came within about a mile of us," receiving "a few bombsels [*sic*]" before stopping and going over toward Fort Stevens where they had "a considerable fight." He did not know "how many of them wer killed but they got pretty badly whipped [*sic*]," fighting "as long as they could see." It was about nine in the evening before they stopped firing, he estimated, but they had "gone up river" thereafter. He also informed her that they could secure cheese at thirty-five cents a pound, butter at seventy-five cents, with four crackers provided for five cents. Interestingly, he also reported that "there has been two Companys of darkeys here but they went off to day I don't know where they have gone to." Marshall was killed later in September.

Fort Gaines—A Vanished Reserve Fort

Location

From the Fort Simmons site, continue on Berkley Street to Western Avenue NW. Turn right onto Westmoreland Circle and three-fourths of the way around the circle go south on Massachusetts Avenue NW into the District of Columbia to the American University campus at Ward Circle. Fort Gaines lies to the left (east) side at the top of the hill before the circle (site of Katzen Art Center).

Visible Remains

None; no interpretive marker.

Description

The fort was probably named for Major General Edmund P. Gaines, renowned U.S. regular veteran of the War of 1812, Seminole War, and the Mexican War.

This early attempt to provide a second line of defense against enemy breakthrough encompassed a perimeter of 171 yards. It mounted five 32-pounder seacoast guns (en barbette) and a single four-and-a-half-inch rifle (en embrasure).

Notes/Anecdotes

Constructed by Pennsylvania Reserves during the autumn of 1861, the land partly belonged apparently to forty-seven-year-old Captain William A. T. Maddox, U.S. Marine Corps, and his twenty-year-old wife Sarah. Owning land also on which Battery Kemble was built, he valued his property overall at $20,000. It was located near the William D. C. Murdock house, "Friendship," not far from Tennallytown. Murdock, at least, protested as inadequate the government's postwar compensation of $7,000 (he wanted $70,000) in damages for wartime timber clearing.

The position was variously garrisoned by contingents of the following:

1st New York Light Artillery
4th New York Heavy Artillery, September–October 1863
  Co. B, July 1863–February 1864 and May–June 1865
  Co. C, November 1, 1862–August 14, 1863
  Co. I, July–August 1864
  Co. K, November 12, 1862–June 1863
9th New York Heavy Artillery
1st New Hampshire Heavy Artillery, Co. B (part), May 1864
1st New Hampshire Heavy Artillery , Co. L (part), December 2, 1864–February 28, 1865
163d and 170th Ohio National Guard (detachments)
55th and 59th New York Infantry
10th Rhode Island Infantry, Co. G

Perhaps Fort Gaines's greatest claim to fame may have been a possible visit by President and Mrs. Lincoln to Colonel Regis de Tobriand's famous "Zous-Zous" of the 55th New York bedecked in French Algerian–style garb and noted for their exquisite French cuisine. They afforded him, said Old Abe, "the best meal he had had in Washington."

James Field of the 10th Rhode Island recalled visiting the fort with friends on their return from a bathing trip to the Potomac in 104-degree heat during the summer of 1862. He graphically described Fort Gaines as an earthwork "about ten or twelve feet thick, with ditch about as wide and six or eight feet deep, on the outside of which were large trees, laid lengthwise, to hinder infantry from going through them to the fort." Noncommissioned officer Thomas A. Bayley of the 4th New York Heavy Artillery wrote in October 1862 how the "accession of 80 recruits from New York who were sent [to the fort]" led to reunion with a fellow sergeant "so as to drive the men up to the standard as soon as possible."

Family legend has Confederate cavalry commander John McCausland infiltrating Union lines in the vicinity of forward Fort Bayard during Jubal Early's 1864 raid on Washington and aided by a member of the local Loughboro family, reaching an unmanned Fort Gaines from which he purportedly viewed the lights of the capital from this high ground.[6]

Fort Bayard—Lost Guardian of the River Road

Location

From the Fort Gaines site at Ward Circle, retrace the route to Westmoreland Circle. Turn right on Western Avenue NW to the park at Western Avenue and River Road. The Fort Bayard site is in the park on the right.

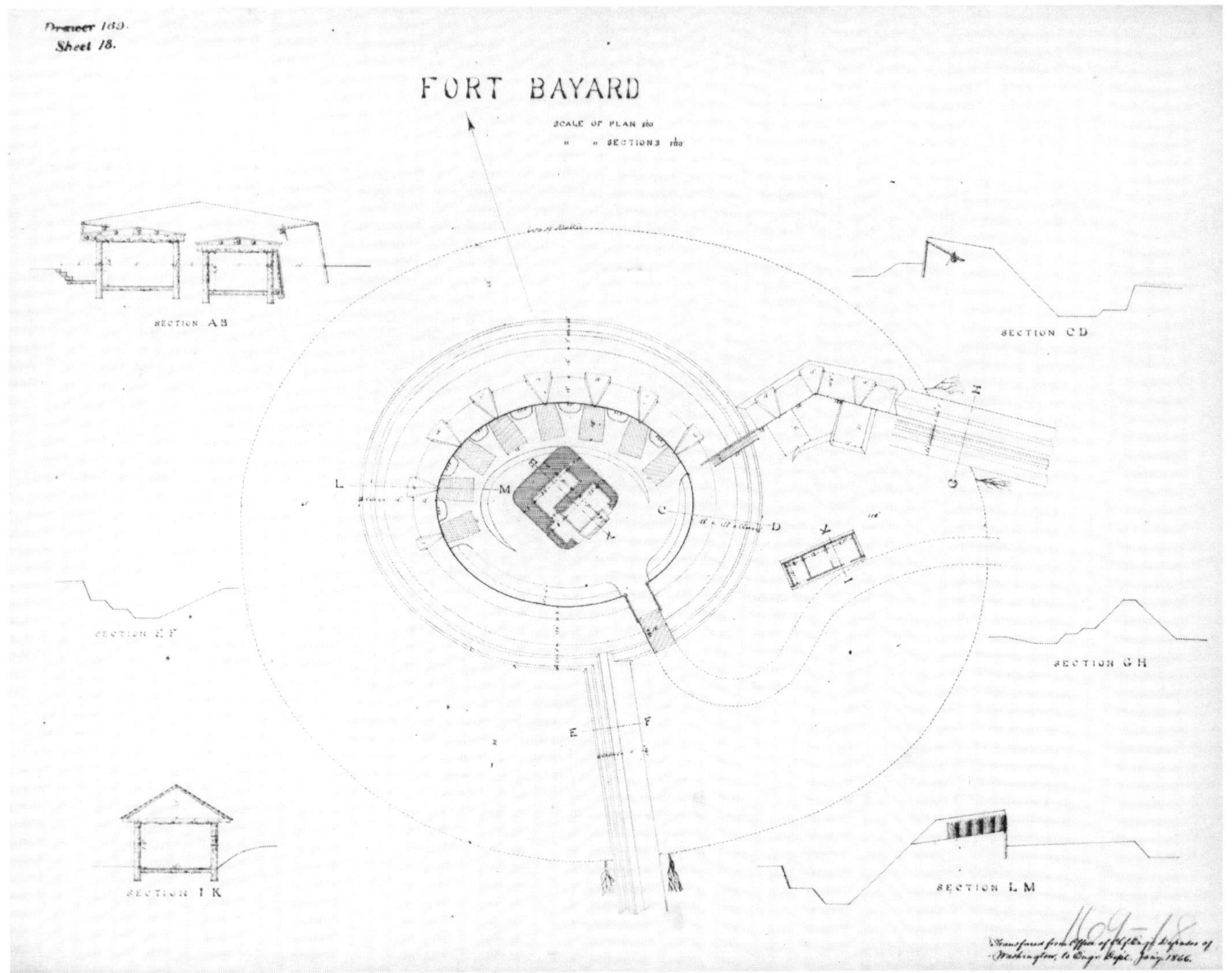

Fort Bayard—Engineer Drawing. *National Archives*

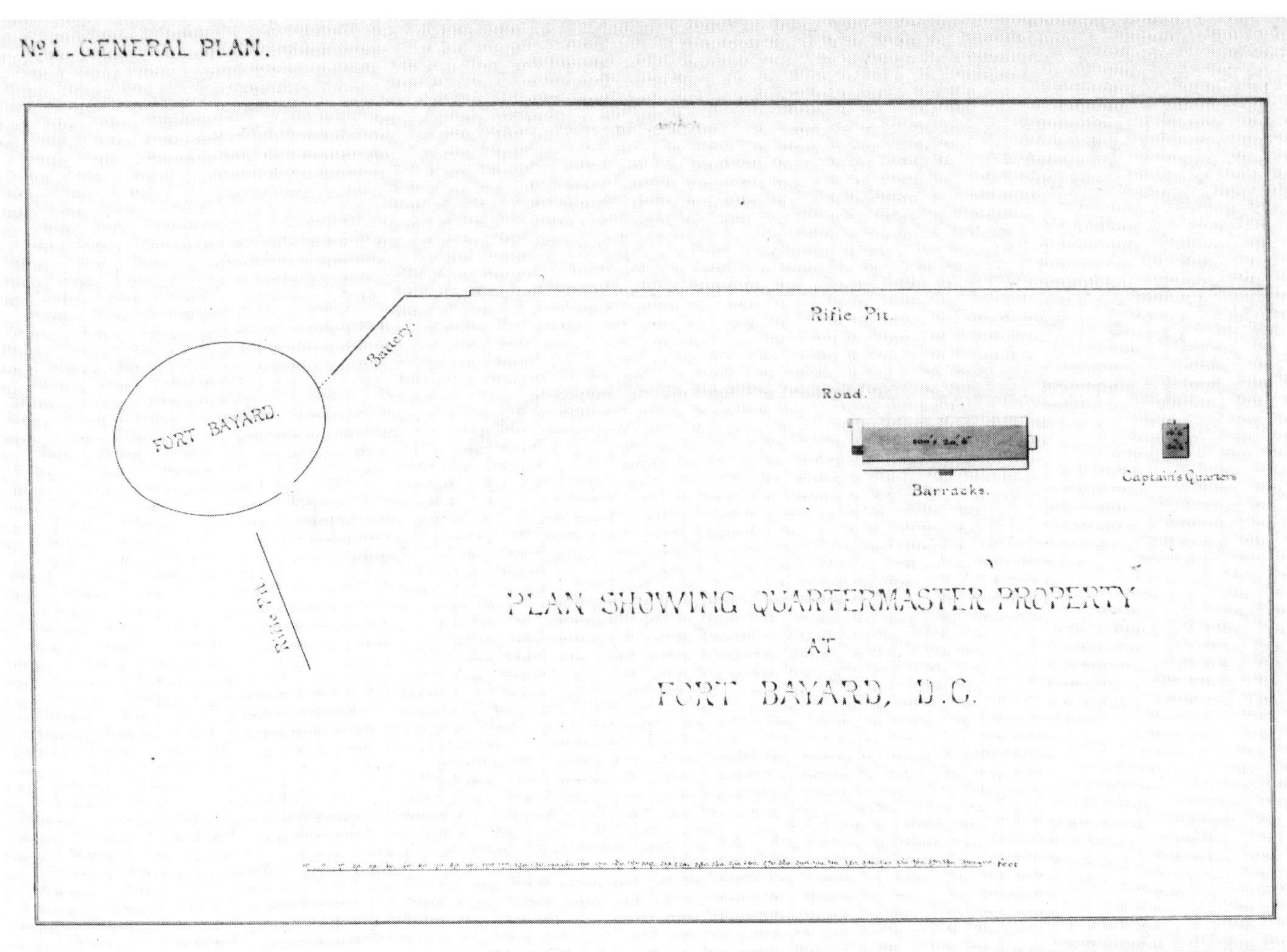

Plan for Quartermaster Structures at Fort Bayard. *National Archives*

Visible Remains

Despite maintenance of the site as a park by the National Park Service, no remains may be seen. A generic National Park Service Defenses of Washington sign is present.

Description

The fort was named for Brigadier General George D. Bayard, 1st Pennsylvania Cavalry, who was mortally wounded at Fredericksburg, December 13, 1862.

The work was a small elliptical earthen fort with a perimeter of 123 yards. It mounted four 20-pounder Parrott rifles and two 12-pounder field howitzers, all firing en embrasure.

Notes/Anecdotes

Fort Bayard commanded the key River Road (a former colonial artery that carried a portion of Braddock's ill-fated expedition to its appointment with disaster in the French and Indian War). Entering the District of Columbia near Tennallytown, the road joined the Georgetown-Rockville Turnpike. The fort was linked by rifle pits to Fort Simmons (775 yards to the west) and Fort Reno (1,250 yards eastward). The work was constructed on the Philip Buckey property, which he valued at $5,000. Details from the Pennsylvania Reserves did the work.

Among units posted here were the following:

9th New York Heavy Artillery
- Co. M, January–April 1863
- Co. F, July 1863–February 1864 and July–August 1864

1st New Hampshire Heavy Artillery
- Co. B, May 1864
- Co. F, September–October 1864
- Co. H

163d and 170th Ohio National Guard (detachments)

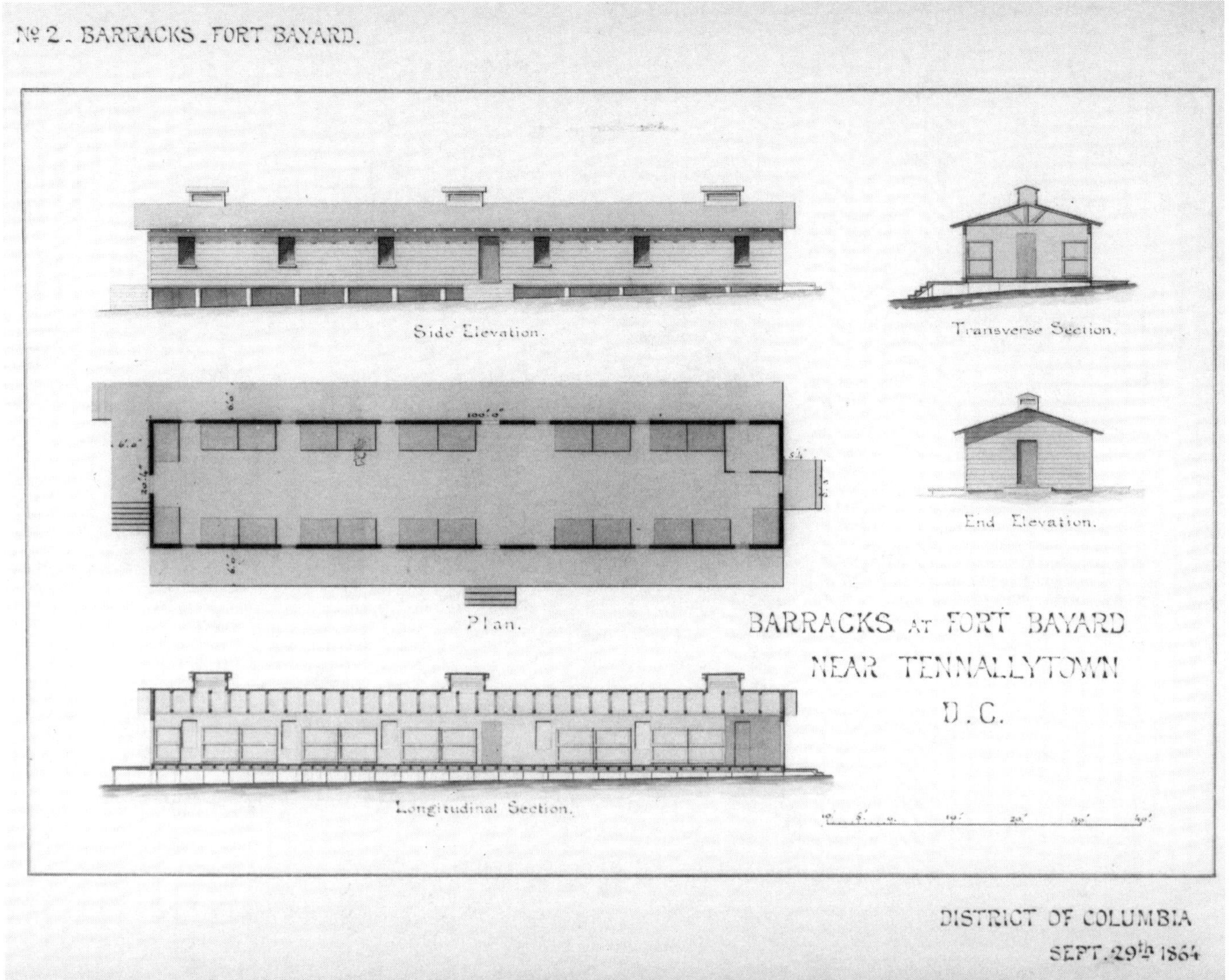

Barracks Near Fort Bayard. *National Archives*

While stationed at nearby "Camp Mud," details from the 117th New York were sent to construct what they styled "Fort Eliptic" or "Soapstone Fort" (because of a particular type of rock indigenous to the area). The unit's historian noted that the regiment received its "beautiful silk banner made by the ladies of Utica" while engaged in digging fortifications in the area.

One inspection report by Major Charles Burgess in March 1864 noted the absence of drinking water within the fort but otherwise declared the position ready for battle with 477 rounds of artillery ammunition, 100 pounds of musket powder, 100 hand grenades, 133 69-caliber Springfield muskets, and 20,850 rounds of small arms ammunition. Three months later, the fort's garrison participated in skirmishing with John McCausland's Confederate cavalry testing Washington's defenses in the Tennallytown vicinity. Post-Early's raid analysis suggested adding two field pieces permanently either in reserve or in unarmed batteries between Forts Simmons and Bayard.

Local residents Joseph and Isaac Shoemaker contracted with the army in 1861 to supply abatis, timber, and lumber in support of fort construction in the area.

Fort Reno and Battery Reno—Defending Tennallytown

Location

From Fort Bayard site, turn right on River Road NW to Wisconsin Avenue NW. Merge to the right and immediately get in the left lane in order to turn left at Albemarle Street (traffic light). Proceed one block, then turn left onto 40th Street/Fort Drive past Woodrow Wilson High School on the right to Chesapeake Street. Ahead lies the recreational area/park and reservoir that denote the Fort Reno site. Connecting Battery Reno extended northward from the reservoir to the

Camp Frieze, Tennallytown, D.C.—Camp of the 9th and 10th Rhode Island Volunteers, June 1862. *Spicer,* History of the Ninth and Tenth Regiments Rhode Island Volunteers and the Tenth Rhode Island Battery

vicinity of 39th and Garrison streets. On-street parking will permit pedestrian visitation of the highest point in District and Fort Reno area.

Visible Remains

None, as the fort was destroyed for construction of the reservoir, and the battery site is now residential. The park is maintained by the National Park Service. A generic Defenses of Washington and small Civil War Centennial plaque provide minimum interpretation.

Description

Having been styled Fort Pennsylvania by the constructing troops from that state, the U.S. government renamed the complex in honor of Major General Jesse L. Reno, who was killed at South Mountain, Maryland, on September 14, 1862.

Fort and Battery Reno rested on the highest point on the defense line (429 feet above sea level calculated from the top of the bombproof). The position had a perimeter of 517 yards. Together, the main fort and battery (connected by a covered or protected way for intercommunication) mounted twenty-seven guns and mortars. There were twenty-two additional vacant platforms for field guns. Among the ordnance at Fort Reno were two eight-inch siege howitzers (en embrasure), nine 24-pounder howitzers (en embrasure), one 100-pounder Parrott rifle (en barbette), four 30-pounder Parrott rifles (en embrasure), and two ten-inch and two 24-pounder Coehorn mortars. Battery Reno mounted an additional seven 20-pounder Parrott rifles (en embrasure).

Notes/Anecdotes

These fortifications commanded three major roads converging at the hamlet of Tennallytown before leading into the city via Georgetown. Thus, Fort and Battery Reno became the initial objective in Confederate general Jubal Early's approach to Washington in July 1864. The area also served as a major campground during the war, and Fort Reno's elevation provided an appropriate place for a major signal station.

The fortifications were built by Pennsylvania Reserve contingents on the land of Giles and Miles Dyer, whose farmhouse became headquarters for the facility.

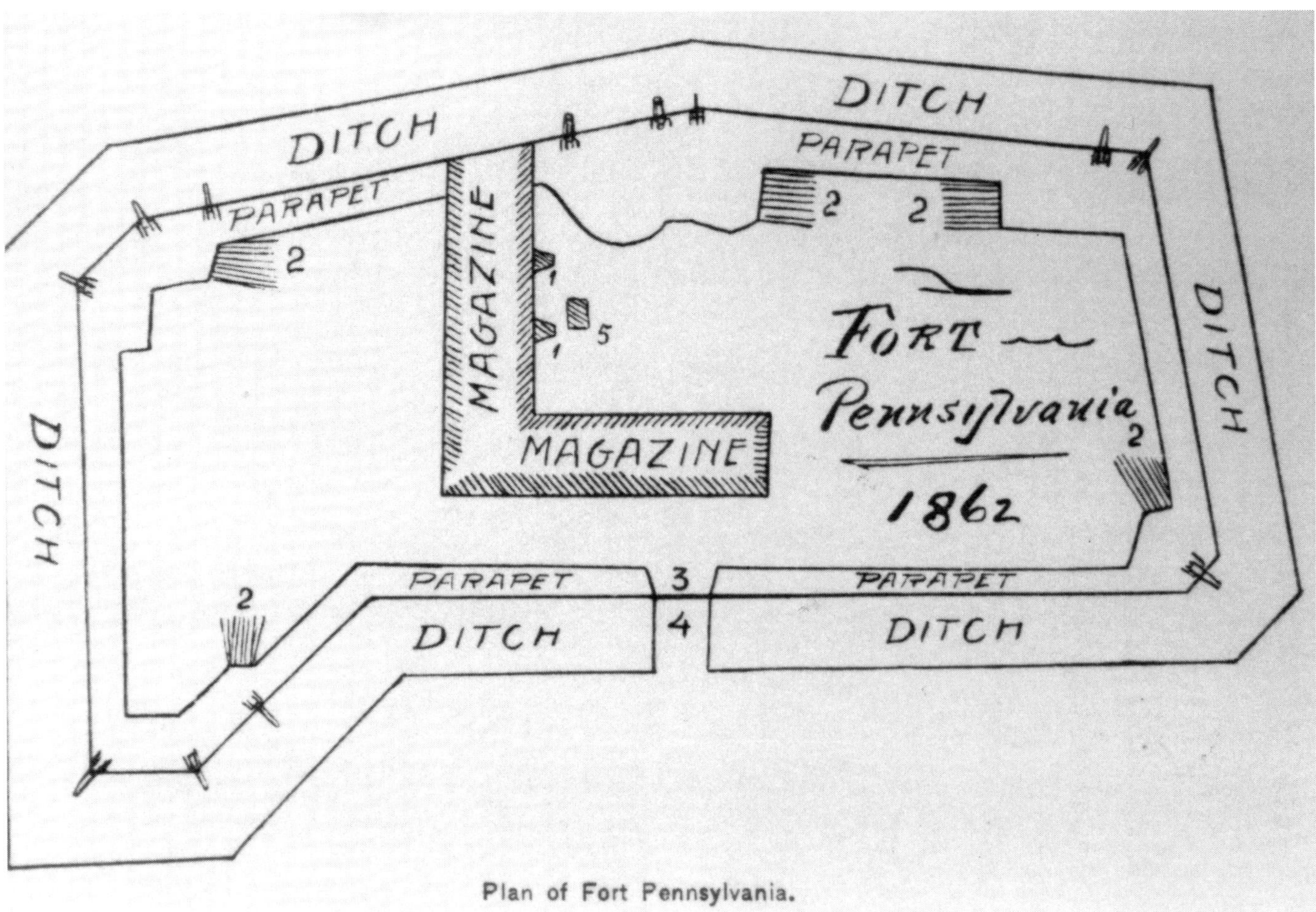

Plan of Fort Pennsylvania. *Spicer,* History of the Ninth and Tenth Regiments Rhode Island Volunteers and the Tenth Rhode Island Battery

The Dyers had purchased "this very desirable farmhouse and acreage" from Isaac Marshall (according to Tennallytown chronicler Judith Helm), who in turn had acquired it from Dr. John Weems. Apparently, the Weems graveyard was destroyed during construction, as was another neighboring house owned by a well-known southern sympathizer, claimed a Rhode Island regimental historian, who possessed some sort of light field howitzers that the Rhode Islanders confiscated on June 18, 1862, "the only rebel cannon taken by the Tenth Regiment Rhode Island Volunteers." The fortification took up some twenty acres of Dyer land with an additional fifty acres given over to barracks, camps, and a parade ground.

One famous visitor to Fort Pennsylvania was President Lincoln, who came to the camp and fort on at least three occasions. On September 10, 1861, he attended a presentation of colors by Keystone State governor Andrew Curtin, followed by a review of Brigadier General George McCall's division. He may also have ridden over from Fort Gaines with Mrs. Lincoln later in January during their visit to the 55th New York camp for a French dining experience. And Captain Oliver Wendell Holmes Jr.—the future Supreme Court justice—wrote home during the Antietam campaign that his 20th Massachusetts was at "TenAlleytown and ready to march in any direction we're wanted."

Writing on August 30, 1861, from Camp Tennally, 3d Pennsylvania Reserve soldier Adam S. Bray told his brother at home in syntax typical of soldier letters of the time, "We ar buzy in building a battery it is mate werry strong & goot to protect our soldiers it holts about too thousand mens it is mounted with three canons one of them wights 48 hundred pounds we expect more canons yet we cut down orchards with fine app and peach trees with fine peaches and also some large corn fields we have destroyed too houses that were in our way to build the battery."

On September 3, William Dunlop Dixon, a Pennsylvania merchant and farmer in the 35th Pennsylvania (6th Pennsylvania Reserves) and promoted to brevet brigadier general for gallantry later in the war, wrote his wife that "our earth Work is about finished[;] it looks fine . . . it is very strong and has in it 11 pieces of Cannon[;] there some of the pieces that looks right over our camps, it is considered one of the strongest

"Corps Badge" for Fatigue Details from 9th and 10th Rhode Island Regiments while Helping Construct Northern Forts in the Defenses of Washington—Pick, Spade, and Broom—Fashioned from Melted Lead Bullets by the Soldiers. *Spicer,* History of the Ninth and Tenth Regiments Rhode Island Volunteers and the Tenth Rhode Island Battery

works about Washington City." Health was improving in camp with the local farmers supplying ample corn meal and milk, which the soldiery turned into mush just about every night. His African American servant had gone home sick with a friend, fearing to venture on his own that he might be "taken up some where along the road" as an escaped slave.

Just a week before, Leo W. Fuller of Carlisle, Pennsylvania, had similarly noted the new fort's progress from his position with the 7th Pennsylvania Reserves. Fuller cited 600 men at work and suggested that "we can throw shell over to Arlington Heights from here." That, he added, should keep the Rebels outside the range "of our Bull Dogs or they might bite them."

Among the units associated with the fort at Tennallytown were the 93d, 98th, 102d, 113th, and 199th Pennsylvania with hardy and diligent Germans of the 98th establishing an officers' school to improve their proficiency before going into the field. Apparently, others were not so minded; in fact, a certain fractious nature could be found when one corporal of the 113th shot at his captain, missing but failing to escape when his foot struck against a stone. Falling, "before he could get up one of the guards pinned him through the hand to the ground, he will probably be shot," noted artilleryman Thomas A. Bayley in the fall of 1862.

Other units soon followed the Pennsylvanians into the camps at Tennallytown. The 55th, 59th, and 69th New York and 63d Indiana, 9th and 10th Rhode Island, and 10th Rhode Island batteries encamped at

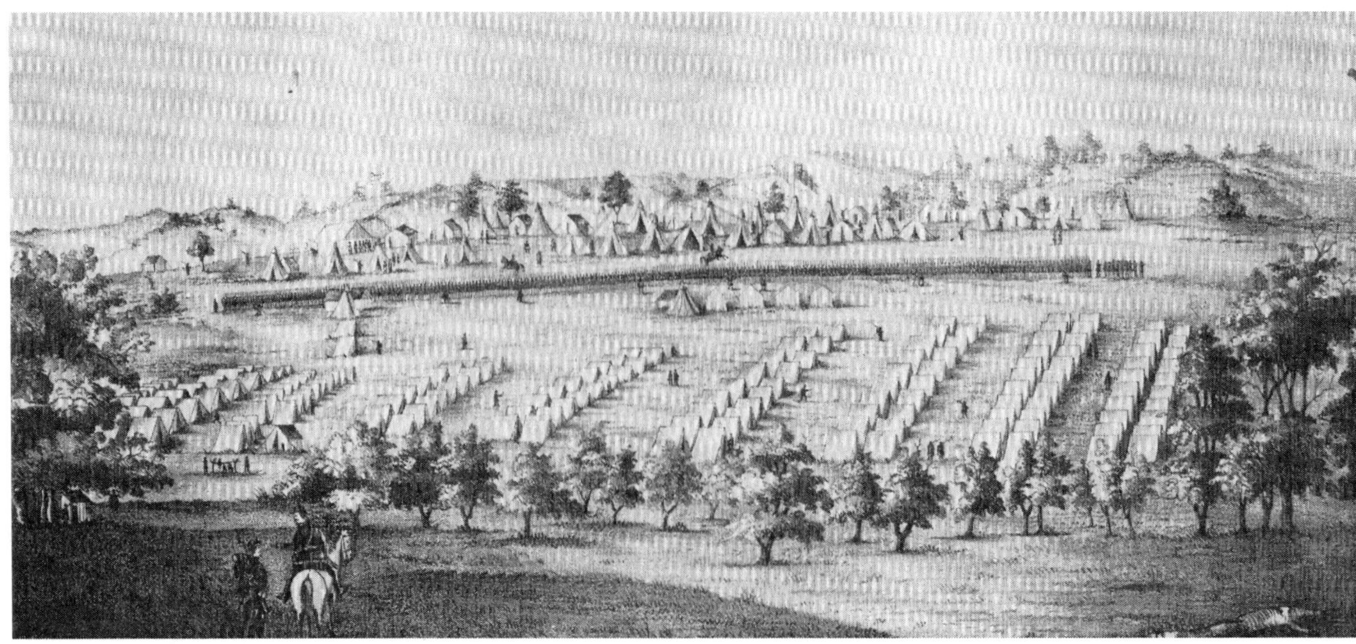

Camp Tennally. *National Archives*

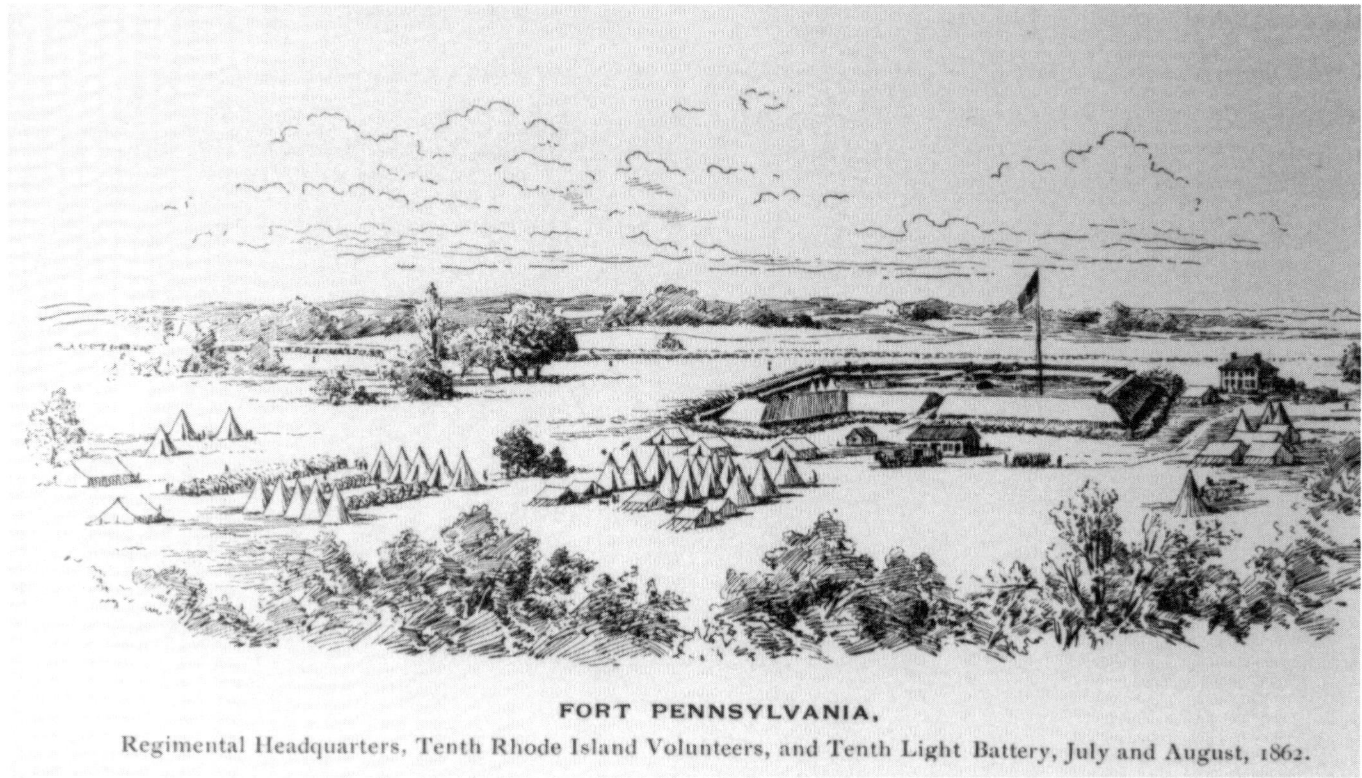

Fort Pennsylvania, Regimental Headquarters, 10th Rhode Island Volunteers and 10th Light Battery, July and August 1862. *Spicer*, History of the Ninth and Tenth Regiments Rhode Island Volunteers and the Tenth Rhode Island Battery

places they named "Camp Frieze." Ensconced in garrison, they joined comrades in periodic jaunts to bathe in the Potomac and to see the sights of Washington City. Rhode Island regimental historian William A. Spicer recounted the story of one officer returning for a visit with the men building Fort Pennsylvania: "They appeared glad to see me back again," he noted. "They say that between heavy artillery drill, garrisoning old forts, and building new ones, their time is pretty well used up."

Among units posted here were the following:

16th Battery, Indiana Light Artillery, August 25, 1862–February 1863
4th New York Heavy Artillery, Co. H, September–October 1862
9th Independent Battery of New York Light Artillery, March 1863
9th New York Heavy Artillery, Cos. A, D, F, G, October 1862–February 1863
11th New York Cavalry, Co. M, October–November 1863
3d Massachusetts Heavy Artillery, Co. H, September–November 1863
Co. E, November 17–30, 1864
Co. I, November 1864–April 1865
Co. L, February 28–April 1865
9th Independent Battery, New York Light Artillery, (Battery Reno) March–December 1863[7]
1st New Hampshire Heavy Artillery, Battery L (Battery Reno), November 1864
10th Rhode Island Infantry, Cos. B, K, L

The latest joke making the rounds of the camps, said Spicer's visiting officer, was "why are the boys of the Tenth in such good company now at the forts?" The answer: "because they are closely associated with so many big guns." Humor aside, this officer suggested that unexciting, hot summer duty had sapped the patriotism of the young soldiers. Some of them, he noted, had derisively fashioned a regimental badge from melted lead bullets. The device represented a pickax, spade, and broom, in combination, reflecting their construction duties.

Eventually the garrisons moved from tent camp into permanent wooden barracks located behind the fort. Yet this brought another set of problems, as the senior brigade surgeon told his superiors in March 1864. The sanitary conditions in the barracks were worse than in the tents, he cited. "Typhoid, pneumonia, and ensypihelas" appeared because "these barracks are altogether too small, they are badly built; improperly ventilated, imperfectly warmed, and apt to leak," claimed Dr. J. F. Pomfret. The records contain no evidence of a

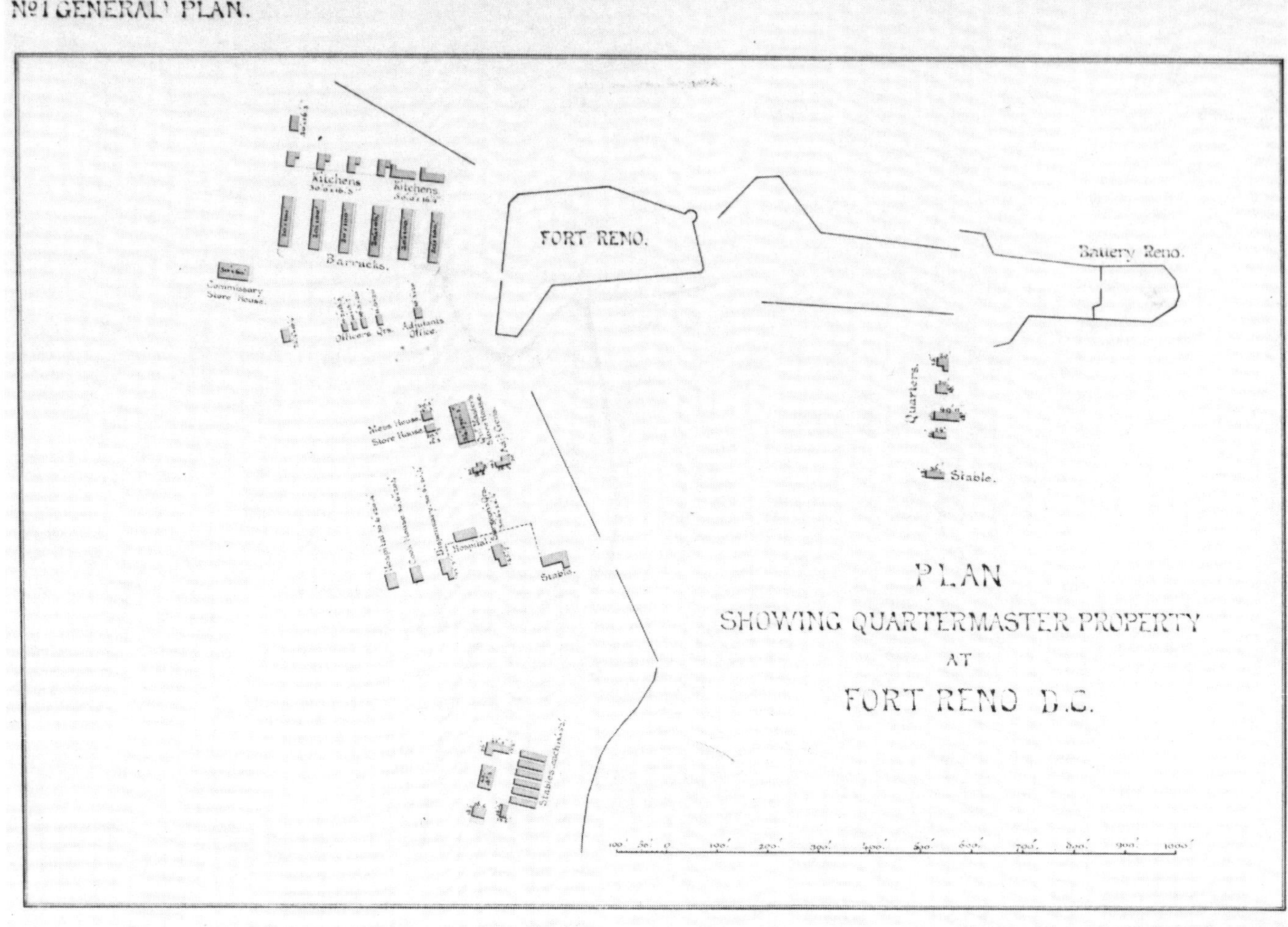

Plan of Quartermaster Property at Fort Reno. *National Archives*

solution. However, the vicinity around Tennallytown being salubrious to recuperation occasioned positioning of a number of army hospitals until some like the one at Tennallytown Methodist Church fell prey to expansion of rifle pits and breastworks.

Later, on July 11, 1864, Fort Reno served as the reconnaissance point for Brigadier General John McCausland's column from Jubal Early's army during the famous raid on the city. He reported the strength of Federal positions in this sector, and Early shifted his focus eastward ending before Fort Stevens on the Seventh Street road. Interestingly, Veteran Reserve Corps Private Alfred Bellard noted reaching Fort Reno and deploying as skirmishers at three feet between men so as to ascertain rebel strength. Had the enemy made an attack on the city that night, he observed, "nothing could have saved it, as there was no troops round the city but our brigade, and we were supposed to be unfit for active service."

Private George Perkins of the 6th New York Independent Battery, however, noted being rushed to the lines at this point from the Camp Berry artillery camp of instruction downtown to find Tennallytown to be a "pretty little village with one tavern" and white cottages "embowered with trees," the fort itself "thoroughly built" with "straw-colored barracks" and threatening black muzzles of its armament peeping just over the works and through the embrasures. To the right and left "in winding courses the rifle pits stretched," filled with infantry. To the rear, guards deterred those without passes from entering the "battle zone," one such civilian enjoining the One Hundred Days sentry to keep cool, there being no occasion for excitement. Certainly, there was "no end of confusion out here, and very little known of the enemy," wrote Colonel Charles Russell Lowell of the 2d Massachusetts Cavalry to his wife on July 11.

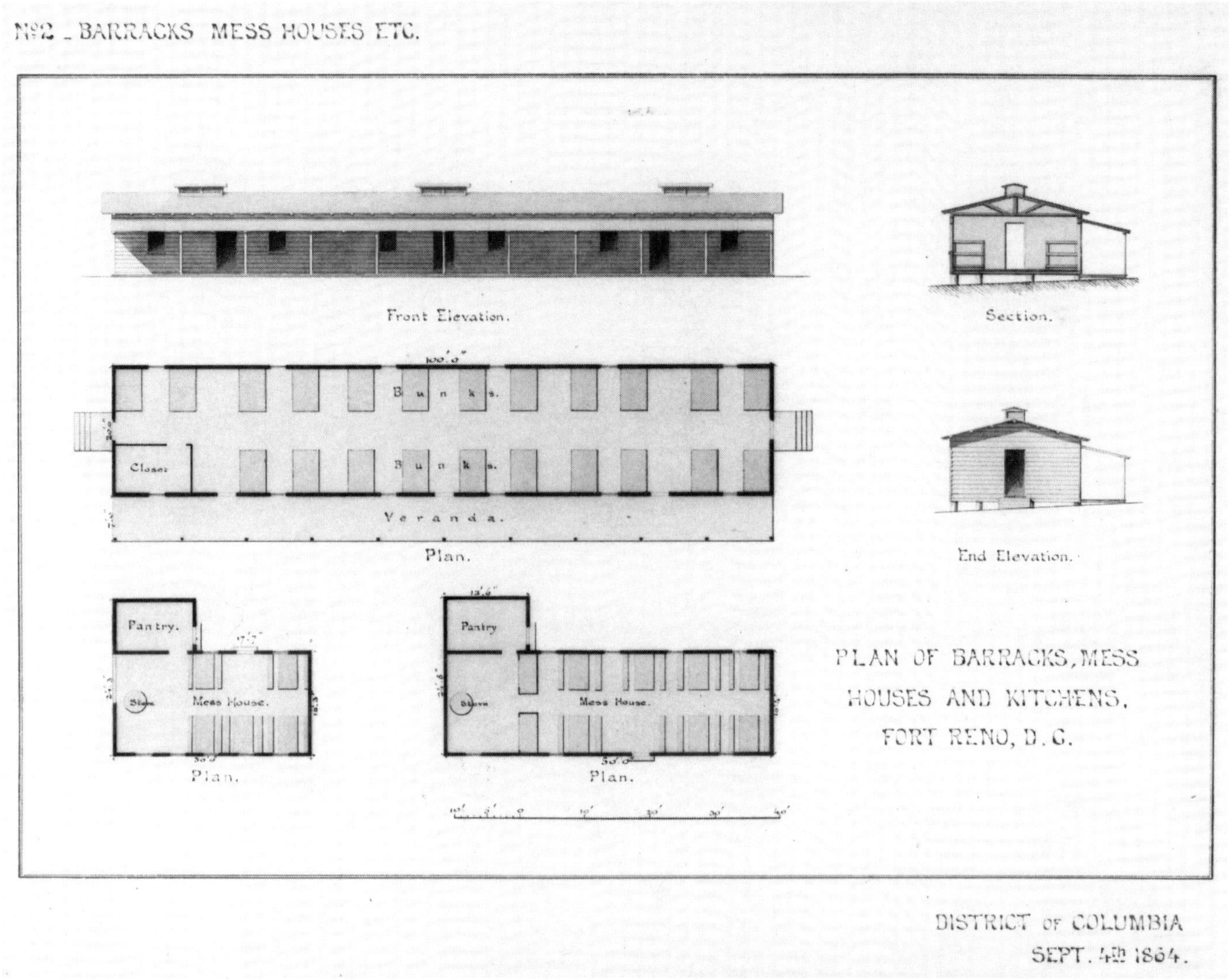
No2 _ BARRACKS MESS HOUSES ETC.
Front Elevation.
Section.
100' 0"
Bunks.
Closet
Bunks.
Veranda.
Plan.
End Elevation.
Pantry.
Stove
Mess House.
Plan.
Pantry
Stove
Mess House.
Plan.
PLAN OF BARRACKS, MESS
HOUSES AND KITCHENS,
FORT RENO, D. C.
DISTRICT OF COLUMBIA
SEPT. 4th 1864.

Plan of Barracks, Mess Houses, and Kitchens at Fort Reno. *National Archives*

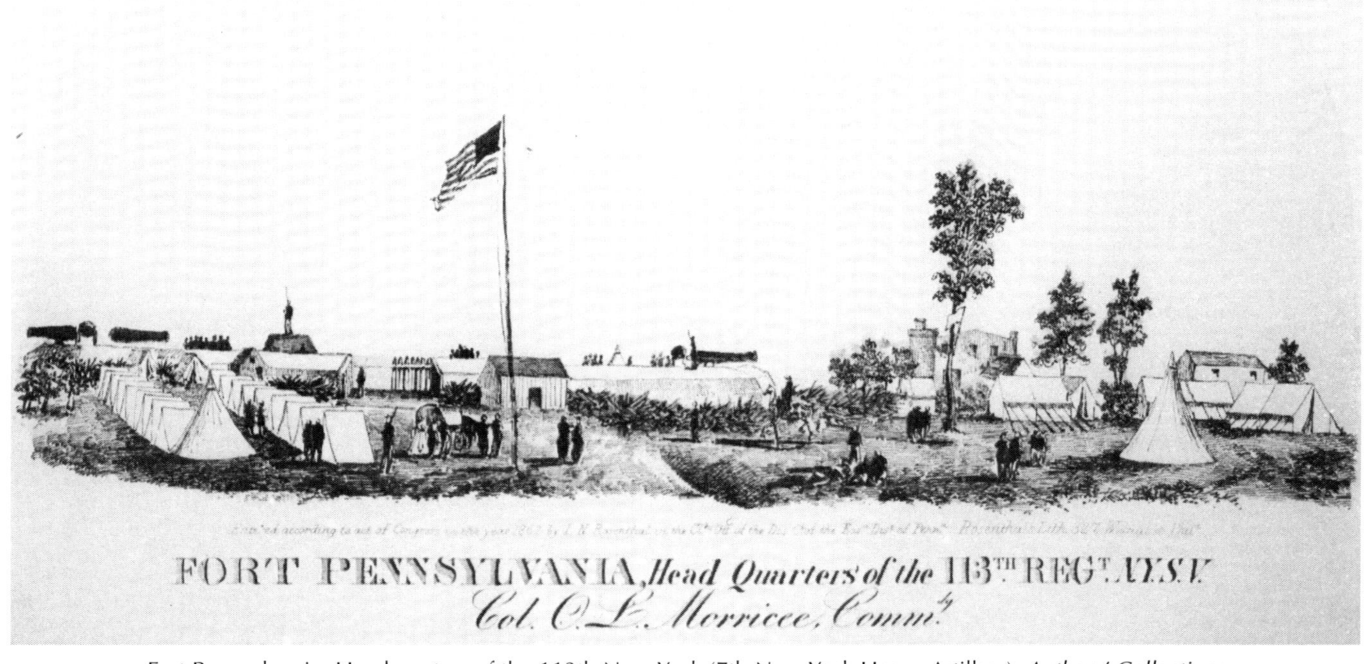

FORT PENNSYLVANIA, Head Quarters of the 113TH REGT. N.Y.S.V.
Col. L. O. Morris, Comm'd.

Fort Pennsylvania, Headquarters of the 113th New York (7th New York Heavy Artillery). *Authors' Collections*

Still, Lowell had it about right when he noted that it appeared at present more like a move "to mask heavier movements" than any "serious effort against this part of the fortifications." Fort Reno's signal station witnessed the dust rising from the marching Confederates and alerted garrisons to the east of this new threat. At that time, Colonel John C. Marble's command in this area comprised Companies C and G of his own 151st Ohio National Guard; Company A, 1st New Hampshire Heavy Artillery; Company L, 9th New York Heavy Artillery; Dayton's regiment of Giles's brigade, Veterans Reserve Corps; and Thompson's provisional regiment of the XIX Corps with the 6th New York Independent Battery illustrating reinforcement.

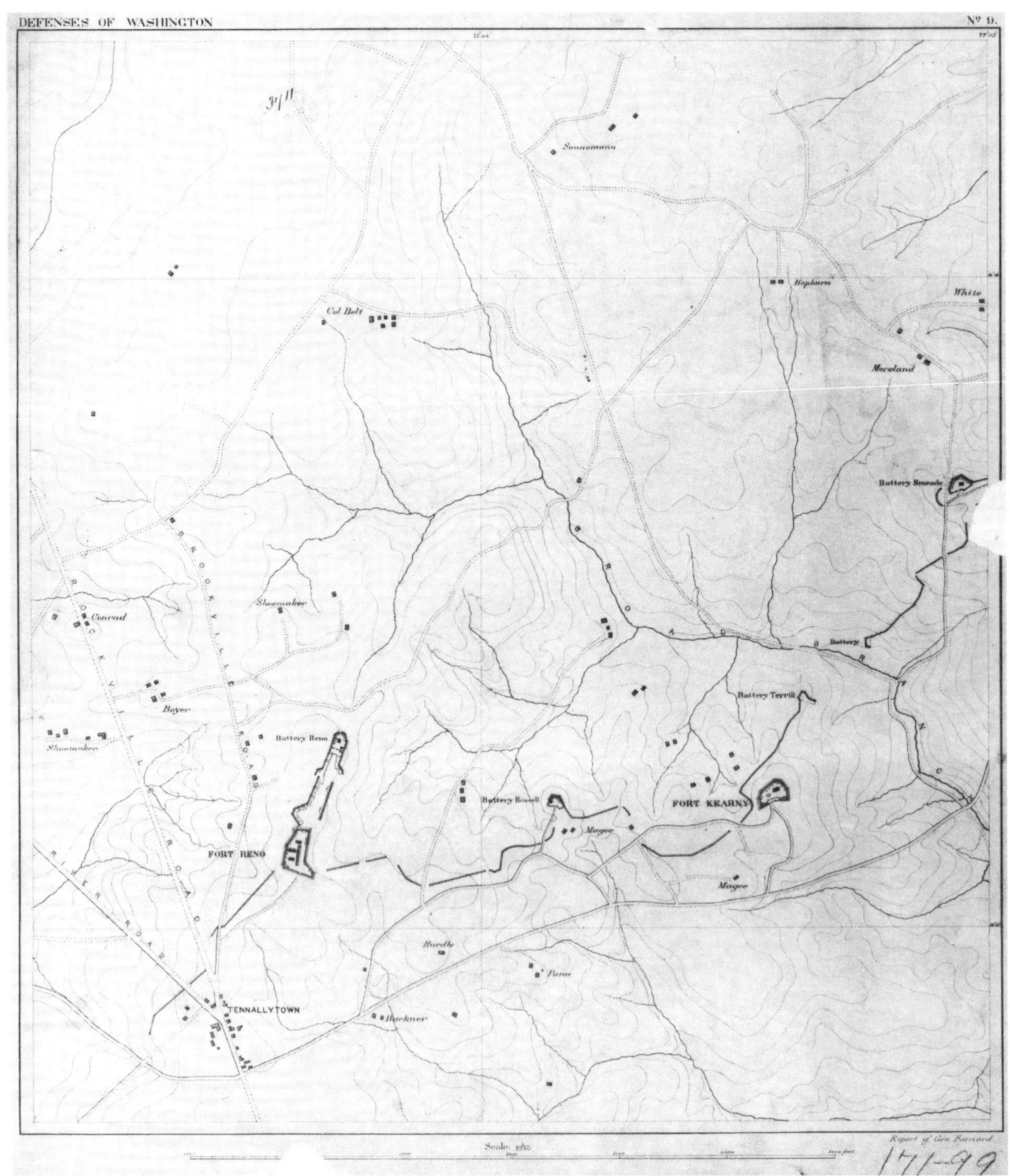

Sector Map—Fort Reno to Battery Smeade. *National Archives*

One postwar anecdote had Tennallytown citizens feeding captured rebels from Early's raid when their captors were less inclined to do so. After Early's raid, Major General Christopher C. Augur, commanding the Department of Washington/XXII Corps, recommended adding four additional field guns to complete Fort Reno's armament. He further noted that "in case of attack two or three light batteries should at once be sent to this important post, taking position at first on the ridge between Tennallytown and Fort Gaines."

As of September 1864, the Fort and Battery Reno complex could be construed as a stronghold, the largest and strongest fort on the northern lines. Three thousand men, a tent city stretching across the ridgeline to Fort Bayard, and the complex of infrastructure supporting this facility were imposing. Six barracks, seven kitchens, a commissary storehouse, four officers' quarters, and an adjutant's office lie on the west side of the fort toward Brookville (or Belt) Road. Next to the east, in the center stood a mess hall, a storehouse, quartermaster's storehouse, an adjutant general's office, two hospitals, a cookhouse, a dispensary, surgeon's quarters, and a stable. On the east side of the fort were six stables and four additional buildings. All this was exclusive of ammunition magazines and the internal infrastructure of the fortifications themselves.

Moreover, Fort Reno, like other federal installations during the war, served as a magnet for Freedmen from the neighborhood who, at the end of the war, built shanties and squatted on the land until able to acquire properties legally. They had loyally served the occupation army, and, while the land reverted to prewar ownership, they steadfastly remained tied to the land, thus forming the basis for postwar urbanization of the area. Even nominally southern-sympathizing residents of Tennallytown often bonded with the soldiery retaining contacts and the memory of their transitory presence. The works at Fort Reno remained in service until January 1866 and could still be viewed by returning veterans until the end of the century when the whole site was leveled for a city reservoir.[8]

THE WORKS OF BROAD BRANCH

Battery Rossell, Fort Kearny, Battery Terrill, "Battery to Right of Broad Branch," and Battery Smeade

Location

From the Fort Reno site, continue on Chesapeake Street NW to Nebraska Avenue (traffic light). Turn left on Nebraska Avenue and continue through three traffic lights to Fessenden Street NW. Turn right on Fessenden Street, crossing Connecticut Avenue (Battery Rossell lies approximately on high ground to the right [south] at this intersection). Continue on Fessenden Street to Linnean Avenue, turn right on Ellicott Street, and take a short left on 30th Place (the approximate site of Fort Kearny was in the 4900 block); continue straight on 30th Place to Garrison Street. Behind the locked gateway to the Peruvian embassy (stone pillars at entrance marked "Battery Terrill" and "3001 Garrison") lie the battery and rifle pits of Battery Terrill. Phone the embassy to ascertain entry since this is private property. From the Battery Terrill site, continue north on Garrison Street NW merging right onto Linnean Avenue to Broad Branch Road. Turn left on Nebraska Avenue (traffic light), right on Military Road (traffic light), and right again on Military Road. Follow Military Road east to 29th Street. Turn right and proceed to the vicinity of 5301–5303 29th Street/Jenifer Street. Earthworks that made up "Battery to Right of Broad Branch" are visible in the park on right. From the "Battery to Right of Broad Branch" site, continue around to 28th Street and follow it back to Military Road. Turn right on Military Road and then left on Utah Avenue (traffic light) at the top of the hill. Turn left on Utah Avenue past St. John's College High School on right. Battery Smeade lay on present site of a running track to the rear of the high school gymnasium on the right.

Visible Remains

Battery Terrill and rifle pits are viewable but lack an interpretive marker—likewise for "Battery to the Right of Broad Branch." No marker for Battery Smeade.

Description

Battery Rossell was named for Major Nathan B. Rossell, 3d U.S. Infantry, who was killed at Gaines Mill, Virginia, on June 27, 1862.

Fort Kearny was named for Major General Philip Kearny, who was killed at Chantilly, Virginia, on September 1, 1862.

Battery Terrill was named for Brigadier General William R. Terrill, who was killed at Perryville, Kentucky, on October 8, 1862.

Battery Smeade was named for Captain John R. Smeade, 5th U.S. Artillery, who was killed August 30, 1862, at the Second Battle of Bull Run (Manassas), Virginia.

Battery Rossell (eight vacant platforms), Battery Terrill (seven vacant platforms), and "Battery to Right of Broad Branch" (three vacant platforms) were all unarmed auxiliary batteries. Apparently, at some point, Battery Rossell, occupying an important position on the right (east) of Fort Reno, became an enclosed work with a magazine.

In contrast, Barnard described Fort Kearny's 320-yard perimeter as "a large lunette with stockaded gorge," mounting ten guns with one vacant platform, including one eight-inch siege howitzer (en embrasure), three 32-pounder seacoast guns (en barbette), three 24-pounder siege guns (en embrasure), and three four-and-a-half-inch rifles (en embrasure).

Battery Smeade was also a lunette with stockaded gorge and had a perimeter of 177 yards, mounting four 20-pounder Parrott rifles (en embrasure) and four vacant platforms.

Running eastward from the Fort Reno complex was a line of rifle pits, broken at intervals by unarmed gun batteries for field guns and Fort Kearny. They commanded the countryside to the front and particularly the valley of Broad Branch, through which ran a road bisecting the defense line.

Notes/Anecdotes

Troops garrisoning Fort Kearny at various times included the following:

9th New York Heavy Artillery, Cos. A. B, C, E, G, H, I, September–October 1862
17th Connecticut Volunteers, Cos. A–K, October 17–November 3, 1862
1st New Hampshire Heavy Artillery, Co. K, November 1864–April 1865
1st New Hampshire Heavy Artillery, Co. L (part), November 20–24, 1864

Regimental historian and chaplain Alanson A. Haines of the 15th New Jersey Infantry recalled twenty years after the war that his unit was among those ordered to construct these works during the "scare" caused by Lee's autumn 1862 campaign. They also engaged in slashing timber, working new military roads (Military Road NW, which continues to serve as a major public artery in the vicinity), and building entrenchments. "Long and wearisome seemed these days," he commented, even though "we enjoy luxuries of which we were soon to be altogether deprived" when sent to the front. He enumerated living in both wall and Sibley tents, full issues of new clothing and ample rations, as well as communications with home from whom the men "received many boxes of delicacies by express."

Apparently, a religious fervor swept across the New Jersey men with open-air prayer meetings every night, organization of a regimental church, and new converts joining the congregation regularly. One blemish came from a whiskey-peddling sutler in the vicinity, but the regimental commander captured the offenders and stifled the sutler by forcing him to sit atop a vinegar barrel and subsist on bread and water for a time.

Haines also noted that a force of 200 freed slaves or contraband arrived, "and we willingly turned over to them our picks and shovels," with the 15th New Jersey departing for the Army of the Potomac at the end of September.

During Early's raid in July 1864, detachments of the 151st and 163d Ohio National Guard garrisoned these works as skirmishing took place all across their front. Afterward, Major General Christopher C. Augur, commanding the Department of Washington/XXII Corps, recognized the importance of Battery Rossell, recommending arming the position with two field howitzers of either 24- or 32-pounder caliber and four 12-pounder field guns. He similarly thought that four light field guns should be permanently placed in Battery Terrill. Moreover, there should be four field pieces added to Battery Smeade with two of them allocated to the "Battery to the Right of Broad Branch." In September 1864, Company I of the 1st New Hampshire Heavy Artillery manned Battery Smeade.[9]

DEFENDERS OF THE ROCK CREEK VALLEY

Fort DeRussy, Battery Kingsbury, "Battery to Left of Rock Creek," and Battery Sill

Location

From Battery Smeade, return to Military Road (traffic light). Turn left and drive one block to Oregon Avenue NW (traffic light). Turn left and park. A National Park Service generic Defenses of Washington sign stands at the trail entrance leading straight up the hill to Fort De Russy. To reach the Battery Kingsbury site, continue on this unpaved trail to the end of the high ground. To reach "Battery to Left of Rock Creek," return to Military Road (traffic light), turn left at the next exit to Beach Drive, take a sharp immediate right at Ross Drive to the head of the "S" curve (enclosing battery), and park. To reach Battery Sill, cross Rock Creek and park on right across from the park police station and proceed up the hillside through the woods across Morrow Drive to the site lying roughly between Morrow Drive and Joyce Road in the park to Manchester Terrace and Manchester Street NW off of 16th Street.

Visible Remains

There are well-preserved (unrestored) earthworks and a Civil War Centennial plaque at Fort DeRussy and earthworks of "Battery to left of Rock Creek." Few tracings exist at Batteries Kingsbury and Sill, and no interpretive markers exist at any of the battery sites—all under National Park Service management.

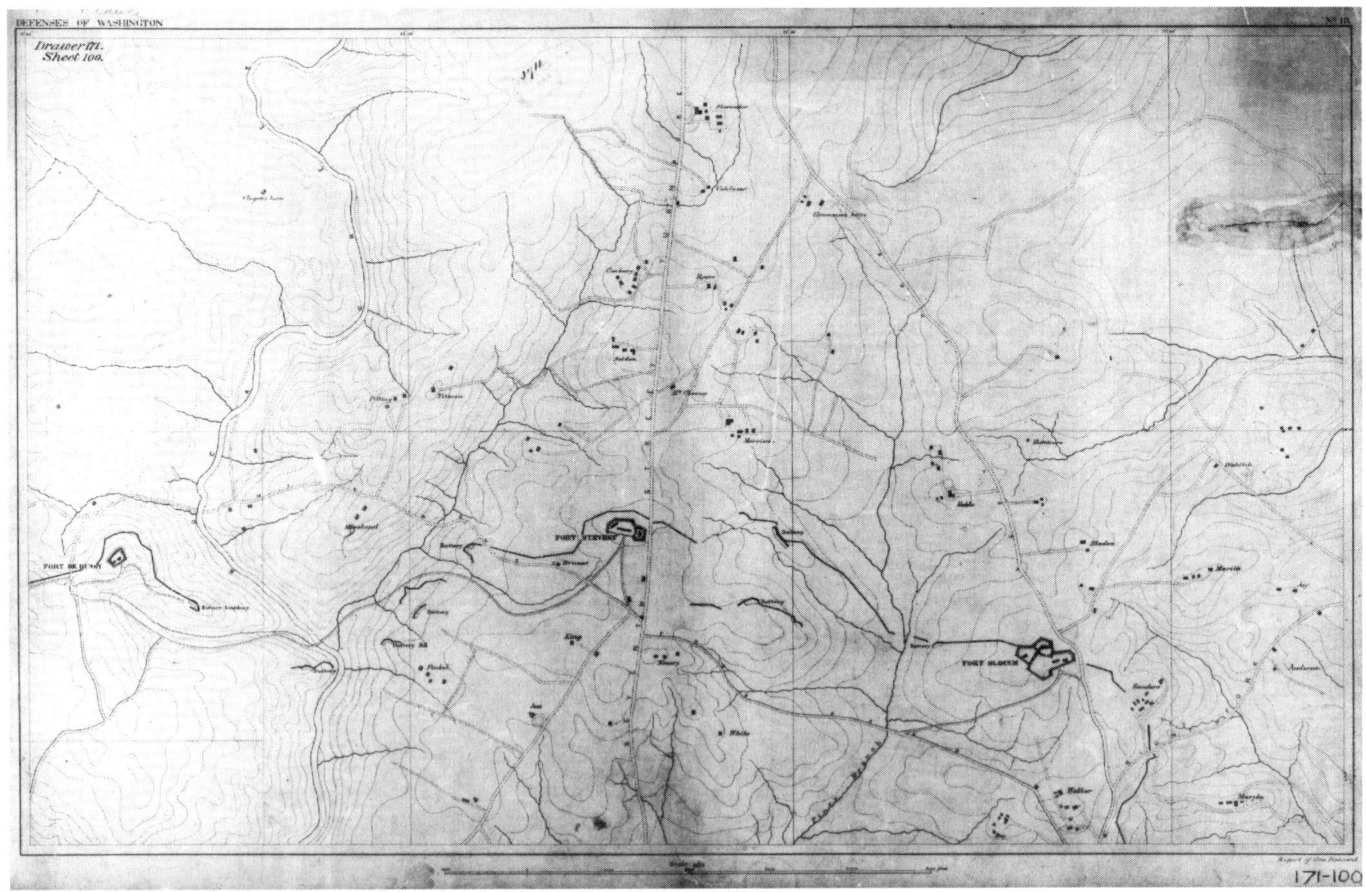

Sector Map—Fort DeRussy to Fort Slocum. *National Archives*

Description

There is some confusion as to whether Fort DeRussy was named for Colonel Gustavus A. DeRussy, whose 4th New York Heavy Artillery provided construction details to build this work as well as others in the system, or for his father, the renowned engineer officer, Brigadier General René Edward DeRussy, superintendent of West Point from 1838 to 1845 and constructor of numerous antebellum coastal fortifications.

Battery Kingsbury honored 1st Lieutenant Henry Kingsbury, 5th U.S. Artillery, who was mortally wounded at Antietam, on September 17, 1862.

Battery Sill was named for Brigadier General Joshua H. Sill, who was killed at Stones River, Tennessee, on December 31, 1862.

Battery Smeade and Fort De Russy, in particular, commanded the Milkhouse Ford Road and crossing over Rock Creek. Fort De Russy was a trapezoidal work with a perimeter of 190 yards with a well-defined line of rifle pits still visible in front. The fort's armament was composed of three 32-pounder seacoast guns (en barbette), one 100-pounder Parrott (en barbette), five 30-pounder Parrott rifles (en embrasure), one ten-inch and one 24-pounder Coehorn mortar, and two vacant platforms. The unarmed field batteries of Kingsbury (nine platforms), "Battery to left of Rack Creek" (six platforms), and Sill (nine platforms) as well as several additional unoccupied batteries and rifle pits could deliver an arc of fire on any enemy attempting to breach the abatis-filled Rock Creek valley.

Notes/Anecdotes

Fort DeRussy was constructed on the farm of Bernard S. Swart, a clerk in the city, and early in the war bore the title Camp Holt. It was an attraction for sightseers because of the picturesque Rock Creek valley. John Collins submitted proposals to the army in 1861 for cutting abatis, timber, and lumber for the posts in this sector.

In addition to the 4th New York Heavy Artillery (with Companies F and G specifically garrisoning from June to September 1862), other units stationed here included companies of the following:

76th, 113th, and 117th New York Infantries
7th New York Heavy Artillery
1st Maine Heavy Artillery

Soldier Sketch of Fort DeRussy from the West. *Spicer,* History of the Ninth and Tenth Regiments Rhode Island Volunteers and the Tenth Rhode Island Battery

10th Rhode Island Infantry, Co. D
1st New Hampshire Heavy Artillery, Co. C, January–April 1865

Units stationed in the works at the time of Early's raid included Captain John Norris's Provisional Pennsylvania Heavy Artillery; Spears' Company A, 1st Wisconsin Heavy Artillery; Howe's Company L, 9th New York Heavy Artillery; and detachments of the 163d Ohio National Guard. A division of the VI Corps bivouacked behind the fort during of the Battle of Fort Stevens, and Confederates were said to have erected protective breastworks in front of Fort DeRussy during the two-day battle during Early's raid in July 1864.

Conditions at the fort varied throughout the war. The 10th Rhode Island remembered having as tenants there, "a thousand ants" in addition to flies, bugs, and lizards, largely because of the deforestation of the area. Some fifty-six acres were denuded to make way for the earthworks. Much of the wood went into construction of quarters and other outbuildings as well as basic earthwork mounding and materials for revetments, and abatis.

Within the eighty-six-acre complex at Fort DeRussy could be found two barracks (lumber, measuring twenty by 100 feet), two mess hails (lumber, twenty by fifty-two feet), five officers' quarters (log), two stables (log), an ordnance sergeant's quarters (lumber), and a guardhouse (log, twelve by eighteen feet). The garrison was well supplied by a spring at the foot of the hill to the rear of the fort. A mixed force of military and hired civilians completed construction and maintained the works.

Fort DeRussy's ordnance was supplemented in the spring of 1863 by shipment of a 100-pounder, center-pintle Parrott rifle from the Washington Arsenal. This heavy piece proved difficult to operate, although it provided useful long-range fire against Early's troop movements and supply trains in the action at Fort Stevens on July 11–12, 1864. In fact, this event marked the high point in the fort's service. Captain F. D. Mather's inspection report of the previous April had noted numerous deficiencies, such as rusty ordnance, disrepair to counterscarp, ditches, and eroded revetments. Yet this fort's guns rendered singular service in the battle with the 100-pounder Parrott rifle alone delivering some thirty-two shells on distant enemy forces at a range of 4,200 to 4,500 yards The smaller guns of the fort likewise kept Early's men at bay beyond Rock Creek and aided the artillery and infantry around Fort Stevens by containing enemy skirmish

Raising the Flag at Fort De Russy.

Soldier Sketch of Raising the Flag at Fort DeRussy. *Spicer,* History of the Ninth and Tenth Regiments Rhode Island Volunteers and the Tenth Rhode Island Battery

lines and preventing a headlong Confederate assault on the defense line.

Major General Christopher Augur, commanding the Department of Washington, recommended after Early's raid that six light field guns be added to Fort DeRussy, "to be placed in Battery Kingsbury, and in a battery now under construction, overlooking the bridge on Rock Creek."

Fort DeRussy was designed for an effective garrison of eleven officers and 233 enlisted men. Ample ammunition supply was considered to be 1,297 prepared "cartridges" for the large artillery, 960 pounds of case shot, 112 grapeshot, 190 canister shells, 1,011 hand grenades, plus 17,842 ball cartridges for the small arms. Such was the state of the fort's readiness in March 1864.

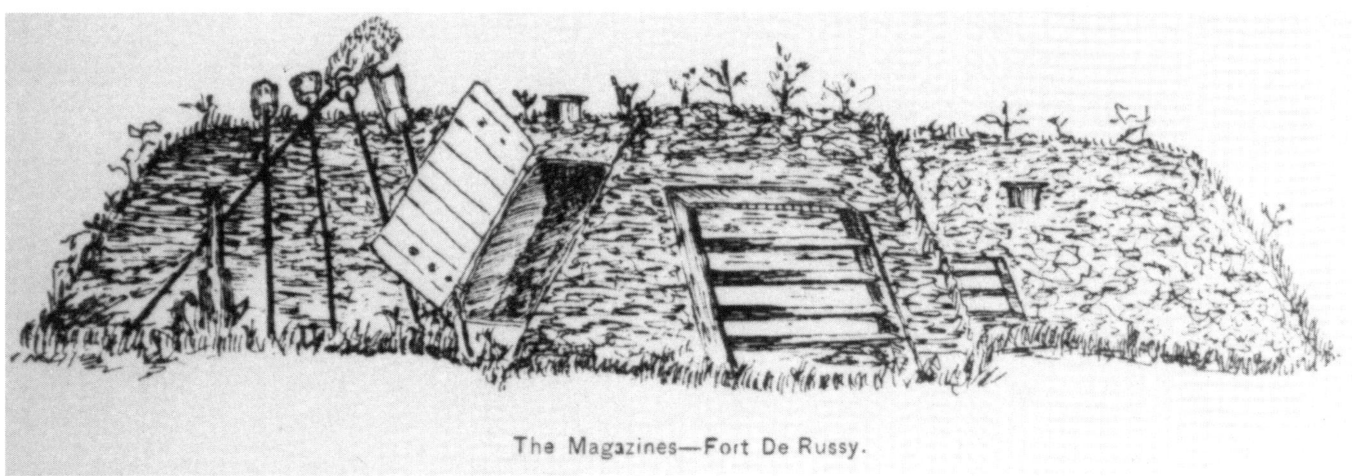

The Magazines—Fort De Russy.

Soldier Sketch of the Magazine at Fort DeRussy. *Spicer,* History of the Ninth and Tenth Regiments Rhode Island Volunteers and the Tenth Rhode Island Battery

Soldier Sketch of Guardhouse at Fort DeRussy. *Spicer,* History of the Ninth and Tenth Regiments Rhode Island Volunteers and the Tenth Rhode Island Battery

Plan for Quartermaster Property at Fort DeRussy. *National Archives*

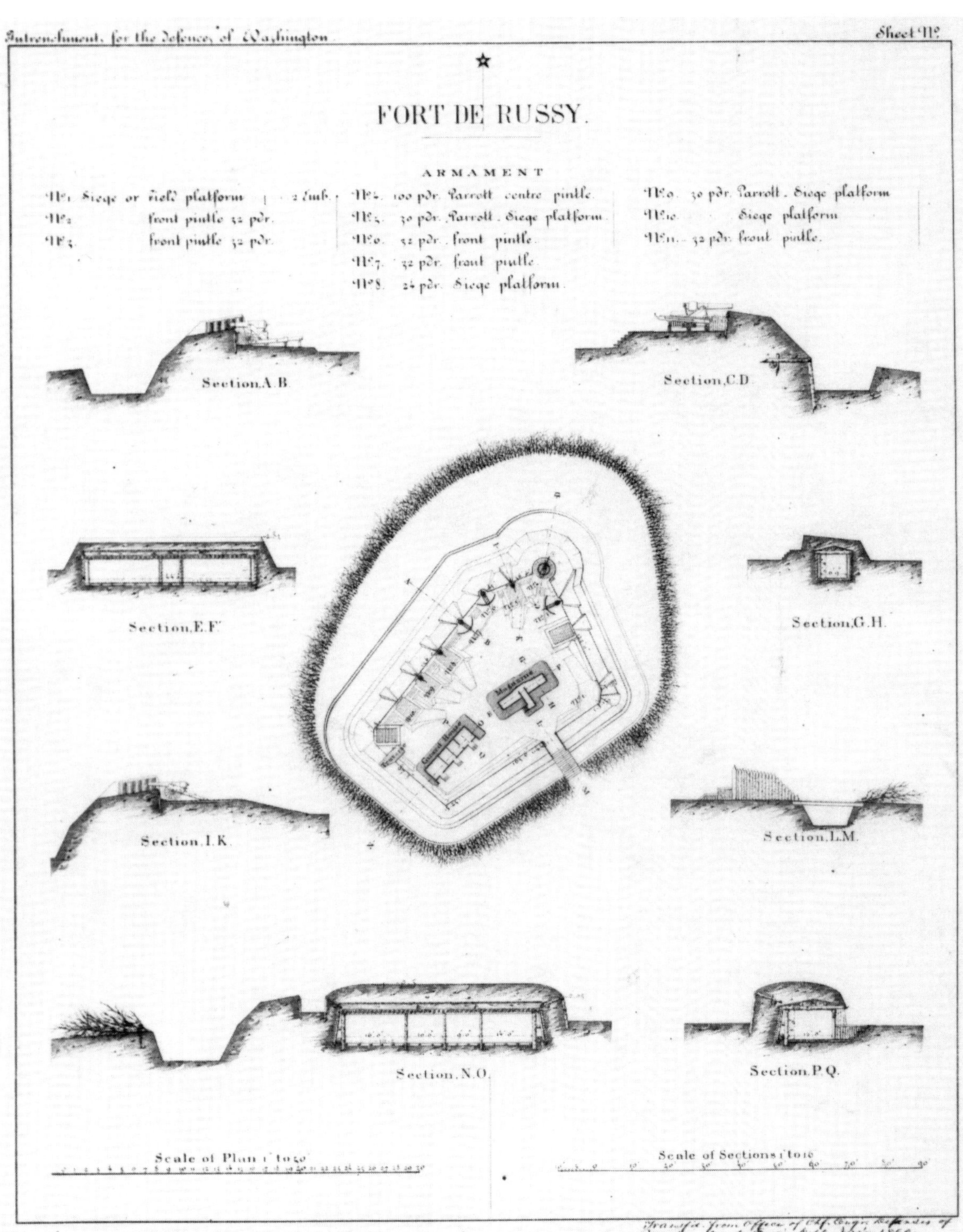

Fort DeRussy—Engineer Drawing. *National Archives*

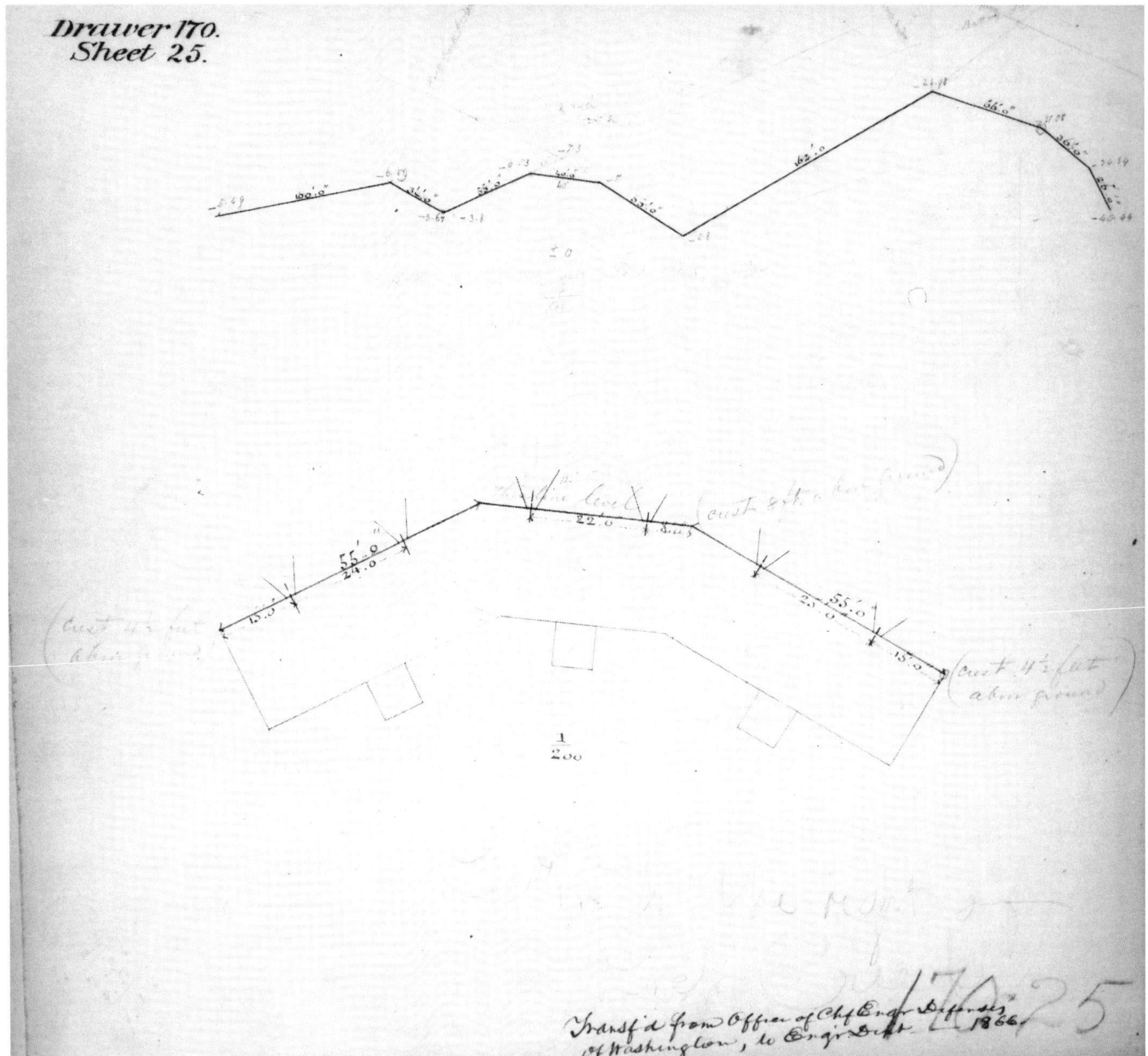

Battery to the Left of Rock Creek—Engineering Drawing. *National Archives*

Aside from the crisis of Early's raid, duty at this work proved quiet and pleasant for the garrisons. The Rhode Island contingents, posted there on July 4, 1862, marked the national holiday with typical patriotic celebrations. Later, similar garrisons were entertained by African American men and women musicians from nearby labor camps. The troops occasionally enjoyed visits from such notables as Major General Ambrose E. Burnside's wife and other ladies, the mail brought delicacies from loved ones, and "passes" could be obtained to visit Washington City and Georgetown. Access to nearby Rock Creek provided opportunities for bathing parties when the stream was not otherwise polluted by human and animal wastes from camp. Major Robert R. Honeyman of the 31st New Jersey noted the following interesting passage in his war journal:

> In The Woods Near Ft. DeRussey, Oct. 10th, 1862. — . . . The 31st is engaged upon a very important military road, which connects the chain of Forts in this part of the District. We turn out 600 men eight hours per day, Lt. Col. [William] Holt and I taking turns in superintending. The superintendence is a mere matter of form,

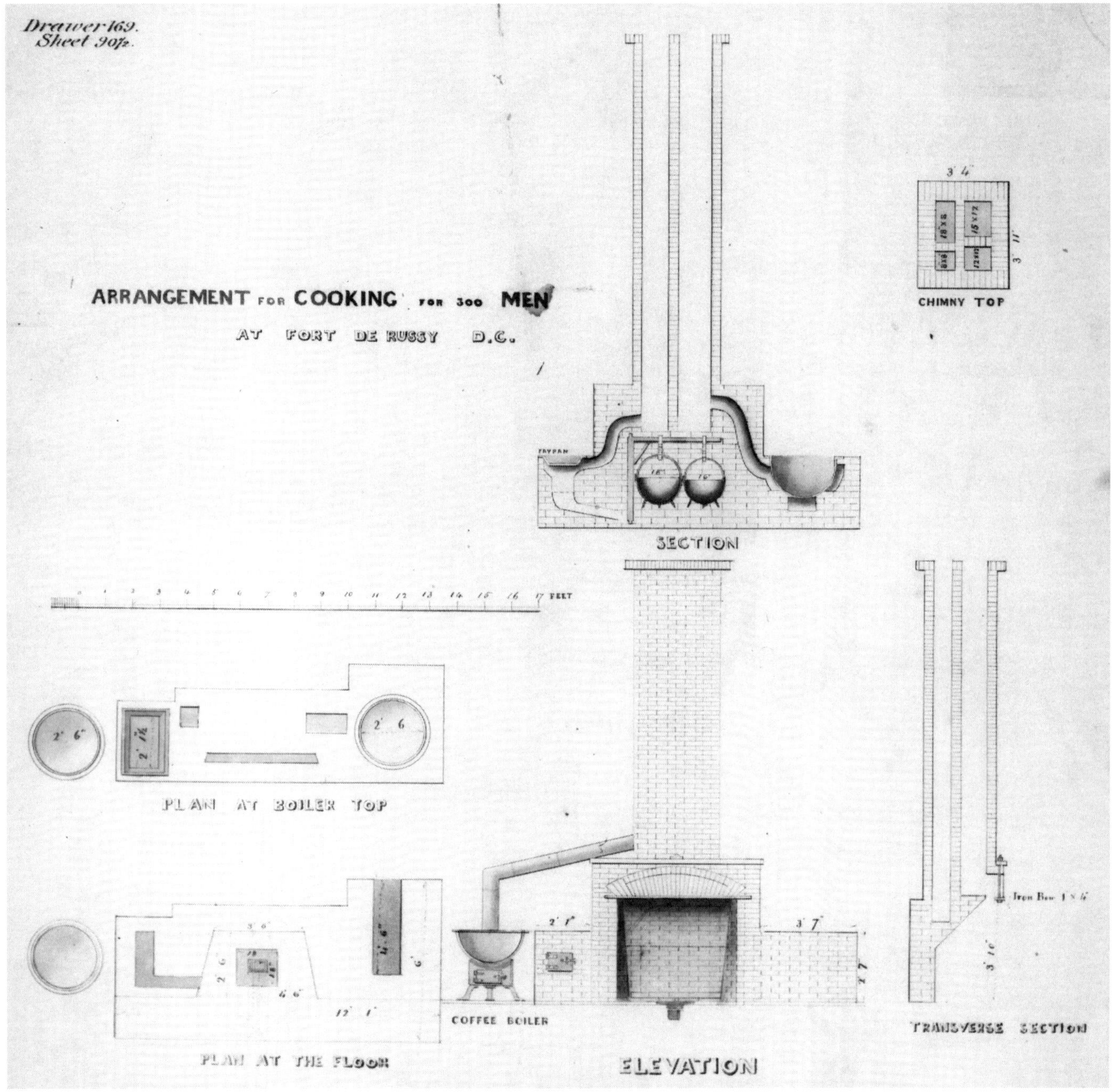

Cooking Arrangement for 300 Men at Fort DeRussy. *National Archives*

the work being conducted and planned by an engineer. The scene before me is enchanting. This is the wildest and most romantic country you were ever in. The road we are making is a splendid affair, going through ravines and fastnesses, and where you would think it impossible a road could be built, so as to be concealed from the observations of the enemy. 600 men at work felling trees, building bridges and digging into the mellow earth presents an animated scene. I am located at a bend of the road upon a high bank overlooking the men, and writing upon my knees. The woods are full of game, and the streams stocked with fish.

Honeyman further noted "exploring" down nearby Rock Creek with the regimental adjutant and a sergeant reaching the famous "Crystal Spring" to the east, "a resort for the festive" but "closed by order of the Prevost Marshal, and, as might be expected, we found the proprietor to be a Secessionist," so the trio promptly liberated a body of wine and reported back to camp about the "champaign country" they had encountered.

Fort DeRussy reverted to civilian ownership at the end of the war. A public sale on October 14, 1865, disposed of barracks, stables, tools, timber, brick, nails, hinges, roofing material, and other commodities from local engineer camps nearby. Eventual incorporation of this section of the Defenses into Rock Creek Park ensured some measure of preservation as the city itself expanded into the vicinity.[10]

Fort Stevens, "The Battle," and Battleground National Cemetery

Location

From the park police station on Beach Drive, turn around, following Morrow Drive out of the park; Morrow Drive becomes Kennedy Street NW. Continue on Kennedy Street east to 13th Street (traffic light). Turn left on 13th Street to Fort Stevens in the park at 13th and Quakenbos streets. On-street parking and pedestrian visitation are available at the restored fort. Auxiliary batteries existed at approximately Rock Creek Ford Road between 14th and 16th streets, Quakenbos and 7th streets, and in the block bounded by Peabody, Oglethorpe, 7th, and 8th streets NW. Rifle pits to the west of Fort Stevens ran approximately through the modern parkland between 13th Street/Piney Branch Road and Military Road.

Visible Remains

A portion of the parapet and one magazine of Fort Stevens were restored by the Civilian Conservation Corps in the late 1930s. A generic Defenses of Washington sign, a wayside sign, and two interpretive bar relief markers can be found at the fort. Battleground National Cemetery on Georgia Avenue contains unit monuments and grave sites but no interpretive markers—all administered by National Park Service. The District of Columbia Office of Cultural Tourism and the Brightwood Neighborhood Association have de-

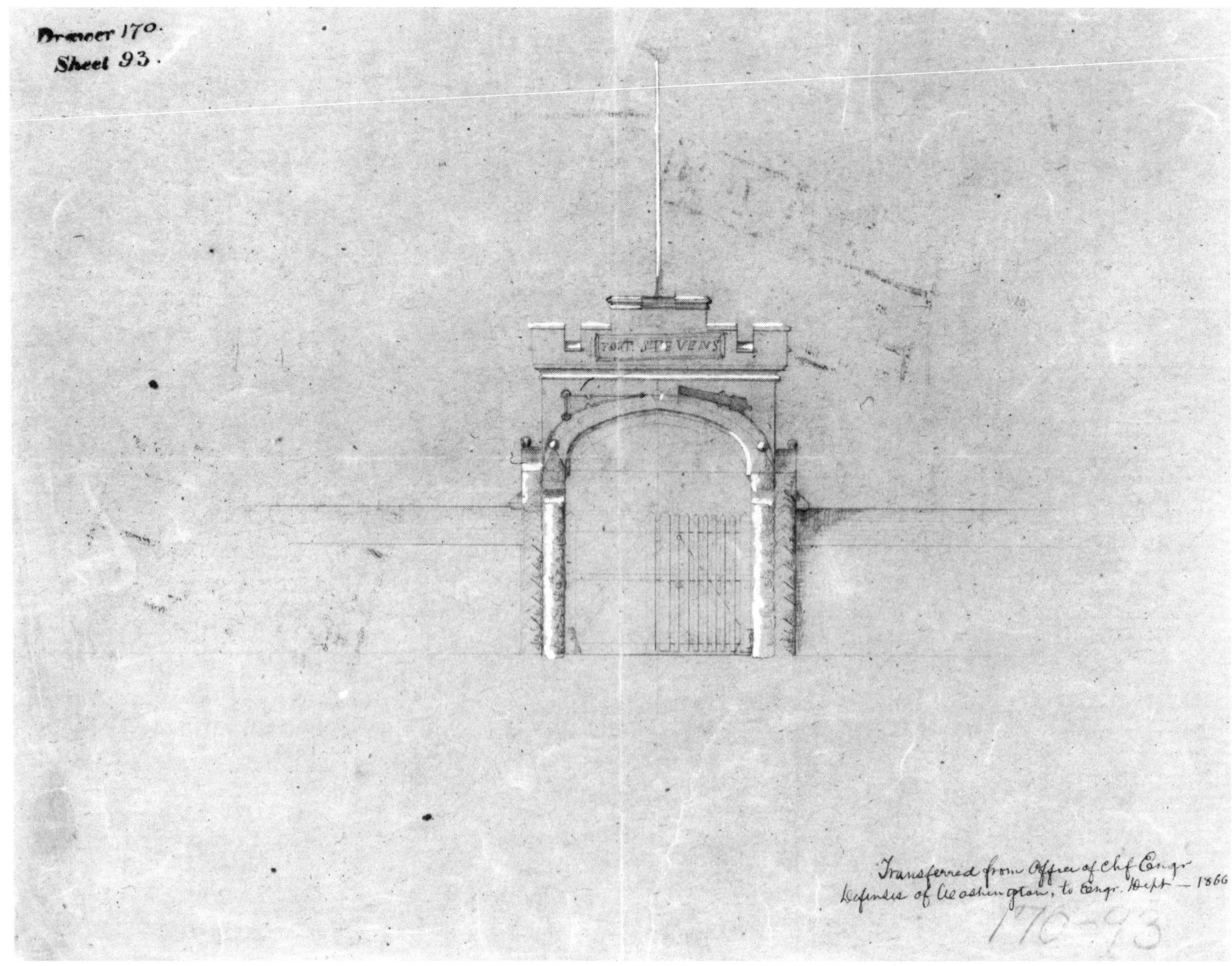

Gate to Fort Stevens—Engineer Drawing. *National Archives*

veloped a walking trail of the area with interpretive signs relevant to the fort, the battle, and local history.

Description

The main battlefield of Fort Stevens encompassed an area roughly bounded by Walter Reed Army Medical Center (north), eastward beyond Piney Branch Road, Oregon Avenue beyond Rock Creek Park on the west, and south to Military Road/Missouri Avenue (behind Union lines). Skirmishing took place across the northern lines from west and north of Tennallytown to Rockville and east to the rail and turnpike to Baltimore at Fort Lincoln. Artillery impact areas reached to the modern Bethesda Naval Medical Center on Wisconsin Avenue and Confederate wagon parks on modern Georgia Avenue in Silver Spring. The epicenter of the action on the afternoon of July 12, affecting President Abraham Lincoln's presence at the battle, was probably in the high ground vicinity of 13th Street and Van Buren Street north of Fort Stevens and south of Walter Reed Army Medical Center, now largely residential but with a District of Columbia recreational area (park) and terrain clearly discernible eastward beyond Battleground National Cemetery and Piney Branch Road.

Fort Stevens was an expansion of Fort Massachusetts, originally constructed on the eastern portion of the site, now occupied by church and other buildings. Constructed by men of Darius B. Couch's brigade from that state, the work was subsequently expanded and renamed in honor of Brigadier General Isaac I. Stevens, who was killed at Chantilly, Virginia, on September 1, 1862. It was constructed near a crossroads called "Brighton" (later "Brightwood") marked by Moreland tavern, a nearby free-black community "Vinegar Hill," abundant springs, and verdant countryside.

Commenced in the wake of the defeat at the First Battle of Bull Run (Manassas) in July 1861, Fort Massachusetts had a perimeter of about 168 yards, ten cannon, and a 200-man garrison. Expansion took place after the Second Battle of Bull Run (Manassas) in September 1862, when the size grew to 375 perimeter yards, and the name was changed to Fort Stevens. The expanded work was a lunette with a stockaded gorge or rear face, and nineteen guns and mortars were mounted in this fort. They included two eight-inch siege howitzers (en embrasure), six 24-pounder siege guns (en embrasure), four 24-pounder seacoast guns (evenly split between embrasure and barbette fire), five 30-pounder Parrott rifles (en embrasure), and one ten-inch and one 24-pounder Coehorn mortar. Like virtually all forts in the system, the armament seems to have changed during the war. In May 1864, Fort Stevens ostensibly mounted four 24-pounder seacoast cannon (en barbette), six 24-pounder siege guns (en embrasure), two eight-inch siege howitzers (en embrasure), and five 30-pounder Parrott rifles (en embrasure).

Fort Stevens was described in 1864 as a "large enclosed work, situated on high ground" overlooking the terrain to its front for several miles. It commanded the vital Seventh Street Turnpike (renamed Seventh Street Road in 1871) artery leading directly into Washington from Silver Spring. It was enclosed by abatis, and behind the fort lies a hollow that could mask large bodies of troops from enemy artillery fire. The fort contained two magazines (one in the original section, one in the expanded part of the fort) and a bombproof for a garrison now calculated at 423 officers and men. Inspectors merely gave the fort a "fair" combat readiness rating.

Fort Stevens was located 5.2 miles from the Capitol and stood 321 feet above sea level.

Notes/Anecdotes

As at Fort Reno, the vicinity of Fort Stevens (Massachusetts) became a favorite campsite for various regiments such as the 7th and 10th Massachusetts, 2d Rhode Island, and 36th New York. "Camp Brightwood" was the name applied to camping areas familiar to such units as Elisha Hunt Rhodes's 2d Rhode Island and today continues as the title for this particular neighborhood in the city. Camp Stetson (1st Maine Heavy Artillery) and Camp Doubleday (76th New York) were also associated with the area, and an invalid camp existed here for soldiers ravaged by malaria contracted during McClellan's Peninsula campaign of 1862. Less formal encampments were those of the 112th and 117th New York on Rock Creek Ford Road, the 136th and 137th Pennsylvania Infantry, and the 2d Pennsylvania Heavy Artillery. The nearby Brightwood Hotel served as a command post during the Battle of Fort Stevens in July 1864, while the palatial summer home of prominent builder and local militia leader Matthew Gault Emery located on higher ground southeast of the fort served as a signal station and headquarters during the war and can be identified in period sketches of Camp Brightwood.

B. W. Sulfrin provided insight into the minds of the soldiery at Camp Brightwood when he wrote his wife and son on October 4, 1861, how "we are not treated half as well as any slave out here" and predicted that "if we was all at home that we could not get five out of a Regiment and to volunteer again, they would have to draft the next time." Still, he would "fight for the Union and the stars and stripes, the Union and my dear family is all I am laboring for, it can't last forever." He was true to his country, so let the authorities "do as they please with us but if at last we can come

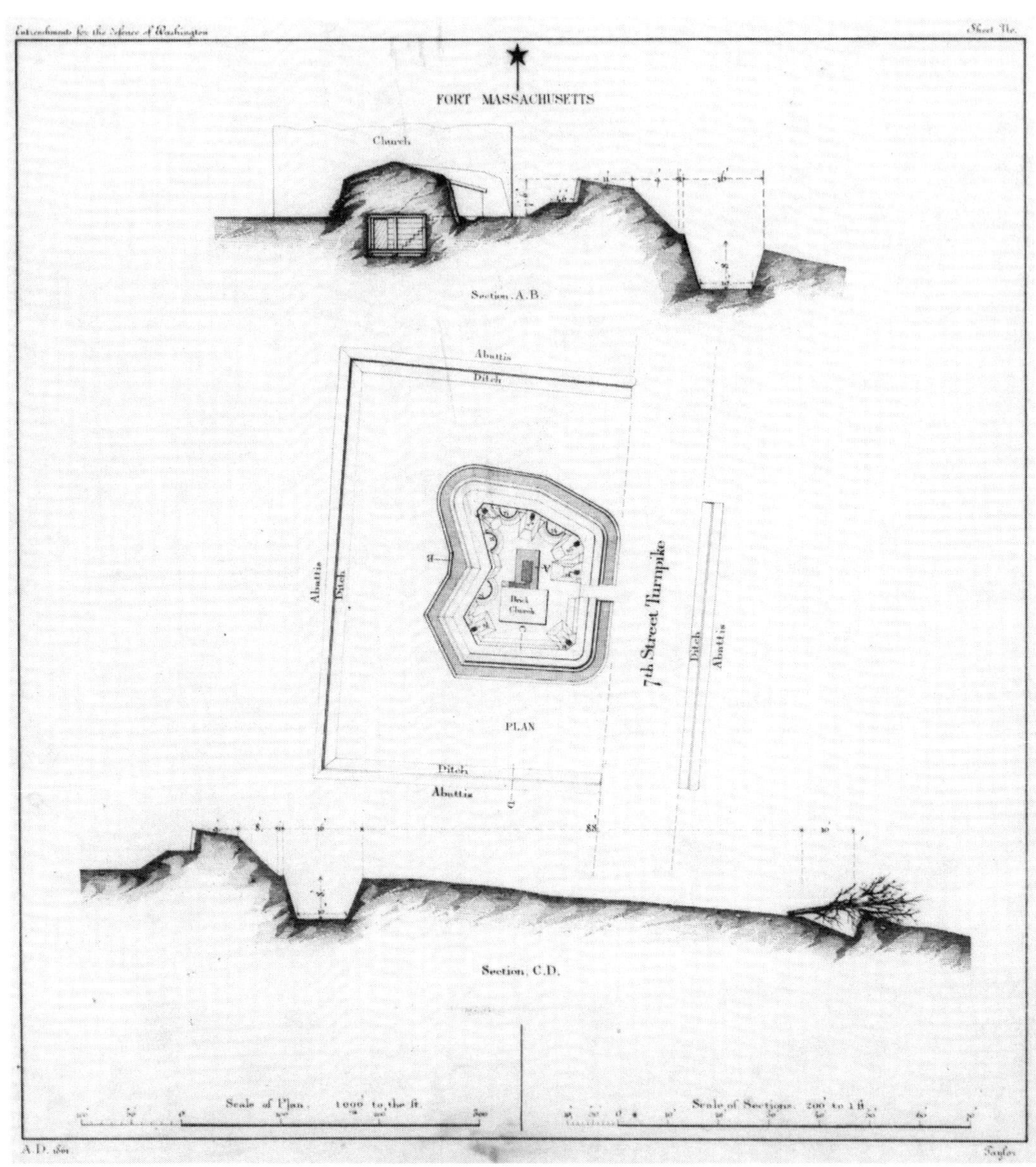

Fort Massachusetts—Engineer Drawing. *National Archives*

out victorious and come home to our dear families it is all I ask. . . . I think I can stand it as long as the rest."

The 2d Pennsylvania Heavy Artillery took particular pride in its role of expanding Fort Massachusetts into Fort Stevens. Companies D and K were stationed here from May through November 1862. The regimental historian declared, "Historians will not likely condescend to give credit to this regiment's part in the defense against Early's advance." But, he contended, "had Fort Massachusetts and Slocum remained as they were in 1862, Gen. Early would have had no difficulty in reaching Washington City by route of the Seventh Street Road."

This expansion of Fort Massachusetts may have contributed another vignette to Lincolniana and the history of Fort Stevens. One of the fort's magazines (that in the original portion) had been constructed from the cellar of the old brick Emory Methodist chapel on the site (ironically where the modern church of that name stands today). When the Pennsylvanians expanded the fort westward, they tore into the house of a free black woman, Mrs. Elizabeth Proctor "Aunt Betty" Thomas, who owned the land in the vicinity, to build a second magazine. She and her husband James farmed the eleven acres that this free black woman owned in the area. Aunt Betty recalled after the war that she could not understand the German speech of the officers and men when they arrived to enlarge the Union fort. They began removing her furniture out of her house and then demolished the structure. That evening, as she sat under a nearby sycamore tree, her only shelter, with her six-month-old baby in her

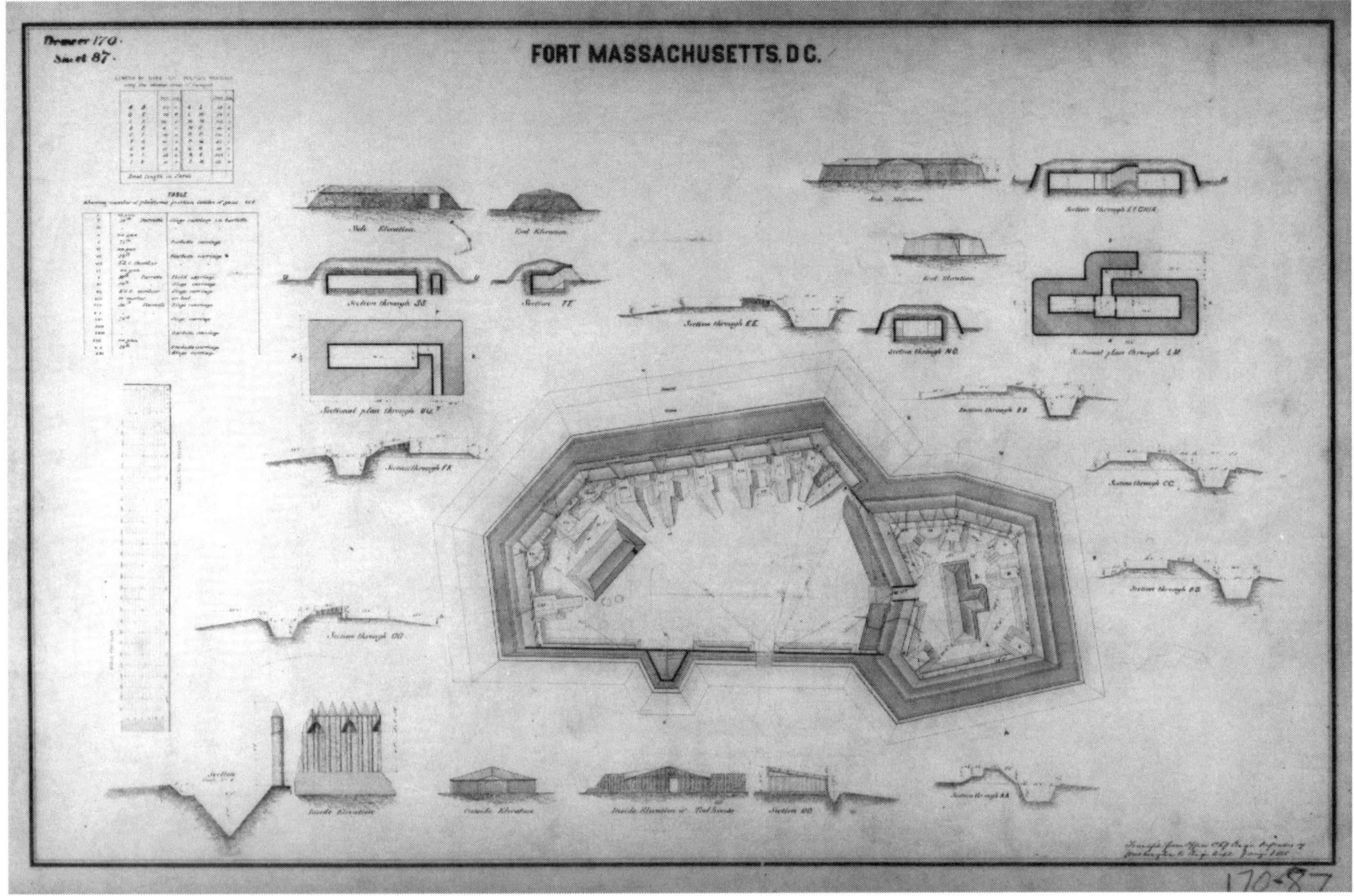

Fort Stevens (Fort Massachusetts Expanded)—Engineer Drawing. *National Archives*

arms, a tall slender man, dressed in black, came up and said to her, "It is hard, but you shall reap a great reward." She claimed that it was President Lincoln. She concluded her tale that she was still waiting for that reward, commenting wryly that if the sixteenth president had lived, she knew her claim would have been honored. Aunt Betty died in 1917 at age ninety-six, the darling of veterans' reunions that gathered at the fort site on her property.

Apocryphal or not, Lincoln returned with his wife and other officials at the height of the battle of July 11–12, 1864, at Fort Stevens. Arguably, he became the only president to actually come under enemy fire while in office. At some point, he mounted the parapet, swept by Confederate sharpshooters' fire. Only when a surgeon was cut down nearby could the president be induced to retire from the exposed perch. The president and First Lady also visited the fort's hospital. All of this so unnerved Mrs. Lincoln that she swooned, prompting Lincoln's laconic comment that she would never make a good soldier if she fainted at the sight of blood.

Postbattle analysis led Major General Christopher Augur, commanding the Department of Washington, to recommend that "in case of threatened attack there should be two field batteries here (twelve pieces), one of them to be a mounted battery. These pieces are to arm the batteries between Rock Creek and Piney Branch, including Battery Sill."

Identifiable units relating to garrisoning Fort Stevens during the postbattle period included the following:

- 150th Ohio National Guard, Cos. B, K, July 1864
- 1st New Hampshire Heavy Artillery, Co. D, September 1864
- 1st New Hampshire Heavy Artillery, Co. L, October–November 1864
- 3d Massachusetts Heavy Artillery, Co. D, November 1864–March 1865
- 3d Massachusetts Heavy Artillery, Co. K, March–June 1865
- 3d Massachusetts Heavy Artillery, Co. F, June 1865

Generally, life at Fort Stevens aptly reflected one soldier's contention on January 30, 1864, that "here it's the same thing over and over everyday, we have to drill and go on inspection every fair day and that is all there is to it." They would periodically march over

Plaque Commemorating Sharpshooter's Tree at Walter Reed Army Medical Center. *Authors' Collection*

Co. F, 3rd Massachusetts Heavy Artillery in Fort Stevens—Battlefield in Distance. *Library of Congress*

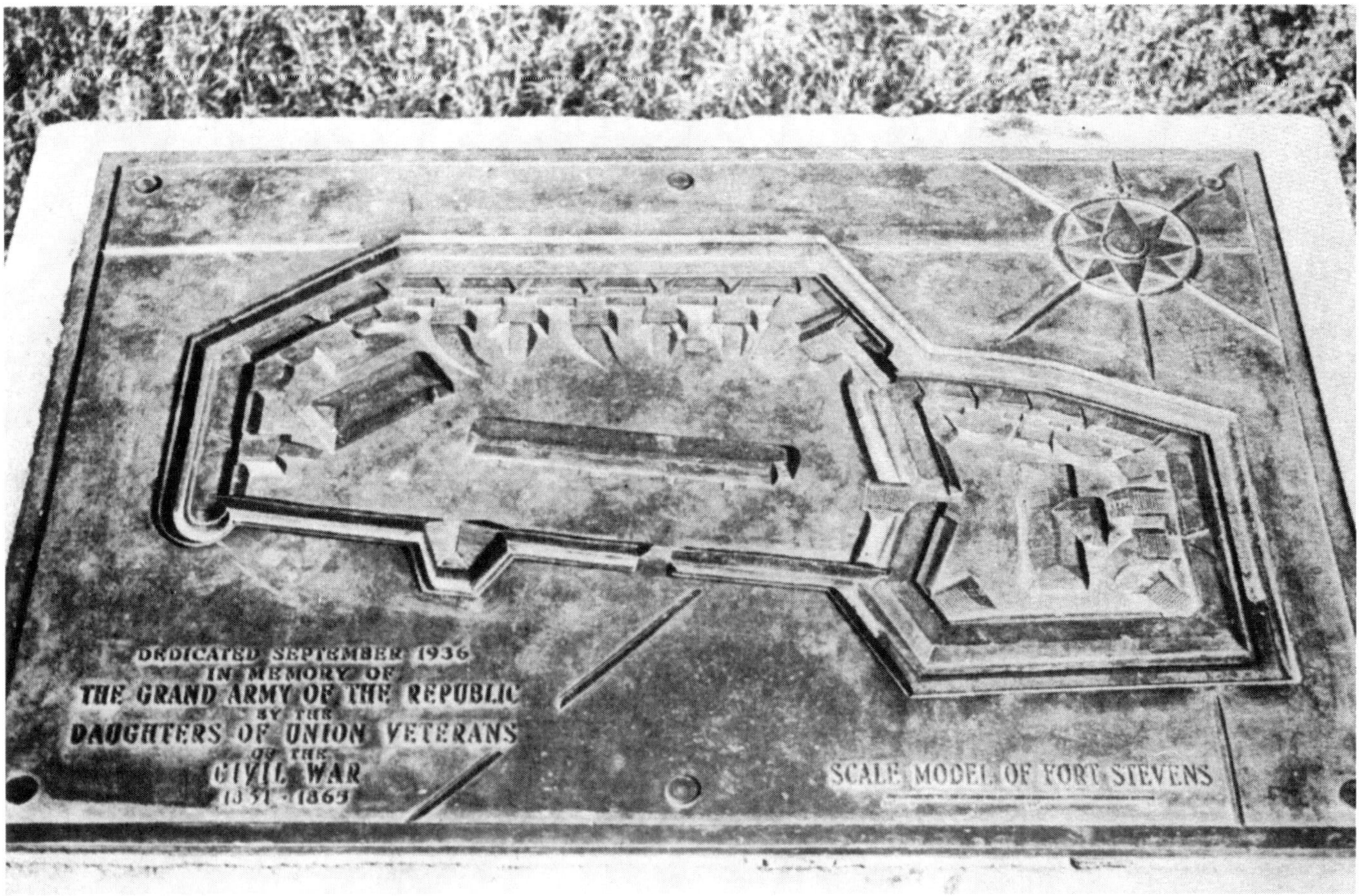

Bas-Relief Map of Fort Stevens. *Authors' Collection*

Unrestored Fort Stevens in 1911. *National Archives*

The Fort Stevens Battlefield and Battleground National Cemetery

Location

The now-urbanized battlefield site embraces Walter Reed on the north, Oregon Avenue west of Rock Creek Park on the west, Military Road/Missouri Avenue on the south, and beyond Georgia Avenue/Piney Branch Road on the east. The epicenter lies in the vicinity of 13th Street and Van Buren Street NW to east of Battleground National Cemetery, all drivable on city streets.

Visible Remains

Marginal, although basic terrain remains identifiable, especially that area encompassed by the Walter Reed Army Medical Center grounds.

Description

The Battle of Fort Stevens lasted either thirty-three hours or five, depending on one's perspective. Skirmishing in the Brightwood section of Northwest D.C. began shortly after noon on July 11, 1864, and lasted until late evening of the next day. Heavy stand-up fighting occupied the latter part of the July 12, commencing around mid-afternoon or 4:00, varying on witness accounts, and did not cease until after dark, or about 9:00 P.M. The battle crossed the full spectrum, from sharpshooter fire to light skirmishing to heavy artillery barrage to crisp firefight, with Union attack and Confederate push-back late on the July 12. Most notably, the president of the United States came under enemy fire possibly for the only time while in office; a former vice president may have witnessed the affair from the other side. The Confederate force comprised hardened veteran "professionals," and their opponents included counterpart seasoned Army of the Potomac personnel as well as hastily recruited government clerks, hospital convalescents, dismounted cavalrymen, and Ohio limited-service men, many of whom were veterans. Preservation/restoration of the ramparts of Fort Stevens directly traces to the actual fighting that threatened Lincoln's life and capture of the nation's capital.

Modern View of Ramparts of Fort Stevens. *Authors' Collection*

Relatively little of the actual battlefield remains. Existing are Fort Stevens and adjacent Federal line traces as well as the Battleground National Cemetery, all owned and managed by the National Park Service, and the outer reaches of Confederate sharpshooter tree site, bivouac and staging, and counterattack departure areas, all on the Walter Reed Army Medical Center grounds (subject to installation rules for access). The expansion of suburban Washington through the Brightwood, Takoma, and Shepherd Park subdivisions and the transition of adjacent areas of Silver Spring, Maryland, in the first half of the twentieth century doomed the battle area and Confederate positions around the Francis Preston and Montgomery Blair mansions along with most other surviving farms and structures from the 1864 scene. Modern Georgia Avenue and Piney Branch Road retain the original Seventh Street Road/Turnpike and Piney Branch Road configurations of the era.

Battleground National Cemetery

Location

From Fort Stevens, proceed north on Georgia Avenue to the cemetery entrance at 6625 Georgia Avenue, NW.

Visible Remains

A well-kept national cemetery containing forty-one grave sites, a cemetery lodge (erected in 1871), a Doric-style rostrum on the east side of the cemetery (erected in 1920–1921), and a flagstaff can be seen. Four granite commemorative monuments to units participating in the battle and twin-cannon entry guards are also notable. The monuments are to Company K, 150th Ohio National Guard (erected in 1907); 122d New York Infantry (erected in 1903); 98th Pennsylvania Infantry (erected in 1891), and 25th New York Cavalry (erected in 1914). Note colorful wayside sign and site restoration.

Modern Entrance to Battleground National Cemetery. *Authors' Collection*

Modern View of Soldier Graves, Battleground National Cemetery. *Authors' Collection*

Description

The cemetery marks the site of the Battle of Fort Stevens, July 11–12, 1864. It contains forty of the fifty-nine dead and 145 wounded Federal casualties suffered in the battle. Barely an acre in size, Battleground National Cemetery is one of the nation's smallest national cemeteries and preserves some of the only surviving ground of Washington's only battlefield. Memorials to units participating in the battle and two 6-pounder artillery pieces can be found near the entrance. The sandstone superintendent's house also provides a monument to battle participant and soldier engineer/architect Quartermaster General Major General Montgomery C. Meigs, who designed the structure as well as the Pension Building (now the National Building Museum) and supervised the Washington Aqueduct and Capitol building completion.

Notes/Anecdotes

The significance of the site may be found in the roll of honor listing burials at Battleground National Cemetery. The last veteran of the Battle of Fort Stevens, E. R. Campbell, was buried there in 1936. Memorial Day ceremonies were long a feature of the community, and in the early twentieth century, surviving veterans of the encounter would gather on the porch of one of their comrades, Lewis Cass White, who had resettled to the neighborhood after the war to eat lunch and swap war stories of their experiences.

President Lincoln, for whom the afternoon battle on July 12 had been conducted and who had witnessed the ultimate sacrifice of the Union casualties in that action, spoke at the cemetery's dedication. Other than Battleground National Cemetery, the only other

Modern View of Unit Monuments in Battleground National Cemetery. *Authors' Collection*

national cemetery so honored was Soldiers National Cemetery at Gettysburg.

The following Union soldiers, killed in action July 11 and 12, 1864, at the Battle of Fort Stevens, Brightwood, District of Columbia, are buried in Battleground National Cemetery. The updated and corrected list is attributable to a nine-year research project finished in 2008 by Ron Harvey of the National Park Service:

Ashbaugh, Andrew (Pvt.), 61st Pennsylvania Infantry, grave 26
Barrett, Edward (Edwin) C. (Corp.), 43d New York Infantry, grave 30
Bentley, John (Pvt.), 122d New York Infantry, grave 4
Bowen, Philip (Pvt.), 61st Pennsylvania Infantry, grave 14
Bavett, E. S. (civilian), Quartermaster Department, grave 9
Castle, Richard [Mark Stoneham] (Sgt./1st Lt.), 43d New York Infantry, grave 2
Chandler, Harvey P. B. (Pvt.), 122d New York Infantry, grave 37
Christ, C. S. (Pvt.), 2d U.S. Artillery, grave 5
Davidson, John (Pvt.), 43d New York Infantry, grave 3
De Graff, Matthew J. (Pvt.), 43d New York Infantry, grave 1
Dolan, Andrew J. (Pvt.), 2d Massachusetts Cavalry, grave 27
Dowen, Andrew J. (Pvt.), 77th New York Infantry, grave 31
Ellis, John (Pvt.), 61st Pennsylvania Infantry, grave 36
Farrar, George W. (Corp.), 43d New York Infantry, grave 8
Frei, Wilhelm [William Tray or Gray] (Pvt.), 25th New York Cavalry, grave 19
Garvin, George (Corp.), 61st Pennsylvania Infantry, grave 11
Gillette, William H. (Pvt.), 49th New York Infantry, grave 39
Gorton, George W. (Corp.), 1st Rhode Island Infantry, grave 6
Hoerle, Bernard (Pvt.), 98th Pennsylvania Infantry, grave 23
Hogeboom, David L. (Pvt.), 122d New York Infantry, grave 16
Holtzman, William (Pvt.), 93d Pennsylvania Infantry, grave 20
Hufletin, Elijah (Pvt.), 25th New York Cavalry, grave 17
Kennedy, John (Pvt.), 122d New York Infantry, grave 13
Laughlin, William (2d Lt.), 61st Pennsylvania Infantry, grave 28
Lovett, Patrick (Pvt.), 37th Massachusetts Infantry, grave 12
Maloney, Jeremiah (Pvt.), 25th New York Cavalry, grave 34
Manning, Andrew (Pvt.), 77th New York Infantry, grave 29
Marquet, George (Sgt.), 98th Pennsylvania Infantry, grave 7
Matott, Ambrose (Corp.), 77th New York Infantry, grave 25
McIntire, H. [Thomas Morrison] (Pvt.), 61st Pennsylvania Infantry, grave 15
Mosier, Alanson (Pvt.), 122d New York Infantry, grave 32
Mowry, Alvarado (Pvt.), 77th New York Infantry, grave 18
Pockett, John (Pvt.), 7th Maine Infantry, grave 8
Richards, John Milton (Sgt.), 139th Pennsylvania Infantry, grave 40
Richardson, Thomas (Sgt.), 25th New York Cavalry, grave 35
Ruhle, William (Corp.), 49th New York Infantry, grave 22

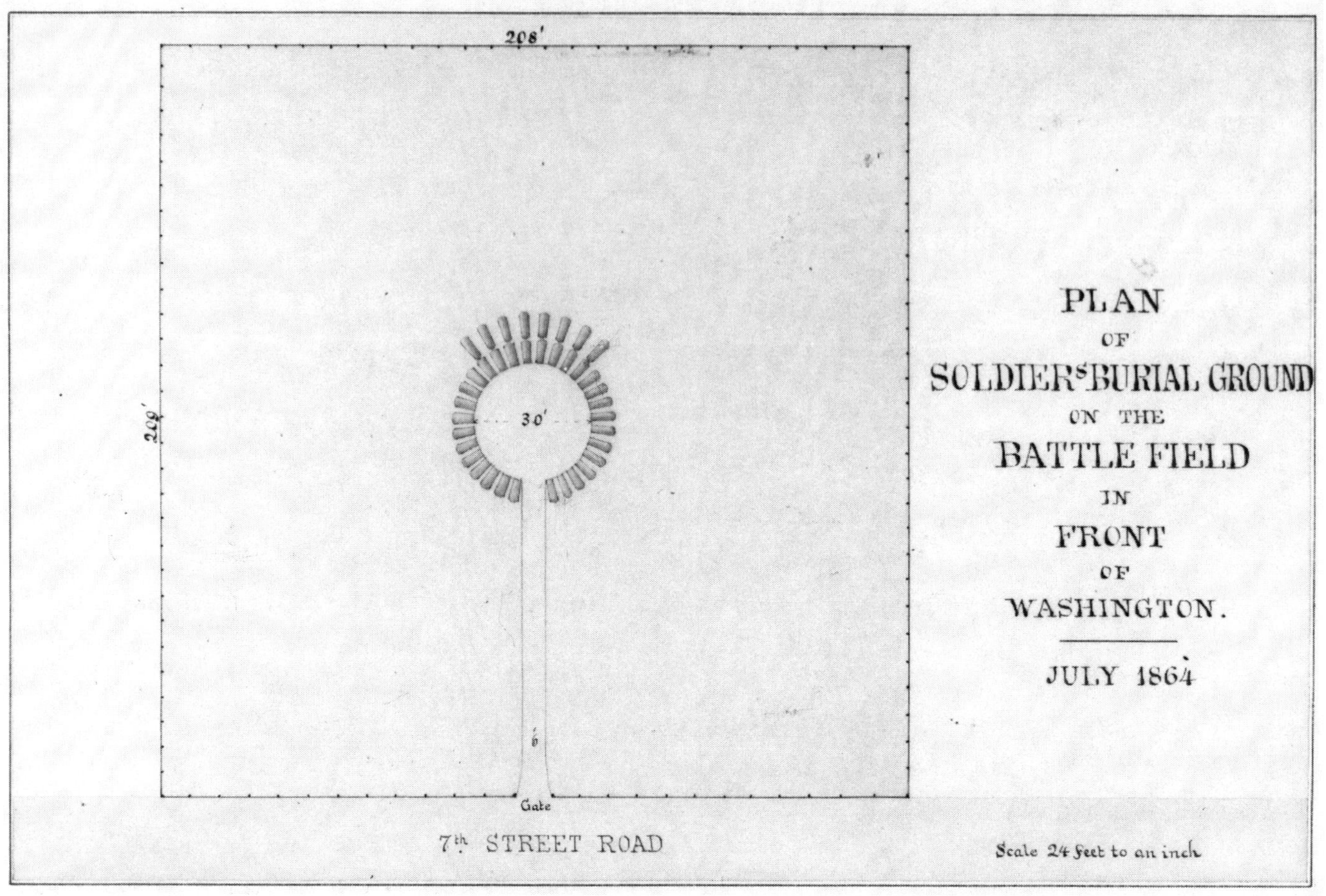

Battleground National Cemetery Plan. *National Archives*

Seahouse, Charles (Pvt.), 98th Pennsylvania Infantry, grave 24
Starbird, Alfred C. (Sgt.), 25th New York Cavalry, grave 33
Stevens, Russell L. (Pvt.), 3d Vermont Infantry, grave 21
Walther, Frederick (Pvt.), 98th Pennsylvania Infantry, grave 10

The last veteran of the battle, Edward R. Campbell, 2d Vermont Infantry (who rose to the rank of major in the postwar U.S. Army), was buried in grave 41 on March 12, 1936, aged ninety-two. Three other graves contain the wife and three children, members of the family of Augustus Ambrecht, loyal cemetery caretaker after the Civil War. They are buried behind graves 28 and 29.

Confederate Monument

Location

To reach the burial site for seventeen Confederate dead from the battle, continue north on Georgia Avenue from the District of Columbia through Silver Spring to corner of Georgia Avenue and Grace Church Road where, on the right, can be found the simple granite Confederate memorial shaft near the church.

Description

The Confederate memorial shaft was erected in the memory of seventeen unknown Confederate dead who fell in front of Washington, D.C., on July 12, 1864.

Notes/Anecdotes

One amusing epitaph to Early's raid was discovered soon after the battle by Federal troops. It supposedly appeared on the flyleaf of one of Lord Byron's works that had been "liberated" from a ransacked local mansion by Early's troops:

> Now, Uncle Abe, you had better be quiet the balance of your administration. We only came near your town this time to show you what we could do, but if you go on in your mad career we will come again soon, and then you had better stand from under. Yours respectfully, The Worst Rebel You ever Saw.

Battleground National Cemetery, ca. August 1865. *U.S. Army Military History Institute*

Fort Slocum—Companion to Fort Stevens

Location

From the Confederate burial site, return via Georgia Avenue NW past Battleground National Cemetery and Fort Stevens to Missouri Avenue (traffic light). Turn left on Missouri Avenue to 3d Street. Turn left on 3d Street to Madison Street and then turn right (an unarmed battery and a connecting trench remain in the park at Madison Street and 2d Place). Continue on Madison Street to Kansas Avenue. Turn left and continue to the top of the hill at Nicholson Street NW. Note the National Park Service generic Defenses of Washington sign on the left side of Kansas Avenue. Fort Slocum occupied the high ground roughly encompassed by Kansas Avenue, Blair Road, Nicholson Street, and Milmorson Place NW.

Visible Remains

The National Park Service preserves the badly eroded field gun battery and rifle pits in the park, labeled "Fort Slocum Park." There is also an interpretive sign on Kansas Avenue.

Description

Fort Slocum was constructed by the 2d Rhode Island Infantry and named for its commanding officer, Colonel John S. Slocum, who was killed at the First Battle of Bull Run (Manassas).

The fort was a strong work with a perimeter of 653 yards. It provided auxiliary fire for Fort Stevens on the Seventh Street Road to the west, and it covered the left and right forks of Rock Creek Church Road (modern Blair Road and New Hampshire Avenue) as they entered the District of Columbia.

Its armament consisted of twenty-five guns and mortars with fifteen platforms for field and siege pieces. Among the heavy ordnance were one eight-inch siege howitzer (en embrasure), two 24-pounder siege guns (en embrasure), two 24-pounder seacoast guns (en embrasure), four 24-pounder howitzers (en embrasure), seven four-and-a-half-inch rifles (en embrasure), six 10-pounder rifled Parrott rifles (en embrasure), one ten-inch siege gun, and two 24-pounder Coehorn mortars.

"The Battery to the Left of Fort Slocum" had four vacant platforms and commanded the valley of Piney Branch between Forts Slocum and Stevens.

"The Battery to the Right of Fort Slocum" (as General Barnard called it) contained six vacant platforms. Its mission enhanced protection of the road junction of the left and right forks of Rock Creek Church Road (in the vicinity of modern McDonald Place and New Hampshire Avenue).

Notes/Anecdotes

The fort was erected partially on the land of John F. Callan, a clerk who had a family of eight children, one of whom listed his own occupation as druggist. Illustrating the early period along the northern lines, Corporal Henry T. Blanchard of the 2d Rhode Island, stationed at Camp Brightwood, regaled his brother Horace back home in Providence on the vicissitudes of guard duty along the northern lines near Fort Slocum in January 1862:

> Company K marched on to the parade ground [at Brightwood] yesterday morn [January 28] for inspection previous to going out. The weather was not the best I have seen, for the rain was falling very fast and freezing as it fell. Inspection lasted about ½ an hour, and 8 ½ oclock we left Camp for Fort Slocum, where the guard were to be divided and sent to their respective post's. We arrived there in a few minutes and after the costomary salutes &c. the Capt began to divide the Co. I was picked out in Company wither. Reynolds and 9 privates to go out to Silver Springs a small village in Maryland about 5 ½ miles from our Camp. [Blanchard may have confused Silver Spring with a larger Bladensburg in Prince George's County as the following will indicate.] So we started, the rain having in the meantime held up a little. The ground was very slippery, and with our knapsacks, canteens &c it was rather hard work. On our way we passed the celebrated Bladensburg Duelling Grounds. It seems as if this place was made expressly for crimes & murder. The grounds are about two acres in extent, and are enclosed in a very thick pine & spruce woods, so thick do the trees grow, that we could not see ten foot inside of them. There are numerous roads leading to this place and it would be impossible to capture a party unless the place was completely surrounded. We reached our destination a few moments after 10 a.m. where we were saluted by the old Guard and then we saluted them in return. The orders were very strict concerning soldiers passing by this post, as it is the last post, of our guard, in Maryland. (That is of our division) We had three posts—one in front of our quarters, and one in a store where they used to sell licquor. The other post was in another store where the man had been sick with the Small Pox, but was so much recovered as to be out of doors. No soldiers are allowed in either store except they have passes signed by Brig. Gen. Couch commanding the Division. At night the men posted as the stores and are drawn in at night and take turns with those in front of the Guard House. Our Guard House or quarters, was once an old tavern or Country Inn and was used in the commencent [*sic*] of the present trouble as an armory by a company of Home Guards. In the room formerly used as a barroom we stoped [*sic*]. There was a large fireplace in the room and outside of the door was some 40 or 50 cords of wood belonging to Uncle Sam, of which we used as much as we wanted. Silver Spring Village [Bladensburg] consists of some 12 or 14 houses two stores and a blacksmith shop. One of the stores is quite a large one, and quite a number of farmers were there trading. I wish you could se some of their teams, some of them with a mule & a horse together and some with two horses and a mule on lead. There was a notice outside of the large store which was calculated to bring a good deal of costoms [customers] I guess. Very good things to eat every day. Good weather and no licquor Bill of fare everything that is good and bad weather and no good grog. If that don't beat every[thing] I ever saw I will give up. There was nothing of especial interest occurred except that we enjoyed ourselves very much. We arrived home about 11 oclock today [January 29], covered with mud.

Blanchard later was killed as a sergeant in the Wilderness, May 6, 1864.

Company C, 2d Pennsylvania Heavy Artillery, garrisoned the fort from May to November 1862. The two months preceding Early's July 1864 raid saw Companies H and K, 150th Ohio One Hundred Days men, posted to the fort. They enjoyed "very good barracks that had been occupied by the 11th Vermont for nearly two years" while watching enviously the strict regular army drill of Company L, 5th U.S. Artillery. They conducted Sunday Bible classes, suffered poor food and blistering May heat, and were shifted eastward to Fort Thayer before returning to Fort Slocum in June. Private James C. Cannon noted how they often went to the Soldiers' Home to see the old Mexican War veterans as well as President Lincoln coming home to the Anderson cottage after a hard day's work downtown. Companies A and G manned the fort at the time of Early's July 1864 raid.

A postraid War Department report stated that "there should be six field pieces sent to this fort, to arm the batteries on the right and left of the fort." Companies A (July–October 1864), D, and H (September) and the 1st New Hampshire Heavy Artillery garrisoned the post in this period. Companies G (November 1864–June 1865) and E (May–June 1865) and the 3d Massachusetts Heavy Artillery closed out the war there.

Victory gardens were located on much of this ground during World War II and may have helped obliterate remnant traces of Fort Slocum and its outworks.

Notes/Anecdotes

Clearly a strong work by the time of Early's raid, Fort Slocum, like Fort Stevens, was dominated by hills two-thirds to one mile distant. Like Fort Massachusetts, this was a small work, subsequently enlarged and strengthened.

Ostensibly, the opening shot of the Battle of Fort Stevens was fired from Fort Slocum at 11:30 A.M. on July 11, 1864, by order of Captain J. N. Abbey, 2d Pennsylvania Heavy Artillery. During the battle, Brigadier General Montgomery C. Meigs, quartermaster general of the U.S. Army, commanded 1,500 employees of his office who were mobilized for the crisis and who were thrown into the rifle pits at this point. Colonel Francis Price's brigade of 2,800 convalescents from nearby hospitals also served near Fort Slocum.

The fort was garrisoned by Company 1, 76th New York Infantry, during the first half of 1862. Other detachments in the Fort Slocum sector during the summer of 1864 included the 1st New Hampshire Heavy Artillery, 150th Ohio National Guard, 14th Michigan Battery, and Companies A and B, Knapp's Pennsylvania Artillery.[12]

FORTIFICATIONS OF THE NORTHEAST: FORTS TOTTEN, SLEMMER, BUNKER HILL, AND SARATOGA AND BATTERY MORRIS

These works exercised a powerful influence on approaches to the city from the north eastward to the Anacostia River.

Fort Totten—Protector of Rock Creek Church Road and Military Asylum

Location

From Fort Slocum, take Blair Road south to Madison Street and then zigzag a short distance to continue on Blair Road. Turn right on Blair Road (note the country-lane dimension connoting the original period artery). This becomes Rock Creek Church Road and then Fort Totten Drive after crossing Riggs Road NW at the traffic light. Continue a quarter of a mile south. The remains of Battery Totten and Fort Totten are in the woods to the left, and access can be made through the clearly marked lane leading to the fort proper.

Visible Remains

Both Battery Totten and Fort Totten have well-preserved, unrestored, but overgrown earthworks and an outer trench line. The site is maintained by the National Park Service. There is a Civil War Centennial plaque.

Description

The fort was named for Brigadier General Joseph Totten, chief of engineers, U.S. Army. The fort and advanced battery to the left occupied a commanding ridgeline position controlling the broad valley and country roads stretching before it to the north and east. A small unarmed battery also existed to the right, commanding a streamlet valley. To the rear lies the Military Asylum, or Soldiers' Home, and the small cottage, the "Summer White House," where Lincoln often relaxed. He often visited the nearby forts and their garrisons from this retreat.

The fort had a perimeter of some 272 yards and was armed with twenty guns and mortars. The armament included two eight-inch siege howitzers (en barbette), eight 32-pounder seacoast guns (en barbette), one 100-pounder Parrott rifle (en barbette), three 30-pounder Parrott rifles (en barbette), four 6-pounder James rifles (en embrasure), one ten-inch and one 24-pounder Coehorn mortars, and two vacant platforms.

The garrison numbered 180 artillerists among a total of 350 officers and men.

Notes/Anecdotes

Troops garrisoning the post and vicinity at various times included the following:

- 76th New York
- 2d Pennsylvania Heavy Artillery, Cos. B, K, March–November 1862
- 136th and 137th Pennsylvania
- 4th U.S. Artillery, Co. A
- 150th Ohio National Guard, Co. F, July 1864
- 1st New Hampshire Heavy Artillery
- 1st Vermont Heavy Artillery
- 3d Massachusetts Heavy Artillery, Cos. A, D, November 1864–June 1865
- 3d Massachusetts Heavy Artillery, Co. B, May–June 1865

Several interesting complaints and observations could be seen in soldier letters in the summer and fall of 1863. Private N. Batchelder of the 1st Vermont Heavy Artillery noted how he and his colleagues would most welcome substitution of new Springfield

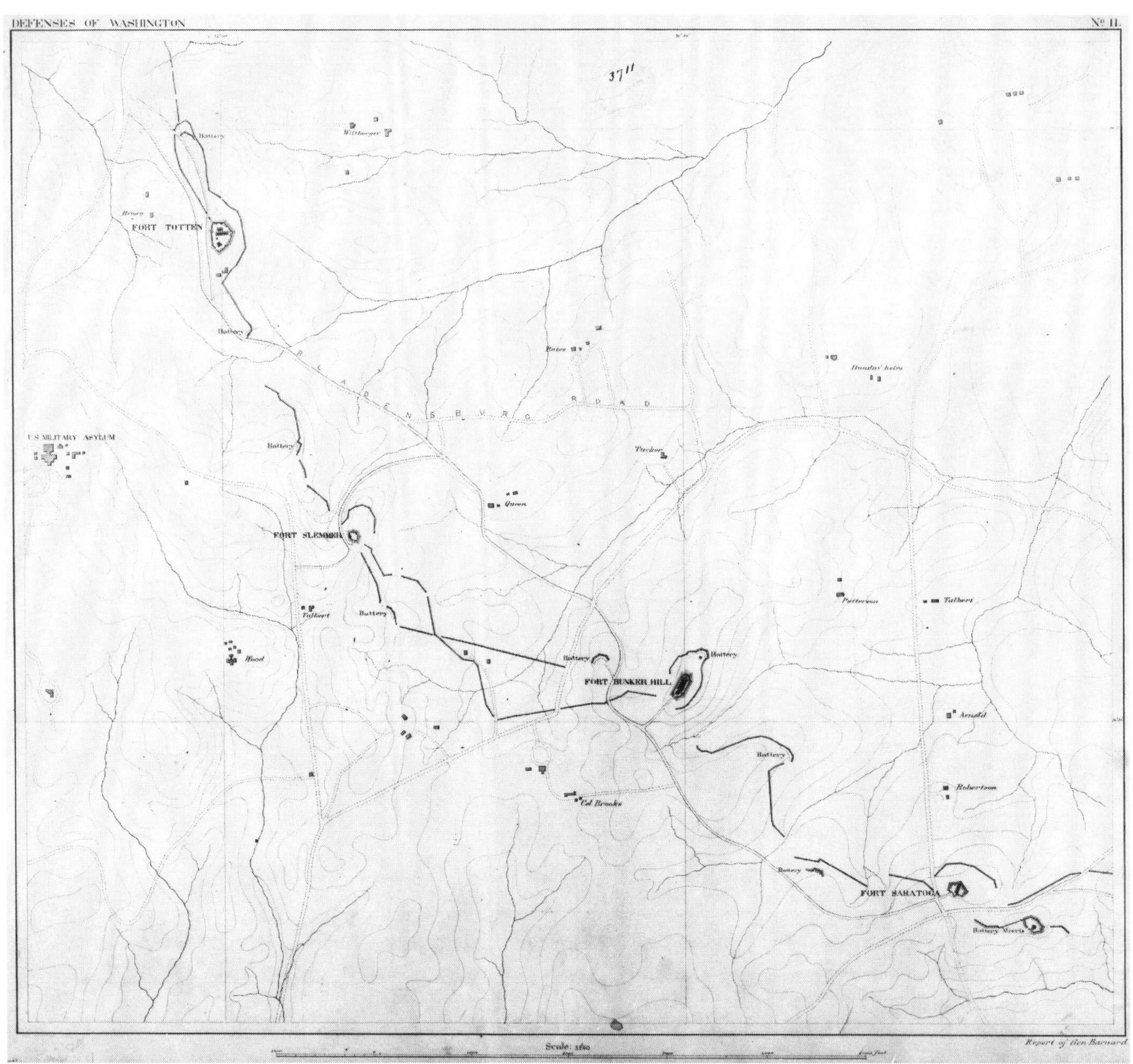

Sector Map—Fort Totten to Fort Saratoga. *National Archives*

rifles for the Austrian firearms issued to them in Brattleboro when they mustered and how he could see no need for doing guard duty in front of the officers' quarters, "but I suppose the Major knows best for a private isent [*sic*] to know anything." Senior 1st Lieutenant John H. Giuesinger of the 2d Pennsylvania Heavy Artillery noted in October how he anticipated commanding the company (since the captain was under arrest for defrauding the government by drawing more rations than he had men) composed mainly of Germans "hard to manage" for which he would first "try kind words" and "if that don't keep them down I will put the screws on them." The forty Americans in the company (by his count) claimed to have not done better because their officers had "never treated them like men should be treated."

Fort Totten illustrates the vicissitudes of earthen fieldworks during the Civil War. The Engineer Investigation Commission, which examined the defense system in the fall of 1862, pronounced the fort as "well built and well armed," with a wood-lined well, and recommended only the addition of the 100-pounder Parrott rifle, sent to the fort from the Washington Arsenal in December of that year. Later, an inspector declared that "the 100-pounder here placed will sweep the sector from Fort De Russy to Fort Lincoln." Still,

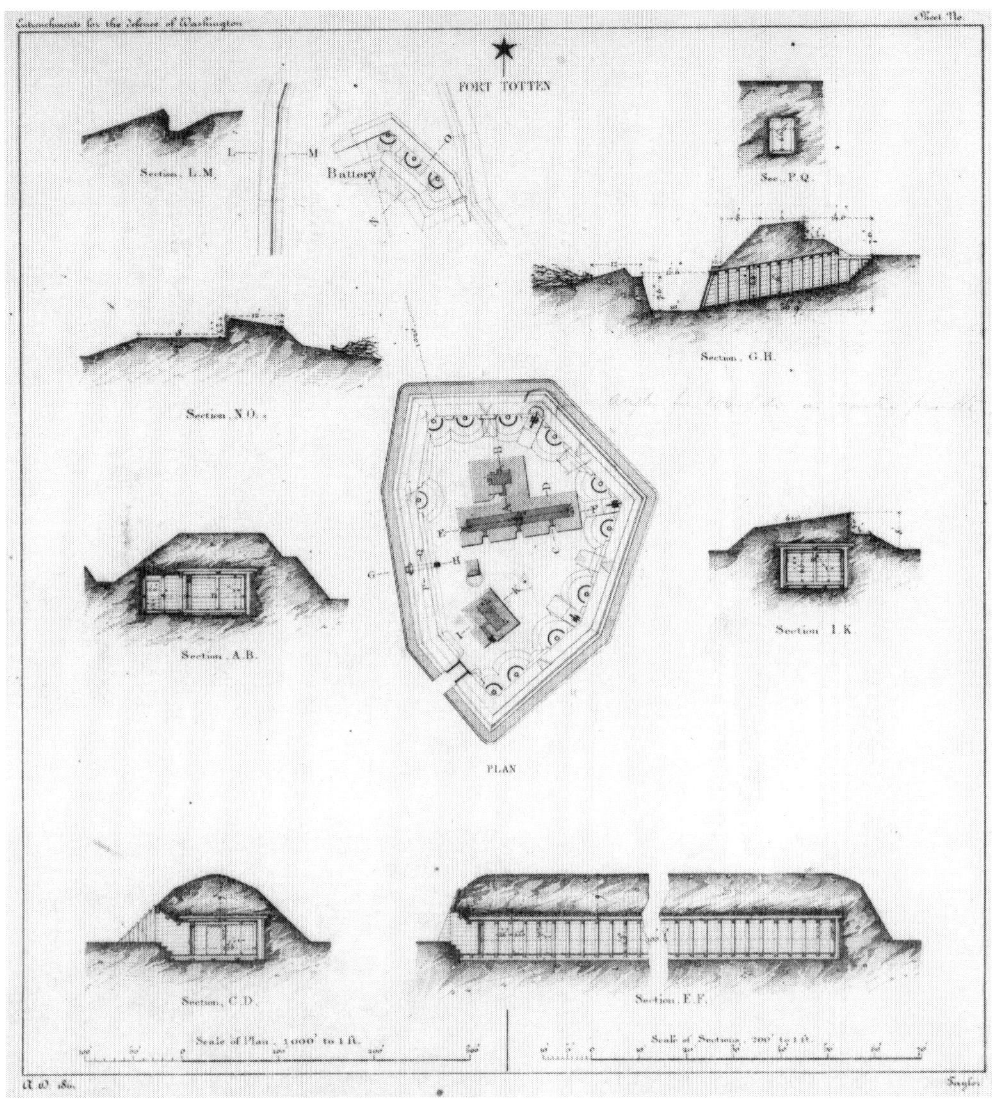

Fort Totten—Engineer Drawing. *National Archives*

by the autumn of 1863, Fort Totten had deteriorated and needed repairs to the magazine, revetments, and parapet. Part of the scarp wall was revetted with stone, a second magazine added, and the abatis renewed, while the parapets were resodded. Nonetheless, by the time that Ulysses S. Grant withdrew veteran artillerists from the works in the spring of 1864, officials rated the Fort Totten garrison as only fair in infantry and artillery drill, although the magazines were admittedly well stocked with powder and ammunition.

An idea of the situation at Fort Totten and nearby Fort Slemmer can be derived from the letters of Major (later Lieutenant Colonel) George E. Chamberlin of the 1st Vermont Heavy Artillery. He commanded Companies A, F, and K of that regiment in March 1864 and reported nine officers, 289 enlisted men, 288 small arms, and 10,000 rounds of ammunition as present. He dutifully wrote his wife about building and improving fortifications in the northeast sector of the lines. He told her of the Yuletide visit by visiting imperial Russian naval dignitaries since Fort Totten had been selected "from among all north of the river as the one for them to see." Bands played, thirteen-gun salutes fired, and there was "quite a crowd to see the strangers," he recounted. Of course, President Lincoln often visited from his nearby summer cottage at the Soldier's Home.

It was not all glamour for officers, however. Chamberlin bitterly complained in January 1863, "I believe I am destined to spend the most of my term of service on military units and boards of some sort." He noted trials for "a Penna. Dutch Capt. for embezzlement of public property, and conduct unbecoming an officer and a gentleman" as well as efficiency hearings for other officers in the fortifications. By the summer, Chamberlin's lot improved, as his rank and social

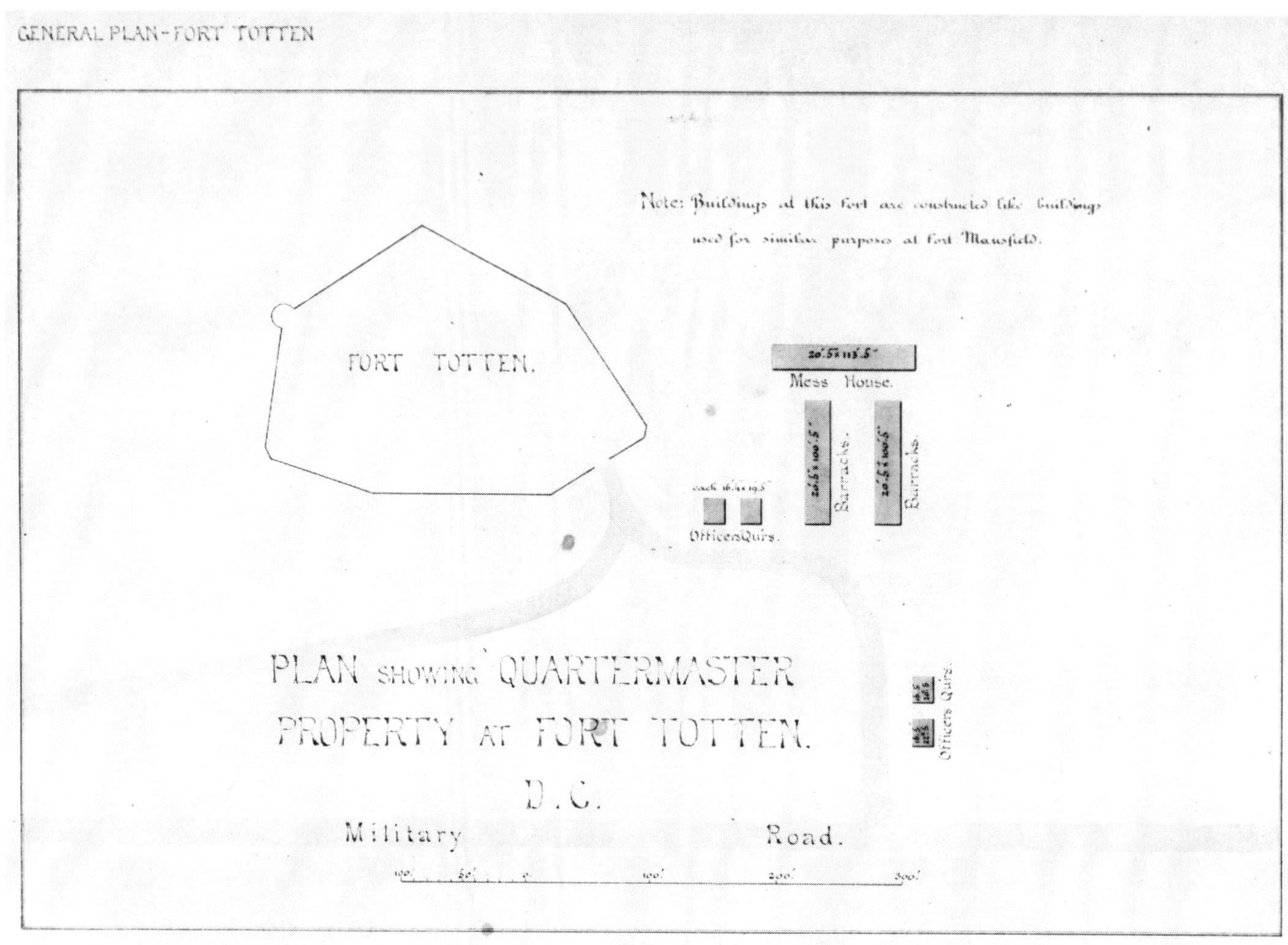

Plan for Quartermaster Property at Fort Totten. *National Archives*

graces had secured entry into the salons of some of Washington's finest citizens, including the famous Blair family and John C. Rives, editor of the *Congressional Globe*. Still, Chamberlin complained bitterly about the paltry politicians of the city, who, "not daring to enlist, hovered around the Capitol, gathering up spoils for themselves, and endeavoring to cheat our officers and soldiers out of their honors." He reflected his men's view that political interference in army affairs had thwarted every general "by some who were afraid he might become too popular."

Fort Totten saw action during Early's raid as the 100-pounder Parrott added long-range supporting fire to the battle in front of Fort Stevens. The guns and supporting troops also skirmished with Confederate cavalry to their immediate front. In his after-action recommendations, Major General Christopher Augur thought that the fort itself was sufficiently armed. But he wanted four field pieces for the battery to the left and two additional pieces acquired for the battery to the right of Fort Totten.

By May 1865, army officials thought that both Fort Stevens and Fort Totten should be retained in a permanent retention, postwar skeletal defense system. But they soon dropped the idea as the nation returned to peace. In April 1866, an inventory at the fort noted the presence of two lumber barracks (100 by twenty-one feet), a lumber mess house (116 by twenty-one feet), two lumber officers' quarters (twenty by eighteen feet), a log kitchen (twenty-five by six feet), three log officers' quarters (twenty-one by eighteen feet), and a log guardhouse (thirty by sixteen feet). This complex of buildings lies south of the fort proper but eventually was simply given to George Thomas, the landowner on whose farm the works had been constructed.[13]

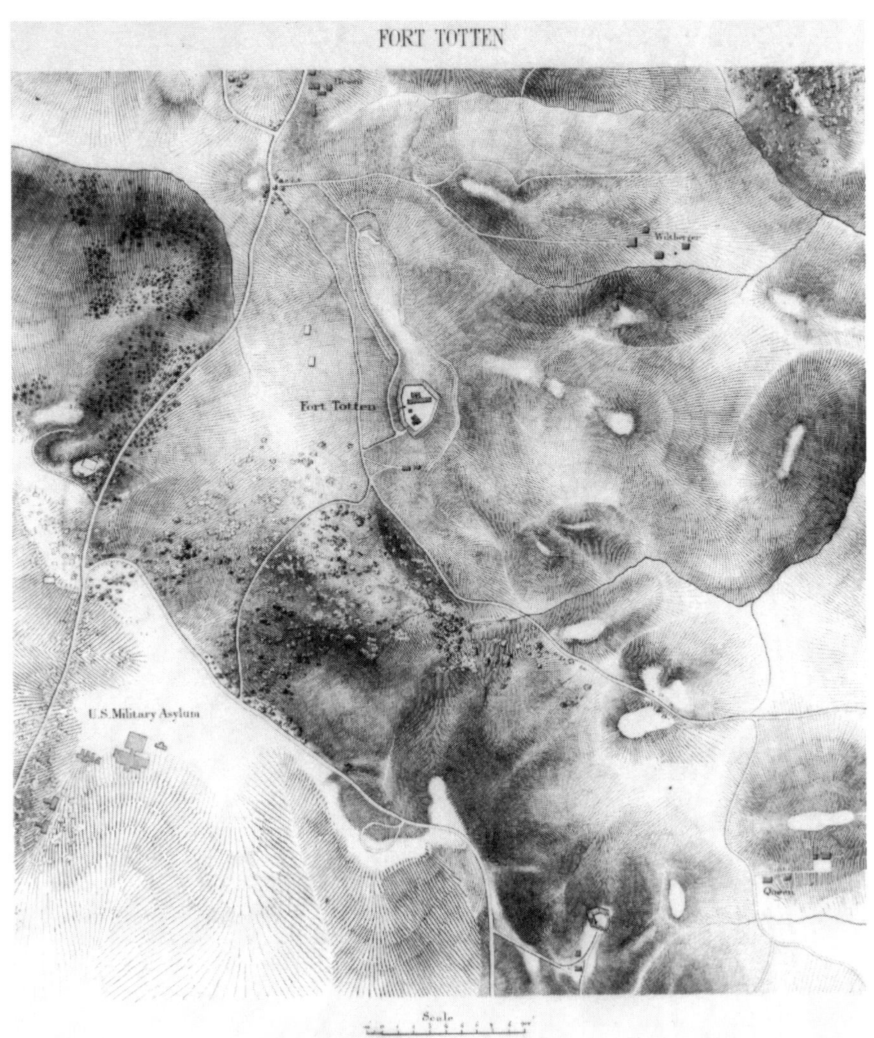

Fort Totten and Environs—An Early Topographic Perspective. *National Archives*

Sally Port at Fort Totten. *National Archives*

Fort Totten's 100-Pounder Parrott Rifle. *Library of Congress*

Gun Drill at Fort Totten Showing Magazine at Right. *Library of Congress*

The Firing Line at Fort Totten. *Library of Congress*

Fort Slemmer

Location

From Fort Totten, continue south on Fort Totten Drive (unarmed battery remains can be seen toward the bottom of the hill to the left), bearing left through the Hawaii Avenue merger to Taylor Street (traffic light). Turn right on Taylor Street and continue to the traffic lights at the top of the hill and turn right into the Brookland Ridge Apartment complex parking lot noting privately preserved and interpreted remains of a rifle trench that linked Forts Totten and Slemmer immediately on the right. Return to Taylor Street and continue straight through the traffic light onto Harewood Road. Turn left on first major street at the edge of the Catholic University campus (note the sign for O'Boyle and Marist halls). Turn left and continue half a block. The site of Fort Slemmer lies on the left of the street north of Marist Hall.

Visible Remains

Modern construction has all but destroyed most of the remaining vestiges of any earthworks; no interpretive markers exist.

Description

Named for Lieutenant Adam Slemmer, a Pennsylvanian and defender of Fort Pickens, Florida, during the Secession crisis of 1860–1861.

The fort was small, with a perimeter of only ninety-three yards, ultimately mounting three 32-pounder seacoast guns and one eight-inch howitzer (all en barbette). The position was supported by an unarmed battery (four vacant platforms) to the left and an unarmed battery (five vacant platforms) to the right of the fort. Following Early's raid, Major General Christopher Augur, commanding the Department of Washington, reported the need for "four field guns to arm the batteries on the right and left" of the fort.

The smallness of the work has led to the mislabeling of official photographs as Fort Massachusetts.

Notes/Anecdotes

Fort Slemmer was constructed on the twenty-four-acre property of florist Henry Douglass. The soldiery destroyed flowers and various plants and bushes, including 1,970 fruit trees, causing great hardship to the property owner.

Units connected with the fort included the following:

1st New Hampshire Heavy Artillery, Co. H, June–September 1863
1st New Hampshire Heavy Artillery, Co. I, March 1862–May 1863
2d Pennsylvania Heavy Artillery
26th New York Infantry
150th Ohio National Guard, Co. H, June–July 1864

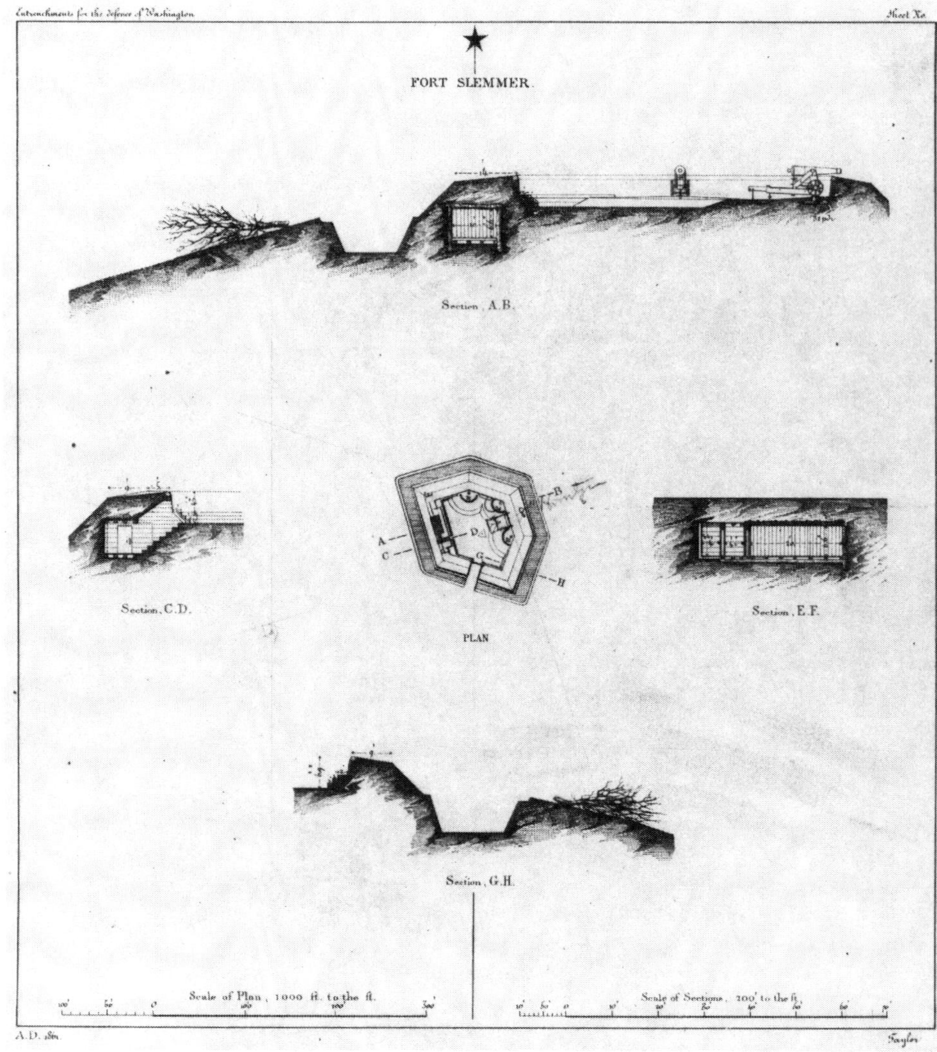

Fort Slemmer—Engineer Drawing. *National Archives*

Garrison returns from the December 1862 report of Lieutenant J. H. Guesinger of Captain G. L. Braaun's company of the 2d Pennsylvania Heavy Artillery at Fort Slemmer provide a capsule of details of interest:

13 caps
102 cap letters
62 feathers
107 crossed cannon insignia
75 eagles
10 sack coats
6 flannel shirts
10 pairs of drawers
1 pair of cavalry boots
76 leather stocks
3 Privates coats
5 Sergeant Shoulder Scales
90 Corporals and Privates Shoulder Scales I Sash
4 Privates Uniform Jackets
7 trousers
7 great coats
11 blankets
114 knapsacks and straps
102 haversacks
107 canteens and straps
3 yards of narrow braid for hats
2 volumes—System of Target Practice
8 Casey's Infantry Tactics Volumes
4 Light Artillery Tactics Copies
3 Bayonet exercises
18 Blank descriptive Lists
4 Heavy Artillery Instruction
1 Monthly Report Book
12 Axes
12 Spades
14 Camp kettles
34 Mess pans
10 camp hatchets

Fort Slemmer (note size, abatis, trimly dressed garrison). *National Archives*

2 bugles and cords
3 Wall tents
4 Wall tent flies
3 Common tents
13 pick axes
14 Sibley tents
7 Sibley tent stoves
7 Sibley tent poles

Forts Slemmer, Bunker Hill, and Saratoga and Battery Morris, together with Forts Thayer and Lincoln and Battery Jameson, were generally manned by various companies of the same regiment. The 2d Pennsylvania Heavy Artillery, for example, provided company-size garrisons for most of the forts in this sector of the defenses.

The unit historian of the 2d Pennsylvania Heavy Artillery (112th Pennsylvania Infantry) described the evolution of his unit while in this sector from a second-rate infantry command with only marginally proficient officers into a crack heavy artillery contingent. Originally equipped with Austrian muskets when assembled at Fort Saratoga, the regiment exchanged them for Springfield rifle muskets and a more rigorous drilling once they became heavy artillerists. An early 1862 purging of subpar officers suggested that higher authorities frowned on lax discipline and the regimental commander's interest in the fleshpots of Washington rather than his post. They replaced him with Colonel A. A. Gibson, former regular army captain of the 2d U.S. Artillery in the Mexican War.

Nonetheless, many of the 2d Pennsylvania "Heavies" took "French leave" when Lee invaded the Keystone State in 1863, going home to defend her "to the letter, as well as the spirit, of their enlistment." They served anonymously but were carried on regimental muster rolls as deserters until well after the war.

Fort Slemmer Sally Port. *U.S. Army Military History Institute*

Pennsylvanians, like their comrades of the 9th New York Heavy Artillery (138th Infantry), also provided construction details for road building and other fatigue details in the area.

The 2d Pennsylvania Heavy Artillery also gained a reputation for running off its first chaplain. The quiet, unobtrusive Reverend John Hassler resigned simply because the men would not respond to his divine services. A new padre appeared—Reverend "Father" Thomas P. Hunt—who appeared "restless in inquiry, his philosophic mind clothed his researches in thought as well as it was solid." Not only did Hunt end Colonel Gibson's hard swearing, but the pair reformed the regiment's tendency toward hard drinking, neighborhood foraging, and abuse of passes. Overall, the Gibson–Hunt team turned the 2d Heavies around. Families of the regiment joined their soldiers in the permanent camps, much as families had followed their soldiers to garrisons to the ancient Roman frontiers.[14]

About mid-July, the heavy artillerists who had remained with the colors in the defenses transferred regimental head quarters from Fort Lincoln to the plateau between Fort Bunker Hill and Fort Slemmer. They began hut construction to replace their Sibley tent abodes under fine shade trees. They built one-story, frame barracks (forty by 100 feet) that were set two or three feet aboveground in hospital style, thus providing good air circulation in every quarter. The

Fort Bunker Hill

Location

From the Fort Slemmer site, return via Harewood Road to Taylor Street NE (traffic light at the top of the hill). Turn right and proceed to 14th Street NE (fifth traffic light). Turn right past the Franciscan monastery grounds on the left to the Fort Bunker Hill site bounded by Perry, Otis, 13th, and 14th streets NE.

Soldier Sketch of Fort Bunker Hill. *McClure,* Guide Leaflet to the Defenses of Washington

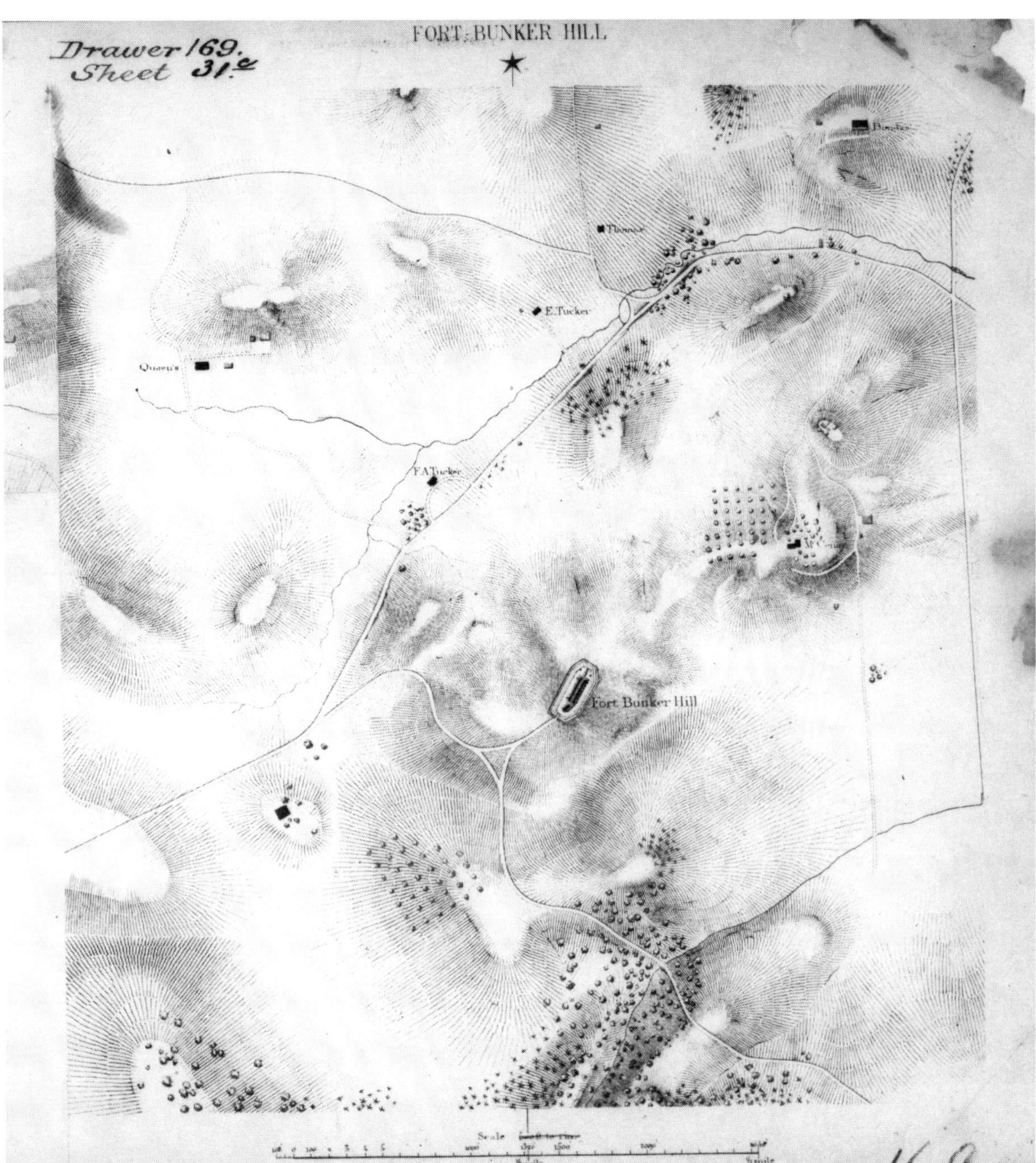

Early Map of Fort Bunker Hill Environs. *National Archives*

Visible Remains

Despite the park setting (overgrown) and National Park Service maintenance, there are few physical remains and no interpretive markers exist.

Description

Constructed by the 11th Massachusetts Infantry during the autumn and winter of 1861–1862, this unit applied the name of Boston's famous Revolutionary War battle site to their work.

The fort had a perimeter of 205 yards and rested atop a commanding hill. The work mounted thirteen guns and mortars, which included one eight-inch siege howitzer (en barbette), eight 32-pounder seacoast guns (en barbette), two 30-pounder Parrott rifles (one en embrasure, one en barbette), and one ten-inch and one 24-pounder Coehorn mortar. There were no vacant platforms.

As with Fort Slemmer, auxiliary unarmed batteries stood to the left (seven platforms) and the right (nine platforms) of the fort and one in front (seven platforms).

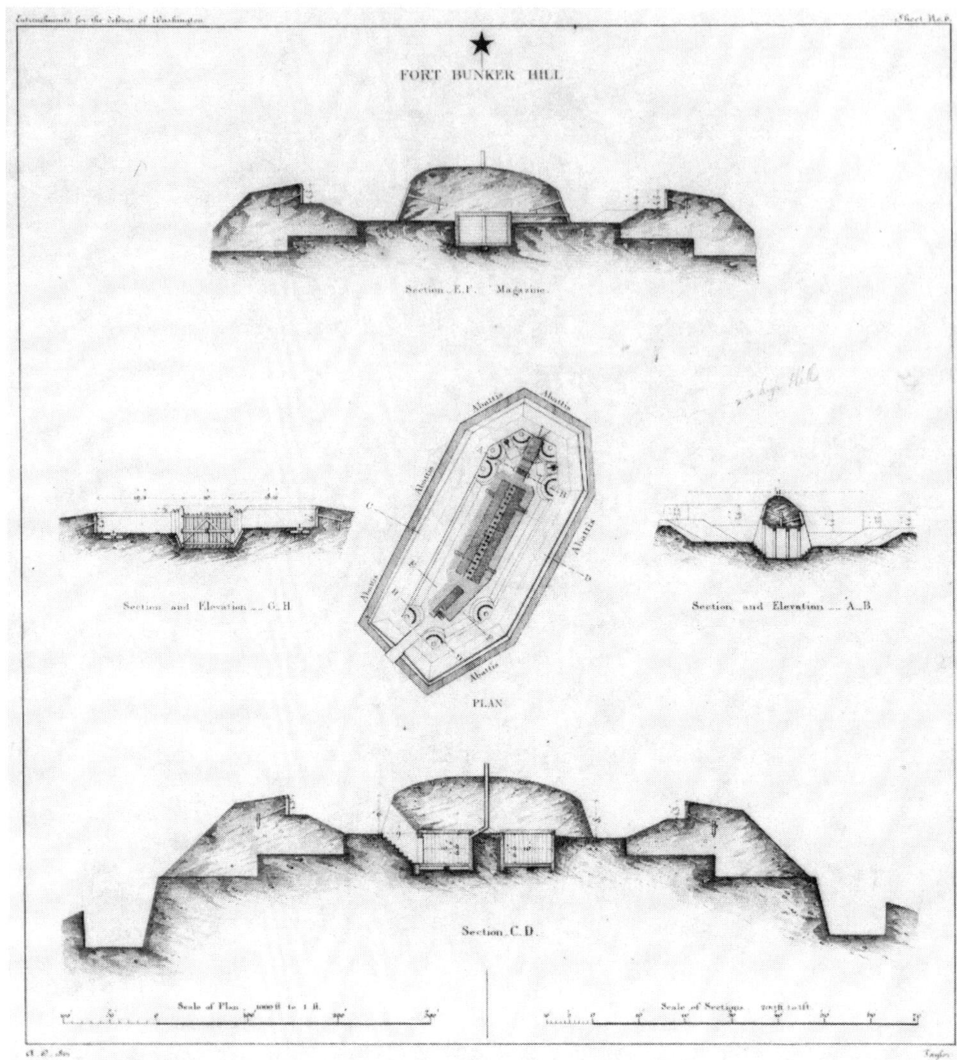

Fort Bunker Hill—Engineer Drawing. *National Archives*

Major General Christopher Augur's post–Early's raid assessment suggested adding eight light artillery pieces to the armament for the three batteries.

Notes/Anecdotes

Other units identified at various times with this position included the following:

- 2d Pennsylvania Heavy Artillery (112th Volunteers), Co. A, June 1862–March 1864
- 2d Pennsylvania Heavy Artillery (112th Volunteers), Co. B, August 1862–March 1864
- 2d Pennsylvania Heavy Artillery (112th Volunteers), Co. C, November 1862–May 1863
- 2d Pennsylvania Heavy Artillery (112th Volunteers), Co. D, June 1863–March 1864
- 2d Pennsylvania Heavy Artillery (112th Volunteers), Co. F, August–September 1862
- 2d Pennsylvania Heavy Artillery (112th Volunteers), Co. M, December 1863–March 1864
- 9th New York Heavy Artillery (138th Infantry), Cos. A, E, F, G, H, I, K, September 1862
- 1st New Hampshire Heavy Artillery, Co. B, May 1864
- 1st New Hampshire Heavy Artillery, Co. L, November 1864
- 3d U.S. Artillery, Co. G
- 150th Ohio National Guard, Cos. B, C, D, F, H, K, June 1864
- 3d Massachusetts Heavy Artillery, Co. K, November 1863–February 1864
- 3d Massachusetts Heavy Artillery, Co. D, March–June 1865

Private James C. Cannon of Company K of the 150th Ohio National Guard recalled on June 17, 1864, that Mrs. Stephen Douglas, widow of the famous Illinois

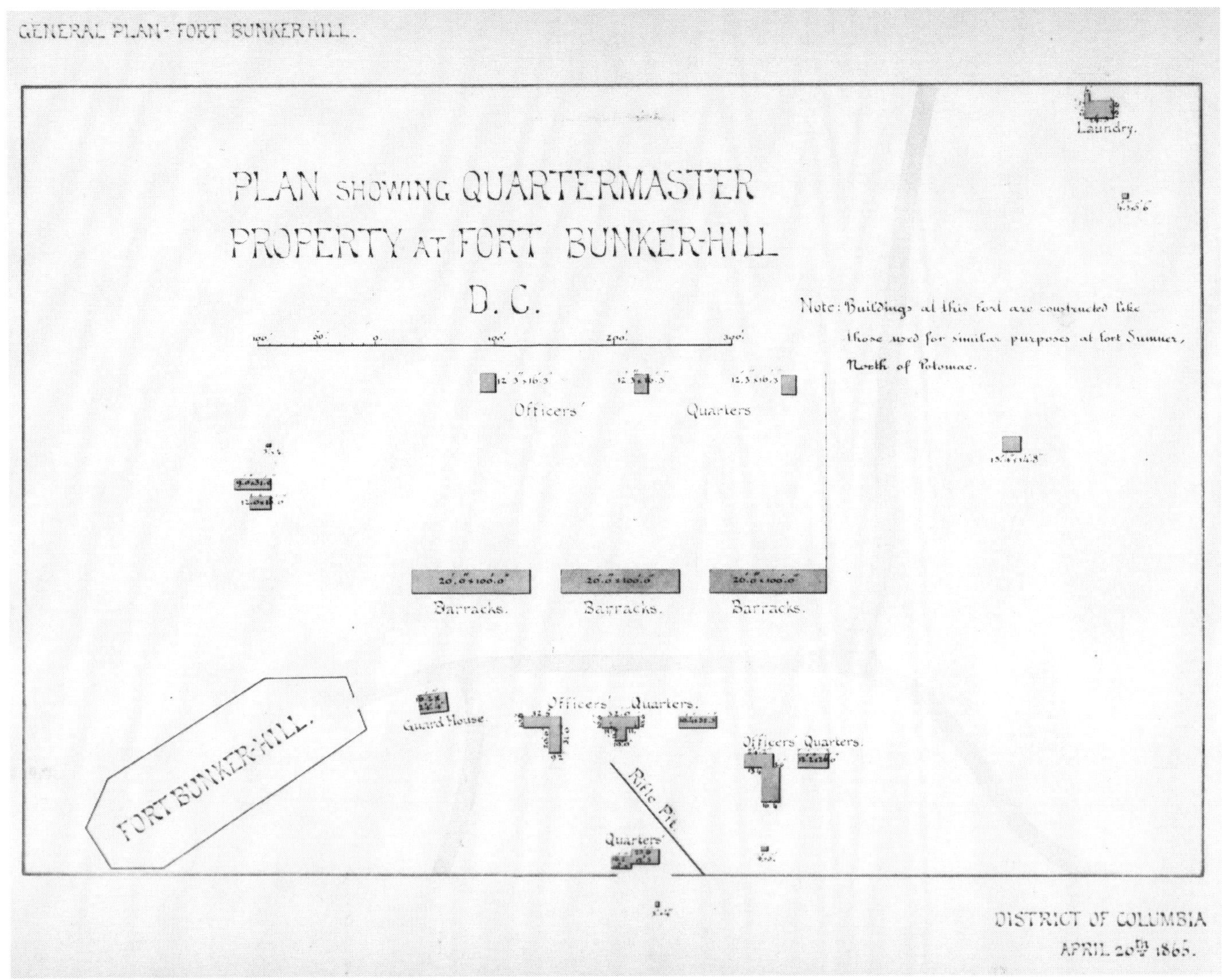

Plan for Quartermaster Property at Fort Bunker Hill. *National Archives*

senator and sometime opponent of Abraham Lincoln, visited the fort, "which afforded an agreeable topic for camp talk." Even more pleasing was the arrival the next day of a cake from home for Corporal Edward Ells. More tragic, however, was a July 4 "friendly-fire" accident that killed Corporal W. H. Wyman by one of the boys trying to play a prank on the noncommissioned officer as he inspected the picket line. Private William R. Reid blithely noted, "It is wonderful the ball did not kill another one of the boys," as they were all together in a crowd.

The park at this site also was used during World War II for victory gardens. After the war, a large monument to the famous father of modern India, Mohandas K. Gandhi, was planned for the hilltop on which Fort Bunker Hill rested. The plan never reached fruition.

Anger at Lincoln's assassination was reflected in Private Henry E. Dunbar's letter to his wife of 10:00 a.m. on April 16, 1865. This Third Massachusetts Heavy Artillerist noted how the joy of war's end "is turned to sorrow—mourning & indignation" for "our loved President is dead, murdered & words cannot express the loathing, yes *hate* that I now feel for *anybody* that even *winked* at this Rebellion." If he and his colleagues had their way, they "would commence *now & hang* without judge or jury not only every outright Rebel but every *sympathizer*, that we could get our hands upon, & I am not certain but we *shall yet*." They were "read here for a *complete annihilation* of the whole *cursed race*," he confessed, and was "about willing to believe that God would justify such a Policy." The Fort Bunker Hill property became another community Victory Garden site in World War II, but postwar plans for a memorial to Indian patriot and peace advocate Mohadas Ghandi atop the hill never came to fruition.[15]

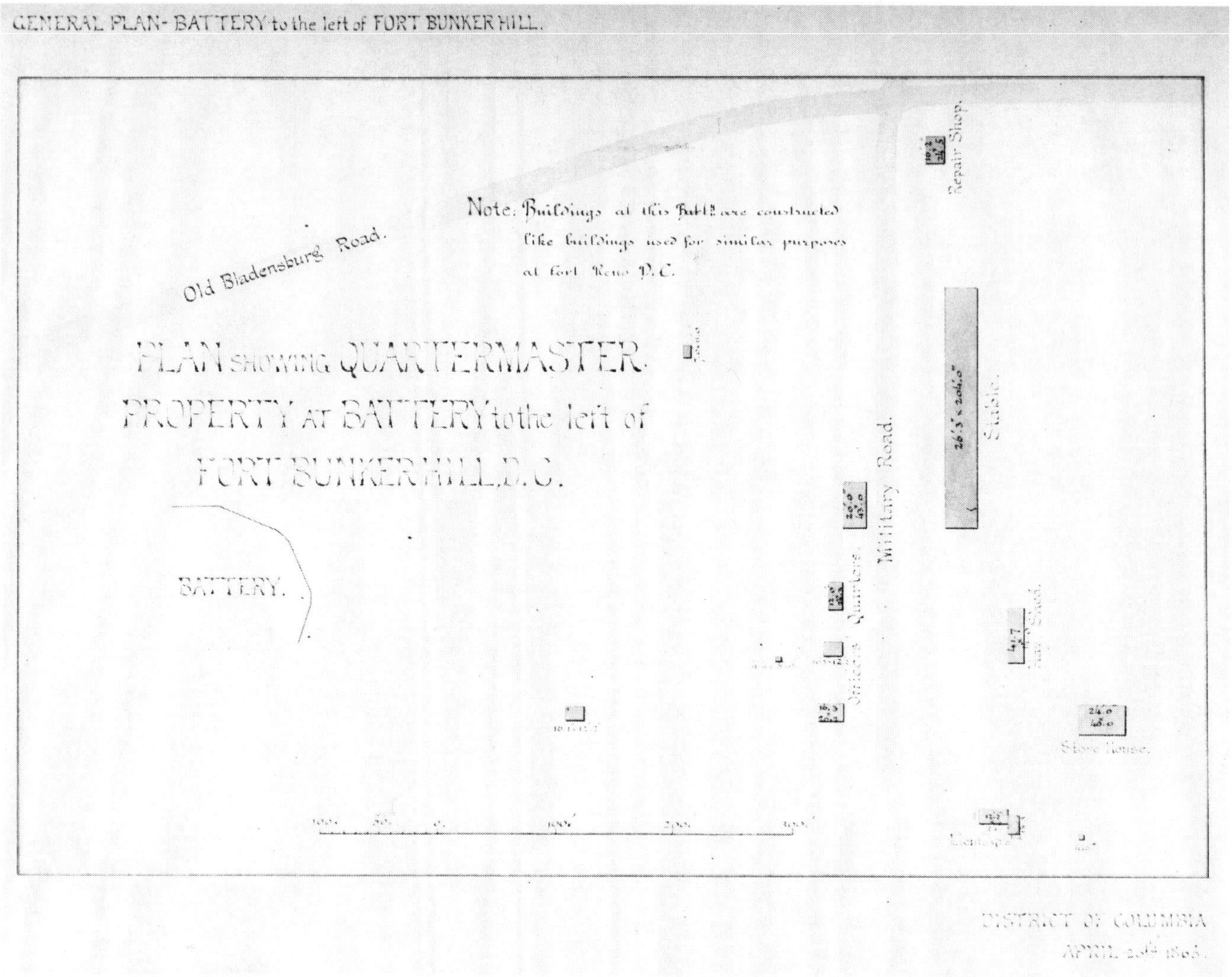

GENERAL PLAN- BATTERY to the left of FORT BUNKER HILL.
Note: Buildings at this Batt'y are constructed like buildings used for similar purposes at Fort Reno D.C.
Old Bladensburg Road.
PLAN showing QUARTERMASTER PROPERTY at BATTERY to the left of FORT BUNKER HILL, D.C.
BATTERY.
Military Road.
Quarters
Stable.
26'3" x 204'0"
Repair Shop.
Store House.
DISTRICT OF COLUMBIA
APRIL 20th 1865.

Plan of Quartermaster Property at Battery to Left of Fort Bunker Hill. *National Archives*

12'
INSIDE VIEW OF GATE AT FORT BUNKER HILL
SCALE 1/30

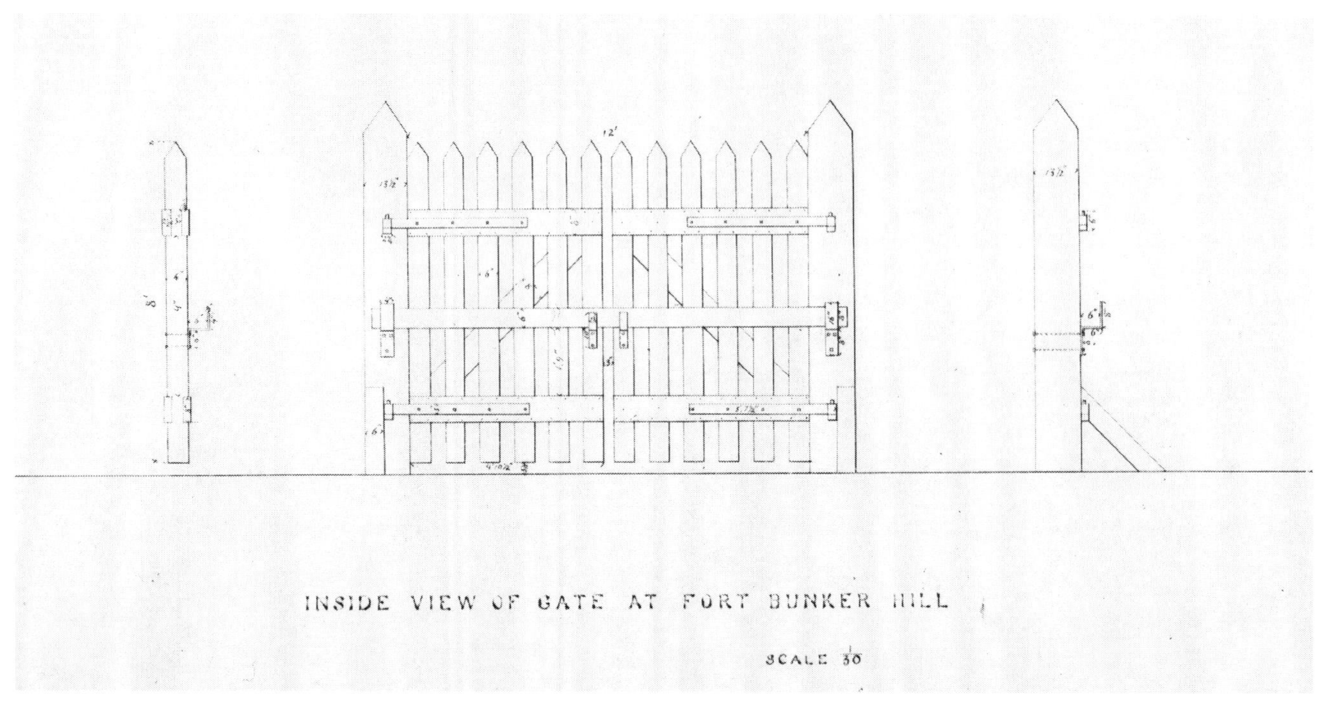

Inside View of Fort Bunker Hill Gate—Engineer Drawing. *National Archives*

Fort Saratoga and Battery Morris

Location

Follow 14th Street NE south to Jackson or Irving Street and turn left to the Fort Saratoga site (bordered by Jackson, 18th, Irving, and 20th Streets with an alley from 20th Street directly into the high-ground site). Turn right on 20th Street and cross Rhode Island Avenue. Battery Morris stood in the block on the left side at the intersection of 20th and Fulton streets NE.

Visible Remains

None; no interpretive markers exist.

Description

Fort Saratoga and Battery Morris were minor works and together with Fort Thayer provided a linkage between Forts Bunker Hill and Lincoln. Fort Saratoga was probably constructed by New York troops in late 1861 and early 1862. This would account for the names applied to the fort and battery—the upper Hudson valley, New York Revolutionary battle site, and Colonel L. O. Morris, who commanded the 7th New York Heavy Artillery (113th Infantry).

Fort Saratoga had a perimeter of 153 yards and mounted eight guns. They included one eight-inch siege howitzer, six 32-pounder seacoast guns (en barbette), and a 24-pounder Coehorn mortar. It had one vacant platform also. Following Early's raid, Major General Christopher C. Augur wanted six light field guns added to the fort for batteries to its left and right. He also sought another four field pieces for what was apparently Battery Morris.

Notes/Anecdotes

Other units garrisoning the works included the following:

- 2d Pennsylvania Heavy Artillery (112th Volunteers), Co. C, May–June 1862
- 2d Pennsylvania Heavy Artillery (112th Volunteers), Co. D, March–June 1862
- 2d Pennsylvania Heavy Artillery (112th Volunteers), Co. E, March 1862–February 1864
- 2d Pennsylvania Heavy Artillery (112th Volunteers), Co. K, November 1862–February 1864
- 1st New Hampshire Heavy Artillery, Co. B (part), May 12–15, 1864
- 150th Ohio National Guard, Cos. D, F, I, May–July 1864
- 1st D. C. Infantry
- Veteran Reserve Corps contingents

Major General Quincy A. Gilmore, commander of the XIX Corps, headquartered here during Early's raid in July 1864. He commanded this sector in the defense line.

GUARDIANS OF RAILROAD AND TURNPIKE FROM BALTIMORE: FORTS THAYER AND LINCOLN AND BATTERY JAMESON

A complex of forts and batteries commanded the upper valley of the Eastern Branch (Anacostia River) as well as the Baltimore and Ohio Railroad and turnpike to Baltimore (Bladensburg Road), all of which entered the District of Columbia from the north at this point.

Fort Thayer

Location

From Battery Morris, return to 20th Street north to Rhode Island Avenue NE, right to South Dakota Avenue, right to 24th Street NE, and right (south) to 24th and Irving streets. Fort Thayer stood in the present block between 24th and 25th streets and Irving and Hamlin streets NE.

Visible Remains

None; no interpretive signs.

Description

Fort Thayer was named for Colonel Sylvanus Thayer, a Massachusetts native and "father" of the U.S. Military Academy.

The fort was a small work of 180 perimeter yards and mounted eight guns and mortars, including two eight-inch siege howitzers (en barbette), four 24-pounder seacoast guns (en barbette), one 24-pounder siege gun (en embrasure), and a 24-pounder Coehorn mortar. After Early's raid, Washington departmental commander Major General Christopher C. Augur wanted to add four field pieces to arm three batteries between the fort and the railroad just to the east. Apparently, an additional new redoubt was planned between Forts Saratoga and Thayer for which Augur wanted four additional field guns.

Notes/Anecdotes

The land on which Forts Thayer and Lincoln and Battery Jameson were constructed belonged to John Veitch, whose family had owned this property under a land grant from Lord Baltimore dating to 1719.

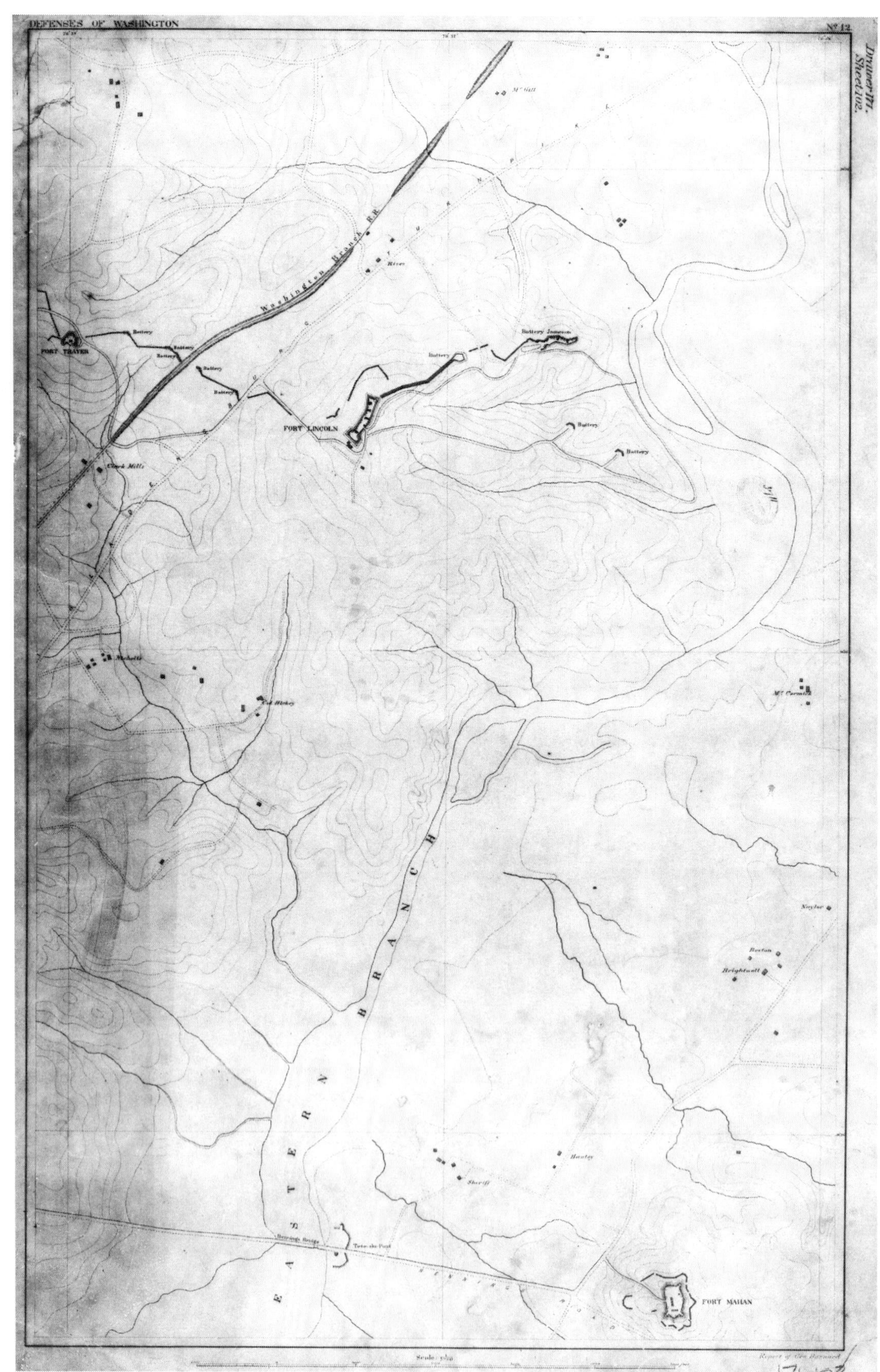

Sector Map—Fort Thayer to Fort Mahan. *National Archives*

Garrisons included the following:

2d Pennsylvania Heavy Artillery, Cos. C, H, February 1862–November 1862
2d Pennsylvania Heavy Artillery, Cos. D, H, November 1862–May 1863
2d Pennsylvania Heavy Artillery, Cos. C, I, July 1863–February 1864
2d Pennsylvania Heavy Artillery, Co. B (part)

In addition to the Pennsylvanians, Fort Thayer was garrisoned during Early's raid by part of Company B, 1st New Hampshire Heavy Artillery, and Company E, 150th Ohio National Guard.

Company K of the Buckeyes remembered best the previous hot May days (ninety-five degrees in the shade on the May 24) that caused mile-and-a-half trips both to the yellow waters of the Anacostia River and to stuffy galleries of the Capitol building, where "the massive frame" of native son Congressman and future President James A. Garfield held forth on merits of an internal revenue bill. Bunking where the 16th Massachusetts Battery had previously resided at the post, James Cannon recalled that one comrade, Sergeant Anson Robbins, tried to buy overalls in the city, only to experience the shopkeeper's refusal to sell on the grounds that he might use them to desert. The One Hundred Days boys went back to Fort Slocum in June and the next month on to a date with destiny in Fort Stevens during Early's raid on the city.

After Early's raid, the fort was garrisoned by the following:

4th Massachusetts Heavy Artillery, Co. B, September 1864
3d Massachusetts Heavy Artillery, Cos. E, H, M, September 1864–April 1865[16]

Fort Lincoln and Battery Jameson

Location

From the Fort Thayer site, return to South Dakota Avenue NE. Turn right to Bladensburg Road or U.S. Route 1 (traffic light). Turn left passing Fort Lincoln New Town on the right and proceed to the Eastern Avenue/Fort Lincoln Drive intersection (traffic light). Turn right to Commodore Joshua Barney Drive. Turn left to the parking lot of Fort Lincoln Elementary School. Park and proceed on foot to the top of the hill behind the school/recreation area roughly shaped as fortress but with no indication that this was site of Fort Lincoln. Traces of other outworks may possibly remain on lower ground to the northwest behind townhouses as well as auxiliary battery sites to the northeast/east. To reach Battery Jameson, return to Bladensburg Road. Turn right to the Fort Lincoln Cemetery entrance and then right onto the grounds past the mausoleum and the Lincoln oak site to the battery.

Visible Remains

No remains exist for Fort Lincoln proper. The battery and trench northwest of Fort Lincoln are overgrown but preserved, and there are no interpretive markers. The Battery Jameson parapet is well preserved and sodded with two guns emplaced, and an interpretive plaque is present. Also marked are a nearby springhouse and the remains of an ancient oak under which President Lincoln allegedly sipped water and conducted strategic planning.

Description

Fort Lincoln was named for the sixteenth president of the United States, Abraham Lincoln. Battery Jameson was named for Brigadier General Charles I. Jameson, whose arduous service at the First Battle of Bull Run (Manassas), Williamsburg, and Fair Oaks, Virginia, contributed to his death of typhoid fever at Old Town, Maine, on November 6, 1862.

Fort Lincoln had a perimeter of 466 yards. Its armament included thirty-four guns and mortars including two eight-inch siege howitzers (en barbette), six 32-pounder seacoast guns (en barbette), one 24-pounder

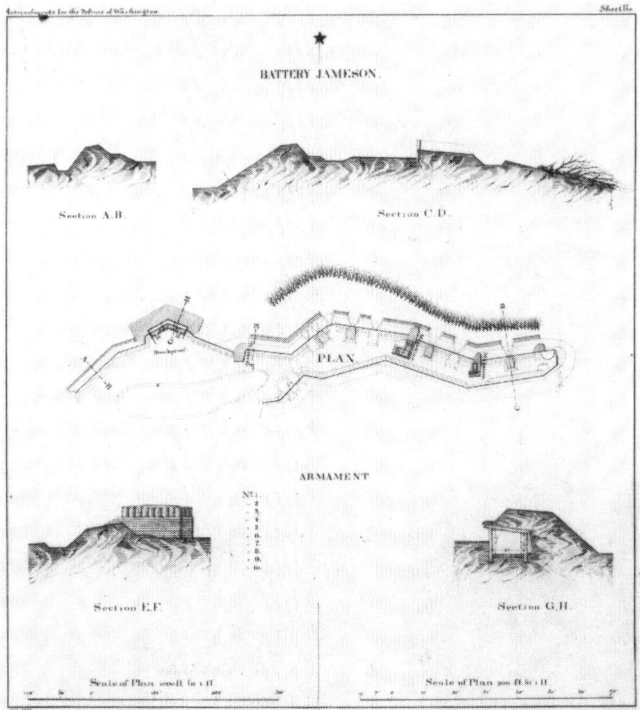

Battery Jameson—Engineer Drawing. *National Archives*

siege and three 24-pounder seacoast guns (en barbette), two 24-pounder field howitzers (en embrasure), four 12-pounder field guns (en barbette), eight 6-pounder field guns (en barbette), four 30-pounder Parrotts (en barbette), one 100-pounder Parrott rifle (en barbette), and one ten-inch and two 24-pounder Coehorn mortars.

Battery Jameson was a powerful auxiliary battery with one emplaced gun (a 24-pounder seacoast gun, (en barbette), and fourteen unoccupied gun platforms.

The interval between Forts Thayer and Lincoln was filled with a field gun battery (three vacant platforms), two batteries immediately beside the railroad (one to the left with seven platforms, the other on the right with three platforms), a three-platform field gun battery to the left of the turnpike, and another unoccupied six-gun battery between the turnpike and Fort Lincoln itself. In the wake of Early's raid, departmental commander Major General Christopher C. Augur stated the Fort Lincoln "ought to have six additional field guns to arm the exterior batteries, beginning on the left at the railroad and ending on the right at Battery Jameson, on the Eastern Branch, making for the line north of the city, eighty-eight additional field guns."

Notes/Anecdotes

The 1st Massachusetts Volunteer Infantry constructed Fort Lincoln in the summer of 1861 with a projected garrison of 750 men, with 150 artillerymen. The fort complex included a system of rifle pits and exterior batteries, compensating for the narrowness of the hill on which the work rested. The investigating commission of late 1862–1863 noted that within the fort, the magazines and bombproofs were arranged as traverses to protect the long and narrow interior from enfilading fire. At one time, an elaborate brick drainage ditch ensured proper runoff and erosion

Modern View of Battery Jameson Ramparts. *Authors' Collection*

Modern View of Battery Jameson. *Authors' Collection*

control for the hillside works. A double-covered way provided communication with the forward battery to the left/front of the fort and adjacent Battery Jameson. Fort Lincoln boasted a 5-foot wide, 175-foot deep well containing 100 feet of water for the garrison.

Among the units prominently mentioned with respect to Fort Lincoln and Battery Jameson were the following:

- 1st and 11th Massachusetts Infantry, Hookers Brigade
- 2d New Hampshire Infantry
- 26th Pennsylvania Infantry
- 1st Rhode Island Light Artillery, Co. D, June 1864
- Maine Light Artillery, 1st Battery, 1st Battalion, May 5–23, 1865
- Maine Coast Guard, Co. A
- 1st New Hampshire Heavy Artillery, Co. B (part), May 1864
- 2d Pennsylvania Heavy Artillery (112th Volunteers), Cos. E, F, G, H, K, L, M, February 1862–February 1864
- 3d Massachusetts Heavy Artillery, Co. E, September–October 1864
- 3d Massachusetts Heavy Artillery, Co. H, October–November 1864, January–June 1865
- 3d Massachusetts Heavy Artillery, Cos. C, L, M, May–June 1865
- Massachusetts Heavy Artillery, 30th Unattached Company, September 22–26, 1862
- 150th Ohio National Guard, Co. I, July 1864
- 7th Michigan Cavalry (pickets drawn therefrom)

Local citizens Franklin Rines, George Mathiot, and Francis Feizer provided abatis, timber, and lumber for fortifications in this sector in 1861. The land on which Forts Thayer and Lincoln and Battery Jameson were erected belonged to various early families, such

Co. H, 3d Massachusetts Heavy Artillery at Fort Lincoln—Village of Bladensburg in Distance. *U.S. Army Military History Institute*

as the Veitch family, dating back to a land grant from Lord Baltimore in 1719. Descendants still lived in the old homestead, located behind the fort, as late as 1912. Subsequent construction of the National Training School for Boys and Fort Lincoln New Town destroyed the last remnants of the fort in the late twentieth century.

The Fort Lincoln complex proved popular for visiting dignitaries, especially the fort's namesake. President Lincoln met his fortification commanders under an ancient oak tree, now called the "Lincoln Oak," near a springhouse dating to 1683.

These fortifications overlooked the famous Bladensburg dueling grounds and lie at the epicenter of the battlefield where British forces routed an American army in August 1814 (viewed by a disappointed President James Madison, possibly the first president to come under enemy fire while in office). The disastrous Battle of Bladensburg led to the only occupation of Washington by an enemy power and accompanying burning of public buildings.

This area adjacent to the District of Columbia was rife with Confederate sympathizers and mischief makers. One local Maryland matriarch wrote her daughter from their nearby Bladensburg and Beltsville home that between the stench of urban Washington and "execrable band from Ft. Lincoln" she was beside herself. The band particularly made night hideous for several hours at local entertainment places Yost's and Barney's as "no two instruments accord, " and they played neither "in time or tune, nor any tune worth hearing, so the only effect they produce is setting one's teeth on edge."

Regimental histories of units stationed at Fort Lincoln carry tales of fraternization with local belles as well as a mysterious poisoning of Union officers and periodic cavalry chases of shadowy characters lurking on the perimeter. Some of the shadowy figures also numbered among Brigadier General Bradley Johnson's raiders, part of Early's force threatening Washington in July 1864. Johnson and company had traversed the countryside from Frederick to Baltimore, bent on ripping up railroad track and telegraph lines before venturing to Point Lookout (at the mouth of the Potomac) to free Confederate prisoners. Returning empty handed from that phase of their mission, they traversed the open country from Beltsville across

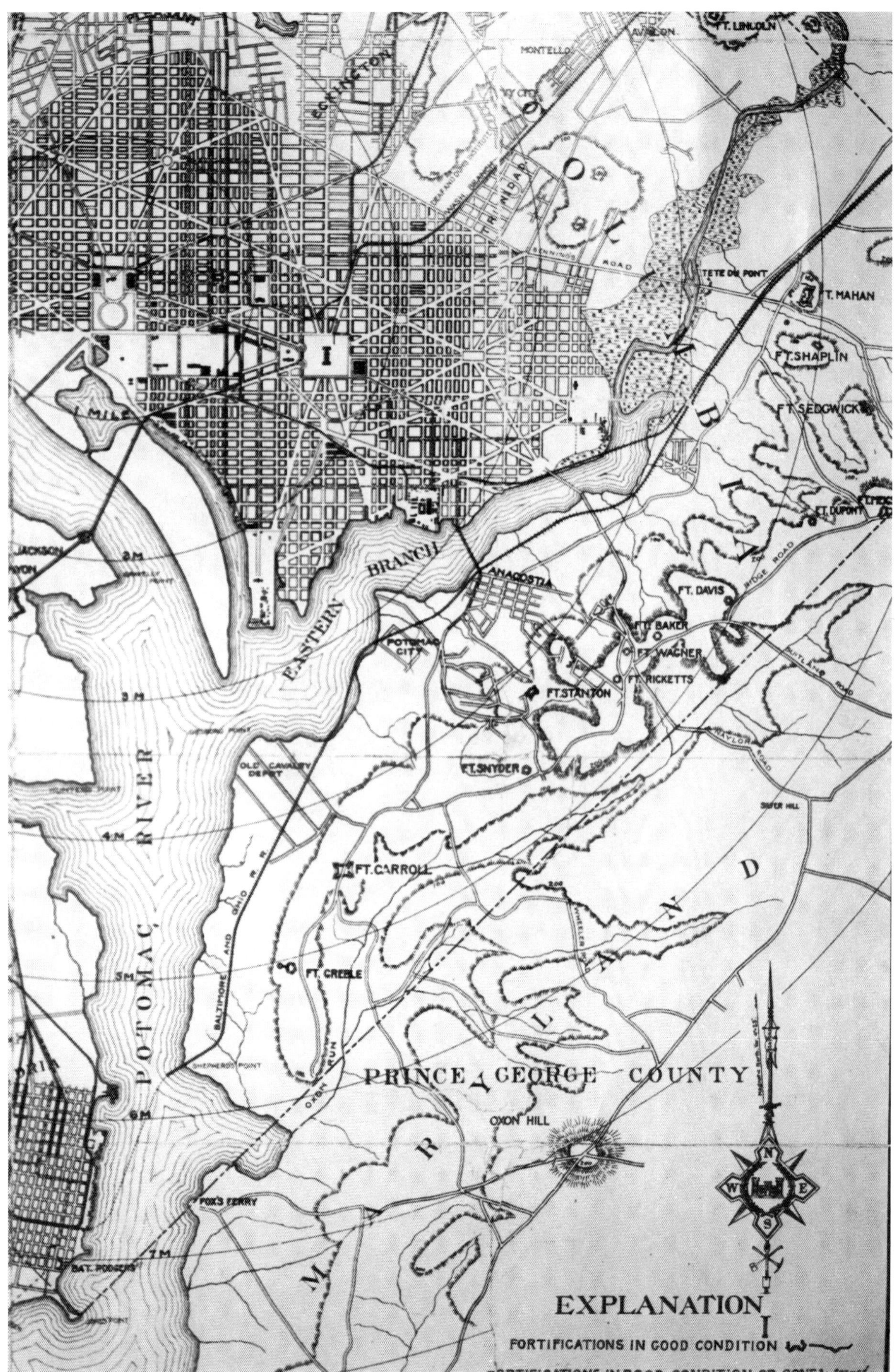

Sector Map—Forts East of the Anacostia. *D.C. National Guard, Engineer Corps, Map of the District of Columbia, 1892*

the northern defense perimeter drawing fire from garrisons like that of Fort Lincoln. In addition, great numbers of officers apparently gathered here and elsewhere along the lines during the two-day "siege" drawing a comment from one Ohio One Hundred Day's soldier that "stars and eagles were at a discount," while a private "was a rarity."

Samuel S. Wint of the 2d Pennsylvania Heavy Artillery left a journal capturing some of the details of garrison life at Fort Lincoln. Coming there from prisoner-of-war guard duty at Fort Delaware in late November 1862, they drew Sibley tents and went to the woods to cut timber to build stockades apparently for protection. Punishment for infractions meant incarceration in the fort's bombproof, and on one occasion the destruction of a runaway sutler's wagon permitted the high-strung soldiers to "liberate" cases of whiskey that neither Sutler J. Wood nor the regimental officers were able to recover. Apparently whiskey—whether the liberated or doled-out legitimate stuff—fortified the men working construction that cold winter. Christmas came with all kinds of games, a pig race, a wheelbarrow race, horse racing, wrestling, and blanket tosses together with band playing for dancers and circus stunts. On the last day of the year, they "raised flag pole in fort 65 feet high." By April, the garrison regularly enjoyed "300 herring, some shad and suckers" from the Anacostia River or Eastern Branch of the Potomac. On April 18, they test fired the fort's artillery with the result that the trunnion broke on the first shot of the ten-inch mortar and the 32-pounders performed poorly. Three days later, some of the regiment attending a horse race in Bladensburg were accosted by a citizen, who shot one of the soldiers. Earlier, Wint had noted a high incidence of desertion from the ranks given the proximity to Washington. At the end of 1863, Wint noted a salubrious holiday visiting a family in Bladensburg with secessionist proclivities, and the Union soldiers causing a whipped black to retaliate with a blacksnake whip that nearly killed his tormentor. Another fine fish haul came in the spring of 1864 that provided 200 pounds of dressed fish for the garrison. By the spring of 1864, the garrison had been transferred to Forts Marcy and Ethan Allen and would eventually join the reinforcement of the Army of the Potomac on the campaign.

One humorous note about Fort Lincoln was recounted after the war by Brevet Major Charles H. Anson of the 1st Vermont Heavy Artillery. It seems that his previous unit, the 11th Vermont, had a very impulsive and dedicated captain in Company E who was plagued by one of the regiment's most ungainly soldiers, a Private Hackett. Hackett could not keep in step and never learned the manual of arms. More at home with the Bible, he could recite Scripture from Genesis to Exodus. Posted one night near the entrance to Fort Lincoln, Hackett was approached by the duty captain, whom he challenged, "Who goes there?" The night being dark and rainy, the captain attempted to cross the dry moat surrounding the fort and promptly fell headlong into the ditch with a loud "Jesus Christ!" Unabashedly, Hackett faced about smartly and called out, "Turn out the Apostles. Jesus Christ is coming." He then helped his captain out of the muck.

Charles Gould of the 11th Vermont Heavy Artillery wrote his brother on October 29, 1862, graphically describing the prescribed drill for Fort Lincoln's heavy guns:

> To handle a barbette gun takes 4 privates, one Corporal & one Seargeant [*sic*]. The Searj. Is "chief of the piece" & the Corporal is gunner & has to thumb the piece while we load it & sights & gives the order when to fire. All that the Searj. Does is to man us to our gun & give the order "in & out Battery" which is back from the wall of the Fort when the order is "from battery" & back to its place when the order is "in battery." The privates are stationed two on each side of the gun. The order "load" from the gunner No.1 seizes the sponge steps onto the front of the carriage [*sic*] & assisted by No. 2 the gun is sponged, No 4 at the same time takes the "pass box" & goes & gets the cartridge which contains nothing but the charge of power, while No.3 gets the Reamer & hands to No. 1 & receives the sponge. After the gun is loaded they all "break off", that is they all face the outside & stand with their legs *straddled* out until after the order fire when they stand back in their places. No. 3 pulls on the gun which is done by placing a "friction tube" in the "vent" & hooking a wire with a string attached & pulling the string.[17]

5

Touring the Forts East of the Anacostia River

The Anacostia River (or Eastern Branch of the Potomac) divided Washington's system of fortifications into two distinct and virtually autonomous sectors north of the Potomac. General Barnard and his engineers regarded the forts "across the Eastern Branch" as the least satisfactory in the system. Yet this was the least-threatened sector, and the Anacostia River itself represented a reasonable barrier to assault on the city from due east, or what is termed southern Maryland. The upper reaches of the Anacostia valley were marshy and would channel any attacker under the guns of Fort Lincoln, Battery Jameson west of the Anacostia, or Fort Mahan on its eastern bank. One-quarter to one-half mile east of the Anacostia rose a six-mile-long, 300-foot-high ridge. It dropped off to a plateau on the south and into the valley of Oxon Run. Various points along the ridge overlooked the Navy Yard, the Washington Arsenal at Greenleaf Point, and the Capitol Hill section of the city. A vast wartime cavalry depot developed at the southern end of the ridge in the flatlands of Giesboro Point beside the Potomac. Roads converged on opposite ends of the ridge to cross the Anacostia at Uniontown and Benning's road bridges. Therefore, distinct defensive problems faced Barnard and the engineers. If southern Maryland lay far from Confederate armies, it remained a festering hotbed of secessionist spirit throughout the war. The Lincoln government could not neglect the Anacostia sector of forts because of possible guerrilla or partisan enemy activity.

Barnard and the army engineers regarded the sixteen forts and batteries that they erected east of the Anacostia as isolated works. They "really guarded against . . . dashes of cavalry against the bridges, or the temporary occupation of the heights by artillery," suggested Barnard in his report. They were erected diligently by the soldiers, who often worked day and night with 100 men per relief, Stuart O. Lincoln told his brother just before Christmas 1861 from an encampment at Camp Lesley above the Navy Yard. One volunteer in the 17th Maine complained about the boring work of drill and fortification improvements at Fort Carroll since his unit had enlisted not to make gabions but to save the Union. "Many of the boys became quite proficient in basket making," he admitted. Probably most of the soldiers in this sector agreed, although one member of the 9th New York Heavy Artillery felt that the experience east of the Anacostia was worth it. He pointed to the superb views of the city from the forts on the ridge (a view still present at Fort Stanton, for example) that could not be replicated elsewhere along the defense line.

Picket details from the eastern forts went out by night to raid chicken coops and civilian gardens. Runaway slaves came into the lines daily with fresh produce and soon attached themselves as servants to the officers (or were hustled off to contraband camps in the city). Service east of the Anacostia was a mixed bag. The regimental historian of the 88th Pennsylvania Volunteers suggested the essential truth of it all. His unit spent its tour guarding nine miles of forts east of the river but saw nothing of any enemy save rabbits, crows, and mud.

Today, some of the best-preserved examples of individual forts in the defense system may be found in National Park Service–managed parks in this section of Washington. But ill kept and located in crime-ridden neighborhoods, they are all but forgotten by students of the war as well as local citizens.[1]

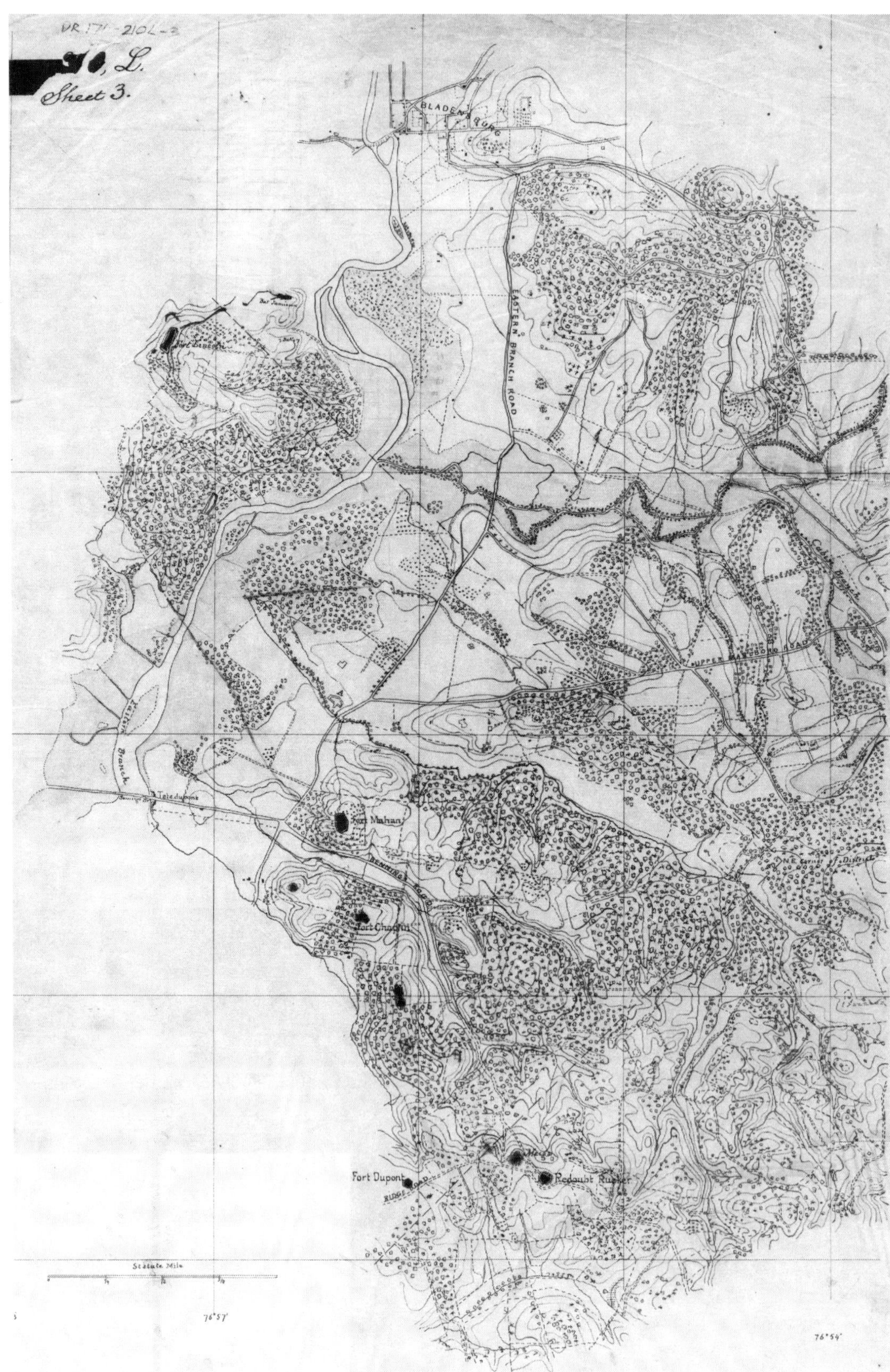

Sector Map—Fort Mahan to Fort DuPont. *National Archives*

GUARDING THE APPROACHES TO BENNING'S BRIDGE: FORT MAHAN, FORT CHAPLIN, "FORT OF CIRCULAR FORM," AND "FORT ON KENNEDY'S HILL"

These finished and unfinished works were to guard the approach to Washington from southern Maryland via the Benning's (Road) Bridge. A small stockaded tete-de-pont and earthwork also guarded the immediate entry to the bridge itself.

Fort Mahan

Location

From Fort Lincoln Cemetery, return to Bladensburg Road (U.S. Route 1) and turn left (south) into Washington. Go approximately two miles (nine traffic lights) and turn left onto 17th Street NE. Drive through six traffic lights to Benning Road NE. Turn left across the Anacostia River and railroad tracks and past Minnesota Avenue (traffic light) to Fort Mahan Park on the left at 42d Street and Benning Road. Turn left at 42d Street (ninth traffic light) and go to the top of the hill. Park the car and use the service road into the fort site.

Visible Remains

Despite National Park Service maintenance, a modern playground has effectively destroyed much of Fort Mahan, although some earthworks can be found north and south and east on hilltop; no interpretive markers exist.

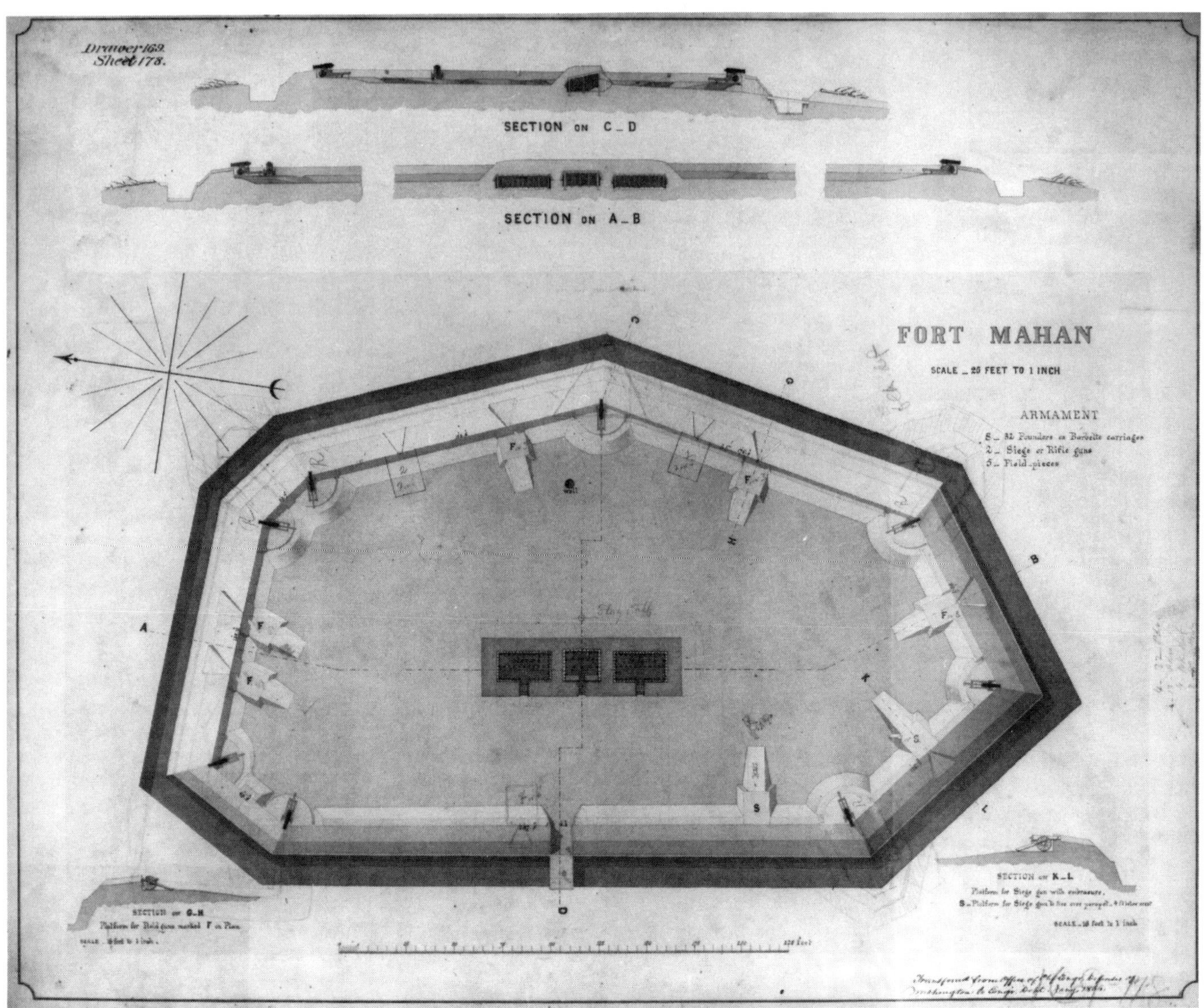

Fort Mahan (original)—Engineer Drawing. *National Archives*

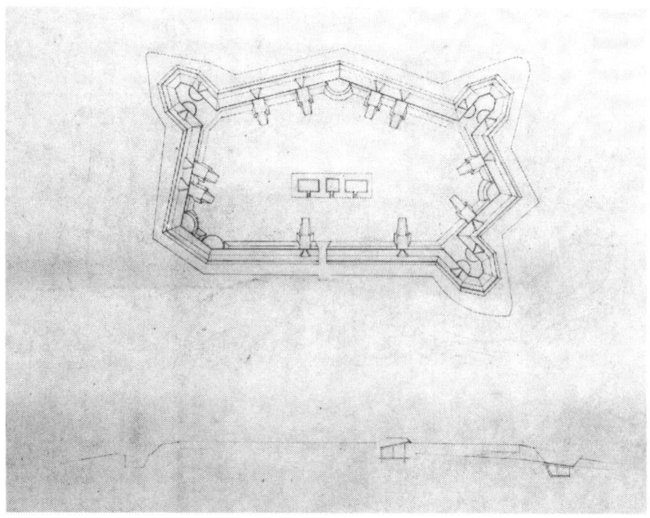

Fort Mahan (reshaped)—Engineer Drawing. *National Archives*

Description

Fort Mahan bore the name of West Point Professor Dennis Hart Mahan (father of the naval strategist Alfred Thayer Mahan), whose teaching helped prepare a generation of military officers for the Civil War.

This work underwent considerable modification during the war. Its final form delineated an irregular nine-sided fortification with a perimeter of 354 yards. The steep hillsides demanded additional rifle pits as well as a battery west of the main work to cover the open ground toward Benning's Bridge, called Battery Mahan.

An additional 400 yards of rifle pits (various "bastionets") were also projected from three angles of the counterscarp to provide reverse and covering fire for these exterior slopes. Early's raid promoted further engineering refinements including the laying of abatis and additional rifle pits toward the river to prevent flanking movements.

The armament of Fort Mahan likewise underwent changes and aptly illustrated the type of evolution and experimentation carried on in the defense system. The 1862 plans called for eight 32-pounder seacoast guns (en barbette) and seven empty platforms. Still another early return listed eight 32-pounder and two 24-pounder field howitzers, three 10-pounder Parrott rifles, and two empty platforms. On January 1, 1863, the listing noted eight 32-pounder, three 12-pounder, and two 6-pounder field guns; one 30-pounder Parrott rifle; one eight-inch siege howitzer; one ten-inch and one 24-pounder Coehorn mortar. Late in 1864, Fort Mahan's armament listed two eight-inch siege howitzers (en embrasure), four 32-pounder seacoast guns (en barbette), four 24-pounder field howitzers (en embrasure), three 12-pounder howitzers (en embrasure), and ten-inch and 24-pounder Coehorn mortars. In the summer of 1865, following abandonment of other forts, this work found its seacoast guns replaced by field guns since Fort Mahan was one of eleven forts in the system scheduled for retention. Battery Mahan had four vacant platforms.

Notes/Anecdotes

Fort Mahan was constructed on the property of Dr. William Manning and commanded the junction of Benning's Road and Eastern Branch Road (now Minnesota Avenue NE). Engineers pronounced that the work "commands the valley of the Eastern Branch as far as Bladensburg." Barnard contended that the fort exercised "a powerful influence in preventing an enemy, coming from the direction of Bladensburg from reaching the margins of the Anacostia opposite Washington." Since it was a relatively isolated work, he felt that it could hold out for a few days without external aid.

Fort Mahan's authorized garrison numbered 531 infantry and 216 artillerymen. Seldom at that strength, among the units stationed there were the following:

- 99th Pennsylvania Infantry, February 19–May 20, 1863
- 2d Pennsylvania Heavy Artillery (112th Volunteers), Co. K, May 20–September 12, 1862
- 17th Maine Infantry, Co. H?, August 24–October 7, 1862
- 19th Maine Infantry, Cos. C, G, August 30–September 27, 1862
- 19th Maine Infantry, Co. F, September 12–30, 1862
- 10th New York Heavy Artillery, Co. G, September 27, 1862–March 24, 1864
- 10th New York Heavy Artillery, Co. E, July 1863–February 1864
- 9th New York Heavy Artillery, Co. B, March 26–May 10, 1864
- 3d Massachusetts Heavy Artillery, 6th Co., May 7–11, 1864
- 3d Massachusetts Heavy Artillery, 11th Co., May 7–September 29, 1864
- Knap's (Knapp's) Independent Artillery Battalion (Pennsylvania), Co. C, May 31–June 1864
- 3d Massachusetts Heavy Artillery, 17th Co., September 17–29, 1864
- 3d Massachusetts Heavy Artillery, 10th Co. (detachment), September 28–October 14, 1864
- 3d Massachusetts Heavy Artillery, 7th Co., October 14–28, 1864, December 1, 1864–June 18, 1865
- Veteran Reserves, November 6–16, 1864
- 3d Massachusetts Heavy Artillery, 9th Co. (detachment), November 17–December 1, 1864

2d Connecticut Heavy Artillery, Co. B, June 6–29, 1865
2d Connecticut Heavy Artillery, Co. D, June 6–27, 1865
1st Maine Heavy Artillery, Co. A, June 27–August 24, 1865

Fort Mahan was the site of numerous additional outbuildings for the garrison and laborers in the area. A guardhouse, two barracks, at least one officers' quarters, a mess house, a stable, and possibly some sheds and about twelve frame and log structures could be found here, with an officers' quarters and barracks located within the earthworks. About one-quarter mile to the rear lay Camp Franklin, an extensive labor camp for workers at the forts east of the Anacostia. Permanent structures included a superintendent's office, cookhouse, mess room, carpenter's shop, blacksmith's shop, and stables as well as a vast "tent city" for laborers. In December 1861, seventy-five pounds of codfish, seventy-five pounds of fresh beef, a barrel of salt beef, a barrel of salt pork, a sack of corn, and two sacks of potatoes were sent to Fort Mahan to feed laborers and soldiers billeted there.

A gale in February 1862 blew down all the tents along the eastern lines necessitating erection of permanent barracks at places like Fort Mahan. That the subsequent permanent barracks spawned dens of vice might be suggested by the arrest on one occasion in 1864 of Jefferson Vantray for selling liquor from his home to the nearby garrison at Fort Mahan.

More praiseworthy was Sergeant Ebenezar Page's daughter, who, while visiting her father in the 9th New York Heavy Artillery, established a school for the soldiers in the Fort Mahan mess hall, charging fifty cents a pupil.

When it was eventually abandoned, Fort Mahan reverted to Mary M. Manning. She had claimed damages in 1864 and the next year purchased the abatis around the fort for $31.00 at auction.

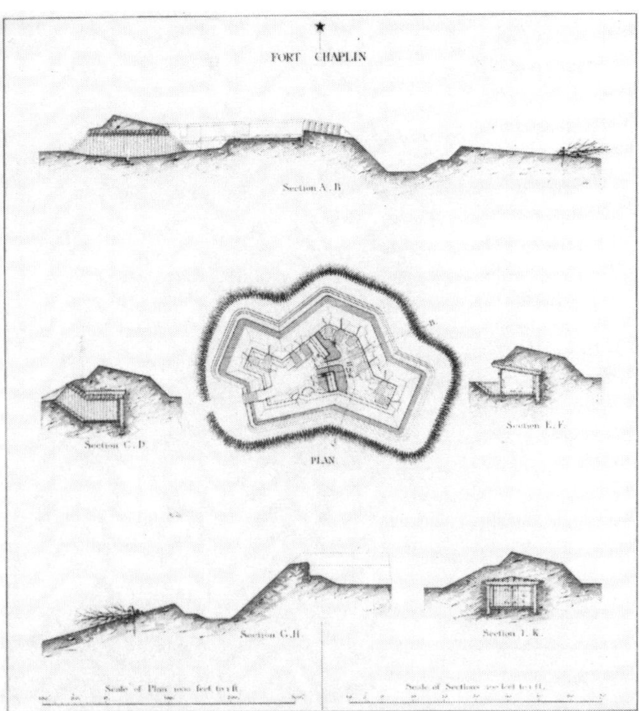

Fort Chaplin—Engineer Drawing. *National Archives*

Fort Chaplin, "Fort of Circular Form" (Craven, Scaggs), and "Fort on Kennedy's Hill" (Sedgwick)

Location

From Fort Mahan, return to Benning Road NE. Turn left and drive through two traffic lights to East Capitol Street. Turn right and immediately take an abrupt left onto Texas Avenue past the Fort Chaplin apartments to Fort Chaplin. Park on the right. Walk into the woods and up the hill to the fort. The "Fort of Circular Form" no longer exists, but its site was between Ames Street and East Capitol Street. The "Fort on Kennedy's Hill" is likewise nonexistent and was situated in the residential area of Chaplin Street and Hilltop Terrace.

Visible Remains

Fort Chaplin is in a good state of preservation but with poor National Park Service maintenance; no interpretive marker exists.

Description

There seems to be some controversy as to how many forts or separate redoubts may have been in this area.

Fort Chaplin was named for Colonel Daniel Chaplin, 1st Maine Heavy Artillery, who was killed at Deep Bottom, Virginia, on August 17, 1864.

The "Fort of Circular Form" was also called Fort Craven or even Fort Scaggs (for the landowner of the property).

The "Fort on Kennedy's Hill" likewise bore the landowner's name as well as "Fort Sedgwick" in honor of the VI Corps commander killed at the Spotsylvania courthouse in May 1864.

Fort Chaplin was never garrisoned, although one piece of ordnance (a 24-pounder seacoast gun mounted en barbette) was noted in Barnard's report, but no dimensions of the fort were given. Fort Chaplin also had eleven vacant platforms. The "Fort of Circular Form" or Fort Craven (Scaggs) contained six vacant platforms and, like the "Fort on Kennedy's

Hill" (Sedgwick), was never completed. Apparently, Selby B. Scaggs owned the 400-acre farm on which the works were constructed.[2]

FLANK WORKS ON THE RIDGELINE

These works guarded Ridge Road from southern Maryland leading to the Navy Yard bridge at Union Town.

Fort Meigs and Battery Rucker

Location

From Fort Chaplin Park, return to East Capitol Street. Turn right onto Benning Road NE and drive to the intersection at the top of the hill with Bowen Road/ Marlboro Pike. Fort Meigs and Battery Rucker were located in the general triangular area bounded by Benning Road, Marlboro Pike/Bowen Road, and Southern Avenue SE.

Visible Remains

No remains of either work or interpretive markers for them exist.

Description

Fort Meigs was named for Union Quartermaster General (Brigadier General) Montgomery C. Meigs. Battery Rucker was named for Major (later Major General) Daniel Rucker, chief quartermaster of the Washington Quartermaster Depot during the Civil War.

Fort Meigs was a strong fort of 500 yards' perimeter and housed eighteen guns and mortars and eight vacant platforms. Among the ordnance were four eight-inch siege howitzers (en barbette), five 32-pounder seacoast guns (en barbette), two 12-pounder howitzers (en embrasure), five 12-pounder field guns (en embrasure), two 30-pounder Parrotts (one en embrasure, one barbette), and one ten-inch and one 24-pounder Coehorn mortar.

No separate listing of ordnance remains for Battery Rucker, also called Redoubt Rucker. Inasmuch as a covered way connected the two works as at Fort Lincoln and Battery Jameson and Fort and Battery Reno, one listing for the work may have accounted for all the ordnance.

Notes/Anecdotes

These works occupied a key ridgeline flank position leading into the District and the Navy Yard crossing of the Anacostia at Uniontown. This was the extreme point from which enemy field batteries could see and reach the Washington Arsenal and Navy Yard facilities.

Units connected with these two works were the following:

New York (Excelsior) Brigade
17th Maine Infantry (various companies)
19th Maine Infantry (various companies)
9th Rhode Island Infantry, Co. B
9th Massachusetts Heavy Artillery
14th Massachusetts Heavy Artillery
Pennsylvania Light Artillery, Independent Co. E (Knapp's)
15th New York Engineers, Co. H, September–October 1862
10th New York Heavy Artillery, Co. F, November 11–December 31, 1862
9th New York Independent Battery, January–April 1864
9th New York Heavy Artillery, Co. H, March–April 1864
9th New York Heavy Artillery, Co. E, May 10–June 30, 1864
9th New York Heavy Artillery, Co. F, July–October 1864, December 1864–June 1865

The 15th and 30th Maine appeared nearby in May 1865, awaiting demobilization after a final grand review. "I suppose at last," wrote one Down Easter, "this 'cruel war' is over." It was, but ironically these veterans soon moved to occupation duty in South Carolina. The same "Down Easter" wrote his sister in Portland on May 19, 1865, how, despite excessive heat, everyone had the baseball fever, his own captain as well as other officers and the men playing every day when not drilling or securing passes into Washington. He recounted how the 133d New York had beaten the National Club of Washington 32 to 27.

Fort DuPont

Location

From the sites of Fort Meigs and Battery Rucker, continue south on Bowen Road as it becomes Alabama Avenue SE to Fort DuPont Park on the right. Note the abrupt right turn into the narrow National Park Service lane leading to the recreational area and fort on right.

Visible Remains

Greatly eroded parapets due to illegal biking activities mar this clearly defined profile maintained by the

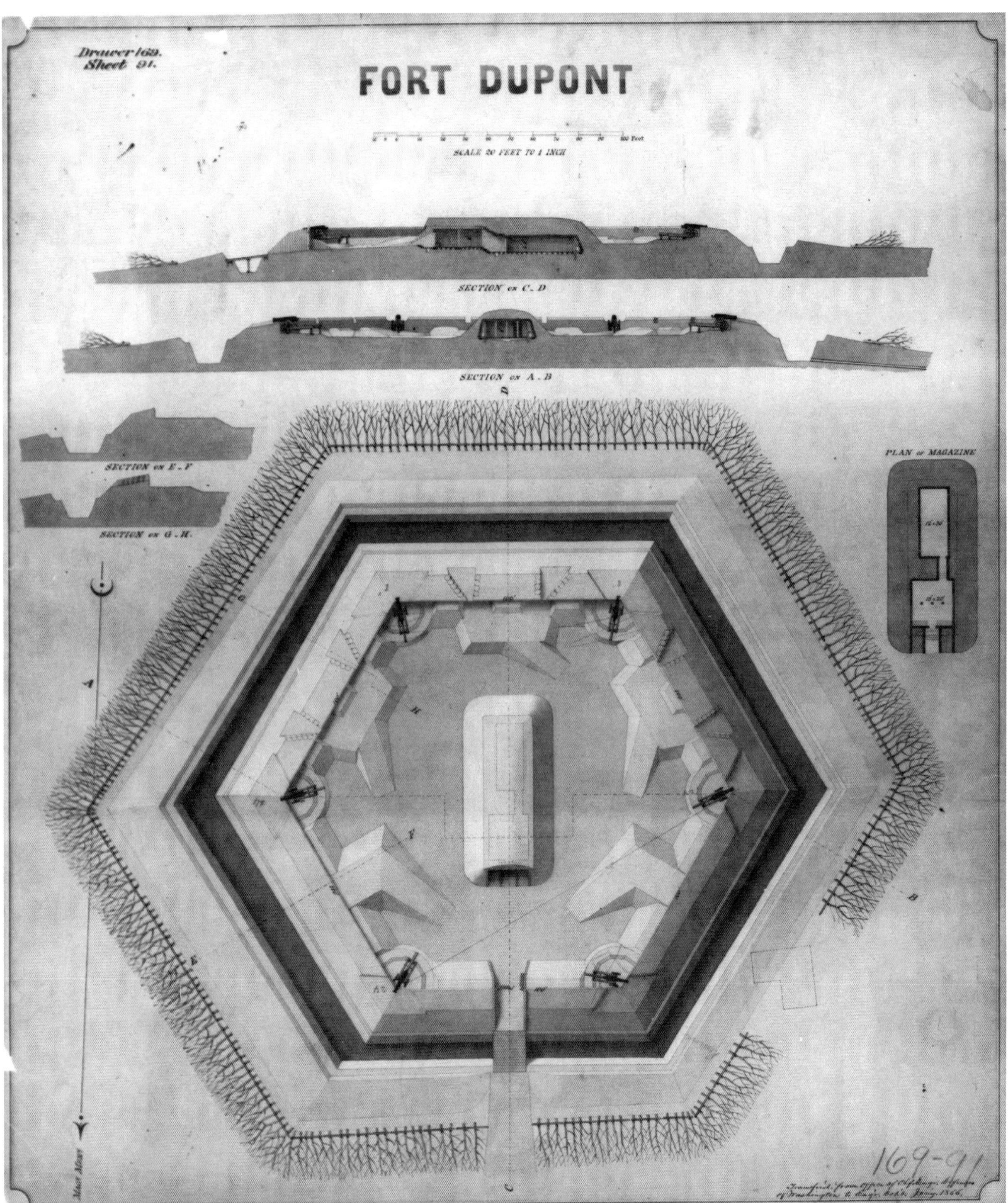

Fort DuPont—Engineer Drawing. *National Archives*

National Park Service. A Civil War Centennial plaque provides the sole interpretive marker.

Description

Fort DuPont was named for Rear Admiral Samuel Francis DuPont. It was a small hexagonal work with a perimeter of 200 yards. Although its armament shifted over the course of the war, it basically included three eight-inch siege howitzers (en embrasure), three 24-pounder seacoast guns (en barbette), two 6-pounder field guns, one 24-pounder Coehorn mortar, and six vacant platforms.

Notes/Anecdotes

Constructed in the fall and winter of 1861–1862, to add coverage of the Ridge Road and open country to the front, Fort DuPont supported a garrison numbering 300 infantry and 117 artillerymen. It was erected on the land of sixty-year-old Michael Caton and family.

Those units in garrison at various times included the following:

88th Pennsylvania Infantry, April 15, 1862
99th Pennsylvania Infantry, April 15–June 28, 1862
9th Rhode Island Infantry, Co. G, June 28–August 25, 1862
17th Maine Infantry, Co. G, August 24–October 7, 1862
9th Maine Infantry, Co. K, August 30–September 27, 1862
10th New York Heavy Artillery, Co. D, September 27, 1862–March 24, 1865
9th New York Heavy Artillery, Co. F (detachment), March 26–May 10, 1864
3d Massachusetts Heavy Artillery, Co. E, May–June 1864
3d Massachusetts Heavy Artillery, Co. F, September–October, December 1864–May 1865
1st Maine Heavy Artillery, Co. F, June–August 1865

Within the walls of Fort DuPont could be found a flagstaff, a magazine, and a deep well. Two officers' quarters (twenty-four by sixteen feet), a barracks (100 by twenty feet), a mess hall (fifty by twenty feet), and a guardhouse stood outside but close to the work.

The engineers never expressed much confidence in this particular fort and, in April 1864, advised abandonment and concentration of effort on larger forts in this sector. However, Fort DuPont was not abandoned until reversion of the site to the land's original owner in 1865.[3]

Fort Davis

Location

From Fort DuPont Park, continue south on Alabama Avenue SE to the intersection (traffic light) with Pennsylvania Avenue. Fort Davis lies to the right in the park area and is readily accessible from on-street parking on Alabama Avenue.

Visible Remains

Like Fort DuPont, the National Park Service maintains this well-preserved, unrestored, and completely overgrown fort; a Civil War Centennial plaque provides an interpretive marker.

Description

Fort Davis was named for Colonel Benjamin F. Davis, 8th New York Cavalry, who was killed at Brandy Station, Virginia, on June 9, 1863.

Like Fort DuPont, this work was a small work (220-yard perimeter) and stood at the same elevation as Fort DuPont: 300 feet above the Potomac's mean tide. It mounted the same ordnance as Fort DuPont except for three additional 6-pounder field guns (en barbette) but had only two vacant platforms.

Fort Davis likewise contained a flagstaff, two bombproof magazines, and a 124-foot-deep well (although the smell and taste of this water caused the garrison to draw water from a spring 300 yards outside the fort). Outside too could be found customary barracks (100 by twenty feet), officers' quarters (twenty-four by sixteen feet), a mess house (fifty by twenty feet), and a guardhouse (twenty-four by eighteen feet).

The fort's magazines held 1,000 rounds of 6-pounder ammunition, nearly the same number for heavier ordnance, and about 120 mortar rounds, plus 12,425 rounds of small arms ammunition. All this sufficed for an estimated garrison of 330 infantry and 144 artillerymen.

Notes/Anecdotes

Units garrisoned at Fort Davis included the following:

88th Pennsylvania Infantry, April 15, 1862
99th Pennsylvania Infantry, February 19–June 28, 1862

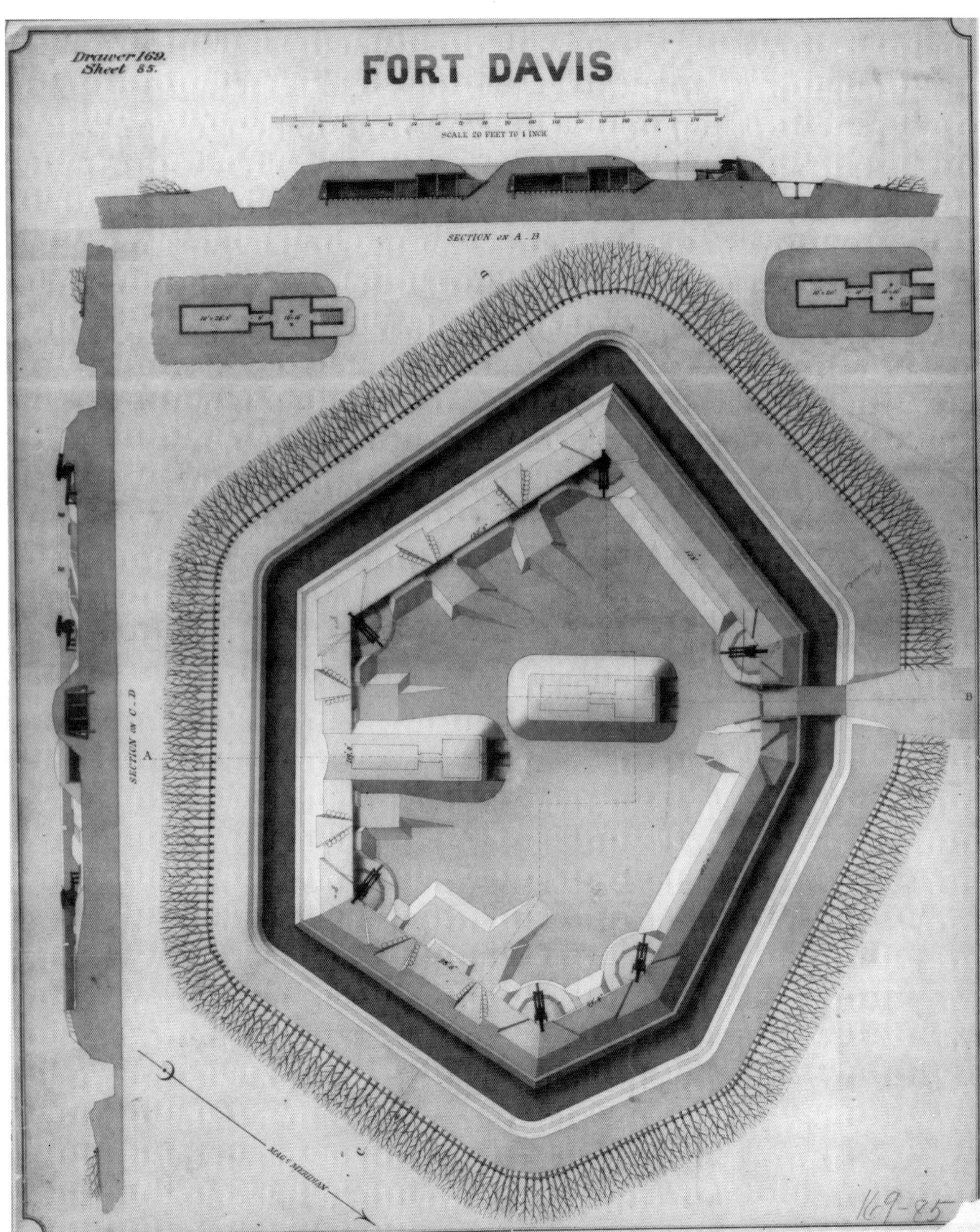

Fort Davis—Engineer Drawing. *National Archives*

- 9th Rhode Island Infantry, Co. L, June 28–August 25, 1862
- 17th Maine Infantry, Co. K, August 24–October 7, 1862
- 19th Maine Infantry, Co. K (detachment), August 30–September 12, 1862
- 19th Maine Infantry, Co. I, September 12–27, 1862
- 10th New York Heavy Artillery, Co. C, September 27, 1862–March 24,1864
- 9th New York Heavy Artillery, Co. I (detachment), March 26–May 10, 1864
- 3d Massachusetts Heavy Artillery, Co. E, May–August 1864
- 3d Massachusetts Heavy Artillery, Co. F, September–October 1864, December 1864–April 1865
- 1st Maine Heavy Artillery, June–August 1865

Tolson Watkins, B. W. Keyser, Marks Henshaw and Co. appeared on a bid to provide the abatis, timber, and lumber for the fort in 1861.

Forts DuPont and Davis provided contrasting views of how the U.S. government handled land claims for the forts around the city in 1865. On August 14, 1865, Michael Caton, original owner of the land at Fort DuPont, received $1.00 and the five quartermaster structures on the site as well as the wooden portions of the fort itself. At Fort Davis, however, Daniel F. Lee, who had purchased the land from Sayls Bowen in 1864, had his claim of $1,500.00 in damages plus all buildings at the work denied by the government. The buildings were sold at auction, and Lee had to buy the abatis at the fort for $33.87.[4]

RIDGE ROAD GUARDIANS OF UNIONTOWN AND NAVY YARD BRIDGE

Fort Baker and Fort Wagner

Location

From Fort Davis, follow Alabama Avenue SE southward to the vicinity of 30th and 32d streets (the approximate site of Fort Baker straddled modern Alabama Avenue). Continue past the triangular grounds of Old Stanton School (bounded by Alabama Avenue, Good Hope Road, and 25th Street). Fort Wagner stood east of the water tower behind the school.

Visible Remains

None; no interpretive markers exist.

Description

Fort Baker was named for Colonel Edward Dickinson Baker, 71st Pennsylvania Infantry, who was killed at Balls Bluff, Virginia, on October 21, 1861.

Fort Wagner was probably named for 1st Lieutenant Orlando O. Wagner, U.S. Corps of Topographical Engineers, who died of wounds suffered near Yorktown, Virginia, on April 21, 1862. It is possible, however, that the fort was named for Colonel Gustav Wagner, 2d New York Heavy Artillery.

Fort Baker was a strong work with a 492-yard perimeter and commanded the direct approaches to Uniontown (the modern Anacostia neighborhood of the city) and the Navy Yard Bridge. It contained twenty-two guns and mortars, including three eight-inch siege howitzers (en embrasure), seven 24-pounder seacoast guns (en barbette), two 24-pounder field howitzers (en embrasure), eight 10-pounder Parrott rifles (en embrasure), one ten-inch and one 24-pounder Coehorn mortar, and three vacant platforms.

Fort Wagner was a smaller work of only 160 perimeter yards and mounted four guns and a mortar including one eight-inch siege howitzer (en embrasure), three 12-pounder field guns (en embrasure), one 24-pounder Coehorn mortar, and no vacant platforms. Like Fort Baker, this work also commanded the road junction (predecessor to the modern street configuration) and the valley to the front.

Notes/Anecdotes

These works were constructed by units of Daniel Sickles's Excelsior Brigade, headquartered at Fort Baker in the fall and winter of 1861–1862, and gave it the name "Fort Good Hope" after the neighborhood appellation in the vicinity. The 86th New York Volunteers was also associated with this post.

Other units stationed at the fort during the war included the following:

- 2d Pennsylvania Heavy Artillery (112th Volunteers), Cos. A, B, C (parts)
- 10th New York Heavy Artillery, Cos. A, C, M, September 1862–February 1864
- 3d Massachusetts Heavy Artillery, Cos. B, E, F, May 1864–April 1865
- 9th New York Heavy Artillery, Co. A, March–April 1864
- 17th Maine Infantry
- 24th Michigan Infantry
- 117th New York Infantry
- Massachusetts Heavy Artillery, 6th Co.
- 9th Rhode Island Infantry, Cos. E, K

Daily artillery and infantry drill occupied the men at these works. Details were drawn from the 117th New York at Fort Baker, for example, to provide guards at the Navy Yard Bridge. "When employed in this capacity they often caused embarrassment to suspicious passengers, all of whom were closely scrutinized and not a few rigidly examined for contraband goods, messages," recorded the regimental historian. Perhaps such guards unknowingly permitted presidential assassin John Wilkes Booth to pass unchallenged on the night of April 14, 1865, and make his way past Forts Baker and Wagner en route to southern Maryland.

Known to have garrisoned Fort Wagner were the following:

- 10th New York Heavy Artillery, Co. I, September 1862–April 1863
- 3d Massachusetts Heavy Artillery, Co. H, May–September
- 3d Massachusetts Heavy Artillery, Co. D, November 1864
- 3d Massachusetts Heavy Artillery, Co. B, January–February 1865
- Pennsylvania Light Artillery, Hampton's Independent Battery F, April–May 1865
- 9th Rhode Island Infantry, Co. H

Various amusing anecdotes were occasioned by the rather loose command arrangements between fort commanders and encamped units nearby. On one occasion, a young captain of the 10th New York Heavy Artillery at Fort Baker was visited by a higher-ranking infantry officer from a nearby camp. The infantryman wanted to "inspect" the garrison and proceeded to severely chastise his artillery victim for allowing the ammunition to become caked and spoiled inside storage sacks within the dark magazine. The regimental ordnance sergeant and other heavy artillery officers of the garrison chuckled at this dressing-down of their comrade, but the garrisons could return the harassment, causing such ad hoc visitors to undergo all types of permission requests before they could leave the works and pass beyond the fort's sentries. Such were the high spirits of youthful volunteers.

The 10th New York Heavy Artillery remained so long in Washington's fortifications that they were dubbed "Uncle Abe's Pets." Their familiar presence on the streets of the city reputedly ensured that no lady would be insulted by ruffians or otherwise disturbed in making her appointed rounds, claimed the unit historian.

Another unit with much to say about service at the eastern forts was the 9th Rhode Island Infantry. Companies of this regiment garrisoned each of the works during the hot summer of 1862. Between target competitions with their Enfield rifle muskets, the men of Company H at Fort Wagner learned the trade of heavy artillerymen and that "it is a mistake to suppose that '32-pounders' weigh only thirty-two pounds in the Washington semi tropical climate." Sergeant H. H. Richardson of that company and his mates periodically went into the city, visiting the Smithsonian Institution and particularly the Capitol. Richardson found it most interesting to listen to House and

Sketch of Fort Wagner and the Richardson House by C. E. Carpenter, 1862. *Spicer,* History of the Ninth and Tenth Regiments Rhode Island Volunteers and the Tenth Rhode Island Battery

Senate debates: "I can hear many of our most noted men, whose names have long been familiar to us." He cited Vice President Hannibal Hamlin specifically.

Proximity to the Capitol meant that politics quite often filled the conversations of the garrison. E. G. Jones of the 117th New York went on at great length to a friend in late January 1863 concerning newspapers and failed Army of the Potomac Major General Ambrose Burnside as well as Empire State politics. He told "Friend Davis,"

> I suppose some of the papers in the north set up a terrible howl after [the battle of Fredericksburg] and demanded that Burnside be removed from the command of the army. It is amusing to see how sudden the tide of public opinion changes. This war I think will inevitably produce on good result. Those who are in the army will learn before they leave it that success is not always the test of merit. For my part I think that Burnside stands better and higher in the estimation of the soldiers today than he did two months ago. A portion of the Northern press has resolved upon a systematic course to weaken the confidence of the people in the Government and they find it suits their purpose well to impress upon the minds of their readers that Burnside is not a fit man to command the army. Their next argument is that Lincoln was influenced by improper motives when he removed McClellan. These men seek to hide their wicked intentions by their hypocritical professions of loyalty. I see by the papers that the New York assembly is at a dead lock. You know it is natural for me to wish for Sherwood's Election but if he is not elected for the sake of the country elect T. C. Callicott or some other loyal and respectable Conservative. As the administration of New York is not constituted our only hope for the maintenance of friendly relations between the state and national governments is the influence exerted by Dean Richmond, S. E. Church, D. R. F. Jones, Callicott and their supporters and no small effort on their part will suffice. Sufficient evidence of this was furnished by the proceedings relative to the Police commissioner of New York City. If these men succeed in rescuing the state from the control of Fernando Wood they will be entitled to the liveliest gratitude of all loyal men. I fear they will not be able to perform this Herculean task.[5]

PROTECTING SOUTHERN APPROACHES TO UNIONTOWN AND NAVY YARD BRIDGE: FORTS RICKETS, STANTON, AND SNYDER

These forts, like those for other bridge crossings into the city, occupied high ground and commanded road arteries leading from the countryside. They also protected against enemy occupation of high ground threatening the vital Navy Yard facility and Washington Arsenal in the city and the Uniontown settlements on the banks of the Anacostia.

Fort Ricketts

Location

From Forts Snyder and Wagner, follow Alabama Avenue SE one block to Ainger Place. Turn right to Bruce Place and left to Erie Place. The remains of Fort Ricketts lie in a corner park across from Raynolds Place at Bruce Place and Erie Place near the Anacostia Neighborhood Museum of the Smithsonian Institution on Fort Place. Park in the museum parking lot to visit Forts Ricketts and Stanton and especially the museum as a rest stop.

Visible Remains

A heavily overgrown earthwork remains visible. A generic National Park Service sign is present, but no interpretive marker exists. The nearby Anacostia Neighborhood Museum has a useful display on the forts as well as the history of the area.

Description

Fort Ricketts most probably was named for Captain James B. Ricketts, 4th U.S. Artillery and later major general, who became famous for the capture of his battery at the First Battle of Bull Run (Manassas) and later

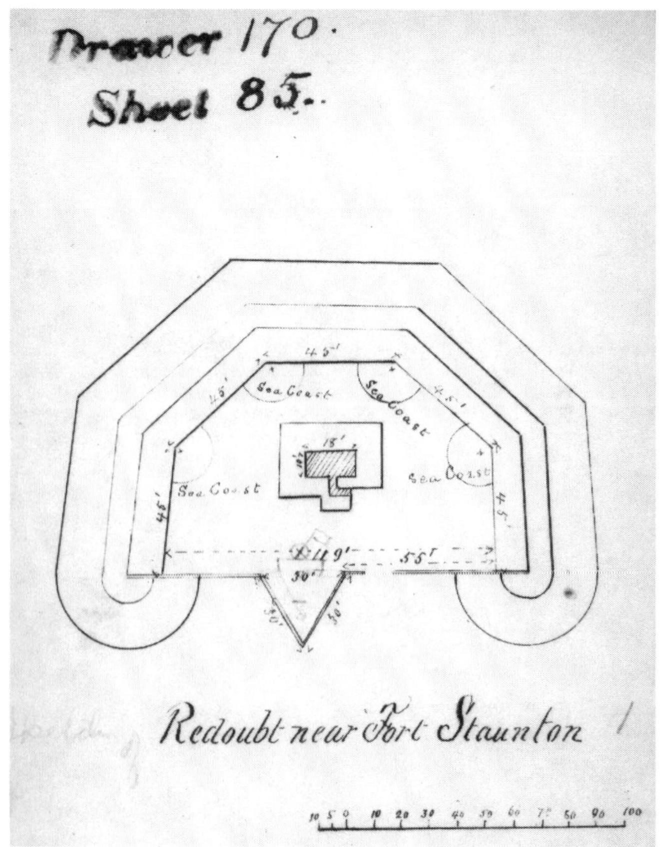

Fort Ricketts—Engineer Drawing. *National Archives*

his service as a division commander in the VI Corps. It may also have been named for Major (Brevet Colonel) Robert B. Ricketts, 1st Pennsylvania Light Artillery, and subsequently chief of artillery for the IX Corps.

This small work had a perimeter of 123 yards and constituted a redoubt or enclosed battery that covered an exposed ravine and minor country road that led toward Uniontown and the Navy Yard Bridge from the southeast.

As evolved, the fort's armament in February 1862 included four 32-pounder seacoast guns (en barbette) but by March 1864 had changed to three 12-pounder howitzers and one eight-inch siege howitzer (all firing en barbette). In March 1865, the ordnance comprised four smoothbore cannon firing en embrasure, an eight-inch siege howitzer (en embrasure), and three 12-pounder Napoleon field guns (en embrasure).

Notes/Anecdotes

Wartime garrisons for this fort numbered 206 men (forty-two artillerists and 164 infantry) and were drawn from the following:

- 59th New York Infantry, February 1862
- 4th New York Heavy Artillery, Cos. E, G (detachment), February–April 1862
- 88th Pennsylvania Infantry, Cos. A, C–E, I (detachment), February–April 1862
- 99th Pennsylvania Infantry, April–August 1862
- 9th Rhode Island Infantry, Co. C
- 17th Maine Infantry, Co. C, August 1862
- 19th Maine Infantry, Co. I, September 1862
- 10th New York Heavy Artillery, Co. I (detachment), September 12–October 31, 1862

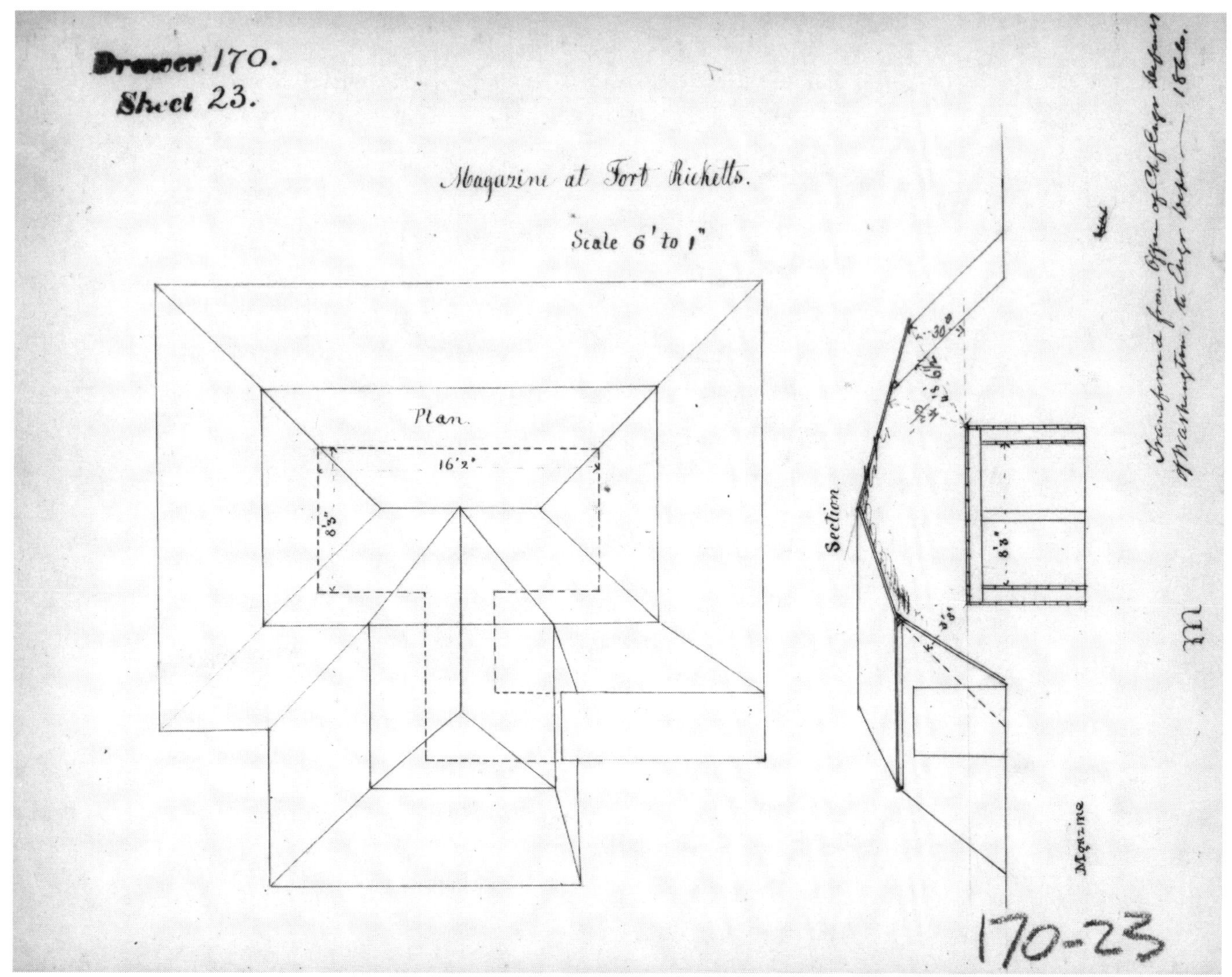

Fort Ricketts' Magazine—Engineer Drawing. *National Archives*

10th New York Heavy Artillery, Co. K, October 1862–February 28, 1864
9th New York Heavy Artillery, Co. F (1/3) March–May 1864
3d Massachusetts Heavy Artillery, Co. H (12th Co.), May 10–June 1864
3d Massachusetts Heavy Artillery, Co. B, January–February 1865
Independent Pennsylvania Artillery, Cos. F, H, April–June 1865
1st Maine Heavy Artillery, Co. B, June–August 1865

Fort Ricketts had four government buildings erected nearby. They included an officers' quarters (twenty by eighteen feet), barracks (fifty by twenty feet), mess hall (fifty by sixteen feet), and log guardhouse. All these structures were sold at war's end.

J. H. Smith bid to supply abatis, timber, and lumber for the fort in 1861.[6]

Fort Stanton

Location

From Fort Ricketts, continue on Erie Street. Fort Stanton lies in the park to the right between the recreation/reservoir area and Our Lady of Perpetual Help Church. Use the on-street parking or recreation center parking.

Visible Remains

Despite a splendid view of Washington in the distance, Fort Stanton has overgrown parapets and a poor capacity for interpretation—a generally neglected site.

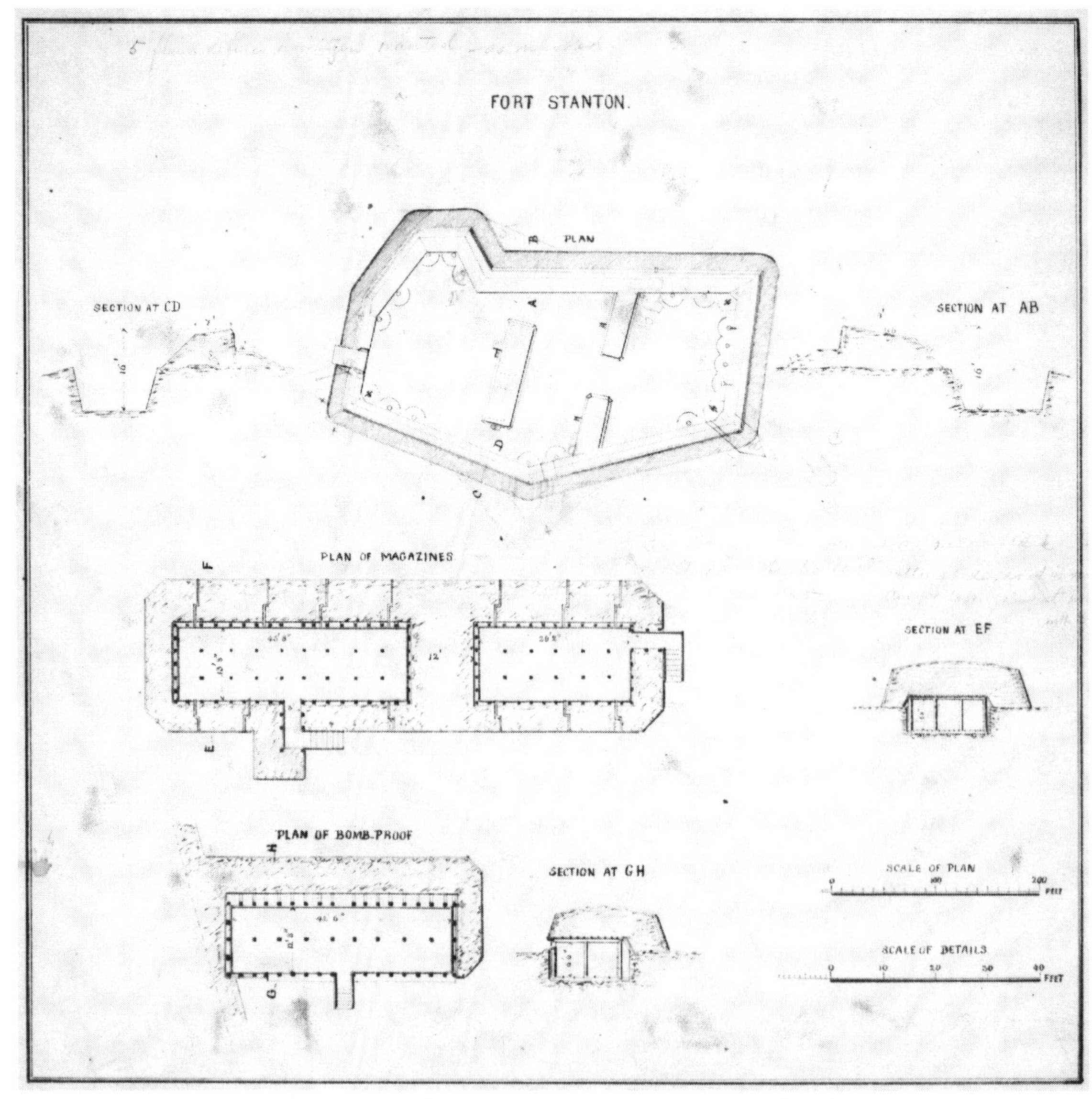

Fort Stanton (original design)—Engineer Drawing. *National Archives*

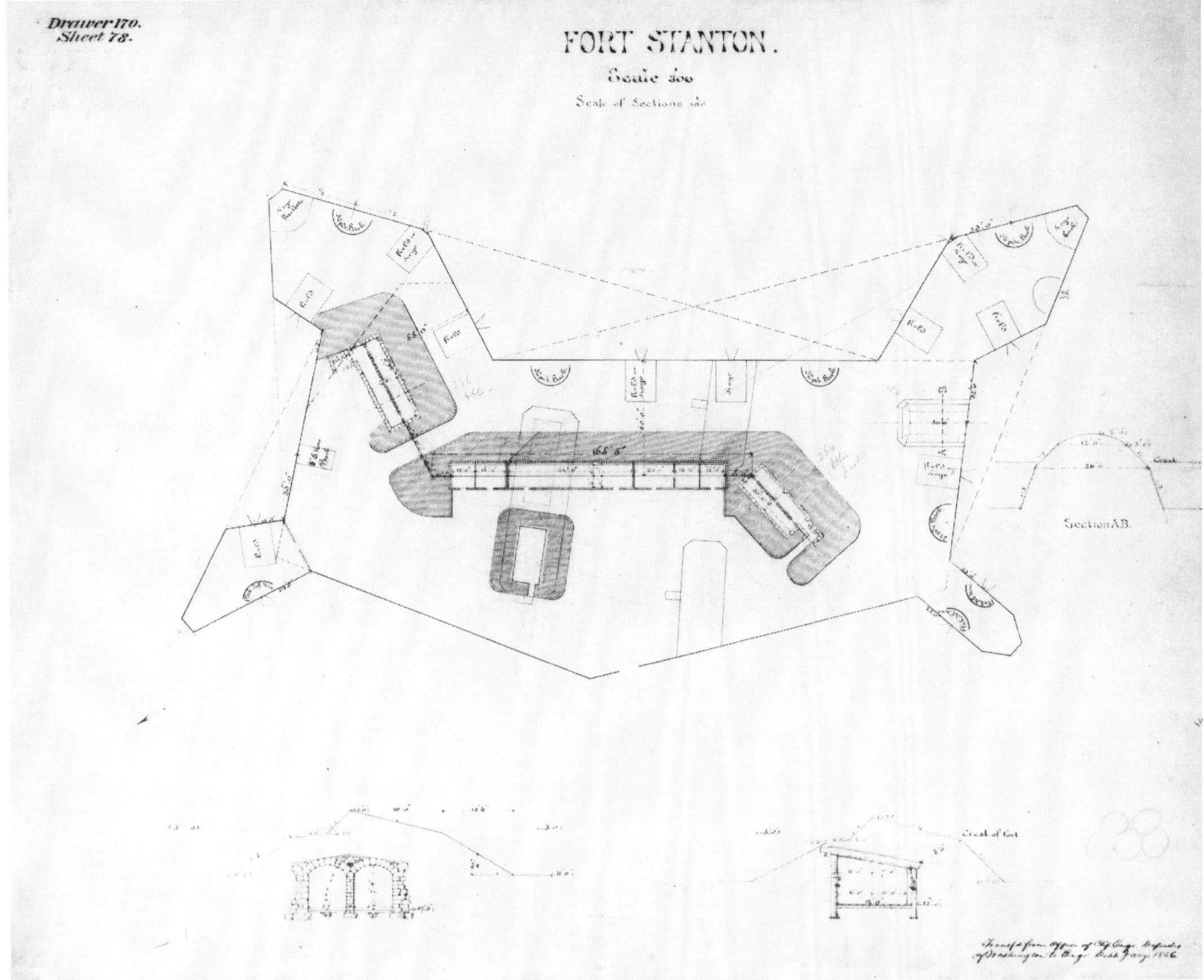

Fort Stanton (planned expansion)—Engineer Drawing. *National Archives*

A generic National Park Service sign is malpositioned facing the parking lot in the rear of Our Lady of Perpetual Help Church and conflicts with "No Trespassing" signs adjacent.

Description

Fort Stanton was named for Secretary of War Edwin M. Stanton. It had a perimeter of 322 yards and was designed for eighteen guns and a garrison of 270 artillerymen and 215 infantrymen.

The fort's commanding position ensured its role as principal work in protecting the Washington Navy Yard across the Anacostia.

Fort Stanton superbly reflects the changing nature of armament for Washington's defenses. As first armed, Fort Stanton held sixteen 32-pounder seacoast guns (en barbette). By January 1, 1863, a four-and-a-half-inch rifle, one eight-inch siege howitzer, and a 10-inch and 24-pounder Coehorn mortar had been added. Barnard's report shows four eight-inch siege howitzers (evenly divided between en barbette and en embrasure placement), six 32-pounder seacoast guns (en barbette), three 24-pounder field howitzers (en embrasure), one 20-pounder Parrott rifle (en embrasure), and two mortars and eight vacant platforms. By March 1864, ten 32-pounders had been withdrawn, and three 24-pounder howitzers and three eight-inch siege guns were added while nine platforms remained vacant. After Early's raid, Major General Christopher C. Augur wanted to add one 32-pounder howitzer, two four-and-a-half-inch rifles, four 12-pounder howitzers, and two 12-pounder Napoleon smoothbores.

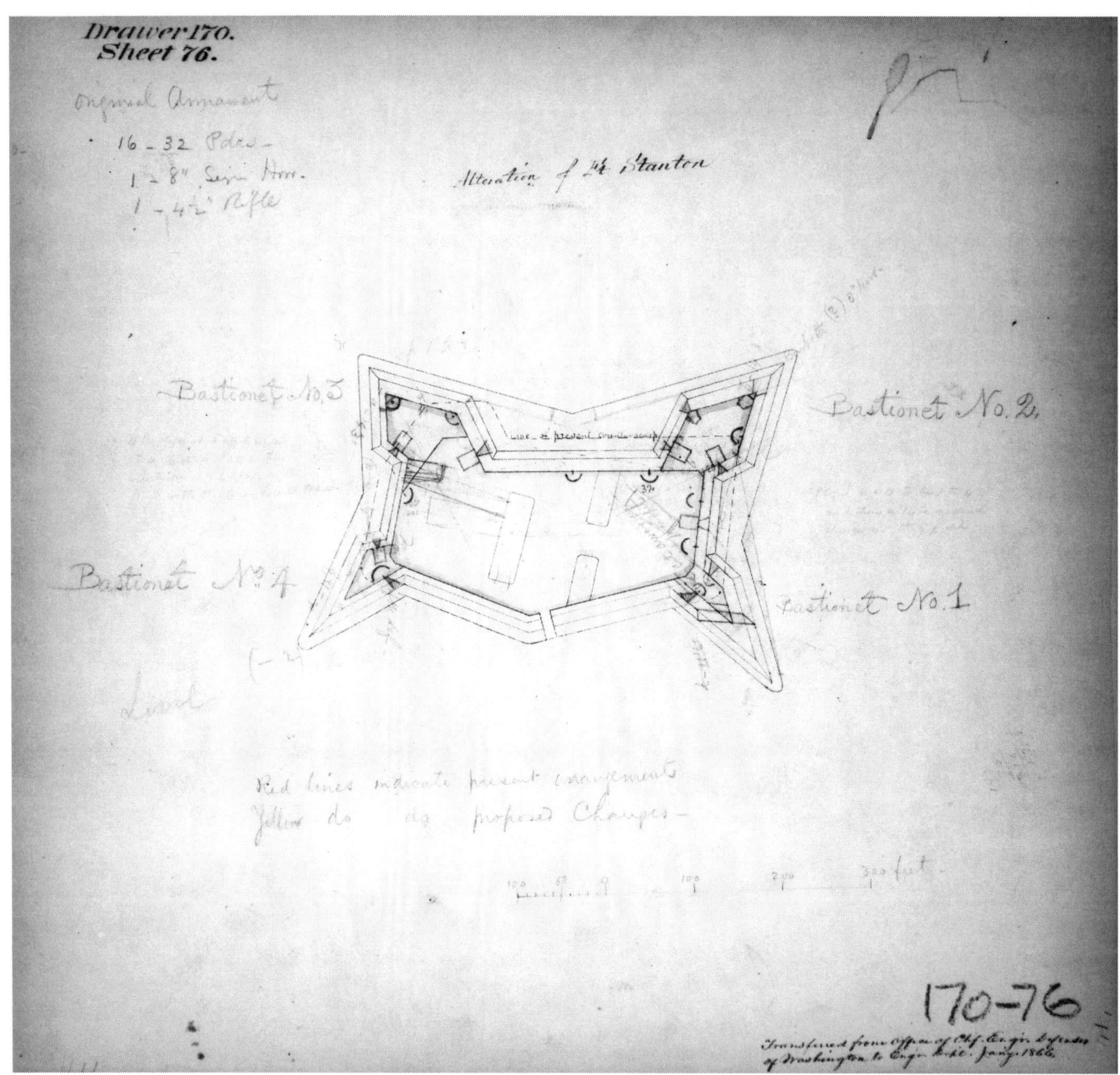

Fort Stanton (expanded)—Engineer Drawing. *National Archives*

Returns at the end of the war listed Fort Stanton's armament as follows:

- Two eight-inch siege howitzers (smoothbore) mounted en embrasure
- Two eight-inch siege howitzers (smoothbore) mounted en barbette
- Six 32-pounder smoothbores mounted en barbette
- Three 24-pounder howitzers (smoothbore) mounted en embrasure
- Six 12-pounder Napoleons (smoothbore) mounted en embrasure
- One four-and-a-half-inch rifle mounted en embrasure
- One ten-inch siege mortar
- One 24-pounder Coehorn mortar
- Eight vacant platforms: one siege platform for guns mounted en barbette
- Five field platforms for guns mounted en embrasure

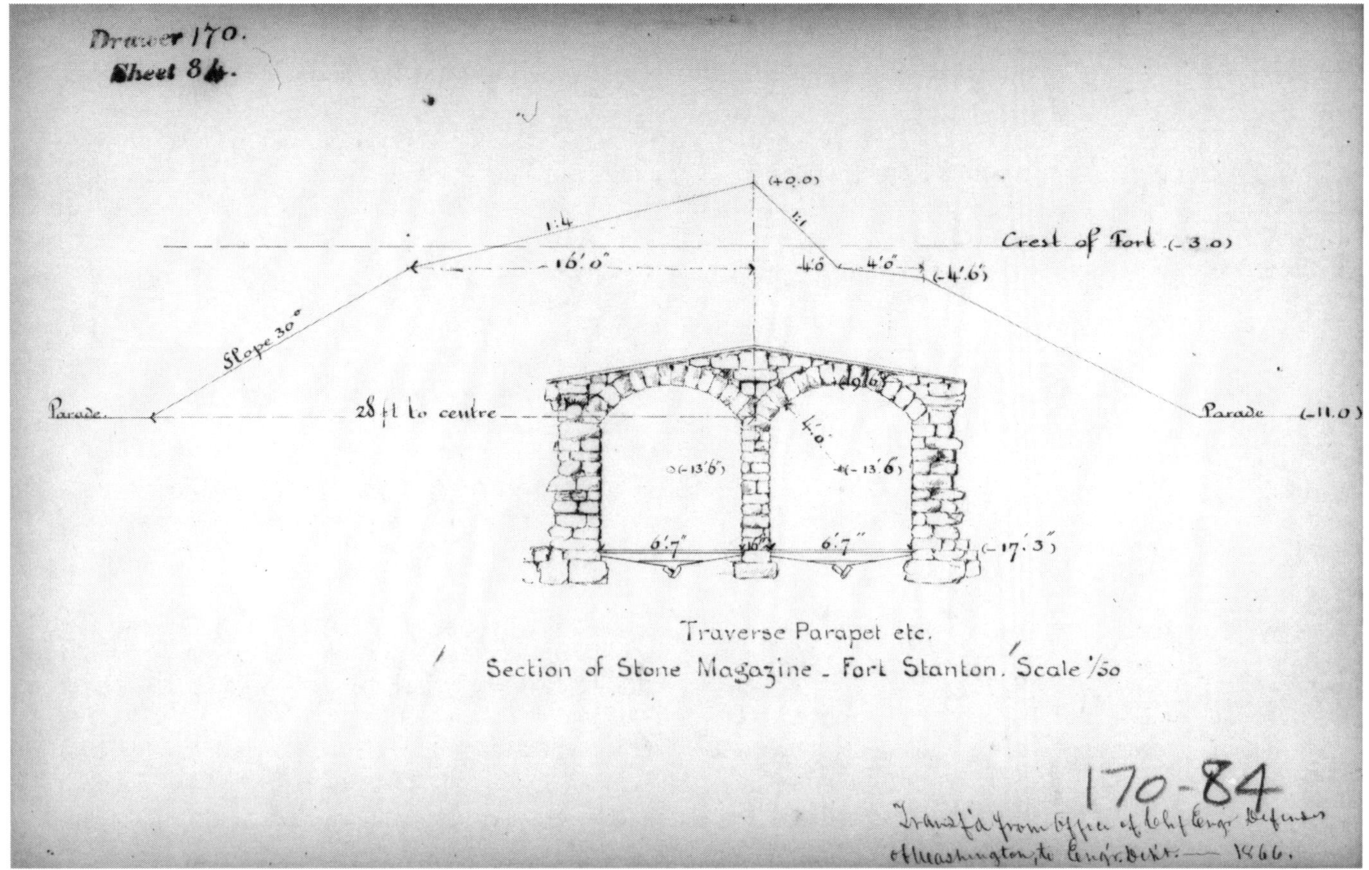

Traverse Parapet Section of Fort Stanton's Stone Magazine. *National Archives*

Two field or siege platforms for guns mounted en embrasure

In addition, 104 small arms and 11,900 rounds of ammunition existed in the magazines.

Notes/Anecdotes

Garrisons at Fort Stanton included the following:

- 4th New York Heavy Artillery, Cos. E, G, February–April 1862
- 88th Pennsylvania Infantry, Cos. A, C–E, I (detachment), February–April 1862
- 99th Pennsylvania Infantry, April–August 1862
- 9th Rhode Island Infantry, Co. I
- 17th Maine Infantry, Co. I, August 1862
- 19th Maine Infantry, Co. I, August 1862
- 10th New York Heavy Artillery, Co. H, September 1862–March 1864
- 9th New York Heavy Artillery, Co. L, March–May 1864
- 3d Massachusetts Heavy Artillery, Co. F, May–June 1864
- 3d Massachusetts Heavy Artillery, Co. K, July–August 1864
- 3d Massachusetts Heavy Artillery, Co. B, November 1864–April 1865
- Independent Pennsylvania Artillery, Cos. F, H, April–June 1865
- 1st Maine Heavy Artillery, Co. B, June–August 1865
- 4th U.S. Artillery, Co. F, September–November 1865

Fort Stanton also reflected the "tinkering" done by both engineers and ordnance officials on various fortifications during the war. Considerable construction work occurred in 1863–1864 as a civilian workforce laid out and constructed "bastionets," altering the appearance of the work. Ninety men took about six months to finish this work. They also constructed stone- and brick-lined magazines costing $2,500 each.

The regimental historian of the 88th Pennsylvania recorded that his unit had engaged in the original construction of a number of the forts east of the Anacostia "and only wanted a few brigades of Johnny Rebs to come along and be knocked sky-high by these big guns, yawning and rusting for something to do." Of course, no Confederates appeared east of the river, "but a couple of nights' guard duty in the rain and mud, without any kind of shelter, chilled to the bone and as miserable and wretched as it was possible to be, took the romance out of the business of taking care of these forts." Units like the 17th Maine recounted their foraging antics and sheltering of runaway slaves as the high points of their tours in forts like Stanton.[7]

Fort Snyder

Location

From Fort Stanton, return to Alabama Avenue SE. Turn right to the vicinity of 13th Street. Fort Snyder lies north and west of the intersection.

Visible Remains

None; no interpretive marker exists.

Description

This moderate-size fort had a perimeter of 210 yards for eight guns. It was probably named for 1st Lieutenant George W. Snyder, Corps of Engineers, who was at Fort Sumter and served with Barnard at the First Battle of Bull Run (Manassas) and in developing the early defenses of Washington before his death from exposure on November 17, 1861.

Ordnance for the fort comprised two eight-inch siege howitzers (en barbette) and six 12-pounder field guns (en embrasure).

Notes/Anecdotes

The fort was designed to protect both Fort Stanton's southeastern flank and a more southerly road leading to Uniontown and the Navy Yard Bridge. Among units garrisoning the fort was Company D, 9th Rhode Island Infantry.

Lieutenant General Ulysses S. Grant's tapping of the fort garrisons for reinforcement of the Army of the Potomac in the spring of 1864 could be seen at works like Fort Snyder. Unattached heavy artillery companies came from Massachusetts to replace trained heavy artillerists, such as Company I (May 1863–February 1864) of the 10th New York Heavy Artillery and Company I (March 26–April 1864) of the 9th New York Heavy Artillery. They had been recruited solely to man coastal fortifications in their home state. Considerable unhappiness within the units and strident protests from state officials were to no avail, and between June 1863 and August 1864, the Unassigned Companies Heavy Artillery was sent to Washington, assigned to the 3d Massachusetts Heavy Artillery and stationed in various forts around Washington. Company H garrisoned Fort Snyder specifically during the crisis of Early's raid. Company I, 4th Massachusetts Heavy Artillery, similarly served in this fort in September 1864.

Fort Snyder also housed a regiment of government clerks during the crisis. Generally known as the Interior Department Regiment, it included two companies from the Government Printing Office. This unit went to "one of the forts in the vicinity of the Insane Asylum" (presumably Fort Snyder) when General Early threatened the city. When the threat abated, "the printers having laid aside their weapons of destruction resumed their places in the office."[8]

PROTECTING THE GIESBORO CAVALRY DEPOT: BATTERY CARROLL AND FORTS CARROLL AND GREBLE

Establishment of a major cavalry depot on the banks of the Potomac at Giesboro Point created the need for forts to cover the vital complex. In addition, southern extremities of the long ridge east of the Anacostia required flank protection. This resulted in erection of Battery Carroll and Forts Carroll and Greble.

Battery Carroll and Fort Carroll

Location

From the Fort Snyder site area, continue south on Alabama Avenue SE as it merges with and becomes Martin Luther King Jr. Avenue. Fort Carroll was located at approximately 3720 Martin Luther King Jr. Avenue, just north of the intersection with South Capital Street SE, with overgrown parkland containing earthwork remains.

Visible Remains

No traces of the fort itself remain. The battery remains poorly preserved. A National Park Service interpretive marker does not exist, but a generic sign does.

Description

The fort and battery were named for Major General Samuel Sprigg Carroll, a native Washingtonian and graduate of West Point. The fort had a perimeter of 340 yards. The evolving ordnance register included the following:

1862
Two eight-inch siege howitzers (one en embrasure, one en barbette)

Camp Stoneman/Giesboro Cavalry Depot—Giesboro Point, D.C. *National Archives*

Four 32-pounder seacoast guns (en barbette)
Six 12-pounder field guns (en embrasure)
One 30-pounder Parrott rifle (en embrasure)
One 24-pounder Coehorn mortar
Six vacant platforms

1864
One 12-pounder field gun
Twelve 32-pounder seacoast guns
One eight-inch siege howitzer
Two 30-pounder Parrott rifles
One 24-pounder Coehorn mortar

Notes/Anecdotes

The fort and battery were built on the estate of George W. Young on what was called the Piscataway Road in Washington County, DC. It commanded the area of Oxon Run to the east and other country lanes leading toward Uniontown and the Navy Yard Crossing.

Garrisons for the works included the following:

70th New York Infantry, July 24, 1861–March 1862
4th New York Heavy Artillery, Co. C, January 1–February 1862
4th New York Heavy Artillery, Co. D, January 12–April 7, 1862
4th New York Heavy Artillery, Co. H, March 1–April 7, 1862
19th Maine Infantry, Co. E, August 3–September 12, 1862
9th Rhode Island Infantry, Co. F
17th Maine Infantry HQ/Field Staff, Co. F, August 18–October 7, 1862
10th New York Heavy Artillery, Cos. B, I, June 2, 1863–February 28, 1864
8th Unattached Massachusetts Heavy Artillery (detachment), May 17, 1864
3d Massachusetts Heavy Artillery, Co. D May 5–August, November 20–27, 1864

Battery Carroll, with four unoccupied platforms, according to Barnard's report, and another small redoubt covered the forward slopes of the original fort and improved interdiction of the Piscataway Road (modern Martin Luther King Jr.). Together, fort and battery became not merely a defensive position but soon also the site of various administrative facilities for the area. As 1st Lieutenant F. A. Sherman, 10th New York Heavy Artillery, reported on March 17, 1864, the fort's drill ground was "much obstructed by hospitals [and] Provost [tents, horses, and cavalry]" and also served as headquarters for garrisons in this sector.

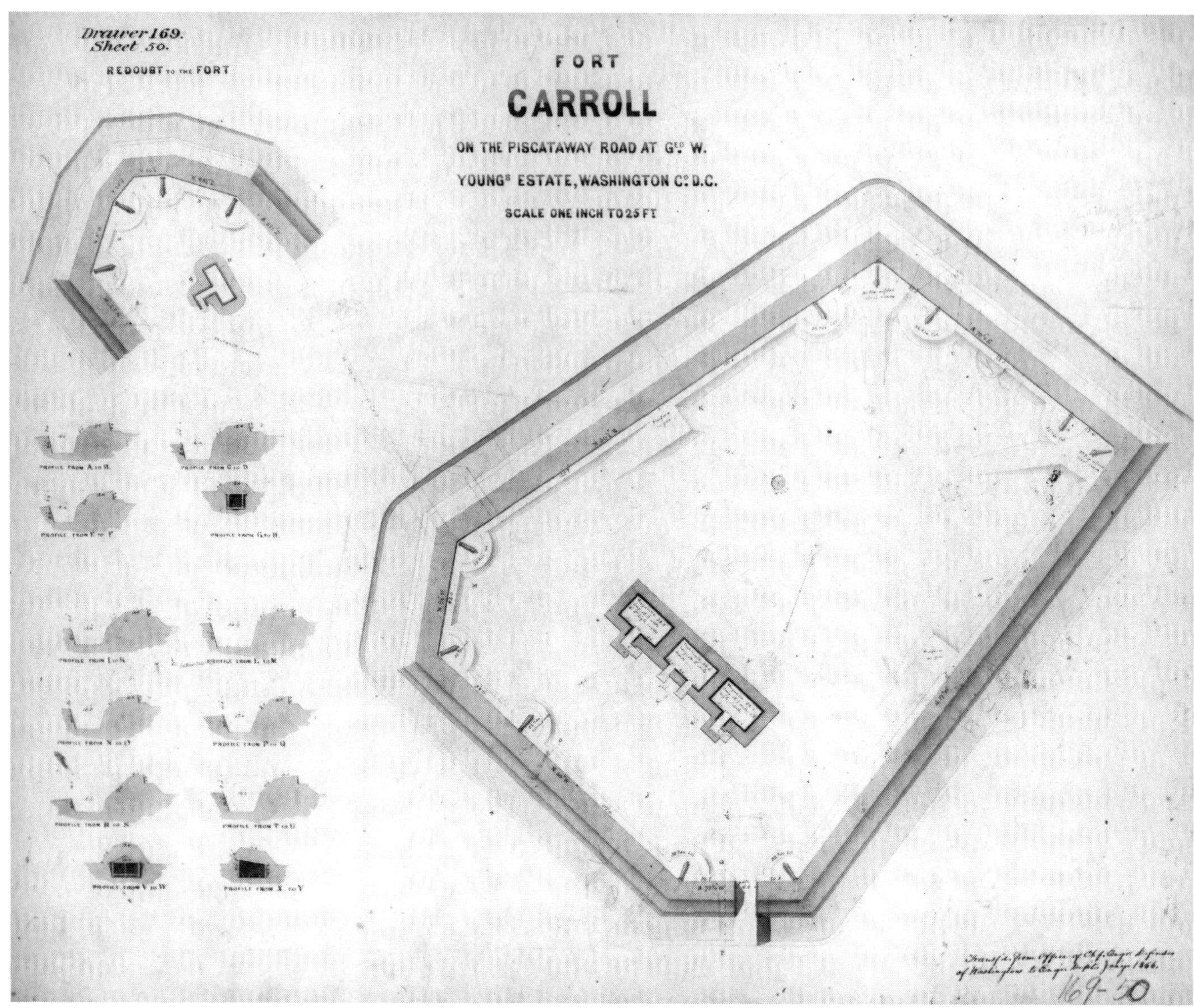

Battery Carroll and Fort Carroll (original configuration)—Engineer Drawing. *National Archives*

Sherman nonetheless noted that Fort Carroll had a good 100-foot-deep well and that the garrisons drilled each day. An adequate supply of ammunition included 1,180 projectiles for the 12-pounders, 508 shells for the 32-pounders, 224 shells for the eight-inch howitzer, ninety-four projectiles for the Coehorn mortar, and 179 projectiles for the 30-pounder Parrott rifle. He further noted 110 Springfield muskets, 14,856 cartridges, and 5,000 blanks in the fort's magazine. At the time, four officers and 112 enlisted men were present for duty.

After Early's raid, Major General Christopher Augur stated that Fort Carroll required addition of one 32-pounder howitzer, two 30-pounder Parrott rifles, and six 12-pounder howitzers.

Possibly the most poignant letter home from anyplace in the Defenses of Washington came from a soldier stationed at Fort Carroll on Thanksgiving 1863. Writing to his wife at Adams Center, Jefferson County, New York, on November 26, 1863, Elias Babcock of the 10th New York Heavy Artillery noted,

> Dear Wife as today is the national thanksgiving let us unit our hearts in thanks and praise to the giver of every good and perfect gift that amongst the ravages of war and the many diseases which nature is heir to[,]

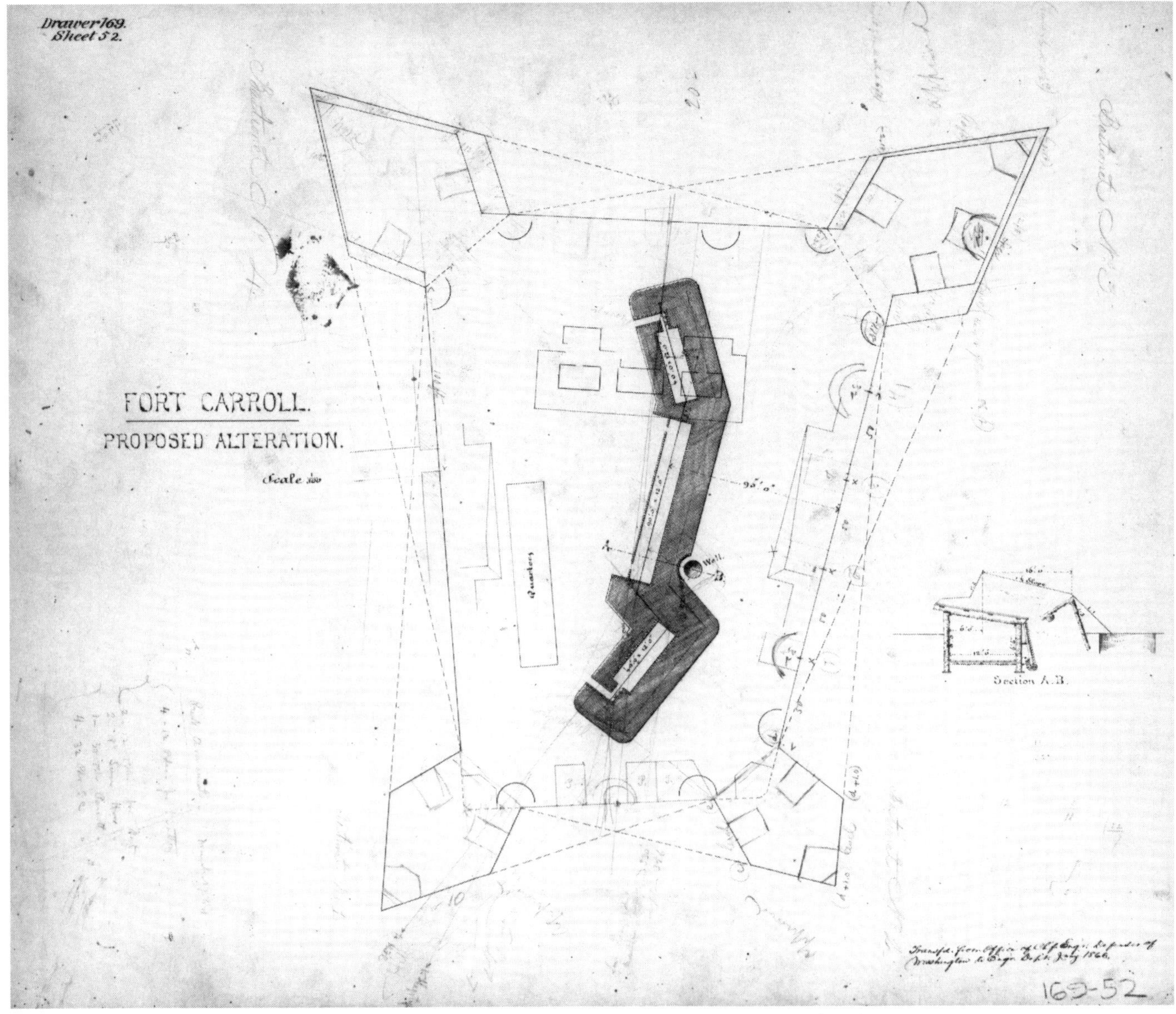

Fort Carroll (proposed alteration)—Engineer Drawing. *National Archives*

> our lives have been precious in his sight and let us live in hopes that before another anniversary of this thing shall roll around we may be permitted to enjoy each others society and with that of our children and may God keep us all from harm the coming year is my sincere prayer and desire.

A month later, on New Year's Day, Babcock wrote, "Another year has gone with its sorrows and its joys and the war is still raging and we are still deprived of each other's society, but for all that we have a great deal to be thankful for." He added that he thought that "this war will end in one year more, and before if they see fit to have it for I am willing to have my part of it stopped any time when they see fit."

Fort Carroll was turned over to the chief signal officer in August 1866.[9]

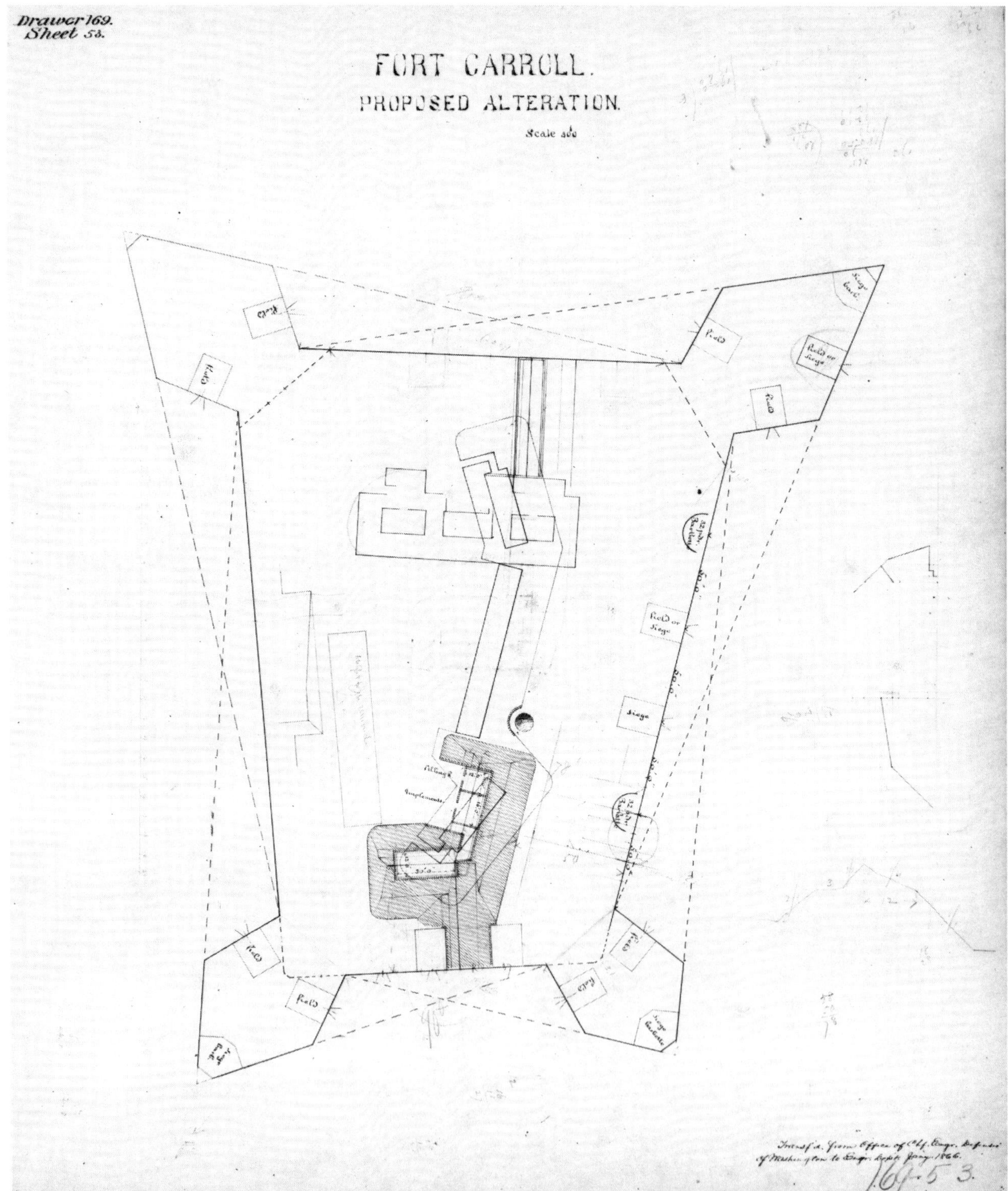

Fort Carroll (proposed alteration)—Engineer Drawing. *National Archives*

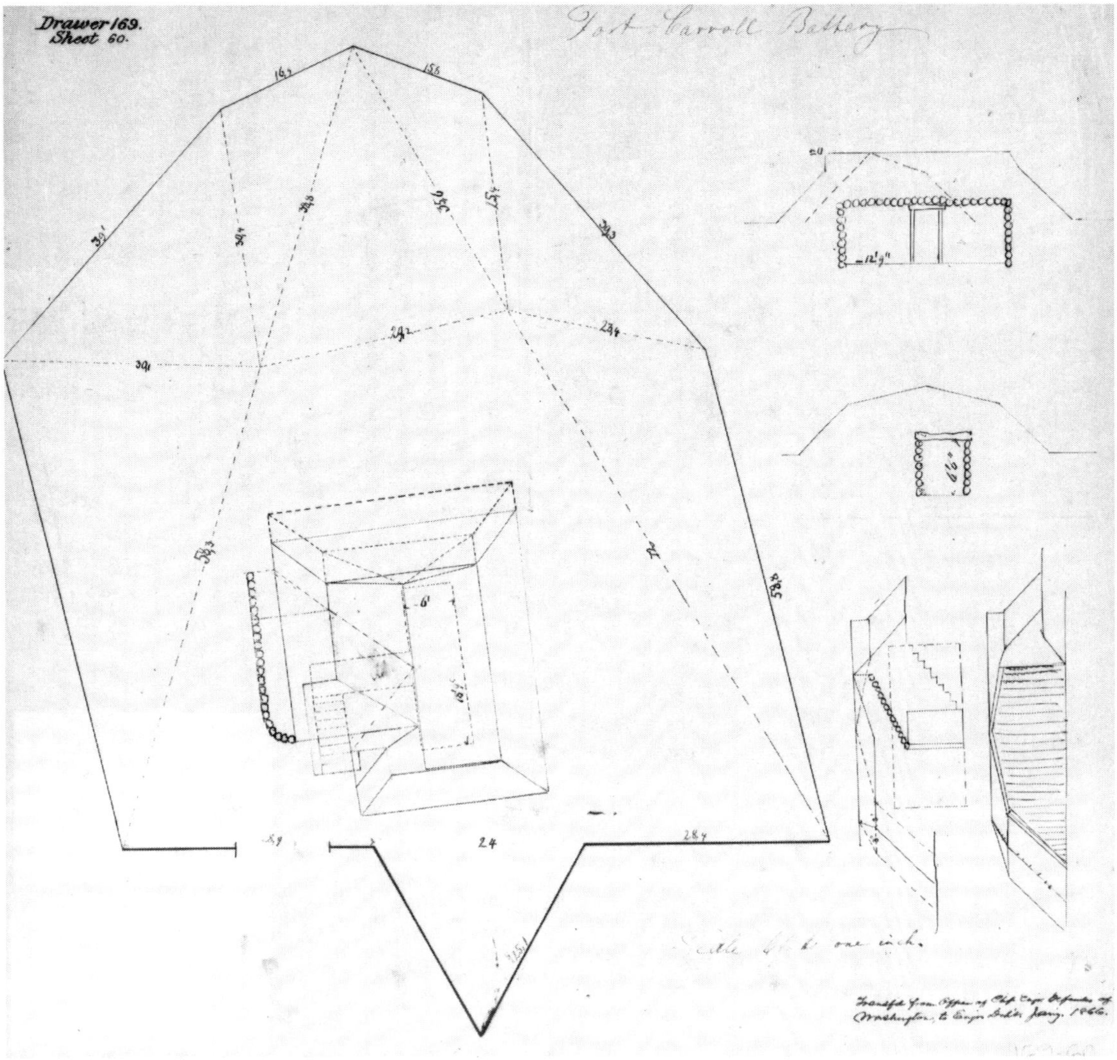

Drawer 169.
Sheet 60.

Fort Carroll Battery

Scale 40 ft to one inch.

Battery Carroll—Engineer Drawing. *National Archives*

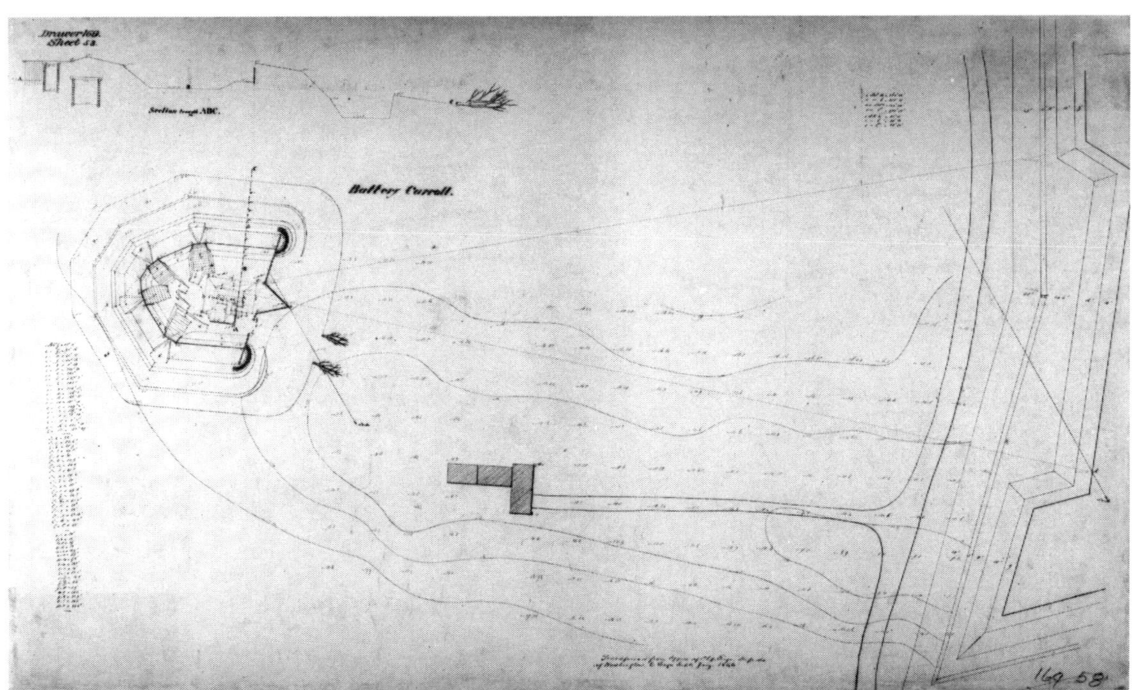

Battery Carroll—Engineer Drawing. *National Archives*

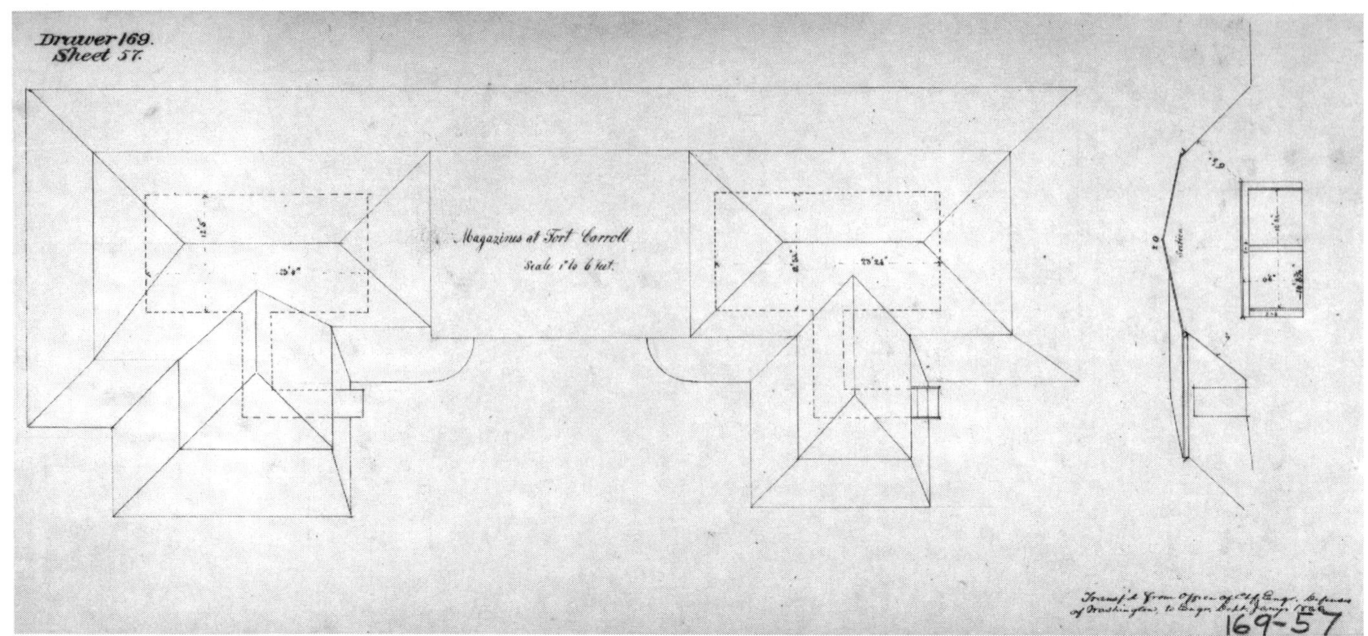

Magazines at Fort Carroll—Engineer Drawing. *National Archives*

Barracks and Hospital Buildings Adjacent to Fort Carroll. *National Archives*

Interior View of Fort Carroll. *National Archives*

Possible View of Fort or Battery Carroll (Piscataway Road in middle; Fort Greble in upper distance). *National Archives*

Fort Greble and Battery Greble

Location

From the Fort Carroll site, continue south on Martin Luther King Jr. Avenue, which merges for two blocks with South Capitol Street SE, to Elmira Street. Turn right and proceed straight to the Fort Greble Park/recreational area behind the apartment complex.

Visible Remains

Few discernible earthen remnants exist. The site is poorly marked and has no interpretive signs.

Description

This irregular, octagonal fort of some 327 perimeter yards was named for Lieutenant John T. Greble of Philadelphia, who was killed at Big Bethel, Virginia, on June 10, 1861.

Fort Greble contained seventeen guns and mortars as follows:

Six 12-pounder field guns (en embrasure)
Six 32-ounder seacoast guns (en barbette)
Two eight-inch siege howitzers (en barbette)
One 30-pounder Parrott rifle (en embrasure)
One ten-inch siege mortar
One 24-pounder Coehorn mortar

Battery Greble nearby to the south had four unoccupied platforms.

Notes/Anecdotes

The Fort Greble garrison included the following units:

4th New York Heavy Artillery, Cos. B, F, January–February 12, 1862–March 27, 1864
19th Maine Infantry, Cos. A, F, August 12–September 12, 1862
17th Maine Infantry, Co. A, August 18–October 7, 1862
10th New York Heavy Artillery, Cos. I, L, May 1863–March 1864
9th New York Heavy Artillery, Co. K, March 26, 1864–April 1864
2d U.S. Infantry, Co. I, December 12, 1864–May 1865
3d Massachusetts Heavy Artillery, Co. C, July–November 20, 1864
3d Massachusetts Heavy Artillery, Co. D, November 11–27, 1864
14th Michigan Battery (detachment), July 1865
12th U.S. Infantry (detachment), September 1867
9th Rhode Island Infantry, Co. A

During the tenure of Company L, 10th New York Heavy Artillery, an average of four officers and 133 enlisted men were present for duty at the fort. Many

Interior View of Fort Greble. *National Archives*

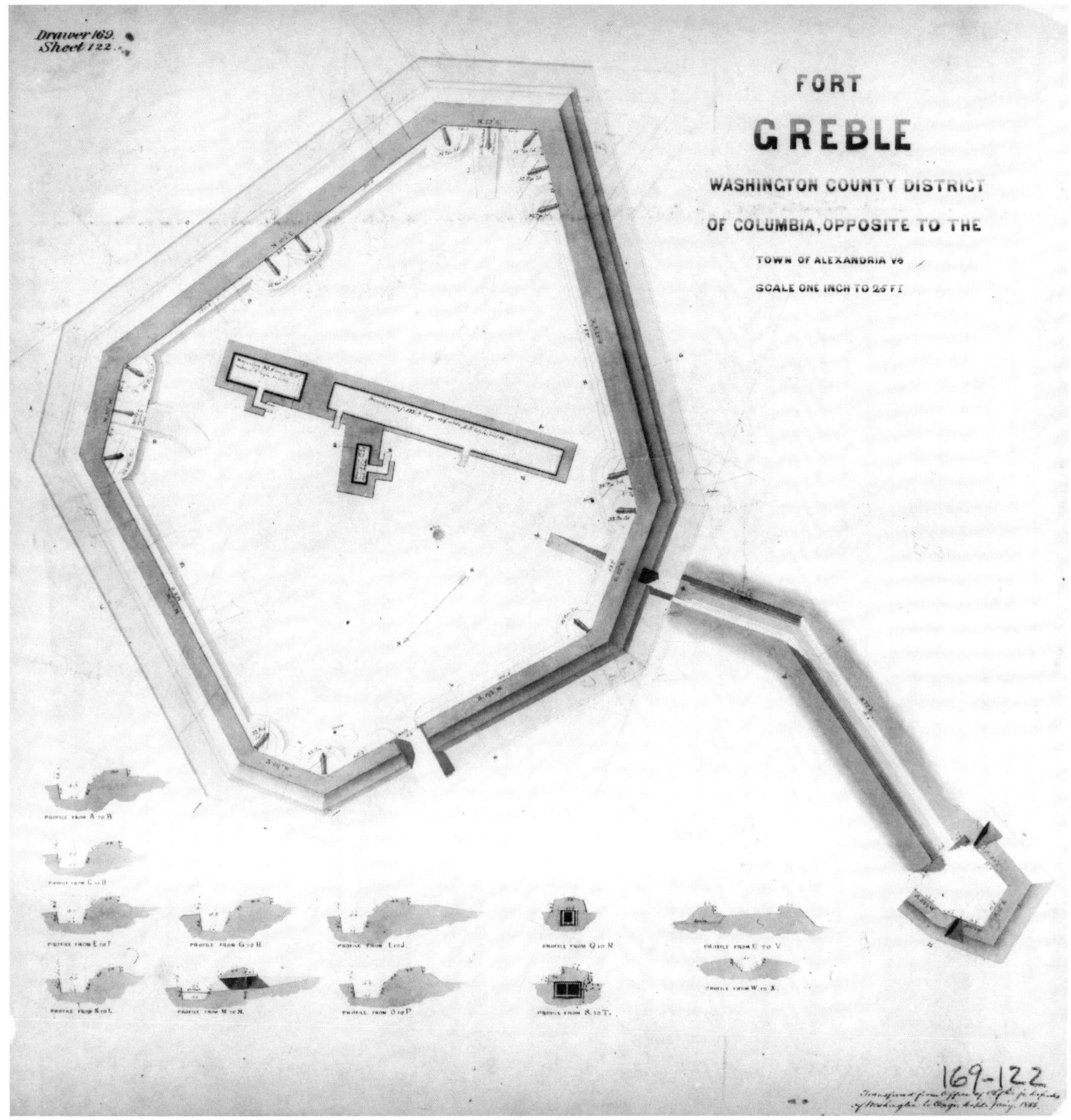

Fort Greble (original)—Engineer Drawing. *National Archives*

of these men recorded their observations of the superb view of the river, Alexandria, and the Virginia shoreline as well as Washington City in the distance. Indeed, not only did Fort and Battery Greble occupy the extreme southern end of the ridgeline cast of the Anacostia, but they also commanded the Oxon Run valley to their front and the Piscataway Road crossing. Their gunfire also could interdict an enemy on the Potomac at this point.

An English immigrant, Thomas A. Bayley of the 4th New York Heavy Artillery (Doubleday's New York Artillery), wrote on his arrival at the post in February 1862, "It is a very strong earthen fortifications mounts 15 guns, 2 of which are rifled and will throw a shot 5

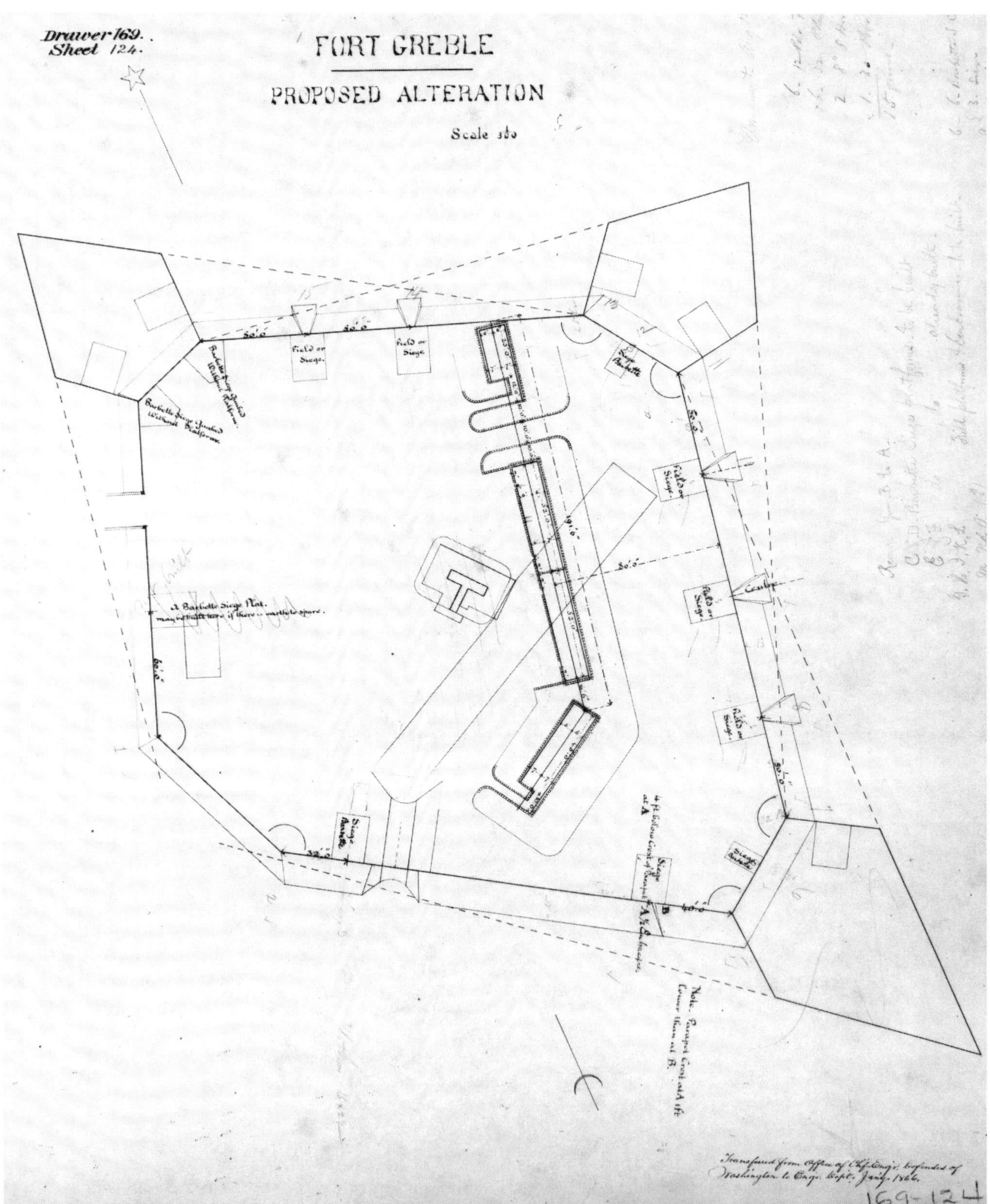

Fort Greble (proposed alteration)—Engineer Drawing. *National Archives*

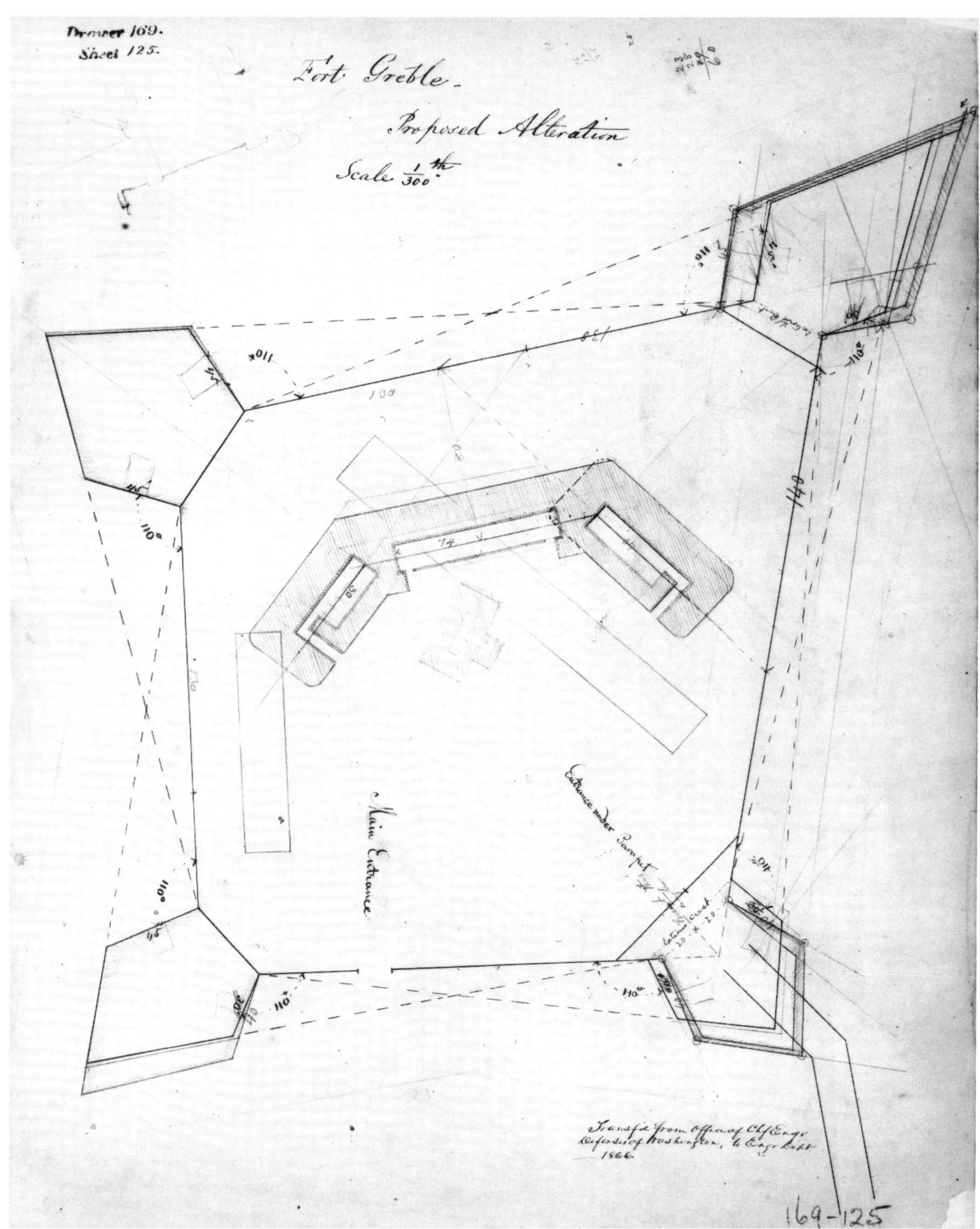

Fort Greble (proposed alteration)—Engineer Drawing. *National Archives*

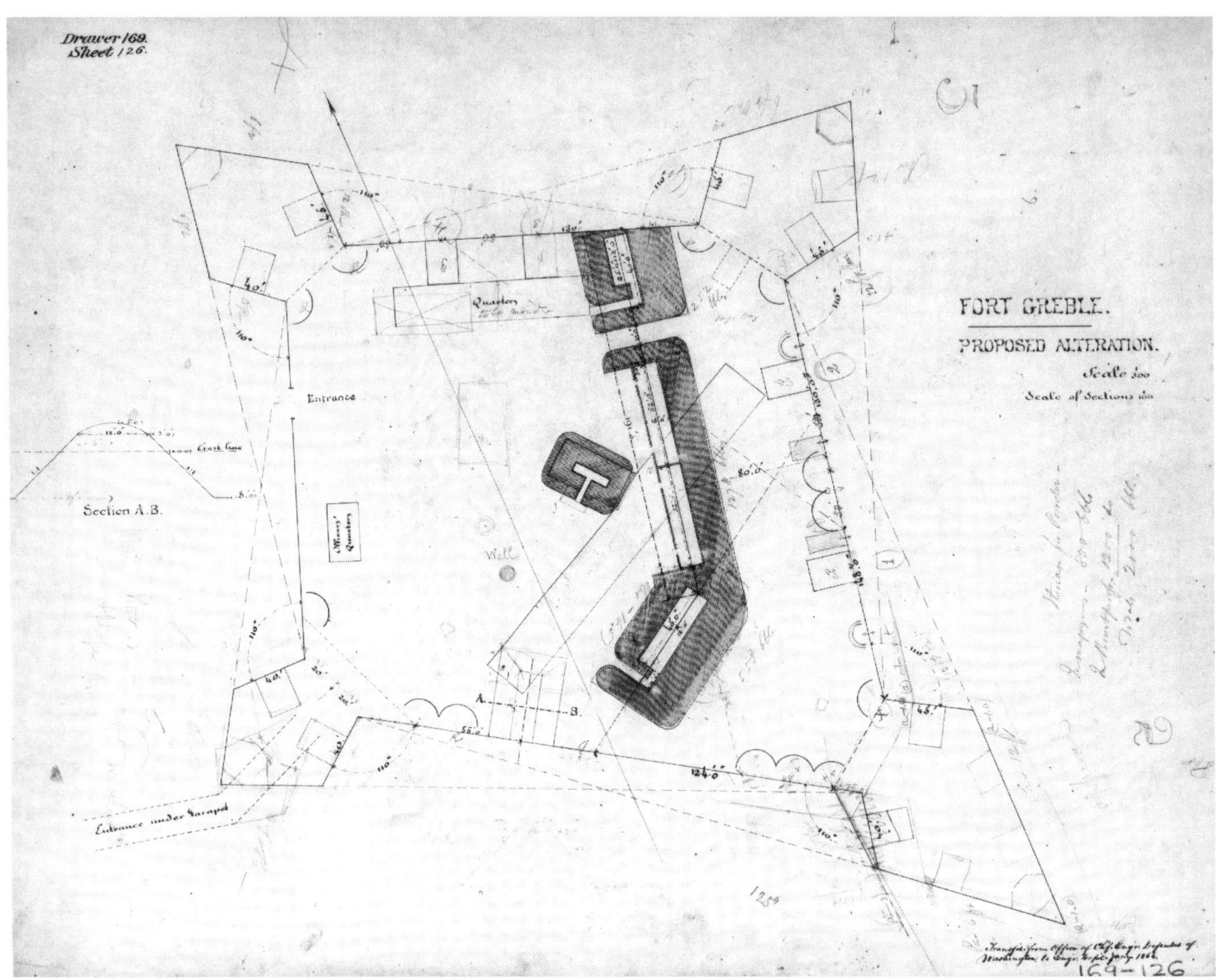

Fort Greble (proposed alteration)—Engineer Drawing. *National Archives*

miles or upwards. . . . We do not stay in the fort but are encamped alongside the beautiful river of the Potomac, with Alexandria on the opposite bank plainly visible for miles, running quietly half a mile below us." Inasmuch as the Confederates had effectively sealed off the river downriver in the Freeport and Quantico area at this time, he noted, "The firing from the Southern blockade can be plainly heard as our vessels run past." He noted how the owner of the land occupied by Fort Greble and 600 additional acres belonged to "a Captain in the Secession army and has been confiscated by the Government." Two months later, he wrote further about the good life in the garrison, with nightly concerts by members of his company, "plenty of coffee, soup, rice, potatoes, pork and beef." They now had a large quantity of shell, powder, and balls; "the men are very efficient in Artillery Tactics," and "we have fired very frequently numerous rounds of blank cartridge and are fully prepared for the Merrimac should she wish to try the effect of her shot on the Capital City of the Union." He further noted the capture of the absent landowner of the Fort Greble property—"a rebel Captain." Parading the captive rebel captain before his former property, they "seemed heart broken but as soon as his back was turned up went their fingers to their noes [*sic*], one fellow jumped off a rail, turned two or three somersaults and began butting his head against a tree, not a much to try its thickness, but his excess of joy." In Bayley's words, "The rebel captain had been a bad master and killed several of his slaves." Soon, however, the Union gunners were transferred across the Potomac to duty in the Arlington lines.

As at Fort Carroll, civilian laborers were employed in the construction of Fort Greble, having been drawn from cities like Philadelphia and New York for wages of forty to ninety cents per day for common laborers, while specialists, such as carpenters and ironmongers, received $2.00 to $3.00 per day.

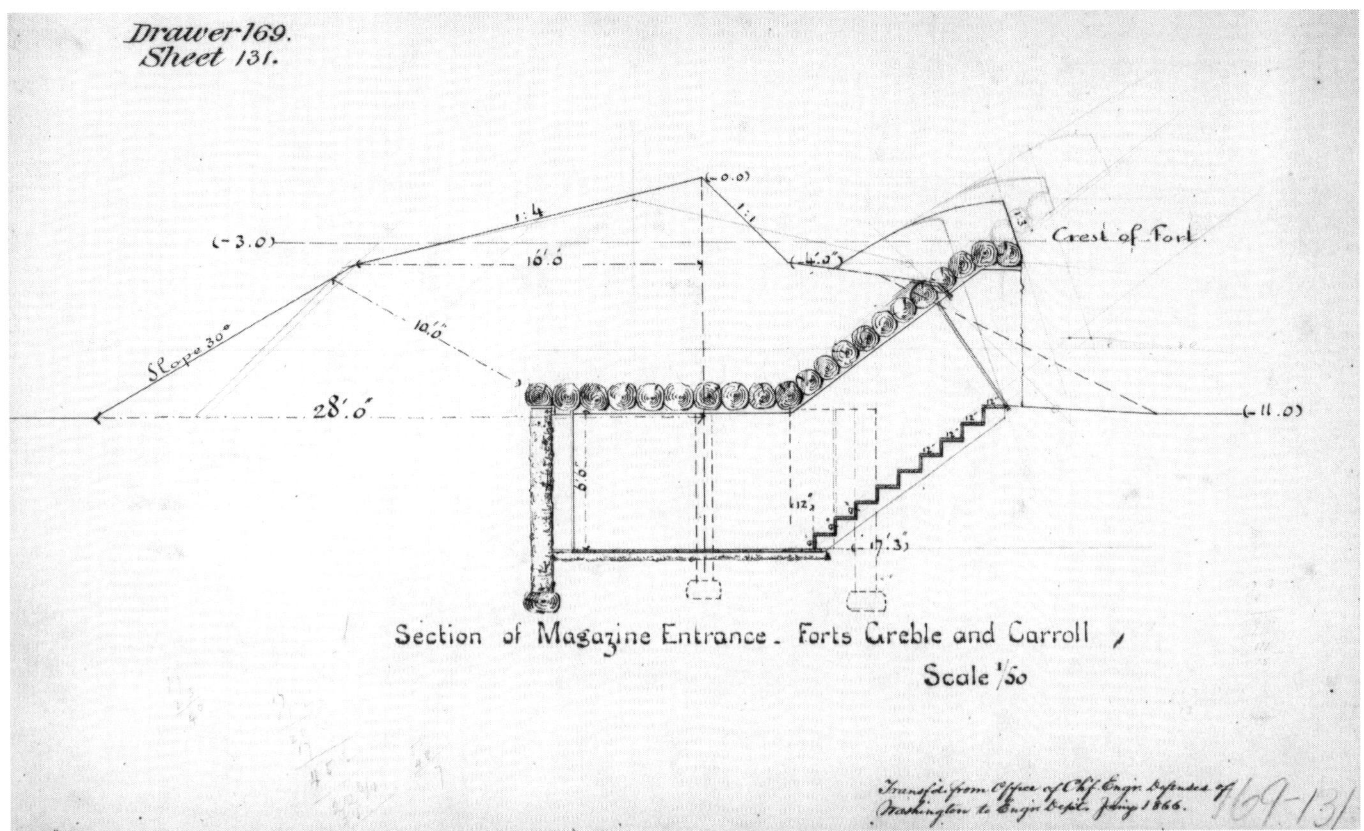

Section of Fort Greble Magazine Entrance—Engineer Drawing. *National Archives*

To provide for both soldiers and civilians working at a place such as Fort Greble, the commissariat sent sixteen days' rations for sixty men in the following ratios: 114 barrels of beef, two and a half barrels of potatoes, and ten pounds of candles. Fresh beef arrived at least once a week, while rations for horses were also furnished for six days at 2,016 pounds of oats and corn and 2,190 pounds of hay.

A picture of the garrison's health emerges from reports at Fort Greble. Depending on the time of year, Companies C and D of the 4th New York Heavy Artillery at Fort Carroll and Companies B and F of that regiment at Fort Greble showed an average of only four to ten men on sick call daily. But in August and September 1862, Companies A and F of the 19th Maine Volunteer Infantry at Fort Greble and Company E of that unit at Fort Carroll showed an average of twenty-five enlisted men on sick call daily. Their officers blamed "the indiscretion of the men in eating improper food purchased by them from hucksters and traders." A crackdown reduced sick call to six to ten men daily.

The regimental historian of the 19th Maine recorded that amid the drudgery of drilling, camp guard, picketing, policing the camps, and garrison, as well as incessant inspections, the unit always welcomed local vendors coming down the winding country lanes in the morning with melons, peaches, and other fruits. Many of the "Down Easters" had never seen melons. "Old black women would climb the hill on the road that led to Fort Greble with a basket of peaches on their heads, a basket of vegetables in one hand and a large bag of fruit in the other, and never wink," he noted. "I have never eaten sweeter or better fruit than in September 1862," claimed another soldier, as "when we were fooling around in the forts. I can taste it yet."

Spiritual as well as physical health of the men came under army scrutiny as religious services took place each Sunday on the parade grounds of both Fort Greble and Fort Carroll. On September 12, 1862, Colonel Thomas A. Roberts, commanding the 17th Maine at Fort Greble, ordered his company commanders to send fifty men and several officers in full dress uniform but without arms and equipment to Sunday service at headquarters. On other occasions, he directed that they appear in full uniform with arms and equipment.

An amusing story emerging from Fort Greble was told after the war by Colonel Thomas B. Van Buren of the 102d New York Volunteer Infantry. Apparently, one night in February 1862, there was a heavy rain. In the morning, one enterprising soldier tied a string to his bayonet, mounted the parapet, and began fishing

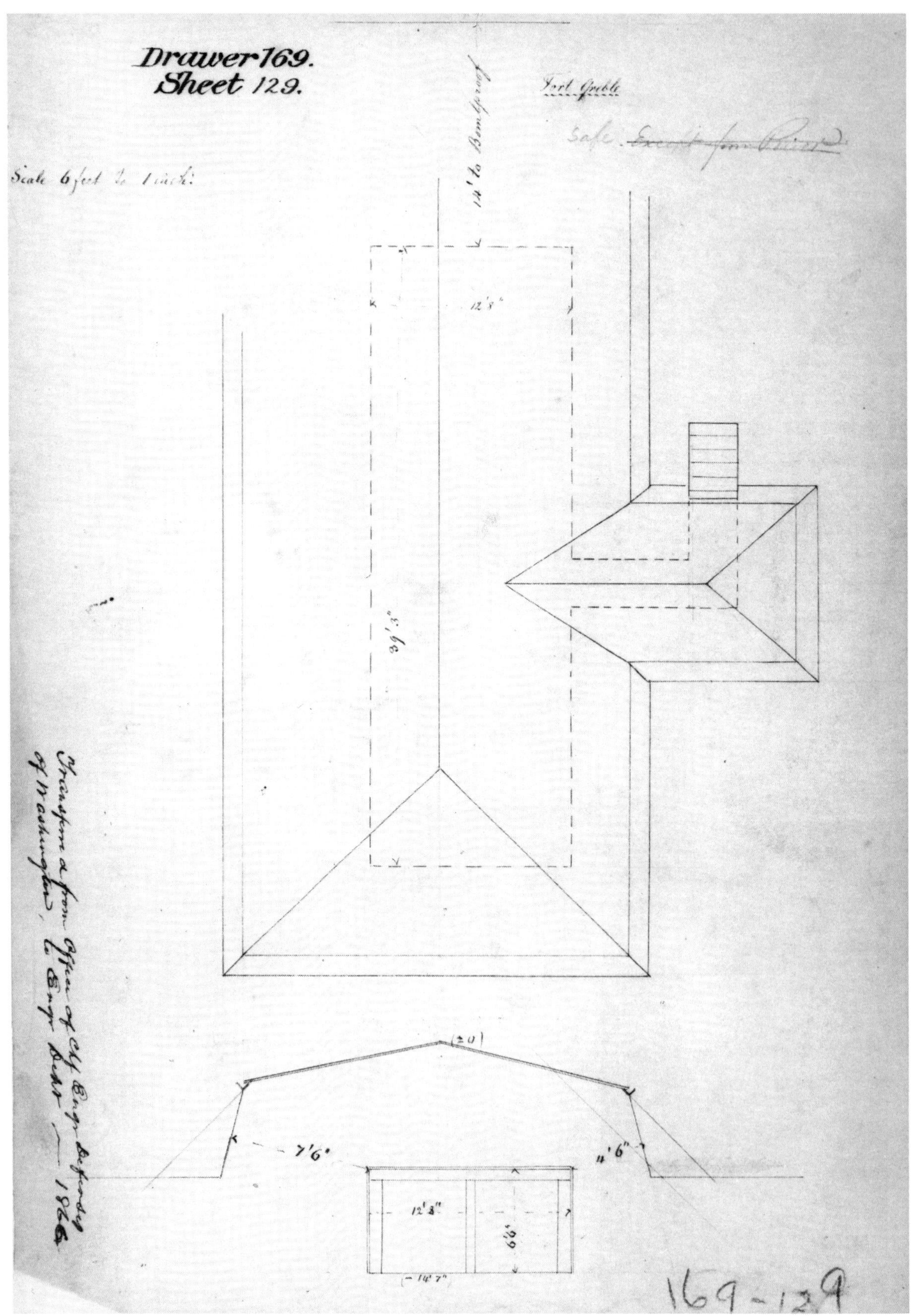

Fort Greble Magazine—Engineer Drawing. *National Archives*

in a shallow pool, entirely unmindful of his surroundings, Quietly but regularly, the soldier would lift his ersatz fishing pole from the pool, and eventually somebody took notice of the strange happening. The soldier's irritated captain could get no answer to his question "What are you doing there?" Neither could the regimental commander, and finally the surgeon was called in. The medical professional recommended a medical discharge for the obviously insane soldier. As the colonel and captain handed the document to the unresponsive soldier-fisherman, the man jumped up, shouting, "That's what I was fishing for," threw down his bayonet, and immediately departed camp much to everyone's chagrin.

At war's end, Fort Greble was offered to Thomas W. Berry of Baltimore, holding the property in trust for its rightful owners. One quartermaster colonel noted on July 29, 1865, that the property consisted of one officers' mess house, a stable, an officers' quarters, a barracks, an enlisted mess house, a guardhouse, a shell room, two bombproofs, and a magazine in addition to the earthworks. In Colonel M. Ludington's opinion, the lumber and shingles used in the buildings and the logs in the stockades would be ample compensation for use of the property. Berry disagreed, stating that the government had occupied the site for four years, had destroyed civilian structures, and had caused loss of rental income from the premises. "We are not disposed to accept the proposition because with the Fort it would be like a Man with an Eliphant."

Temporarily retained for Signal Corps purposes, the battery and fort finally were abandoned despite the advisability of retaining both Fort Greble and Fort Carroll for part of the river defense of the capital.[10]

6

Touring the River Forts

THE RIVER DEFENSES: FORT FOOTE, BATTERY RODGERS, AND FORT WASHINGTON

Washington's traditional point of greatest danger until the advent of airpower was the Potomac River. Fear of Confederate or even British and French flotillas steaming up the river during the Civil War caused army engineers to perfect three main positions at Battery Rodgers, Fort Foote, and old Fort Washington.

Fort Foote

Location

From Fort Greble Park, return to South Capitol Street SE. Turn right and follow as it becomes Indian Head Highway (Maryland Route 210). Immediately beyond the Capital Beltway (I-495), move to the right lane and proceed to the second traffic light (Kerby Hill Road). Turn right and proceed to Oxon Hill Road (next traffic light atop the hill fenced National Harbor complex to front). Turn left onto Oxon Hill Road and proceed one block to Fort Foote Road. Turn right and follow Fort Foote Road to Fort Foote Park. After passing through a wooded ravine, look for an abrupt right turn into the parking lot and walk straight ahead to the fort.

Visible Remains

The National Park Service has cleared and preserved here some of the best Civil War fort remains in the national capital area. They have also remounted cannon and restored the river view while providing various interpretive markers.

Description

Constructed between 1863 and 1865, Fort Foote was pronounced a "model" fortification by the engineers. It was named for Rear Admiral Andrew Hull Foote, who died in 1863 after arduous service on western rivers.

Fort Foote had a perimeter of 472 yards and mounted two fifteen-inch Rodman guns, four 200-pounder rifled Parrotts (all en barbette), and six 30-pounder Parrott rifles (en embrasure), and eleven vacant platforms according to Barnard's report. After Early's raid, Major General Christopher Augur recommended additional armament for the fort to include two 24-pounder flank defense howitzers, one 12-pounder mountain howitzer, and four 12-pounder Napoleons.

Fort Foote became the only "permanent" fortification for the defense of Washington after the Civil War, continuing in active service until 1878 although mostly in neglected condition. The fort's long service is attested by the full scope of ordnance that was in place during its existence.

For the guns marked by asterisks, there was apparently some confusion between the 12-pounder field gun and the 10-pounder field gun in the post returns of May and July 1877. While the 12-pounder is shown in the returns prior to these two and again in the October 1878 return, it does not appear in those of May and July 1877, and the 10-pounder appears only in those two returns.

Notes/Anecdotes

Fort Foote was constructed on Rozier's Bluff (the land of Francis W. Rozier and wife) eight miles downriver from Washington by Lieutenant Colonel William Henry Seward (son of Secretary of State William Henry Seward) and the 2d Battalion (four companies), 9th New York Heavy Artillery. Companies C, D, E, and G constituted the garrison from August 1863 to April 1864.

Other units garrisoning the work at various times included the following:

Date	*Unit*	*Size of Garrison*	*Officer Commanding*
May 17–October 1864	Co. B 1st New Hampshire Heavy Artillery		
April 27, 1865	Battery G 1st Pennsylvania Light Artillery		
December 13, 1864, May 1865	Co. I 2d U.S. Artillery Co. G 3d U.S. Artillery	2 Off 71 EM 2 Off. 105 EM	Lieutenant Colonel Alicock Captain Conant Major Reed
May 23, 1864, June 1865	Co. B, Maine Coast Guard	3 Off 45 EM	"
May 1865–June 1865	Co. G 14th Pennsylvania Reserves	13 Off. 375 EM	Major D. W. Stafford
June–August 1, 1865	1st Vermont Heavy Artillery Consoldiated Battalion (4 companies)		
June 1865	Co. I, 14th New York	"	"
June 1865–September 24, 1865	Cos. E, G 1st U.S. Artillery	6 Off. 195 EM	"
September 24–November 26, 1865 1867	Co. E 4th U.S. Artillery	3 Off 56 EM	Captain Marcus P. Miller
November 26, 1867–January 15, 1868 1871	Co. I 4th U.S. Artillery	3 Off 66-115 EM	Captain Richard Lodor to April 1870; 1st Lieutenant Robert Craig, May 1870; Captain Lodor, June–December 1870
January 15–June 19, 1871 1872	Co. F 4th U.S. Artillery	3 Off 66 EM	Captain Joseph B. Campbell
June 19–October 24, 1872	Co. M M, 4th U.S. Artillery 4th U.S. Artillery	3 Off 44 EM	Captain C. B. Throckmorton
October 24–December 1872	Co. I 5th U.S. Artillery	?	Lieutenant J. E. Sawyer
December–August 20, 1872	Co. B	3 Off	Lieutenant James Eastman, December 1872–August 1873; Major James M. Robertson, August 1873–July 1874; Captain J. C. Breckinridge, July–October 1874; Major James M. Robertson, October 1874–May 1875
1878	2d U.S. Artillery	58 EM (June 1873) 2 Off 45 EM 4 Off 37 EM (July 1877)	 Captain J. C. Breckinridge 1st Lieutenant George Mitchell, August–September 1877 Capt. J. C. Breckinridge, October 1877–August 1878
August 20–November 10, 1878	Co. I 2d U.S. Artillery	3 Off 54 EM	Capt. Frank B. Hamilton August–November 1878
November 10, 1878	Co. I (withdrawn and not replaced) Post discontinued		

Fort Foote provided a varied experience for its garrisons. Visits by dignitaries included President Lincoln and many of his cabinet members. They marveled at the sophistication of the works and the size of the cannon and enjoyed having Secretary of State Seward's son and his regiment play host. Lincoln led a party downriver on August 20, 1863, for example, with Secretary of War Stanton, Quartermaster General Meigs, Barnard, and others in tow. They toured the fort and dined on local peaches and crackers and cheese,

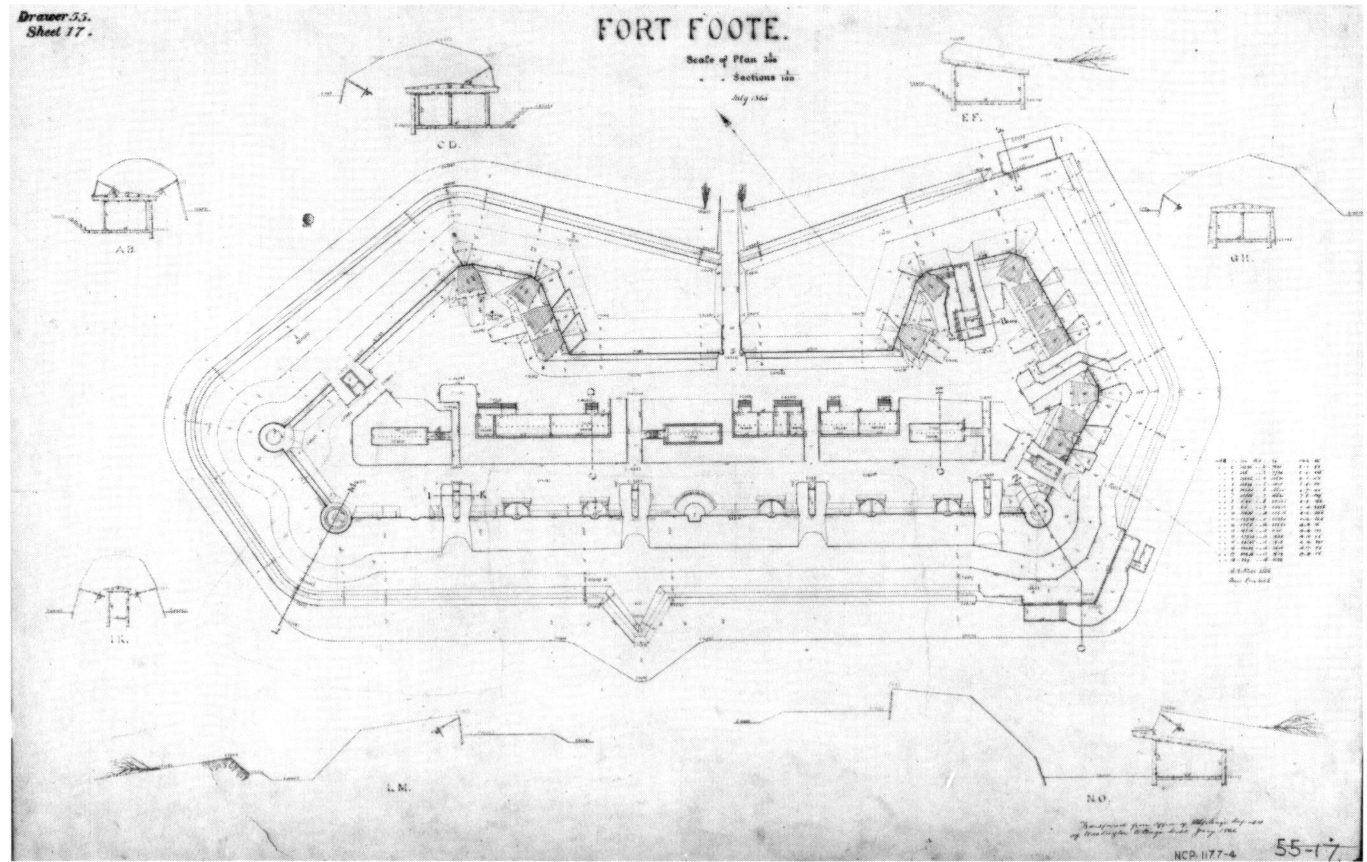

Fort Foote—Engineer Drawing. *National Archives*

washed down with champagne. They returned well fed and entertained to the city on the stern-wheeler *General Hooker* after dark. Young Seward's wife, Janet, especially enjoyed entertaining visitors in the ample bombproofs and once in April 1864 provided a sumptuous feast of sandwiches, raw and steamed oysters, pickles, cake, and coffee.

Russian warships steamed past the fort on an official visit in December 1863, and Seward squired the squadron's officers around his post.

The main attraction seemed to be the firing of the heavy guns. Weighing 49,000 pounds, the fifteen-inch Rodman guns were great objects of curiosity as they fired 500-pound solid cannonballs three miles downriver. Requiring 300 to 400 soldiers to move the cannon up the bluffs from the river (they had been transported from the Washington Arsenal by boat since the country roads could not bear such traffic), these cannon fired at targets anchored in midstream. They required fifty pounds of powder to make the range at

Description of Gun	*March 1865*	*December 1867*	*May 1868*	*March 1871*	*November 1872*	*December 1874*	*May 1877*	*July 1877*	*October 1878*
Fifteen-inch Rodman	1	2	2	2	2	2	2	2	2
200-pounder Parrott rifle	2	4	4	4	4	4	4	4	4
30-pounder rifled Parrott	6	7	7	7	7	7	7	7	7
Ten-inch siege mortars		5	5	5	5	5	5	5	6
12-pounder Coehorn Mortar		5	5	5	—	5	5	5	5
12-pounder field gun*		6	6	6	6	6	—	—	6
6-pounder field gun		0	1	1	1	1	1	1	1
Eight-inch siege mortars							2	2	2
Gatling gun, one-inch caliber							1	1	1
10-pounder field gun*							6	6	—
Four-and-a-half-inch rifled gun								2	2
Three-inch rifled field guns								4	4
Gatling gun .45-caliber									1

*There was apparently some confusion between the 12- and 10-pounder field gun in the May and July 1877 post returns. While the 12-pounder is shown in the returns prior to these two and again in October 1878, it does not appear in May and July 1877 and the 10-pounder only appears in those two returns.

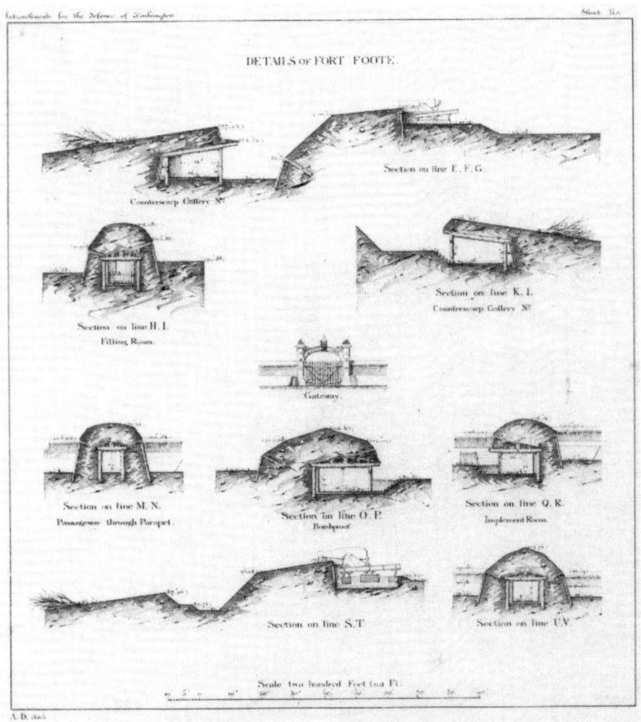

Details of Fort Foote—Engineer Drawing. *National Archives*

a twenty-five-degree elevation. The heavy concussion of their firing caused viewers to stand on tiptoe and open their mouths to lessen the effect. On at least one occasion, Confederate sympathizers rowed out from the Virginia shore and stole one of the targets from the river. After 1865, budget constraints dictated that only twenty shells per year could be used in target practice, and the garrison turned to drill mostly with the 30-pounder Parrott rifles.

Garrison life during and after the war posed a typical round of drill, maintenance, repair, and static garrison duty. Malaria and typhoid made Fort Foote the pesthole of Prince Georges County in southern Maryland. One of the most singular points about service at Fort Foote was the high incidence of men on sick call. Even young Seward was absent for many mouths with malaria, finally returning to upstate New York for his convalescence. None of this lessened normal activity for the fort.

The pattern remained unvarying after the war except for seasonal variations in daylight hours. Reveille came first at daylight or about thirty minutes before sunrise. Breakfast followed half an hour later and lasted thirty minutes. The garrison moved to an hour's drill, followed by sick call, guard mount, fatigue call, police call, and first sergeant's call. By 8:30 or 9:00 A.M., the troops were again ready for drill. About 1:00 P.M., the troops again conducted police or fatigue call followed at 2:00 or 3:00 by more drill. Recall was sounded between 4:00 and 5:00, and dress parade or retreat occurred about fifteen minutes before sunset, followed by supper. That meal occasionally came before retreat. Tattoo was sounded between 8:30 and 9:00 in the evening, and taps came about fifteen minutes thereafter. Inspection would occur on Sunday morning between 8:30 and 9:00 followed by church call at 10:30.

Monthly parades for inspection and muster took place in the early 1870s. By this time, most of the soldier's life was spent in caring for disintegrating buildings and wooden gun carriages, removal of trash, and infantry and artillery drill, and periodically a noncommissioned officer school would be offered. Only by 1876 would the swamp north of the post be drained, solving the malaria problem. The threat of fire spreading about the post was contained by 1877 with the introduction of a portable force pump for use at the cisterns, six Babcock and six U.S. patent extinguishers, and fifty-three buckets, fourteen tire hooks, and five ladders. Extensive postwar modifications were planned for buildings and the earthworks, and a brick and concrete magazine was constructed after 1872.

Indeed, by 1864, Fort Foote mirrored the "state of the art" for Civil War field fortifications. Barnard maintained that "it was a powerful enclosed work, and the most elaborate in its internal arrangements of all the defenses of Washington." However, his successor, Colonel Barton S. Alexander, advocated addition of river obstructions moored in the stream and held together by a 400-foot chain and twenty-three anchors—a $300,000 project that might "detain" any enemy flotilla up to an hour or more under the direct fire from the fort. This "Alexandrine Chain" was never tested, for the war ended, and while discussions continued as late as 1868, the navy championed its own ironclads and torpedoes (mines) as the proper river defense for the city.

Secretary of the Navy Gideon Welles disdained the whole scheme of Fort Foote both during and after the war. He claimed in a passage from his famous wartime diary that the position was a strong one but that it was all a frightful waste of money and labor. "In going over the works a melancholy feeling came over me," he noted, "that there should have been so much waste, for the fort is not wanted, and it will never fire a hostile gun."

Welles's prediction held. No hostile fleet has ever ascended the Potomac after the British invasion of 1814. The works at Fort Foote were abandoned finally in 1878, and by the turn of the century, the site was a tumbled-down ruin of earthworks, half-filled and overgrown ditches, and bunkers, while the two Rodman guns dismounted, their carriages broken among the weeds.

Briefly reactivated as an engineer training and practice site during World War I, the neglected Fort Foote once more sprang to life as a historic site in the mid-1980s. Today, visitors can once more view the Civil War parapets and remounted ordnance much as they can at Forts Ward and Stevens. The National Park Service and Youth Conservation Corps have worked to restore and maintain this particular fort site in the Defenses of Washington.[1]

Hauling Fifteen-Inch Rodman Gun by Ox Team and Cart. *National Archives*

Interior of Fort Foote during the Civil War. *National Archives*

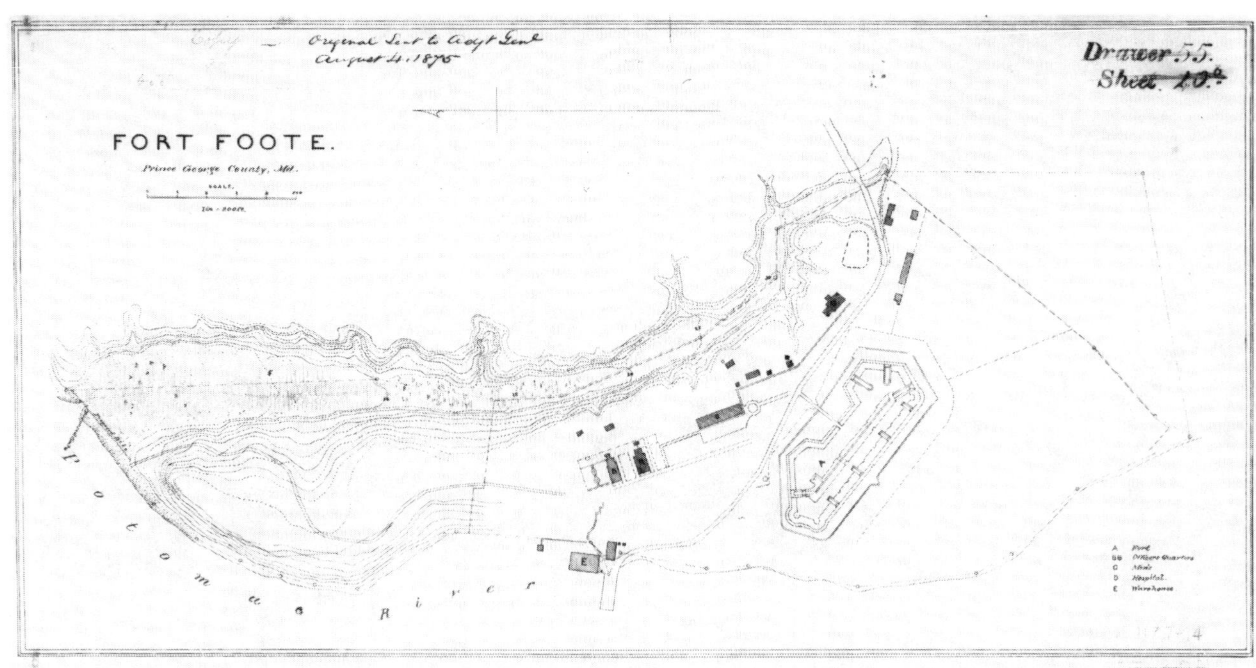

Fort Foote and Environs—Post–Civil War—Engineer Drawing. *National Archives*

Modern View of Remounted Fifteen-Inch Rodman Gun—Fort Foote. *Authors' Collection*

Fort Washington. *London ILLUSTRATED NEWS, May 18, 1861*

Fort Washington—Original Defender of the Nation's Capital

Location

Leaving Fort Foote, turn right and follow Fort Foote Road south to the intersection (traffic light) with Oxon Hill Road. Turn right back to Indian Head Highway (Maryland Route 210). Turn right on this highway to the next traffic light at Fort Washington Road. Turn right straight ahead to Fort Washington Park. Note the entrance fee to the National Park Service site.

Visible Remains

Well preserved and interpreted, Fort Washington, including masonry fort and buildings, contains nineteenth- and early twentieth-century gun batteries and garrison structures all administered by the National Park Service.

Notes/Anecdotes

While this sole guardian of Washington in 1860–1861 did not constitute one of the formal Civil War Defenses of Washington, it was garrisoned during the war. Constructed on the ruins of old Fort Warburton (1809–1814), which its own garrison destroyed on the approach of the British naval squadron after the British army had captured the city, Fort Washington stands in tribute to the engineering skills of Major Pierre L'Enfant, its designer. It stood for nearly half a century as an example of state-of-the art, nineteenth-century brick and masonry coastal fortifications. Abandoned to caretaker status in 1853, the sole "garrison" of the

General View of the Potomac toward Washington from Off Fort Washington. *London ILLUSTRATED NEWS, May 18, 1861*

View toward Mount Vernon from Off Fort Washington. *London ILLUSTRATED NEWS, May 18, 1861*

post in the Secession winter of 1860–1861 was a watchman who reputedly could be bought for a bottle of whiskey. The secretary of the navy rushed a contingent of forty marines to regarrison the place on January 5, 1861. Later, detachments of the 4th U.S. Artillery and volunteer regiments occupied the work during the remainder of the war.

Units identified with wartime Fort Washington included the following:

37th New York, Cs. H, I, July–August 1861
New York Light Artillery, 9th Independent Battery, May 1862–February 1863
Indiana Light Artillery, 16th Independent Battery, March 1863–April 1864
Maine Coast Guard, Co. A, 1864

The strong earthworks of Fort Foote and Battery Rodgers in addition to the wartime experience with heavy rifled ordnance against masonry fortifications doomed Fort Washington's utility. Nonetheless, Private George Perkins of the Sixth New York Independent Battery noted the imposing fortress "built of dark blue stone and bristling with cannon" while passing downstream with his unit in August 1862. He suggested that the grounds and lawn between the fort and river were very beautiful and neatly kept. The channel ran right under the guns, and "it would be difficult even for a Monitor to get by such an obstacle," in his opinion.

The fort was abandoned once more in 1873. Later, Fort Washington served as headquarters for the Defenses of the Potomac from 1896 until 1921 with the placement of eight modern, concrete batteries for ten-inch disappearing rifled guns and other ordnance at the post. With batteries located across the river, it helped protect the city from naval attack during this period. Resembling other local army posts such as Fort Myer (behind Arlington National Cemetery) and Fort Leslie J. McNair (the modern title for Civil War–era Washington Arsenal, later Fort Humphreys on the river in downtown Washington), Fort Washington in this period contained typical brick and frame quarters and other garrison facilities. Even after the eclipse of its coastal defense function in 1921, Fort Washington housed the 12th U.S. Infantry until the post was transferred to the Department of the Interior in 1939. The advent of World War II saw reconversion to military use until finally, in 1946, the fort and reservation returned permanently to historic site status under National Park Service care and control.[2]

Appendix A

John Gross Barnard: "Father of the Defenses"

Writing on June 28, 1878, in response to a request for his biography, Brevet Major General John Cross Barnard penned the following as a modest synopsis of his accomplishments:

> I graduated the Military Academy in 1833 aged 18.
> Bvt. 2d Lieut. July 1, 1833
> Commissioned 2d Lieut. of Engineers May 15, 1835
> Captain—July 7, 1838
> Brevet Major (Mexican War) May 30, 1848
> Major Eng. Dec. 13, 1858
> Lieut. Col. Engrs. May 3, 1863
> Colonel Engrs. Dec. 28, 1865
> Brevet Colonel. U.S. Army June 30, 1862
> (Gallant & Meritorious Services in the Campaign of the Peninsula, Va.)
> Brevet Brigadier General U.S.A. Mar. 13, 1865.
> (Gallant and Meritorious Services in the campaign terminating Lee's Surrender)
> Brevet Major General U.S.A. Mar. 13, 1865
> (Gallant & Meritorious Services in the field during the Rebellion)
> Brigadier General U.S Volunteers Sep 23, 1861
> Brevet Major General U.S. Volunteers July 4, 1864 (Meritorious & distinguished services during the rebellion)
>
> I was present and under fire of the first guns opened upon Gen. McDowell's Army Blackburn's ford July 18 1861—at the subsequent battle of Bull Run July 21. 1861 (See Johnson's Cyclopedia Art. Bull Run)—was Chief Engineer at the Siege of Yorktown—present at battle of Williamsburg—at most of the combat on the Chickahominy, called the "Seven days" battles, losing a horse under [me] the first day, June 26, 1862. Was in Command in the City of Washington during the 2d Bull Run battle and subsequently till June 1864 Chief Engineer of the Defenses of that City. Was on Gen Grant's staff June 64 to April 1865 as "Chief Engineer of the Armies in the field" being present at many of the combats that occurred around Petersburg—especially at the Capture of Fort Harrison—and at the surrender of Genl. Lee, Appomatox Court House—thus being at the last, as I had been at almost the first battle of the war.

While this capsule biography may tell much about how Civil War officers viewed their life's achievements, it by no means does justice to John G. Barnard's varied career of forty-eight years of service with the Corps of Engineers. Born May 15, 1815, in Sheffield, Massachusetts, he secured his appointment to West Point through the effort of his great-uncle, General Peter B. Porter, secretary of war under President John Quincy Adams. Nonetheless, displaying brilliance at this early age, he graduated second in his class, gaining him appointment to the coveted Corps of Engineers. His early service involved coastal fort construction. Similar duties attended his service in the Mexican War. Subsequently, he led a survey commission investigating a commercial route to California via the Isthmus of Tehuantepec. Despite tropical illness and inherited deafness that gave the appearance of premature aging, Barnard achieved acclaim as an authority on American coastal defense. He authored *The Dangers and Defense of New York* (1859), *Notes on Sea-Coast Defense* (1861), and *Fabrication of Iron for Defensive Purposes* (1872). A professional soldier who enjoyed high esteem in the scientific community, Barnard was one of the original incorporators of the National Academy of Sciences. He received AM and LLD degrees from the University of Alabama (1838) and Yale (1864) and following the Civil War contributed other scientific writing concerning the *North Canal of Holland* (1872) as well as interrelationships of the gyroscope, equinoxes, and the pendulum (1872). The federal government relied on his scientific and engineering expertise, and he served as president of the permanent fortification, river, and harbor improvements board prior to retirement in 1881. He died

Brigadier General John Gross Barnard. *National Archives*

a year later in Detroit, Michigan, but was returned to his birthplace for burial.

John Gross Barnard remains an overlooked figure of the Civil War. Not only did he see service in many major eastern campaigns, but he counseled military and civilian leaders on military problems, based largely on his reputation as one of the U.S. Army's foremost engineers. As McDowell's engineer at the First Battle of Bull Run, Barnard's flank reconnaissance dictated the course of the Union battle plan, as he explained in his apologia, *The C.S.A. and the Battle of Bull Run* (1862). As McClellan's chief engineer on the Peninsula, he advised returning the Army of the Potomac to Washington and later penned an account, *The Peninsular Campaign and Its Antecedents* (1864), which emerged as a subjective political tract during an election year in which the principal field commander of that operation ran as opposition candidate to the incumbent, President Abraham Lincoln, McClellan's commander in chief.

Nonetheless, Barnard's preeminent contribution during the Civil War came as architect for the Defenses of Washington (explained in his 1863 report, which was published by the Corps of Engineers in 1871). This system, embracing thirty-five miles of fieldworks, earned him the sobriquet "Father of the Defenses of Washington." Yet he also planned the defenses of Pittsburgh, Pennsylvania, during the conflict and later returned to the Army of the Potomac as its chief engineer officer during the terminal campaigns in the east. Then Grant dispatched Barnard as his personal envoy to William T. Sherman to ascertain the state of the latter's army following its dramatic march to the sea.

While Barnard possessed undisputed engineering skills, his military reputation remains enigmatic. Neither General in Chief Henry Halleck nor Secretary of War Edwin Stanton professed confidence in "his judgment on practical military matters" because of Barnard's perceived identity with the McClellan faction in the Army of the Potomac. Still, Barnard declared his political allegiance to the Union and the Lincoln administration in an 1862 *National Intelligencer* panegyric to West Point professionalism as standing above partisan and sectional politics in the secession crisis. This may have returned him to favor coupled with his yeoman-like service building Washington's forts. In the end, Barnard's contribution to his country was in engineering—particularly the protection of the nation's capital, which withstood Confederate threats and preserved the symbol of the Union.[1]

Appendix B

Selected Ordnance Statistics for the Defenses of Washington

Based on Barnard's tables of ordnance in the Washington forts, the following compilation will provide an approximate idea of firepower capabilities. For further information on characteristics of artillery and ammunition, readers should consult sources cited in this table.

Ordnance Type	*Pound Weight*	*Weight of Charge*	*Type of Projectile*	*Range (Yards)*
Smoothbore guns:				
6-pounder field	820–910	.25	Shot, case, shell	1,500–1,700
12-pounder Mountain howitzer	200	.5	Case, shell	800–1,500
12-pounder field	l,200–1,800	2.0–2.5	Shot, case	1,100–1,600
12-pounder howitzer	780–880	.5–.75	Case, shell	1,050–1,072
24-pounder Field and Deck howitzer	1,300–1,475	2.0–2.5	Case, shell	1,200–1,322
24-pounder seacoast	5,500	6	Shot	1,900
24-pounder siege	5,720	6	Shot	1,900
32-pounder seacoast	7,200	8	Shot	1,922
42-pounder James	8,300–8,400	10.5	Shot	1,955
Eight-inch siege howitzer	2,550–2,650	4	Shell	2,280
Eight-inch seacoast howitzer	5,740–5,800	6	Shell	1,800
Fifteen-inch Rodman	49,000–50,000	40	Shell	5,000–8,000
Rifled guns:				
6-pounder James	884	1.25	Shell	1,700
10-pounder Parrott (3.3 in.)	890–904	1	Shell	2,970–5,000
12-pounder Whitworth	1,090–1,100	1.75	Bolt	1,100
12-pounder	1,227	2.0–2.5	Shot, case, shell	1,100–1,600
20-pounder Parrott (3.67 in.)	1,750	2.25	Shell	4,400
30-pounder Parrott (4.2 in.)	3,550–4,200	3.25	Shell	4,800–6,700
Four-and-a-half-inch Rodman	1,450	3.25	Shell	3,265
(Barnard uses term 4½ in Rodman, which may be more accurately styled a 4.62 rifle, although Ripley, *Artillery and Ammunition of the Civil War*, p. 374 notes, "4.5-in. Siege Rifle M.1861," and "4.62 Siege Rifle M.1862.")				
100-pounder Parrott (6.4 in.)	9,700	10	Shell, shot	6,820–8,453
200-pounder Parrott (8 in.)	16.500	16	Shell	4,272–8,000
Mortars:				
24-pounder Coehorn	164	.5	Shell	1,200
Eight-inch siege	900–1,000	1–2	Shell	2,225
Ten-inch	1,852–1,900	4	Shell	2,028–2,065[1]

100-Pounder Parrott Rifle Firing *En Barbette*—Fort Totten—August 1865. *U.S. Army Military History Institute*

Fifteen-Inch Rodman Gun Firing *En Barbette*—Battery Rodgers. *Library of Congress*

32-Pounder Seacoast Gun Firing *En Barbette*—Fort Gaines. *National Archives*

Field and Siege Carriage Artillery Firing *En Embrasure*—Fort Ramsay. *Authors' Collection*

Appendix C

Engineer Glossary[1]

ABATIS. Obstacles formed by cutting trees, sharpening and entangling the branches, and positioning them pointing toward the enemy.

ARTIFICER. A soldier or civilian mechanic who performed skilled labor with troops in the field.

BANQUETTE. A step on the inside of the parapet for troops to stand on when firing.

BARBETTE. A raised platform enabling guns to fire over a parapet rather than through an opening cut in the parapet, hence term *en barbette*.

BASTION. That part of a fortification that projects at an angle toward the field, enabling defenders to fire along the face of the fort's main wall.

BATTERY. A smaller, often unenclosed fortification for artillery.

BERM. A narrow ledge between the ditch and the parapet serving as both a passageway and an impediment to earth eroding into the ditch.

BLIND. A screen made from tree/brush branches for concealment.

BREACH. An opening by the besiegers in a fortification prior to a direct assault.

BREASTWORK. A hastily constructed breast-high defensive work on the ground's surface.

CASEMATE. A fortified chamber in a fortification.

CHAIN (SURVEYING). An engineering tool: a chain with standardized links used in distance measurement on the ground.

CHEVAL-DE-FRISE. A timber frame inserted with iron-tipped lengths of wood designed to impede troops/vehicles on land. The marine version weighted and sunk to the river bottom to obstruct the passage of enemy vessels. Most often used in a series, hence term *chevaux-de-frise*.

CIRCUMVALLATION, LINE OF. An earthen wall and trench placed between besieging troops and the field to guard against attack by a relieving army.

COUNTERSCARP. The exterior slope of ditch in front of the fort.

COUNTERVALLATION, LINE OF. An earthen wall and trench placed by besiegers between themselves and the fortress to provide protection from counterattack.

COVERED (COVERT) WAY. A flat space above the exterior slope of the ditch, usually with its own banquette and wall terminating in a slope toward the field.

CURTAIN. The part of a wall that joins two bastions or towers.

DEMI-BASTION. A bastion with one face and one flank.

DEMI-LUNE (RAVELIN). A crescent-shaped outwork, usually between two bastions.

DITCH. A deep, often water-filled trench surrounding a fortification.

EMBRASURE. An opening cut in the top of a fort wall through which cannon may fire, hence term *en embrasure* as opposed to *en barbette*.

ENCEINTE. The main wall or "body" of a fortress, including the rampart with its parapet.

ENFILADE. A position exposed to fire along its whole length; to fire along the length of a battle line or trench.

EPAULEMENT. A type of breastwork providing cover from flanking fire.

ESCALADE. An attack on a fortified position using ladders.

FASCINE. A bundle of small sticks or branches used to fill ditches or strengthen earthworks.

FLANK. The part of a bastion extending from the curtain to the face.

FLECHE. A V-shaped earthwork erected in the field.

FOSSE. A ditch or moat, usually filled with water.

FRAISE. A defense made of pointed stakes generally placed obliquely or horizontally on the outward slope an earthwork.

GABION. A bottomless, cylindrical wicker basket tilled with earth used in field fortifications.

GALLERY. An underground passage connecting the inner and outer works of a fortification; also the largest type of mine tunnel.

GLACIS. An earthen bank gradually sloping toward the field from the top of the counterscarp or covered way helping make attackers visible from the parapet.

HORNWORK. An outwork of two bastions joined by a curtain.

HURDLE (GABION). A rectangular wicker construction used to strengthen batteries, aid in crossing shallow water, and protect workmen.

LUNETTE. A work consisting of a salient angle with two flanks that can be open or stockaded to the rear.

PALISADE. A fencelike defense formed of pointed stakes (also known as palisades) set several inches apart in the ground.

PARALLELS. A series of trenches placed in front of and parallel to the face of a fortress to provide cover for the attachers.

PARAPET. An elevation of earth or other material forming the main wall.

PIONEERS. Troops detailed to clear obstructions placed in the line of march or before fortifications, dig trenches, and construct bridges and roads.

PLANE TABLE. An instrument, used to plot maps, consisting of a wooden panel mounted on a tripod.

RAMPART. The broad earthen wall on the interior side of a ditch surrounding a fortification.

RAVELIN. A crescent-shaped outwork, usually placed between two bastions, also called a *demi-lune.*

REDAN. A V-shaped work often joined with other works to form a simple fortification.

REDOUBT. An enclosed work used temporarily to defend a point.

REENTRANT. An angle projecting into a fortress from the field.

REMBLAI. Material, usually the earth excavated from the ditch, used to erect the rampart and parapet.

REVETMENT. A facing (masonry, stone, or wood) covering that provides support and protection for an earthen embankment.

SALIENT. An angle projecting from a fort into the field.

SAP. A deep, narrow trench providing an approach to a besieged location.

SAPPERS. Engineer troops employed to dig trenches (saps) or mine galleries. Usually referred to as sappers and miners.

SAUCISSON. A large fascine.

SCARP. The inner slope of the ditch.

SLEEPER. The undermost timber of a gun battery.

SOUTERRAIN. An underground passage.

TALUS. The slope of the face of a work.

TERREPLEIN. The level part of the fortification wall on which cannon are placed.

TRACE. The ground plan of a fortification and to render such a plan.

TRAVERSE. A embankment providing protection from the sweeping fire of the enemy, usually placed across the covered way.

TRIANGULATION. A surveying technique using triangles to determine distances between points.

VERTICAL PROFILE OF A FORTIFICATION. The mass of earth (a–h) forms the rampart with its parapet (e–g). (a, b) The interior slope of the rampart. (b, c) The terreplein. (d, e) The banquette. (g, h) The exterior slope of the parapet. (h, i) The revetment. (h, k) The scarp. (i–m) The ditch. (l, m) The counterscarp. (m, n) The covered way. (n–p) The covered way banquette. (r, s). The glacis.

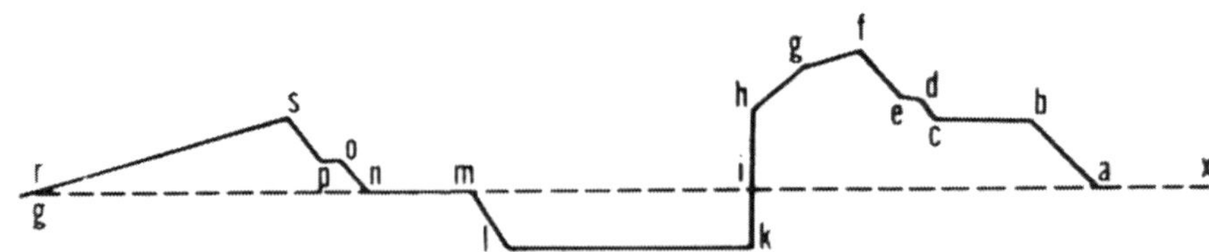

VERTICAL PROFILE OF A FORTIFICATION. *The mass of earth,* a-h, *forms the rampart with its parapet,* e-g; a, b *is the interior slope of the rampart;* b,c *is the terreplain;* d, e *is the banquette;* g, h *is the exterior slope of the parapet;* h, i *is the revetment;* h, k *is the scarp;* i-m *is the ditch;* l, m *is the counterscarp;* m, n *is the covered way;* n-p *is the covered way banquette; and* r, s *is the glacis.*

Vertical Profile of a Fortification

Signal Station at Prospect Hill, Virginia. *Brown,* The Signal Corps, USA in the War of the Rebellion

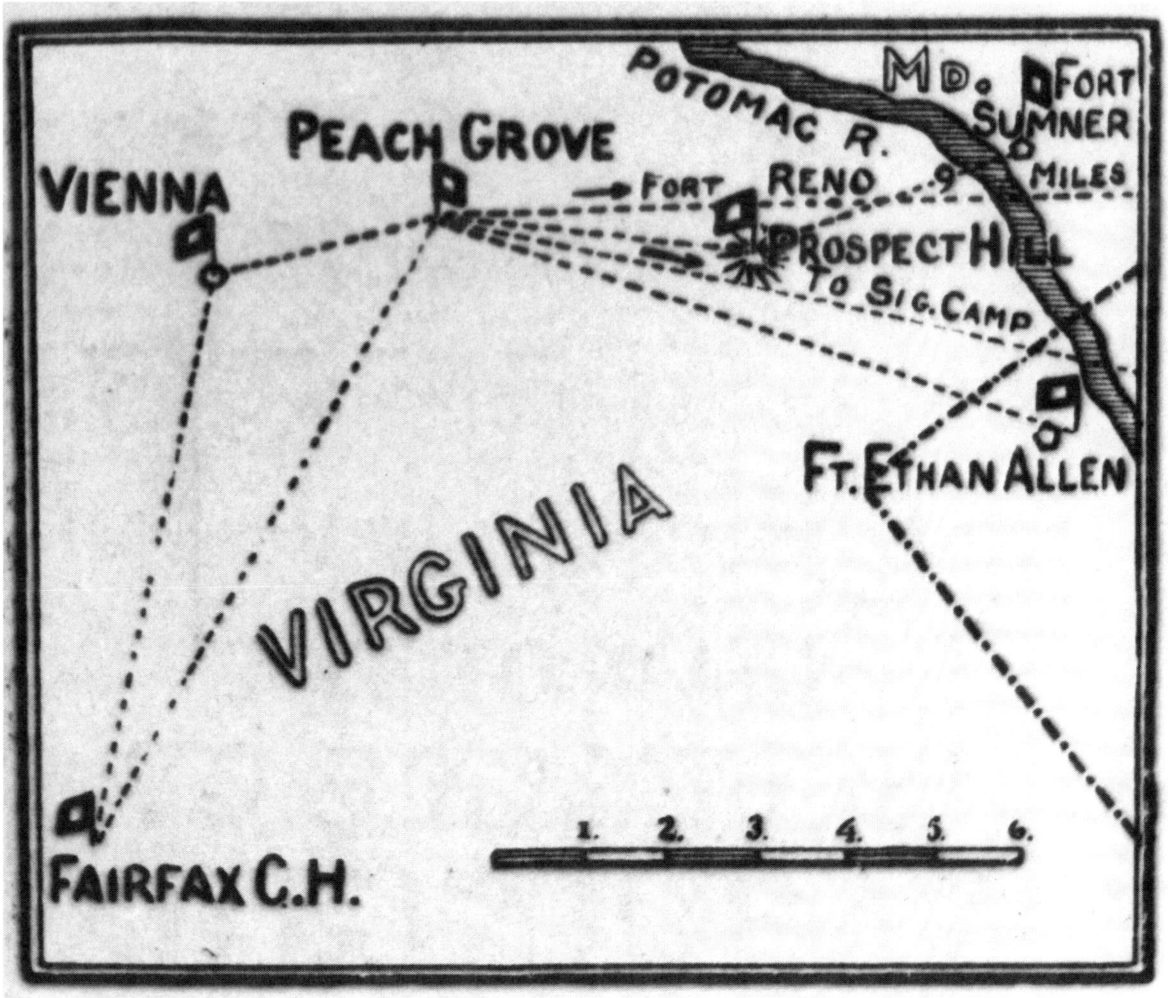

Sketch Map of Signal Stations in Virginia. *Brown,* The Signal Corps, USA in the War of the Rebellion

Appendix D

Communications in the Defenses of Washington[1]

In addition to couriers and the system of military and public roads linking the forts around Washington, a series of signal stations (for flag and torch relay of information) connected the system. Signal officers determined the locations for signal stations in each fort in case of serious enemy threat. Various subsystems of stations existed, particularly on the outer defense perimeter in Virginia, linking outposts at Prospect Hill, Peach Grove, Vienna, and Falls Church with the main defenses. Communication from Washington was also transmitted to the key forts by a large number of telegraph lines. A detail record of the signal locations can be seen in the listing from the U.S. Coast Survey of the stations in 1863, which listed them as follows:

1. U.S. Coast Survey Office, Corner New Jersey Avenue and C Streets SE.
2. Kengley's House, Georgetown, opposite Causten Signal Station.
3. Causten's Station, Georgetown Heights.
4. U.S. Naval Observatory (circa Civil War period).
5. Blunt's House, ¼ mile south of Tennallytown (used as triangulation point?).
6. Fort Corcoran, ½ mile south of Aqueduct Bridge, station between guns 7 and 8.
7. Fort Gaines, ¾ mile southwest of Tennallytown, station on parapet between guns 5 and 6.
8. Battery Cameron, above distributing reservoir ¾ mile from Georgetown College Observatory, station atop magazine.
9. Battery Kemble, ¾ mile southwest of Fort Gaines, station atop right parapet.
10. Navy Yard, benchmark on upper surface of stone wall of pier in front of Navy Yard office, used for plane of reference by tidal observer.
11. Fort Marcy, ½ mile from Little Falls Bridge on south side of Potomac, station to left of flagstaff facing northwest bastion.
12. Fort Ethan Allen, ¾ mile south of Fort Marcy and ¾ mile from bridge across the Potomac, station in southwest bastion.
13. Battery Parrott, located between Batteries Cameron and Kemble, station on parapet nearly in front of gun as mounted February 21, 1863.
14. Fort Alexander, 1¼ miles north of Fort Marcy, near the Little Falls of the Potomac on Maryland side, station adjacent to flagstaff at northeast rear of fort where parapet joins stockaded gorge.
15. Fort Bennett, ½ mile west of the south end of the Aqueduct Bridge, close to Fort Corcoran, station in northwest portion of fort.
16. Fort DeKalb (Strong), 1 mile west and south of end of Aqueduct Bridge, station on top of parapet between guns 8 and 9.
17. Fort McDowell (C. F. Smith), station located in northeast bastion.
18. Fort Woodbury, ½ mile southwest of Fort Corcoran, station located in northwest corner of fort on banquette inside parapet.
19. Fort Cass, ⅓ mile south of Fort Woodbury, station on parapet near flagstaff in north corner of fort.
20. Fort Tillinghast, ½ mile west of Arlington House, station atop magazine.
21. Fort Franklin, short distance north of Fort Alexander, within line of entrenchments connecting Forts Alexander, Franklin, and Ripley, with station atop magazine.
22. Fort Ripley, within line of entrenchments connecting Forts Alexander and Franklin, station atop magazine.

23. Langley Church or Meeting House, nearly two miles from either Fort Alexander or Fort Marcy on Virginia side, and painted red (used as triangulation point?).
24. Hall's House, 1⅓ miles from Fort Ethan Allen and 3 miles from Falls Church, station centered in cupola.
25. Battery Martin Scott, above Little Falls Bridge (Chain Bridge), a little over 3 miles from Aqueduct Bridge, station atop right side of parapet.
26. Battery Vermont, near eastern end of receiving reservoir, not far from Little Falls Bridge, station on parapet near flagstaff.
27. Fort Mansfield, located nearly midway between Blunt's House and Fort Alexander 1½ miles distant from each and same to Fort Pennsylvania (Reno), station atop parapet near flagstaff and stockaded gorge.
28. Fort Lincoln, ¼ mile east of Bladensburg Road, 4 miles from Capitol, station located on parapet in south bastion on southwest face of fort.
29. Fort Thayer, situated ¾ mile west of Fort Lincoln, 3¼ miles from Capitol, on west side of Baltimore and Ohio Railroad, station on southwest parapet near gun 6.
30. Fort Totten, located ½ mile northwest of U.S. Military Asylum (Soldiers' Home), station located on a banquette at the first magazine to rear of fort.
31. Maryland Agricultural College, a stone structure, 2¾ miles north of Bladensburg (used as triangulation point?).
32. Buck House, 1 mile southwest of Agricultural College (used as triangulation point?).
33. Fort Bunker Hill, 1⅜ miles to south and east of Military Asylum, station atop magazine.
34. Fort Saratoga, 2 miles to south and east of Military Asylum, station atop parapet between guns 5 and 6.
35. Military Asylum (Soldier's Home), station atop tower.
36. Fort Slocum, 1¼ miles north of Military Asylum, station atop magazine.
37. Fort Reno, north of Tennallytown, station atop bombproof, near flagstaff.
38. Fort Kearney, 1 mile east of Fort Reno, station atop magazine near flagstaff.
39. Fort DeRussy, 2½ miles northwest of Military Asylum, station atop parapet of gun 4.
40. Fort Stevens, 1¾ miles northwest of Military Asylum, station is in interior enclosure on parapet opposite flagstaff near gun 1.
41. Fort Bayard, ¾ mile west of Tennallytown, between Forts Reno and Simmons, with station in middle of central magazine.
42. Fort Simmons, ⅜ mile distant from either Forts Mansfield or Bayard, station atop bombproof nearest flagstaff.
43. Montgomery Blair's House, on Seventh Street Road (used as triangulation point?).
44. Yellow Roof, White Cupola House near Bladensburg (used as triangulation point?).
45. Bladensburg Church (used as triangulation point?).
46. U.S. Lunatic Asylum, opposite side of Eastern Branch facing Navy Yard station atop highest tower.
47. Fort Ramsay, situated on Upton's Hill, 4½ miles from Aqueduct Bridge and 1½ miles from Falls Church, station atop bombproof in corner nearest to flagstaff.
48. Fort Buffalo, ½ mile west of Fort Ramsay, station atop parapet on right near corner where parapet joins stockaded gorge,
49. Fort Craig, 1 mile southwest of Arlington House, station atop right magazine.
50. Fort Albany, located on first range of hills on road from Long Bridge, 3½ miles from Capitol, station atop bombproof.
51. Fort Richardson, ¾ mile southwest of Fort Albany, station atop bombproof.
52. Fort Barnard, 2 miles north of Alexandria Seminary, 1 mile from Fort Richardson, station on top middle of bombproof.
53. Fort Blenker, 1½ miles north of Seminary, station atop bombproof.
54. Fort Mahan, situated across Eastern Branch in direction of Bennings Bridge, 3½ miles from Capitol, station located atop wooden building within fort opposite flagstaff.
55. Fort Ward, situated ⅞ mile northwest of Seminary, station atop bombproof.
56. Fort Worth, ½ mile southwest of Seminary, station atop parapet in south angle.
57. Fort Lyon, 2 miles southeast of Seminary and southwest of Alexandria, station located on traverse near flagstaff.
58. Fort Scott, on a spur of hills 1¼ miles southeast of Fort Albany, station atop right bombproof.
59. Fort Ellsworth, short distance west of Alexandria near outskirts of city, 1¾ miles from Seminary, station atop magazine near flagstaff.
60. Fort Meigs, located across Eastern Branch, 1¾ miles from Fort Mahan, 4½ miles southeast of Capitol, station atop magazine.
61. Fort DuPont, situated across Eastern Branch, ½ mile from Fort Meigs, approximately 4 miles from Capitol, station atop magazine.
62. Fort Davis, located across Eastern Branch about 3½ miles southeast of Capitol, ¾ mile from Fort DuPont, station atop magazine.

63. Fort Baker, located across the Eastern Branch about 3 miles southeast of Capitol, 7/8 mile from Fort Davis, station atop magazine.
64. Fort Wagner, situated across Eastern Branch, 3 miles from Capitol, ¼ mile from Fort Baker, 1/3 mile from Fort Ricketts, station atop parapet between guns 1 and 2.
65. Fort Ricketts, situated on same range of hills with Forts Baker and Wagner, 3 miles from Capitol, station atop wooden roof of magazine.
66. Fort Stanton, 1 mile east of Lunatic Asylum, atop parapet to left of entry gate.
67. Fort Snyder, 1 mile from Lunatic Asylum, station atop long magazine.
68. Fort Carroll, 1 1/3 miles southwest of Lunatic Asylum, station atop parapet to left of entry gate.
69. Fort Greble, 2¼ miles southwest of Lunatic Asylum, station atop parapet to right of entry gate.
70. Smithsonian Institution, station atop highest tower.

Appendix E

Regulations for Care of Fieldworks and Government of Garrisons[1]

GENERAL ORDERS, No. 42 — WAR DEPARTMENT
Adjutant General's Office
Washington, February 2, 1864

The following Regulations for the care of Field-works and the government of their Garrisons, prepared by Brigadier General Barry, Inspector of Artillery, U.S.A., are published for the government of all concerned:

1. It is the duty of the Commanding Officer of each work to provide for the care of the armament and the safety and serviceable condition of the magazines, ammunition, implements, and equipments; and, by frequent personal inspections, to secure the observance of the rules prescribed for this purpose.
2. The fixed armament, consisting of the heavy guns and those the positions of which are prescribed, will be numbered in a regular series, commencing with the first gun on the right of the entrance of the main gate. Where there are platforms temporarily unoccupied by guns, they will be numbered in the regular series. The ammunition will be kept in the magazines, with the exception of a few stands of grape, canister, and solid shot, which will he piled near the guns.
3. The gun-carriages will be kept clean, and all axles and journals well lubricated. They will be traversed daily, and never be allowed to rest for two successive days on the same part of the traverse circle. If the gun-carriage does not move easily on the *chassis*, the tongue will be occasionally greased. The upper carriage should not rest habitually on the same part of the chassis.
4. The elevating screw and its box will be kept clean and well greased. When the guns are not in use, the screw will be run down as far as it will go, the breach of the piece being first raised until the muzzle is sufficiently depressed to prevent water running into it, and kept in that position by a wooden quoin or block. The *tompion* should be kept in the muzzle, and the apron over the vent.
5. The piece is not to be kept habitually loaded. It will be time to load when the enemy appears, or when special orders to that effect are given.
6. The Commanding Officer will see that a shed is constructed for the implements and equipments. For each drill these will be issued to the gunners by the ordnance sergeant, or other non-commissioned officer acting as such, who will receive and put them away after the drill is over, and be at all times responsible to the Commanding Officer for their safety and serviceable condition, and that the supply is adequate. When sheds cannot be provided, the implements will be kept near the pieces, or in the bombproofs. The *equipments* (haversacks, tube-pouch, etc.) may be kept at the entrance of the magazine, where they will be sheltered. Platforms for projectiles will be laid near the guns; for canisters, a couple of pieces of scantling for skids will answer. A water-shed, made by joining two boards together at the edges, should be placed over them. When the wooden sabots become wet they swell and burst the canisters, so that they cannot be put into the gun. When this happens, dry the sabot until it shrinks sufficiently for the canister edges to be brought together and tacked.
7. When not supplied by the Engineer Department, materials for constructing the sheds and for skidding will be furnished by the Quartermaster's Department, on requisitions made to the Chief of Artillery.
8. The magazines must be frequently aired *in dry weather*. For this purpose, ventilators and doors

must be opened after 9 a.m., and must be closed, at latest two hours before sunset. The ammunition for different classes of guns will be carefully assorted, and the shelves, boxes, or barrels, containing each kind, plainly marked. When there is more than one magazine, the ammunition will be so distributed as to be near to the particular guns for which it is provided. Cartridges must be moved, and, if necessary, rolled once a week, to prevent *caking* of the powder. In doing this, care must be taken not to pulverize the grains. *Friction primers* must be kept in the tin packing boxes and carefully protected from moisture. They will be frequently examined, and dried by exposure to the sun. This must always be done immediately after wet weather of long continuance. The supply of friction primers for each gun must be fifty per cent greater than the number of rounds of ammunition provided for it. A dozen primers will always be kept in the tube pouches in use at each gun. Three lanyards will be provided for each gun, one of which will be kept in store; the other two in the tube-pouches. As soon as received, the *hooks* will be tested to see if they are sufficiently small to enter the eye of the primer, and yet strong enough for use.

9. In order that practice may be had in the use of friction primers, authority is given to expend on drill five per gun each month. These primers will always be taken from those longest at the post.
10. There should be one lantern for every three or four guns, and two *good globe lanterns* for each magazine.
11. No person will be allowed to enter the magazines except on duty, and then every precaution against accidents will be taken. Lights must always be in glass lanterns, and carried only by the person in charge of the magazine. Swords, pistols, canes, spurs, etc., will not be admitted, no matter what may be the rank of the person carrying them. Socks or moccasins will be worn, if they can be procured; if they cannot, then all persons must enter with stocking feet. No fire or smoking will be allowed in the vicinity when the doors or ventilators are open. *Too many precautions cannot possibly be taken to avoid the chances of an explosion.*

    A copy of this paragraph, legibly written, will be conspicuously posted near or on the doors of every magazine.
12. Companies will be assigned to guns in such proportions as will furnish at least two, preferably three, reliefs in working them, and sufficient men in addition for supplying ammunition from the magazines. From fifteen to twenty men should therefore be assigned *to each gun* and instructed in its use. Companies should habitually serve the same gun, each man being assigned a special number at the gun, and thoroughly instructed in all its duties. As occasion offers, all of the officers and enlisted men should be instructed at each of the different kinds of gun at the post, as well as in the duties of all the numbers at each gun. Every night at retreat or tattoo, the men who are to man the guns in case of a night attack should be paraded at their pieces and inspected, to see that all their equipments, implements, and ammunition are in good order, and the gun in serviceable condition and easy working order. The men so stationed should "call off" their numbers before being dismissed. In case of alarm at night, all should repair at once to their posts, equip themselves, and await orders, without losing time by forming upon their company or battalion parade grounds.
13. Each gun should be under charge of a non-commissioned officer, and to every two or three guns should be assigned a Lieutenant, who will be responsible to the Captain for their serviceable condition at all times. The Captain will be responsible to the Commanding Officer for the condition of the pieces, and the instruction of the men of his company. Artillery drills will be frequent until all of the men are well instructed, and there will never be less than *one artillery* drill per day when the weather will permit, nor will any officer be excused from these drills unless it is unavoidable. For action, all the cannoneers not actually serving the guns will be provided with muskets, and will be stationed near the guns to which they belong, for service on the banquettes or elsewhere, in case of assaults.
14. Each company should be supplied with three copies of the *Tactics for Heavy Artillery*, and rigidly adhere to its directions. *Tables of Ranges* will be found in the work. One copy of *Instructions for Field Artillery* should be supplied to each company. All authorized books can be obtained on written application to the Chief of Artillery, who will obtain them from the Adjutant General of the Army. The books so drawn are the property of the United States for the use of the company, and will be accounted for on the Muster Rolls.
15. The Commanding Officer will make himself conversant with the approaches to his work, the distance to each prominent point commanded by his guns, the nature of the ground between them and his post, and the most probable points of attack upon it. He will also make it his duty to see that all of his officers, and, as far as possible, his non-commissioned officers, are thoroughly acquainted with these matters. The distances will be ascertained by actual measurement and not left to conjecture. *Tables of Ranges* or *Distances* for each point,

and the corresponding elevation, according to the nature of the projectile, with the proper length or time of the fuze, when shell or case-shot are used, will be made out for *each gun*, and furnished to the officer and non-commissioned officers serving it. These tables should be painted upon boards, and securely fastened in a conspicuous place near the gun. As these tables differ for different kinds of gun, the same men should be permanently assigned to the same piece.

16. The projectiles should be used in their proper order. At a distance, *solid shot*; then, *shells* or *case-shot*, especially if firing at troops *in line*; *canister* or *grape* is for use only at short ranges. When columns are approaching so that they can be taken in direction of their *length*, or *very* obliquely, solid shot is generally the best projectile, because of its greater accuracy and penetrating power. If the column consists of cavalry, some shells or case-shot will be useful, from the disorder their bursting produces among the horses; but shells and case-shot should not be used against any troops when moving *rapidly*. The *absolute* distances at which the projectiles can be used with effect vary with the description and calibre of the gun, and be ascertained only by consulting the Tables or Ranges. The prominent points on the approaches to the works should be designated, their distances noted, and directions drawn up for the different kinds of ammunition to be used at each gun for these different points. During the drills the attention of the chiefs of pieces and gunners should be frequently drawn to this subject.
17. Commanding Officers will pay special attention to the police and preservation of the works. All filth will be promptly removed, and the drainage particularly attended to. No one should be allowed to walk on the parapets, or move or sit upon the gabions, barrels, or sand bags that may be placed upon them. When injuries occur to the earthworks, they should be repaired as quickly as possible by the garrison of the work. If of a serious nature, they should be at once reported to the *Engineer Officer* in charge of the work. *All injuries to the magazines or platforms of the guns will be promptly reported as soon as observed.* The *abatis*, being a most important portion of the work, must be always well looked to and kept in perfect order.
18. Special written or printed instructions as to the supply of ammunition at the different posts, and the proportion for the different classes of guns, will be furnished by the Chief of Artillery to the Commanders of posts. Instructions will also be furnished as to the special objects of each work, on proper application for this purpose to the Chief Engineer or Chief of Artillery.
19. No persons not officially connected with the garrisons of the fieldworks will be allowed to enter them, except such as visit them on duty, or who have passes signed by competent authority; nor will any person except commissioned officers, or those whose duty requires them to do so, be allowed to enter the magazine, or touch the guns, their implements or equipments.
20. The garrison can greatly improve the work by sodding the slopes of the parapet, and those of the ramps and banquettes, or by sowing grass seed on the superior slope, first covering it with surface soil. The grass-covered or sodded portions of the parapets, traverses, magazines, etc., should be occasionally watered in dry weather, and the grass be kept closely cut. Early in the spring and late in the autumn they should be covered with manure.
21. As a great deal of powder is wasted in unnecessary salutes attention is called to paragraph 268 of Army Regulations, edition of 1861–'63:

    Paragraph 268. — A General Officer will be saluted but once in a year at each post, and only when notice of his intention to visit the post has been given.
22. The practice of building fires on the open parades, for cooking and other purposes, is prohibited, as it endangers the magazines.
23. The armament of a fort having been once established, will not be changed except by authority of the Commander of the District, Geographical Department, or Army Corps, and then only on consultation with the Chiefs of Engineers and Artillery.
24. The machinery of the Whitworth, or other breech-loading guns, will not be used except by special orders from the Commanding Officer of the post.
25. Experience having conclusively shown that rifled guns, of large calibre especially must be subjected to most careful treatment and skillful management in order to secure their maximum efficiency, both in range and penetration, and especially their maximum endurance, the attention of all officers using rifled guns of large calibres is called to the following rules: Sponges well saturated with oil shall alone be used; and for this purpose the necessary supply of oil shall be provided for all batteries of position in which rifled guns form the part or whole of its armament. A little grease or slush upon the base of the projectile adds much to its certainty, and should be always used when possible. The bores of the guns should be washed, and the grooves cleaned of all residuum and dirt subsequent to the firing, after the gun has cooled. Great care must be taken to send the projectile home in loading, that no space be left between the projectile and the cartridge.

Before using shells, unless already loaded and fuzed, they must be carefully inspected both on their exterior and interior; and scrapers should be used to clear the cavity of all moulding sand before charging the shell. Special attention should be given to the insertion of the fuses, and the threads of the fuze hole should be carefully cleaned before screwing in the fuze. In all Parrott projectiles it should be carefully observed that the brass ring or cup is properly swedged, and that, in the case of the ring, the cavities between it and the projectile are not clogged with dirt or sand.

In loading shells care will be taken to fill them entirely with powder, leaving no vacant space after the fuse is screwed in.

For the 10, 20, and 30-pounder Parrott guns, powder of too large a grain should not be used. The best powder for the projecting charge of these guns is what is called "mortar powder."

26. Pole straps and pole-pads of field limbers, not belonging to horsed batteries, are to be kept in the implement-room or in the trays of the limber chest, they should be occasionally washed and oiled, as prescribed for the care of harness in field artillery tactics.
27. The forts will be inspected daily by their Commanding Officers; and by the Brigade, Division, District, or Department Commanders, and by the Chief of Artillery, as frequently as possible. Particular attention will be paid, at all inspections, to the drill and discipline of the garrison and police of the work; to the condition of the armament, ammunition, and magazines; and as to whether the proper supply of ammunition, implements, etc., is on hand at the post.

INSTRUCTIONS FOR FIRING

1. The firing in action should be deliberate — never more than will admit of accurate pointing. A few shots effectively thrown is better than a larger number badly directed. The object of killing is to inspire terror so as to deter or drive off the enemy, and precision of fire and consequent *certainty* of execution, is infinitely more important in effecting this than a great noise, rapid firing, and less proportional execution.
2. To secure accuracy of fire, the ground in the neighborhood must be well examined, and the distance to the different prominent points within the field covered by *each* gun *measured* and *noted.*

   The gunners and cannoneers should be informed of these distances, and in the drills the gun should be accurately pointed at the objects noted in succession, the gunner designating it, calling the distance in yards, and the corresponding elevation in *minutes* and *degrees,* until all the distances and corresponding elevations are familiar to the men. When hollow projectiles are used, the time of flight corresponding to the distance must be given to the man who goes for the projectile. He tells the ordnance sergeant, or the man who furnishes the ammunition, and the latter cuts the fuze to burn the required time.
3. The gunner is responsible for the aiming. He must therefore know the distance to each prominent object in the field covered by his gun, the elevation required to reach that point, and the time of flight of the shell or case-shot corresponding to each distance or elevation. He must have a table of these ranges, taken from the Heavy Artillery Tactics, pages 236 to 247, (edition of 1862).
4. These tables will be promptly prepared under the direction of the Commanding Officer, and copies furnished for each gun, and used habitually in the drills. They will be examined and verified by the Chief of Artillery.
5. The attention of all officers in charge of artillery in the works is directed to the articles in the Tactics on "*Pointing guns and howitzers,*" "*Night firing,*" etc., pages 76 to 90.
6. Commanding Officers of the works will keep themselves accurately informed of the amount and kinds of ammunition in the magazines. The supply must always be kept up to the amount prescribed by the Chief of Artillery or other competent authority. When it is less than that amount, a special report of the fact will be made to the Chief of Artillery, with requisitions for the ammunition necessary to complete the supply. Commanding Officers will also see that the necessary equipments are always on hand for the service of all the guns, as prescribed in the Tactics or in General Orders.
7. Hand grenades are intended to be used against the enemy when he has reached such parts of the defenses (the bottom of the ditch for example) as are not covered by the guns, or by the muskets of the infantry posted on the banquettes.
8. After the enemy has passed the abatis and jumped into the ditch, hand grenades will be used; and then, if he mounts the parapet, he must be met there with muskets. A resolute defense against assault must also be made by posting men with muskets so as to fire over the tops of traverses, bomb-proofs, or magazines.

By Command of Major General Halleck:
E. D. TOWNSEND,
Assistant Adjutant General.

Appendix F

Engineer Drawings of Selected Forts with Existing Earthworks

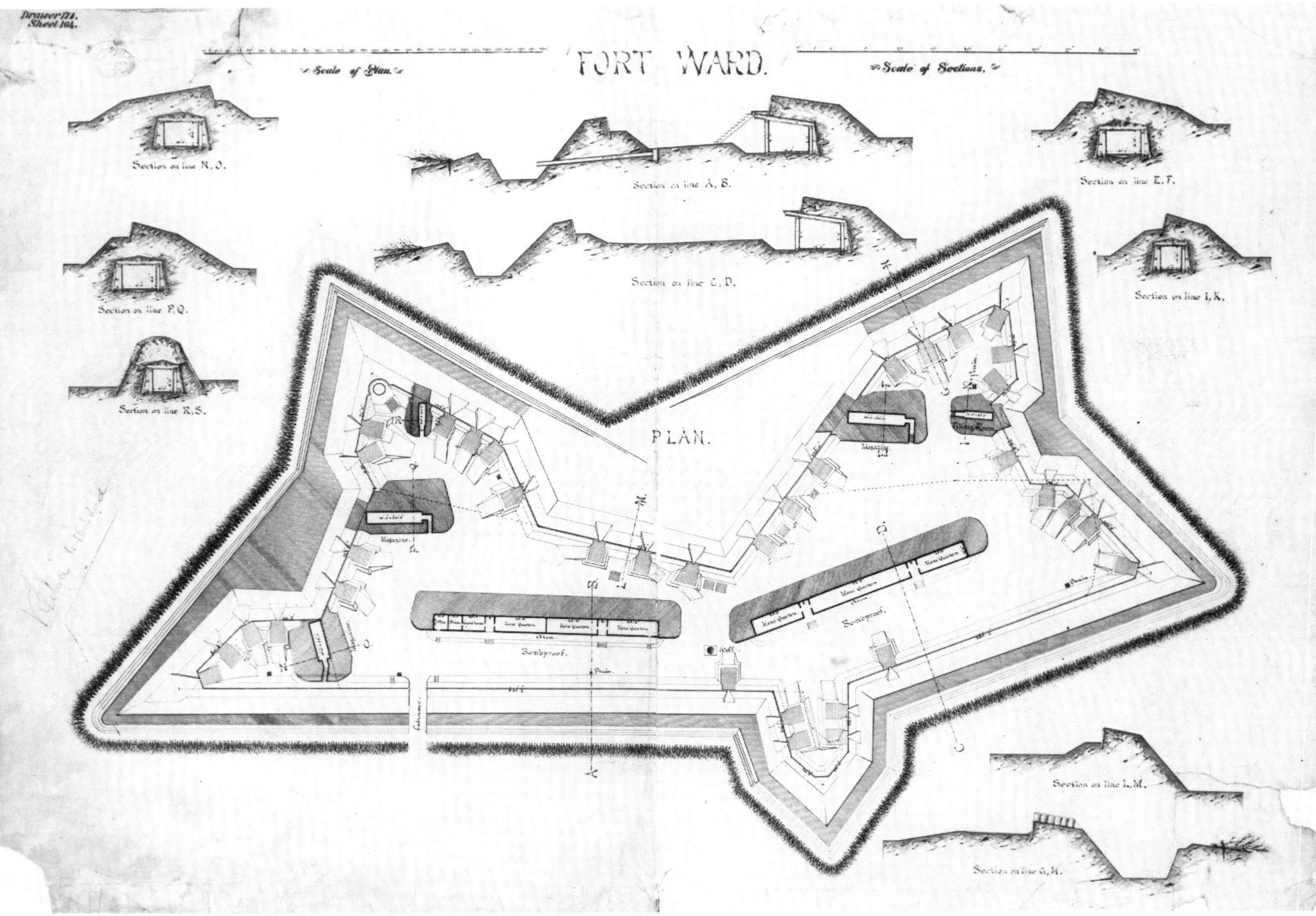

Fort Ward Engineer Drawing, 1864. *National Archives*

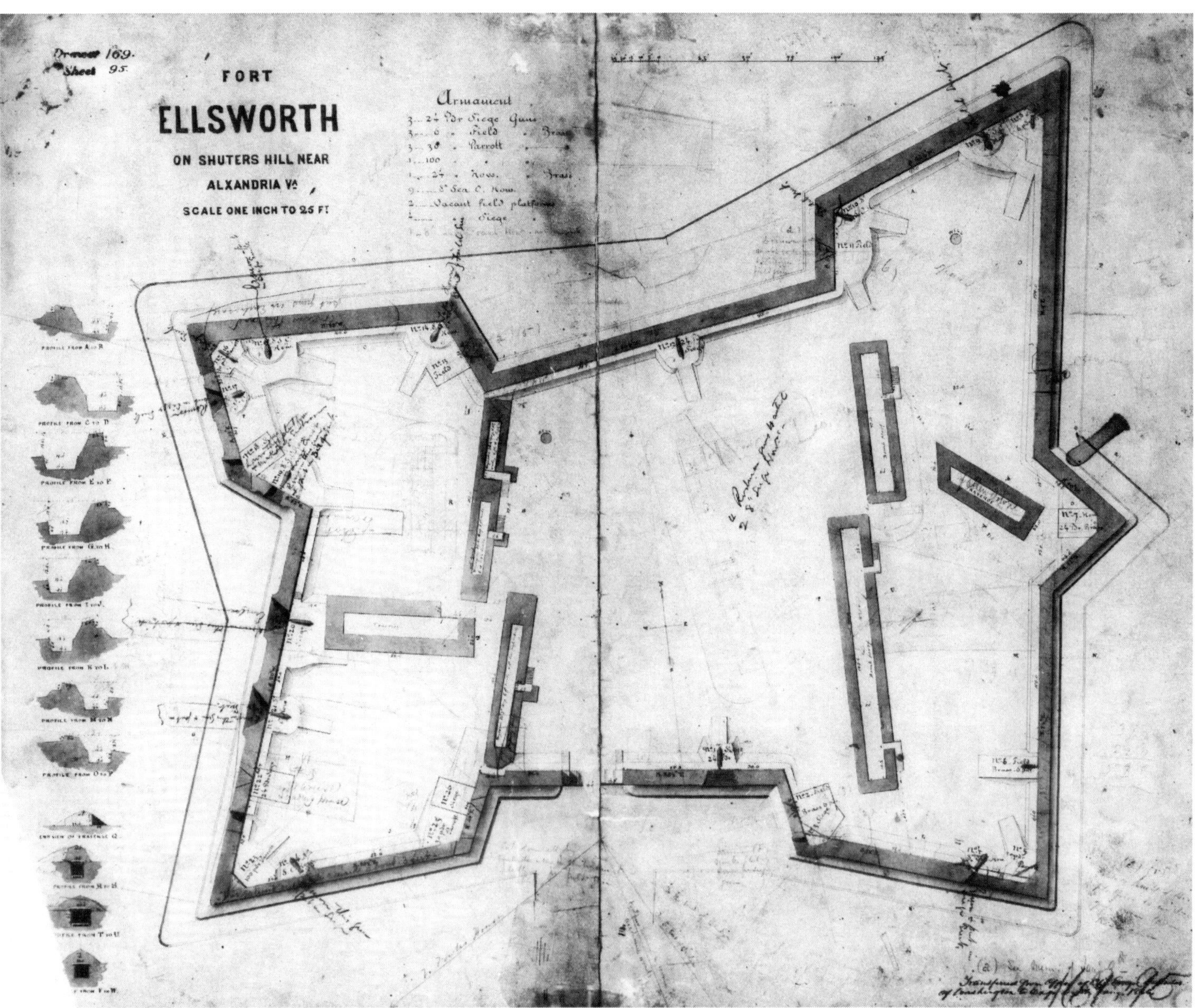

Fort Ellsworth—Engineer Drawing. *National Archives*

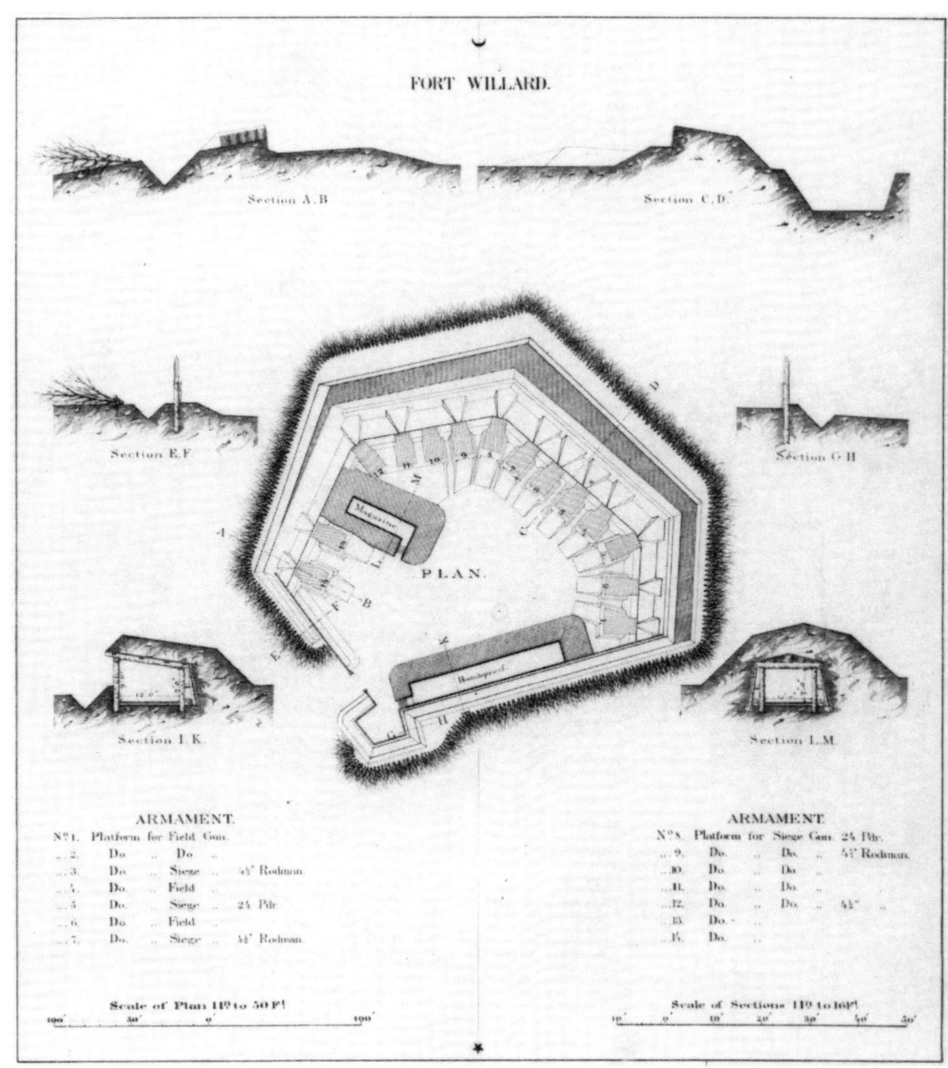

Fort Willard—Engineer Drawing. *National Archives*

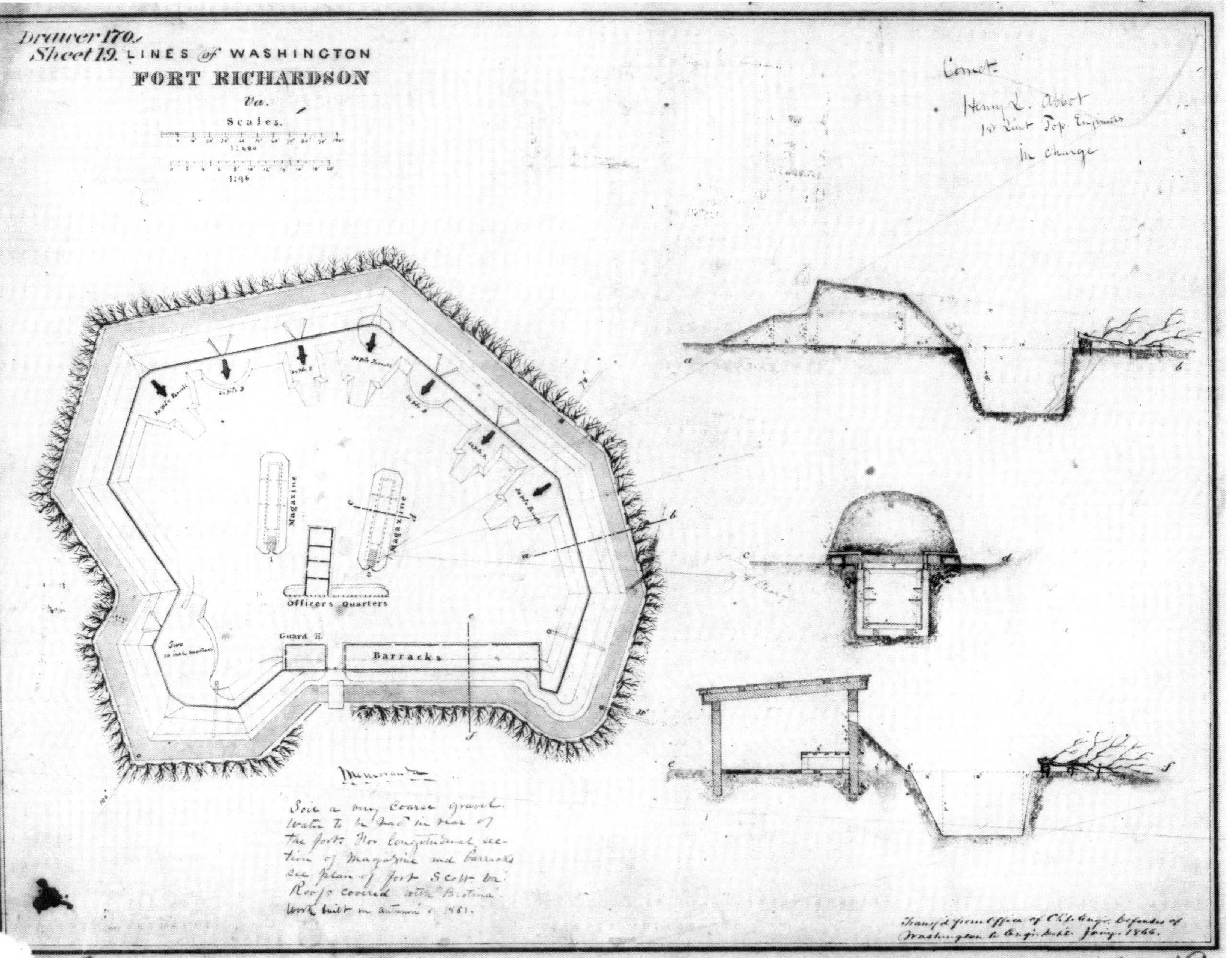

Fort Richardson—Engineer Drawing. *National Archives*

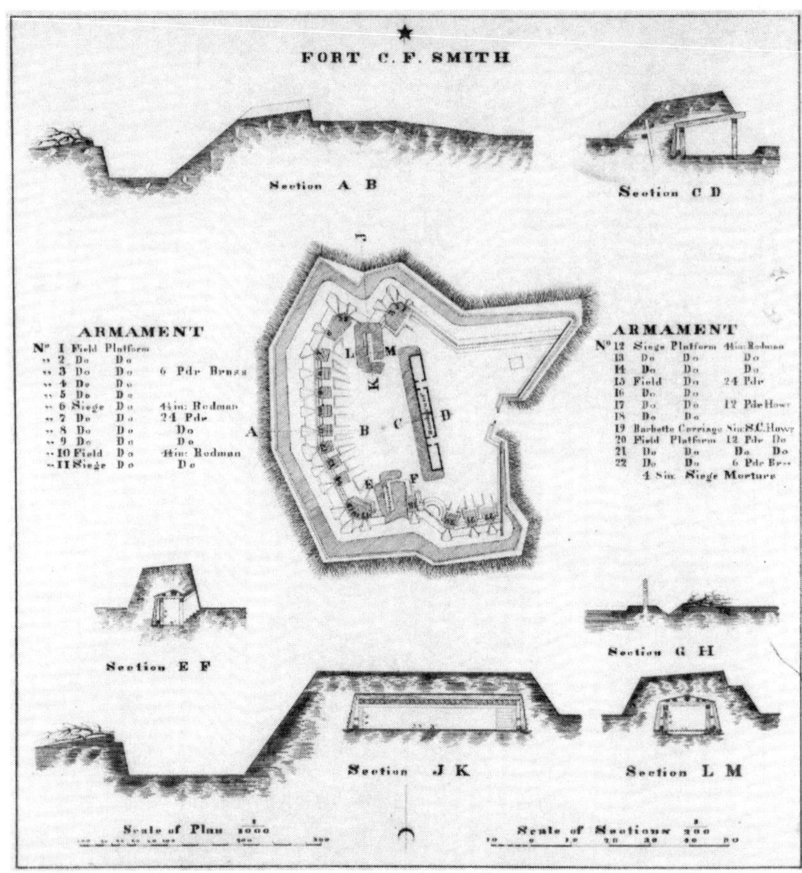

Fort C. F. Smith—Engineer Drawing. *National Archives*

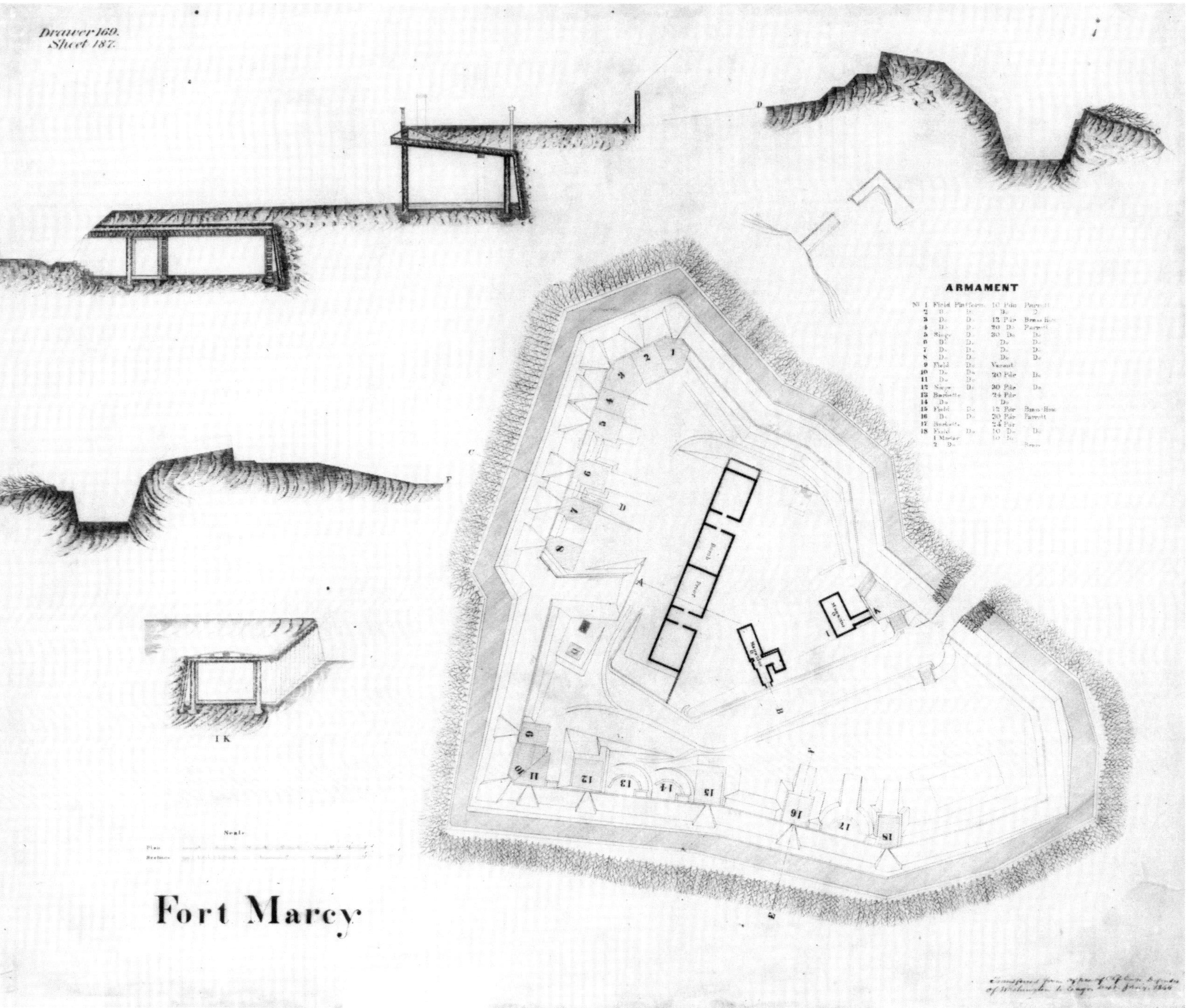

Fort Marcy—Engineer Drawing. *National Archives*

Fort Ethan Allen—Engineer Drawing. *National Archives*

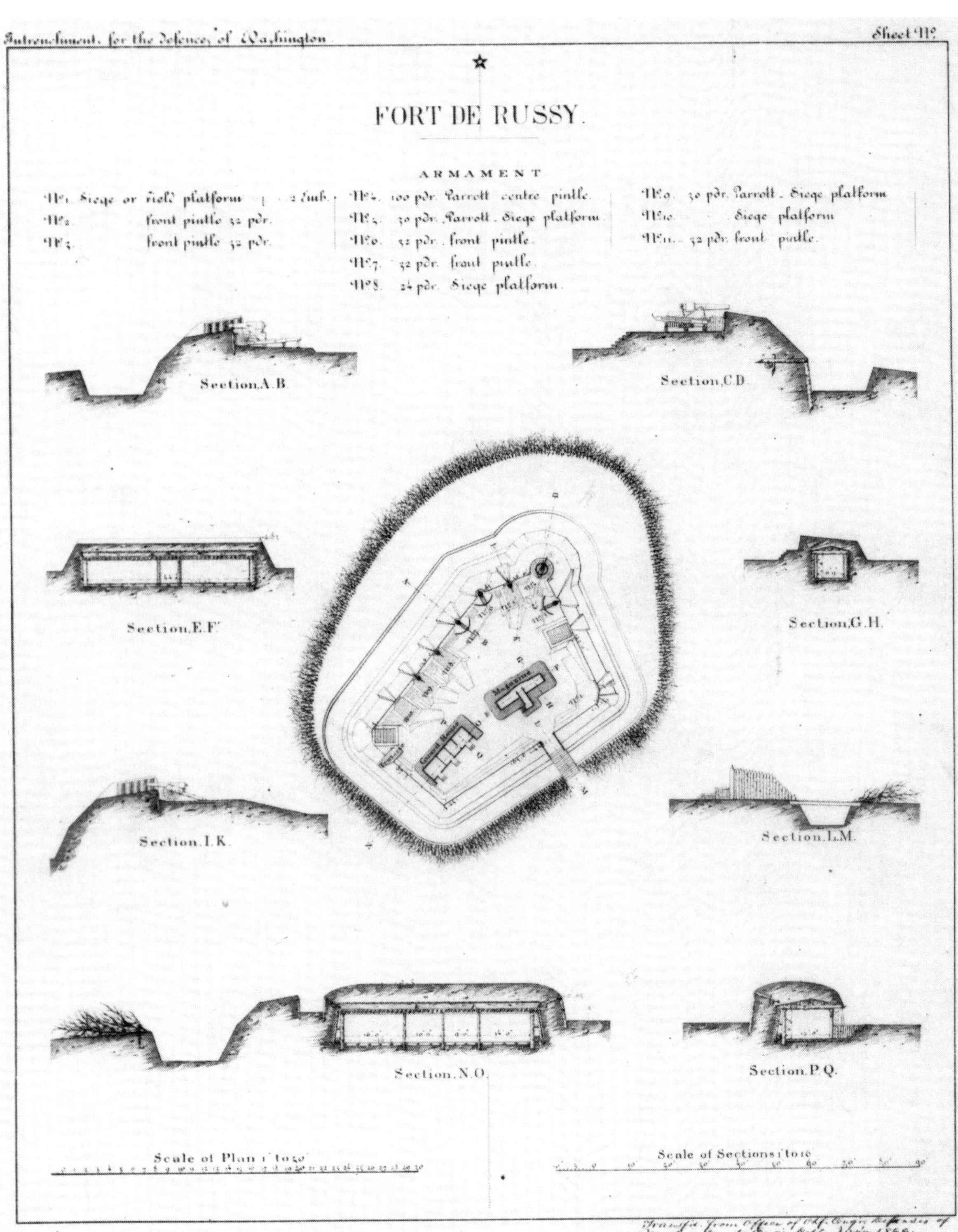

Fort DeRussy—Engineer Drawing. *National Archives*

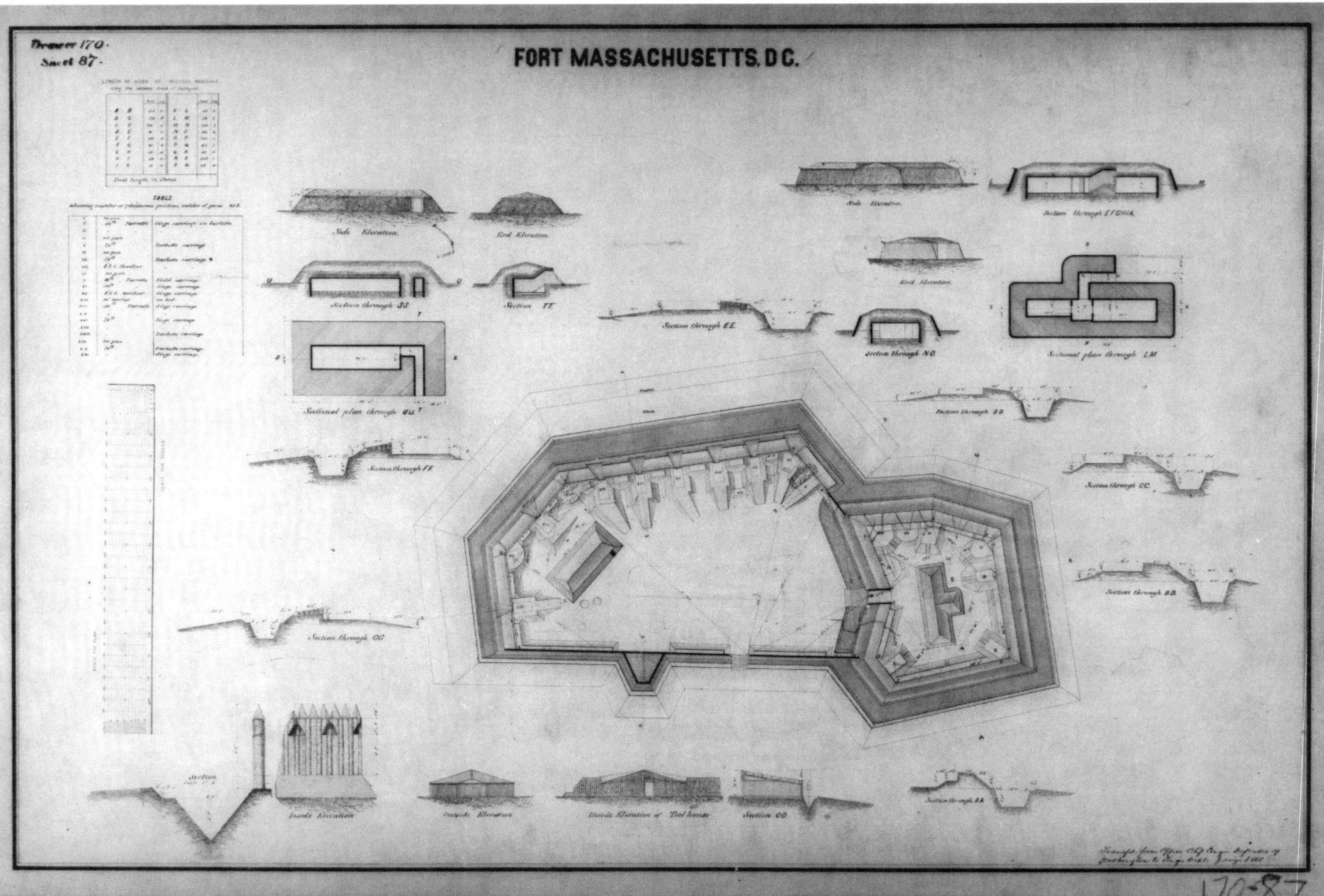

Fort Stevens (Fort Massachusetts Expanded)—Engineer Drawing. *National Archives*

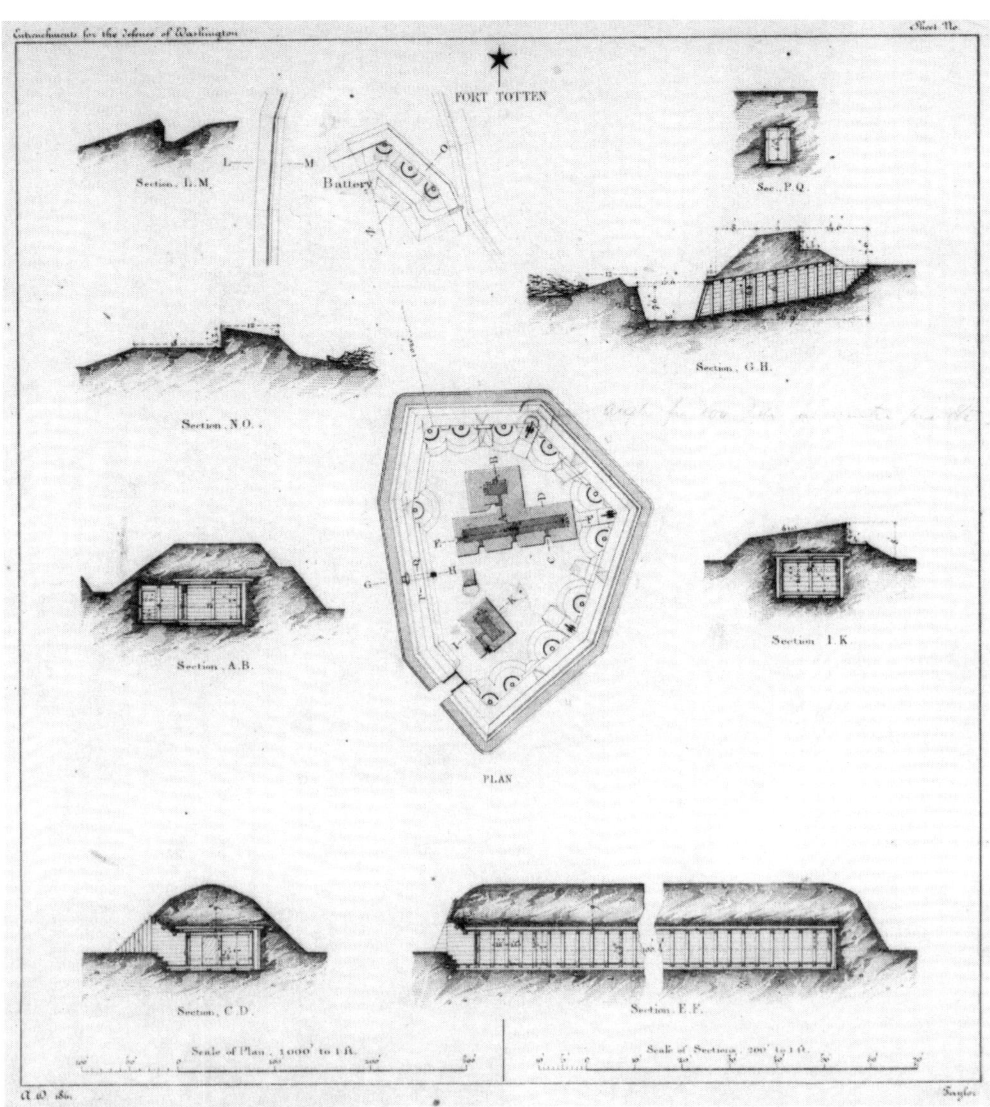

Fort Totten—Engineer Drawing. *National Archives*

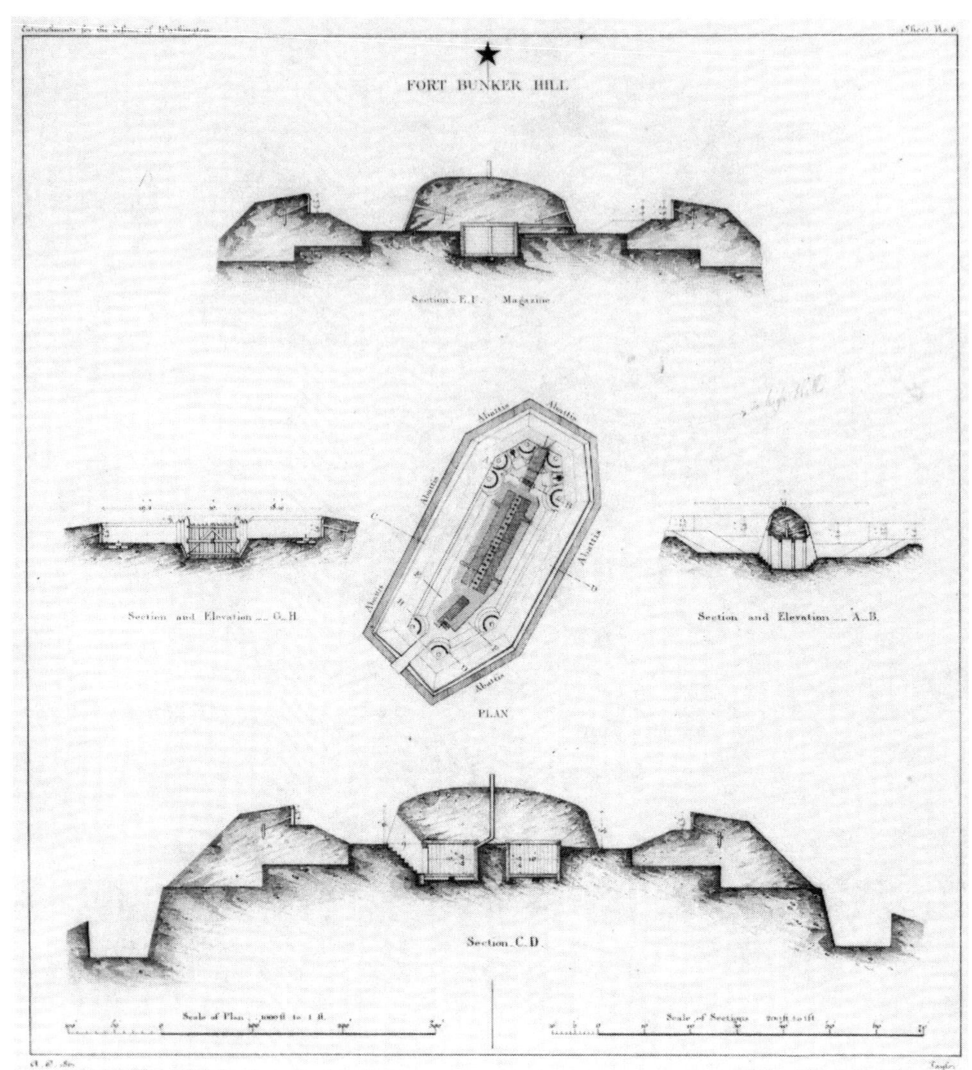

Fort Bunker Hill—Engineer Drawing. *National Archives*

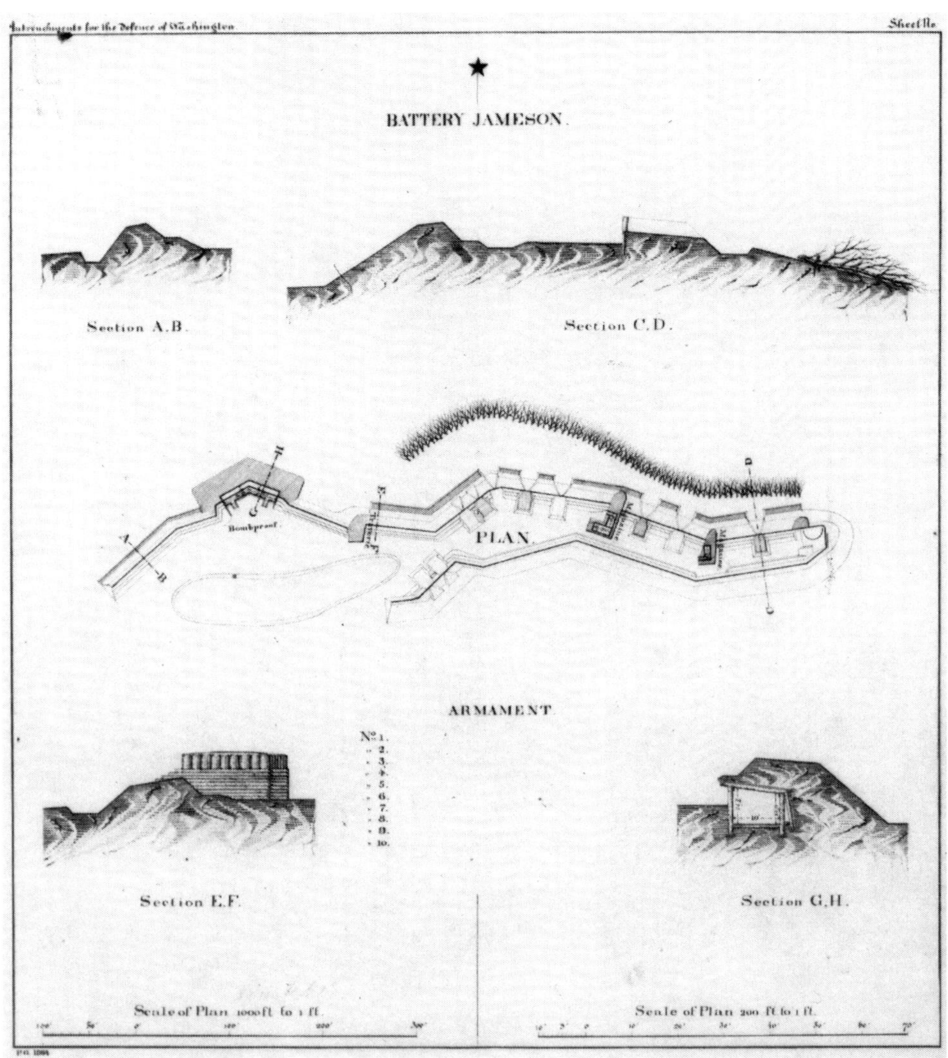

Battery Jameson—Engineer Drawing. *National Archives*

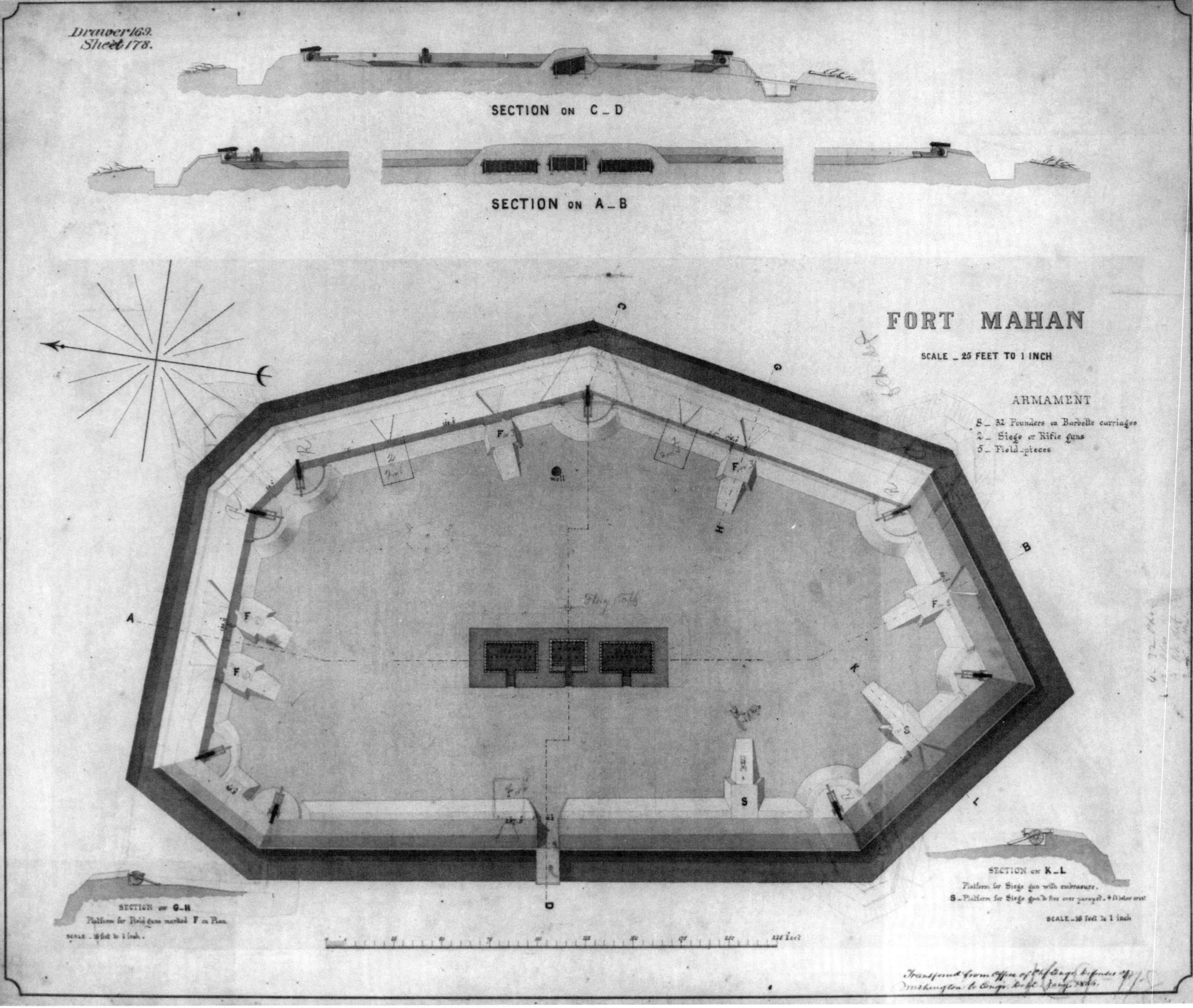

Fort Mahan (original)—Engineer Drawing. *National Archives*

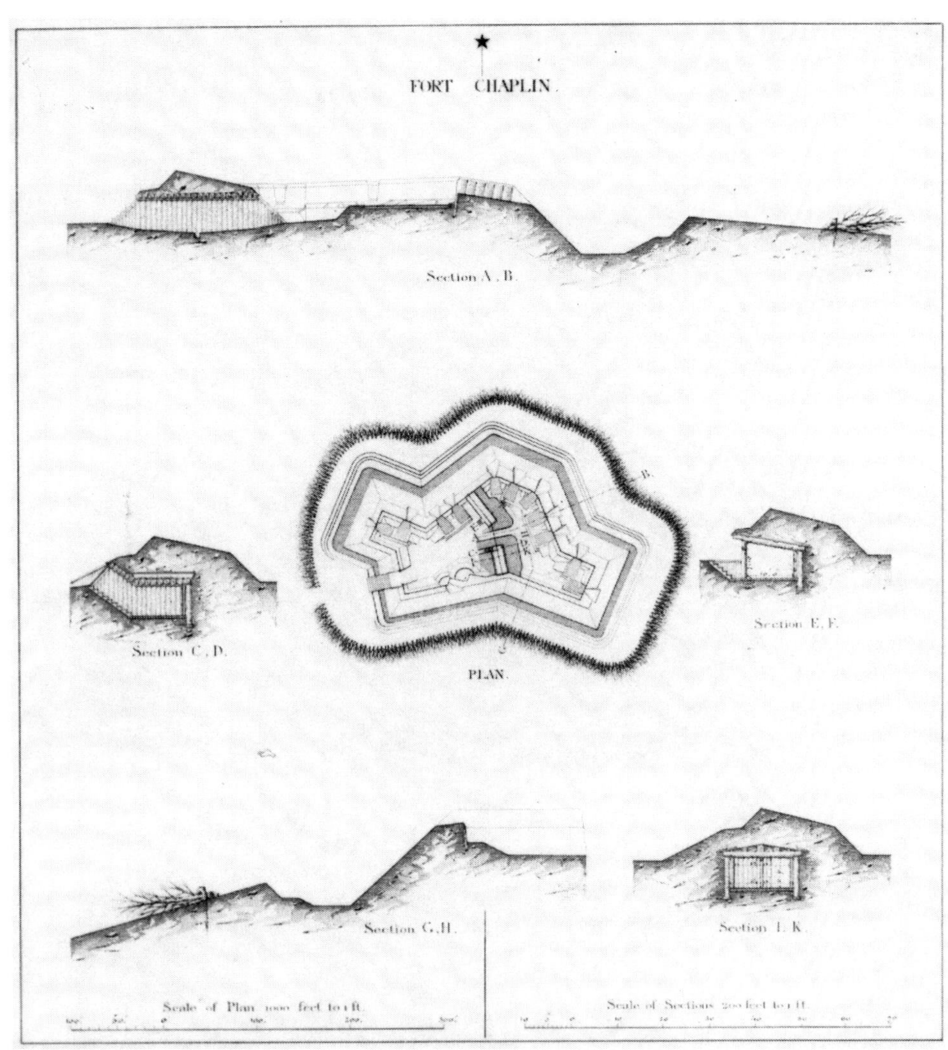

Fort Chaplin—Engineer Drawing. *National Archives*

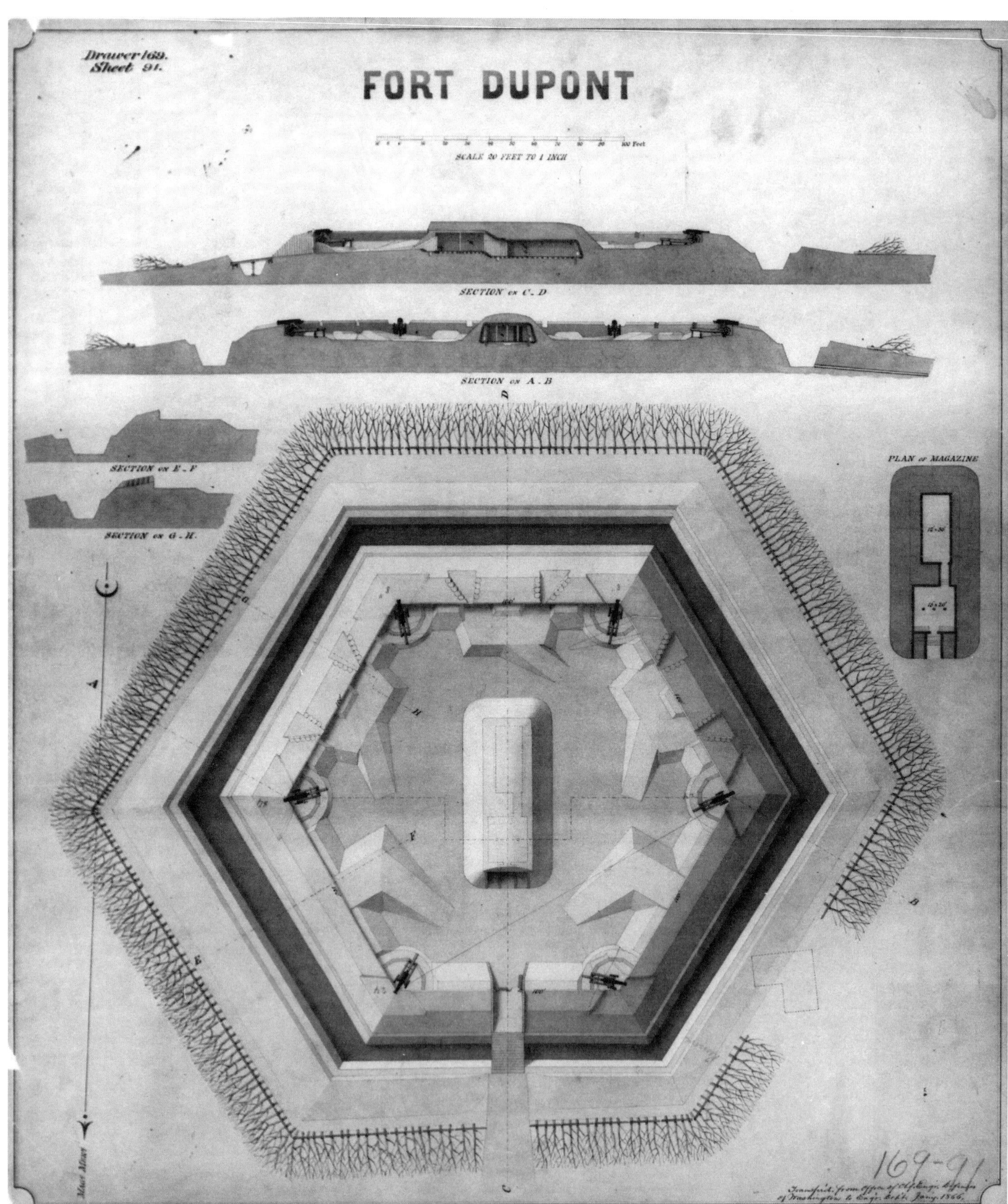

Fort DuPont—Engineer Drawing. *National Archives*

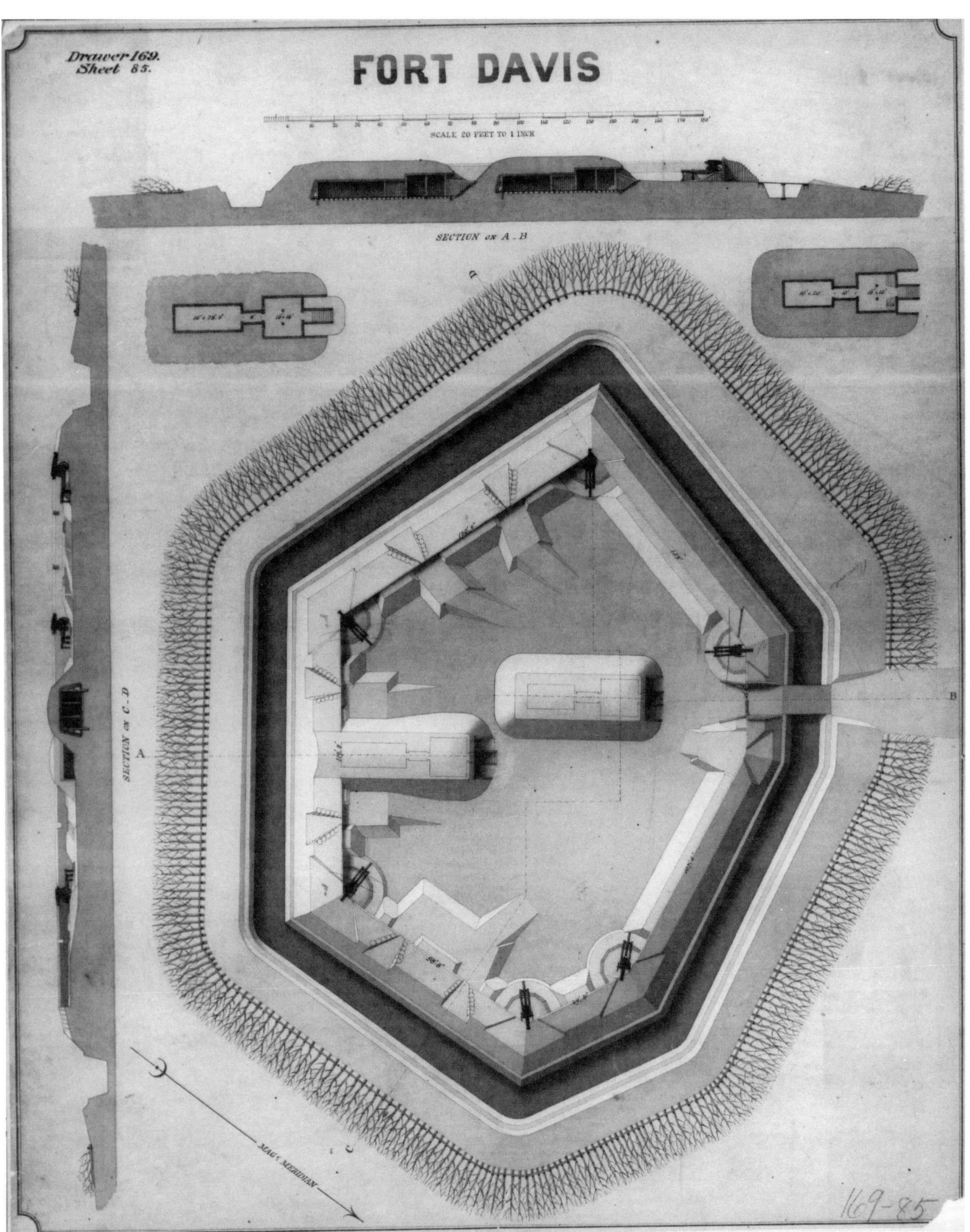

Fort Davis—Engineer Drawing. *National Archives*

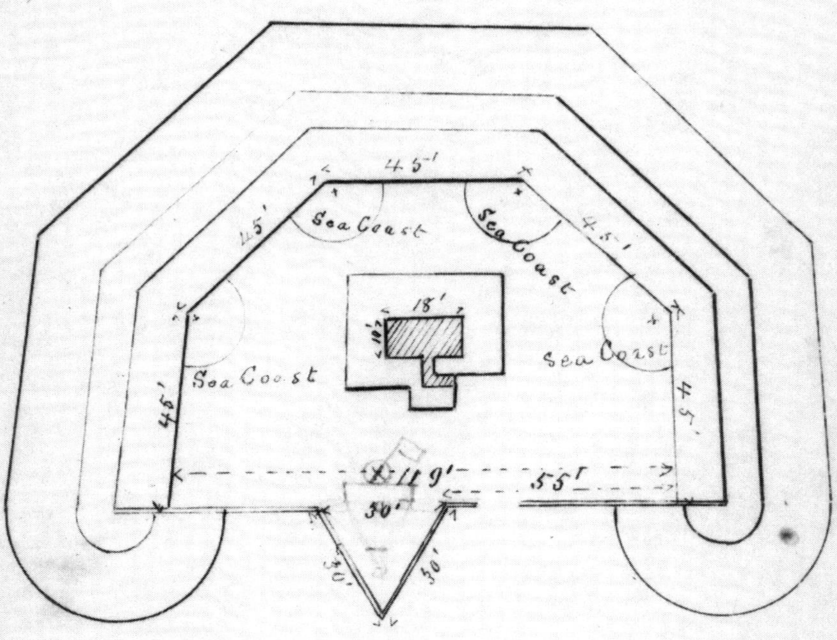

Fort Ricketts—Engineer Drawing. *National Archives*

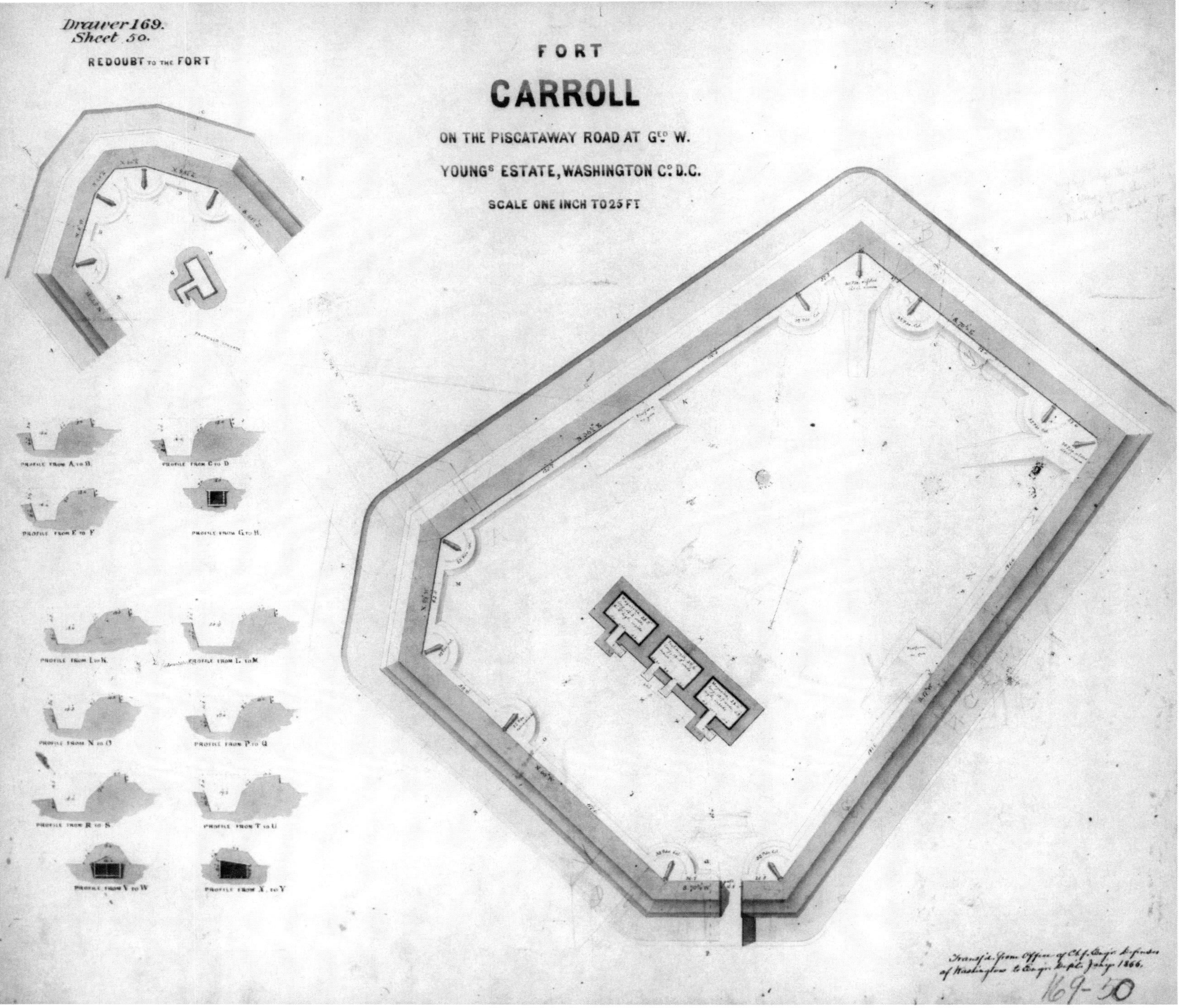

Battery Carroll and Fort Carroll (original configuration)—Engineer Drawing. *National Archives*

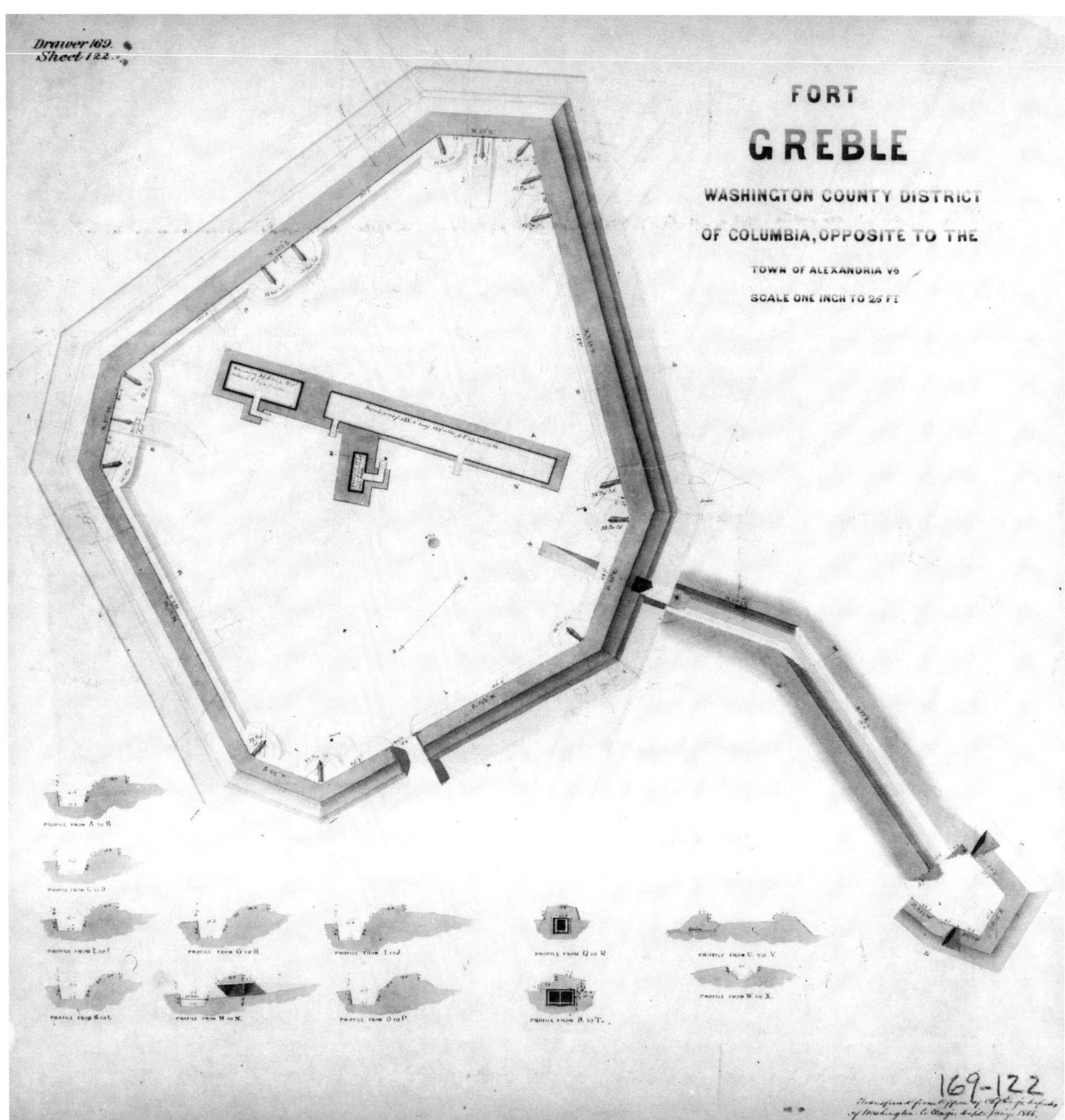

Fort Greble (original)—Engineer Drawing. *National Archives*

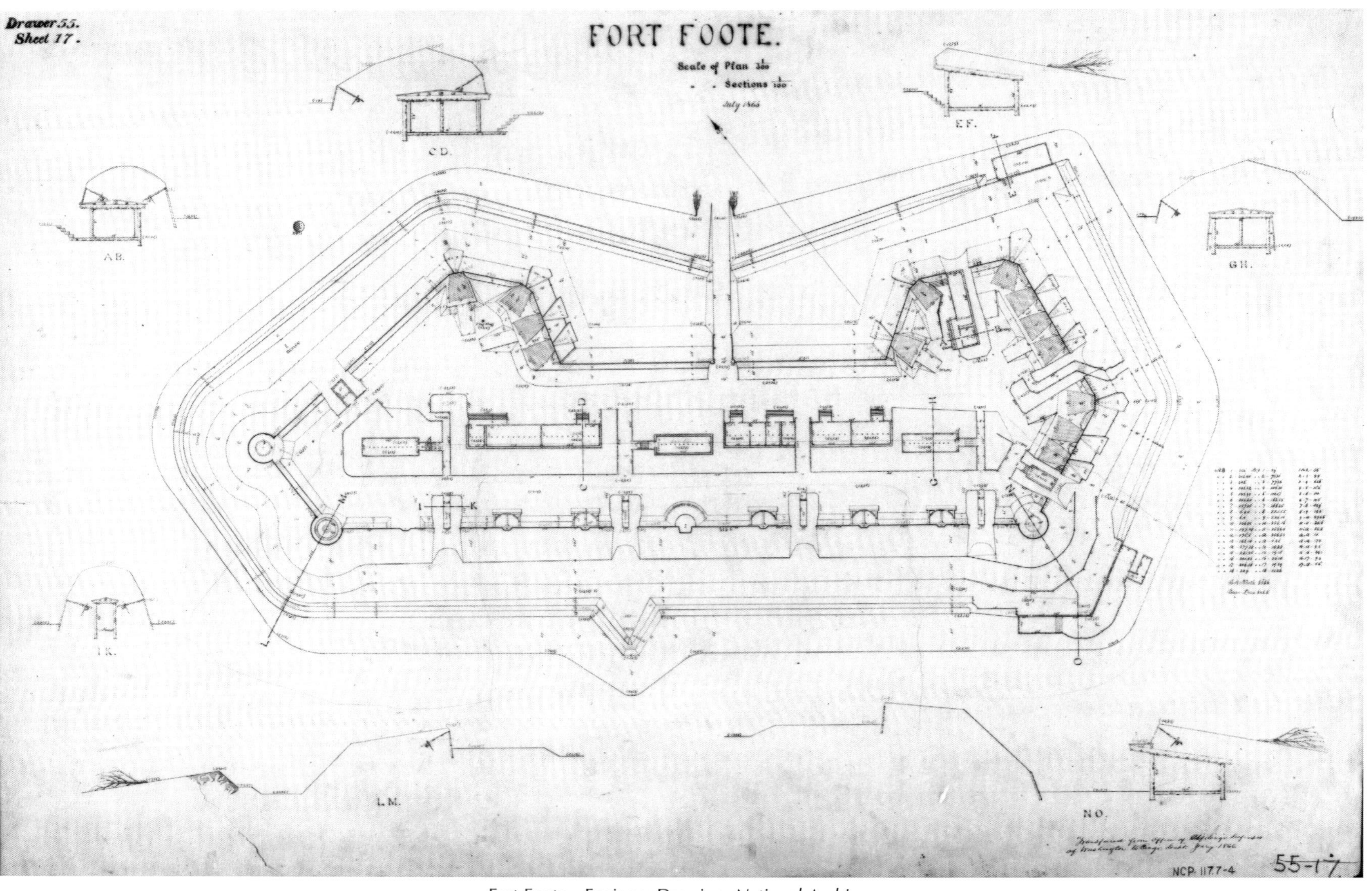

Fort Foote—Engineer Drawing. *National Archives*

Notes

CHAPTER 1

1. Bvt. Maj. Gen, John G. Barnard, *A Report on the Defenses of Washington to the Chief of Engineers, U.S. Army*; Professional Papers of the Corps of Engineers Number 20 (Washington, DC, 1871), 6, hereinafter cited as Barnard, *Report*, with appropriate page. See also Marcus Benjamin, "The Military Situation in Washington, 1861," in *Washington during Wartime* (Washington, DC: National Tribune, 1902), 19.

2. Charles W. Davis to Gideon Welles, April 11, 1861, Gideon Welles Papers, Library of Congress (LC), v. 44, no. 27, 449.

3. Statement of Stone with regard to D.C. Militia in House Report 3336, 49th Cong., 1st sess.; also letter of Lambert Tree in Chicago *Post*, May 1, 1861.

4. Washington *Evening Star*, April 24, 1861.

5. Reports of Maj. Gen. C. W. Sandford, May 28, 1861, and Maj. Gen. S. P. Heintzelman, July 20, 1863, U.S. War Department, *The War of the Rebellion: A Compilation of the Official Records of the Union and Confederate Armies* (Washington, DC, 1880–1901), ser. I, vol. 2, 37–39, 40–41 (hereinafter cited as *ORA* with all references to series I unless otherwise noted).

6. Washington *Evening Star*, May 24, 1861.

7. Barnard, *Report*, 9.

8. Report Col. J. F. K. Mansfield to Lt. Gen. Winfield Scott, May 3, 1861, *ORA*, vol. 11, 618–19; letter, D. L. Dalton to Jefferson Davis, June 29, 1861, authors' collections, copy, Defenses of Washington files, Fort Ward Library.

9. See extract embracing the "First Period" from Maj. Gen. George B. McClellan's report of the operations of the Army of the Potomac, July 27, 1861, to November 9, 1862, *ORA*, vol. 5, 11. In August, McClellan estimated 20,000 men sufficient for the defenses (p. 7), and by October, he had raised this figure to 35,000 and forty guns (p. 9). See also report of Barnard and W. F. Barry (chief of artillery) to G. S. Williams, Asst. AAG, October 2. 1861, in Box of Miscellaneous Records pertaining to Defenses of Washington, Record Group 77, National Archives and Records Service (NARA).

10. Barnard to Col. J. C. Kelton, January 15, 1864, and Barnard to Edwin Stanton January 16, 1864, both in Letterbook—Letters Sent August 19, 1862, to May 1, 1864, Headquarters Defenses of Washington, RG 77, NARA, as well as Barnard to Abraham Lincoln, August 10, 1863, vol. 120, August 9–17, 1863, Lincoln papers, LC.

11. Hon. Francis P. Blair to Commanding General Military Defenses of Washington, September 22, 1862, and Maj. Gen. C. C. Augur to Commanding General Defenses of Washington, January 17, 1865, both in Letterbook—Letters Received August 1862 to January 1865, and Barnard to Blair, September 29, 1862, Letterbook—Letters sent August 19, 1862, to May 10, 1864, all RG 77, NARA.

12. Dennis Hart Mahan, *A Treatise on Field Fortifications* (New York: Wiley, 1861); see also Barnard, *Report*, 63.

13. William Todd, *The Seventy-Ninth Highlanders: New York Volunteers in the War of the Rebellion 1861–1865* (Albany, NY: Brandon, Barton and Co., 1886), 72–73.

14. Barnard to Brig. Gen. J. G. Totten, December 10, 1861, *ORA*, vol. 5, 678–85; Barnard, *Report*, 12–13.

15. Barnard to Maj. Samuel Breck, AAG, January 13, 1864, Letterbook—Letters Sent August 19, 1862, to May 10, 1864, RG 77, NARA, mentions specifically one other engineer officer, Maj. B. S. Alexander, and Lt. H. L. Abbott of the Topographical Engineers. Other officers were available for assistance, but apparently at no time during the war did Barnard's assistants number over a dozen officers. See also Barnard to Totten, December 10, 1861, *ORA*, vol. 5, 678–85.

16. Barnard, *Report*, 15; Barnard to Totten, *ORA*, vol. 5, 678–85.

17. President's Special War Order No. 1, January 31, 1862, *ORA*, 5, 41, and President's War Order No. 3, March 8, 1962, *ORA*, vol. 5, 52, and as Attachment A, Stanton to L. Thomas and E. A. Hitchcock, April 2, 1862, *ORA*, vol. 11, pt. 2, 57–58.

18. Keyes, Heintzelman, and McDowell felt that "a covering force in front of the Virginia line of 25,000 men would suffice." Sumner noted that a total of 40,000 could defend the city. Report of Council, March 31, 1862, Attachment B, Stanton to Thomas and Hitchcock, April 2, 1862, *ORA*, vol. 11, pt. 2, 58.

19. McClellan to Brig. Gen. Lorenzo Thomas, April 1, 1862, Attachment D, Council Report, *ORA*, vol. 11, pt. 2,

59–60, and extract from McClellan's report, July 27, 1861, to November 9, 1862, *ORA*, vol. 5, 60, 62, 63.

20. J. S. Wadsworth, Thomas and Hitchcock to Secretary of War, April 2, 1862, Attachment E, Council Report, *ORA*, vol. 11, pt. 2, 61–62.

21. Lincoln to Stanton, April 3, 1862, *ORA*, vol. 11, pt. 2, 65–66.

22. Barnard, *Report*, fn. 15 .

23. Barnard to Halleck, August 28, 1862, Letterbook—Letters Sent August 19, 1862, to May 10, 1864, RG 77, NARA.

24. Barnard to Brig. Gen. U. W. Cullum, August 19, 1862, in Letterbook—Letters Sent August 19, 1862, to May 10, 1864, RG 77, NARA.

25. Report of General Robert E. Lee of Operations, August 13, to September 2, 1862, *ORA*, vol. 12, pt. 2, 558.

26. E. O. Wentworth to wife, September 16, 1862, Edward O. Wentworth Papers, Library of Congress.

27. Barnard to Brig. Gen. D. P. Woodbury, September 13, 1862, Letterbook—Letters Sent August 19, 1862, to May 10, 1864, RG 77, NARA.

28. Report of Brigadier Generals J. Totten, M. C. Meigs, W. F. Barry, J. G. Barnard, G. W. Cullum to Secretary of War, December 24, 1862, *ORA*, vol. 11, pt. 1, 904.

29. The Headquarters letterbooks of the Defenses contain numerous urgent requests for laborers, pleas to superiors in the War Department to allow convalescents to work, and frustrated notes to troop commanders in the forts concerning the need for work details. By 1864, Confederate deserters were pressed into service. With respect to the laborers from New York City, see Lt. Col. B. S. Alexander to W. P. Trowbridge, Esq. Engineer Department, New York, January 14, 1863; Alexander to Trowbridge, March 16, 1863; and Barnard to Mayor George Opdyke, April 6, 1863, all in Letterbook—Letters Sent August 19, 1862, to May 10, 1864. On Confederate deserters, see Col. T. Ingraham to Commander of Defenses of Washington, March 12, 1864, Letterbook—Letters Received August 1862 to January 1865, all RG 77, NARA.

30. Grant A. Childs to John C. Calymes, March 8, 1863, U.S. Army Engineers, Frost's Letterbook, AC Number 7609 111-19-C.3, LC; Alexander to Barnard, November 3, 1862; Letterbook—Letters Sent August 19, 1862, to May 10, 1864: Affidavit of John Collins, Superintendent of Fortifications North of Potomac, July 5, 1865, both in Box of Miscellaneous Records, RG 77, NARA.

31. The river approach became a major concern to the engineers from 1863 to 1865. See Barnard to Stanton, June 2, 1863; September 1, 1863; September 23, 1863; and October 13, 1863, all in Letterbook—Letters Sent August 19, 1862, to May 10, 1864, RG 77, NARA. On Jones's observation, see E. G. Jones, Friend Davis, January 21, 1863, authors' collections, copy, Defenses of Washington files, Fort Ward Library.

32. Stephen F. Blanding, *In the Defenses of Washington or Sunshine in a Soldier's Life* (Providence, RI: Freeman, 1889), 5. See also E. O. Wentworth to wife, September 25, 1862, Edwin O. Wentworth Papers, LC.

33. Caroline Chamberlin, ed., *Letters of George E. Chamberlin* (Springfield, IL: Rokker, 1883), 246, 266, 280.

34. Barnard to Kelton, January 15, 1864, Letterbook—Letters Sent August 19, 1862, to May 10, 1864, RG 77, NARA.

35. B. S. Alexander to Barnard, June 5, 1863; Barnard to Heintzelman, June 25, 1863; Alexander to Barnard, July 2, 1863; Barnard to Heintzelman, July 4, 1863, all in Letterbook—Letters Sent August 19, 1862, to May 10, 1864, RG 77, NARA. See also Lee to Davis, June 23 and 25, 1863, in ORA, vol. 27, pt. 3, 925, 931 as well as July 8 and 24, 1863 in Clifford Dowdey and Louis H. Manarin, eds., *The Wartime Papers of R. E. Lee* (New York: Bramhall House and Virginia Civil War Centennial Commission, 1961), 544, 558

36. Abstracts Department of Washington Strength Returns, June 20 and 30, and July 10, 1863, *ORA*, vol. 27, pt. 3, 242, 440, 638.

37. Standard modern works on Early's raid (including the battles of Monocacy and Fort Stevens) are Frank E. Vandiver, *Jubal's Raid: General Early's Famous Attack on Washington in 1864* (New York: McGraw-Hill, 1960); B. F. Cooling, *Jubal Early's Raid on Washington, 1864* (Baltimore: Nautical and Aviation Press, 1989; Tuscaloosa: University of Alabama Press, 2007); Joseph Judge, *Season of Fire: The Confederate Strike on Washington* (Berryville, VA: Rockbridge Publishing, 1994); B. F. Cooling, *Monocacy: The Battle That Saved Washington* (Shippensburg, PA: White Mane, 1996); and Marc Leepson, *Desperate Engagement: How a Little-Known Civil War Battle Saved Washington, D.C., and Changed American History* (New York: St. Martin's Press, 2007). See also William V. Cox, "The Defenses of Washington—General Early's Advance on the Capital and the Battle of Fort Stevens, July 11 and 12, 1864," *Records of the Columbia Historical Society*, vol. IV, 135–65; for Perkins's comments, see Richard N. Griffin, ed., *Three Years a Soldier: The Diary and Newspaper Correspondence of Private George Perkins, Sixth New York Independent Battery, 1861–1864* (Knoxville: University of Tennessee Press, 2006), 248, 250, 251.

38. Thomas Swan et al. to President of United States, July 9, 1864, and Lincoln to Swann et al., July 10, 1864, *ORA*, vol. 37, pt. 2, 140, 173.

39. Vandiver, *Jubal's Raid*, 174.

40. B. S. Alexander to Delafield, August 9, September 5 and 17, and October 7, 1864, in Defenses of Washington Letterbook—Letters Sent 1864–1866, RG 77, NARA.

41. *ORA*, vol. 37, pt. 2, 492–95. The principal outposts were located at "Prospect Hill" on the Georgetown and Leesburg Turnpike, at Vienna on the Loudoun and Hampshire Railroad, at Fairfax Courthouse on the Little River Turnpike, and at Fairfax Station on the Orange and Alexandria Railroad. See Alexander to Delafield, December 3, 1864, Letterbook—Letters Sent 1864–1866, RG 77, NARA.

42. Barnard, *Report*, 86.

43. Alexander to Delafield, May 1, 1865, *ORA*, vol. 47, pt. 3, 1063–64.

44. *ORA*, vol. 47, pt. 3, 1064.

45. Delafield to Stanton, May 6, 1865; General Orders 89, June 23, 1865, *ORA*, vol. 47, pt. 3, 1099–100, 1293–94.

46. Alexander to A. J. Childs and W. Gunnell, July 14, 1865; Circular to Publishers of *National Intelligencier*, Washington *Evening Star*, Baltimore *American*, and Alexandria *Gazette*, September 26, 1865; and Alexander to Delafield, November 29, 1865, all in Letterbook—Letters Sent 1864–1866, RG 77, NARA.

47. Alexander to Delafield, October 18, 1865—Report of Year Ending September 30, 1865, and Alexander to Delafield, July 14, 1865, both in Letterbook—Letters Sent 1864, RG 77, NARA.

48. On the McMillan report, see Charles Moore, ed., *Report of the Senate Committee on the District of Columbia on the Improvement of the Park System of the District of Columbia (Plan of 1901)* (Washington, DC: U.S. Government Printing Office, 1902), 75–77, 91–93, 111–12, 167–68; Frederick Gutheim and Antoinette J. Lee, *Worthy of the Nation: Washington, DC, from L'Enfant to the National Capital Planning Commission* (Baltimore: Johns Hopkins University Press, 2006), 204–5.

CHAPTER 2

1. Reprinted from J. G. Barnard, *A Report on the Defenses of Washington to the Corps of Engineers, U.S. Army: Professional Papers of the Corps of Engineers Number 20* (Washington, DC, 1871), 62–85.

2. At this period the forests, which had originally occupied much of the surface had been destroyed, partly by the direct agency of the troops and partly by injudicious clearings by the engineers—such, for instance, as that of the *entire* mass of valuable timber that surrounded Fort Scott.

3. Had there been an interior retrenchment or "reduit" at Fort Fisher, from which a fire could have been delivered in reverse upon the crest of the land front, our assault would most certainly have failed. As it was, the garrison, by aid of the perpendicular traverses, disputed possession of the work for several hours—our own troops being compelled to avail themselves of the cover the same traverses afforded on account of oblique fire, which came from other parts of the extensive works.

4. The proposed transformation of the aqueduct into a roadway excited considerable opposition at first, not only from the canal company, but even from officers in the administrative departments of the Army of the Potomac, and in consequence the alternative of a boat bridge (the depth and character of the river forbidding any other) was seriously studied. The great depth, the floods, the powerful currents, and the ice were insuperable objections to dependence on such a bridge to subserve so vital an object.

5. The *actual disbursements*, both for the purchase of materials and for monthly payment of laborers and employees, were made by Mr. James Eveleth, clerk in the Bureau of the Chief Engineer United States Army, who in addition to his office as clerk, was, as long ago as June, 1837, specially appointed disbursing agent of the Engineer Department, and in that capacity has, continuously to the present time, rendered valuable services, and disbursed large sums of public money, including more than a million of dollars for the Defenses of Washington, *on his personal responsibility*, without having received any compensation for that, at times laborious, and highly responsible service. His own statement in reference to service relating to the Defenses of Washington may properly be quoted here: "The onerous and responsible duty of paying for all purchases, together with the monthly payments of all the mechanics and laborers and other employees, demanded every moment of my time after regular office hours not indispensable to sleep, including Sundays and nights. . . . It is not to be supposed that in disbursing the hundreds of thousands of dollars paid by me in small sums to large numbers of workmen at a time, and generally *at night*, occasional losses did not occur. . . . It is a source of great pleasure for me to be able to add that every cent of the large amount (over a million of dollars) advanced to me from the Treasury has been accounted for, to the satisfaction of the accounting officers."

CHAPTER 3

1. Barnard, *Report*, 37–38.

2. Letterbooks, May 30, 1863, Defenses of Washington, RG 77, NARA.

3. Letterbooks, February 17, 1865, Defenses of Washington, RG 77, NARA.

4. Letterbooks, April 6, 1865, Defenses of Washington, RG 77, NARA.

5. Letterbooks, December 6, 1865, Defenses of Washington, RG 77, NARA.

6. Letter, Charles F. Lee to Mother, July 14, 1864, copy, Defenses of Washington files, Fort Ward Museum Library.

7. Letterbooks, June 4, 1865, Defenses of Washington, RG 77, NARA.

8. Fort Ward Quarterly Return of Ordnance Stores, September 31, 1864.

9. David V. Miller, *Defenses of Washington during the Civil War* (Buffalo, NY: Mr. Copy Inc., 1976), 14.

10. Barnard, *Report*, 9, 12, 20.

11. Howard J. Kitching, *"More Than Conqueror" or Memorials of Col. J. Howard Kitching* (New York: Hurd and Houghton, 1873), 26.

12. William Adrian Brown, *The George Washington Masonic National Memorial* (Alexandria, VA: History House, 1980), 3, 100–101.

13. William S. Lincoln, *Life with the Thirty-Fourth Massachusetts Infantry in the War of the Rebellion* (Worcester, MA: Noyes, Snow, 1879).

14. Letter, William A. Smith to Mother, July 31, 1864, copy, Defenses of Washington files, Fort Ward Museum Library.

15. Barnard, *Report*, 60.

16. Barnard, *Report*, 35, 36.

17. CEPH, Inc., *Civil War Defenses of Washington: Historic Resources Study* (Washington, DC: Department of the Interior, National Capital Region, 2004), app. A.

18. Barnard, *Report*, 36.

19. Letter, Leroy Stafford to "Lydia," December 28, 1864.

20. Letter, Elias Babcock to his Wife, in Defenses of Washington Files, Fort Ward Museum Library.

21. Regimental Letter and Order Book, 1st Wisconsin Heavy Artillery Regiment, NARA.

22. Barnard, *Report*, 36.

23. Newton M. Curtis, *From Bull Run to Chancellorsville: The Story of the Sixteenth New York Infantry Together with*

Personal Reminiscences (New York: G. P. Putnam, 1906), 61, 62, 63.

24. Barnard, *Report*, 36.

25. Mark Olcott, *The Civil War Letters of Lewis Bissell* (Washington, DC: The Field School Educational Foundation Press, 1981), 138.

26. Lincoln, *Life with the Thirty-Fourth Massachusetts Infantry in the War of the Rebellion*, 38.

27. Barnard, *Report*, 19, 35–37.

28. Charles B. Fairchild, comp., *History of the Twenty-Seventh Regiment, New York Volunteers* (Binghamton, NY: Carl and Mathews, 1888), 22.

29. Olcott, *The Civil War Letters of Lewis Bissell*, 126–28, 161.

30. New York *Times*, June 11, 1863.

31. Washington *Post*, September 9, 1883.

32. Barnard, *Report*, 36–37.

33. Letterbooks, A. G. Childs, April 20, 1963, Defenses of Washington, RG 77, NARA.

34. Letter, Edward "Ned" Hopson, January 12, 1863, authors' collections, copy, Defenses of Washington files, Fort Ward Museum Library.

35. Joseph Laycox Papers, U.S. Army Military History Institute, Carlisle Barracks Pennsylvania.

36. Barnard, *Report*, 20, 21, 36, 39.

37. Mrs. Burton Harrison, *Recollections Grave and Gay* (New York: Charles Scribner's Sons, 1911), 39.

38. T. F. Vaill, *History of the Second Connecticut Volunteer Heavy Artillery* (Winsted, CT: Winsted Printing Co., 1868), 26, 27.

39. Delavan S. Miller, *Drum Taps in Dixie: Memoirs of a Drummer Boy 1861–1865* (Watertown, NY: Hungerford-Holbrook Co., 1905), 62–63; Kitching, *"More Than Conqueror" or Memorials of Col. J. Howard Kitching*, 31–39; Olcott, *Civil War Letters of Lewis Bissell*, 43, 75–109.

40. Barnard, *Report*, 21.

41. Barnard, *Report*, 21.

42. Letters Received, September 1862 to March 1869, box 1, 1863, C143, A. G. Childs to Ensign Bennett, April 20, 1863, RG77, NARA.

43. Engineer Platoon, Engineer Corps, D.C. National Guard, *Guide to the National Capital and Maps of Vicinity Including the Fortifications* (Washington, DC: n.p., 1892), 18; CEHP, *Civil War Defenses of Washington*, pt. I, chap. 4, 42; *ORA*, vol. 21, 906.

44. Barnard, *Report*, 21.

45. Alfred S. Roe, *The Ninth New York Heavy Artillery, 1862–1865* (Worcester, MA: Author, 1899), 61.

46. Edgar B. Bennett, comp., *First Connecticut Heavy Artillery: Historical Sketch and Present Addresses of Members* (East Berlin, CT: Star Printing Co., 1889), 18.

47. Miller, *Defenses of Washington during the Civil War*, 17.

48. Barnard, *Report*, 39, 40.

49. Barnard, *Report*, 22.

50. Edward A. Walker, *Our First Year of Army Life: An Anniversary Address Delivered to the First Regiment of Connecticut Volunteer Heavy Artillery* (New Haven, CT: Thomas J. Stafford, 1862), 56.

51. Roe, *The Ninth New York Heavy Artillery, 1862–1865*, 25–35.

52. Barnard, *Report*, 9, 22.

53. Abner R. Small, *The Sixteenth Maine Regiment in the War of the Rebellion* (Portland, ME: B. Thurston and Co., 1886), 27–28.

54. Letterbook, Thomas R. Tannatt to Capt. Carroll H. Potter, April 3, 1863, RG393, pt. 1, box 2, NARA.

55. Barnard, *Report*, 22.

56. Emmons Clark, *History of the Seventh Regiment New York 1806–1889* (New York: Regimental Association, 1890), vol. II, 28–29.

57. Sheldon B. Thorpe, *The History of the Fifteenth Connecticut Volunteers in the War for the Defense of the Union 1861–1865* (New Haven, CT: Price, Lee and Adkins, 1893), 24.

58. CEHP, *Civil War Defenses of Washington*, app. A.

59. Barnard, *Report*, 11, 22.

60. Warren Ripley, *Artillery and Ammunition of the Civil War* (New York: Van Nostrand Reinhold, 1970), 57.

61. Letter, G. W. Vail, November 30, 1862, Arlington Historical Society.

62. Roy C. Brewer, "Fort Scott—Past, Present, and Future," *Arlington Historical Magazine* 3, no. 1, (October, 1965): 40–47.

63. Barnard, *Report*, 33, 43; Miller, *Defenses of Washington during the Civil War*, 19.

64. Miller, *Defenses of Washington during the Civil War*, 20.

65. Barnard, *Report*, 42–43.

66. Massachusetts, First Infantry, *Souvenir of First Regiment Massachusetts Volunteers Excursion to Battle Fields . . . Historical Sketch of Regiment* (n.p., 1907), 43, 44.

67. Barnard, *Report*, 22, 23.

68. M. H. Macnamara, *The Irish Ninth in Bivouac and Battle; or Virginia and Maryland Campaign* (Boston: Lee and Shepard, 1867), 62–63.

69. Barnard, *Report*, 22, 41.

70. Barnard, *Report*, 22, 41, 44; Miller, *Defenses of Washington during the Civil War*, 21.

71. Hyland C. Kirk, *Heavy Guns and Light: A History of the Fourth New York Heavy Artillery* (New York: C. T. Dillingham, 1890), 48–49.

72. Letter, G. J. Clark, April 23, 1865, authors' collections, copy, Defenses of Washington files, Fort Ward Museum Library.

73. Barnard, *Report*, 9; Miller, *Defenses of Washington during the Civil War*, 22.

74. Miller, *Defenses of Washington during the Civil War*, 22.

75. Barnard, *Report*, 9.

76. Letters received April 6, 1865, Barton S. Alexander to Col. J. H. Taylor, RG393, pt. 1, box 4, 1865, NARA.

77. Barnard, *Report*, 8–9.

78. Frank Moore, ed., *The Civil War in Song and Story* (New York: P. S. Collier, 1889), 217–18.

79. Kirk, *Heavy Guns and Light*, 56–57.

80. Barnard, *Report*, 9, 22–23.

81. Letter, Unidentified Soldier to "Miss Anna N. White," January 7, 1863, copy, Defenses of Washington files, Fort Ward Museum Library.

82. Barnard, *Report*, 22–23.

83. Eleanor L. Templeman, *Northern Virginia Heritage* (Arlington, VA: privately published, 1966), 58.

84. Kirk, *Heavy Guns and Light*, 52.

85. Barnard, *Report*, 43.

86. Thomas Jewell, Abstract from the Southern Claims Commission: Claim 20709. (General Records of the Department of the Treasury, 1877), NARA.

87. Roe, *The Ninth New York Heavy Artillery, 1862–1865*, 267.

88. Miller, *Defenses of Washington during the Civil War*, 25–26.

89. Miller, *Defenses of Washington during the Civil War*, 25–26.

90. Miller, *Defenses of Washington during the Civil War*, 25–26.

91. Miller, *Defenses of Washington during the Civil War*, 25–26.

92. Barnard, *Report*, 24, 45, 47.

93. Kirk, *Heavy Guns and Light*, 52, 55.

94. Augustus C. Brown, *The Diary of a Line Officer* (New York: Author, 1906), 4–6.

95. George W. Ward, *History of the Second Pennsylvania Heavy Artillery* (Philadelphia: n.p., 1904), 44.

96. Barnard, *Report*, 24, 45.

97. Charles H. Banes, *History of the Philadelphia Brigade* (Philadelphia, PA: J. B. Lippincott & Co., 1876), 20.

98. Tent 24, National Alliance, U.S. Daughters of Civil War Veterans, "Signal Service Station at Fort Ethan Allen, Virginia," University Libraries, Pennsylvania State University; J. Willard Brown, *The Signal Corps, USA in the War of the Rebellion* (Boston: U.S. Veteran Signal Corps Association, Department of Washington Chapter, 1896), 655.

99. William C. Davis, ed., *The Image of the War 1861–1865* (Garden City, NY: Doubleday, 1981), vol. III, 275, 278, 279.

100. Letter, John Carpenter to Mother, November 2, 1862, authors' collections, copy, Defenses of Washington files, Fort Ward Museum Library.

101. Roe, *The Ninth New York Heavy Artillery, 1861–1865*, fn. 59.

102. Ward, *History of the Second Pennsylvania Veteran Heavy Artillery*, 39–44.

CHAPTER 4

1. Barnard, *Report*, 14, 15; William A. Spicer, *History of the Ninth and Tenth Regiments Rhode Island Volunteers and the Tenth Rhode Island Battery* (Providence, RI: Snow and Farnham, 1892), 15.

2. CEHP, *Historic Resources Study*, pt. I, chaps. 3, 5.

3. Spicer, *History of the Ninth and Tenth Regiments Rhode Island Volunteers and the Tenth Rhode Island Battery*, 221; Unidentified Note of Inspection, Misc. Records, HQ Defenses of Washington, RG 77, NARA, copy, Defenses of Washington files, Fort Ward Library.

4. Letter, Thomas A. Bayley to "Dear Emmeline," October 13, 1862, authors' collections, copy, Defenses of Washington files, Fort Ward Library.

5. J. A. Mowris, *History of the One Hundred and Seventeenth New York* (Hartford, CT: Case, Lockwood, 1866), 43–44; Horace H. Shaw and Charles J. House, *The First Maine Heavy Artillery* (Portland, ME: n.p., 1903), 97, 104–7; Spicer, *History of the Ninth and Tenth Regiments Rhode Island Volunteers and the Tenth Rhode Island Battery*, 270; Letter, E.G. Jones to Friend Davis, January 21, 1863, authors' collections, copy, Defenses of Washington files, Fort Ward Library.

6. Mowris, *History of the One Hundred and Seventeenth New York*, 46–48; Spicer, *History of the Ninth and Tenth Regiments Rhode Island Volunteers and the Tenth Rhode Island Battery*, 260; Judith Beck Helm, *Tenleytown, D.C.: Country Village into City Neighborhood* (Washington, DC: Tennally Press, 1981), 116–17, 120; Letters, Thomas A. Bayley to "Dear Emmeline," October 13, 1862, and Benjamin F. Marshall to Mother, July 17, 1864, both authors' collections, copies, Defenses of Washington files, Fort Ward Library; CEHP, *Historical Resources Study*, pt. I, chap. 3, 5, 6.

7. Mowris, *History of the One Hundred and Seventeenth New York*, 4; Shoemaker proposals, 1861 Misc. Files, and Burgess Report, 1864, Misc. Files, both in RO 77, NARA; Letters, Adam S. Bray to Brother, August 30, 1861; William Dunlop Dixon to Mary, September 3, 1861; and Thomas A. Bayley to "Dear Emmeline," October 13, 1862, all authors' collections, copies, Defenses of Washington files, Fort Ward Library.

8. Milton E. Flower, ed., *Dear Folks at Home: Civil War Letters of Leo W. and John I. Fuller with an Account of Andersonville* (Carlisle, PA: Cumberland County Historical Society, Hamilton Library Associates, 1963), 26–27; Letter, Pomfret to Col. L. C. Morris, March 15, 1864, Misc. Records, box 1864, HQ Defenses of Washington, RG 77, NARA, copy, Misc. Letters, Defenses of Washington files, Fort Ward Library; Spicer, *History of the Ninth and Tenth Regiments Rhode Island Volunteers and the Tenth Rhode Island Battery*, 240–41; Griffin, *Three Years a Soldier*, 257, 259, 261; Edward Waldo Emerson, ed., *Life and Letters of Charles Russell Lowell* (Columbia: University of South Carolina Press, 2005), 321; David Herbert Donald, ed., *Gone for a Soldier: The Civil War Memoirs of Private Alfred Bellard* (Boston: Little, Brown, 1975), 270–71; Helm, *Tenleytown, D.C.*, chap. 3, 167–74.

9. Alanson Haines, *History of the Fifteenth New Jersey* (New York: Jenkins and Thomas, 1883), 15–17.

10. Lenard Brown, *Forts De Russy, Stevens and Totten: General Background. National Park Service Historical Sites Survey* (Washington, DC: Department of the Interior, National Park Service, February 1968), 16, 30–34; Spicer, *History of the Ninth and Tenth Regiments Rhode Island Volunteers and the Tenth Rhode Island Battery*, 259–69.

11. Cultural Tourism DC, *Battleground to Community; Brightwood Heritage Trail* (Washington, DC: Cultural Tourism DC, 2008), intro., stops 2, 5–7, 11, 13, 15, 17; Stephen F. Blanding, *In the Defenses of Washington or Sunshine in a Soldier's Life* (Providence, RI: Freeman, 1889), 31, 35; Brown, *Forts De Russy, Stevens and Totten*, 9–19, 34–37; L. E. Chittenden, *Recollections of President Lincoln and His Administration* (New York: Harper, 1891), 415–16; Shaw and House, *The First Maine Heavy Artillery*, chap. 9; A. P. Smith, *History of the Seventy-Sixth New York* (Cortland, NY: n.p., 1867), 44–57; Ward, *History of the Second Pennsylvania Heavy Artillery*, 21–26; Ron Harvey, *Buried in History: The Five Misidentified Graves at Battleground National Cemetery* (Washington, DC: National Park Service, 2008); Letters, B. W. Sulfrin to Wife and Son, October 4, 1861, and "Sargt A. F. S to Friend Frank," January 30, 1864, authors' collections, copy, Defenses of Washington files, Fort Ward Library.

12. Miller, *Defenses of Washington during the Civil War*, 35–36; Jim Leeke, ed., *A Hundred Days to Richmond: Ohio's "Hundred Days" Men in the Civil War* (Bloomington: Indiana University Press, 1999), 51; Letter, Henry T. Blanchard to Brother, January 29, 1862, authors' collections, copy, Defenses of Washington files, Fort Ward Library; CEHP, *Historic Resources Study*, pt. I, chap. 3, 5.

13. Barnard, *Report*, 13, 53; Brown, *Forts De Russy, Stevens and Totten*, 38–41; Chamberlin, *Letters of George E. Chamberlin*, 246–47, 253, 266–68, 271, 296, 304; Statement of Troops, North of Potomac, August 30–September 1, 1862; Monthly Statement, Maj. George F. Chamberlin, March 1864, Misc. Records, HQ Defenses of Washington, RC 77, NARA, copies in Defenses of Washington files, Fort Ward Library; Letters, N. Batchelder to Sister, June 11, 1863, and John H. Giuesinger to Uncle, October 26, 1862, both authors' collections, copies in Defenses of Washington files, Fort Ward Library.

14. Roe, *The Ninth New York Heavy Artillery, 1862–1865*, 25–35; Ward, *History of the Second Pennsylvania Heavy Artillery*, 14–37; copy, Giuesinger quarterly return, Defenses of Washington files, Fort Ward Library; Leeke, *A Hundred Days to Richmond*, 52, 105; CEHP, *Historic Property Study*, pt. I, chaps. 2, 5.

15. Jeffrey D. Marshall, ed., *A War of the People; Vermont Civil War Letters* (Hanover, NH: University Press of New England, 1999), 302–303.

16. Leeke, *A Hundred Days to Richmond*, 51–52.

17. Charles H. Anson, "Reminiscences of an Enlisted Man," in *War Papers*, vol. IV, Military Order of the Loyal Legion of the United States, Wisconsin Commandery (Milwaukee, WI: Burdick and Allen, 1914), 288; Miller, *Defenses of Washington during the Civil War*, 37–38; Ward, *History of the Second Pennsylvania Heavy Artillery*, 26–38; Leeke, *A Hundred Days to Richmond*, 242, fn. 18; Samuel S. Wint Journal, 1862–1864, authors' collections, copy, Defenses of Washington files, Fort Ward Library; CEHP, *Historic Resources Study*, pt. I, chap. 3, 5; Charles M. McGee Jr. and Ernest M. Lander Jr., *A Rebel Came Home: The Diary and Letters of Floride Clemson, 1863–1865* (Columbia: University of South Carolina Press, 1989), 129; Letter, Charles M. Gould to Brother, October 29, 1862, Special Collections, University of Vermont Library, Burlington, VT.

CHAPTER 5

1. Barnard, *Report*, 14, 30–32, 55–56; Edwin B. Houghton, *Campaigns of the Seventeenth Maine* (Portland, ME: Short and Loring, 1866), 7–8; Misc. Letters, Defenses of Washington files, Fort Ward Library; Roe, *The Ninth New York Heavy Artillery, 1862–1865*, 78; John D. Vautier, *History of the Eighty-Eighth Pennsylvania* (Philadelphia: Lippincott, 1894), 24.

2. Charles McCormick, *General Background, Forts Mahan, Chaplin, DuPont, Davis* (Washington, DC: National Park Service Division of History, Office of Archeology and Historic Preservation, July 15, 1967), 24–30, 77; Roe, *The Ninth New York Heavy Artillery, 1862–1865*, 78; Letter "John" to Sister, May 19, 1865, authors' collections; CEHP, *Historic Resources Study*, pt. I, chap. 3, 5.

3. Barnard, *Report*, 14, 56; McCormick, *General Background, Forts Mahan, Chaplin, DuPont, Davis*, 24–36, 54–57, 76–77; CEHP, *Historic Resources Study*, pt. I, chap. 3, 5.

4. Barnard, *Report*, 14, 56; McCormick, *General Background, Forts Mahan, Chaplin, DuPont, Davis*, 24–36, 54–57, 76–77.

5. Mowris, *History of the One Hundred and Seventeenth New York*, 53–54; Spicer, *History of the Ninth and Tenth Regiments Rhode Island Volunteers and the Tenth Rhode Island Battery*, 92–115; Edward P. Webb, *History of the Tenth New York Heavy Artillery* (Watertown, NY: Post Book and Job Printing Establishment, 1887), 19–21, 61; Letter, E. G. Jones to Friend Davis, January 21, 1863, authors' collections, copy, Defenses of Washington files, Fort Ward Library.

6. Barnard, *Report*, 14, 30, 56–57; Lenard Brown, *Fort Stanton, Fort Foote, Battery Ricketts, Historic Structures Report* (Washington, DC: National Park Service, Office of History and Historic Architecture, Eastern Service Center, May 1970), chaps. 2, 3.

7. Edwin B. Houghton, *Campaigns of the Seventeenth Maine* (Portland, ME: Short and Loring, 1866), 7–8; Vautier, *History of the Eighty-Eighth Pennsylvania*, 24–25; Ruth L. Silliker, ed. *The Rebel Yell & Yankee Hurrah; The Civil War Journal of a Maine Volunteer* (Camden, ME: Down East Books, 1985), 34–35.

8. R. W. Kerr, *History of the Government Printing Office* (Lancaster, PA: Inquirer Printing and Publishing Co., 1881), 49–52; Adjutant General of Massachusetts, *Massachusetts Soldiers, Sailors, and Marines in the Civil War* (Norwood, MA: Norwood Press, 1932), vol. V, 770.

9. Letters, Elias Babcock to Wife, November 26, 1863, and January 1, 1864, both authors' collections, copy, Defenses of Washington files, Fort Ward Library; Barnard, *Report*, 30, 56; George J. Olszewski, *Forts Carroll and Greble: Washington DC* (Historic Structures Report). (Washington, DC: National Park Service, Office of History and Historic Architecture, Eastern Service Center, June 1970), pt. A; Sherman's Report, Misc. Records, box, HQ Defenses of Washington, RG 77, NARA, copy, Defenses of Washington files, Fort Ward Library.

10. John Day Smith, *History of the Nineteenth Maine* (Minneapolis: Great Western Printing Co., 1909), 8–9; Spicer, *History of the Ninth and Tenth Regiments Rhode Island Volunteers and the Tenth Rhode Island Battery*, 111; Washington Davis, *Camp Fire Chats of the Civil War* (Chicago: A. B. Gehman, 1888), 259–61; Letters, Thomas A. Bayley to Mrs. Kinsey, February 23, 1862, and Bayley to "Dear Emmeline," April 2, 1862, both authors' collections, copies, Defenses of Washington files, Fort Ward Library.

CHAPTER 6

1. Barnard, *Report*, 31–32, 58–62; Brown, *Fort Stanton, Fort Foote, Battery Ricketts, Historic Structures Report*, chaps. 4, 5; Roe, *The Ninth New York Heavy Artillery, 1862–1865*, 58–65.

2. Griffin, *Three Years a Soldier*, 58.

APPENDIX A

1. Barnard biographical folder, Defenses of Washington files, Fort Ward library.

APPENDIX B

1. Albert Mauncy, *Artillery through the Ages* (Washington, DC: U.S. Government Printing Office, 1949), 19; Harold L. Peterson, *Notes on Ordnance of the Civil War, 1861–1865* (Washington, DC: American Ordnance Association, 1959), 6–7, and *Round Shot and Rammers* (New York: Bonanza Books, 1969), 106; Ripley, *Artillery and Ammunition of the Civil War* (New York: Van Nostrand Reinhold, 1970), 366–79.

APPENDIX C

1. Reprinted by permission from Paul K. Walker, *Engineers of Independence: A Documentary History of the Army Engineers in the American Revolution 1775-1783* (Baltimore: Office of Chief of Engineers, Historical Division, 1981), 380–82.

APPENDIX D

1. Description of signal stations in and near the District of Columbia used in the survey of the fortifications of Washington 1863 by U.S. Coast Survey, drawer 170, sheet 186, RG 170, Engineer Records, Cartographic, Branch, NARA, copy, Defenses of Washington files, Fort Ward Library; Brown, *The Signal Corps, USA in the War of the Rebellion*, Department of Washington chapter.

APPENDIX E

1. U.S. War Department, Adjutant General's Office, *Compendium of General Orders, Adjutant General's Office, 1864* (Washington, DC: U.S. War Department, 1864), 13–32.

Bibliography

UNPUBLISHED SOURCES

Most of the unpublished sources cited in this guide have been deposited in the Defenses of Washington files at Fort Ward Library, Alexandria, Virginia, where they may be used by those seeking further information.

PUBLISHED SOURCES

Abbot, Catherine C. *Family Letters of General Henry Larcom Abbot, 1831–1927.* Gettysburg, PA: Thomas Publications, 2001.

Adams, F. Colburn. *Siege of Washington D.C. Written Expressly for Little People.* New York: Dick and Fitzgerald, 1867.

Anson, Charles H. "Reminiscences of an Enlisted Man." In *War Papers.* Vol. IV. Military Order of the Loyal Legion of the United States, Wisconsin Commandery. Milwaukee, WI: Burdick and Allen, 1914.

Banes, Charles H. *History of the Philadelphia Brigade.* Philadelphia, PA: J. B. Lippincott & Co., 1876.

Barnard, John G. *A Report on the Defenses of Washington to the Corps of Engineers, U.S. Army.* Professional Papers of the Corps of Engineers, U.S. Army, No. 20. Washington, DC: U.S. Government Printing Office, 1871.

Bartlett, A. W. *History of the Twelfth Regiment New Hampshire Volunteers in the War of the Rebellion.* Concord, NH: Ira C. Evans, 1897.

Benjamin, Marcus, comp. and ed. *Washington during Wartime.* Washington, DC: National Tribune, 1902.

Bennett, Edgar B., comp. *First Connecticut Heavy Artillery: Historical Sketch and Present Addresses of Members.* East Berlin, CT: Star Printing Co., 1889.

Berg, Scott W. *Grand Avenues: The Story of the French Visionary Who Designed Washington, D.C.* New York: Pantheon, 2007.

Blanding, Stephen F. *In the Defenses of Washington or Sunshine in a Soldier's Life.* Providence, RI: Freeman, 1889.

Brewer, Roy C. "Fort Scott—Past, Present, and Future." *The Arlington Historical Magazine,* Vol. 3, No. 1 (October 1965): 40–47.

Brown, Augustus C. *The Diary of a Line Officer.* New York: Author, 1906.

Brown, J. Willard. *The Signal Corps, USA in the War of the Rebellion.* Boston: U.S. Veteran Signal Corps Association Department of Washington chapter, 1896.

Brown, Lenard. *Fort Stanton, Fort Foote, Battery Ricketts, Historic Structures Report.* Washington, DC: National Park Service, Office of History and Historic Architecture, Eastern Service Center, May 1970.

———. *Forts De Russy, Stevens and Totten: General Background. National Park Service Historical Sites Survey.* Washington, DC: Department of the Interior, National Park Service, February 1968.

Brown, William Adrian. *The George Washington Masonic National Memorial.* Alexandria, VA: History House, 1980.

Bundy, Carol. *The Nature of Sacrifice; A Biography of Charles Russell Lowell, Jr., 1835–1864.* New York: Farrar, Straus and Giroux, 2005.

CEPH, Inc. *Civil War Defenses of Washington: Historic Resources Study.* Washington, DC: Department of the Interior, National Capital Region, 2004.

Chamberlin, Caroline, ed. *Letters of George F. Chamberlin.* Springfield, IL: Rokker, 1883.

Chittenden, L. E. *Recollections of President Lincoln and His Administration.* New York: Harper, 1891.

Clark, Emmons. *History of the Seventh Regiment New York 1806–1889.* New York: Regimental Association, 1890.

Cooling, Benjamin Franklin. "Civil War Deterrent: The Defenses of Washington." *Military Affairs,* 20 (Winter 1966): 164–78.

———. "Defending Washington during the Civil War." In *Records of the Columbia Historical Society of Washington D.C., 1971–1972,* edited by Francis C. Rosenberger. Washington, DC: Columbia Historical Society and University of Virginia Press, 1973.

———. *Jubal Early's Raid on Washington, 1864.* Baltimore: Nautical and Aviation Press, 1989; Tuscaloosa: University of Alabama Press, 2008.

———. *Monocacy: The Battle That Saved Washington.* Shippensburg, PA: White Mane, 1996.

———. *Symbol, Sword and Shield: Defending Washington during the Civil War.* Hamden, CT: Archon, 1975.

Cramer, John Henry. *Lincoln under Enemy Fire: The Complete Account of His Experiences during Early's Attack on Washington.* Baton Rouge: Louisiana State University Press, 1948.

Cultural Tourism DC. *Battleground to Community; Brightwood Heritage Trail.* Washington, DC: Cultural Tourism DC, 2008.

Curtis, Newton M. *From Bull Run to Chancellorsville: The Story of the Sixteenth New York Infantry Together with Personal Reminiscences.* New York: G. P. Putnam, 1906.

Davis, Washington. *Camp Fire Chats of the Civil War.* Chicago: A. B. Gehman, 1888.

Davis, William C., ed. *The Image of the War 1861–1865.* 6 vols. Garden City, NY: Doubleday, 1981.

Dickman, William J. *Battery Rodgers.* Alexandria, VA: privately printed, n.d.

Donald, David Herbert, ed. *Gone for a Soldier: The Civil War Memoirs of Private Alfred Bellard.* Boston: Little, Brown, 1975.

Dowdey, Clifford and Louis H. Manarin, eds. *The Wartime Papers of R. E. Lee.* New York: Bramhall House and Virginia Civil War Commission, 1961.

Dyer, Frederick H., comp. *A Compendium of the War of the Rebellion.* 3 vols. New York: Thomas Yoseloff, 1959.

Emerson, Edward Waldo. *Life and Letters of Charles Russell Lowell.* Columbia: University of South Carolina Press, 2005.

Engineer Platoon, Engineer Corps, D.C. National Guard. *Guide to the National Capital and Maps of Vicinity Including the Fortifications.* Washington, DC: n.p., 1892.

Fairchild, Charles B., comp. *History of the Twenty-Seventh Regiment, New York Volunteers.* Binghamton, NY: Carl and Mathews, 1888.

Flower, Milton E. ed. *Dear Folks at Home: Civil War Letters of Leo W. and John I. Fuller with an Account of Andersonville.* Carlisle, PA: Cumberland County Historical Society, Hamilton Library Associates, 1963.

Fort Myer, Va. (originally Fort Whipple). *Historical Sketch.* N.p., 1934.

Furguson, Ernest B. *Freedom Rising; Washington in the Civil War.* New York: Knopf, 2004.

Griffin, Richard N. ed. *Three Years a Soldier: The Diary and Newspaper Correspondence of Private George Perkins, Sixth New York Independent Battery, 1861–1864.* Knoxville: University of Tennessee Press, 2006.

Gutheim, Frederick and Antoinette J. Lee. *Worthy of the Nation: Washington, DC, from L'Enfant to the National Capital Planning Commission.* Baltimore: Johns Hopkins University Press, 2006.

Haines, Alanson. *History of the Fifteenth New Jersey.* New York: Jenkins and Thomas, 1883.

Hall, Isaac. *History of the Ninety-Seventh Regiment New York Volunteers.* Utica, NY: L. C. Childs and Son, 1890.

Hanson, Joseph Mills. *Bull Run Remembers . . . The History, Traditions and Landmarks of the Manassas (Bull Run) Campaigns before Washington 1861–1862.* Manassas, VA: National Capitol Publishers, 1953.

Harrison, Burton, Mrs. *Recollections Grave and Gay.* New York: Charles Scribner's Sons, 1911.

Harvey, Ron. *Buried in History; The Five Misidentified Graves at Battleground National Cemetery.* Washington, DC: National Park Service, 2008.

Helm, Judith Beck. *Tenleytown, D.C.: Country Village into City Neighborhood.* Washington, DC: Tennally Press, 1981.

Hess, Earl J. *Field Armies and Fortificaition in the Civil War: The Eastern Campaigns, 1861–1864.* Chapel Hill: University of North Carolina Press, 2005.

Houghton, Edwin B. *Campaigns of the Seventeenth Maine.* Portland, ME: Short and Loring, 1866.

Jacob, Kathryn Allamong. *Testament to Union: Civil War Monuments in Washington D.C.* Baltimore: Johns Hopkins University Press, 1998.

Judge, Joseph. *Season of Fire: The Confederate Strike on Washington.* Berryville, VA: Rockbridge Publishing, 1994.

Kerr R. W. *History of the Government Printing Office.* Lancaster, PA: Inquirer Printing and Publishing Co., 1881.

Kiefer, W. R. *History of the One Hundred and Fifty-Third Pennsylvania.* Easton, PA: Chemical Publishing Co., 1909.

Kirk, Hyland C. *Heavy Guns and Light: A History of the Fourth New York Heavy Artillery.* New York: C. T. Dillingham, 1890.

Kitching, J. Howard. *"More Than Conqueror" or Memorials of Col. J. Howard Kitching.* New York: Hurd and Houghton, 1873.

Konsoulis, Mary, et al. *Brightwood to Community: Brightwood Heritage Trail.* Washington, DC: Cultural Tourism DC, 2008.

Laas, Virginia Jeans, ed. *The Civil War Letters of Elizabeth Blair Lee.* Urbana: University of Illinois Press, 1991.

Lancaster, Mary H. and Dallas Lancaster. *The Civil War Diary of Anne S. Frobel of Wilton Hill in Virginia.* Birmingham, AL: Birmingham Printing and Publishing Co., 1987.

Lee, Richard M. *Mr. Lincoln's City: An Illustrated Guide to the Civil War Sites of Washington.* McLean, VA: EPM Publications, 1981.

Leech, Margaret. *Reveille in Washington, 1860–1865.* New York: Harper and Brothers, 1941.

Leeke, Jim, ed. *A Hundred Days to Richmond: Ohio's "Hundred Days" Men in the Civil War.* Bloomington: Indiana University Press, 1999.

Leepson, Marc. *Desperate Engagement: How A Little-Known Civil War Battle Saved Washington, D.C., and Changed American History.* New York: St. Martin's Press, 2007.

Lincoln, William S. *Life with the Thirty-Fourth Massachusetts Infantry in the War of the Rebellion.* Worcester, MA: Noyes, Snow, 1879.

Mahan, Dennis Hart. *A Treatise on Field Fortifications.* New York: Wiley, 1861.

Macnamara, Daniel O. *The History of the Ninth Regiment Massachusetts Volunteer Infantry.* Boston: E. R. Stillings, 1899.

Macnamara, M. H. *The Irish Ninth in Bivouac and Battle; or Virginia and Maryland Campaign.* Boston: Lee and Shepard, 1867.

Marshall, Jeffrey D., ed. *A War of the People; Vermont Civil War Letters.* Hanover, NH: University Press of New England, 1999.

Massachusetts, Adjutant General of. *Massachusetts Soldiers, Sailors, and Marines in the Civil War.* 8 vols. Norwood, MA: Norwood Press, 1932.

Massachusetts, Fifth Battery Light Artillery. *History of the Fifth Massachusetts Battery.* Boston: Luther E. Cowles, 1902.

Massachusetts, First Infantry. *Souvenir of First Regiment Massachusetts Volunteers Excursion to Battle Fields . . . Historical Sketch of Regiment.* N.p., 1907.

Mauncy, Albert. *Artillery through the Ages.* Washington, DC: U.S. Government Printing Office, 1949.

McClure, Stanley. *Guide Leaflet to the Defenses of Washington.* Washington, DC: National Park Service, 1956.

McCormick, Charles. *General Background, Forts Mahan, Chaplin, DuPont, Davis.* Washington, DC: National Park Service Division of History, Office of Archeology and Historic Preservation, July 15, 1967.

McGee, Charles M., Jr., and Ernest M. Lander, Jr., eds. *A Rebel Came Home: The Diary and Letters of Floride Clemson, 1863–1866.* Columbia: University of South Carolina Press, 1989.

McLean, James. *California Sabers: The Second Massachusetts Cavalry in the Civil War.* Bloomington: Indiana University Press, 2000.

Miller, David V. *Defenses of Washington during the Civil War.* Buffalo, NY: Mr. Copy Inc., 1976.

Miller, Delavan S. *Drum Taps in Dixie: Memoirs of a Drummer Boy 1861–1865.* Watertown, NY: Hungerford-Holbrook Co., 1905.

Miller, Francis Trevelyan, ed. *Photographic History of the Civil War.* 10 vols. New York: Review of Reviews, 1911.

Mitchell, Mary. *Divided Town: A Study of Georgetown, D.C. during the Civil War.* Barre, MA: Barre Publishers, 1968.

Moore, Charles, ed. *Report of the Senate Committee on the District of Columbia on the Improvement of the Park System of the District of Columbia (Plan of 1901).* Washington, DC: U.S. Government Printing Office, 1902.

Moore, Frank, ed. *The Civil War in Song and Story.* New York: P. S. Collier, 1889.

Mowris, J. A. *History of the One Hundred and Seventeenth New York.* Hartford, CT: Case, Lockwood, 1866.

Newman, Mac. *Potomac Diary: A Soldier's Account of the Capital in Crisis, 1864–1865.* Charleston, SC: Arcadia, 2001.

New York, Fifth Heavy Artillery Veterans Association. *Roster and Report of Eleventh Annual Reunion.* New York: n.p., 1889.

Olcott, Mark. *The Civil War Letters of Lewis Bissell.* Washington, DC: The Field School Educational Foundation Press, 1981.

Olszewski, George J. *Forts Carroll and Greble: Washington DC.* Historic Structures Report. Washington, DC: National Park Service, Office of History and Historic Architecture, Eastern Service Center, June 1970.

Parker, Francis, J. *The Story of the Thirty-Second Massachusetts.* Boston: C. W. Calkins, 1880.

Parson, Thomas E. *Bear Flag and Bay State in the Civil War: The Californians of the Second Massachusetts Cavalry.* Jefferson, NC: McFarland, 2001.

Pelka, Fred, ed. *The Civil War Letters of Colonel Charles F. Johnson, Invalid Corps.* Amherst: University of Massachusetts Press, 2004.

Peterson, Harold L. *Notes on Ordnance of the Civil War, 1861–1865.* Washington, DC: American Ordnance Association, 1959.

———. *Round Shot and Rammers.* New York: Bonanza Books, 1969.

Pinsker, Matthew. *Lincoln's Sanctuary: Abraham Lincoln and the Soldiers' Home.* New York: Oxford University Press, 2003.

Ray, Fred L. *Shock Troops of the Confederacy: The Sharpshooter Battalions of the Army of Northern Virginia.* Asheville, NC: CFS Press, 2006.

Rhodes, Robert Hunt, ed. *All for the Union: The Civil War Diary and Letters of Elisha Hunt Rhodes.* Lincoln, RI: Andrew Mobray, 1985.

Ripley, Warren. *Artillery and Ammunition of the Civil War.* New York: Van Nostrand Reinhold, 1970.

Roe, Alfred S. *The Ninth New York Heavy Artillery, 1862–1865.* Worcester, MA: Author, 1899.

Shaw, Horace H., and Charles J. House. *The First Maine Heavy Artillery.* Portland, ME: n.p., 1903.

Sherman, W. T. *Memoirs of General W. T. Sherman.* 4th edition. New York: Charles Webster and Company, 1891.

Silliker, Ruth L., ed. *The Rebel Yell & Yankee Hurrah; The Civil War Journal of a Maine Volunteer.* Camden, ME: Down East Books, 1985.

Small, Abner R. *The Sixteenth Maine Regiment in the War of the Rebellion.* Portland, ME: B. Thurston and Co., 1886.

Smith, A. P. *History of the Seventy-Sixth New York.* Cortland, NY: n.p., 1867.

Smith, John Day. *History of the Nineteenth Maine.* Minneapolis: Great Western Printing Co., 1909.

Spicer, William A. *History of the Ninth and Tenth Regiments Rhode Island Volunteers and the Tenth Rhode Island Battery.* Providence, RI: Snow and Farnham, 1892.

Standlee, Mary W. *Borden's Dream: The Walter Reed Army Medical Center in Washington, D.C.* Washington, DC: Office of the Surgeon General, Borden Institute, 2009.

Stevens, George T. *Three Years in the Sixth Corps.* Albany, NY: S. R. Gray, 1866.

Templeman, Eleanor L. *Northern Virginia Heritage.* Arlington, VA: privately published, 1966.

Thorpe, Sheldon B. *The History of the Fifteenth Connecticut Volunteers in the War for the Defense of the Union 1861–1865.* New Haven, CT: Price, Lee and Adkins, 1893.

Todd, William. *The Seventy-Ninth Highlanders: New York Volunteers in the War of the Rebellion 1861–1865.* Albany, NY: Brandon, Barton and Co., 1886.

U.S. Army, Board of Officers. *Instruction for Heavy Artillery.* Washington, DC: Gideon and Company, 1851.

U.S. War Department, Adjutant General's Office. *Compendium of General Orders, Adjutant General's Office, 1864.* Washington, DC: U.S. War Department, 1864.

U.S. War Department. *War of the Rebellion: A Compilation of the Official Records of the Union and Confederate Armies.* 130 vols. Washington, DC: U.S. Government Printing Office, 1880–1901.

Vaill, T. F. *History of the Second Connecticut Volunteer Heavy Artillery.* Winsted, CT: Winsted Printing Company, 1868.

Vandiver, Frank E. *Jubal's Raid; General Early's Famous Attack on Washington in 1864.* New York: McGraw-Hill, 1960.

Vautier, John D. *History of the Eighty-Eighth Pennsylvania.* Philadelphia: Lippincott, 1894.

Walker, Edward A. *Our First Year of Army Life: An Anniversary Address Delivered to the First Regiment of Connecticut Volunteer Heavy Artillery.* New Haven, CT: Thomas J. Stafford, 1862.

Ward, George W. *History of the Second Pennsylvania Heavy Artillery.* Philadelphia: n.p., 1904.

Webb, Edward P. *History of the Tenth New York Heavy Artillery.* Watertown, NY: Post Book and Job Printing Establishment, 1887.

Whitt, Jane Chapman. *Elephants and Quaker Guns—Northern Virginia: Crossroads of History.* Arlington, VA: Vandamere Press, 1984.

Wills, Mary Alice. *The Confederate Blockade of Washington, D.C. 1861–1862.* Parsons, WV: McLean, 1975.

Woolsey, Jane Stuart. *Hospital Days.* Roseville, MN: Edinborough Press, 2001.

Index